CASEY

PENGUIN BOOKS

CASEY

Joseph E. Persico is the author of *Edward R. Murrow: An American Original*, *The Imperial Rockefeller*, and *Piercing the Reich*.

JOSEPH E.

PERSICO

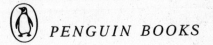 PENGUIN BOOKS

CASEY

From the OSS

to the CIA

PENGUIN BOOKS
Published by the Penguin Group
Viking Penguin, a division of Penguin Books USA Inc.,
375 Hudson Street, New York, New York 10014, U.S.A.
Penguin Books Ltd, 27 Wrights Lane, London W8 5TZ, England
Penguin Books Australia Ltd, Ringwood, Victoria, Australia
Penguin Books Canada Ltd, 10 Alcorn Avenue, Suite 300,
Toronto, Ontario, Canada M4V 3B2
Penguin Books (N.Z.) Ltd, 182–190 Wairau Road,
Auckland 10, New Zealand

Penguin Books Ltd, Registered Offices:
Harmondsworth, Middlesex, England

First published in the United States of America by
Viking Penguin, a division of Penguin Books USA Inc., 1990
Published in Penguin Books 1991

10 9 8 7 6 5 4 3 2 1

THE LIBRARY OF CONGRESS HAS CATALOGUED THE HARDCOVER AS FOLLOWS:
Persico, Joseph E.
Casey: from the OSS to the CIA / by Joseph E. Persico.
p. cm.
ISBN 0-670-82342-2 (hc.)
ISBN 0 14 01.1314 2 (pbk.)
1. United States. Central Intelligence Agency.   2. Casey, William
J.   3. Intelligence officers—United States—Biography.   I. Title.
JK468.I6P455   1990
327.1′2′092273—dc20   90–50121

Printed in the United States of America
Set in Aster
Designed by Barbara Bachman
Photograph on title page by James Nachtwey/Magnum

To the memory of my mother, Blanche,

and the role of my wife, Sylvia

Preface

The life of William J. Casey presents a dilemma to the biographer. Paint him a sinister, behind-the-scenes, above-the-law operator right out of spy fiction and you will find a receptive audience. Paint him an old-fashioned patriot, an avatar of anticommunism, the director who restored a demoralized CIA and you will please a small audience of conservatives and few others. Take a middle course and paint him as a man of considerable accomplishment who was also capable of colossal blunders, a man possessed of vision and blindness (at times simultaneously), and you perhaps begin to strike closest to the truth—and you probably risk displeasing all sides, right and left, friend and foe, critic and champion, who prefer their heroes pure and their enemies pure evil.

As his biographer, I had both the advantage and the disadvantage of knowing the man personally. I first met Casey in the course of writing an earlier book, *Piercing the Reich*, which dealt with the penetration of Nazi Germany by the Office of Strategic Services during World War II. Casey figured prominently in that story. He had had, as the British say, "a good war," and he left it having served his country honorably in an unambiguously honorable conflict—not only honorably but excitingly, since his experiences in that war were indeed the stuff of spy thrillers.

The man I met in 1977 was in his mid-sixties and looked even older. I blithely assumed that I was dealing with someone at the tag end of his life, little imagining that Casey's most spectacular chapters lay ahead of him. Yet, even then, behind the washed-out eyes, the slumped posture, the pouched, gray face, something lurked, something in the brusque manner, the machine-gun speech, the palpable ego, that bespoke an unspent energy, like that of a prize fighter forced into premature retirement.

I interviewed Casey several times. Out of this contact came a casual, friendly acquaintanceship of the kind he collected by the hundreds. The association was just close enough to give me a flesh-and-blood man against which to measure the Casey others were to describe to me during my later interviews for this book.

The private man I knew possessed considerable charm of a rough-and-ready sort. Casey could be generous of his time, his friendship, his connections, and, by all accounts, his money. And he was good company to boot. Thus, if you shared his politics, you had it all—the loyal friend, the lively companion, and the ideological soul mate. I did not share his politics, though I have tried within the limits of human neutrality not to let that fact prejudice my portrayal of the man, any more than the fact that I enjoyed his company.

I began work on this biography some six months after Casey's death. I had the good fortune to be granted exclusive access to his personal papers by his widow, Sophia Casey—letters going back to his youth, thousands of files kept throughout his multiple careers as lawyer, venture capitalist, publisher, author, and government official in four high federal posts. These files, located in the Casey homes on Long Island and in suburban Washington and totaling over three hundred thousand pages, were made available to me through Mrs. Casey's generosity, no strings attached to their use. I was also fortunate that scores of Casey's associates and friends were willing to talk to me about the man—indeed, were eager to talk about him.

Casey's leadership of the CIA was the controversial capstone but hardly the whole of an extraordinary life. There were several earlier chapters and other Caseys. There was the lower-middle-class kid from Queens who amassed a fortune, mostly as a high-diving venture capitalist, yet cared little for money per se, except for score keeping and as a key to the club of power. There was Casey the World War II American intelligence chief for Europe, who managed to penetrate Nazi Germany with 102 secret agents and then tried to walk away from the clandestine game he loved. There was Casey the publisher of books on legitimate greed (*How to Raise Money to Make Money*), the tax lawyer who invented the gambit and the term "tax shelter" and then stunned Wall Street by becoming the little guy's champion as chairman of the Securities and Exchange Commission. There was Casey as undersecretary of State for economic affairs, miserable under the heel of an overweening Henry Kissinger, later reveling in the sweet satisfaction of having Kissinger come to him when he wanted to reenter the power circle. There was the Casey who just skirted contamination during Watergate, riding out the storm while Nixon and his court went under.

There was the Casey who, at an age when most men retire, took over the failing presidential campaign of Ronald Reagan in 1980 and redirected it to victory—the same politico who, for all his brains, energy, and money, could not get himself elected to a seat in Congress.

Then there was Casey of the CIA, beloved (the word is not too strong) by intelligence professionals and credited by even his harshest critics with restoring the morale and effectiveness of a cowed and crippled

CIA after the investigations of the seventies, yet whose role in the Iran-contra affair left the agency in virtually the same cowering state in which he had found it.

And there was Casey of the Reagan inner circle, who leveraged what traditionally had been a staff post—the President's intelligence officer—into a role as a coarchitect of American foreign policy; a director of intelligence who shaped these policies as much as the secretaries of State and Defense, the national security adviser, even the President he served; a Casey who held, in effect, two portfolios, clandestine minister of state and of war.

He was a bundle of contrasts: a man often accused of shady business deals, yet one to whom honorable men would happily entrust the estates of their widows and children; a Catholic who was a pillar of his church, its universities, and its charities, who would go to astonishing lengths not to miss mass, yet a pragmatic who could tell his daughter to go ahead and get married—if it didn't work out, she could always get out of it; a descendant of Tammany Hall Democratic politicians who found the power and influence he sought in the Republican establishment.

He was a man whose Dickensian appearance, sartorial disarray, shambling manner, and mumbled speech totally belied the man beneath, a man possessed of considerable intellect, scholarly erudition, and a facile pen, all coexisting alongside rigid moral and religious certitudes never reexamined from his Catholic youth, when he concluded that he already possessed the truth.

He was a man who reveled in politics, government, and public affairs but rationed himself to dabbling in them until he had made his bundle and could move into the public arena at the top.

He was a man whose public persona stirred deep animosities because of his archconservatism, knee-jerk anticommunism, heavy-handed foreign interventionism, alleged deceptions of Congress—and, for some people, simply because he was the head of the CIA. Yet, as an individual, he had a great gift for friendship and a surprising capacity to hold on to the grudging admiration, even affection (if not always the trust), of his adversaries. This ambivalent group includes opposition members of Congress, the press, and old liberal comrades from World War II.

He was a man who, stretching the credulity of even his closest friends, started out as a social worker determined to serve a suffering humanity, who during the early years of the Depression could indict the failures of capitalism as eloquently as any Union Square radical; a future multimillionaire who in his twenties wrote essays on the superiority of the spiritual over the material life that would have delighted Saint Francis. He would later enjoy saying, however, "Anybody who isn't a Democrat at the age of twenty has something wrong with his heart. If he's still a Democrat at the age of thirty, there's something wrong with his head." Casey was well ahead of schedule.

He was a man who virtually over a weekend could knock out a lawyer's desk guide on how to cut inheritance taxes (books that made another fortune for him) yet he hungered to be taken seriously as a scholar and historian, and was in fact the author of two respectable books of history.

In the end there is the Casey whose death, at the very height of the Iran-contra revelations, was exactly like his life—melodramatic, controversial, cloaked in speculation, rumor, and mystery.

His life is worth our attention because it is a story of how power is acquired in this country, even by those who begin with none, and how that power is exercised at the pinnacle. Casey's story is particularly intriguing and instructive because, at the end, it involves possibly the most serious challenge to the United States's democratic institutions since the country's founding. Iran-contra struck at the vitals of the Constitution. The sanctity of the President's duty to uphold the laws? Iran-contra suggested that the President may ignore laws he does not like. The system of checks and balances that one branch of government exercises over another? Evade it by the simple expedient of leaving one branch in the dark about what another branch is doing. The separation of powers? Carry out by presidential fiat whatever Congress refuses to pass into law. And in all this, by the force of his character, by his activist conception of the CIA, by the freedom he enjoyed under the lightly held reins of Ronald Reagan, Casey was to play a leading role. Sorting out his role in Iran-contra—accomplice, silent partner, mastermind—is a principal objective of this book.

The study of Casey's life offers one final attraction. He was virtually the last of the cold warriors, a bridge spanning the Stalin and Gorbachev eras. Casey was a quintessential representative of the breed who, for well over a generation, stood in the wings of American foreign policy determining how far the actors in that drama dared veer to stage left before they were yanked right. Understanding what shaped and drove Casey may help illuminate the origins of the cold war mentality, which was, for America, either a necessary vigilance or the greatest miscalculation of the second half of the twentieth century.

Acknowledgments

A work of biography best comes to life through the eyewitness recollections of those who knew the subject as family member, friend, colleague, superior, subordinate, adversary, or even foe. In writing about the life of William J. Casey, I was fortunate to talk to dozens of people who fell into all the above categories. Many of those from the world of intelligence who agreed to talk to me did so under pledges of confidence. I am therefore unable to acknowledge my debt to them publicly. They know who they are; and they must know as well my gratitude for their indispensable contributions.

Among those who helped and can be identified, first and foremost was Sophia Casey, the widow of Bill Casey. Mrs. Casey was unstinting in her assistance to me, with no demands placed on me as to the use of her many contributions to this work.

I received invaluable assistance from that unique repository of foreign policy documents, the National Security Archive. For this help, I thank the archive's executive director, Scott Armstrong, and his impressive staff, particularly Malcolm Byrne, Jeff Nason, Peter Kornbluh, and Eddie Becker.

I am grateful as well for so much time given to me by Malcolm Wilson, former governor of New York and a valued friend, and Father Edward Duffy, S.J., both Fordham University alumni who helped me re-create Casey's critical college years.

I received inestimable help in researching facts from my college classmate and a fine librarian, Joan Barron. Facts that are wrong are my responsibility alone. My longtime political colleague, Tanya Melich, gave my manuscript the benefit of her close reading, discerning eye, and shrewd judgments, for which I am in her debt. Dan Frank, my editor, buoyed me at the beginning by his enthusiasm for the project and at the end by his editorial wisdom. I also thank my literary agent, Clyde Taylor, for his role. Clyde is as good an advocate and friend as a writer can have. Further, I thank my wife, Sylvia, who labored endlessly over the manuscript, all the while giving it the benefit of her sharp insights. I am grateful to all those friends who offered me hospitality on the road to this book, including the Russianoffs, the Gagans, Bill Shepard, Mary Stuart, and Wolfgang Neumann.

Finally, I thank all those who alone know what they did for me. They include John Bross, Howard Cady, Larry Casey, Robert Gates, David Halevy, Harv Morgan, Bernadette Smith, Owen Smith, Jim Redden, and Maurice Rosenblatt.

Contents

Abbreviations

CIA—The Central Intelligence Agency; conducts foreign intelligence collection and analysis and covert foreign operations for the United States.

DA—The Directorate for Administration; the CIA branch responsible for the Agency's administrative, management, and procurement needs.

DCI—The Director of Central Intelligence, appointed by the President; the head of the CIA, the President's chief intelligence adviser and the coordinator of all other U.S. intelligence operations besides the CIA.

DDA—The Deputy Director for Administration; the chief of the DA.

DDCI—The Deputy Director of Central Intelligence; the DCI's deputy and the second in command of the CIA.

DDI—The Deputy Director for Intelligence; the chief of the CIA directorate charged with the collection and analysis of intelligence.

DDO—The Deputy Director for Operations; the chief of the CIA directorate charged with conducting covert operations.

DI—The Directorate for Intelligence; headed by the DDI (see above).

DO—The Directorate for Operations; headed by the DDO (see above).

HPSCI—The House Permanent Select Committee on Intelligence; the committee in the U.S. House of Representatives overseeing intelligence operations.

IBP—The Institute of Business Planning; the business publishing company established by William J. Casey.

IOB—The Intelligence Oversight Board; a three-member body charged with advising the President as to the propriety and legality of intelligence operations.

NIC—The National Intelligence Council; a body, under control of the DCI, which coordinates and produces National Intelligence Estimates.

NIE—National Intelligence Estimate; a projection, produced by the NIC, of likely political, economic, and military developments in a particular country or region; also an NIC-produced assessment of a foreign leader or foreign policy issue.

NIO—National Intelligence Officer; a senior analyst, working usually as part of the NIC, specializing in a particular country or subject.

NSA—The National Security Agency; the agency that monitors satellite and other communications worldwide for intelligence purposes; also the code-breaking agency and the organization responsible for protecting U.S. secure communications and codes.

NSC—The National Security Council; composed of the President and other key foreign policy officials; it is charged with coordinating U.S. foreign and national security policies and run by the President's assistant for national security affairs.

NSPG—The National Security Planning Group; a smaller group drawn from the NSC; the chief body responsible for the formation of foreign policy during the Reagan administration.

OSS—The Office of Strategic Services; the U.S. intelligence service established in World War II; forerunner of the CIA.

PDF—The President's Daily Brief, a digest of key intelligence developments prepared by the CIA for the President and a few key officials.

PFIAB—The President's Foreign Intelligence Advisory Board; a prestigious, nonpartisan body appointed from outside the federal government to advise the President on the efficacy of intelligence operations.

RIA—The Research Institute of America; a business research and publishing organization where William J. Casey was employed.

SI—Secret Intelligence; the branch of the OSS charged with collecting and analyzing intelligence.

SO—Secret Operations; the branch of the OSS charged with carrying out paramilitary and other actions against enemy forces and installations.

SSCI—The Senate Select Committee on Intelligence; the committee in the U.S. Senate overseeing intelligence operations.

VOSS—Veterans of the OSS; an organization of former members of the OSS in which William J. Casey was an early member and longtime power.

CASEY

1.

Lawyers, Guns, and Money

The stooped figure peering out of the hatch of the chopper looked utterly out of place. He was a generation older than the next-oldest man aboard. The younger men wore bush jackets and olive drab pants bloused into jungle boots. He wore a plaid, short-sleeved sport shirt that exposed the wiry white hair on his arms. The shirt was not tucked in but hung out over a pair of baggy blue cotton slacks ending in brand-new white tennis shoes. His face was puffed and pale with fatigue. With its sagging jowls, tired eyes, and gray flesh, it seemed composed of old molten wax and cobwebs—an arresting face, a face out of Dickens, rendered all the more incongruous by the suburban weekend dress. The heavy lower lip hung loose and his head drooped as he gazed down at the moving shadow the helicopter towed across the jungle canopy. Undisciplined wisps of hair fluttered from beneath an army cap perched on top of his head. Blazoned across the front of the cap were the words "Tegoose Station— Send Lawyers, Guns and Money."

He had changed clothes aboard the C-141 on the flight down from Washington. His security people always found it hard to get him to dress down. In tropical rain forest or Pakistani mountain outpost his inclination was to wear the uniform of his generation and rank—a business suit, striped shirt, and tie.

The chopper belonged to the Central Intelligence Agency. Everyone aboard was CIA, including the pilot. They did not trust Air Force crews—not experienced enough, not reliable enough. This was tree-top-level flying over trackless jungle, and the principal passenger this day was the director of Central Intelligence.

William J. Casey moved away from the hatch and resumed his seat beside the pilot. Alan Fiers breathed a relieved sigh that the man had not fallen out. The past three days would have been punishing enough for a man half Casey's age—a man like Fiers, an ex–Big Ten football star, a smart, seasoned, energetic officer whom Casey, on a hunch, had plucked from covert operations in the Middle East to run the Central American show.

In two years of close association, Fiers had become accustomed to the indefatigable Casey, gruff, abrupt, decisive, quick of mind, ceaselessly questioning, always pressuring Fiers to do more, more, more for the contras, the Casey-built guerrilla army that was fighting the Sandinista regime in Nicaragua. Alan Fiers had loved working for Bill Casey. But the present listless figure was a Casey he had never known. The trip was to last only four days, and so they had decided to drop the agency doctor who always accompanied the director abroad. Now Fiers regretted the decision.

They had arrived in El Salvador three days before, November 16, 1986—Casey, Fiers, and a senior agency official not to be identified. They met first with the CIA station chief and his people in the capital, San Salvador. Casey had been impatient and distracted during the briefing; he had asked none of the piercing questions that station staffs around the world had learned to fear. Next, they had moved on to a meeting with Salvadoran officials, where Casey sat slumped with eyes half-closed, barely enduring their elaborate Latin courtesies and slow circumnavigation of the points they wanted to make. He wanted to get out into the *campo,* to see the impact of the aid and attention that the United States had lavished on El Salvador in propping up the current regime against a dogged leftist insurgency.

Then it had been off to Costa Rica for another round of briefings— except that in this tiny, precariously positioned democracy, President Oscar Arias Sánchez had flatly refused to see Bill Casey. Word was leaking out about unidentified Americans using installations on Costa Rica's northern border to harass the Nicaraguan Sandinistas. It would not do for Arias's standing among his Central American *compadres* to look like a CIA lapdog.

They arrived next in Honduras, and Casey dozed through another round of briefings with the local CIA staff. He then granted an audience to Honduran officials, who were so adept at extracting tribute from the United States for allowing the contras sanctuary that Senator Daniel Patrick Moynihan referred to them as the "Honduran Department of Extortion."

Finally, they had boarded the helicopter out of Honduras's Toncontín Airport for the final leg of the journey, the true purpose of the trip.

Congress's ban on aid to the contras, the Boland Amendment, had only just been lifted. "Why don't we wait until we've got all the restrictions cleared away," Fiers had argued, "when we'll have a really clean deal?" Casey had given Fiers that dismissive back-of-the-hand wave that meant end-of-discussion. He wanted to see the army that he had fathered.

Three days before their departure, the President had addressed the nation and essentially confessed that the United States had been selling arms to Iran—the country that had humbled and humiliated America, that had in effect brought down the previous American President by holding fifty-two Americans hostage for over a year; a country that had ordered the truck bombing that killed 241 young American marines in Beirut; a country that was tied to the bombing of the U.S. embassy in Beirut, with seventeen Americans dead, and the later bombing of the embassy annex, with twenty-four people killed; a country ruled by a religious fanatic whose hatred of America inspired these atrocities. This was the country with which the Reagan administration had sought to trade weapons for hostages. The President had publicly admitted to what he had sworn could never happen: "Americans will never make concessions to terrorists—to do so would only invite more terrorism. Once we head down that path, there would be no end to it. . . ."

The American people were suspended between disbelief and outrage. It was Watergate all over. What did the President know, and when did he know it? For Casey, it was not only what did he know and when did he know it but how deeply was he involved—how fully were he and his agency the authors of this deceit? Congress was getting ready to investigate. During the meetings in Central America, Casey had been constantly popping in and out to take calls on the secure phone from his deputy, Bob Gates, back in Langley, about his own forthcoming testimony on the Hill. Casey found himself once more where he had been so often in his life, hungering for respectability, teetering on the brink of disgrace.

It was at this point that he had inexplicably chosen to leave the country and fly off to Central America. Bob Gates wondered why the trip had been laid on so hastily. He finally concluded it was another instance of a pattern he had observed: "When things got hot, when the pressure built up, Casey liked to get out, get away from the bureaucratic bullshit in Washington and go to the cutting edge so he'd remember what his job really was."

The chopper was floating through undulating terrain down a steep valley where the jungle in places was double and triple canopy. Casey sat slumped in his seat, one arm limp at his side. He could well be thinking of what he called the Good War, the one he had fought before most of the men on this helicopter had been born. Then it had been chill nights in England when the moon was right and he had driven through the blacked-out villages of Surrey to see off the agents he was parachuting into Nazi Germany.

He had been thirty-two then, and he had put the whole thing together himself, the penetration of the enemy heartland by American spies. Now he was old, and it was steaming jungle instead of manicured England. But below that verdant cover was another army, one that he had created to fight the archenemy of the latter half of his life, the communists.

He had no business on the chopper. He knew it. The station chief in Tegucigalpa had blanched when he learned that the director wanted to go to a contra camp. The last offensive had been fought up this very valley. The Sandinistas were now deploying Soviet-equipped hunter-killer teams to down helicopters. The month before, further south, they had shot a contra supply plane out of the sky. The only survivor had been an American named Eugene Hasenfus, a man with apparent ties to the CIA.

The pilot coaxed the chopper toward a clearing hacked out of the jungle. Casey peered out and saw the welcoming committee standing in a rutted road alongside a convoy of jeeps. They were, Fiers told him, the Contra Council of Comandantes and CIA advisers attached to the contras. As the chopper settled to earth, even before the rotor had sputtered to a stop, a stocky figure in starched, immaculate camouflage fatigues came striding forward. Casey recognized Colonel Enrique Bermúdez, commander of the FDN, the Nicaraguan Democratic Force, the contra leader. The director got stiffly out of the chopper, took Bermúdez's extended hand, and clapped him on the back like the New York politico he had once aspired to be. As he headed for the jeeps, Casey's arms and legs moved disjointedly; still, he walked with a purposeful stride—a jerry-rigged contraption that worked. One of the advisers directed him into the second jeep, in case the road had been mined. Bermúdez sat next to him.

The rainy season was just beginning, and the muddy, twisting route that they bounced along resembled an unhealed scar inflicted on the jungle. Casey studied the man next to him, thick-set, muscular, black haired, handsome in a coarse way. The sleeves of his shirt were rolled up, revealing a Rolex watch. Enrique Bermúdez had been a colonel in the Nicaraguan National Guard, under the dictator Anastasio Somoza Debayle. He had been a servant of the corrupt regime whose excesses had helped bring the Sandinistas to power. Casey could

remember the judgment of David Halevy, an Israeli journalist working for *Time* magazine: "Bermúdez is a Somocista. He was a good
military attaché at their embassy in Washington. But he's no soldier,
no field commander." Looking over the man on whom the United
States had placed its bet, Casey wondered.

The jeeps wound up a hill and past the first solid structure, a low,
rude building constructed of logs peaked by a tin roof, the hospital.
Lounging in front were a half-dozen bandaged and wounded contras.
One, a boy of perhaps sixteen, was sitting in the open doorway, swinging the stump of a leg back and forth. The jeeps rolled into the center
of the camp. Clusters of small, lean, brown, bare-chested men sat
cleaning AK-47 assault rifles, designed, ironically, in the Soviet
Union. Others were assembling and disassembling American M-60
machine guns and Belgian FAL rifles. Piled between the buildings
were caches of antitank rockets, 60-millimeter mortars, and RPG
grenade launchers—a formidable-looking arsenal, but, to Casey, still
not enough for a guerrilla army that had been starved by the U.S.
Congress for the previous two years.

During that hiatus the CIA had been virtually sidelined by law from
operating against Nicaragua. The Reagan administration thereafter
entrusted the job of keeping the contras afloat to a Marine Corps
lieutenant colonel. Casey had deep affection and admiration for Oliver
North. Ollie North and Bill Casey attended the same parish, the
Church of Can-Do. Virtually all the people that Casey admired were
self-starters, people who delivered deeds, not excuses. He was also
aware of the liability of the breed, the price paid for their tendency
to follow their zealousness out a tenth-story window. He had known
dozens of Ollie Norths during the other war. They had their value;
he had often made long-shot bets on them. He still did. But they
reminded him of the V-2s that fell on London those last months of
the war: they packed a tremendous wallop, but you could never be
sure where they would land.

Casey eased himself out of the jeep, and Fiers followed behind him.
After the jolting ride, the last shred of jauntiness had fled the director.
Fiers thought, "Hell, no wonder—he's 73."

An adviser pulled alongside Casey: "We'll be inspecting the facil-
ities first. Then you'll troop the line, sir. We'll hold the briefing last."
Casey grunted his approval.

They followed a path back to the hospital, passing by gnarled old
men with skin like leather who were unloading sacks of grain from
mules. They walked between small plots of corn, beans, and tomatoes.
Casey's new tennis shoes began to accumulate clots of red mud. After

visiting the wounded in the hospital, they toured another shack, the com center, silent but for the incongruous click of computer keyboards and the rasp of printers in the middle of the jungle. The equipment was Radio Shack. "What we call low-cost high-tech," Fiers joked to Casey.

Casey glanced briefly through the door of a primitive machine shop where old rifles were being repaired and where the heat of a homemade forge almost knocked him over. Casey had been to Vietnam. He remembered seeing similar crude arsenals that the Viet Cong guerrillas had concealed in their jungles. And they had won.

The party returned to the center of the camp to the sounds of military commands shouted in Spanish and mocked by the caw-cawing of parrots overhead. A company of contras, ranging in age from fourteen to forty, had been deployed at attention on the packed earth in the center of the camp. They were dressed in obviously new combat utilities, floppy jungle hats, and calf-length jungle boots, also creaky new. The spigot of U.S. aid had only recently been turned on again.

Casey had heard all the worst about them, that some contra leaders, like Bermúdez, were motivated by greed more than anything else, that some were dealing in drugs, little better than criminals. Still, to Casey, you could not argue with survival. Actually, it was far more than survival: this force had managed, through the wavering support of the U.S. Congress, not only to stay alive but to grow from a handful five years before to some fifteen thousand men now. They had made of themselves an irritant to the Sandinistas. They had drained off precious Sandinista resources. They had diverted Daniel Ortega Saavedra, the Nicaraguan leader, and his *junta* from what Casey saw as their clear intention, to spread communism throughout Central America.

Casey remembered what his people had reported. Why did the Nicaraguan peasant leave his patch of earth to join up with the contras? Because the Sandinistas had forced him into cooperatives, told him what he could grow and what he could sell it for. One middle-aged peasant said he had joined the contras after the Sandinistas confiscated his pigs "to give to worthless, lazy people."

The latest figure the contras had given him for battle deaths was more than five thousand, almost certainly inflated. But there was no doubt they were dying for their cause—*his* cause. That was what Casey had wanted to hear, needed to hear. That was what his life was about—saving people from the coils of communism. This was Casey's secular religion. David Halevy remembered what Casey had answered when he asked him what was so important about a tiny, poverty-stricken country like Nicaragua, with a population less than that of two boroughs of New York City: "I'm looking for a place to start rolling back the Communist empire."

Casey reached the end of the formation and the company commander gave him a smart salute. Even slouched, Casey towered over him. He grinned. "Your men look good," he said. Hell, maybe they were not the 82nd Airborne. But they were the stone in Ortega's shoe.

"C'mon," Casey gestured with his head toward another shack. He was anxious to get on.

Bermúdez opened the briefing, welcoming the Americans, particularly this statesman, their steadfast comrade-in-arms, *El Jefe* Casey. The briefing was conducted in Spanish. An American adviser translated. Using a map pinned to a bare wall, Comandante Tono explained the strategy, the strength and deployment of the contras and the Sandinistas, the fighting going on, even as he spoke, on the Nicaraguan border less than ten miles away.

Fiers observed the director uneasily. He had witnessed this scene so often back in Langley: Casey visibly sinking into his chair, feet propped on his desk, poking the straightened end of a paper clip between his teeth, his eyes half-shut or gazing off at some invisible horizon. The difference between then and now was that at Langley the supine figure, the sagging cheeks, the glazed eyes would suddenly harden into a fierce attention. He would fire off questions in machine-gun bursts. "What's the enlistment rate? Is it up? Down? What arms do they need? Are they getting them? How long does it take? Why so long? What about training? What's the operation going to cost this year? Next year? The following year?" And always, "Why aren't you guys doing more?" It was the performance of a lizard on a rock, seemingly sluggish under the hot sun, suddenly snatching insects from the air with lightning speed.

This trip it had been different. In the meetings in San Salvador, San José, and Tegucigalpa, Casey had looked dazed, had missed his cues, forgotten the script, failed to ask questions that went begging. Fiers had found himself running the show, picking up the slack, saying, "What the director means . . . What Mr. Casey wants to know . . . What you haven't told us yet . . ."

Comandante Tono was wrapping up the briefing with a passionate plea for more firepower and faster delivery. Fiers leaned over and whispered to Casey. Casey nodded absently and started to rise. He looked around him as though uncertain where he was. Then his eyes took on something of the old light. "When the Congress cut you off in 1944 . . . ," he began. The interpreter fixed the wrong year in his translation. Yes, 1944, Fiers thought—the war that would never end for Casey. ". . . You've done a remarkable job under impossible conditions. Now the United States is back in this war. We're going to do everything we can to help you. Your struggle is our struggle." The man was genuinely moved; Fiers could see that. Still, his voice was a low rumble, the words thick and clotted. He could barely be understood.

Afterward, Bermúdez invited Casey and his party to share their rations. Fiers thought it would be good for morale. Casey agreed. A rough plank table was cleared, and two Nicaraguan girls, lost in oversized fatigues, began to set plastic plates and tin spoons before the men. They served a stew with rice from a terra-cotta bowl. The base joke was that meals consisted of rice and beans at noon and beans and rice at night. Fiers noted with relief that Casey shoveled in the food with his customary gusto.

The day before, Casey had taken a phone call on a secure line from the President's national security adviser, Admiral John Poindexter. The center was not holding on the Iran problem, Poindexter told him. They were both going to have to testify before the oversight committees; maybe they ought to meet first and get their stories straight. Casey had then cut a day off his trip. Norman Gardner, a special assistant in the CIA operations directorate, was dispatched to Honduras to bring Casey background material. It was time for the director to leave the relative calm of a guerrilla camp and return to the Washington jungle.

It was six-thirty by the time the helicopter returned to Toncontín Airport in Tegucigalpa. The days were growing short this time of year, and the sky was already turning a tropical purple. Fiers jumped out of the chopper first and offered Casey his hand. Casey ignored him. The unlovely bulk of the C-141 loomed nearby. The tail dropped from the rear of the plane to the tarmac like the seat of a pair of long johns. Casey seemed to be veering away from the plane. Fiers gently steered him back on course. He had been in virtual nonstop motion for seventy-two hours, up this morning at five, the trip to the camp, and with a five-hour flight ahead of him before he reached Washington.

Casey walked up the ramp toward the portable VIP living compartment that had been shoehorned into the hull of the transport. Gardner came forward to meet him. Under his arm were three thick three-ring binders.

"When am I on?" Casey asked. He was told that he would be going before the House and Senate in two days.

Fiers followed Casey into the living compartment, watched him sit down and draw the seat belt across a slight paunch. Casey resignedly held out his hand for the briefing books. Fiers was staying behind and started to back out of the plane. His last sight was of the ashen figure already bent over the notebooks.

2.

The Boy Is Father
to the Man

Family photographs show a pugnacious-looking little boy, stance defiant, lips puckered, sand pail in hand, standing protectively alongside his little sister on a Long Island beach. Long Island is where he was born, in Elmhurst, Queens, on March 13, 1913. He weighed at birth an astonishing fourteen pounds.

He was named after his father, William Joseph Casey. Casey senior was thirty-one when his first child was born, and working in the Queens Street Cleaning Department. A slight man of medium height, with blue eyes and wavy blond hair that was never to turn gray, he resembled a smaller, finer version of the silent movie star Francis X. Bushman. His handsome face was usually set in a serious mien, for he was a serious man, devoted to pulling himself and his family up one more rung on the ladder of American success. His route was the same one that had worked for his father before him and for ambitious Irish immigrant families for nearly half a century—the Democratic party.

The Caseys in America had followed an almost stereotypical Irish-American odyssey. George C. Casey, the grandfather of the man who was one day to become the director of Central Intelligence, had come to America in 1849 at age two on the flood tide of the Irish fleeing the potato famine. The Caseys had been shoemakers back in Daingean, County Offaly; and there they were starving to death along with the peasants, who could not afford to eat, much less buy shoes. Many of these immigrants washed up on the eastern shore of Queens, in Astoria, just across the East River from Manhattan, among them the Caseys. The arrival of the Irish sent a shudder through this established Protestant community. "Popery and Romanism"—that was what these wretches presumably carried in their cheap, tattered luggage.

At age eighteen, George Casey happily escaped the shoemaking trade and ran off to catch the last year of the Civil War as a seaman on a Union gunboat. He came home from the war and discovered Democratic politics. He became a ward heeler, then the fire chief of Astoria. He opened a saloon, Casey's Place, which became a hangout for the Queens Democratic organization.

George Casey died before his grandson was born. But the boy was raised on his legend. The family album contained photos of the fire chief at the head of his company, with four hand-drawn pumpers, seven horse-drawn carriages, and three horseless hook-and-ladder carriages, all with brass fittings burnished to a fiery finish. There were photos of the ward heeler in striped vest and white apron, presiding over his saloon behind an oak bar, serving up mugs of Imperial Beer and Evans Ale, his patrons, feet resting on the brass footrail, wearing bow ties, celluloid collars, and derbies, forever talking politics. Across the street was another bar, fancier, catering to the carriage trade. Part of the Casey family lore recorded how Grandpa would direct customers who ordered Manhattans and gin fizzes across the street: "Sorry, we don't carry that sort of thing here." The Caseys were plain people.

Family lore also preserved the story of how a new administration tried to fire Grandpa as fire chief. George Casey was having none of that. He rallied his friends; he enlisted his cronies; he lobbied City Hall; he went to the state capital in Albany—and he got his job back. The Caseys were scrappers.

Grandpa Casey lost his wife in childbirth when she was thirty-seven years old, and raised his five children on his own. The Caseys were survivors.

The eldest of these children was William Joseph. With his father's help, he entered politics and became correspondence secretary of the First Assembly District Democratic Club. He wanted no part of saloon keeping, and through the party he managed to land the job in the street-cleaning department. But the fastidious Bill Casey did not haul other people's garbage. He became a clerk. He proved quick, reliable, hard-working, modest, and unassuming. And at the time of the birth of his son and namesake, Bill Casey senior had risen to supervisor of the department with a reputation for making Queens's streets shine.

His son was later to play the Irishman to the hilt whenever it suited him. But it was only half-true. Bill Casey junior's mother was Blanche Lavigne, the daughter of a French Canadian chef who came down from Ontario and settled in New York City. The Lavignes too were whole-souled Democrats. At the time she met her future husband, Blanche Lavigne had worked herself up from saleslady to buyer in May's Department Store. They were married in 1910, when she was twenty-three and Bill twenty-eight. She never held another job the rest of her life. Casey wives did not work.

The newlyweds left Astoria and moved to Elmhurst, a more fashionable Queens neighborhood. Three years later, Bill junior was born, followed in a year and a half by Dorothy, and three and a half years after that by George. A fourth child, Blanche, lived for a day.

Elmhurst was then a community of single-family homes, close-packed but comfortable. The borough of Queens had been swallowed by New York City twenty-five years before. But the tide of urbanization had not yet overwhelmed what was then called "the Cornfield Borough." There were still woodlands within walking distance of the Casey home.

In 1920, the Casey family fortunes took an even sharper turn upward. Bill Casey senior managed to extricate himself from the sanitation business. In a burst of reform, New York City had decided to create an employees retirement system to straighten out the mess in pensions. Though a thoroughgoing Tammany man, Bill Casey was known as an honest, able official, a rare combination in the organization. He was brought in to help organize the new pension system, and there he remained for the rest of his life.

Four years into the job, he bought his first automobile, a Model T Ford. The following year, he decided to move his family out to the country, to Bellmore on the south shore of Queens, into a brown-shingled Dutch colonial at 422 Midwood Avenue, purchased for $7,500. The Caseys' new neighbors were mainly second-generation families, Irish, Scandinavian, Italian, all moving up in the world.

At the time of the move, Bill junior was twelve years old and had completed the sixth grade. On entering a new school district he had to take a placement test. Bellmore school officials took a look at the results and decided to put him in the eighth grade, which Bill entered at Saint Agnes Academy, a parochial high school, in September of 1926.

Blanche, his mother, was a large, handsome woman—what the brassiere ads of that era called "a full-figured lady." She possessed a regal imperturbability. She ruled at home firmly but good-naturedly and allowed her husband to concentrate his energies on his work. She made of their house on Midwood Avenue a tranquil harbor for him from the pressures of the city. The devotion between the

couple was apparently total. Dorothy Casey was later to sa[y]
could not remember a cross word between her mother an[d]
the while she was growing up.

On Sundays, the Caseys attended ten o'clock mass together at Saint
Barnabas, where tough old Father Rattigan ruled as a benevolent
despot. There, Blanche flushed with pride: the altar boy, with black
cassock and white surplice, swinging the incense burner, looking like
a miniature priest, was her boy Bill. He was to serve mass for Father
Rattigan until he graduated from high school.

On Sunday evenings the Caseys had friends and family over.
Blanche would lay out a supper with the good china and crystal. Bill
senior, the sober bureaucrat, would sit at a baby grand, where the
usually compressed mouth dissolved into a broad smile as he banged
out old tunes and show tunes of the day. He could hear a Broadway
musical once and come home and play virtually the entire score.
Guests gathered around the piano and followed Bill's silky baritone
in "Bye Bye Blackbird," "Oh Johnny," and "Always."

The Caseys appeared regularly in the Bellmore *Courier:* "Mr. and
Mrs. William J. Casey are spending their vacation at Shrub Oak, N.Y.
this month." . . . "Dr. Albert Neil was the week-end guest of Mr. and
Mrs. William J. Casey of Midwood." . . . "Bill Casey, popular and ef-
ficient pension expert of the New York City Employees Retirement
System, left this week for a vacation trip by auto through the Adi-
rondack Mountains."

Bill senior was not a robust man. As he grew older and his hours
longer, he became thin, and his complexion took on a sallow color.
Still, he drove himself uncomplainingly. His younger son, George, in
a later letter to his brother, Bill, wrote:

I guess our father didn't have much time . . . but what he had I
think he squandered on us . . . [He took] the 6 a.m. ferry from Fire
Island . . . and the 9 p.m. ferry back . . . two months in a row . . . so
he could spend August with his vacationing family. God only knows
why he squandered a very promising career for us. I guess that's
the way he was. I was the guy he came back to when I was sick in
Bellmore, in obvious pain himself, stuffing his hand under his belt
and singing "You're my pal." It ain't easy to forget. I only know
he was the guy who gave us the most beautiful memories kids
can have . . . a whole month of country . . . on less than 5 grand a
year. He was my pal. I try to emulate him. I haven't found a better
model.

Two qualities surfaced early in the elder son: Bill Casey was smarter than most of the other kids, and he demonstrated a compulsion to thrust himself ahead of the pack. Then as now, every year around Christmas, the *New York Times* printed its "Hundred Neediest Cases," accounts of poor people in desperate straits. His fifth-grade teacher picked one of these cases out and asked the children what they might do to help. Ten-year-old Bill pointed out that the class had raised four dollars and thirty-six cents for its Christmas party. "Send 'em the party money," he said—and the class did, along with a note drafted and signed by "William Casey, Room 312."

He attended Saint Agnes's parochial school through his junior year. But he was increasingly unhappy. There were no interscholastic sports and only two boys left in his class. He had become a baseball nut, one of those kids constantly spouting statistics—batting averages and pitchers' win-loss records—going back to the days of Honus Wagner and Christy Mathewson. He won a newspaper contest for predicting the lineups for the All-Star Game. The prize was a bat signed by Babe Ruth. Bill kept it in his room for years; when he returned from World War II and found out that his mother had thrown it out, he was devastated.

He persuaded his parents to let him transfer to the public high school in Baldwin, a fifteen-minute train ride away. At Baldwin, kids were soon pouncing on Bill Casey the moment he arrived in the morning, eager to copy his homework. It was always done and it was always right. Still, he was not particularly studious; school came easily to him. These kids, hurriedly scribbling down his answers without even knowing the questions, puzzled him. What was the point? he wondered. What were they learning? He *liked* learning, enjoyed seeing his store of knowledge grow. Didn't it say in the stained-glass ceiling of the school auditorium, "Knowledge Is Power"?

He got into a fight one lunch hour in the school cafeteria after an Italian boy called him a "mick bookworm." The English teacher was aghast at this unruly streak in her star pupil. She assigned Bill to memorize Kipling's "If"—"If you can keep your head when those about you/Are losing theirs and blaming it on you . . ." She made him recite the poem in class. He mumbled and raced through the recitation—even then, his thoughts poured out more quickly than his mouth could handle. Nonetheless, he liked Kipling's call to self-responsibility. He framed a copy of the poem, and it was still hanging in the library of his home in Roslyn Harbor sixty years later.

His Italian tormentor was right. Young Casey had contracted an incurable virus—and at an early age: when he was two years old, his mother had been astonished to find little Bill sitting on the floor, a book of nursery rhymes in his hands, apparently reading them out loud. He had memorized what she had read to him.

He had a fixed routine in high school. He would come home and put his books on the kitchen table, along with a loaf of bread and a jar of jam. He would then become totally absorbed in his homework, all the while absently spreading jam on one slice of bread after another, until the loaf was demolished.

There was a newsstand on Bedford Avenue where he liked to stop on the way home. He would start at one end of the magazine rack and work his way to the other. The owner once hollered at him, "Hey, kid, did you get to the Z's yet?" He was used to boys coming in and furtively thumbing through the girlie magazines, but this kid actually read the stuff.

The undersized twelve-year-old had sprouted to over six feet by the time he was sixteen. Casey was gawky, all knees, elbows, and appetite. Though he had started late at Baldwin High, he was eager to get into high-school sports. He tried out for the football team in his senior year and was cut.

He was not a natural athlete, more dogged than gifted. Ray Murphy, a close friend, recalled: "There was a gang of us got caught up in boxing one summer. Roy Tuck's yard was just about the size of a ring. So we'd put on the gloves and go at it there—a bell, a timer, the works. Old Casey sure as hell didn't look like a boxer—all skin and bones. But the way he flailed away with those long arms, we called him 'Cyclone.'

"One of the guys, Pete Drew, never took it easy on anybody, even a friend. Drew and Casey were in the ring one day and Drew threw a haymaker at Casey's chin. It missed and caught poor Casey right in the throat. His face turned every color of the rainbow. He went down on his knees. He was gasping, his eyes popping, blood running out of the corner of his mouth. He couldn't make a sound. We thought he was a goner. Damned if he wasn't back the next day, his neck all black and blue, ready to put on the gloves again."

The blow to the neck and the consequent damage to the muscles of the throat marked the beginning of speech problems that plagued Casey the rest of his life.

The boxing fad also revealed another lifelong pattern: if you like it but cannot do it well yourself, then manage those who can. Among the boxers in Roy Tuck's yard, the one with the most natural aptitude was Eddie Busher, thickly built and a powerful puncher. Professional fights were held at nearby Mitchell Field, with five- and ten-dollar purses for the preliminary bouts. Casey talked a wary Busher into letting him become his manager and booked him into a fight. On a Saturday night, Casey, Busher, and the rest of the gang took the train out to Mitchell Field, with Casey talking confidently out of the side of his mouth like a real fight manager. Eddie Busher was knocked out in the first round, and Casey abandoned his managing career.

As graduation neared, everyone was talking about the senior prom. Casey, involved in every other school activity, was unaccustomedly silent. He was painfully shy around girls; he was awkward in their company, an ungainly string bean with irregular features and a heavy mouth, certainly no prize in looks. He was also the product of a culture that made the sensual stirrings of adolescence suspect, even shameful. Puritanism was a central fact of the Irish-American character. An Irishman could be expansive over drink, sports, gambling, politics, friendship; but, as one Irish-American writer put it, "Of all Catholic countries, only Ireland came up with men who believed what the Church told them about sex."

Ray Murphy knew that Casey wanted to make the prom, and so he pleaded with his sister, Viola, a pretty, fun-loving girl known as "Sunshine," to be Casey's date. As Murphy later recalled, "Sunshine tried to teach Casey to dance. He had two left feet, no coordination at all. After the prom she told me, 'Never again!' "

He was otherwise a confident boy. He was his mother's favorite; Bill imbibed self-assurance like mother's milk from Blanche's preferential treatment of him. She remarked years later, "I never knew my Bill to undertake anything where he didn't rise to the top."

Her favoritism was not lost on the other two children, however much she loved them. As Dorothy was to put it, "Bill was Mother's fair-haired boy. Mom was always bragging about his accomplishments. That bothered George. Later, Bill helped George with his business problems. And, down deep, that made George all the more resentful." Young George was a lovable boy, but he lacked Bill's swift intellect, his compulsive drive. Ironically, in the genetic crap shoot of life, it was George who inherited what young Bill wanted most— great natural prowess as an athlete.

Bill's inheritance from his father was different but decisive. His father's example taught young Bill that men work hard, take responsibility for themselves, and do not complain. In his father, Bill also had a male model who felt love but did not express it easily. The physical restraint was evident even in his father's discipline. Bill Casey was physically punished only once in his life: he had sassed his mother, and his father gave him a hard slap across the face. At the end of the day, the father took his son into his bedroom and, with eyes glistening, begged Bill to forgive him.

The Caseys were hardly rich. But wealth is relative to what one's neighbors have. The Depression had arrived and was deepening as Bill prepared to graduate from Baldwin High; yet his father was earning a considerable five thousand dollars a year in a fire-proof civil service job. As Dorothy put it, "I don't recall ever feeling the Depression. It never touched our family. Around 1933, I remember telling my father how much I hated the cold. And he went out and bought me a fur coat."

Still, young Bill did work. He held his first job at age nine, helping out at a nearby nursery, coming home covered with dirt from head to toe and carrying leftover lilies home to his mother. He picked vegetables at nearby farms, and he caddied during the summer at the Salisbury Club—fifty cents for eighteen holes, seventy-five cents if he carried a double. He fell in love with the game. And he was impressed by the confident air of the prosperous men who played golf. They were a breed apart from his father's Democratic clubhouse cronies, whose pastimes were softball and horseshoes.

Though Bill worked, he never had to; and he never worked during the school year, when his father wanted nothing to interfere with his children's education. A boy's chores in the Casey household were more a matter of character building than of economic necessity. There would later develop a myth about Casey the street-smart kid from the sidewalks of New York who pulled himself up by the bootstraps to achieve wealth and power. He would indeed acquire much wealth and wield great power; but he did not have to bend as far down as his bootstraps to pull himself up.

He was raised in a world buttressed by two religions, the Democratic party and the Catholic Church. The party had looked after the Caseys' daily existence, lifting the family from impoverished immigrants to solid, middle-class burghers; the Church took care of life everlasting. Bill Casey would never lose faith in the latter religion. The other he was to abandon with a vengeance.

On the night he graduated from Baldwin High, Mom and Dad had their friends and family over for a celebration. At one point, Bill senior drew his son into the kitchen alone. They made an odd, unlikely pair, one slightly built and sensitive of face, the other towering over him, gangly, his features raw and petulant. His father retraced the family saga: the passage over the Atlantic like cattle, the Caseys who had stayed behind and starved to death in Ireland. And when he finished, he said, "Your grandfather chased fires and ran a saloon. That's fine. And I've done all right, too—I'm a respected man in my profession. You can go farther, Bill. And I expect you to."

The route was to be a good Jesuit college one borough away, Fordham University in the Bronx. Bill would be the first Casey to go to college.

3.

In the Hands
of the Jesuits

A cynic might argue that Bill Casey was indoctrinated rather than educated at Fordham University. The study of philosophy, ordinarily thought to be an opening of the mind to differing systems of thought, was described in these words by a Fordham teacher and Jesuit priest during Casey's time:

> The main purpose of teaching philosophy is to defend the faith. However strongly we may insist on its cultural value, down in our hearts we know very well that our controlling motive is to implant those principles which we have received from a higher source than mere reason—to render our students immune from those infections of skepticism and materialism that are in the air we breathe.

Young Casey arrived at the Fordham campus on September 15, 1930, via the Third Avenue el, getting off at the Fordham Road stop in the Bronx. Other than that big-city touch, he might as well have been entering the most verdant, secluded New England campus. Fordham University offered a reprieve from the asphalt and concrete, the tenements and traffic of New York. One quick turn through the main gate on East Fordham Road and the city's din was left behind. Casey walked up a brick path that curved gently under the shade of tall oaks and elms to the administration building, a former manor house dating from the eighteenth century, when these grounds had been Fordham Manor. The other buildings were made of handsome gray fieldstone, appropriately ivy-clad. Dealy Hall, the main dormitory, had a crenellated roof, like a castle's, and windows in the shape of fleurs-de-lis. A tower rose from the college library, giving it the aspect of a Gothic cathedral. Even the gym, with its copper roof gone green, suggested a medieval fortress.

Casey was entering a school that had been founded not quite ninety years before to train priests. The lay college had originally been an annex tacked onto the seminary almost as an afterthought. But by Casey's time, Fordham had an enrollment of twelve hundred. It was a school for city boys, with day trippers outnumbering boarders by nearly two to one.

The entering freshmen were much like Casey, Irish Catholic. A random check of any Fordham yearbook of the era reveals close to 60 percent Irish surnames. The next-largest bloc was Italian, followed by a sprinkling of Germans, Poles, and other ethnics. There was a handful of Protestants but no blacks in Casey's class. They were nearly all lower-middle-class boys, the sons of cops, firemen, middle-range civil servants. Casey came from slightly more privileged circumstances. He started as a day student, though it was not a matter of money. Tuition and fees totaled $180 a year, well within his father's means. But the boarders, mostly boys from the small towns and rural areas of upstate New York, Pennsylvania, and Connecticut, were looked on as "apple-knockers." Bill Casey was a city boy, and so he spent over two hours a day that first year just getting to and from school. He planned to become a doctor and enrolled in the science department as a pre-med major.

The class of '34 was issued maroon beanies and matching ties, lopped off in the middle. They were given instructions for Hell Week, the period of freshman hazing: freshmen seeing an upperclassman approach were supposed to step into the gutter. A junior spotted Casey, without his beanie, striding down the middle of the road, and had started to gig him. Casey gave him a withering stare, said, "Why don't you grow up?" and walked off.

There were a few lay professors on the faculty, but the majority of teachers were Jesuits, as was the entire administration. Casey was entering a system of learning that had scarcely changed in the previous four hundred years, since Saint Ignatius of Loyola had created the Society of Jesus and set forth its *ratio studiorum*, the Jesuit plan of study. Besides the science courses expected of a budding physician, Casey, over the next four years, was expected to ingest a heavy diet of Greek, Latin, mathematics, philosophy, religion, ontology, ethics, and Catholic-style psychology. Electives at Fordham were few. Discipline was strict. In the classroom the teacher's rule was absolute. And Fordham students came to class dressed properly; if they came without a jacket and tie, they were tossed out.

Casey early favored the humanities over the sciences. He was drawn to the irresistible logic of Father Joseph Murphy, his philosophy and religion professor. Logic was the sharpest tool the Jesuits employed, and Father Murphy wielded it like a scalpel. He was a neat, fleshy man, with a smooth, full face, a dimpled chin, a primly set mouth, and wore rimless glasses. He had little humor and spoke in precisely chiseled phrases. It was a time when the teaching of evolution had unleashed an educational firestorm across the country, culminating in the Scopes "monkey trial." Casey, on a dare, asked Father Murphy, "Is it possible, Father, that the creation of the universe may have happened by chance?" Father Murphy strode to the blackboard, seized a piece of chalk, and began scribbling one equation after another, explaining over his shoulder as he chalked away. Down the blackboard he went, filling it with formulas that began to look like the theory of relativity. When he finished, he threw down the chalk, rubbed the dust from his hands, and said, "There you have the proof. Logic demonstrates beyond any possible doubt that chance could not produce creation."

Another Casey favorite was Father Ignatius Cox, his ethics teacher, steel-haired, hard-eyed, rich-voiced. Casey forever remembered Father Cox closing a lecture on courage: "God give us men who will not shrink from the battle . . . God give us men who will not flee the fray . . . God give us *men!*" In a lecture on poverty, Father Cox boomed, "So long as there is hunger in India, nakedness in China, ignorance in Africa, men will cry out, 'Peace! Peace!' " Then in a dramatic whisper he added, "But . . . there . . . will . . . be . . . no . . . peace!"

Sunday afternoons, Father Cox would go downtown to a Protestant church on Park Avenue and debate the redoubtable columnist of the New York *World Telegram* Harry Barnes. Monday mornings, he was back at Fordham regaling his classes with how he had demolished agnosticism with logic.

The Jesuits awed Casey. "They are brilliant," he wrote a friend. "I'm absolutely convinced that they have the right dope on this world."

There was another religion on the Fordham campus—football. The game seemed to displace the academic purpose of the college. Fordham football in that era was big-time; its "Seven Blocks of Granite" had already entered gridiron legend. Fordham played home games at the Polo Grounds and Yankee Stadium, drawing crowds of upwards of eighty thousand when it faced its archrival, New York University. The year before Casey entered Fordham, the Rams had gone undefeated. The players were demigods who seemed to float above ordinary mortals on the campus.

On the eve of his first Fordham-NYU game, his high school pal Ray Murphy begged Casey for a ticket. "If I give you my ticket, how the hell am *I* supposed to get in?" Casey asked. Then he had an inspiration. Murphy was a clarinet player; he could come up to Yankee Stadium the day of the game and walk in with the Fordham marching band. Murphy came to the stadium and met Casey outside, but as the band approached, he lost his nerve. An annoyed Casey shoved his ticket into Murphy's hand and said, "Gimme the goddamn clarinet!" He then joined the musicians and strode through the gate—holding the instrument upside down. Recalling the incident years later, Murphy remarked with lingering wonder, "Nothing ever seemed to faze Bill Casey."

Fordham also excelled in track. In 1930, Joe McClusky, the Fordham Flash, one year ahead of Casey, was about to set the intercollegiate record in the two-mile, and would make the U.S. Olympic team in 1932. To Casey, Joe McClusky walked around the Fordham campus in a nimbus of glory. Casey, long-legged and possessing endurance, if no great speed, figured that the two-mile was his distance too. A classmate who saw him pounding the Fordham oval along Southern Boulevard remembered, "He looked like Ichabod Crane in shorts."

Casey made the track team and ran in all the meets his freshman year. He once finished eleventh in a field of seventeen, his best performance of the season. The following year, deciding that he had less speed but more endurance than the two-mile required, he went out for cross-country. The main meet of the cross-country season was a six-mile race around Van Cortlandt Park. Casey trained for it for weeks, using the usual cross-country strategy—training at ten miles so that the six miles would seem short. What little flesh he had left melted during the exhausting weeks of conditioning.

The day of the Van Cordlandt Park race came. After the first mile, Casey felt that his lungs were going to explode. At three miles, the cramps in his calves were excruciating. At four miles, he thought he would have to drop out. But by mile five, a merciful numbness set in. He plowed on and crossed the finish line in an insensate fog. He had finished tenth in a field of twelve. Still, in the New York papers the next day, there was his picture, his face a tortured mask, a Fordham cross-country man.

He coolly looked over his running career and concluded that there was always going to be more sweat than glory, more cramps than prizes. He did not have it. By the end of his sophomore year, he decided to abandon college athletics. He began to explore the possibilities of rising in the Athletic Association, the student organization that set sports policy. Next to the jocks, the biggest men on campus were the association's officers.

A change was also in order in his studies. His biology teacher, Father Joseph Asmuth, was a bald, bearded German with an accent thick as *schlag*. Father Asmuth was a distinguished entomologist who had discovered seven new agents of disease. "Yeah," Casey cracked in biology class, "five of 'em in his beard." He had not minded dismantling and assembling Horizontal Charlie, the dummy Father Asmuth used in his anatomy lectures. But the first time Casey came into the lab and saw an eviscerated cat, a wave of nausea sent him reeling from the room. His medical aspirations, already weakened by mediocre grades, died on the spot.

Part of his academic problem was that he had decided to end the arduous commute from Bellmore to the Bronx. The prejudice that only apple-knockers lived on campus had proved wrong—the students having the best time were those living away from home. Casey had moved near the campus during his sophomore year and, to the detriment of his grades, was indeed having a good time.

The Jesuits seated the students alphabetically in every class. Consequently, Casey often found himself next to a fun-loving redhead named Cornelius Cassidy. "Red" Cassidy had already made something of a splash on campus as a high-stepping drum major and virtuoso baton twirler with the Fordham marching band. Casey also knew and liked Tom Buckley, an affable fellow Long Islander. With these two he rented an apartment at 2580 Bainbridge Avenue for forty-five dollars a month.

One more Irishman rounded out his circle of intimates: Eugene Duffy, handsome, with a profile like Scott Fitzgerald's, a serious lad, devout even by Fordham standards. Bill Casey had finally given up being an altar boy after high school, but Gene Duffy continued to get up well before eight o'clock classes to serve mass at Fordham's Our Lady of Mercy Church throughout college. The two of them became "Case-man" and "Duff-man," and the friendship was to last until Casey's death.

Prohibition was still the law of the land, which Casey and his fellow Gaels believed worked a particular hardship on them. But it was a hardship easily borne: bootleggers made direct deliveries to Fordham and were viewed as practitioners of an honorable profession.

Bill fell easily into the illicit boozing. On weekends, Casey, Cassidy, Duffy, and Buckley, along with a stream of other Fordhamites, headed for Barney Clark's speakeasy across from the Paradise Theater. The main attraction was an Irish-born bartender, Bernie O'Reilly. With his rimless glasses and quiet manner, O'Reilly suggested an English parson. But to these Irish-American youths, he was a hero, a veteran of the rebel Sinn Fein movement in the old country and an alumnus of British gaols.

After downing schooners of Owney Madden's etherized beer, they would head for one of the good Italian restaurants in neighboring Belmont. Afterward, they would call a meeting of the "Hell of a Feller's Club" at somebody's apartment, an excuse for consuming more bootleg beer, and vile gin concocted by students in the chemistry lab. Then it was a rollicking saunter home, down Fordham Road, singing IRA songs at the top of their lungs.

Casey kept pace with the best of them, writing to a friend: "I have acquired no mean proficiency at deriving inspiration from the bottle." By his junior year, the partying and boozing had not diminished. But Casey, unhappy with his grades, imposed a discipline on himself: from now on, the hell raising began only when his schoolwork was done. He finished the junior year with a 92 average and took the silver medal for academic distinction.

He also began giving Casey's Quarterly Cram Course. "It would start on a Friday night at the end of each quarter," Gene Duffy recalled. "There were certain subjects we all had to take—psychology, philosophy, ethics, religion. We'd gather in Bill's apartment. He'd get up in front of us and say, 'Philosophy II—here's all you gotta know.' Then he'd start rattling off the high points, *bing, bing, bing.* And we'd be scribbling as fast as we could. If you started to ask a question, he'd say, 'Shut up. Why are you asking me that? I'm giving you everything you're gonna need. We haven't got time to waste. Just pay attention.' He'd spend no more than fifteen minutes on each course. And, damn, if you *did* pay attention, you had it. You'd pass probably with an 85 or better. I was stunned by the clarity of his mind. He seemed to be able to brush aside anything that wasn't relevant and home in on exactly what the profs wanted. And he knew how to put it across to us in a few choice words. But he would brook no interference—you had to do it his way." Red Cassidy recalled, "Casey pulled half of us through Fordham with those seminars."

Casey joined the Fordham debate team. But his performance was peculiarly split. The debate coach was delighted, even astonished, by his logic, by his obvious talent for marshaling an argument—on paper. But his performance was poor. He would start out strongly; then his voice would tire, sink lower, and degrade into an incoherent mumble. During the drive back to Fordham after an abysmal showing against Boston College—a debate that Casey's side should have won on points but which he lost on articulation—the coach said, "Open your mouth. Let me take a look." Casey obeyed. The coach looked in, shook his head, and said, "Just as I thought—a thick palate."

He was a student at a time when American colleges were in political ferment, and nowhere more fervidly than in New York City. As the Depression deepened, as more people were thrown out of work, as the government seemed incapable of stemming the collapse, thousands of the young indicted capitalism. Students at City College of New York and New York University were turning to new gods, socialism and communism. Virtually none of this fervor penetrated Fordham University. There were no organizations of young Democrats or Republicans, much less the Young People's Socialist League. Malcolm Wilson, a year behind Casey and later to become New York's governor, remembered one attempt to bring politics to the Fordham campus. Joseph McCabe, a Fordham alumnus himself, was running for mayor of New York on the Recovery ticket against the organization Democrat, John F. O'Brien. Young Wilson sent out a letter on college stationery urging McCabe's election. He was summoned to the office of Fordham's president, who wanted to know "by what authority had I done such a thing," Wilson later recalled. "I was practically kicked out of school for working for political reform in the middle of the Depression."

Though at Fordham Casey was insulated from the radical passions roiling other campuses, he was absorbing another, older brand of politics. The Seabury Commission was then investigating the corrupt administration of Mayor Jimmy Walker. When Judge Samuel Seabury's investigators lifted a rock and the crooked pols underneath were exposed to the light, the intelligent thing for them to do was to retire and save their pensions. Occasionally Casey would stop by his father's office downtown and witness the game in progress. The gambit was known as "throwing down the papers." Sober, honest Bill Casey senior was the resident expert. As he explained it to his son, "Most of these lads aren't bad. They get a little careless, a little greedy. But they've put their time in with the city. They've got families. You don't just throw them out in the street. Bill, we never break the law, do we? And you must never. But sometimes we have to bend it a bit."

While students downtown were pulling strikes and staging marches, students at Fordham were attending meetings of the Sodality of the Blessed Virgin. Religion pervaded the campus almost as deeply as football. Every school year began with the entire student body turning out for the Solemn Mass of the Holy Ghost. Every morning in May, the month of Mary, classes were suspended promptly at eleven while the student body gathered in the little park where statues of the Sacred Heart and Our Lady stood. Each day, a junior or a senior was chosen to speak on one of the invocations in the Litany of Mary. When the honor fell to William J. Casey, he spoke on "Mary, Mother Most Pure."

The Jesuits' rational arguments in favor of Catholicism were critical in shaping Casey's outlook. He had come to college with the blind, untested faith of a child who has memorized his catechism. The Jesuits provided Casey with an intellectually respectable foundation for what he already took on faith. The Jesuits allowed him to bolster, with logic and reason, the memorized answers of the catechism, the rote beliefs of the Apostles' Creed. Yes, it often appeared that there were many sides to an argument; the danger lay in allowing this complexity to engulf you, in becoming confused by a wilderness of competing answers. The Jesuits proved to him that in the midst of seeming moral chaos, there was one everlasting, changeless truth— the Catholic Church. As his wife was later to observe, "Bill got his self-assurance from the Jesuits. They let him know who he was. And they made him comfortable with who he was."

Casey's roommate from Long Island, Tom Buckley, had a girlfriend in West Hempstead. Since Casey often went home on weekends, Buckley suggested, in the fall of their junior year, that they go out together to his girl's house. Loretta Kurz had sisters.

Casey was twenty years old, still backward with girls, an innocent, certainly a virgin. Occasionally, he had let the football players use his apartment to entertain their girlfriends while he was away. The ease of these fellows around good-looking girls was beyond him.

On the weekend of Buckley's invitation, Casey's father let him borrow the Model T for the drive out to West Hempstead. Casey was immediately taken by Loretta Kurz's infectious good humor. He felt completely at ease with this girl—a novel sensation for him. And then he met Sophia Kurz, Loretta's sister. The quick-tongued Casey of the Quarterly Cram Course became the thick-tongued Casey of the debate team in her presence. Sophia was then nineteen, the oldest of the eight Kurz children. She was petite, delicately featured, a beautiful young woman with a heart-shaped face, short hair, and an aura of serenity about her.

The Kurzes were also Catholic. The father was of German descent, but by blood Sophia Kurz was as Irish as Bill Casey—her mother had been a McCaddan. Her name was pronounced "Soph-eye-a," but to her family and friends she had been "Tootsie" since childhood.

The Kurzes were modestly but comfortably off; in spite of the

Depression, Sophia's father was doing reasonably well as a housing contractor. Sophia contributed to the family's support, working as a telephone operator, earning twenty dollars a week.

Casey became a regular at the Kurzes. It was a more innocent age, and their pleasures were simple. The young men played cards; the girls baked biscuits and cookies. At an appropriate hour, Father Kurz would take a big pitcher and disappear into the cellar; he would return with the pitcher brimming with homemade wine. Occasionally, the young people would put a record on the Victrola and dance to the singing of Russ Colombo and Bing Crosby.

For months Sophia regarded Bill merely as one of the gang. Then, one day he asked her to a Fordham dance. Over the next months they went out often, usually with others—to Long Island night spots, to hear the big bands at the Glen Island Casino or to the Roadside Inn in Valley Stream to catch the popular crooner Jack Leonard. Sophia would sip one ladylike glass of beer. Bill liked that. And the old aphorism "Love teaches even asses to dance" came true. Awkward Bill Casey began to look rather graceful on the dance floor.

Love did for Casey what no one—not even his mother, who had been a fashion buyer before her marriage—had ever been able to accomplish. He had gone through twenty years oblivious of his appearance, and usually looked as though he dressed in the dark. Sophia was astonished to have him appear on her doorstep one weekend in a derby and a velvet-collared chesterfield. The outfit had been the rage on the Fordham campus for a year. Now Bill Casey had discovered it.

He began writing to her. He was tentative in his first letter: "I've been thinking about the swell time I had Easter vacation. I really enjoy your company immensely. I have ideals covering every imaginable situation. But you are the only one I've actualized." Soon, however, an unexpected romantic streak emerged: "I'm not going to try to tell you what I think of you. For I know from experience that my vocabulary is pitifully inadequate for such a task. A further reason is that such an extravagant appraisal as I would find necessary to express myself would seem like empty flattery no matter how much sincerity underlay it." And for the first time, he signed a letter, "Love, Bill."

One night in Barney Clark's speakeasy, he dashed off a note to her on a napkin, apologizing for having gotten drunk in her presence the previous Saturday. He finished with, "No intoxication can compare with seeing your beauty with a clear eye."

Sophia was not swept off her feet. She had many young admirers, several more poised and certainly better-looking than William J. Casey. But she liked him well enough, and she was flattered by his attentions—the note on the napkin had been quite romantic, she thought. And, working most in his favor, she detected behind the ungainly façade deeper sentiments, a finer intelligence, a more substantial person than her other suitors.

Toward the end of his junior year, Casey launched another campaign along with the quest for Sophia's heart. He still hungered for the recognition on campus that had been denied him in athletics. He had been reconnoitering the Athletic Association—the AA—for over a year. The most prestigious student office at Fordham was not a class presidency, not even the presidency of the student body, but president of the AA. With his trusted pal Gene Duffy, Casey started to plot the route to AA power. The first task was to pick a realistic target. Edward A. Malloy had been president of Casey's class in the freshman, sophomore, and junior years. Now, in his senior year, popular Eddie Malloy was going to run for president of AA. The presidency was obviously foreclosed. But if president of AA was the most prestigious student office, then the vice-president was second—and the vice-presidency was wide open.

Casey and Duffy holed up in Casey's current apartment, a second-floor walk-up on 194th Street, and began to plan. The first hurdle was to get enough signatures on the nominating petition to put Casey on the ballot. Casey paced the room rather in the way he conducted the cram course, thinking out loud. "Who are the most influential guys on campus? The football players, right? Who's next? The track guys. Next? Basketball. Then the baseball team. Here's how we do it: I'll take the football and track guys. You take basketball and baseball. We get the biggest names we can to sign the petition first—the stars. Take a pen with you—with black ink. And tell them to sign big. Then we take the petitions to the other guys in the dorms and classes."

Casey won a place on the ballot for VP of the AA with three times the number of signatures required, a fact duly reported in the *Ram*, the student newspaper.

The week before the election, Duffy suggested that Casey was home free. "Nah," Casey said. "We've gotta hit the dorms again, and cover every gate for the day trippers."

He went downtown to see his father, who arranged a discount printing of a flyer with a printer who held a city contract: "Casey at Bat for AA VP. This Time a Home Run!" He collected IOUs from all the friends who had benefited from the cram course, enlisted old teammates from track, and recruited members of the debate club. By seven-thirty on the morning of class elections, Casey partisans were manning each of the five major entrances to the campus, handing out his flyer. Boarding students in Dealy Hall awoke to find the flyer slipped under their doors. Bill Casey was elected vice-president of the AA by a vote of 757 to 183.

For three years, he had sat with the unanointed at the annual Block F dinner, for which Fordham took over the grand ballroom of the Hotel Pennsylvania. He had watched the athletes troop up to the stage to be awarded the coveted maroon *F*. He had not watched with jealousy; he accepted that they came by their laurels fairly. But he had watched with envy. Now, as VP of the Athletic Association, he sat with the coaches and players in the place of honor. And he was awarded his *F* as vice-president. The athletes performed before cheering thousands, covering themselves with glory. But he learned through the AA that there were movers behind the scenes, privy to confidential matters, pulling the strings that influenced the lives of these more visible heroes. And he learned that unseen power had its subtle satisfactions.

After he had engineered his election to the AA, he confided an ambition to Duffy. He had just finished reading the memoirs of Colonel Edwin House, Woodrow Wilson's confidant and trouble-shooting ambassador-at-large. "That's what I want to be someday, Duff-man," he said, "a Colonel House, the guy behind the throne, advising the President of the United States."

His senior year was an idyll. He was a big man on campus. The schoolwork he could virtually do with his left hand. And he was in love with a beautiful girl who had not totally ruled out his prospects.

The romance ran the unsmooth course that true love is destined to follow. The previous summer he and Tootsie had wandered away from a beach party and stood on a hotel balcony watching the stars above and a shimmering pool below. She had allowed him an unrestrained kiss. "That was," he later wrote, "the golden moment of my life. I have tasted heaven."

Yet a casual word of hers could plunge him into despair. She answered his letters infrequently. In one response, she suggested that he ought to "develop broader interests." He spent tormented days deciphering the possible meaning of those three words. She had found someone else. She did not want him to be so possessive. His adoration had become a bore. He was an underdeveloped personality.

At one wild party he got drunk and began to curse like a dock walloper. Sophia Kurz was a deeply religious young woman; some friends suspected that her secret ambition was to become a nun. There was also in her, under the unwaveringly sweet disposition, a steely streak. She told Bill, "A fellow going to college ought to have a little better means of expressing himself than that kind of language." She left the party and went home alone.

She was an avid reader, with a taste for the romantics, Rostand, and the Rossettis. Occasionally, when Bill could scrape together the price of a ticket, they enjoyed the theater and the opera. Afterward, they would go to the Silver Grill in the Hotel Lexington and talk over what they had just seen. Sophia was intelligent, but she was a working girl, not a philosophy major; she did not always recognize the authors Bill quoted, or understand the latest syllogism picked up from Father Murphy, or keep up with the torrent of ideas tumbling from Bill's mind. If he had been drinking, he might berate her. Afterward, he would be mortified by what he had said and torture himself with remorse. After one such occasion, he wrote, "Whenever I have the slightest disagreement with you, Toots, I'm utterly miserable for days."

Nevertheless, he had found someone with whom he felt comfortable confiding the deepest longings of his spirit, thoughts he could never have shared with anyone else, certainly not his college pals. He could bare his soul to her. As the end of his days at Fordham approached, he wrote her what amounted to a state-of-his-spirit message. He had been sitting in Father Beglan's class, trying to stay awake during a stupefying lecture on cosmology. He began to write Sophia:

Spring makes me dislike that word "material" and all that it stands for. I resent being confined by the narrow boundaries of the material realities of our mundane sphere. I much prefer to roam in the boundless areas of the ideal, unhampered and unchecked by hard realities and too often bitter actualities. What I seek answers the description of heaven advanced by our Catholic theologians— unlimited space, unlimited freedom and unlimited possibilities, all perfection and no imperfections or obstacles. That is where mere thinking has it over heaven, because the presence of obstacles adds to the fun of striving and their defeat adds to the enjoyment of an ultimate victory. In one's thoughts, no obstacle is too difficult to hurdle.

I suppose to ramble on like this lays one open to the charge of being a dreamer and an idealist. Well, I'm willing to expose myself to such a charge and to admit its validity, with some reservations. I maintain with many other eminent men that one who lives entirely on a practical plane is not deriving the most out of life. I don't see how we can afford to miss any little pleasure to be gotten or even to be squeezed out of a drop of existence. I'll admit that I'm not entirely impervious to the natural human craving for power and wealth, nor am I entirely oblivious of the necessity for securing and utilizing some of the world's goods. But I am sure that a relentless struggle for power and position would be unbearable and even maddening if it were not tempered and softened by friendship, quiet talks, dreaming and soliloquizing.

In the spring of Bill's senior year Fordham staged a symposium on social justice. The purpose was to show the students that the Church was alert to the suffering abroad in the land and to make clear that there was a Catholic alternative to communism. On Friday night, Casey went to Collins Hall to hear the most learned Jesuits, Catholic lay leaders, economists, social scientists, and captains of industry take the Reds head-on in a panel discussion: "Communism: A Contradiction of Liberty and Natural Law." The next morning he attended a panel called "Property Rights: A Corollary of Liberty and Natural Law." That afternoon, the topic was "Economic Liberalism: A Perversion of Natural Law." And that night he heard satisfying answers during a panel entitled "Can a Thinking Man Be a Catholic?" He came away filled with gratitude at his good fortune in being born in the true faith. The symposium stoked a growing desire to devote his life, not to material gain, but to alleviating human suffering.

On the afternoon of June 13, 1934, a sunny Wednesday, the voices of the Fordham Glee Club floated over the quad in front of the physics building:

> Thy winding elms, thy hallowed halls,
> Thy lawns, thy ivy-mantled walls—
> O Fordham, alma mater,
> What memories each recalls.

All the Caseys were there. Bill senior pointed out to his wife the asterisk alongside their son's name in the list of graduates. William J. Casey, Jr., was graduating cum laude, and he had never mentioned it to anyone.

The Jesuits had done their work well. He knew what was false and what was true, what was right and what was wrong, what was within the reach of logic and what had to remain within the realm of faith. He was armored in his religion.

And thanks to a notice he had just seen on a bulletin board, he now knew what he wanted to do. Catholic University of America in Washington, D.C., was launching a new two-year School of Social Work. Qualified college graduates were invited to apply for admission and for a fellowship worth two hundred dollars per annum. Not only would the Catholic University program serve his idealism: it satisfied his practical streak, too. As Casey analyzed it, virtually the only growth industry in the midst of a depression was poverty. Where would a 1934 college graduate more likely find a professional position in these hard times? It was a cold world beyond Fordham Road in 1934. Shortly before graduation, a friend of Casey's, who had himself been a big man on campus two years before, came to him looking for his help. His friend wanted to know if Casey could use his father's influence to get him an audience with the Bronx clubhouse. Afterward, he wrote to Sophia, "I waited outside for an hour while this honor graduate of Fordham talked to a bunch of petty politicians. And he came out with a job pumping gas!"

And so he applied for the Catholic University fellowship. Two weeks before graduation, he was accepted.

Red Cassidy warned him, "Bill, with your brains, you're crazy. A school of social welfare? The highest-paid welfare official in the country is Warden [Lewis Edward] Lawes up at Sing Sing Prison—and he's lucky if he's making ten grand a year. Go to law school. You could earn that much on one case."

"I can't do it, Red," Casey told his friend. "The old man's not well. I couldn't put the financial strain of law school on him." Besides, he was not interested in piling up bucks for bucks' sake. Bill Casey had decided what he wanted: "I want to devote my life to remedying the crying injustices of our blind economic system." He was going to be a social worker.

4.

The Unmaking of
an Idealist

B ill Casey arrived in Washington full of the idealism and
the certitudes of youth. He would leave not much older
but far warier.

He kissed Sophia goodbye at a Manhattan bus station on September 24, 1934, and, at midnight, boarded the Nevin Line bus for
Washington, and Catholic University's School of Social Work.

He would live at the National Training School, an institution for
juvenile delinquents convicted of federal offenses. The dean of the
school, Father Joseph O'Grady, believed that his students should live
with those whom they were eventually going to have to help. Casey
wrote in his first letter home, "I am hob-nobbing with a bunch of
young Dillingers."

But NTS was no ordinary juvenile prison. It was an early New Deal
social experiment, an attempt to steer boys from a life of crime
through enlightened rehabilitation. The school grounds covered acres
of lush farmland and woodland. The boys lived in comfortable cot-
tages. As Casey described NTS, "It's like being away at boarding
school. They have academic classrooms, industrial classrooms, agricultural classrooms, athletic teams, debate club, dramatics, the
works."

Bill Casey had been raised in a white world among white friends,
white neighbors, white classmates, white teammates; blacks were
people he saw on the Third Avenue el. On the bus ride to Washington,
passing through New Jersey and Maryland in the middle of the night,
he had struck up a conversation with a black across the aisle. The
man, he was astonished to learn, taught mathematics at a North
Carolina high school and was headed home after spending the summer working on his master's degree at Columbia University. Of this
encounter, Casey wrote Sophia: "His undoubted and unaffected cul-

ture and sincerity broke down my racial prejudices. I do try to keep that to a minimum. But I doubt if any of us are entirely free of it. I made the startling discovery that it is not necessary to be white to be happy."

His newfound tolerance, however, underwent an immediate test. One of the comforts of life at NTS was that inmates were assigned to clean the rooms of the social-work students. Casey was watching his money carefully, hoping to get a weekend home with Sophia. Just before he was to leave, he went to his room and discovered that "one of those Negro candidates for the electric chair swiped my wallet containing my driver's license and $21. I am mad enough to take that African and tear him to pieces. There goes my trip home." The language falls with a special harshness on the contemporary ear. But a half-century ago, bigotry was voiced more openly, with little risk of disapproval. Casey was exhibiting the attitudes of a class and a time as much as of an individual.

From the beginning, tremors of discontent began to assail him at CU. He had been looking forward to weighty courses—economics, industrial relations, statistics, criminology. Instead, they were feeding him physical hygiene, mental hygiene, social-work techniques— "sissy stuff," as he described it. The very name "school of social work," he wrote a friend, "gives me the willies." When he went home on weekends, particuarly if he ran into Fordham buddies, he told them, "I'm doing graduate work in sociology in Washington."

He was nevertheless as quick as ever at sponging up the course work, and soon he was Father O'Grady's favorite, a student on whose future the priest set great store. Casey was elected class president, as he put it, "through techniques I learned in that cradle of Tammany Hall, Fordham University."

The habits of self-discipline begun during his junior year at Fordham now ruled him, became virtually reflexive. He rationed his time as though a stopwatch ticked in his head. Minutes waiting for his roommate to get out of the bathroom, minutes on a bus ride, minutes between classes added up to hours—productive hours if he used them, hours forever lost if he wasted them. He did not waste them. The sports fanatic of yesterday was now saying of the 1934 World Series: "I can't see spending three hours in front of a radio when a newspaper will supply all the salient information in fifteen minutes."

The college-era boozing fell off abruptly, as though it had no more place in his present life than the pranks of Hell Week. He was never again to be more than a social drinker.

Until now, save for family vacations, he had known little of the world outside New York, and nothing at all of other cities. At Catholic University, he began to explore the city that would provide the stage for so many of the future dramas of his life. He liked to hitchhike down Bladensburg Road to the Capitol. A favorite perch was the visitors' gallery in the House or the Senate, where he would watch the debates. The legislators, so various in origin, accent, style, and character, presented a crosscut of America. He wrote home: "I like the composition of society here. I do believe in class distinction to an extent. But I do object to its being based on wealth and wealth alone. Here is an aristocracy of real distinction consisting of persons of real intellectual, cultural attainments and not vapid scions of wealthy families."

What he enjoyed most was entering the hushed chambers of the U.S. Supreme Court, to sit quietly and listen to the arguments before the robed justices. "Justices [Charles Evans] Hughes and [Louis] Brandeis have magnificent minds," he wrote Sophia. "It strikes me that their dignity, distinction and opportunity for public service are far more desirable than the millions of a Rockefeller or a Morgan."

What he saw on the streets of the nation's capital pleased him less. "I had a few illusions go up in smoke," he wrote. "I pictured Washington as composed of splendid white structures and rolling lawns plus a few Japanese cherry trees. Never thought of all the negroes, tenements and gin mills."

The worst part of Catholic University for Bill Casey was being away from New York, being separated from Sophia. Whenever a classmate or teacher was going up to New York, he begged him to bring back the *New York Times*. Yes, Washington had the Congress, the Supreme Court, the White House. But New York was civilization. "How wonderful it would be," he wrote Sophia, "sitting across from you at the Silver Grill exchanging our opinions of *Rigoletto*."

They had made a pledge when he left. Every night at nine p.m., no matter what else they might be doing, they were to pause and say a prayer for each other. Just before nine, Bill would temporarily close his books and begin strolling the grounds of NTS, "thinking of you, my eyes lifted toward the sky and a look of exaltation on my face. I find I can pray much more intelligently, with more feeling, with the stars shouting to the human mind the story of creation."

He was the more faithful correspondent. He complained bitterly that he had counted her last letter and "there were only 117 words!" He went with friends to see *The Barretts of Wimpole Street* and was inspired to attempt poetry. He wrote:

> I see thy smiling, radiant face,
> Thy trilling, thrilling voice I hear,
> and happier scenes and hours retrace,
> too fleeting, but how dear.

In his next letter, he told her he was embarrassed by his audacity and retreated to prose in likely the most eloquent letter he ever wrote her:

> I have decided that since I couldn't possibly do justice to sweetness and goodness so ethereal and ineffable, I could only outrage it by my feeble attempts. The spirit is there, but I fear poverty of expression will, for the duration of this life at least, smother the flame of devotion which burns so intensely within me. I can only hope that the mute adoration of eyes and demeanor convey more than language. They cannot do less. Would that the hand of the creator had touched me with the lyric genius of a Browning or a Byron with which to sing and shout your glory. But will you not understand something beyond expression—even beyond the god-like expression of a Keats, a Shelley. I live in hope that when we rise above this sphere of human limitation, we will all be poets.

He went to the movies as often as his straitened circumstances permitted. The Catholic Church had recently launched the Legion of Decency, a form of voluntary movie censorship for the flock. Casey wrote a former classmate: "I am glad for the Legion of Decency not so much for cleansing the films, although that is a boon, but for elevating the artistic standards of the movie moguls. They used to figure that a liberal supply of smutty cracks plus a bedroom scene or two was all the public wanted. They neglected the dramatic qualities of their productions. I figured the indecency would not influence me. Although I did consider it an insult to my mental maturity." A bit of a critic, a bit of a prude.

As he started his second semester at Catholic University, his doubts deepened. He was beginning to detect distinctions among the poor. In February of 1935 a heavy snowstorm paralyzed Washington. He wrote home, "We had a hard time getting the unemployed to clean the streets. They couldn't see why they should shovel snow for sustenance when the government doles out sustenance to them anyway. Some of these negroes of a certain attitude won't ever work again."

He now believed that there were two kinds of poor, the deserving and the undeserving: those who were poor as a result of circumstances beyond their control—true victims of the Depression—and those who were poor out of failings of character. He tried not to let this conviction shake his commitment. He told Tom Buckley, "I can still stand Catholic University because I know at least I'm still better off than the guys trying to make it in the business world. Look what they're going through in this depressed economy. At least, in my field, I'm trying to get at the roots of the problem." It struck some of his friends that the person he was trying most to persuade was himself.

Still, his outrage at the suffering he saw around him was authentic. He wandered through Hoovervilles, the tar-paper and tin-roof shanty towns scarring the edge of America's capital. And he wrote home:

> A social or economic system that permits such conditions is positively immoral and indefensible, if one accepts our religion which places the purpose of life in a reward after death to be gained by the practice of virtue in this life. Communism, socialism, fascism and the other isms offer still worse evils and no hope. All the constructive measures that have ever been offered are contained and systematized in the encyclicals of Leo XIII and Pius XI. I'm no utopian. The lazy, the shiftless, the alcoholics are always with us. Original sin and fallible human nature are realities. But certainly there is enough to make everybody desirous of work happy by giving them what they want—a job.

And so he tried to stick to his calling. He also wrote home to his father that he still intended to enroll as a Democrat.

He was increasingly unhappy at Catholic University. He missed Sophia. He missed home. The prospect of another year of courses like "Social Agency Organization" depressed him. He began cutting classes and overstaying his weekends in New York. In one respect, however, his earlier appraisal of social work proved dead right: there were plenty of jobs for trained social workers. On one trip to New York, he found out that the city's Department of Welfare would hire him as a "home relief invesigator."

He mustered his courage and went in to see Father O'Grady and confessed that he would not be back for the second year. O'Grady admitted that he was disappointed, but added, "I understand, William. You do lack the illusions necessary for this kind of work." Casey went home and took the job with the New York City Welfare Department.

A home relief investigator was a welfare cop. Casey's job was to audit armfuls of welfare case files to see if the case worker had properly determined eligibility and benefits. He had to become expert at knowing how much a family of four should be allowed for rent and what an old woman living alone rated for food. He was expected to make spot checks of the homes of people on relief. It meant poking his nose into the personal lives of the aged, the sick, and the destitute. It meant going into urine-stinking slums and finding drunks, wife beaters, child molesters, and idlers living off the taxpayers. It meant searching out who was hiding sources of income.

And he hated every minute of it.

He invited Sophia to join him for lunch at the field office where he worked in Brooklyn. She arrived to find pickets parading in front. Casey was a tough but fair-minded investigator. If an application was legitimate, he approved it. If people were incorrectly paid too little, he upped the benefit; if they were paid too much, he cut it. If they were frauds, he threw them off the rolls. The marchers, Sophia discovered, were picketing against William J. Casey.

Over lunch at an Italian restaurant, he confessed his unhappiness. The job was bureaucratic, routinized, uncreative. It was dulling his social conscience instead of satisfying it. He was embarrassed prying into kitchens, toilets, and piggy banks. "This is women's work," he told her. He had made a career blunder, he admitted. But what was he to do? You did not walk out of civil service jobs in the America of 1935.

He had a plan, and he confided it to Sophia. Of all the professionals he had observed thus far, none had impressed him more than the lawyers and judges he witnessed at the Supreme Court. He enjoyed the combat of competing logic, the way smart lawyers marshaled evidence to make their arguments. He admired the profound learning the justices brought to the tangled issues before them. The law's use of logic and rhetoric were jesuitical. Red Cassidy had been right— he should have become a lawyer. It was not too late.

He applied to Saint John's Law School in Brooklyn. Saint John's was close to Bellmore, and it offered a three-year course compared with Fordham's four. He could save money by living at home. And if he was willing to work like a dog, he could go to Saint John's at night and still continue full-time at the Welfare Department. He began his classes in September of 1935.

Bill Casey senior died that October at age fifty-two. He always had been a frail man, and his heart had finally given out. The pension expert's death was reported in the obituary columns of the *New York Times* and every other New York daily.

He had been the breadwinner. Now he was gone. The responsibility now fell to his elder son. At first it seemed the death of Bill's hopes as well. He would probably have to leave Saint John's and spend the rest of his life at the Welfare Department. He thought hard. His sister, Dorothy, was working as a nurse. His brother, George, a high-school senior, could probably win an athletic scholarship to college. By pinching every penny, Bill could still support his mother, give George some help, and put enough away for his law school tuition. He was not turning back.

It would be unfair to say that Bill Casey's social conscience died with his father's death. His idealism had already been badly battered at Catholic University. The exposure to the bureaucratized charity of the Welfare Department had soured him further. His firsthand contact with the hard-core poor, what he considered the undeserving poor, the cheats and loafers, had disillusioned him. Too much of what he had seen of Roosevelt's New Deal struck him as promoting parasitism. And now fate had intervened to reorder his priorities. At this point, charity had to begin at home. His aim now was to get through law school and start earning serious money. He was twenty-two years old, the man of the house, the new breadwinner.

He had loved his father, that quiet, unassuming, modest, admirable man. But he confided to Red Cassidy soon after the funeral what he regarded as a miscalculation in his father's life: "My old man worked hard enough so that he should have gone farther. But he always hid his light under a bushel. You won't catch me doing that."

Saint John's was not Fordham, an education-cum-party; it was hard work. He also had his full-time case load with the department. He managed both by virtually chiseling in stone for all time two salient work habits: he absorbed great masses of information in furious bursts of concentration, and he never wasted time. By going to school summers and overloading his schedule, he finished the three-year course in two years. He graduated in September of 1937, and one month later he was admitted to the bar. In no résumé that Casey prepared during the rest of his life were his days as a social worker ever mentioned.

5.

The Research Institute of America: A Graduate Education

Life was good for Leo Cherne. Not yet twenty-six years old, he had discovered an enterprise that thrived on hard times. Born Leopold Chernetsky, son of a Jewish socialist printer who fled Russia for anticzarist activities, young Leo had initially hoped to become a journalist; but a family friend, Judge Albert Cohn (the father of Roy Cohn), persuaded Leo that there were few jobs available for reporters in the Depression and that a legal career would be more promising. Cherne graduated first in his class from New York Law School. But he hated the path he had chosen; and his unhappiness grew when he began clerking at a firm and realized how far he had strayed from his youthful ideals: one of the firm's clients was Lucky Luciano.

He soon met the publishing entrepreneur Carl Hovgard. Hovgard had an idea. Businessmen all over the country were bewildered by the blizzard of New Deal legislation—Social Security, unemployment compensation, new disability laws. Hovgard asked Cherne to try his hand at a reference book to help businessmen thread their way through this maze.

The book succeeded. In 1936 the two men founded, with Hovgard as the owner-publisher and Cherne as the chief executive, what would ultimately be called the Research Institute of America. And businessmen lined up for their newsletters. The firm prospered. Its ads for bright young attorneys frequently appeared in the classified section of the *New York Law Journal*. Among those responding in April of 1938 was a recent graduate of Saint John's Law School.

Years later, Cherne recalled that first encounter with Bill Casey. "He was at that time still very much a Long Island boy. New York seemed not to have touched him, except for his speech, which was rapid and poorly articulated.* He was tall and thin, stooped, and dressed with not the slightest evidence of care. We were then hiring lawyers from fifteen to twenty-five dollars a week. I detected intelligence and confidence underneath the less than overwhelming presence. We were shorthanded. I offered him twenty dollars. One newsletter we published was the *Federal Tax Coordinator*. Casey had no background in taxation, but I threw him in to sink or swim. Not long afterward, I was in the hospital recovering from appendicitis. Three of our secretaries came to see me. They said they couldn't work for Mr. Casey. We used Ediphone disks for dictation in those days. And they said they dreaded putting on the earphones for Casey's work—they couldn't understand a thing. So I suggested he start doing his drafts in longhand.

"Well, an extraordinary thing happened. He revealed one of the clearest pens I've ever read. You could give Casey an impenetrable piece of federal law and he could reduce it to a paragraph or two that any meagerly educated factory manager in Akron could understand. Not only did Bill have the gift of synthesis, he had an instinct for the intent of a law. He could strike at the heart of it and identify those minimal actions that an employer could take to comply. He soon soared ahead of our other people. He outworked everybody. We raised him to thirty dollars a week.

"I enjoyed him. Bill had a roving, curious mind—possibly the most widely read person I've ever known. Yet his mind presented a peculiar blend of inquisitiveness and orthodoxy. He absorbed new information and new ideas like a sponge. Yet he clung to the moral prejudices of a middle-class Irish Catholic. We would have lunch and talk about anything and everything. But he was an embarrassment in a restaurant. There he'd be, expressing brilliant thoughts through a mouthful of food. He personified a Yiddish expression of my youth—a *graubyon*, a coarse young fellow."

Casey seemed to be born free of exaggerated reverence for presumed expertise. He was spared the overestimation of the difficulty of things unknown that so often cripples novices. As he later put it, "At the Research Institute of America, I was digesting, analyzing, synthe-

---

*New York was never to leave Casey's speech. "Years" was "yihz." "Saw" was "sore." "Florida" was "Flahrida." "War" was "waw." "Washington" was "Wash'nun." "Certain" was "sittin."

sizing complicated laws. They're written by guys like you and me. Not by geniuses. They're not handed down from Mount Sinai. One fallible human being is doing the drafting. Another fallible human being is doing the interpreting. There was nothing God-like to me about a piece of legislation. Interpretation was everything. And I interpreted them in the best interests of our business subscribers."

Like any bright, questing youth, he had searched for meaning in his life. Earlier, he thought he had found his purpose in spiritual fulfillment: "I much prefer to roam in the boundless areas of the ideal, unhampered and unchecked by hard realities." The collision with reality since he had written those words as a student left him philosophically adrift. But in his new job he discovered a new self. Practical, intellectual problem-solving replaced his earlier milky abstractions. By age twenty-five, he had abandoned philosophic musing. A pragmatist was born.

The Research Institute of America was more than a business. Leo Cherne described it as "a cross between a seminar and a college fraternity bull session." On the staff were Republicans and Democrats, conservatives and socialists, interventionists and isolationists. At the end of the day, in front of a great stone fireplace in the office, battles royal waged, debates that caught in microcosm the issues of the 1930s. The hottest topic was the Spanish Civil War. The American Left cheered the Loyalist republican government and admired the Soviet Union for supporting that side. The Right favored General Franco and his Phalangists, pro-Catholic, anticommunist, though undeniably fascist. Both sides were represented at the Institute.

Casey was drawn to the flames of this combat. His position reveals in embryo the political religion that was to guide him throughout his life. As Leo Cherne remembered: "I opposed Franco for his assault on a fragile Spanish democracy, for allowing Hitler and Mussolini to help crush his enemies, and for letting himself be used so they could test their war machines on his own people. Later, I became less supportive when it became clear the Soviet Union was exploiting the other side. But Bill, from the beginning, was to the right of Attila the Hun. He was one hundred percent for Franco and one hundred percent against the Loyalists. To understand this, you had to understand his Catholicism."

Casey saw the issue with jesuitical logic. The Loyalists were being aided by the Soviet Union; the Soviet Union was communist: communists were atheists, murderers of priests, desecrators of churches. General Franco was pro-Church and anticommunist. The Spanish Civil War thus pitted atheism against religion, communism against

Catholicism, God against the Antichrist. That, to Casey, was an easy choice.

"Our fights were violent shouting matches," Cherne remembered. "I saw certain of Casey's habits surface early. He did not suffer fools gladly. He would dismiss the arguments of weak adversaries with that contemptuous back-of-the-hand wave. He might get furious at able opponents, absolutely apoplectic. But I noticed, no matter how enraged he became, he listened and he tried to rebut them. He did not simply block them out. He never closed his ears."

Cherne noticed something else about Casey. He could curse and bellow at Cherne in the evening, yet amble into his office the next morning with a new idea for the newsletter. The slate was wiped clean.

The two men were studies in contrast. Cherne, small, finely made, mustachioed, dapper, speaking in beautifully articulated phrases; Casey, gawky, stooped, untidy, his speech tumbling forth. Cherne was also a bit of a renaissance man, an aesthete, an artist, a sculptor, a singer possessed of a silvery voice good enough for the Metropolitan Opera. Casey had fancied himself something of a student of the arts, but Cherne was out of his league. "Never in his life," Cherne recalled, "did Bill discuss with me a play, an opera, a novel, a work of art." Yet the chemistry worked. The friendship deepened. When Cherne's first child, Gail, was born in 1939, the man he chose as the child's godfather was Bill Casey.

Casey tried to stay true to the party of his father, to the party that had made the Caseys. But he grew increasingly leery of Franklin Roosevelt's New Deal. He told friends, "I believed in distributive justice when I was at Catholic University." Distributive justice: new economic jargon for a romantic old notion, take from the rich and give to the poor—Robin Hood. But what Casey thought he was seeing was: take from the toiler and give to the idler. He remembered sitting in the Kurzes' kitchen talking to Sophia's parents, hard-working, self-made people like the Caseys, and hearing Mrs. Kurz say, "I think from now on we're all going to have to be Republicans." By the time of the 1940 election, Casey had made the switch.

Daniel Patrick Moynihan, as much social scientist as United States senator, and who would later battle with Casey over the CIA, commented on the young Casey's political odyssey: "When I wrote *Beyond the Melting Pot* with Nathan Glaser, I looked up the children of great Brooklyn Democratic leaders. What were they doing in the 1956 election? They were up in Westport, Connecticut, canvassing for Eisenhower. This had more to do with economic than political succession.

As people in this country move from the working class to the middle class, they begin to feel more comfortable in the party of the middle class. This was particularly true of American Catholics in the twenties and thirties. They failed to develop an intellectual class to guide them through the intricacies of contemporary public issues. The New Deal and its solutions were very hard for them to understand, even when they were voting for Roosevelt. Casey is a product of that history. There is nothing aberrational about his politics. Casey's emergence as a conservative Republican was a perfectly natural political progression."

Casey's initial favorite in 1940 was the freshest face on the Republican scene, the racket-busting New York County district attorney, Tom Dewey. Exactly what Casey did in that campaign is not clear. The waters are muddied by his own claims. Newspaper profiles of Casey written years later would report that he had been a delegate to the Republican National Convention in Philadelphia. Not so, though Casey never said anything to correct the record.

One of Dewey's financial advisers, John Burton, had heard about a bright young fellow at the Research Institute of America and arranged to meet him. Burton was impressed. Bill Casey was full of statistics that proved the failure of the New Deal. He was full of ideas for putting a sick American economy back on its feet, not through socialist fantasies, he said, but by restarting the stalled engine of the free market. Burton passed the ideas to Dewey, along with advice from a dozen other sources. The Burton experience emerges in Casey's résumés as "tax and fiscal advisor to presidential candidate Thomas E. Dewey in the 1940 campaign." It was true and it was not true. He had given advice on tax and fiscal matters that found its way to the Dewey camp; ergo, he could be called a "Dewey adviser." If he had become expert at anything, it was learning what he could say and still remain technically within the bounds of truth.

That summer of 1940, Gene Duffy got a call from Casey. They were still seeing a good deal of each other since Fordham, and Duffy always looked forward to hearing from Casey, never knowing what it might lead to. "Duff-man," Casey said, "pack your bags. We're going to the Republican convention." "As what?" Duffy wanted to know. He reminded Casey that he had no particular credentials; also, he had a job. That did not matter, Casey said. Duffy would go as his associate. And what was Casey going as? "To represent educational interests on Long Island."

There was a sliver of truth in his claim, since, through his mother's long service to the PTA, he had become the attorney for the Bellmore

Board of Education. Casey and Duffy arrived in Philadelphia just in time to see Dewey defeated for the Republican nomination by Wendell Willkie. Casey was undaunted. He went back to New York, made himself known to the Willkie people in the state Republican organization, and began promoting the same tax and economic prescriptions he had offered to Dewey. He went further. He submitted proposed language for Willkie's speeches incorporating his ideas. Thereafter, he described himself in his curriculum vitae as "Willkie speechwriter in the 1940 presidential campaign."

Unknown to Leo Cherne, Casey had another professional life. While still at Saint John's he had occasionally picked up a few bucks on weekends by parking cars at Jones Beach. There he met another budding lawyer, Jerome H. Doran. After law school, before going to work for the Research Institute of America, Casey had teamed up with Jerry Doran and two other lawyers to found the firm of Backer, Casey, Doran and Siegel, specializing in labor law. Casey carried out his law practice nights, weekends, and holidays. His high-school friend Ray Murphy recalled, "Any time any of us had a legal problem, we went to old Case. And he wouldn't take a dime from a friend. He'd wave you away and say, 'Aaah, don't worry about it.' "

Casey's failure to tell Cherne that he was practicing law had nothing to do with ethics. It was simply, as Cherne later concluded, that "Bill Casey was a remarkably private man. As close as I liked to think we were, in fifty years of friendship he never confided a single personal matter to me. We talked constantly, but never about him."

Back in the spring of 1939, Cherne had invited Casey to lunch at a French bistro around the corner from the office. The Institute had arrived at the right place at the right time, with the right product. Now a new opportunity was looming. "Bill," Cherne said, "before this year is out, we're going to have a war in Europe. How long before the United States gets involved is problematical. This is an enormous challenge. How do you take a country like ours, stuck in a depression, and convert it into an arsenal? How do you shift our industrial plant from Chevys to tanks, from washing machines to bombers? Who gets the steel? Who gets the aluminum? The manganese? The manpower? This is an opportunity for the Institute. I want to start putting together a book, a counterpart to what we put out for coping with the New Deal. But the military people I've been dealing with down in Washington, the Army and Navy munitions boards, just aren't up to it. I want you to start pulling this thing together."

Casey leaped to the assignment. He and Cherne spent months on the project; and in one furious six-day burst, working RIA's secretaries in relays around the clock, they produced the first edition of a thick, squat volume, *The Business and Defense Coordinator*. They finished on September 1, 1939, the day war broke out in Europe.

The preface suggested Casey's research style:

> The cost of killing one enemy soldier was 75 cents for Julius Caesar; during the 17th century, the cost of killing a man in the Thirty Years' War had risen to $50; the mortality expense of the American Civil War was $5,000 a man; the vast change effected by the World War can be realized from the fact that it cost $25,000 to kill one man then; and in the current era it is already roughly estimated at over $50,000. All this is a result of the fact that war has become a conflict of economics in which financial and material resources are the chief weapons.

The volume quickly jumped from the historic-esoteric into bread-and-butter intelligence for businessmen. Chapters were entitled "How to Sell to the Army," "Government Construction Opportunities," "Selling the Military Horses and Mules," "What the Medical Corps Buys."

He and Cherne predicted in the Institute's newsletter in the fall of 1941, "The United States is unlikely to get involved in the war in Europe until a triggering event occurs in the Pacific." The *Saturday Evening Post* did a disparaging story on what it called "the rover boys at RIA." The *Post*'s story came out on December 2. Pearl Harbor was bombed five days later. The Institute's reputation soared.

Casey's own success at the Institute finally freed him to fulfill the secret longing of his heart. By 1941, he had been in love with Sophia Kurz for seven years. The romance had begun in white heat, as his letters to her testify. After he came home to New York, the ardor did not cool, but the time to express it shrank as he was swallowed up in his ambitions.

It had become an odd courtship. They had never, in the phrase of that era, gone steady. Sophia occasionally dated other men. As she later described the relationship, "Bill would call me up during the week—'Do you want to catch a movie, have some dinner?' He probably hadn't thought about me all week. We'd go out maybe on a Friday or Saturday. Mostly, he'd talk about his job. I might not see him again for a couple of weeks. We were never engaged. He never gave me a ring. We never talked about marriage. On holidays, we'd alternate going to each other's families. He was just always there. He was like my cousin."

Then, toward the end of 1940, he simply said to Sophia, "Toots, I think we ought to get married." She agreed.

"If you want to understand Casey in love," his friend Red Cassidy later observed, "you have to know the Irish. Bill had become the head of the family. He was responsible for his mother, for helping his brother, George, get through college. He was afraid of working himself into an economic trap. He wanted the security that comes with the bucks." By any comparative standard, Bill Casey had little reason to feel insecure. Between the raises at the Institute and his law practice, he was earning $10,000 in 1940, when the median income of an American family was $1,231.

Bill and Sophia were married on George Washington's birthday, February 22, 1941. George Casey was best man. The wedding pictures show a steady physical change taking place in Bill. The once raw, angled face had begun to fill out. The hairline was starting to retreat. He wore glasses now. After a wedding breakfast at the fashionable Garden City Hotel on Long Island, Casey took his bride on a three-week honeymoon cruise to Havana and ports of call in the Caribbean. None of his friends had done anything so grand. Red Cassidy accompanied the newlyweds to the pier to see them off and asked, "Jesus, Bill, how the hell did you pull it off?" Casey gave him a wink and a knowing smile. "Just the old bullshit, Red—just the old bullshit."

Sophia Kurz was what Bill Casey wanted and needed—a good Catholic woman who would now become a good Catholic wife, forever beautiful in his eyes. The marriage seemed to heed the advice of the sage who said, "If you would have a successful marriage, then marry a friend." They had become exactly that to each other. Sophia was his closest, indeed his only, confidante.

She had seen her early assessment borne out. He had been a cut—several cuts—above the other young men she knew, serious, intelligent, ambitious, and, toward her, forever thoughtful. Now, as she watched him start to rise in the world, she sensed that she was marrying more than a good man and a good provider. She thought she saw the seed of a big man, possibly a great man. And the best part, for her and for him, was that she was unawed.

By the summer of 1941, Bill was spending most of his time in Washington. Cherne and the Institute's owner, Carl Hovgard, decided that Casey should move there and run the office. "You're going to need more horsepower," Cherne told him. "We'll make you chairman of the editorial board." "There *is* no editorial board," Casey noted. "So? You'll still be chairman," Cherne told him. It was a gambit Casey understood. He and Sophia moved to Washington that June, eventually living in the Carlyn Apartments at 2500 Q Street.

Red Cassidy was also in Washington, working for the Internal Revenue Service. Soon after Casey's arrival, Cassidy got a call that opened with the usual Casey delicacy: "What are they paying you over there?"

"I just got a raise to twenty-one hundred."

"Peanuts. Come on over and work for us. We'll double your salary. This outfit is going places. You better get on board."

What Casey wanted was Cassidy's considerable charm, his gift of gab. As he put it to Cherne, "This guy can get us past the secretaries and into the clients' offices." Cassidy came to work for RIA as a "contact man," in effect a salesman of the Institute's publications.

"I hadn't been there long," Cassidy recalled, "when Casey comes running into the office, intense as hell. He opened up his briefcase and dumped what looked like trash onto his desk—wadded-up papers, carbons, torn-up sheets. Jesus, there may have even been orange peels. He'd been over to the Office of Price Administration for an interview with the director, Leon Henderson. While he was waiting to see Henderson, the secretary left the office. Casey went straight for her wastebasket and stuffed everything into his briefcase. We stayed up all night smoothing out those sheets, pasting the torn-up pages together, combing this junk for every scrap of information. We put out a scoop on price controls in the next RIA newsletter.

"Another time, Bill took me with him to a meeting in a federal agency that allocated resources to defense industries. The secretary takes us into a conference room to wait for our man. She said, 'Just a minute, I'll tell the boss you fellows are here.' They'd just finished a meeting. There was one of those steno pads on the conference table where somebody had taken notes.

· "No sooner is she out the door than Casey grabs the pad. 'Christ,' he says, 'just listen to this . . . and listen to *this*.' I was getting nervous. But Bill just kept on flipping through these pages, marveling at what he was reading. Then we had the meeting with this official and he wasn't giving us the time of day. As soon as we got back to the Institute, Bill called in his secretary and he started dictating an insider story off the top of his head. He seemed to remember everything in that steno pad. And we had another scoop for the newsletter— where raw materials were being allocated over the next six months."

Bill and Sophia were having Sunday dinner at his mother's house on December 7, 1941. The radio was on, and suddenly the music was interrupted for a news flash. Pearl Harbor had been bombed. "I remember," Sophia later recalled, "that nobody said a word. But I knew what Bill and his mother were thinking." George Casey, fresh out of Hofstra College, had been called up three months before in the first peacetime draft.

A letter he wrote to George the month after Pearl Harbor tells a good deal of the Casey character at that time:

I feel moved to do just a little bit of brotherly advising, something I do too much of and not at all well. . . . You'll recall, or do you, how I used to work with you in the back lot to interest you in football and teach you what little I knew and watch you go miles past me while I acted as a stalking horse, chasing your passes and punts. I was gloating in your achievements while scolding you and riding you as my inept way of pushing you still further. You recall my one-man campaign to all the papers on your behalf [to have George named a little All-American at Hofstra]. Then came the army for you and I wouldn't be surprised to find myself with a bayonet too. . . . Suppose you don't come out? I constantly worry and pray over that. But I'm becoming a fatalist. One of those planes I ride may crash any day. . . . I'm afraid that if you're shipped out, we may not see you again on this planet. . . . So George, stay good and clean. Don't take any chances on missing a reunion in the next life if your number is up . . . use your religion to keep you going. If there is anything to this heaven business, as we believe there is, don't let anything interfere with your being on deck. . . . I hope this doesn't sound like sob sister stuff. Remember that it comes from a hard-headed, practical guy. . . . I've taken out $10,000 worth of insurance for Mom. I'd hate to see both of us check out and leave her without something of a sock. Do you want to take some of that cheap army insurance for mother? I'll pay the premium. I'm enclosing a check for you for $50, let me know if you need more. . . .

The letter was signed, "Love and Kisses, Bill."

It was a revealing letter. Almost all of the character is exposed: the pushing and striving; the difficulty in praising, which expresses itself instead in more pushing; the sense that one makes things happen rather than relying on a capricious fate, as when Bill promoted George's football prowess; a faint defensiveness about his safe civilian status; his literal conception of heaven and hell; the total awareness of, and a certain pride in, his pragmatism—a hard man, yet with the unabashed streak of sentiment revealed in his closing.

Bill Casey was then twenty-eight years old, in good health, and his country was at war. He was quickly classified 1A by his draft board. His mother already had one son in uniform. And Leo Cherne was telling him, "You can't go into the army. That would be foolish romanticism. There is probably not another man in this country who knows any more than you do about how the hell we're going to mobilize for war. Do you think you'll be more helpful lugging a rifle around Fort Dix? That would be the real loss." Reluctantly, uncomfortably, Casey let the Institute get him reclassified from 1A to 3A. He was safe, for as long as he wanted.

The Washington that he and Sophia had moved to was like a somnolent southern belle who had been stirred from her lassitude and told suddenly to behave like a Valkyrie. The population of the once-drowsy city—barely six hundred thousand when Casey was attending Catholic University—had spurted to over a million. Government employees doubled overnight. It was a national capital with one legitimate theater, no restaurants of any distinction, and a major-league baseball team with a near death grip on last place in the American League.

Economists from Harvard, film makers from Hollywood, agronomists from Illinois, military personnel from every corner of the country came flooding into the city. Blacks came pouring in, fleeing the sharecropper servitude of tobacco and cotton farms in Virginia and South Carolina for good jobs in the capital.

Everything in Washington was short—housing, office space, cabs, trolleys. With the government now on round-the-clock shifts, the city never slept. Traffic was almost as congested at midnight as at noon. Casey had had to pull all of the Institute's considerable strings to find the apartment in the Carlyn.

It had also become—for all the congestion, shortages, heat, and confusion—the most exciting city in America. If one was not on the field of battle but wanted to be part of the war, Washington was the place. This arsenal, however, produced not mortars or ships, not medals or glory, but paper. And Casey found himself increasingly uneasy. Theoretically, he was capable of recognizing that his role in the war effort was worthy. And yet passing the lowliest private on Constitution Avenue made him uncomfortable. A national test of manhood was under way, and Bill Casey was not, in his mind, part of it.

In September of 1942 he became a consultant to the Board of Economic Warfare—the BEW. As he later described this experience, "My job was pinpointing Hitler's economic jugular and investigating how it could be squeezed by blockade, preemptive buying, and other economic warfare." It sounded crucial, even exciting. But it was in truth dull, and it failed to relieve his unease about being out of the fight. His contemporaries were turning the war around in the Pacific at Guadalcanal, being bloodied in the North African campaign, flying B-17s over Europe. His kid brother had been rushed through officer training, a ninety-day wonder, and was now a lieutenant of artillery headed for the Pacific. Backer, Casey, Doran, and Siegel had been dissolved as his partners went off to the war. In the spring of 1943, Casey told Leo Cherne, "I don't give a goddamn how essential I'm supposed to be. I'm going in."

He was not, however, so blinded by duty that he was ready to take orders from some semiliterate Okie in a rifle company. He expected a direct commission, and at a high level. He was still under thirty, but he had been telling top industrialists and Cabinet officials how to mobilize the country for war. He was an officer of unspoken rank in civilian life. He expected no less from the military. He went first to the Army. He was told that he was too young for a direct commission, but that if he was willing to take his chances and enlist, his talents would doubtless quickly be spotted. Casey was taking no chances. Instead, he turned to the Navy; and he made it—just barely. On June 15, 1943, he was commissioned a lieutenant junior grade.

When his orders came, he was devastated: he was not even leaving town. He was assigned to the Office of Naval Procurement on Constitution Avenue to figure out how to break bottlenecks in the production of landing craft. As he described his reaction in his later war memoir, "I longed for action and did not want to sit out the war as a civilian in uniform. But the Navy was not about to waste my Washington experience on a ship." What his ego would not allow him to add was that he was not fit for sea duty; his eyesight was too poor.

The Office of Naval Procurement was deadly. It was the Board of Economic Warfare minus the $12,000 a year he had been earning in his last year as a civilian. He refused, he said, "to spend this war goosing ship builders into turning out more LCIs."

There was something new, something mysterious, exciting, and glamorous, emerging. He noticed that when well-connected associates went into uniform, it was often into the Office of Strategic Services—the OSS. "Oh So Secret" was the half-envious gibe around Washington when the name of the new outfit came up. Casey did not know much about the OSS, except that it was virtually the country's virgin effort in clandestine warfare.

But he had had one glimpse of how the intelligence game must be played. The United States had become the last haven for scores of German Jews—intellectuals, academics, experts of all kinds—fleeing Hitler's Germany. A few had found their way to the Institute, among them Dr. Julius Hirsch, an economist who had worked on price controls during the runaway German inflation of the twenties. Casey had pumped Hirsch to find out how Germany had mobilized its industry for war. Here was the sort of knowledge the OSS must certainly collect. At the Institute they called it "information"; the OSS called it "intelligence." But the game was the same.

Still, one did not show up at a recruiting station and say, "I'd like to be a spy." How was the OSS wired? he wondered. Who mattered? How could he run a line into it? He knew only that the organization was the child of William J. "Wild Bill" Donovan of the fabled Fighting 69th in the last war. Donovan had until recently been the senior partner in the New York law firm of Donovan, Leisure, Newton and Lombard. And Donovan's old law office, Casey knew, served as the OSS old-boy net. Life is largely chance, and because Casey had once parked cars at Jones Beach, he now had his line into Donovan's firm: his former fellow car parker and law partner, Jerry Doran, had moved over to Donovan, Leisure, Newton and Lombard.

On a sweltering Washington afternoon late in August of 1943, Bill Casey shoved aside a stack of shipbuilders' contracts he had been reviewing and made a phone call to Doran that was to change his life.

6.

Casey's War

The most influential figure in the life of William Joseph Casey was William Joseph Donovan. Here were two descendants of impoverished Irish immigrants, two devout Catholics, two successful lawyers, two fervid Republicans—and ultimately, and much to Casey's satisfaction, two chiefs of American intelligence.

William J. Donovan was one of those corklike individuals who unfailingly bob to the top no matter how far down they start or how often they are submerged. He was in his mid-thirties, a successful attorney, when America entered the First World War. Donovan was impatient for action and found it. Twenty-seven days before the war ended, by then a lieutenant colonel, he led a charge of the Rainbow Division against the Hindenburg Line, waving his pistol overhead and urging his men forward like the central figure in some military tableau—until a German bullet in his right leg brought him down. The wound was serious, but Donovan refused to leave the field; he directed his troops for five hours as he lay on the ground, and halted a German counterattack. For this feat he won the Congressional Medal of Honor, which, added to the Distinguished Service Cross, the Croix de Guerre, and other honors he had already won, made Donovan the most decorated American soldier of the war.

He was imbued with a deep sense of public service and served for a time as the U.S. attorney for Buffalo, rising eventually to head the antitrust division of the Justice Department. Along the way, he also developed a taste for power and influence. Power and influence, he knew, did not come readily to a legal bureaucrat. And so he established a law practice in New York City and used his government-gained knowledge to work the other side of the fence. He became phenomenally successful as a lawyer for corporations beset by antitrust suits, defending 24 oil companies and 135 coal companies. Bill Donovan became rich, powerful, and influential.

A fellow Republican, Frank Knox, a former newspaper publisher and Franklin Roosevelt's Navy secretary, brought Bill Donovan to

FDR's attention. The President, a man of boundless enthusiasm and mental energy, recognized a kindred soul in Donovan. In the year and a half before Pearl Harbor, FDR bypassed his own diplomats and twice sent Donovan on fact-finding missions to Europe.

These two European journeys by a lone corporate lawyer on his President's business were the seeds of America's first espionage service. Donovan offered more than observations; he argued, from what he had seen abroad, that the United States had to have its own intelligence agency. Donovan pressed his case on Roosevelt with quiet persistence until FDR at last allowed him to prepare a paper describing just how America would go about entering the spy trade. Donovan leaped to the challenge. On July 12, 1941, Roosevelt named Donovan to head the determinedly anonymous Office of the Coordinator of Information, which a year later became the equally opaque Office of Strategic Services.

Jerry Doran had come through handsomely for Casey. Donovan's right hand at the OSS was Otto C. Doering, a former law partner. Doran arranged a lunch meeting for Casey and Doering. Ole Doering, as he was called, was a talker who never seemed to conclude a point; but at the end of the lunch, he scribbled a name and address on a slip of paper. "See this fellow tomorrow, about ten," he told Casey.

On a September morning in 1943, Bill Casey, in Navy summer khakis that Sophia had insisted on pressing before he left home, found himself in a downtown Washington office building searching out a Colonel Vanderblue. He eventually located him on the fourth floor behind an unmarked frosted glass door. Vanderblue, an amiable man, was a New York shoe manufacturer turned OSS recruiter. While Casey was interested in action, Vanderblue kept questioning him about his experience in pushing paper. "We've got a mess over in London," Vanderblue told him. "Good people, but nobody knows what anybody else is doing. Donovan leaves chaos wherever he goes, but at least here in Washington he's got a secretariat that picks up the pieces. I'm thinking of somebody who can do that in England."

Casey's heart leaped. Paperwork or no, the man was actually considering him for an OSS job abroad. "We'll get back to you," Vanderblue said. And the interview ended.

As soon as he was back in his own office, Casey began to lobby. He called Leo Cherne and his former chief at the BEW and asked them to draft letters of recommendation. He called Doran and told him, "Jerry, I want you to lay it on with a trowel. Write to Vanderblue and tell him I'm the greatest paper shuffler on the Atlantic seaboard."

He waited what seemed an eternity. It was not: in two weeks he received a call to see Ole Doering again, this time at OSS headquarters. He reported to a building on the corner of E and 25th streets, Northwest, in what had been a part of the National Institutes of Health. The top floor was still a lab where monkeys were kept for disease research.

"We'll arrange with the Navy for your transfer." Doering told him. "You'll come over here for a couple of months and see how we run this circus. And then you can take all our tricks over to London." Doering rose and took Casey down a corridor painted battleship gray and cluttered with file cabinets. He gestured toward a room. "That's the General's office. We'll introduce you as soon as he's done roaming the world. The man can't stay put."

The chief of American intelligence, whom Casey met a few days later, was then sixty years old. He was five feet ten inches tall, but his dumpy, soft-edged body and twenty excess pounds made him look shorter. His face was squarish, his chin dimpled, his mouth determinedly set, and his eyes a pale blue. His hair had remained full and was now silver. His skin had the ruddy glow of either good health or drink—the former in Donovan's case, since he was a teetotaler. He had a soft, agreeable voice. In a cassock he would have passed nicely as an Irish-American parish priest.

The external appearance was deceptive. The humpty-dumpty figure possessed rare vigor. He moved lightly on the balls of his feet. His blood pressure, 115 over 70, was that of a twenty-year-old. His gaze was mesmerizing. One of his officers remembered, "Donovan would grab your hand, fix you with those blue eyes, and say softly, 'I'm counting on you.' And I always believed him." Another aide recalled, "He would preface an order with 'Would you like to . . . ?'—in effect, 'Would you like to go off and get yourself killed?' And we always answered, 'Yes.' "

Donovan had a restless, devouring mind that leaped from enthusiasm to enthusiasm, giving brilliant and crack-brained schemes an equal hearing, as though all ideas were innocent until proven faulty. He was immune to conventional patterns of thinking, preferring to rely on his intuition. He told one bewildered assistant, "You know, we've got to get into the Far East. Intelligence is like the weather— weather comes from the East, and so does good intelligence."

The courage that the wounded officer had displayed on the Hindenburg Line did not fade with age. He was fearless, or more likely, he submerged his fears in flamboyant bravado. He flew 150 miles behind the Japanese lines in Burma in a Gypsy Moth aircraft, with most of the nation's intelligence secrets in his head. An aide asked him if he had not acted rashly. No, Donovan explained—he was carrying his L pill and was fully prepared to take it if captured. "L" stood for "lethal": the capsule was filled with potassium cyanide.

The organization that he had created was not universally loved. His bid for a separate intelligence service had been fought by the Army, the Navy, the Joint Chiefs of Staff, the secretary of War, the secretary of State, and the FBI. But the steeliness under the soft contours had prevailed. Donovan not only survived; he thrived. He managed to weave his way through the bureaucratic thicket until, by the time Bill Casey joined, the OSS was an organization approaching a strength of fifteen thousand people, with a budget nearing sixty million dollars. It had won a role in the battles then waging in the Pacific and North Africa and in the preparations for the invasion of Europe. Roosevelt became Donovan's shield against his domestic enemies. Still, even FDR said, "We must find a way to harness Bill— because if we don't, he will be doing a lot of things other than what we want him to do."

Partly Donovan's problems were turf rivalries. But something else rankled—a suspicion, not entirely mistaken, that the OSS was a place where the well-born and well-connected could play at war. Far more appealing to wangle an OSS commission and say smugly at Washington soirées, "Sorry, I'm just not in a position to talk about what I do," than to crouch in a foxhole on Guadalcanal. And many of Donovan's recruits did read like the Social Register: Junius and Henry Morgan of the house of Morgan, Alfred Du Pont, Lester Armour of the meat-packing fortune, the diplomat David Bruce, and Paul Mellon among them. "If you should by chance wander in the labyrinth of the OSS," Austine Cassini, gossip columnist for the Washington *Times Herald* wrote, "you'd behold ex–polo players, millionaires, Russian princes, society gambol boys, and dilettante detectives." One OSS veteran confessed after the war, "In half of my OSS comrades, I knew the bravest, finest men I would ever meet. The rest were phonies." Casey had a term for the latter. Remembering certain members at Long Island country clubs from his caddying days, he called them "white-shoe boys."

Casey functioned at headquarters as something of a fly on the wall. He worked with a half-dozen other officers, all young lawyers, who ran the secretariat. They arrived early in the morning and waded through cables that had accumulated during the night from OSS outposts around the world, determining which matters required Donovan's personal attention and which could be handed off. They screened requests for Donovan's time from thirty competing branch chiefs. From this privileged perch Casey quickly learned how both the OSS and Wild Bill Donovan functioned.

"The first thing I remember," Casey later recalled, "was an expression the General was always using. 'The perfect is the enemy of the good.' At first the meaning wasn't so clear to me. But I watched the way he operated, and after a while, I understood. You didn't wait six months for a feasibility study to prove that an idea could work. You gambled that it might work. You didn't tie up the organization with red tape designed mostly to cover somebody's ass. You took the initiative and the responsibility. You went around end, you went over somebody's head if you had to. But you acted. That's what drove the regular military and the State Department chair-warmers crazy about the OSS."

Casey soon concluded that the white-shoe boys were an OSS minority. Beyond the café-society habitués and Virginia huntsmen was another breed. Donovan believed in expertise. He had raided academia, industry, and journalism for economists, geologists, psychologists, writers, physicists, political scientists, and engineers. Evidently aware of the lab animals at headquarters, Berlin radio described Donovan's OSS as "fifty professors, twenty monkeys, ten goats, twelve guinea pigs, and a staff of Jewish scribblers."

"When Donovan defended all those oil and coal companies against antitrust charges," Casey later recalled, "he wasn't relying on his social connections. He used information. He collected eighteen tons of documents to defend the oil companies alone. He had a task force of lawyers to go through this stuff, organize it, analyze it, and summarize it. He pieced it together until he had the facts at his fingertips. This was the same approach I'd used at the RIA. It's not the layman's romantic notion of intelligence, but it's 75 percent of the game. I'd been in it all along.

"I was just a boy from Long Island. Sure, I had worked with high-level government officials, generals and admirals. But never had I been in personal contact with a man of Donovan's candlepower. He was bigger than life. I reveled in my association with that man. We all glowed in his presence."

Early in November of 1943, Casey received secret orders to report to OSS London. The parting would be harder now that he was a father. His first child, Bernadette, had been born six months before, on May 5. For the first time in his life, he found himself impatient to put the work aside and get home at a decent hour. There he took the baby in his arms, dancing her around the apartment, squealing when she squealed. He liked to bring her out on the sun deck, where he knew the neighbors would fuss over her.

On November 14 he left the apartment and tossed a seabag containing his rolled-up uniforms into the backseat of a Navy sedan, bearing a letter from General Donovan to Colonel David Bruce, the European chief of OSS. The letter explained that this raw-looking lieutenant junior grade was to establish and run a secretariat for the London operation.

Bruce, a tall, aristocratically lean forty-five-year-old, was the sort of American to whom the British upper classes were immediately open—lawyer, legislator, diplomat, gentleman farmer, a proper American cousin. He had furnished his office, at 70 Grosvenor Street, OSS headquarters in London, with Ming pottery and Sheridan furniture. And it was here that Casey presented Donovan's letter to Bruce. "This is a splendid letter, Lieutenant," Bruce said. "I'll just put it in my file, and I'm sure we can find something useful for you to do around here." He had expected a key role, but Casey suddenly felt like a night-school lawyer barely tolerated in a prestigious Wall Street firm.

He moved into an apartment at 87 Harley House with four other officers. Every walk he took through London's streets reminded him that he was on the rim of the war. Scar tissue from the blitz of '40 was everywhere apparent, though air raids were rare now. Even undamaged buildings, drab and unpainted, betrayed four years of wartime neglect.

After he had been in London over a month, he wrote to Ole Doering: "The secretariat has not yet been established. When I arrived, I met some skepticism as to its value. I deemed it wise not to argue for its establishment for now. As a result, I have been operating as sort of a special assistant in the Director's office. I would not be fully candid if I did not say that I have not yet found the scope or opportunity to use my energy and whatever ability I have on the level or scale which I enjoyed as a civilian."

He was determined not to be depressed. He just had to find a strategy for infiltrating the citadel of power at 70 Grosvenor. The key, Casey decided, lay in his experiences with the RIA and the Board of Economic Warfare. He had a deep understanding of how a country's economy supports its wars. He had described his job at the BEW as "pinpointing Hitler's economic jugular." That job dealt with external pressure on an enemy. But what about internal pressure? In a memorandum he urged Bruce to recruit agents from among businessmen in neutral countries like Sweden, people who moved easily in and out of Germany. They would have firsthand knowledge of the German industrial plant: What was Germany importing? From whom? How was this material transported? Where were the plants located? Where were the goods delivered? This kind of intelligence could be fed immediately to bomber command and Allied warships. His paper displayed the fine-edged Casey pragmatism. He argued that the neutrals had nothing to lose by this clandestine cooperation. The more ships sunk and the more plants bombed, the more the Germans would have to buy from them.

There was another side to the coin. These neutrals could pass along demoralizing intelligence to the Germans—real or fabricated, it did not matter—about the flood tide of ships, tanks, guns, and planes rolling off U.S. assembly lines. The neutrals could also ferret out anti-Nazis among the German businessmen. They might be able to persuade potential dissidents to carry out slowdowns, work stoppages, and sabotage, through a simple, powerful argument: they would make more money in the postwar world with Hitler out of the way.

Casey lifted another leaf from the RIA. He proposed a newsletter to be published by sympathetic or properly rewarded neutral Swedes but secretly underwritten by the OSS. Most of the news would be factual items on materials, markets, prices, and transport. But defeatist propaganda would be woven between the lines, again playing up the theme of superior Allied productive power and Germany's comparative weakness. The Swedes would see that visiting German businessmen got copies of the newsletter. And on their trips into Germany, the Swedes would leave copies behind.

Donovan did not seem particularly concerned that the secretariat scheme had not taken hold. His enthusiasms skipped from idea to idea like a flat pebble hurled across the surface of a pond. And he liked Casey's new ideas. Bruce too, a perceptive and fair-minded man, came to accept that this Casey was a promising chap. His suggestions were adopted.

Casey was invited to attend a budget meeting chaired by Junius Morgan, a direct-commission Navy captain who handled the London office's finances. Casey, the junior officer present, stood by as the others filed into the conference room. Among them was Raymond Guest, who had stepped from the polo fields of Long Island and Virginia into the Navy as a lieutenant commander. "Get me a chair, Lieutenant," Guest ordered Casey. "Get it yourself," Casey replied.

As Casey described the moment years afterward, "You could have cut the tension with a knife. Later that day, Junius Morgan called me into his office. He looked very uncomfortable. He told me, 'Raymond's been in here and he wants me to bring you up on charges at captain's mast. In the future, Bill, do try to be nicer to Raymond.' " The story made the rounds, and a Casey legend began to take root.

Better assignments began to come his way. When piles of raw intelligence had to be shaped into concise reports for dispatch to Washington, Casey was the man chosen. He had done the same thing for years at the RIA. Donovan used Casey's reports to pry ever-larger budgets from Congress. Howard Cady, not long out of the Doubleday publishing house in New York, worked as an OSS civilian under Casey and recalled, "I'd watch this avalanche of paper descend on him from all over the building. Bill would be at his desk around the clock, disappearing behind heaps of cables, graphs, statistics. His powers of concentration were frightening to behold. He'd tear into this mishmash and somehow make it sing. Out would come a logical, concise report. Even though it was 75 percent horse shit, it read like the gospel. And once Bill finished one of these magnum opuses, he believed every word of it."

Casey had learned Donovan's lesson well. He was not afraid to stick his neck out, to risk mistakes. The perfect was the enemy of the good.

"Bill was terribly impatient," Cady remembered. "He wouldn't bother to finish a thought once he figured you'd gotten it. When someone was briefing him, he would rush them along, snapping his fingers—'Gotcha, gotcha, gotcha. What else, what else, what else?' "

When somebody said something that displeased him or tested his credulity, he would make a drawn-out groan, accompanied by rolling eyes and the dismissive wave. People who failed him or crossed him were "sons of bitches" or "bastards," or "no goddamn good" but never "pricks" or "fuck-ups." Casey used profanity, but rarely obscenity. His ultimate insult was "The guy's a jerk—a jerk!"

"He was tough to work for," Cady recalled, "but I found Bill stimulating. And his demands stretched me. He had a wonderful habit of turning aside obstacles or excuses or complaints with that Irish humor of his. When some not particularly deserving comrade had to be written up for a medal, Bill would say, 'Howard, old boy, won't you do a waffle on the gallant major?' "

Cady found, beneath the hard-driving, crusty exterior, an unexpected sympathy. "I was a civilian, so I couldn't get into any of the officers' messes. In those days, in London, there was barely any other decent place to eat. I thought I was going to starve to death. Casey was the only one who seemed aware of my situation. Two or three times a week, he'd stand me to a good lunch at the navy officers'

mess. I think he took a liking to me because I had been a book editor
and he revered books."

In early June of 1944, General Donovan materialized unannounced
in London. Casey pieced together the significance of his sudden arrival. Donovan had previously shown up on the eve of the invasions
of Sicily, Salerno, and Anzio. Obviously the invasion of Europe could
be no more than days off. "It was a deadly serious time," Casey
recalled of the period, "and yet there was an air around headquarters
of excitement, like a big football weekend at Fordham."

Donovan—rashly, foolishly, typically—rode an amphibious truck
onto Omaha Beach on D day plus one. On D plus 19, Casey came
ashore with David Bruce. They had been sent to see how well OSS
teams infiltrated into France were supporting the invasion. The two
men threaded their way by motor launch through blasted landing
crafts and burned out half-tracks littering the beach. His arrival in
Normandy was, Casey later confessed, "the most exciting moment of
my life."

His formal responsibilities in London were still ambiguous—nominal control over a still-sketchy secretariat, the report writing. But
he was emerging with a more formidable unofficial portfolio. He had
managed to break through the mask of generalized cordiality that
Donovan presented as his face to the world. In Casey, Donovan spotted
a younger reflection of his own roving imagination and restless energies. Casey had been admitted to the inner circle. He became Donovan's troubleshooter in Europe.

"Donovan would come bursting into town," Casey remembered of
those days. "He'd take a suite at Claridge's and hold court. He'd put
pressure on us in that quiet way of his. Had we worked the bugs out
of photo interpretation? Was anybody thinking about postwar planning? He'd jump all over the lot. We'd be with him until the small
hours. Then he'd dismiss us and take a stack of books to bed. He used
to send me over to the Bumpus bookshop on Oxford Street to pick
up anything new in military science, biography, politics, diplomacy.
I'd show up at his suite the next morning, and while he shaved and
dressed, I'd thumb through the books I'd brought over the day before.
Passages would be underlined; the margins were filled with his notes.
He had actually read the damn things. He had a strong influence on
my awareness of how much one individual could pack into a day."

Casey was much amused by Donovan's tolerance of human fallibility. "We had Wacs assigned to us in London, and one of them got

pregnant. We had to ship her home. Before we did, the General got in touch with Colonel Doering in the States and he told him, 'Ole, I want you to welcome that young woman personally on her arrival. And I want you to treat her like a casualty of the war.' "

Some of Donovan's enthusiasms breezed right past reality. Just before departing London, he told Casey, "I want one copy of everything in the files so I can read it on the flight back." Casey coughed uncomfortably and said, "We can do it, General, but we won't be able to get the plane off the ground."

Donovan had a favorite poem and gave Casey a copy, a sentiment from an earlier age, which in truth was where Donovan had been formed. It began:

> Say not the struggle naught availeth,
> the labor and the wounds are vain,
> the enemy faints not, nor faileth,
> and as things have been they must remain.

Forty years later, Casey still kept the poem in his Long Island home.

He had taken to writing letters to his infant daughter so that when she grew up, she would have a record of the years stolen from them. On Bernadette's first birthday, he wrote, "This ocean was placed between us by forces you never knew which the generation before mine failed to control and which mine must defeat. . . . So today, much as I miss being with you, I am glad that I am privileged to do my small part in making our world a decent, peaceful and free one. If I had been with you these months, I would always have felt the uneasiness of reaping the benefit of someone else's sacrifice. . . ." The words ring with an almost embarrassing sentimentality. But it was a different age and a different war, before the stalemate in Korea and the failed, uncertain crusade in Vietnam. The people of Casey's era, whether they fought the war bravely or fearfully or because they wanted to or were compelled to, at least had one clear advantage: they knew why they were there.

As an extension of Donovan's eyes and ears, Casey found himself in places that would acquire historic resonance: Normandy after D day; Algiers on the eve of the invasion of southern France; Grenoble in time to watch a field-gray sea of German prisoners marched into Allied cages.

Toward the end of August, he was to fly back with Donovan to London. He found the General unusually animated. At the airport, they were to pick up Allen Dulles, already a storybook figure in the

OSS. Dulles had been trapped inside neutral Switzerland, surrounded by Nazi-occupied territory, and had taken advantage of his situation to run highly productive agents inside Germany. Donovan was eager for a firsthand report.

The three men boarded a DC-3 that began cruising up the valley of the Loire. Casey looked uneasily at the General and at Dulles, neither of whom seemed to share his concern: the chief of American ingelligence was aboard a plodding aircraft, with no fighter escort, prey to any German fighters in the neighborhood, as vulnerable as a duck in a shooting gallery. The Donovan sangfroid was one quality Casey had not yet mastered.

Allen Dulles was fifty years old, mild-looking, with graying hair, rimless glasses, and the manner and speech of a country lawyer. He was, like Donovan, a figure of the American establishment. He and his brother, John Foster Dulles, were partners in Sullivan and Cromwell, a New York law firm even more prestigious than Donovan's. They moved effortlessly from high-powered clients to high-level government posts. Casey sat quiet and observant. Dulles was giving Donovan fresh details on the failed plot the previous month to assassinate Hitler, information garnered from Dulles's agents in Germany. Hitler's revenge, Dulles reported, was sweeping and brutal. Anyone remotely connected to the plotters was being arrested, summarily tried, and executed. A national bloodletting was under way that would ultimately take the lives of 4,980 Germans.

Donovan's interest quickened as Dulles began speaking of conditions inside Germany. Order was breaking down, he said. The Third Reich was beginning to crumble.

"You've had a few people in there, Allen," Donovan observed. "I wonder if the time isn't ripe for penetration en masse? Agent drops from England—the way we infiltrated France."

Casey said nothing. He knew that the British forbade the use of their soil as a launch pad for American intelligence operations against Germany. They considered any such efforts futile. Clandestine operations required a friendly population—Frenchmen, Belgians, Dutchmen chafing under Nazi occupation, who could provide safe houses and communications routes, none of which could be expected inside Germany. Casey knew all this but kept his counsel. Wild Bill was not the sort of man who liked to hear what could not be done. He wanted to hear how it could be done anyway.

It was only since D day that the British had allowed OSS London to mount any independent operations at all. As Casey described the climate, "We'd arrived in London as the new kid on the block, untested, unknown, scorned, derided and ignored." But the OSS, in Donovan's eyes, had proved itself in Operation Anvil, the invasion of southern France. The assault had been preceded by brilliant intelligence. When the landing craft hit the beaches, the American army knew the location, with pinpoint precision, of virtually every enemy unit, coastal defense, mine field, artillery emplacement, roadblock, even search light. Donovan was ready to declare his independence from Great Britain. "Bill," he said to Casey, "maybe we ought to start taking a closer look at getting into Germany."

When they landed in England, they learned that Paris had just fallen. The General's quicksilver attention was distracted. The Allied offensive in France was to roll on irresistibly, over the rivers Marne, Aisne, and Meuse, taking in a few days ground that had been blood-soaked in seesaw trench warfare for four years in the last war. Soon the Allies would reach the German border. And then it would be over. Donovan's mind had already leapfrogged to the postwar world.

When they got back to London, the General summoned his senior staff and told them that this war had forever ended the isolation of the United States. He directed an OSS colonel, J. Russell Forgan, to head up a committee, as he put it, "to study the need for our country to establish on a permanent basis, as an integral part of the military, a strategic intelligence organization." Bill Casey was to serve as the committee's secretary. The assignment was to bring Casey in at the creation of what would ultimately metamorphose into the Central Intelligence Agency. As he would tell his staff at Langley thirty-seven years later, "I was there in the beginning. Nobody saw me. But I was there."

Casey was selected to deliver the London recommendations to Donovan in Washington. There he was made part of the drafting group that pulled together contributions from OSS outposts around the world. Donovan's chief argument for a permanent central intelligence organization was one that few Americans were thinking about at the time. The Soviet Union was an ally in the struggle to defeat the Nazis. But that war was almost over, and Donovan was looking ahead, with scant trust, to Russia in the aftermath. He told Roosevelt: "There are common-sense reasons why you might want to lay the keel of the ship at once."

Donovan and Casey saw eye to eye on the Soviet Union. Of course, Nazism was a barbarity; it had to be crushed. But only the naive would assume that the alliance with Stalin was anything but a necessary and temporary pact with evil.

His duties in Washington over, Casey took a train to New York and another out to Long Island, where Sophia and seventeen-month-old Bernadette were staying with Sophia's family. All too soon, he found himself at night on a fog-shrouded pier in New York harbor, where a launch took him out to the Pan American clipper for a flight to neutral Lisbon, from whence he would make his return to London.

Back at 70 Grosvenor, Casey found himself for the first time under enemy fire. Since the week after D day, the Germans had been launching "vengeance" weapons against London: first the V-1s, remote-controlled, pilotless aircraft, the buzz bombs that exploded with scant warning; then rocket-propelled V-2s, which exploded with no warning at all. Two of Casey's roommates were responsible for plotting the points of impact of the V-2s. "Every time those fellows heard one of them go off," Howard Cady recalled, "they'd rush out to find out where it landed. One time they invited Casey along, and he dragged me too."

The V-2 had scored a direct hit on the Smithfield market, the whole-sale meat supplier for London butchers and restaurateurs. "The place was just a charred, smoking mess, with the smell of a burnt roast," Cady remembered. "These two fellows started clambering up through the wreckage of the building while the timbers were still smoking so they could get a bird's-eye view of the damage. And Bill was trailing along after them."

Bill Casey was no Wild Bill Donovan, no nerveless courtier of death. He was simply reacting to peer pressure. His dresser top at Harley House was a home pharmacy of nerve pills and antacids. Of the V-2 explosions, he confessed to a friend, "I can pretty much control my exterior. But I have a little more trouble with my insides."

By mid-October, he was back on the Continent, this time in Paris. The situation could not have been more sanguine. France was essentially liberated. For the past month, Allied troops had stood at the German border, and in a few places crossed over. The Russians were advancing from the east, about to break out of Poland and onto German soil. The Third Reich was trapped in a vise. In the last war, the Germans had been sensible enough not to bring destruction down on their homeland. They had surrendered first. This war was lost too; surely they would behave as sensibly this time. GIs dug in along the Siegfried line began talking about being home by Christmas.

Since its liberation, Paris had become a magnet. As Casey saw it, "Every guy in the OSS with an ounce of pull thought his presence in Paris was indispensable. I could just see David Bruce's elbow testing the mahogany at the Ritz Bar." On his own arrival, Casey found that the OSS had taken over fashionable offices at 70, avenue des Champs-

Elysées offering a view of the Arc de Triomphe and the place de la Concorde. OSS personnel filled up the Elysée Park Hotel, then the Gallicia, then the Powers.

Walter Lord was among them. Years later, Lord would gain fame as the author of *A Night to Remember*, the story of the sinking of the *Titanic*. In the fall of 1944, he was a thin, pale, scholarly civilian employee of the OSS in Paris. He described Casey's arrival: "Half of our people there thought the war was over with France liberated. The first team had all gone back to the States for the show in the Far East. A lot of ineffectual people were left, people who just liked the idea of being in Paris. The place had gone slack. There was no creative tension, no sense of purpose. General Donovan had sent Casey to shake the place up, to clean out the deadwood. And he turned Paris upside down. He came into my office and started firing off questions. He was blunt and impatient. But he knew exactly what to ask.

"He took an interest in me because I had been classified 4-F. I could have beaten the war but I chose not to. Casey liked that. He invited me to dinner at the officers' mess. He was already something of a legend and I was completely taken with him. He always looked disheveled in a marvelous way. The uniforms never quite fit. He wore his Navy officer's cap flat, without a trace of style. He had a contagious, almost innocent eagerness and idealism. Before the dinner was over, he told me I was going back to London to work for him."

As Casey diagnosed OSS Europe at the time: "We had staff, organization, but no mission. We had lost momentum and we didn't seem to know how to restore it. I was trying to figure out how."

And then Hitler provided the mission. The Germans balked at playing the role assigned by Allied strategists of defeated but reasonable men. All along the Siegfried line German resistance stiffened. General Patton's headlong race across France stalled along the Moselle River. Field Marshal Montgomery's rash gamble, Operation Market Garden—a northerly bypass of the Siegfried line and a dash through Holland straight on to Berlin—failed utterly. And on December 16, the Germans struck back through the Ardennes with an offensive of blitzkrieg scale, to be known to history as the Battle of the Bulge. Casualties on the Western Front had been a relatively light 2,529 in September. In October they reached 44,535; in November, 61,724; and in December, the first month of the Bulge, 153,250, including 24,291 dead. Winston Churchill was telling the British people, "The truth is no one knows when the German war will be finished."

To Donovan, here was the golden moment to prove to Allied generals in the field and to his critics back home that the OSS had fully matured. The penetration of Nazi Germany would be the ultimate test. The British had said the job could not be done. Here was a chance to break away from their domination and go it alone. What better way to prove the arrival of the OSS? Donovan decided to infiltrate the Third Reich. The next question was who would carry out the mission.

7.

His Finest Hour

In December of 1944, Bill Casey's formal title was Chief of the OSS Secretariat in the European Theater of Operations. More accurately, he was Donovan's man, one of the General's roving cage-rattlers, an extension of his eyes and ears. Donovan had given Casey authority to skip channels and deal directly with him.

From the moment Casey had first heard Donovan mention the idea of penetrating Germany, during the plane ride up the Loire, he had started turning the idea over in his mind. That September, he had sent Donovan a secret cable headed "An OSS Program Against Germany." Casey described what he saw as a Trojan horse: "There are some two million Russians, more than a million and a half Poles, a million and a half Belgians, between 300,000 and 400,000 Dutch, and on and on inside Germany, an explosive potential for us that we must not overlook."

On December 17, the day after the American First Army was caught flat-footed by the German drive through the Ardennes, Casey sent Donovan another secret message urging him to shift gears: "It must be assumed that the Germans will be able to maintain resistance throughout the winter. . . . Intelligence on order of battle, defense installations, air targets, morale, military plans, and other conditions inside Germany should carry the highest intelligence priority. Controls over movements and food are now so tight that the establishment of agents inside Germany is likely to be an extremely slow and uncertain process. However, when these controls begin to break down, OSS must be ready to place agents within Germany." Shortly afterward, Donovan made the policy decision to attempt a full-scale penetration of the Reich.

The London office was divided into two major branches: Secret Operations, or SO, the blow-up-the-enemy-bridges end of the business, and Secret Intelligence, or SI, the clandestine collection of information—traditional spying. SI was now paramount. Few American agents were going to be planting mines under German troop trains outside Munich, as they had done in the occupied countries.

John Haskell had headed SI in London. But Haskell, a West Pointer, had grown weary of spycraft, had managed a combat command at the front, and by December of 1944 his SI job was vacant. Haskell's deputy, Alan Scaife, was his presumed successor. Casey's judgment of Scaife was brutal: "He was one of the original white-shoe boys. He'd done it all in a day. He'd married one of the Mellon heiresses. And that took care of Alan. The guy didn't have much steam. His people were rattling around with nothing to do. SI was falling apart."

Just before Christmas, while the Battle of the Bulge was still raging, Donovan came to London with Whitney Shepardson, the worldwide SI chief. The two men closeted themselves with David Bruce, Lester Armour, London's "coordinator," and J. Russell Forgan, who was getting ready to take over Bruce's job as OSS chief for Europe. The meeting went on for the better part of the afternoon. "When they finally came out," Casey recalled, "Donovan took me aside and said, 'Bill, you're the new chief of SI for Europe. I'm giving you carte blanche.' 'To do what?' I asked him. Those blue eyes of his twinkled and he said, 'Why, to get us into Germany.' "

Casey was thirty-one years old. Nineteen months before, he had been a civilian; fifteen months before, he had been reviewing Navy contracts for landing craft. He was now in charge of American intelligence in a continent at war. His lack of awe before the unknown and untried was to undergo a formidable test.

As a still-junior partner of the British, the OSS had dropped over a hundred teams into France in advance of D day. But these agents had landed in friendly lands, welcomed by an occupied people as eager as themselves to drive out the Nazis. But an agent sent into Germany would be parachuting into the enemy heartland. No resistance fighters would greet him on the ground. No safe houses would be waiting. No communications channels existed. And the Gestapo's control over the German people, in the wake of the plot against Hitler, had been tightened like a garrote.

Even the Allies' grand strategy worked against penetration of the Reich. The Allies demanded unconditional surrender. Roosevelt had further asked his confidant and Treasury secretary, Henry Morgenthau, to devise a plan for pacifying Germany after the war. Morgenthau had come up with a scheme for dismembering and turning Germany into "a country primarily agricultural and pastoral in character." The Allies had handed Nazi fanatics a convincing reason to spur the German people to fight on. What was to be gained by surrender? Total prostration before the victors, while, in Joseph Goebbels's phrase, their country was reduced to "a potato patch."

Casey moved into the office vacated by John Haskell and began to inventory his assets. "We had nothing at all on Germany," he later recalled. "Until now, all we had thought about was how the hell did you get on those Normandy beaches without being thrown off. We had not thought beyond France. Then, all of a sudden, that war is over. We had this apparatus and didn't know what to do with it. The army hadn't always wanted our help. But they saw what we could do in southern France. And they were taking a beating in the Ardennes—terrible casualties. And why? A colossal intelligence failure. So now the brass was more receptive to us.

"As soon as I had SI, while the Bulge was still being fought, I went to see two top Brits in intelligence, Sir Stewart Menzies, who later became 'C,' the head of MI-6, and Sir Gerald Templer, who headed up the German desk for Special Operations Executive. I was disappointed. 'It can't be done, Mr. Casey. We're sorry. You won't be able to get your people in, and if you do, you won't be able to get their intelligence out. This is Germany, not Holland or Yugoslavia.'

"But Donovan wanted it. Penetrating Germany was to be our first totally OSS show. We'd lose people, sure, but nothing compared to the casualties our troops were taking along the Siegfried line. It didn't matter what the British said. It didn't discourage me. I never entertained for a minute any thought of not going ahead. And I accomplished one thing at least: I got the Brits to lift their ban on operations by us against Germany. At least they wouldn't stand in the way."

Casey realized that he already had the skeleton of a German operation upstairs, over his office. Compared to the units that directed saboteurs and spies, this one, the Labor Division, lacked any shred of glamour.

Among the early casualties of Nazism was the German trade-union movement, which Hitler replaced with a paper organization. The deposed trade unionists, mostly socialists and Communists, had been herded into concentration camps or fled the country. Arthur J. Goldberg, general counsel for the CIO at the beginning of the war, had persuaded Donovan that these labor refugees represented priceless intelligence assets. They possessed an unrivaled knowledge of Germany's economic infrastructure. Workers knew what made a country work. Donovan had immediately grasped the point and persuaded Goldberg to exploit this potential by creating a labor organization within the OSS.

The London Labor Division was run by George Pratt, before the war the chief trial counsel for the National Labor Relations Board. While other offices at 70 Grosvenor parachuted spies and saboteurs into occupied Europe, the Labor Division went about its humdrum chores. Pratt would give a few pounds to some half-starved Düsseldorf railroad-union exile who could tell him exactly how coal cars were loaded in the Ruhr. His people studied bills of lading which revealed what German war materiel was moving on Rhine River barges. Labor Division staff pored over German newspapers smuggled in through neutral Sweden and Portugal. They filed away odd bits of information that slowly began to yield an X-ray of daily life inside Germany— the ration cards issued, the curfew hours, the travel permits required. A German news story about a woman arrested for selling cigarettes to a foreign worker revealed the location of a conscript labor camp, a possible site for harboring an agent.

Pratt was then in his mid-forties—an ancient by OSS standards— a small, neat, sandy-haired man with a little half-smile that suggested a secret understanding of life. Casey called Pratt down to his office. "George," he said, "those Reds you're harboring upstairs are the only people around here who know a damn thing about Germany. I'm going to use the Labor Division as the cadre for the German opera- tions. I'm going to create a whole new organization around it. We'll call it the Division of Intelligence Procurement. Nobody will know what the hell that means. But the DIP is going to put agents inside Germany. And you're going to run it under me. Anything, anybody you want, you get. You're going to have to learn how to recruit, how we train agents, how we invent cover stories that will fly, how we paper the agents, how we get them into Germany, and how we get the intelligence out."

Casey gave him the priorities passed along by the Army. "First, we want troop movements through rails centers. The next thing we need are targets for the Eighth Air Force. After that we want to know industrial output, especially anything on new kraut wonder weap- ons—and if you've got any time left, anything that will tell us if the Nazis are serious about the Alpine Redoubt, this last-ditch stand in Bavaria we keep hearing about."

It was as if a man and a mission had been waiting a lifetime to be mated. Richard Helms, then an OSS Navy lieutenant, one day to be the director of Central Intelligence himself, roomed with Casey at the time. "The man had a natural bent for what the Germans call *fin-gerspitzengefühl*," Helms remembered, "a feel for the clandestine. He had enormous drive too. Bill could set a goal, get people fired up to do it, and then give them their heads." Walter Lord, now working for Casey in London, recalled: "Bill had a healthy contempt for bureaucracy, for form and protocol. He was like a breath of fresh air. Suddenly everybody wanted to work for Casey. He was a feet-on-the-desk, get-the-job-done-I-don't-care-how-you-do-it executive. I was under his spell."

Casey may have inspired those under him, but he still wore only the uniform of a Navy lieutenant. And he now had to deal on equal terms with men ranks above him—army generals, air corps brass, chiefs of Allied intelligence services. Casey took his problem to Lester Armour, who, as a captain, was the senior OSS naval officer in the London office. "Let's go see Admiral Stark," Armour suggested. "He's just across the street. Maybe we can get you a little more braid."

Harold Stark was not eager to put Navy noses out of joint by jumping Casey over scores of officers with actual naval experience. He had another solution. As Casey recalled the visit, "The Admiral took one look at me and said, 'The best thing we can do for him is put him in a gray suit.' So Captain Armour walked me around the corner to Selfridge's, and I bought two gray suits." On January 5, 1945, Casey was mustered out of the Navy, but he retained his OSS position, now as a civilian. He was Mr. Casey again, a supple enough rank to deal with any amount of gold braid.

He was concerned about the potential agent pool. Americans, no matter how fluent in German, were out of the question. If young and healthy, why weren't they in the *Wehrmacht?* If old or unhealthy, how could they parachute? A more promising source was the prisoner-of-war cages. Here were tens of thousands of native Germans, and among them, inevitably, anti-Nazis. But General Eisenhower, as Supreme Allied Commander, had forbidden the recruitment of POWs as secret agents; it violated the Geneva Convention. The best single source were exiles in London who could be infiltrated into that huge body of foreign conscript workers in Germany. They did not have to be German or even to speak German. But cover as workers limited them to a low-level perspective of the Reich.

Far more ticklish was the question of using German Communist refugees living in England. On one hand, the Communists possessed model credentials. They were German. They hated the Nazis and had brawled with Hitler's brownshirts for years to see who would rule thier country. When they lost, the least lucky Communists wound up in concentration camps, and the more fortunate escaped Germany.

Casey gagged at the prospect of using Communists as American spies; the prospect was viscerally repugnant. On one of his trips to

Paris, Casey had met Albert Jolis, a dashing and sophisticated scion of an old diamond-merchant family. Jolis had been recruited into the OSS because his business had given him a wide acquaintance with European labor leaders. Jolis, too, was horrified at the prospect of recruiting German Communists as agents: at the end of the war, they would be in place, positioned to seize power—and myopic liberals would have put them there. The affinity between the two men was instant. "Here, at last," Jolis thought, "is someone who sees communism the way I do."

In the end, Casey's trust in Donovan proved stronger than his abhorrence of the Left. It was all too clear what Donovan felt in his heart. But Donovan had said he was ready to deal with the devil to beat Hitler. Was Casey to be more Catholic than the Pope? "Look," Casey told a disappointed Jolis, "I think it's wrong. But the old man wants it." And so Casey began to prepare Communist exiles for a trip home to Germany as U.S. spies.

Casey also managed to find a way around the ban on recruiting prisoners of war. German-speaking OSS officers would go into the POW cages and strike up conversations. They might profess a grudging admiration for Hitler and wait to see who disagreed. Prisoners who had served in *Strafbataillonen*—German army punishment units—were often receptive. But no matter how they approached the prisoners, the Americans in the end always asked, "Are you saying you want to volunteer to fight against the Nazis?" An answer in the affirmative left a legalistic crack of light between recruitment and volunteering. Not for nothing had Casey known how to educate RIA's clients in minimum compliance with the law.

The agent pool was now defined: Europeans who could pass as foreign workers, anti-Nazi German prisoners of war, and willing refugee Germans of any political stripe, including Communists.

Casey found two men in the Labor Division to manufacture cover stories. Privates Lazare Teper and Henry Sutton were unlikely soldiers, two soft-looking men, already in their thirties, both speaking with foreign accents. Teper was big, dark-haired, shambling, with an engaging lopsided smile. Sutton was fat, with apple cheeks, undisciplined tufts of blond hair, and a high-pitched Viennese accent. (He had been born Heinrich Sofner.) Teper was the senior private and chose to name the new cover-story unit, of which he and Sutton were the entire roster, the Bach Section, after his favorite composer.

The section's cubicles were jammed with cabinets containing alphabetically filed facts on hundreds of German cities. From these accumulated minutiae, Teper and Sutton began to construct a person, giving him or her a family history, an authentic address, schools attended, a profession, dates and places of employment. They included the color of the buses in the agent's hometown and the burial place of deceased parents (a favorite question that the Gestapo posed to suspected enemy agents). The identity chosen dictated what papers the agent would need: a foreign worker's passport for a conscript laborer, a paybook for an ersatz soldier, a hospital pass for a phony nurse, ID and ration cards for everybody.

The Bach Section passed along these requirements to Willis Reddick, Casey's chief counterfeiter. Reddick was a neat, mustachioed man who had run a printing business in Springfield, Illinois, before the war. He had a simple, useful approach to his work: anything that could be printed could be counterfeited. Reddick would locate servicemen who had previously worked for the U.S. Bureau of Printing and Engraving or the American Bank Note Company and commercial artists from the staffs of *Collier's* and the *Saturday Evening Post*, and Casey would arrange to have them transferred to London. Actual forgers who could have been sprung from prison held no interest for Reddick. "How good could they be?" he said. "They got caught."

Reddick's people never lacked for cigarettes; they simply counterfeited ration stamps. Carl Strahle, who ran the print shop, once came worriedly to Reddick. "Suppose these guys decide to start knocking out the British five-pound note?" Strahle asked. "They could do it, you know."

The documents were given an aged patina by leaving them on the floor, where they were walked on all day; or they were worn for a time under the armpits. Reddick's models were authentic German documents scavenged by OSS teams from captured towns, from POWs, from the enemy dead.

Nearby, on Brook Street, was the OSS clothing depot, a brownstone that looked inside like a used-clothing store run by the Salvation Army. Some of the clothes literally came off the backs of refugees from Germany. OSS people asked if they would be willing to sell their suits, dresses, shoes, hats, combs, razors, shaving brushes, wallets, even the suitcases they carried—anything made in Germany. German uniforms could be found among the detritus of battle or acquired in POW cages. OSS officers would enter a cage and have the prisoners fall in for "inspection." The demands of the Geneva Convention were technically observed. If a man's tunic or cap was taken, he was given a replacement. If the item did not fit, the Convention was not specific on sizes.

For the last, most critical link in the chain of penetration, where error meant almost certain capture or death, Casey relied on a former Brooklyn photographer. Lieutenant Anthony Turano's job was to choose the pinpoints where the agents were to be parachuted. The ideal pinpoint, Turano learned through hard experience, was a flat field, away from antiaircraft batteries, near to a woods where an agent could hide, close to a back road he could travel, and with a major feature visible from the air by night—a lake, a bend in a river, or the ever-burning lights of a German POW camp. Turano's chief headache was the air corps. Pilots hated dropping agents. They dreaded flying low enough or slow enough to make safe, accurate drops—which from their perspective felt like playing clay pigeons to German guns.

Casey liked to go out to Area F, the training facility outside London, to see it all coming together. Area F was part trade school and part Fagin's classroom. The curriculum included burglary, bribery, and blackmail. Agents were taught how to use short-wave radio; how to remember what they saw and how to report it; how to copy a signature from a real document to a false one by using the damp surface of a freshly hard-boiled egg; how to parachute (taught in three days, compared with six weeks for army airborne units); how to kill with a newspaper (fold it into a square, then fold it diagonally to make a point; shove the point into the soft flesh just under the chin). They learned that if a policeman seemed to be watching them, the best thing was to ask him for directions to disarm his suspicions. If captured, agents were to endure torture for forty-eight hours; by then, their accomplices should have had time to get away. If they could not stand the torture, their alternatives were escape or the L pill. If an agent did not make it, the U.S. government would pay his designated beneficiary a $2,500 death benefit.

Casey, unlike Donovan, was a man whose sense of adventure was vicarious. Watching the trainees, he was filled with a mixture of awe and puzzlement. What made them do it? What would induce a man to jump out of an airplane to spy inside Nazi Germany? Their cover was thin at best—10 percent hard fact, the rest invention, often pure guesswork. Pushed hard enough, any cover story could crack. In the end, the agent's greatest protection lay in his mind, in quick-wittedness, in a talent for lying, in the vigilance, the fear, and the loneliness that honed his senses.

As Casey left Area F, he would tell the agent handlers, "Give these guys anything they want. They're the kings around here. We work for them."

On a moonlit evening late in January of 1945, Casey and George Pratt climbed inside an army panel van at Area O, the staging area.

The two men made desultory small talk. Reddick, Pratt said, was having trouble getting the watermarks right on foreign worker passports. The Polish recruits were an undisciplined lot, but they were tremendously eager. It looked like a clear night. If the weather held over Germany, finding the pinpoint should be no problem.

Leon Grell, an OSS escort officer, appeared with two men. They wore mismatched suit jackets and pants, dingy white shirts buttoned at the neck, worn cloth caps—virtually the uniform of working-class Europeans. Grell introduced the agents to Casey and Pratt as the "Doctor" team, the code name for their mission. They were two Belgians going in as conscript workers.

They began the two-hour drive to Harrington Field, guided in the pitch-black night only by parking lights. Casey studied the men out of the corner of his eye. One kept making gallows humor, followed by a nervous giggle that died in the unresponding silence. In a few minutes he would try again. The other agent remained grim-faced and said nothing.

At Harringon, Grell led them into a Quonset hut, where he ordered the agents to empty their pockets to make sure that they were not bringing British railway ticket stubs, matchbooks advertising the Kit-Kat Club, or Players cigarettes into Germany. He sealed their personal possessions—money, letters, photographs, and keys—in an envelope and said cheerily that he would return them soon, when they came back. He went through a checklist of their forged documents. He gave each man a money belt with the equivalent of seven hundred dollars in reichsmarks and two gold pieces. They were also given Smith & Wesson .45s. The pistols had little practical value, but the handlers had found them a great boost to the agents' morale. Finally, they were issued three packets of pills. The blue pills were a sulfate to overcome fatigue; the white were knockout pills; the third packet contained the L pill.

Grell told the agents to take off their shoes. He bandaged their ankles and fixed rubber cushions under their heels to help break the force of the jump. They were handed jumpsuits, baggy affairs that fit easily over their clothes, with a zipper that ran the entire length of the suit. The agent could step out of it in an instant. In the big, baggy pockets were a flashlight, a knife to cut the chute if he should get hung up in a tree, and a short spade to bury the parachute and the jumpsuit. The two men slipped on helmets lined with sponge rubber cushioning, goggles, leather gauntlets, and, finally, the parachute. Grell fluttered around them, tugging at the straps, like a mother dressing a bride. When he finished, he nodded to Casey, who shook hands with the men. He watched them climb into a B-24 painted black to melt into the night sky. And he watched the plane take off. Casey's first mission was on its way to Germany.

Months before, in the fall of '44, Casey had had dinner with a Navy lieutenant commander named Steven Simpson. They were discussing a key obstacle should they ever reach the point of penetrating Germany. Spies in occupied Europe could communicate via shortwave radio from safe houses. The signal was diffuse, however, and could be picked up by the German radiogoniometry vans that cruised city streets and the countryside. Agents solved this problem by frequently changing safe houses. But since there were no assured safe houses inside Germany, shortwave radio would be terribly risky.

Simpson, an RCA engineer before the war, began describing to Casey his solution. Since joining the OSS, he had been working on a system that would let an agent on the ground communicate directly to a plane flying overhead. Simpson had wanted to see Casey because he knew that the man had a reputation for getting things done. "You give me the people, the equipment, and the right plane," he told Casey, "and I can give you a way to communicate from Germany."

Casey had managed to get Simpson the support he needed. Early in 1945, the engineer produced his system. The agent on the ground carried a battery-powered transmitter-receiver small enough to fit into the palm of his hand. Its signal rose on a beam no wider than a pencil at the point of origin, and widened gradually until it reached the plane circling overhead. The narrow signal was virtually undetectable on the ground. Aboard the plane a radio operator talked directly to the agent on the ground and recorded their conversation on a new gadget, a recorder that captured sound on a spool of wire. Simpson called his invention Joan-Eleanor, "Joan" for a Wac officer he admired, and "Eleanor" for the wife of a colleague.

Casey assigned a young, quietly effective officer, Lieutenant Colonel John Bross, to get Simpson the aircraft he needed to test the system. Bross cajoled, wheedled, begged, and finally managed to get the Air Force to provide a lightweight attack bomber, the A-26, which had a range of fourteen hundred miles. "Do you know what that means?" Simpson asked Casey. "Sure," Casey said. "It means we can drop a team into Berlin."

By now, Casey had resigned himself to consorting with Communists the way a once-virtuous woman abandons herself to sin. The first attempt to parachute agents near Berlin was assigned to a team of two Communists who had worked together in an anti-Nazi labor organization. They had ultimately made the Gestapo death list and managed to escape to England. Pratt designated their mission "Hammer," but Casey liked to refer to it as "Hammer and Sickle." Hammer, equipped with Joan-Eleanor, flew an A-26 out of Watton airfield on March 1, 1945.

Casey had to deal with egos that were simultaneously delicate and powerful. One belonged to Henry Hyde. Hyde, a patrician American raised in Europe, was the SI officer working with the Seventh Army along the German border. Nominally, Hyde fell under Casey's command, since Casey was SI for all of Europe. Hyde was a charismatic man, as effective at persuading German POWs to spy against Hitler as he was at commanding slavish loyalty from his subordinates. He had been every bit as qualified as Casey, and certainly more experienced, to take over SI for Europe. (He had, in fact, been one of Donovan's candidates.) Hyde ran his own show in France, recruiting, documenting, and putting agents behind enemy lines. But with Casey now launching missions out of England, conflicts and competition over targets, aircraft, communications equipment, and personnel were inevitable.

Two men could scarcely have been less alike: Hyde, cosmopolitan, devilishly handsome, speaking in crisp aristocratic accents, fluent in French, a man captured by the word "dashing"; Casey, blunt, rough-edged, an artless speaker even in English, for whom "dashing" would be the last word imaginable. Their conflicts could not be left hanging; too much was at stake. A showdown was unavoidable.

Casey handled the issue in his customary unadorned fashion. He flew to Hyde's headquarters in France and told him, "Henry, I'm in charge—you work for me. Let's have that understood." It was just the heavy-handed pulling of rank that Hyde had feared.

"Now, I'll tell you what the intelligence requirements are," Casey said, "and you just tell me what you need—people, planes, equipment, whatever's necessary to get the job done. You know a damn sight more about this business than I do. You run your show any way you see fit, and I'll get out of the way. The only thing I expect are results."

Casey caught Hyde off guard. Hyde later described this encounter: "I was astonished at his lack of pretense, the absence of vanity, his willingness to subordinate his ego to the mission. My father and my grandfather were both cold fish. That's why I suppose I've always been drawn to the opposite—the warmer people, Latins, Catholics, Jews. I can tell a decent man from a shit the minute he walks into a room. I liked this man right away."

By March, the missions began to clog the pipeline. More than fifty teams were backlogged, waiting for the next moon. Casey became impatient and took a calculated risk: he tried test-dropping agents by the dark of the moon. The result was a surprise. Virtually the same percentage of teams hit the pinpoint whether they jumped in the dark or by moonlight. Thereafter, agents parachuted every night the weather permitted planes to fly. By the end of April, Casey had fifty-eight teams inside Germany.

The job became his graduate education in geopolitics. He had formed sixteen teams of highly motivated Poles, men who had witnessed Nazi barbarism in their homeland. Then, earlier, in February of 1945, at Yalta, the Western Allies ceded part of Poland to the Soviet Union. Allied leaders buckled to Russian pressure and backed away from the democratic Polish government-in-exile in London in favor of Stalin's proxies, the Lublin provisional government. Overnight, Casey recalled, "the morale drained right out of our Poles. I could see it happening before my eyes. After that, they just went through the motions. They weren't worth a damn. I never forgot what caving in to the Russians did to those people."

Dropping agents was roughly comparable to planting a garden. One sowed seeds, then hoped something came up. The DIP dropped teams near Bochum, Regensburg, and Stuttgart, then waited for the first shortwave transmission, the first message to be brought out by courier, the first successful Joan-Eleanor connection. The seeds began—some to flower, some to be crushed underfoot, some to disappear entirely. The first team that Casey had seen off, Doctor, set up in Kufstein in the Austrian Alps and became downright garrulous, transmitting over fifty messages to London. Doctor reported that there was no evidence that the Germans intended to hole up in an Alpine redoubt.

Eleven days after they had been dropped near Berlin, the Hammer team began talking via Joan-Eleanor to an A-26 circling overhead. The agents identified a power plant on the Rommelsbergsee still operating and feeding key war industries despite daily allied bombing raids over Berlin. The agents pinpointed for the Eighth Air Force two still-functioning tank factories in the suburbs.

The Chauffeur mission established itself in Regensburg, where the agents recruited two French girls who had been forced into prostitution by the German army. The girls were eager to betray their clients. They slipped the agents into a closet, where the men wrote down the postcoital revelations of German officers. Later, from a field outside of town, they reported via Joan-Eleanor the movement of units moving west to meet the Allied advance. They located the headquarters of the general staff in Regensburg as a possible bomber target.

A team called Luxe virtually ordered up a bombing raid on the railhead in Weilheim. The air corps sent in P-38 Lightning dive bombers, and the after-action report read: "Heavy damage to tracks, rolling stock on the Munich-Garmisch-Partenkirchen line...." What the Luxe team saw on the ground was that one building of an aircraft-manufacturing plant had been slightly damaged. But the rest of the American bombs had struck houses in a residential neighborhood and hit a clearly marked hospital train, killing or further injuring over three hundred and fifty wounded men.

Hilde Meisl had been code-named Crocus. She was recruited in London, where she was living as a refugee member of a puritanical sect of German socialists who did not smoke, drink, or eat meat. She was a remorselessly plain woman in her early thirties, with a scrubbed face that had never known makeup. She wore her hair pulled back in a bun and wore drab dresses of the type favored by American Shakers. She had been flown to a point near the French-Swiss frontier, slipped over the border, and eventually made her way over the Austrian border to Vienna.

In February, George Pratt reported to Casey on Crocus. Hilde Meisl had succeeded in setting up an intelligence network among fellow socialists in Vienna. She had been returning over the Austrian-Swiss border when an SS patrol spotted her, and she had been brought down by a shot that shattered both her legs. Before anyone could reach her, Meisl had bitten into her L pill. Pratt remembered that Casey's expression seemed to suggest a certain surprise that all this activity back in the relative safety of 70 Grosvenor could have such deadly consequences.

A team called Chisel was dispatched in an A-26 with a defective navigation system during foul weather, and the plane vanished. Another team was dropped prematurely by a pilot impatient to get home and parachuted into the full view of an SS unit that was watching an outdoor movie. The missions ran from the useless to the priceless; their fate, from the heroic to the farcical. Casey knew it and accepted early on the essential nature of warfare—a disorderly tragedy, tinged with black comedy.

On April 12, he boarded a DC-3 to Paris. The mood among the passengers and crew was subdued: just hours before, news had reached London that Franklin Roosevelt was dead. Casey had been no champion of FDR and the New Deal. He also thought that Roosevelt's insistence on unconditional surrender was righteous bluster elevated to misguided military policy; in his judgment, it was only lengthening the war. But Casey had a history student's eye for the value of charismatic leadership. And it was also Roosevelt who had shown the vision to back Donovan in creating an American intelligence service when virtually every other element of his administration was ready to choke the OSS in its cradle. At the news of Roosevelt's death, Casey had watched the tears stream down the faces not only of Americans at 70 Grosvenor but of Poles, Czechs, Frenchmen, and the ordinary Londoner-in-the-street. A great American figure on the stage of history had passed on, and Casey found himself choking back tears.

The next morning, Casey met with Donovan over breakfast at the Ritz. The General was uncharacteristically glum as Casey reported his successes so far in penetrating the Reich. Finally, Donovan spoke, gazing off in the distance. "You know, he was the only one protecting me from the wolves at home."

"What do you think it means for the organization?" Casey asked.

"I'm afraid it's probably the end."

Less than a month after FDR's death, the war in Europe was over. The London staff applied its ingenuity to an appropriate celebration. They drafted Thomsen, the Norwegian chef at Claridge's, to prepare a victory banquet. The turnout of white-shoe boys was near 100 percent. The party ran for a night and a day. And for the first time in years, Casey allowed himself to get tipsy on champagne.

Donovan had been in London just before the German surrender, and he asked Casey, "Bill, what do you want to do after we've beaten the Boche? You know, there'll be a big job for SI in occupied Germany."

"I don't want garrison duty," Casey said. "When it's over here, I'd like to go home to my wife and kid."

Donovan looked at him, surprised, disapproving.

"And then," Casey went on, "I want to get into the show in the Pacific."

Donovan beamed. "That's fine. How would you like to pull your whole team out of here and take them to Yenan in China? I'd like you to do the same thing behind the Japanese lines that you've been doing in Germany."

Casey made one last tour of OSS posts on the reconquered continent before he prepared to transfer to the Pacific. He visited Dachau and later commented, "That was my most devastating experience of the war." Nevertheless, just because the Nazis were pure evil did not, in his practical mind, make their Communist adversaries necessarily good. He complained to Lazare Teper, a Jewish liberal, with whom he had been discussing Nazism versus communism, "Every time anybody tries to criticize the Communists, some liberal starts telling you how much worse the Nazis were. Don't people understand? The Nazis are finished. But the Communists are still unbeaten." He had been keeping a little tally, he told Teper. "We made seventy-four requests to the Russians for intelligence. They granted twenty-one. We granted twenty-three of twenty-four of their requests. Those are allies?"

On Casey's last Paris visit, Bert Jolis—if anything, more anticommunist than Casey—had told him a horrifying tale. Not for a moment had Jolis bought the pragmatic arguments that Casey had bowed to in using Communists as agents. Now Jolis was telling him about liberated Russian POWs and Russians who had fought with the Germans and who did not want to go back to the Soviet Union. They were being forcibly repatriated by the American army, and to an obvious fate.

As for those Communist agents still working for OSS, waiting to be parachuted into Germany when the war ended, they were simply released. The OSS also washed its hands of Red agents who already had made their missions. One of Casey's aides prepared a memo on their final disposition: "These men did render extremely valuable service to our organization during the hostilities period . . . but because of their political background, there is serious doubt as to whether they could fit into our postwar German operations."

Just four days after the German surrender, Casey listened to Winston Churchill speaking over the radio on the Soviets' likely behavior in the postwar world: "What will be the position in a year when the British and American armies have melted, when Russia may choose to keep two or three hundred divisions on active service? An iron curtain is drawn down upon their front, and we do not know what is going on behind it." That, to Casey, was the warning of a statesman.

He was gratified to hear the latest sounds coming out of OSS headquarters in Washington. One officer returning to London told him, "Do you know what our next target is? Mother Russia."

On a day in mid-July, he went into his office and disappeared behind masses of after-action reports, debriefings, statistical analyses, bombing surveys, and agent interviews. He kept firing out copy to Wac secretaries working in shifts around the clock and emerged two sleepless days later with a document, classified secret and entitled: "Final Report of SI Operations Inside Germany." Given Casey's gift for embellishment, this document is remarkable for its understatement, for revealing the triumph of the analyst over the promoter in Casey. He made no heroic claims. He was, he said, submitting the report with a mixed sense of "satisfaction and dissatisfaction." Of 102 missions originating under his command, he rated 62 as successes, 29 as failures, and 11 as "results unknowable." Five percent of the agents dropped had become casualties, a figure far below expectations. He later remarked, "When I'd see those guys off, I have to admit, I never expected to see any of them again." Knowing what he knew now, he said, the OSS could have attempted the penetration of Germany earlier, possibly by a year. That had been his greatest disappointment.

He described the bombing raids, the bomb damage wrought, the enemy troop movements revealed to Allied ground forces, the identification of local Nazi leaders, all achieved through intelligence procured by agents inside Germany. But he made no claim that the enterprise he commanded had shortened the war by a week, a day, even an hour. The most he would say was, "We probably saved some lives." The greatest value of these operations, he concluded, was that "for the first time, we operated under our own steam." Penetrating the Third Reich, after the British had opposed and derided the objective, represented the maturation of U.S. intelligence during the war. Donovan's determination that the United States could and ought to maintain its own intelligence service, Casey said, "has been vindicated in Germany."

If a companion document had been prepared, "Final Report on William J. Casey After the German Operations," it might have read: "Casey went into this job as a solo operator, a man who previously had attacked problems singly: digesting laws for the RIA, problem-solving for the BEW, counseling law clients, drafting reports for OSS London, troubleshooting for Bill Donovan. He came out of the German experience with his fuller potential realized. He had found that given a mission, he knew how to marshal the personnel, the organization, the technology and hardware. He could mobilize people, command their loyalties, inspire them and stretch them. The lone operator, in those last six months of the war, had found another self, the leader."

His confidence was maturing quietly within. But outwardly he remained diffident. For years afterward, he delighted in telling how he won the Croix de Guerre: "One day in July of '45, I was in Russ Forgan's office. A liaison officer from French military intelligence stopped by. He dropped a brown paper bag on Forgan's desk and said the French wanted five officers in our service to have the Croix de Guerre. After he left, Forgan dumped the medals on his desk and said to me, 'Who should we give the other three to?' "

Casey acquired a new roommate in the last months of the war. Milton Katz was a former Harvard law professor, now a Navy lieutenant commander whom Casey had made his deputy in SI. Katz was a man possessed of qualities Casey prized—intelligence, clarity of thought, and a high energy level. Katz later described Casey during this period: "Bill would come back to the apartment late. I'd say to him, 'Well, today is K day minus sixty-one or fifty-three or forty-two.' It was my way of estimating how much longer the war would last before I got home to my wife and children. Bill was too keyed up to get to sleep. He'd start talking about what we'd all do when it was over. He'd say, 'Milt, you're a helluva bright guy. So am I. We could team up after the war. We could get into new enterprises. That's what we could call our business—New Enterprises, Inc. They're going to be hungry for new products and new services back home. Think of all the civilian spin-offs from radar, from Joan-Eleanor. I've got an idea for a product that would burn off weeds without harming the garden. Or we could buy a piece of a ball player or a prizefighter. We'd raise capital through our talent. We'd sell a piece of ourselves to the investors. We'd give them a quarter or a tenth interest for putting up so much. These things are only fun at the beginning when you're building and creating. Once they're on their feet, the fun is gone, and then we move on to another enterprise.' " Katz would listen, amazed at the restless imagination, the raw enthusiasm, recognizing that he was in the presence of an incorrigible entrepreneur. Finally he said, "Bill, this war has given me all the excitement I need for the time being. I've got a nice job waiting for me back on the Harvard law faculty."

Six weeks after the war in Europe ended, Casey found himself on a plane with Donovan, headed back to Washington, playing gin rummy with Russ Forgan while the General mulled over his plans for the war still being fought in the Far East.

Bill was vacationing with Sophia and Bernadette in August, expecting to leave for China by Labor Day, when the word came about Hiroshima on August 6. Nagasaki was hit by the second atomic bomb three days later, and by August 15 the war against Japan was over.

He faced a wrenching decision. Bill Casey had found in the OSS an all-too-rare convergence: a thing he loved to do and the talent to carry it off supremely. What tempted him most was to stay on, to make a career of intelligence—in effect, to marry his true love and settle down for life.

But the mind was too clear, too calculating to be lured by immediate gratification. The OSS had been his graduate school in the ways of the world. During those years in London he had worked with the American power elite. His comrades-in-arms had been the Brahmins—the Bruces, the Morgans, the Armours, the Dulleses. And he had held his own with the best of them. "Bill *appeared* to be on an intimate basis with all those people," Walter Lord later observed. "But it looked to me, putting perhaps a harsh light on it, that they were using him. The establishment types were only too happy to have this bright, hardworking guy around. He was with them. But he wasn't *of* them."

Casey knew this too. And he knew the difference. These people moved easily from civilian power to military power and back as though it was their birthright. His hero, Donovan, had not laboriously climbed the rungs of some civil service career ladder to become the head of American intelligence; he had left the Justice Department long years before and gone out and made his name and fortune. He had been chosen to create the OSS because he was a man who, along with his other admitted gifts, possessed wealth, connections, and influence. It was that way with all the resonant names Casey had come to know—the Whitney Shepardsons, the Raymond Guests. An able junior officer might get away with telling Guest to get his own chair once. An equal could do it forever.

"I didn't really want to leave," Casey was to say years later. "But, from what I had seen, I thought I'd better establish my financial independence first." As he put it later, life was "a little like a thousand-dollar-a-plate dinner. You don't get to go unless you can afford the thousand dollars."

He submitted his resignation from the OSS on August 15, the day the war ended. Almost immediately, he felt twinges of doubt. Russ Forgan and some of his other admired comrades, he learned, were staying on. Two weeks after sending Donovan the resignation, he wrote him, "I began to feel like something of a slacker in having asked your blessing to return to private life." He was also feeling a little like the fellow who thinks he may have left the party too early.

But one week after writing this letter to Donovan, his decision seemed positively prescient. Donovan's earlier fears were fulfilled. With Roosevelt's death the April before, the General's enemies had come crawling out of the woodwork. From rival federal agencies, from the military, from Capitol Hill, stories were leaked to the press: the OSS had employed Communists; the OSS was a tool of British intelligence; the OSS wanted to become a peacetime American Gestapo.

On September 20, with the war over barely a month, President Truman signed an executive order that gave Donovan a humiliating ten days to disband his organization. Truman's accompanying letter of appreciation sounded more appropriate to a retiring civil service drone: "I want to take this occasion to thank you for the capable leadership you have brought to a vital wartime activity in your capacity as Director of Strategic Services. You may well find satisfaction in the achievements of the office and take pride in your own contribution to them."

The War and State departments picked up what pieces were left. State took over the OSS Research and Analysis branch. The War Department stowed away the remaining OSS survivors in a "Strategic Services Unit," commanded by a one-star general whose orders were "Wind it down."

Long years afterward, before he became director of the CIA, Casey was asked what the war had meant to him. "Maybe it was because I was young," he answered, "but I'd never known such responsibility. I had five hundred people under me, a couple of air force squadrons at my disposal, a dozen French chateaus where we kept agents. I could walk into Patton's or Bradley's briefings any time I wanted to. I felt part of something larger than myself. I was making decisions that were a part of history." A Casey not given to visible displays of emotion looked out the window across Long Island Sound. His eyes clouded over. "It was the greatest experience of my life."

8.

The Making of William J. Casey

Three years after the war, Bill Casey was living in a Long Island mansion. In July of 1948, he purchased Mayknoll in Roslyn Harbor, a steeply peaked Victorian Gothic on nine landscaped acres of land that sloped gently to the water's edge and offered a splendid view of the harbor. One approached Mayknoll through an ivy-clad stone gateway, then followed a circular drive implanted over a heart-shaped lawn that led to the porte cochere. The main entrance opened onto an arched center hallway. The floors were in Italian terrazzo tile, the ceilings twelve feet high. The house had been built in the previous century and exuded a fusty Teddy Rooseveltian charm.

Casey bought Mayknoll virtually on an impulse for a then considerable $50,000. He could afford it. He had made a modest killing by selling a little microfilming company he had started, called Film Sort, to the Minnesota Mining and Manufacturing Company. He was also back working at the Research Institute of America, practicing law, and, as he had discussed with Milton Katz, promoting new enterprises.

Casey had stopped by 292 Madison Avenue soon after he came home from the war and Cherne had asked, "What do you expect to do with yourself now?" "I think I'd like to get into investment banking," Casey answered. Cherne was not sure what "investment banking" meant, but he was relieved to learn that in the meantime Casey was willing to return to the Institute. He came back at a salary of $12,000 a year, which soon rose to $24,000.

His energy had, if anything, increased. One young assistant remembered, "I'd see him working three secretaries at once, dictating to one while the others were off typing up the last batch. One would come back for more dictation while the other girl went to type, the way they keep painting the Golden Gate Bridge continuously from one end to the other."

Casey's London aide Walter Lord had finished up a law degree at Yale after the war and then came to Casey for career advice. Casey's reaction was instantaneous: "Come to work for me." Lord did and soon observed how the RIA functioned. The suave and silver-tongued Leo Cherne was Mr. Outside, attending the conferences, the big client lunches, and business community banquets. Casey was Mr. Inside, riding herd on the staff and pumping the work out. Lord also noticed that Casey was gaining renown as a tax and finance expert. "At first, Bill always seemed to be going down to Wall Street. But before long Wall Street was coming up to him." He recognized something else: no matter how important Casey was, "he was still distinctly in Leo's shadow"—a condition that struck Lord as impermanent, given the Casey he had come to know in London.

Still, Bill and Leo were obviously more than colleagues. Among Cherne's endless enthusiasms, flying was the latest. He had earned a pilot's license and wanted to take Casey up in a single-engine four-seater Beechcraft Bonanza. Cherne was a slapdash pilot; he forgot to replace the gas cap, and the fuel gauge soon dived toward empty. He managed to get the plane down, and Casey climbed out of the plane, ashen. If he was going to risk anything, it was his capital, not his life. This was more danger than he had faced in the entire war, he told Cherne. He did not fly with him again.

Cherne had fallen in love with a devout Catholic. He went to Casey for counsel. "Bill explained the elements of converting to Catholicism," as Cherne remembered, "without a trace of emotion, with all the detachment he'd bring to an elucidation of the tax code. No mention of my soul intruded on this discussion." And the confidences still flowed in only one direction.

Though Casey was set on piling up a fortune, he still yearned for public service. In 1948, his London roommate Milton Katz had left Harvard to become general counsel to the Marshall Plan in Paris. "I had a sense that Bill was getting restless at the RIA," Katz recalled. "So I said, 'Why don't you come over and work with me as associate general counsel?' "

Casey gave it a try. That July, he took leave from the Institute and went to Paris. His job was to get American industrialists and investors to build plants in a shattered and prostrate Europe. By then, pragmatism had settled into Casey's bones. He could support the loftiest ideals—as long as he could locate a no-nonsense rationale. He told a group of skeptical American businessmen who looked on the Marshall

Plan as a giveaway, "Well, you can invest your money in Europe, or you can have the government tax away your dollars to pay for a large military establishment to hold back the Soviets. A sick Europe can't do it itself, What'll it be?"

He proved a fair soothsayer: "I am now really hepped on American travel as the answer to Europe's dollar repayment problems. If we can just get air fares cut in half and get Americans traveling over here, we would get a lot of buying power over here."

But he quickly sized up the situation in Paris. There was only one job he wanted in the Marshall Plan—the top one, held by W. Averell Harriman, who had no plans to leave. Within less than six months, he was back at the RIA.

Two years later, during the summer of 1950, Casey staggered Leo Cherne: he was going into business for himself. Not only was he going into business for himself, but he was going into a *competing* business. And not only was he going into a competing business, but he was taking some of the Institute's stars with him, among them the firm's hottest salesman, and that prolific writer, now editor-in-chief of the Institute's foreign report, Walter Lord.

Of this bombshell Cherne later said, "Bill Casey totally set aside friendship and went by the ethics of the competitive system. I, a romantic, felt his breaking away and competing against me was an act of utter betrayal. I was confusing ethics, philosophy, and friendship with business. He became a ruthless and not terribly sensitive former friend."

Casey told Lord, " 'Walter, I've discovered that the world is divided between editors and publishers. And the publishers get all the money." He offered Lord a raise from $8,000 to $10,000 to become editor-in-chief of his new firm, ultimately to be called the Institute for Business Planning.

Casey's intention was to reproduce the success that the RIA had created out of war planning. As Walter Lord explained Casey's aim, "The Korean War had just broken out. We were going to tell businessmen how to deal with the new wartime controls. Bill told me, 'The prospects are unlimited. You'll move a lot faster with me than with Leo.' "

Casey sent Lord to Washington, while he himself intended to run the business out of offices on Long Island. "Bill had taken a seedy office for me at 1805 F Street, behind the Willard Hotel," Lord recounted. "When I got there, a guy was painting a sign on the window of the next-door office, 'Film and Fun.' Hmmm, I thought, this could be interesting. It was a mistake. It was supposed to be Film and File, which turned out to be another Casey microfilm operation that he'd told me nothing about."

Casey established the IBP offices at 14 Plaza Road in the town of Greenvale, about a mile from Mayknoll. He eventually hired a dozen bright young law-school graduates and more than twenty salesmen to provide newsletters, loose-leaf reference services, and desk manuals targeted to businessmen, lawyers, and accountants. In order to cut out middlemen, he acquired his own printing plant.

One young man whom Casey hired was Robert Walsh, a nephew of his old college pal Red Cassidy. Walsh described Casey's publishing philosophy: "He saw a gap and he was going to fill it. We were going to recommend to businessmen and investors how they could legally beat the system, how they could push the law to its outer edges, how they could profit from the law's ambiguities." Out of this philosophy came Casey's perhaps most notable invention. One of IBP's highly successful reference books was entitled *The Tax Shelter in Real Estate*. In it Casey described legitimate tax-beating angles in real property investments. William J. Casey was the originator of the tax shelter—both the name and the game.

He displayed an extraordinary facility for cranking out the stuff. He would leave the Greenvale office on a Friday night with an armful of research. He would then park himself at the kitchen table and begin writing furiously on yellow legal pads, in a barely legible hand. All of Sophia's efforts to set up an office for him in the huge house failed; he preferred the kitchen. By Monday morning, he would drop a complete handwritten first draft of a new reference book on the desk of one of his subordinates, saying, "Here. Clean it up." In this manner were born such works as *How to Build and Preserve Executive Wealth*, *How to Raise Cash and Influence Bankers*, and *How Federal Tax Angles Multiply Real Estate Profits*.

But no matter how successful the individual publications, IBP was losing a fortune. Casey had made a fundamental blunder: there was simply not enough editorial work to keep the costly presses and printing crew busy. The printing plant was an albatross. Aggravating the situation, the Korean War ended before the war planning services really got off the ground. Walter Lord quit to go into advertising and later to write highly successful books of his own.

Just as the losses from the IBP were becoming alarming, Casey spotted a life raft. In the mid-fifties, he went to R. P. Ettinger of Prentice-Hall Publications. He pointed out to Ettinger that he obviously had tapped a ready market with his desk reference books. Ettinger was a little old man, courtly, gracious, and tightfisted with a Prentice-Hall buck. After one of his lunches with Casey, he insisted on walking four blocks back to the restaurant to get a free-parking ticket stamped. Yet Casey managed to get a sweetheart deal out of the old man. Prentice-Hall, in effect, bought Casey out. The publisher set up a separate subsidiary for his books, still called the Institute for Business Planning, and left him with complete editorial control. Casey was to get 50 percent of the net profits, far superior to an author's usual 10 percent royalty. And he was free of the losing printing business.

He kept pouring out the books (*The Mutual Funds Desk Book*, *The Accounting Desk Book*), and the arrangement was instantly profitable. In time, he was running the operation with his left hand, leaving the bulk of the work to his editors. By the time he ended the arrangement some fifteen years later to go into government, Casey had earned more than $2,000,000 from the Prentice-Hall arrangement—$450,000 in the last year alone.

In his heart, he harbored more elevated literary ambitions. A reporter interviewing him in his book-lined study at Mayknoll asked him about a whole shelf on religion. Casey told him, "I get tired of churning out that other stuff. I'm planning to do a book on missionaries. That's the best story of organization and salesmanship in the world."

What he had seen in Europe while working on the Marshall Plan had confirmed Casey's loathing of communism. The Soviet Union had liberated Eastern Europe from the Nazis, then never let go. China had gone to the Communists in 1950. Cold war had become the persistent state between the West and the Soviet Union. And by June of 1950 the United States was involved in a hot war with the Communists in Korea. Senator Joe McCarthy found political gold in a vein of national political paranoia. True, McCarthy destroyed careers and innocent lives by his reckless, almost whimsical accusations of communism in government. True, his charges never flushed out a single Communist in the State Department, where he said there were 205. Fair-minded Republicans, even rational conservatives, cringed at the man's crude character assassinations. But Bill Casey supported Joe McCarthy.

Walter Lord was puzzled. "I always wondered," he later said, "how an essentially good man like Bill Casey could support this bully and liar. When I put the question to him one night at Mayknoll, he said, 'Walter, this isn't patty cake we're playing with the Russians. You need a McCarthy to flush out the enemy.' "

"Oh, Bill knew McCarthy was a horse's ass," Milt Katz concluded, "but in his judgment, a useful horse's ass. He picked up some of this zealotry from General Donovan. I once asked the General why he wanted to take a potentially boring job like ambassador to Thailand. 'Milt,' he said, 'because the cloven hoof is there, and I've got to find it.' Bill was always looking for the Communist hoof too. He was not a hater. He hated few things, and fewer people. But he did find one thing to hate just as you must find something to love. And it was communism."

One night, Casey invited all his old college pals out to Mayknoll. "I got there late," Red Cassidy remembered. "The whole gang was already there—Gene Duffy, everybody. I went up to say hi to Bill. He was involved in some kind of a discussion about McCarthy and his boys, and he says, 'What do you think of Roy Cohn?' I said, 'I don't think much. But maybe you could find him out at Fire Island.' 'Fire Island?' Bill roars at me. 'Yeah,' I said, 'with the rest of the queens.' All of a sudden, Bill took a shot at me and knocked me right over a table. I got up and let him have it. The other guys finally pulled us apart. Bill's practically frothing at the mouth, screaming at me, 'Get out of my house! Out! Out!' I didn't hear from him for over a year. Then one night he calls and invites me to be his guest at the big Fordham alumni dinner at the Waldorf. He never said a word about the Cohn incident. That was Casey's way. The invitation to the Waldorf was the apology."

He became a regular at Republican National Conventions. He was at the 1948 convention, which emerged in his résumé as "researched and hunted delegates for Thomas E. Dewey." The Republicans' selection of Dwight Eisenhower in 1952 did not please Casey. He told Milt Katz, who was moving from the Democrats to support Ike, "Eisenhower's a lightweight. Bob Taft has real weight." He went to Chicago for the convention, "hell bent," he said, "to get Bob Taft nominated." He set up an underground paper. Every morning on the hotel doorstep of every delegate, alternate, and hanger-on, the newspaper appeared as if from nowhere, like the "Swedish" newsletter that he had wanted to slip into Germany during the war. Headlines read, WE ALL LIKE IKE, BUT IKE CAN'T WIN and IKE'S A ME-TOO REPUBLICAN—LET'S NOMINATE A REAL REPUBLICAN.

The moralist Casey had his own explanation for why Eisenhower could not win, a reason known to few Americans at the time. Red Cassidy's nephew Bob Walsh was still working for Casey. Why was he for Taft, Walsh wanted to know, with an attractive candidate like Eisenhower available? "Because Ike can't make it," Casey said. "He had a skirt over his head during the war. He had a girlfriend, his Army chauffeur—that Summersby dame. That will sink him."

The now prosperous Casey became the angel to young, fragile conservative movements. He was a director on the board of the right-leaning publishing house of Henry Regnery. He had been pleasantly startled by the cleverness of a Regnery book entitled *McCarthy and His Enemies*, written by William F. Buckley, recently out of Yale. He and the author became fast friends. Bill Buckley occasionally anchored his sailboat in the little inlet at Mayknoll. They had lunch together. "We were always relaxed with each other," Buckley remembered of his visits, "the way it is with people who are Catholic, anticommunist, and conservative."

Buckley's magazine, the *National Review*, was having trouble staying afloat, and so Buckley went to Casey. "Here's what you do," Casey explained. "You sell the investors a bond for eighty dollars that matures at one hundred in ten years. See, if people just loan you the hundred outright, they'll have to pay taxes on the interest. But if a bond matures at a hundred dollars, they're just getting back the amount they put in, so there's no tax bite. And in the meantime, you'll have the working capital." As Casey's idea tumbled out in a torrent, young Buckley was surprised at how little he and the other intellectual champions of capitalism actually understood about how the system worked. The Casey plan was adopted, and the *National Review* survived.

By 1957, Buckley was urging formation of a New York State Conservative party, to counter the state's Liberal party. Buckley wanted Casey to be the new party's chairman. He wanted him, he said, "because he was deeply informed and literate. He was also a man of affairs who knew his way around the world—altogether, a logical, ideal choice." Casey knocked the idea down. He told Buckley that a state Conservative party could never match what the Liberal party had—"Dave Dubinsky's treasury at the International Ladies Garment Workers Union and thousands of garment workers."

A few years later, he was asked to save another conservative organ, *Human Events*. James Wick, the magazine's publisher, was on his deathbed. Casey had represented Wick as he bought up a small empire of periodicals, including *Human Events*. As he lay dying, Wick feared that this conservative voice would be stilled with his own. He asked Casey to take over as executor and to find a way to perpetuate the magazine. "I spent the better part of a year selling off Wick's publications for his estate, including *Human Events*," Casey remembered.

"But I sold *Human Events* to its employees—that kept the magazine alive, and Jim's conservative views along with it."

Casey was still practicing law solo. A later FBI background check on him for a seat on the Arms Control and Disarmament Commission reported: "He is regarded by his peers as one of the leading tax attorneys in the United States." When two heirs of the Du Pont fortune, brothers Eugene III and Nicholas Du Pont, faced a horrifying tax bill, they brought in Casey. Their father's death had left each brother with a huge block of Du Pont stock, and it looked as if they were going to have to sell off to pay the inheritance taxes. Casey had a solution. He created a new corporation for each brother. The corporations sold warrants—promises to pay a specified amount at a future date—backed by their stock. The proceeds from the sale of the warrants were used to pay off the estate taxes, and the Du Ponts' stock was saved.

The brothers liked this smart New Yorker. They brought him in as a partner in a company that dabbled in oil leases. When Ridgely Oil was liquidated, Casey's settlement totaled $771,000, for which he had put up nothing but his legal savvy.

He was a hot property, sought after by law firms, a "rainmaker," who knew how to generate business. Leonard Hall wanted Casey in his firm. Casey had met Hall in 1952 at the Republican National Convention. Hall was a former six-term congressman from Long Island who had just wrapped up four years as the Republican national chairman when he first approached Casey. One of Hall's law partners had gone on the bench. Why didn't Casey come aboard and take his place? Casey could run the New York office of the firm, and Hall would run the Garden City end. Len Hall was a power and an appealing man to boot. Casey happily accepted. In July 1957 he became a partner in a firm ultimately called Hall, Casey, Dickler and Howley.

Casey was in his mid-fifties, and his appearance and manner had begun to harden into caricature. All the gangling leanness of youth was gone, replaced by a fleshiness. The face had started to acquire its pouched, puckered appearance. The hair on his pate thinned, and what was left turned frizzy. He remained an unconscious dresser. And Gerry Dickler, one of his new partners, noted, "Bill was a shoveler when it came to food."

He had developed odd tics, mostly ways of working off nervous energy, that became familiar to everyone who knew him. When people talked to him, he would listen with a deceptive distractedness, gazing off, his feet on the desk, chewing on the end of his tie, or opening a paper clip and jabbing at the spaces between his teeth. Then, suddenly, he was all motion, behaving like an absentminded professor on uppers as he dashed from office to airport to board room. There was always too much on his schedule, too much on his mind. Once, he and Hall were to meet in Washington's National Airport. Casey failed to show. An annoyed Hall was on the point of leaving when he was paged. On the phone was Casey. He was sorry, he said—he had boarded the wrong plane and was in Chicago. "But it's okay," Casey added, "I sat next to the CEO of an insurance company and signed him up as a client."

Besides handsome fees, Casey's most important reward in the new partnership was Len Hall's friendship. Hall was thirteen years older than Casey, a bald, portly, moon-faced, jovial man who was virtually impossible to dislike. Hall too was a Long Island native, the youngest of eight children of Teddy Roosevelt's coachman. He liked to say that there were two classes where he grew up, "the people who owned the estates and the people who worked on them. My people worked on them."

They were superficially similar: self-made men with old-shoe looks, plain-talking and unpretentious. And both of them loved politics. But Casey loved the politics of ideas—conservative ideas. Hall loved the politics of people, doing favors and asking favors, cobbling a compromise that made everybody feel a winner and nobody a loser, attending wakes, baptisms and bar mitzvahs. Casey could not swallow Hall's all-embracing bonhomie, but he admired his practical knowledge of politics, his zest for the game, the sensitivity in Len's fingertips for the public pulse, which the intellectualizing Casey still lacked. They found that their differences stimulated rather than grated. "He's my brains," Hall would say of Casey. "I'm the guy who holds Len's briefcase," Casey would say of Hall. They had a standing date that was to last until Hall's death in 1979: every Saturday they lunched together at Caminari's Restaurant in Locust Valley, and for over two hours they talked politics.

In the late spring of 1958, Hall decided to pursue the dream of a lifetime: he was going to run for governor of New York, an office Teddy Roosevelt had held. Averell Harriman was just finishing out his term as New York's first Democratic governor in twelve years. Harriman was an able governor but a lifeless and inept campaigner. Harriman's party was split between reformers and regulars. Hall thought he saw a clear shot at the State House. He told Casey at one of their Caminari lunches, "You're the smart one. I want you to work up the issues, the position papers, my speech themes."

The powerful Nassau County organization lined up behind Hall, its favorite son. When President Eisenhower called Republican House members together to give Hall an award for his services to the party, Ike's signal was unmistakable. Hall began to travel New York, a state where he had friends and IOUs in every town. Most promising, L. Judson Morehouse, the state Republican chairman, seemed to be in Hall's corner.

And then something strange happened. Malcolm Wilson, a Fordham contemporary of Casey's, now a popular and powerful Republican state assemblyman, was showing up in all the locales that Hall visited, and with another candidate—a new face on the Republican stage, Nelson A. Rockefeller. Soon, "secret" polls were finding their way to the press that showed Rockefeller to be the stronger candidate. Rockefeller had paid for the polls. Casey was furious. "That's just name recognition," he complained. "These pollsters don't know if people are responding to the Rockefeller Foundation, Rockefeller Center, or Nelson Rockefeller. And he doesn't give a damn."

Len Hall was glum. Rockefeller, then a vital fifty-year-old, was fresh, handsome, rich. Hall told Casey, "Can you believe it, Bill? My best friends are asking me to release them. They want to go over to that guy. Do you know what we're fighting? A money machine! I feel like I've been run over by a gold-plated steamroller." Hall dropped out before the state nominating convention.

Casey was more bitter than Hall. Men like himself and Len had paid their dues, earned their power and positions through merit and struggle. Len Hall had pulled his way up from folks who waited on people like the Roosevelts and the Rockefellers. Now, a generation later, were the sons of the privileged simply to brush them aside like upstart servants? To Casey, Nelson Rockefeller was just another white-shoe boy—worse still, a graduate of Roosevelt's New Deal school of tax and tax, spend and spend.

Casey was not done with Rockefeller. He went to Daniel G. Buckley, a Long Island lawyer and conservative activist, and quietly persuaded him to create a "Committee for Republican Victory." The committee took a room in the Hotel McAlpin in New York. Its only function was to send letters attacking Rockefeller to delegates attending the New York State Republican gubernatorial nominating convention. Casey approved the text, which was standard right-wing political apoplexy: "As far as we know, Rockefeller never officially moved into the Democratic Party. But we do know that his socialite wife, who said she was also fed up with our party, registered in New York's socialistic Liberal Party. . . . Do you want the Republican Party to become a captive of left-wing liberals?"

The letterhead of the Committee for Republican Victory listed ten names, but Bill Casey's was not among them. He did, however, Daniel Buckley reported, pay Buckley "four or five thousand dollars in cash" to cover the costs of the committee's effort to defeat Rockefeller—an unsuccessful effort, for Rockefeller was nominated, and went on to defeat Averell Harriman handily.

Bill Casey was a pragmatist, and pragmatism suggested courting a powerful new Republican governor of his state, especially one with hot-eyed presidential ambitions. But Casey's pragmatism was not bottomless. He could not swallow Nelson Rockefeller then, or ever.

Casey had turned away from intelligence after the war to pursue his fortune. It was to be a prosperous era for Casey, but not—not immediately—for American espionage. With the coming of peace, the enemies of the OSS were not content that they had reduced it to a puny Strategic Services Unit buried in the War Department. They wanted to stamp out even this spore—it might grow. Early in 1946, while still at the RIA, Casey had received a call from General Donovan, asking Casey to come to Washington to David Bruce's house. The General was also inviting Russ Forgan, Lester Armour, and other OSS luminaries. The meeting was to be secret, which did not detract from its appeal. Donovan himself would not be coming: he would be a lightning rod, he said. The SSU was in danger of being run out of town. They had to do something to keep this skeleton outfit alive, weak as it was.

To Casey, the gathering over dinner at Bruce's was a bittersweet moment, like seeing an old lover again too soon after the breakup. But he was flattered that Donovan had welcomed him into the old-boy net. Before the group adjourned, they drew up a quiet plan to lobby influential friends in Congress to save the SSU. They did their work well, and the SSU was able to retain its meager assets for another day.

At the meeting, Casey met Bill Quinn, then executive officer of the SSU, a canny G-2 veteran of the Seventh Army campaigns in France. Quinn was scouring his ingenuity to keep the SSU afloat and grateful for the help of the old hands. Before Casey left town, he told Quinn, "Give me a call once in a while. Let me know what's going on. Tell me how I can be helpful."

In 1947, the Cold War achieved what Bill Donovan had failed to do. Harry Truman was compelled to eat a ration of crow and, instead of sinking the SSU, establish the Central Intelligence Agency.

Casey's association with old comrades-in-arms was to be fleeting, casual, mostly social, until late in the fifties. He was still close to Bert Jolis, now back in the diamond business, working out of New York and Paris. John Bross, the officer who had managed to scrounge the A-26s for the Joan-Eleanor missions, was now a Long Island attorney and neighbor. And he would occasionally see Henry Hyde, who had a place on Fire Island. One afternoon, Hyde told Casey that he, Whitney Shepardson, and some of the other fellows were forming an organization, the Veterans of the Office of Strategic Services—the VOSS. Of course, the country had a permanent intelligence service; but who could tell when the VOSS might be needed, as a cadre, or a lobby, should support for intelligence ever flag again? The new association would also offer an opportunity to see everybody, to relive their glory days. Hyde was an attorney, with a posh practice in Manhattan. And for lawyers like himself and Casey, the VOSS could be a splendid source of clients.

Casey, the indefatigable joiner, quickly made himself a stalwart of the VOSS. In the summer of 1959, fifteen years after D day, he arranged for thirty-five members of the French resistance to come to America as guests of the VOSS. The following year, the French reciprocated. Casey was now president of the organization. On May 21 he led a party on what he called the "second invasion of France." The Americans were guests of Action Amicale, the veterans' organization of the French resistance. It was a journey drenched in nostalgia—a visit to an American cemetery outside of Paris where the war had ended for some of their comrades, and to Mont-Valerian, the shrine of the resistance. In Lyons, Casey made a bold decision: he would speak in French at the dinner honoring the VOSS. After all, he had studied the language in college. The conclusion of Casey's speech was greeted at first by a perplexed silence, broken at last by polite applause. The next day a Lyons newspaper reported: "Monsieur William J. Casey spoke a language of his own."

One figure was missing on the return to France. Through the years, Casey had been among the regular visitors who called at 4 Sutton Place, Donovan's home in Manhattan. Donovan could still exercise his almost mystical power over men who somehow forever remained his loyal subordinates; and in Casey, the old man found a son who shared his historical vision of espionage. Donovan had amassed a collection of documents on intelligence operations that George Washington had carried out during the revolution. He told Casey that there was a book to be written here, a book with pertinence for the present, the proof that espionage was not foreign to the American character—

it was there at the very founding. Casey begged off. He had his own books to write, books that were making his fortune.

If he failed to call on Donovan, the old man would call him, faintly querulous, like an aging parent who felt neglected. And then the calls stopped. Donovan had a stroke in 1958. Within a year, on February 8, 1959, he was dead.

Casey flew to Washington for the funeral at Arlington National Cemetery. He went with Sophia, John Shaheen, and Shaheen's wife, Barbara. Shaheen was a friend in the Casey mold, a self-made oil operator and an OSS veteran who had had a colorful OSS career running agents in the Mediterranean.

John Shaheen recalled the gray, joyless day. Casey was uncharacteristically quiet, almost numb; at times during the ceremony, he would shake his head, as though Donovan's passing was something he could not accept. Shaheen knew Casey for another business hard-nose. But this was a father they were putting away. Donovan was "part of Bill's heart," Shaheen said. "Bill buried a part of himself that day."

9.

Wealth and Power

O n a fall day in 1962, at five o'clock in the morning, Carl Paffendorf was awakened by a phone call from William J. Casey. Paffendorf was a thirty-year-old Cincinnati lawyer with a flourishing practice in estate planning. Casey said he wanted to have lunch with Paffendorf; where could they meet? At the Colony Restaurant at twelve-thirty, Paffendorf answered drowsily, and went back to sleep. It was not until they sat down at the Colony that Paffendorf realized that Casey had not been in Cincinnati when he called. He was still home on Long Island, and flew out later that morning. This was Paffendorf's introduction to the Casey style.

A month before, Casey had heard Paffendorf make a speech at the American Bar Association Convention in St. Louis. Paffendorf had described a potential breakthrough enterprise—preparing income tax returns by computer. Casey had long ago decided that rapid processing of data was the modern equivalent of the Industrial Revolution; here was where the great advances and fortunes would be made. Paffendorf, a tall, lean, rugged, quietly confident man, was clearly on to something.

"Look, kid," Casey told Paffendorf over the lunch, "I've been in on a hundred venture-capital deals. It always takes more time and money than you think. You're going to run out of capital. Come and work for me at the Institute for Business Planning and I'll stake you."

"I don't want to work for anybody else," Paffendorf answered, politely but firmly.

"All right. Take a six-month sabbatical. I'll provide you with office space and help," Casey went on. "I've got a good technical library you can work in. If you run out of money, I'll give you whatever you need. Then, when you've got your system operational, just give me a piece of the action—whatever you think my help was worth. Think it over. Now, take me out to the airport."

Carl Paffendorf was a bachelor earning more than thirty thousand dollars a year in 1962, with six other lawyers working for him and more business than he could handle. But his dream was to perfect his computerized tax-returns system. If he could just stop the phones from ringing, the meetings with clients, the constant interference, and set aside ten thousand dollars to support himself for six uninterrupted months, he knew he could make this system work. And here was this odd stranger dangling that very opportunity before him. Within six months, Paffendorf wrapped up his Cincinnati law office and went to work full-time on his project out of Casey's IBP offices in Greenvale.

Casey had gone into venture capitalism the very month he left the OSS. An uncle, Robert Lavigne, had developed a formula for making concentrated frozen orange juice. Casey had bought into the firm. He took several cans of the juice on a business trip, but they leaked and the juice went bad. Undaunted, he invested in a company producing a handgun that could be converted into a rifle. Some schemes worked; some failed. He dropped $91,000 on a deal for publishing quickie college texts. He got in early on a company with a dry system for developing film by heat instead of a liquid solution. He reportedly made at least $500,000 on the sale of the company's stock.

He went to a stockholders' meeting of another company and there met a Greek-American who had worked with the OSS in the Aegean. They traded war stories, and, intriguing to Casey, he learned that George Doundoulakis was an inventor.

At the time he met Casey, Doundoulakis had recently won a contract from the Army Signal Corps to produce a radar that could measure the trajectory of a mortar shell. But he lacked the capital to follow through on his bid. He had had only this single encounter with Casey; but on a hunch, he called him and explained his problem. Casey said, "Meet me in front of the Franklin Bank in Garden City at eleven o'clock tomorrow." Casey was standing there when Doundoulakis arrived. He handed the inventor a check for $100,000. "I was stunned," Doundoulakis remembered. "Nothing to sign. No collateral. No interest. Not even a handshake. He gave me the check and left. I gradually paid him back, but he never seemed to have any idea how much I owed him."

Casey essentially had bought himself an inventor the way another man might buy a yacht. He gave Doundoulakis space in Greenvale for a laboratory, charged no rent, paid him a $50,000-a-year salary, and let the inventor putter. "He never asked what I was doing—never even asked me for a piece of the patents," Doundoulakis recalled. "I'd never dealt with anybody like him."

Casey's sponsorship of Carl Paffendorf and his computerized tax returns was to last not six months but six years. Casey never faltered; he soon had $100,000 invested in Paffendorf—and still Paffendorf needed more. "I can't keep tapping you," Paffendorf finally told Casey after he had spent two years on the project. "Why don't we incorporate and sell shares?" Paffendorf suggested. Casey agreed and said, "All right. I'll take twelve and a half percent of the business."

Paffendorf went home and thought over the deal. It was not fair. He called Casey and said so. "He hollered so loud, I thought he was coming through the phone," Paffendorf recalled. "I let him rant for five minutes about all he'd done for me and what an ungrateful little bastard I was. Finally I said, 'Bill, it's not fair because you should get at least twenty-five percent interest.' There was this sudden silence. And then he said, like a little kid, 'Gee, nobody ever did anything like that for me before.' I'd made a friend for life."

In the serendipitous ways of business, Paffendorf's tax-return service itself did not make much money, but it led indirectly to a fortune. The service was included in a new company that Paffendorf formed, called COAP, for Computer Oriented Analysis and Planning. Casey took back all the money he had loaned Paffendorf in stock in the new corporation. The public offering of COAP stock was oversubscribed by three times. Paffendorf had to send money back. The stock opened at one dollar and was trading at fifteen dollars three months later. Casey had gambled one hundred thousand dollars on Paffendorf, but he later made another instant million just selling off part of his COAP holdings.

If it was that easy to raise money for COAP, why would it not be just as easy to raise money for other entrepreneurs? Paffendorf concluded. Why didn't they combine capital formation with Casey's invention, the tax shelter? They could form a corporation that would raise money for new ventures. The scheme offered investors attractive tax savings on essentially paper losses, plus the potential for capital appreciation. Thus was born what came to be called Vanguard Ventures, which Paffendorf ran and in which Casey became a heavy investor. "We raised an awful lot of money. We did maybe thirty deals over the next few years," Paffendorf recalled. "We were copied all over the lot. Eventually these tax-shelter investments nationwide became a ten-billion-dollar industry.

"Bill Casey had the two absolutely essential traits of the venture capitalist," Paffendorf concluded. "He could pick horses *and* jockeys. He could spot a promising company, an idea, an invention, and he could judge if the people running it were any good.

"There were so many unexpected sides to him," Paffendorf recalled.

"I was working late one night and Bill came into my office and poured himself a cup of coffee. I was going with a girl at the time and couldn't decide if I wanted to get married. So I asked Bill's opinion. He said something that stayed with me: 'It doesn't have to be one hundred percent in a marriage. None of my deals are one hundred percent. Marriage isn't even based all that much on love, either. It's mutual affection, mutual help, putting together a lifetime of memories.' That helped me, because I was afraid of not achieving some kind of perfection in marriage."

There was another side to Casey's character that Paffendorf had not counted on—a hair-trigger temper. And he could never tell when he would trigger it. "Once I casually mentioned to him that I thought the game where there was real money was insurance. He blew up! He started swearing at me and pounding his desk. 'The law! The law! That's where the goddamned money is!' I had no idea what set him off. I never saw such a performance. I was astounded."

Another business associate recounted: "I was at Casey's house with my wife and another couple. Bill was talking about a friend of his, a liberal Democrat. I said I was surprised Bill Casey had a liberal Democrat for a friend. The man went absolutely crazy. He started screaming at me. 'You sound like an idiot! I must have sold my brains when I got involved with somebody like you!' When we left that night, I thought, 'Well, there goes the deal.' But I saw him the next day and it was as if nothing had happened. He didn't even seem to remember."

Within fifteen years after the war, Casey was a millionaire several times over. His most profitable investment dwarfed all the others. There was in the city of Albany, New York, the Hudson Valley Broadcasting Company, which owned a radio station, WROW, and a sister television station, WROW-TV. The company had gotten off to a rocky start; the directors had had to hit up the original investors twelve times for additional capital. Casey's law firm represented the Hudson Valley Broadcasting Company. At one point, Hudson Valley issued stock to raise capital to buy another radio station, in Raleigh, North Carolina, and thus it became Capital Cities Broadcasting Corporation. Casey, as the lawyer for the corporation, came to know the founder of the company, Frank Smith, and drew a quick conclusion: problems apart, Frank Smith was a good jockey. And so he started buying shares in Capital Cities. They were virtually penny stocks—he initially was paying thirteen cents a share. He also began giving the company the benefit of his tax expertise, which saved huge sums as Capital Cities acquired more and more stations. By 1957, he was a member of the board.

Frank Smith was eventually followed by his hand-picked successor, a younger man named Tom Murphy. Bill Casey spotted another jockey. Tom Murphy was a graduate of the Brooklyn Preparatory Jesuit School and Cornell, tall, broad-shouldered, balding, as unpretentious and plainspoken as Casey. And his father had been Thomas Murphy, the judge who tried Alger Hiss. Casey liked that.

"Bill's intelligence background never completely left him," Murphy recalled. "Frank Smith hated to fly. I was coming up in the company, so Frank sent me with Casey to negotiate the acquisition of KOVR-TV in San Francisco. We were in a conference room with their people. Their guy would propose something and I'd say, 'That makes sense to me.' I'd said it several times when Casey popped up and asked where the men's room was. On the way out he tapped my shoulder, so I followed him. As soon as we got there, I was shocked to see him get down on his hands and knees on the floor—he was looking under the door of the toilet stalls! Finally, he got up and said in a whisper, 'For chrissake, Murphy, will you stop agreeing!' 'But,' I said, 'their positions *are* reasonable.' 'I know that,' Casey said. 'But we don't give anything away without getting something for it. That's why it's called negotiation!' "

Capital Cities continued to thrive. At one point, Casey had 51,000 shares, which he had acquired for something over $10,000. When the company went public, Capital Cities Broadcasting opened at 37.5—and Casey's shares were worth just under $2 million.

The road of the entrepreneur, however, could be rock strewn, Casey learned. In 1956 he went to the Republican National Convention in San Francisco. A Prentice-Hall salesman had asked him if, while there, he would see an aspiring business writer named Harry R. Fields. Casey agreed. Fields came to his hotel room bearing a manuscript that he hoped Casey would publish. He also wanted to write on a regular basis for the Institute for Business Planning. Casey told him, "If we take your piece, it'll probably be for two hundred and fifty dollars. And if it works out, we'll pay you the same for any other pieces on assignment." According to Casey, when he got back to Greenvale, he handed the Fields manuscript to his chief editor to review. The editor told him it was just a rehash of law and regulation and of no interest.

In April of 1957, Casey received a letter from Fields complaining that several pages of his manuscript had appeared in a supplement to one of Casey's desk reference books, entitled *Pay Plans*. Casey later claimed that he checked into the matter and found out that one of his stable of lawyer-writers had in fact lifted a chunk of Fields's material and dropped it intact into the *Pay Plans* supplement. Casey called Fields and offered to pay him $250. Fields was not appeased; instead, he sued William J. Casey for $175,000 for plagiarism. The case came to trial in March of 1962.

J. Braxton Craven, Jr., was relatively new to the federal bench. He had been sent up temporarily from the South to hear cases at the federal court on Foley Square in Manhattan. The case of *Fields* vs. *Casey and the Institute for Business Planning* was one of the first New York cases he heard. Judge Craven found the attorney that Casey had retained cocky, overbearing, and contemptuous. "I had the feeling from the beginning of the trial," Craven remembered, "that it was going for the plaintiff." But if Fields did win, he thought, the man would be lucky to get $250.

To Casey's shock, the jury found for the plaintiff and awarded Fields, between compensatory and punitive damages, $41,425. He could handle the financial loss with the stroke of his pen on a checkbook. But the potential damage to his reputation was horrifying.

He was, by now, not only a financial success but a budding philanthropist, a pillar of his community. He contributed heavily to Catholic Charities, to hospitals, to the United Fund, the Boy Scouts, the United Jewish Appeal, the Fordham Fund. He had apologetically told Arthur Hug, a business associate who hit him up for a charitable cause, "I'm sorry, Art, I can only give five thousand dollars. That's my customary limit." He belonged to honorable and exclusive societies—the Knights of Malta, the Friendly Sons of Saint Patrick. He had begun his own philanthropy foundation, the William and Sophia Casey Foundation, which made awards to children to carry out projects over summer vacation. One girl had wanted to make her own clothes but did not have a sewing machine; Casey's foundation bought her one. The whole thrust of these years had not been simply to build a fortune but to make himself a figure of respectability and influence—and certainly not to have his name dragged through the mud by an offense as vulgar as plagiarism.

Casey huddled with his lawyers and came to a conclusion. They had lost on first hearing of the case; they would quite likely lose on appeal, thus doubling the risks of bad publicity. The objective now was damage control. Two days after the verdict, both parties met in Judge Craven's chambers, and Casey made an offer. He would not appeal, and he would pay the judgment—if the record of the trial was sealed and the verdict sheet destroyed. No one, including the plaintiff, was ever to discuss the verdict with the press.

After obtaining the consent of all parties, Judge Craven ordered the court reporter not to transcribe his notes and that no record of the trial be made available. "I then held up the verdict sheet," Craven later recounted, "and said, 'What do I do with this?' Everybody said, 'Tear it up.' I folded it two or three times into several pieces, walked to the judge's bathroom adjacent to the robing room, put the pieces in the toilet, and flushed them into the Hudson River."

Technically, the case had not been sealed; still, Casey thought, here was an end to it. In sending the papers into the Hudson, however, all the judge had done was to convert a land mine into a floating mine—one that would bob up years later and very nearly sink William J. Casey's quest for dignity.

The Casey of Mayknoll was an often remote, distracted master. "We had an expression in the family," his daughter, Bernadette, recalled. "Dad would be all tied up in his work. We'd ask him a question and he'd ignore us. We'd say, 'Sorry, the line is busy.' Five minutes later he'd look up and give you the answer.

"We'd usually have all our relatives over to our house for Christmas. I remember after one dinner, all the cousins got together in the living room to practice the Christmas show we were going to put on. Some of us were reciting our lines. Other kids were singing; somebody else was dancing. And Dad was sitting in the middle of all this, with the legal pad on his lap, writing. My mother came in and said, 'Bill, how can you concentrate in here?' He looked up—and finally noticed we were in the room."

Red Cassidy's nephew Bob Walsh was summoned to Mayknoll from the IBP offices. "Bill was suffering from an allergic reaction to penicillin," Walsh recalled. "So he wanted me to bring the mail and some papers out to him. There were huge red welts all over his face. He had a week's growth of beard. His temperature was one hundred and two degrees, and he could hardly talk. But the minute I stepped into his room, he was rasping orders at me and didn't stop until I left. He seemed totally oblivious of his condition."

Oblivious he may have appeared, but his self-awareness was acute. At age fifty-two, he wrote his family doctor, who had advised him to take it easier: "Don't you know I lead about as strenuous a life as anybody I know? I don't exert myself physically very much, but I almost always have something going on. I don't do very much except talk to people and cope with problems, most of which involve a fair degree of pressure and mental strain. This goes on all the time." And he popped antacid tablets all day long.

Connie Kirk was Casey's personal secretary for more than fifteen years, beginning in the early fifties in the days of his solo law practice. Her recollections of Casey leave a vivid portrait: "I answered a placement agency ad in the paper and went for an interview at his office at 122 East Forty-Second Street. Within five minutes, he said, 'Okay, you're hired,' and he started giving me dictation. The first thing he dictated was an eighty-six-page brief. Five o'clock came and he was still dictating. Eight o'clock, still dictating. About midnight, he said, 'I gotta go. I'm going to the Republican convention. Here, take care of this while I'm gone.' He handed me the petty cash box and ran out the door. The next day I went back to the employment agency and I said, 'I can't stay there. I can't understand him. And the hours!' The manager begged me, 'Stay. He's a wonderful man.' "

Connie Kirk was thirty-nine years old and unmarried when she went to work for Casey. She was a tall, stately woman, raised in Brooklyn, with an appropriate accent. She was capable, quick, and took no guff from anyone, beginning with Casey. George Doundoulakis remembered coming into the middle of a Casey rampage: "Bill was shouting at Connie, 'Where the hell is the contract? What the hell did you do with the contract?' " Connie, Doundoulakis recalled, looked at Casey with the amused contempt of Alice answering Ralph Kramden: "With that trash heap you call a desk, it's a wonder I can find anything." Doundoulakis was astounded: "I had been raised in Europe. I had never heard a secretary talk to a boss like that and stay on the job."

The hours never slackened. Kirk once had to remind Casey that it was Christmas Eve. "But what about finishing your work?" he asked her. She threw on her coat and stormed out, shouting, "And Merry Christmas to you too, Scrooge!" He later told her, "You got more spirit than most of the men around here." He had found the perfect foil. He liked people who shot back.

Connie Kirk was also to discover an unexpected sensitivity. His distractedness, the wrong planes taken, the misplaced papers, the mumbled orders were becoming legendary and had created an image that Casey resented. On one occasion he had gone out to lunch and lost his wallet. His driver told Kirk what had happened, and she later said, sympathetically, "Hey, I hear you lost your wallet." "Who said so?" he snapped back. "Who told you that?" When she had to ask him to repeat himself again and again while he was dictating, he would shout, "You know your trouble? You've got a hearing problem." "He just couldn't admit to any faults," Connie Kirk concluded. "You had to pretend he never made a mistake."

He was a bellower and a hollerer, brusque and impatient, hard as nails in a negotiation but soft toward people in their personal travails. Owen Smith had first met Casey during the ill-starred Len Hall gubernatorial bid, when Owen was a big, cherubic, affable college kid who ran the mimeograph, ran errands, and traveled with the candidate as a one-man advance team. In 1960, he found himself rooming in Washington with Casey while they both worked in the Nixon campaign. Casey thought Owen ought to become a lawyer and made him an attractive offer: work part-time at IBP at the then-handsome salary of one thousand dollars a month while attending Casey's alma mater, Saint John's. The deal ran for the full four years that it took Smith to get the degree. Owen Smith became close to Casey—an aide-de-camp, a surrogate son. And Owen fell in love with Casey's daughter, Bernadette.

"He was not really tough as a boss, just tough-acting," Owen recalled. "I'd say, 'Bill, this guy's a drunk. We can't carry him anymore.' Then he'd tell me all about the guy's problems at home. Finally, when a situation became intolerable, he'd send me to lower the boom. He couldn't bring himself to fire anybody."

Casey had hired a chauffeur, a flashy Colombian with a string of women. The chauffeur came to Casey and asked for a thousand-dollar loan. Casey made a business decision: the man looked like a poor risk. He turned him down—thereupon the Colombian stole the petty cash fund and skipped out. "Aren't you going to prosecute him?" Connie Kirk asked. "Nyaaah," Casey answered. "What's the use?"

He rarely criticized anyone openly. "Whenever I'd start finding fault with my friends," Bernadette recalled, "Dad wouldn't put up with it. 'You don't know everything about them,' he'd tell me. 'Give people a chance. Give 'em three strikes. Maybe you caught 'em on a bad day.' "

But the moment the issue was business, it was as though the bell rang and he was in the ring. George Doundoulakis found the businessman Casey frightening. "I'd see the change as soon as he'd start to negotiate. It didn't make any difference if the man was his best friend five minutes before—he became a tiger. He could be rough. When I'd say, 'Bill, you didn't have to be so tough in there,' he'd say, 'I won't lose any sleep over that one.' "

Casey and Leo Cherne had eventually repaired their friendship. But after the split of 1950, Cherne understood the man better: "To Bill, business was about business. It was not about going to church on Sunday. That's why he had no problem with stealing my people. He never saw an ethical dimension to business. Is it illegal? If not, then you can do it. You don't defraud investors. You don't break the law. But bare-knuckled competition? That's the American way. That was what *made* America. Besides, nothing had ever been handed to him— why should he hand anything to anyone else?"

He had learned from his father the political currency of favors. When someone asked him for a favor, if he could, he did it. Bread upon the waters—it was a language he understood. He was always writing letters: to get an old veteran into a VA hospital, to help an alien stay in the country, to find a job for an out-of-work friend. Milton Katz remembered an incident involving Kingman Brewster, a thoroughgoing New England Yankee, then president of Yale. Casey had known Brewster during the Marshall Plan days. He complained to Katz: "I've got a friend trying to get his son into Yale. I called Kingman and told him, 'The kid's having a little difficulty—can we give him some help?' Jeez! He treated me like dirt. He made me feel as if I'd committed a crime. He practically hung up on me. What the hell's going on here?" His idea of ethics was personal, not institutional. Friends helped friends. He could not understand the bloodless honor code of Yankee Kingman Brewster.

He had made a rich man of Carl Paffendorf; they had cut dozens of profitable deals. Yet when an interviewer asked what, after twenty years of association with Casey, stood out most in his mind, Paffendorf thought at length and then answered, "He had a profound influence on my religious beliefs. I'd gone through periods of doubt, of agnosticism. I was always questioning my faith. I drifted away from the church. At first I was surprised to find that Bill was a religious man. He was such a tough guy. He had the most questioning, unaccepting mind I'd ever come across. You could never get anything past him. But when I mentioned my crisis of faith, he said, 'Carl, you can question business deals. But if you start questioning your faith, you're a hollow man.' I started thinking, 'If a guy this brilliant can stop questioning his God, why can't I?' Because of him, I went back to the church. I found my faith again."

He was not only the squire at Mayknoll but chieftain of a clan. His mother lived with him in the main house. His mother-in-law and one sister-in-law lived in the "carriage house." The "shore house" was occupied by another sister-in-law, the "horse barn" by a brother-in-law, and the "chicken coop" by still another sister-in-law, all with their respective families, all in buildings that had been converted from their original uses to comfortable dwellings. On holidays, the relatives came up to the big house for huge dinners. At Easter the children romped over the heart-shaped lawn looking for Easter eggs.

The Casey marriage rolled on, steady as an ocean liner. Of it Casey's friend William Safire observed: "Sophia had a marvelous irreverent strain. She never took Bill too seriously. She reminded me of Judy Holliday in *Born Yesterday*—the dumb blonde who isn't dumb at all. She was also a very safe repository of all his confidences. You could ask her a question and she could look through you as though she'd never heard a thing in all her years with Bill Casey." He might not be the smitten lover of their youth, but Casey continued his unspoken adoration of his wife. Len Hall once observed, "Anything that woman wants, she gets."

One reason that the marriage worked well was a clear division of labor. Casey was like the ship's captain who once in home port never lifts a finger. "She ran the home, and Bill never got involved in anything," Owen Smith remembered. "Besides, Bill was mechanically hopeless. He couldn't screw in a light bulb." Bernadette remembered, "From the time I was ten, I had to put my own Christmas toys together."

Casey could have afforded any car, but he was as oblivious of the American love affair with the automobile as he was of his appearance. "He just didn't care," Bernadette recalled. "He'd let me pick out our cars—any good, solid American make. Then he'd keep it until it fell apart. He had a driver, and it was just as well, because Dad was a terrible driver." On a family vacation abroad, Casey rented a car and drove up a Corsican mountainside, the car lurching and bucking all the way—he had forgotten to shift out of high for the entire drive. On another occasion, he drove from the Nice airport to Monte Carlo in low gear.

He and Sophia had wanted to have more children, but they were unable. And so his attentions were lavished on his daughter. Bernadette grew up a pretty, happy, uncomplicated girl, with huge saucer eyes set in an ever-smiling face. Little of the adolescent angst that makes child rearing so anomalous a pleasure seems to have infected the Casey household. Mother, father, and daughter all seemed to live in harmony. At home, Casey was easy about his fortune as few self-made men are. "I must have been thirty," Bernadette remarked, "before I realized that we had money. Dad never talked money around the house. I had the sense he liked the game of making money more than the money itself—the wheeling, the dealing, the operating."

He liked to play chess with Bernadette. The board was kept set up, ready to go. Chess taught you to think several moves ahead. It taught you that all of one's actions are eventually interrelated, that the moves we make today determine the moves we can or cannot make tomorrow. But he could not bear to lose, not even to his beloved daughter. That would have been a misleading and dangerous lesson about life—to expect unearned victories.

His relationship with his brother, George, was predictable for siblings of unequal talents. After the war, George, a good writer, had gone to work for Bill's IBP. He decided eventually to break free and take a job in Detroit; but when a baby came along, George had to come back to Bill's employ. Then he went off to become circulation director for *Forbes* magazine; but again he came back, this time to try a new business venture with Bill. In and out of dependence on big brother—an ego-bruising cycle. George's son, Larry, read the relationship well: "My dad was immensely proud of his brother, Bill. He basked in his achievements. He even kept a scrapbook on him. Yet there was always a tinge of envy. He wished he could have provided as well for his family as Bill had. He also felt terrible frustration trying to communicate with Bill. My dad would start a conversation and it always seemed to end up with Bill lecturing him. Or he'd go to see Bill on a piece of business, and that mind of my uncle's would spew out ten other ideas. My dad would come away in a daze, with the original problem still unsolved. He would see his brother in constant motion, plunging from one project to another, never coming up for air; and he used to say, 'What makes Sammy run? What makes him go like that?' "

George also felt the conflicted emotions of watching his son set his brother as his model. Larry Casey was drawn, through his uncle, into law and politics. Bill Casey was the formative force in his life. "Even when I was just a kid," Larry remembered, "I'd go over to Mayknoll and the first thing he'd ask me is 'What are you reading?' As soon as I'd tell him, the grilling would start. If I took a position, he'd make me defend it—'Why? . . . Why? . . . Why?' He never accepted an easy answer. I'd have to back it up. When I read something he didn't know about, he'd use me to learn about it. 'Where did you get that? What's your source? Tell me more about it.' Then, when we'd finish talking about my reading, he'd start on goals. What were my goals? I always had to have goals."

The inventor of tax shelters, the crafty lawyer, the venture capitalist, revealed in his few free moments an incongruous secret side. He wrote to a monsignor:

Some years ago, when I read Fulton Oursler's book about St. Paul, *The Greatest Faith Ever Known*, I thought that a great story could be developed by going on from there to weave together a continuous history of the work of Martin of Tours, Augustine of England and his followers, Patrick, Columbanus, Boniface, Xavier, Ricci, Nobili, Serra, the Franciscans in Central and South America, and so on, until we pretty well cover the globe. I know the whole story. I have a lot of the reading done. I have quite a library brought together. I'd like to do it as a contribution to the cause. All I need is time, which is my problem. Maybe some research help might cut down some of the time needed and I would be glad to pay for it if I could find the right people. You may have some ideas on that. In any event, I would like to just talk to you about it.

He told another visitor who had marveled at the bookcases that now rose from floor to ceiling at Mayknoll: "My hobby is something I call 'not writing books.' I think of a subject I'd like to do a book on. I do research and collect books on the subject and mull it over for a while. Then one day I decide I've had it. Most of the fun is doing the research and thinking about it, and I decide to spare myself the pain of writing."

Casey worked hard. He prayed hard. And he played hard. Casey family vacations were usually taken abroad and resembled travel seminars. In advance of a trip, he stocked up on armfuls of guide books and devoured them. "It was exhausting," Sophia recalled of their travels. "Every morning, early, it was 'Everybody up! Two museums and three cathedrals today!' Then the next morning it was up again early for more museums, more cathedrals, more sights, more history."

When Len Hall was going on a vacation to France, Casey prepared a five-page single-spaced guide. "Be sure to visit Sainte-Chapelle. It's much more dazzling than Notre Dame. . . . Another little gem is the Musée des Plans, a collection of models of French villages, towns and cities . . . Don't drive directly from Paris to Geneva. That takes you away from Burgundy, the chateau country, Normandy and Provence. . . . The cathedral at Autun contains the work of a sculptor called Giselbertus, who I consider the first modern artist. . . . " "I got tired just reading the damn thing," Hall remarked.

And Casey prayed hard. Religion permeated his life and his home. When he had first bought Mayknoll, there was a niche in the great staircase that led from the main hall to the upper story. In another age it had been used as a place to set candles. Sophia had placed a statue of the Virgin Mary on it. She collected statues of Mary; they appeared on mantels, on shelves, on sills around the house. Father Giles Webster was a frequent guest at Mayknoll; Casey referred to the Franciscan as "my in-house chaplain." "I'd stop over on a Sunday morning to see Bill on some business matter," Carl Paffendorf remembered. "Sophia would come in and announce, 'Mass in two minutes.' And Father Giles would start setting up his portable altar." Church, family, friends, fortune. His life, Casey felt, rested on stout pillars.

10.

Casey for Congress

In 1960, Casey's thoughts returned to politics. The campaign for the Republican presidential nomination had narrowed down to Richard Nixon and Nelson Rockefeller—an effortless choice for Bill Casey. William F. Buckley shared Casey's wish to bring Rockefeller, a liberal comet streaking across the Republican sky, crashing to earth. "Our principal anti-Rockefeller article in the *National Review*," he admitted years later, "was ghosted by Bill Casey. The thrust of Bill's article," Buckley said, "was that Rockefeller wanted to lead New York State and then America away from anticommunism and toward collectivism."

Casey happily gave his services to Nixon gratis. His strategy of fifteen years before was working out; as he later wrote, "I had the necessary financial independence to do it and spent substantially full time in Washington for fifteen months on the Nixon campaign."

Cliff White, whom Casey regarded as a conservative strategist without peer, remembered coming to the Nixon campaign offices in Washington: "There was Bill, doing the issues. No fanfare, no publicity, no interest in self-promotion, just a guy working anonymously behind the scenes."

"He thought he saw in Nixon what he saw in himself." Leo Cherne concluded, "an analytical mind, a creative capacity." But it went deeper: they shared a religion—anticommunism. Nixon, like Joe McCarthy, had come into the national consciousness as a Red hunter, albeit with more finesse.

William Safire was then a young public-relations man in the Nixon camp. "I had drafted a gut-kicking anti-Kennedy ad," Safire recounted, "and I took it to Len Hall. Hall sent me to Bill Casey, whom I knew slightly. Bill looked at my ad and immediately started firing off phone calls. With one he got a wad of cash from a fellow who would later head up the FBI. With another he set up a bank account. With another call he got the ad placed. His head was full of names for paper organizations—the Committee for Economic Freedom, the

Committee for a Sound Defense. Within hours, the ad was sponsored, placed, and paid for. He'd given the dirty deed the coloration of law. When you went to Bill Casey, things got done."

But Nixon disappointed Casey. After winning the nomination, the candidate had trotted like a yeoman up to the manor house to get the blessing of the lord of the manor—in this case, to Nelson Rockefeller at his triplex apartment on Fifth Avenue. There, in Casey's judgment, Nixon sold out to win the rich man's support.

Cliff White once commented on the roots of Casey's antipathy toward Rockefeller: "It wasn't just that Nelson was too liberal. It went beyond ideology. It was the Rockefeller arrogance that Bill couldn't stomach—the raw power, the phony camaraderie. Bill's attitude toward Nelson was dislike bordering on contempt."

Nixon lost, and Jack Kennedy was elected President. Casey's reaction was immediate and allergic. Soon after Kennedy took office, Casey wrote his OSS friend Bert Jolis, "After twelve days in office, Kennedy has overtaken the Russians in space. It took him eight more days to close the missile gap. Our old OSS comrade Arthur Schlesinger has announced that the welfare state is the most potent weapon against communist imperialism. What a wondrous New Frontier we've reached."

He assumed that the popular Kennedy would serve two four-year terms; the White House was probably foreclosed to the GOP until 1968. But Kennedy was slain; Lyndon Baines Johnson assumed the presidency in November of 1963 and 1964 would be another presidential election year.

In mid-January of 1964, Blanche Casey died suddenly of a heart attack. Bill's father had willed him a tolerant, practical view of people and the world. His mother, by her doting, had bred in him an unconscious confidence, the inner certainty that in the end, all must turn out well for Bill Casey. A couple of weeks after his mother's death, he brought all the sympathy cards into the office to dictate to Connie Kirk responses to each one. Soon, the dam broke. He kept dictating. But the tears rolled down his cheeks.

Around the time of Blanche's death, Barry Goldwater was emerging as the first modern conservative to be seriously considered for the White House. Goldwater's chief Republican opponent for the nomination was Casey's nemesis Nelson Rockefeller. Bill Buckley asked Casey to come to work for Goldwater. But, to Buckley's astonishment, he refused. Instead, Casey traveled around the country trying to breathe life into the political corpse of Richard Nixon, still his favorite. He helped organize Nixon's primary campaign in Oregon. An episode on the financing of this effort sheds some light on the Casey political methods of that era. As Connie Kirk recalled: "It was like one of those OSS stories he always used to tell me. He sent me to the bank to get ten thousand dollars in hundred-dollar bills. The bank officials wanted to send me back to the office with armed guards. I said, 'Are you crazy? Do you want to draw attention to me?'" She shoved the one hundred bills into her purse and marched back alone. Casey gave her an unfamiliar name to whom she was to send the money in Oregon. She simply stuck the bills in an envelope and sent them by regular mail.

Days later, Casey followed the money to Oregon. It was a bitter journey. The Nixon corpse stayed dead. More galling, the Oregon primary was won by Nelson Rockefeller. Later, Casey went to the Republican convention in San Francisco and thoroughly enjoyed the spectacle of Rockefeller being booed during his speech. Still, his heart could not warm to Barry Goldwater. He effectively sat out the 1964 campaign.

Cliff White was puzzled. Casey was a devout conservative, and the conservatives, at last, had a presidential candidate. But as Casey explained it to White, Barry Goldwater was all wrong. Goldwater's simplistic right-wing sloganeering gave conservatism a know-nothing tone, a kooky flavor. Casey, a lover of books and learning, knew that Goldwater had not even written his own bible, The Conscience of a Conservative. "He just didn't think Barry had enough gray matter for the job," Cliff White observed. After Goldwater's stunning defeat, which took Republican candidates all across the country in its undertow, Casey concluded that he had been right to sit out that year.

A seed began to sprout in his mind. Couldn't conservatism be rescued from extremism? Couldn't you have conservatives who discussed issues sophisticatedly instead of sounding like political yahoos? Couldn't you have conservative candidates who would attract voters instead of frighten them? The more he thought about it, the more he concluded it was time for such a candidate to come out of the wings.

Ben Frank was a thirty-one-year-old lawyer bitten by the political virus. He had managed the winning campaign of another Long Island lawyer, Sol Wachtler, for supervisor of the town of West Hempstead in November of 1965. That December Frank received a call to stop by and see Len Hall at Hall's offices in Garden City. To Frank, a call from Long Island's premier Republican was like being summoned to the majors.

Hall briefly worked his genial charm on Frank and then got to the point: "My law partner, my brains, wants to run for Congress here in the Third District. I tried to talk him out of it. He's a brilliant man—I think he's overqualified. But he's determined to go ahead, and he wants to go first-class. You're a comer. I've told him about you. I'd appreciate it if you'd stop by and see him." Frank left Hall's office floating.

Days later, Frank headed for the Blue Spruce Inn in Roslyn, where he was to have lunch with William J. Casey. "My head was filled with the Nelson Rockefellers of the world, and attractive Republicans like John Lindsay, who'd just been elected mayor of New York," he remembered. "I was not expecting Bill Casey. I was expecting some-one . . . well, a little more dashing, someone a little more understand-able when he talked. But the longer the lunch went on, the more fascinated I became. He had a global outlook and a clear idea of what he wanted to accomplish in Congress." Casey also hinted to Frank that he ultimately had his eye on a United States Senate seat.

To Frank, the race in Nassau County's Third District looked like a good bet. The district was almost congenitally Republican. It had been represented for six straight terms by Steven B. Derounian, until 1964, when Derounian, along with Republicans all over the country, had been swept out by the Goldwater disaster. The district was cur-rently represented by a Democrat, Lester L. Wolff. Derounian had declared for his old seat, which meant that Casey would have to face him in a Republican primary. In his twelve years in the House, Steve Derounian had been an old warhorse, a lackluster, conservative water carrier; and he had already been beaten once by the incumbent. Surely, Frank thought, Casey could make a better race against Lester Wolff than Derounian.

What Casey saw on this first meeting was a boyish, curly-haired, blue-eyed native Canadian who looked too young for a campaign director. But Frank spoke knowledgeably and possessed a convincing confidence. They struck a deal. Frank came aboard as Casey's cam-paign chairman.

Why did Bill Casey want to run for Congress? Winston Churchill once said that for all things people do, there is a good reason and the real reason. For Casey, promoting his world view in the House of Representatives was the good reason. And the real reason? He had set a goal for himself when he had reluctantly walked away from the OSS in 1945: he had opted for the independence and power that came with money. Now, at age fifty-two, he had the money; he had con-nections and influence. In the 1960 presidential election, he had been in a position virtually to give Richard Nixon a year of his life. Up to now, however, he had been influential but anonymous, the insider known only to a handful of other insiders. The desire had been building in Casey to go public, to taste recognition.

Political courtesy demanded that Casey inform Derounian of his intentions. For this thankless errand, Casey selected his protégé, Owen Smith. He had made Smith the number-two man, behind Frank, in the campaign organization. The task was especially unappealing to Smith: he was a Republican committeeman and district leader and had already promised Derounian that he would work for him. A surprised Derounian complained, "I don't know why Bill is doing this to me. Doesn't he realize it could cost the party the seat?"

In March, Casey swallowed his first dose of political reality. The Nassau County Republican organization met, voted, and decided to stick with Derounian. "Bill was shocked when he found out they preferred a man of the past to him," Ben Frank recalled. "But they all knew Steve. And they didn't know Bill Casey, except as this guy who talked to them about how he wanted to reshape the world. He had no interest in yakking with some district leader about getting federal funding for a sewage treatment plant."

With or without the party regulars, the Casey team entered the contest with high hopes and impressive advantages—virtually unlimited cash, for one thing. Casey was prepared to spend what it took. Indeed, his fund-raisers' only problem was to conceal the source of the funds. It was unseemly for a candidate to appear to be buying his seat; so Casey gave money to relatives and friends who then contributed it to the campaign. Here was a candidate for a Long Island seat in Congress who could afford to take out full-page ads in the *New York Times*. Casey also went first-class on his official campaign photograph: he hired Fabian Bachrach. The photo showed a fleshy-faced man with glasses, an engaging, lopsided grin, and a light fuzz on his pate that looked like a semisuccessful hair-growing experiment.

Another resource was quickly evident along with the candidate's money—his energy. A Derounian brochure appeared in voters' mailboxes on a Friday. Casey read through it, called in Connie Kirk, and started dictating a rebuttal. He interrupted himself only long enough to bark instructions to Owen Smith to get a printer ready and to Ben Frank to assemble a mailing list. By Saturday afternoon, a crew, including Sophia and Bernadette, was stuffing envelopes. They raced to the post office and just before closing time got out seventy-five thousand pieces, first-class, which were in the voters' mailboxes that Monday.

If the Casey campaign could not have the old-line party organization, it would have something better. The Third District was home to young lawyers, bankers, and Wall Streeters who commuted daily to Manhattan, energetic, sophisticated people fascinated by politics. Ben Frank had mobilized them for the successful Wachtler campaign. He now sold them on this man of the world, this student of world affairs, this hero of the OSS, and began to build a Casey organization from the ground up. A friend of Casey's remodeled the back of a truck so that it looked like a caboose. Casey intended to speak from the back of it at the commuter stations in Great Neck, Manhasset, Port Washington, Plandome, and Hicksville—an old-fashioned whistle-stop campaign. Commuters were served free coffee from the back of "Casey's Caboose."

The endorsements started coming in. U.S. Senator Jacob Javits of New York broke a lifelong rule of remaining strictly neutral in Republican primaries and came out for Casey. Another Senate giant, Pennsylvania's Hugh Scott, and an upcoming presidential aspirant, Governor George Romney of Michigan, declared for Casey. The *Long Island Press*, the *Manhasset Press*, and the *Long Island Commercial Review* all endorsed Casey.

Casey wrote to dozens of influential friends: "To me, it's like seeing my name in neon. But you get adjusted. After you take the plunge, you divest yourself of your natural modesty the first day. The second day, you like to hear about yourself. The third day you start to believe it."

The endorsement of a liberal like Jack Javits raised a nettlesome question. What was Casey running as? Leo Cherne observed drily, "I didn't think you could find anyone on Long Island more conservative than Bill Casey." He was not flying under his old colors. Casey had been able to hire one of the country's leading pollsters, the Opinion Research Corporation of Princeton. The poll revealed that district voters were mostly undecided—54 percent of them. But among remaining voters, a "progressive" Republican was preferred. A pragmatic Casey accepted that he had to position himself to the left of Derounian.

Tanya Melich was a thirty-year-old liberal Republican who had come off the successful Lindsay mayoral campaign the year before and was looking for another congenial candidate. A friend of Casey's had spotted Melich as politically savvy and suggested that she talk to Bill about working in his race. The idea appealed to Melich. Two years before, she had seen her father's moderate Republican campaign for governor of Utah fall victim to the Goldwater debacle. If

Casey was opposing a right-winger like Derounian, she assumed, he must at least be middle-of-the-road.

She had gone to see Casey at his law office on East Forty-second Street for an interview. The Casey charisma was not immediately evident. She recalled her first reaction on meeting this tie-nibbling mumbler: "This is a man who expects to run for political office?" He struck Melich as "gruff and friendly, sympathetic and impatient all at the same time." She was clearly a political intellectual, and Casey made sure that she understood that he too was a man of letters, pointing to a shelf filled with the "how to" desk manuals he had written. He hired her to write and research issues for the campaign.

"At that point I had no idea the man had any connection with the right wing of the Republican party," she remembered. Indeed, Casey was telling the voters, "My political philosophy is progressive Republican, like the people I've worked for—Willkie, Dewey, Eisenhower, and Nixon. My complaint with Derounian is that he's a reactionary." Derounian, he said, had embarrassed reasonable Republicans by a speech linking the *New York Times* and Walter Lippmann with *Pravda*. Derounian, he said, had campaigned in California for Congressman John Rousselot, a member of the John Birch Society, an outfit that considered Dwight Eisenhower a Communist dupe.

His old allies of the Right were flabbergasted. Bill Buckley, learning that Casey was running against a fellow conservative, called Barry Goldwater and asked in disbelief, "Barry, can this be our Bill Casey?" Buckley told a reporter, "Nobody, not a battalion of angels, could persuade me that Bill Casey is a liberal. The notion that he is identified with the progressive wing of the Republican party is just laughable."

"We broke when Bill declared himself a Rockefeller Republican," Buckley later recounted. "And he called me a Bircher!"

"A couple of weeks before the election," Tanya Melich recalled, "I went over to the Garden City Hotel on kind of an intelligence mission. I'd learned that the *National Review* crowd and people like Brent Bozell, who ghosted Goldwater's book, were over there helping Derounian. I slipped quietly into the back of the room and took notes on all this right-wing stuff—their opposition to civil rights legislation, the usual paranoid anticommunism. It seemed like wonderful ammunition for Casey to use against Derounian.

"When I got back to headquarters, I briefed him on what I'd heard. I talked to him about his opportunity to win over moderate voters in Oyster Bay, and about the Teddy Roosevelt traditions of progressive Republicanism. But he didn't seem to be listening. I began to think, 'Maybe this guy isn't what I thought.' "

Derounian's people accused Casey of raw hypocrisy. They dredged up Casey's single-handed engineering and financing of the conservative Committee for Republican Victory that had attacked Nelson Rockefeller during the gubernatorial campaign in 1958. Casey nervelessly denied that he had ever been associated with any conservative causes. He told a *New York Times* reporter, "My record is clear. I'm not a conservative. I hardly know Mr. Goldwater and I've only seen Bill Buckley five or six times in ten years. They warned me that I would be smeared if I went up against Derounian in the primary."

Political inconsistency, however, was not Bill Casey's major problem. Ben Frank remembered, "I'd fired up all those eager young lawyers and professionals so they were ready to go through stone walls for Bill. I brought them all together at Patricia Murphy's Restaurant to hear him for the first time. Bill started speaking and got all wrapped up in the fine points of tax reform. They physically could not make out what the man was saying. You could see the enthusiasm drain out of them as he droned on. By the time he finished, the most I could hope for was that they would still vote for Bill Casey."

Casey's Caboose did not work either. Commuters waiting for the 7:46 were not about to leave their spot on the platform to go and listen to a politician. And the free coffee outraged vendors at the station who made their living selling it. Ben Frank persuaded Casey that he would have to come down from the caboose and wade into the crowds. Casey looked ill at the prospect. With practice, he developed a passable train-side manner, working the crowd, pressing the flesh.

But Frank had other problems. "Bill didn't really want to campaign. He wanted to write. He wanted to stay at headquarters and draft position papers. He wanted to do all the ads himself. I'd say, 'Bill, you're late for the shopping center rally.' And he'd still be writing draft five of his paper on Red China.

"When he'd finish a day on the hustings," Frank recounted, "he'd come back to headquarters late at night when we were all exhausted and start sticking his nose into everything—the speeches, the brochures, the financing, the printing. Bill Casey did not take direction easily."

His low tolerance of fools was not a political advantage. Tom Murphy of Capital Cities came out to lend a hand and was in the audience when Casey addressed a conservative organization. After his speech, Casey took questions. As Murphy remembered, "One of these earnest-looking right-wingers gets up and says, 'Isn't fluoridating the water the first step on the road to socialized medicine?' Bill said, 'Anybody who believes that crap is stupid!' I put my hand over my eyes and thought, 'My God, he's dead.' "

Len Hall had lined up a lunch for Casey with a wealthy, politically influential socialite who might make a heavy campaign contribution. He poured out his concern to Connie Kirk. "She could be very important," Hall said. "But his table manners—they're atrocious! What am I going to do?" "Don't serve him any soup," Kirk answered.

A friend who saw Casey on television wrote: "I must compliment you. You are handsome and well attired. However, I must point out:

(A) Your tie was disorganized.
(B) Your pockets were bulging with papers.
(C) Your suit was not pressed.
(D) You made Leonard Hall look good."

Since the Nixon campaign of 1960, Casey had been a mentor and friend to Bill Safire. Safire then ran a public-relations business, and Casey had steered clients his way. When Casey began the congressional campaign, he called Safire and said, "I need you. I want you to handle my public relations."

Safire was pleased to help. He came out to Long Island and told Casey: "Let me explain something basic to you. Politics is communication. And you don't even know how to speak. I want you to see Betty Cashman."

"Who?"

"Betty Cashman. She's the best speech coach in the business. She did John Lindsay last year."

"Teach me to talk? Jeez-zus!" Casey moaned.

Nevertheless, he went. Betty Cashman had an impressive list of actors, politicians, and performers who had benefited from her coaching. She later described the arrival of her newest pupil at her studio at 1860 Broadway: "He stood in the doorway, head hanging low like an unhappy Saint Bernard. He mumbled something like, 'What are ya gonna do, make me a movie star?' I thought, 'Oh, my God—this one is going to need a complete overhaul.' I told him, 'You don't know how to stand. You don't know how to dress. You've got holes in your shoes. Who do you think you are—Adlai Stevenson?'" She let him talk at length to get an idea of his speaking. The voice alone was a serious problem. It lacked resonance; it had a throaty, muffled sound, as though he were speaking through a pillow.

Cashman was an astute woman. She detected that the poor voice complemented traits of Casey's character. "Part of the reason he mumbled and spoke half-words was because he was speaking to his own mind. He wasn't thinking about the listener," she concluded. "But when others spoke, he was a good listener." He was, she realized, more interested in hearing someone else than in hearing himself. "He already knew what he thought," she observed. An odd quirk, it struck her, in a world of extrovert politicians. "When I did get him to speak out, it was as if I was invading his privacy. I finally told him, 'The way you shuffle and shamble, the way you stand, the way you talk—everything about you says that you don't really care what people think of you. That's fine—except for a guy who wants to win an election.' "

They were together for two hours twice a week. She found Casey engaging, even playful. She would stand before him, showing him how to put his weight on one foot, how to match the gesture to the word. "And he would be throwing spitballs at me," she remembered. "I found both the lion and the lamb in this man."

She also told him how to dress. And so he returned to the campaign trail looking better but, as far as Safire could tell, not sounding any better. For years afterward, Safire loved to tell how he had sent Bill Casey to a speech teacher, and when Casey finished, the teacher mumbled.

Casey continued to get up every morning before dawn to meet the trains, work the shopping centers, attend communion breakfasts and bar mitzvahs. His energy and spirit never flagged. But, Safire concluded, "Bill was Coriolanus as a candidate. It was hard for him to bend, to ask people to support him. With two or three guys in a backroom dreaming up some new Concerned Citizens for Casey Committee, he was in his element. But outside, he was . . . well . . . Coriolanus."

That spring of 1966, as Casey was running for Congress, Vietnam was emerging as the controversy that would sunder America. He had been, up to this point, the hawk of hawks. Two years before, he wrote to an old friend, a veteran of the French resistance, "I'm for throwing Castro out of Cuba and out of South America. I'm for encouraging Russia and China to feud with each other. I'm for putting on the pressure so we can open up Eastern Europe. I'm for pushing Russian and Chinese influence out of Africa. And I'm for winning in Southeast Asia rather than neutralizing it."

But now he had to maintain that space to the left of Derounian. For years, he had been a major figure in the International Rescue

Committee, and he was now chairman of the organization's executive committee. For thirty years the IRC had been saving political refugees. Vietnam was full of refugees. And so, in the midst of his campaign, Casey decided to acquire Vietnam credentials. He went there on a refugee fact-finding mission for the IRC in mid-May.

He came back with his position. Jack Javits inserted Casey's position paper in the *Congressional Record*, under the thin veil of a report from the International Rescue Committee. Javits prefaced the piece by saying that Casey was a "progressive Republican and his views are in many ways in accord with my own views."

Of Vietnam, Casey said, "Don't extend and escalate the war . . . do not send ships in or mine Haiphong harbor or bomb the population of Hanoi. To escalate the war in this way could involve us in a major land war in Asia. It could force the North Vietnamese to send against our men the 300,000 trained troops they now have in North Vietnam." In radio spots on Vietnam, he said, "We should be ready to negotiate with anyone at any time."

The Third District went to the polls on June 28, 1966. Frank had set up telephone banks for a last-minute blitz. Casey made a final round of six field offices scattered around the district. That night some three hundred visitors jammed his headquarters, where a caterer had set up a buffet and bar for the victory celebration.

Soon after nine p.m., early returns came dribbling in. The bellwether districts did not look good. Casey appeared indifferent, almost bored. He already knew the outcome: a few days before, Ben Frank and Owen Smith had brought him the results of the latest poll. He was going to lose. "He just brushed it aside with that wave of the hand," Smith remembered. "All he said was, 'Don't tell anybody yet. We have to put a good face on it and see it through. Especially don't tell Tootsie.' "

At ten o'clock, Casey got up and made a graceful little speech of concession. Then he circulated among the campaign staff, thanking everyone. Sophia, Bernadette, Connie Kirk, and some of the other women were crying. Ben Frank felt like crying. Casey looked, if anything, relieved. He motioned Frank outside. "Where are we going?" Frank wanted to know. Casey answered with a mirthless grin: "To congratulate the winner."

Casey lost to Derounian by 22,000 to 15,000 votes—borderline respectable, considering that he had gone up against the party. "He wouldn't show it," Bill Safire recalled, "but he took that defeat hard. Bill Casey didn't like to lose. He wasn't used to losing. But the big difference after a Casey campaign was at least the bills were paid."

The staff had been able, the organization sound, the positions thoughtful, the financing lavish—and he had lost anyway. There was evidently something more to this game, something beyond merit and brains. Politics, Casey concluded, was not a civil service exam. He faced the truth that whatever that indefinable quality was that made a candidate shimmer, he lacked it. His campaign for Congress did not kill his zest for politics, only for facing the electorate.

The day after the defeat, he appeared as usual in his IBP office. He called Owen Smith in to discuss a new desk-reference book. He never mentioned what he had given his life to for the previous six months.

11.

The Man Who Liked Richard Nixon

After the failed congressional campaign, Casey threw himself back into his other interests with a fury. He played his part in Capital Cities' relentless acquisition of more and more stations. He was still helping Carl Paffendorf make a go of COAP. He had his hand in a dozen other new enterprises. And his law practice was flourishing. Still, the siren song of politics sounded in his ear.

He found Lyndon Johnson's Great Society repellent, the New Deal approach to problems without Roosevelt's magnetism or his Brain Trust. By early 1968, the subject of the Saturday lunch with Len Hall at Caminari's was which Republican could best oust the Democrats that year. Hall was too forgiving by half, in Casey's estimation: he was trying to get his old opponent Nelson Rockefeller to run again. Casey virtually gagged on his lunch. Later that year, when Rockefeller dropped out, Hall signed on with George Romney. Romney, another successful businessman, a management whiz who had kept little American Motors afloat, had turned his ambitions to presidential politics. Bill had to appreciate Romney, Len said—birds of a feather.

Casey's heart still belonged to Dick Nixon, and Nixon was starting to sound like a candidate again. But after Nixon's defeat by JFK in 1960, his defeat for governor of California in '62, and his virtual nonshowing in '64, even the faithful Casey was losing hope. Casey sent Nixon a handsome five-thousand-dollar contribution but otherwise sat on the sidelines.

George Romney proved an inept politician. He declared that he had supported the Vietnam War only because he had been "brainwashed" by the military—not the sort of brain the American people wanted in a President. Early in 1968, Romney dropped out, and ultimately Nelson Rockefeller changed his mind and decided to reenter the GOP race. As Casey wrote a friend, "The Rockefeller thing was too much for me, so in June I came out full blast to do whatever I could for Dick Nixon."

A close business associate was having a cup of coffee late at night at Casey's office and the talk turned to politics. The friend later recounted: "Bill had a short fuse. And I lit it. I said I thought Nixon was untrustworthy and the best Republican in America was Nelson Rockefeller. He went crazy. He got up and practically frothed at the mouth. He screamed at me. He got very personal when he got into these moods. He could be mean as hell. I was 'a second-rate idiot! A first-rate ass! A man identifiable only by the smallness of his testicles!' "

Casey gave another substantial contribution to Nixon that summer. In the end, he would contribute seventeen thousand dollars to the man. He began phoning other wealthy Republicans and displayed a genius for estimating just how much could be squeezed out of a prospect. "R. P. Ettinger at Prentice-Hall," he advised a Nixon fund-raiser, "has about twenty times as much money as I do, but he is more attached to it than I am. He is good for five thousand dollars"—which indeed was what the publisher contributed.

Casey went to the Republican National Convention in Miami and, as was his custom, made a social outing of it. Besides Sophia and Bernadette, he liked to bring relatives, favored in-laws, Connie Kirk, old college and OSS pals and their wives. He would fly them all out, lodge them, and pick up the tab. This year his guests included Gene Duffy and his wife. "Bill had taken a big apartment in a building where the New York Republicans were staying," Duffy recalled. "But the phones hadn't been installed yet. Bill couldn't survive an hour without a phone. He was going crazy. So he just walked out and moved the whole crew over to the Hilton."

Casey came back to Long Island from the convention doubly satisfied. His hero, Richard Nixon, had been crowned. His bête noire, Rockefeller, had been humiliated, beaten on the first ballot.

There would be a dead spot between Nixon's nomination and the traditional Labor Day kickoff of the campaign. Casey chose the time to make a trip for the International Rescue Committee to Czechoslovakia, which had just been invaded by the Soviet army. Before leaving, Casey made his bid to John Mitchell, Nixon's closest adviser. He complained to Mitchell that because he had made a fortune and was a tax expert, he was only consulted on finance. "I know Dick wants me to work on tax reform ideas," he told Mitchell. "But I can do much more." What nobody seemed to recognize was what he saw in himself: a geopolitical strategist, a defense policy thinker, and a student of intelligence.

Then he was off for Europe with Leo Cherne, another power in the International Rescue Committee. The trip meant much to Casey. He had had a hot-and-cold relationship with the IRC going back over twenty years. At one point, he had quit in disgust. The IRC had been formed in the years before World War II to save persecuted German intellectuals from Hitler; but after the war, Casey felt the IRC needed a course change. "Bill was bored by the IRC's efforts to help poor old Loyalists who had fled Spain after Franco," Leo Cherne recalled. "He thought we were being silly and wasting our resources." He had already served his time in welfare as a young man. Casey wanted the IRC to become political, an instrument in the holy war against the Communists.

Years before, in 1951, Casey had met a young college professor, Frank Barnett, who was on a one-man crusade to recruit disaffected Czechs, Poles, Ukrainians, and White Russians into an anticommunist army, the Legion of Freedom. Casey lured Barnett from the faculty of Wabash College in Indiana to come to New York and set him up in something he, Burt Jolis, and Eugene Lyons, a conservative from the *Reader's Digest*, had put together, American Friends for Russian Freedom. The idea was to get Red Army personnel in Berlin and Vienna to desert, to get them papers, find them jobs, resettle them in the West, and make propaganda hay out of their defections. Casey sank a fair amount of money into the enterprise, but the idea did not prosper. In time, Casey returned to the International Rescue Committee.

What was happening in Czechoslovakia in this summer of 1968 was more to his taste—not refugees fleeing some tinhorn, right-wing *caudillo* in Central America, but a small, brave nation standing up against Soviet tanks, trying to free itself from communism. Casey and Cherne wanted to see for themselves what was happening in Prague. On a Saturday afternoon, they rented a car and driver and, posing as businessmen, managed to bluff their way past the Russian soldiers at the Austro-Czech border. They were almost to Bratislava when they ran into a roadblock. Fifteen tanks frowned on them. From a watchtower, Red soldiers trained a machine gun on the car. A Soviet officer pulled up alongside on a motorcycle.

Cherne sprang out of the backseat and said to the officer, "We demand to be taken to your superior." The Russian was taken aback, and a long, hot negotiation ensued during which Cherne refused to budge. At one point, he realized he was carrying the fight alone: Casey was sitting in the backseat of the car reading a novel. "I was furious," Cherne recalled. "I leaned into the car and I said, 'For God's sake, Bill, how can you sit there, with the fix we're in, reading that damned book!' He looked up at me and spoke in the calmest voice I have ever heard in my life: 'Is there something more useful you think I might be doing?' "

They were interrogated for two hours and finally sent back to Austria.

Casey was back in New York the first week in September. He stopped by to see John Mitchell at the Nixon campaign headquarters. No one had snapped up his offer to shoulder a major campaign role. Instead he found himself shunted to underlings. He sent a bristling letter to Mitchell on September 16:

> Somebody named J. M. Keogh called me. He had me pegged as some kind of a tax expert. I said I'd rather work a little more broadly and explained what you and I had talked about. He suggested passing a couple of papers by me. I said I was rather hoping to be in the mainstream work. He started to tell me about his space problems. I resisted saying that I've already paid a lot of the rent for that space.

He finally managed to get a foot in the door, but wrote Jack Javits ruefully, "I am handling the rear echelon of the research and speech writing operation of the Nixon campaign organization." His young friend Bill Safire was now at the upper echelon of the operation as a principal speech writer. "When I needed input into the speeches," Safire recalled, "I'd go into the bull pen where the researchers worked and there was Bill. It was so odd—this older guy who had achieved so much, who'd made so much money, doing campaign research. It was beneath him."

Then came a chance to shine, to place himself inescapably in Nixon's line of vision. On October 12, Casey flew to the candidate's home at Key Biscayne, Florida, for a research strategy session. Nixon was angry. He was tired of being attacked as a hollow man, a political cipher without substance or ideas. He had taken positions on *everything*, he said, but the media just ignored that fact. Why couldn't he have a book published that established his stand on the issues?

The election was twenty-four days off. Publishing books was, with the research, writing, editing, proofing, typesetting, printing, binding, and distribution, an enterprise of months, even years, not of days.

Certainly Nixon meant a handout listing his positions, one aide said. No, Nixon insisted with the petulance he favored under stress. He wanted something solid to throw at the press. He wanted a book.

"I'll take care of it," Casey said.

Martin Anderson, Nixon's issues man traveling on the campaign plane, alerted the disbelieving researchers back in New York.

On Sunday night, Casey left Key Biscayne for New York and went directly to the campaign headquarters, where he found the research staff waiting. He began immediately to organize the effort. He rode hard on the researchers, pushed the writing, and had a courier come by every two hours, around the clock, to pick up fresh copy and drop off the latest page proofs. Richard V. Allen, heading Nixon's foreign policy research, had his first brush with Casey at this time. As Allen later recalled, "I wondered, 'Who's this guy to come in here and push us around?' He'd burst in saying, 'How ya doin'?' I'd say, 'I'm doing fine, how *you* doing?' And he'd shoot back, 'Don't give me that stuff. You know what I mean.' "

The final batch of copy went to the printer on Wednesday. As the Nixon campaign plane touched down at La Guardia Airport the next morning, four days from the start, a young woman was standing by with a box of finished books. Marty Anderson stepped out of the plane and took the box on board. The books were bound in a deep green cover with the title *Nixon on the Issues*. Casey had arranged a special leather-bound copy with the title printed in twenty-four-carat gold leaf for the candidate. Nixon, beaming like a child, said, "Okay, give 'em to the press."

Election Day arrived, and Richard Nixon narrowly defeated Hubert H. Humphrey. Casey waited. He confided to Ben Frank what he was looking for: State, Defense, the CIA. At the very least, he expected a major embassy, Great Britain or France. And he wanted to be asked; he expected that Nixon would call him personally. He heard nothing.

He hated the idea of having to plead. He persuaded his old London OSS boss, J. Russell Forgan, to write to Nixon's finance man, Maurice Stans, who knew how many bucks Casey had pumped into the campaign, along with his labor, gratis. Forgan wrote Stans, "I have a feeling that Bill would be available for government service if the right kind of job were offered." Casey next wrote directly to Bryce Harlow, a talent scout close to Nixon, to head off being pigeonholed in a finance job. "I'm interested," he wrote Harlow, "in the foreign or national security area."

A month went by; still Casey heard nothing. He swallowed his pride, lowered his sights, and wrote to Robert Finch, the lieutenant governor of California and a close Nixon operative, "I can do the Secretary's job in Army, Navy or Air, or I can handle Europe or South East Asia at State, or run the CIA." He also reminded Finch, "I was one who made *major* financial commitments *before* Miami," and ended, "It's awful to have to toot your own horn this way."

It is interesting that among the jobs pitched to Finch, the CIA was last. It would fit a simple, romantic notion to believe that, after his experience in the OSS, the CIA would have been the culmination of Casey's fondest hopes. There he could become what his hero Bill Donovan had been—America's spymaster. Casey had not lost his fascination with intelligence. But he now found himself in the position of the fellow who had not been good enough for the hometown beauty queen, who then goes out into the world to prove himself worthy and becomes so successful that he realizes that he has outgrown her. The director of Central Intelligence had developed essentially into a staff position. The director was not a cabinet member, not a policymaker. He was primarily the President's intelligence officer. Casey would take the job if offered, but he would rather have his hands directly on the policy levers.

Still he waited. "He looked like a little lost boy when nothing came through," Connie Kirk remembered. "He was writing letters all over the place."

Dick Allen, by now a Casey friend, had an explanation: "There was no loyalty in Dick Nixon. The day after the election, he took off for California and no one heard from him." Bill Safire reminded Casey of a badge that a mutual New York friend, Jack Wells, always put on after a campaign; it read: "Nice work, kid. Now get lost." Casey did not find the story funny.

At last, it seemed the long drought was over. On December 9, Casey attended a dinner for the board of one of his philanthropies, the Boys Clubs. The President-elect was also there. As Nixon worked his way through the crowd of well-wishers, he clapped Casey on the back and said that at some point he needed to know what Casey wanted to do in the Administration. The next day, Casey had a letter hand-delivered to Nixon at his headquarters in the Hotel Pierre. "I have been hoping and working for this for a full ten years," he wrote. "Now I want to turn my back on all those six-figure fees and dedicate the next eight years to your Administration."

Shortly thereafter came the first solid offer. Casey was shocked: deputy director of the Internal Revenue Service.

The next offer was, if anything, more galling, because it brought him close to the banquet table, but not close enough: deputy director of the CIA. The Nixon people no doubt thought they were doing the old spook a favor; after all, the job was in the national security field that he was always yammering about. Casey was furious. Richard Helms, appointed director of Central Intelligence by Lyndon Johnson in 1966, was being held over by Nixon. Casey was being asked to serve under Helms. It was not that he did not respect Helms; he had great regard for him and thought he had been an excellent Johnson appointment. But didn't these people understand? Dick Helms had worked *for* Casey more than twenty-five years ago. He had been a junior officer in London when Casey was the U.S. intelligence chief for all of Europe. This was the master plan turned upside down. Helms had followed the very course that Casey had rejected, working his way up the career ladder, promotion by promotion, while Casey had gone out and made himself rich and powerful. People like Casey were supposed to be brought in at the top. People like Helms were supposed to work for *him*. Casey rejected the offer before Helms ever learned that it had been made.

What had gone wrong? Primarily, Casey did not cut the figure of an eminent personage. The Dickensian face, the rumpled clothes, the ungainly movements, the abrupt manner, the speech that sounded like a bail bondsman's all worked against him. He was seen as one of those figures perennially on the periphery, handy to have around, good in the backrooms of campaigns. Need to raise funds? Get Casey—he knows everybody with money. Got a tough job? Give it to Bill—he'll get it done. The virtuoso overnight production of *Nixon on the Issues* had not broken him out of the mold; it hardened him into it.

While the newly minted appointees of the Nixon administration began to run America, Casey returned to New York. With a mind-distracting burst of energy, he fired off a memo to his IBP staff with ideas for a dozen new publishing subsidiaries. He went into a new business with Ben Frank and a man who had invented a way to reproduce oil paintings that were virtually indistinguishable from the originals. He helped Capital Cities expand into newspapers along with broadcast properties.

He had made his bid for a foreign policy post in the Nixon administration without one credential he particularly would have savored. One of his wartime comrades, Milton Katz, was prominent in that establishment firmament, the Council on Foreign Relations. Casey never had been asked to join. In July of 1967 he had written Katz for help in becoming a member. Katz thought Casey was eminently qualified. He put together a blue-ribbon list of sponsors for Casey, including Allen Dulles, Kingman Brewster, Jack Javits, and Frank Stanton of CBS—support as high-powered as any nominee could hope to muster.

The nominating procedure dragged on, with Casey prodding Katz continually to find out what was happening. Finally, after six months, Katz told Casey that he had received a reply from the chairman of the membership committee. Of course, Casey would be considered for membership, the chairman had written; but "the press of applicants for the new vacancies has become greater than ever, and also the committee is now trying to reduce the average age of new members to age forty-five, which does put someone even at the age of fifty-four at a disadvantage." The explanation had a tinny ring to Casey's ear. He told Katz bitingly, "I'm glad to have them remind me I still have twelve years to catch up with Winston Churchill when he took over Great Britain."

His rejection by the Council on Foreign Relations was humiliating. Were the badges of respectability always to elude him? Still, he was a resilient man. He spotted a modest opportunity to function in the national security arena. High on the Nixon defense agenda was an antiballistic missile system. In April of 1969, with Nixon a little over three months in office, Casey wrote him, "I thought the ABM decision would be your first important one and you made it clearly and brilliantly." He got no reply. He pressed on. ABM was going to be a hard sell in Congress. Casey informed Peter Flanigan, the White House personnel man, that he was taking it upon himself to launch a campaign to win public support for the ABM. He contacted other sympathetic Republicans and happily shelled out enough of his money to set up headquarters and a staff in the Plaza Hotel. Casey called this movement the Citizens' Committee for Peace and Security. He took out full-page ads in major newspapers, sponsored by the committee, listing dozens of prominent names. The headline read: 84 PERCENT OF THE AMERICAN PEOPLE SUPPORT AN ABM SYSTEM.

Ben Frank casually mentioned to Casey that he knew somebody who knew George Meany, then head of the AFL-CIO. "Fix it up so I can see him," Casey said. Frank arranged a meeting at Meany's Washington headquarters. George Meany, in 1969, was hardly a fan of Richard Nixon. "But Bill was very clever with Meany," Frank remembered. "He told Meany that here was a rare occasion when national interest and self-interest coincided." He had done the research to show Meany that the ABM system could mean thousands of jobs for the AFL-CIO. Casey left the meeting with Meany's pledge of support. He went directly from the union's headquarters to the White House to make sure his win was posted.

ABM was defeated, but Casey won a minor personal victory; he had managed to play a bit part in the Nixon national security arena. Nixon thus named him to the Arms Control and Disarmament Commission, a power lineup that included John J. McCloy as chairman; retired General Lauris Norstad, former Supreme Allied Commander, Europe; Dean Rusk, former secretary of State; Cyrus Vance, former deputy secretary of Defense; and similar luminaries, among whom Casey was pleased to move.

It was only a membership on an advisory body, but the post required Senate confirmation. At his appearance before the Senate Foreign Relations Committee Casey collided head-on with Senator William Proxmire of Wisconsin. Proxmire had been appalled by Casey's tactics in support of the ABM. Did 84 percent of Americans *really* support the ABM? he asked Casey during the hearing. And the senator provided his own answer: "The six past presidents of the American Association for Public Opinion Research say that the 84 percent claim is by no means proved on the basis of opinion poll results presented in the advertisement." Proxmire then asked whether the signers of the ad could honestly be described as "disinterested public-spirited citizens." Was it not true, Proxmire went on, "that sixty-four signers of the ad were officers or directors of companies which would benefit financially from the installation of the ABM?"

Casey was not about to be rolled, not even in his first appearance before the U.S. Senate. He shot back, "Do you know that for a fact, Senator?"

Proxmire began again, "Sixty-four—"

Casey broke in. "Do you know that to be a fact?" It had been a part of his life for so long now, this embellishing of a kernel of truth, that it was difficult for him to appreciate the niceties that troubled a Bill Proxmire.

He was eventually confirmed. But the public recognition he hungered for had come out soiled: Proxmire's line of questioning made him out a corner cutter, a manipulator of facts, a dealer in doctored truths. And he had made an enemy in what was to prove not an isolated skirmish but a long battle.

The U.S.-supported invasion of Cambodia and the bombing of North Vietnam in 1970 signaled to the doves that instead of winding down the Vietnam War as he had promised, Richard Nixon was expanding it. Strikes and demonstrations flared across college campuses. In May, thirty-seven college and university presidents signed a manifesto urging Nixon to get the country out of Vietnam. Among the signers were the presidents of Princeton, Columbia, Bryn Mawr, Amherst, Notre Dame, Johns Hopkins, Dartmouth, and Cornell, and, to Casey's horror, the Reverend Michael T. Walsh, president of Fordham University.

Casey was a Fordham trustee; he made large contributions to the university. He sent Father Walsh a letter. By signing the manifesto, Walsh was, Casey said, "calling for a course of action on matters of the gravest consequence on which you are neither informed or charged with responsibility." Walsh must think, Casey went on, that "judgments involving national security and the lives of soldiers should be resolved—by mob action on the campus." In other words, Padre, you don't know what you're talking about. And you let yourself be stampeded by a bunch of hippie kids.

The letter bordered on the offensive. Still, Father Walsh beat a swift retreat. He wrote Casey: "Dear Bill, Needless to say, we college presidents are not sufficiently informed or knowledgeable, as you indicated, to be charged with any responsibility with regard to the matters which President Nixon must resolve. . . . Your comments and the points you make, Bill, will be very helpful to me in the future and alert me to be more cautious. . . ."

In 1971, two years into the Nixon presidency, Casey received a call from Peter Flanigan. The White House head hunter began by describing how deeply the President was concerned about problems in the capital markets. It did not sound to Casey like a foreign policy bid. And then Flanigan made the offer: Nixon wanted Casey to become chairman of the Securities and Exchange Commission.

Casey knew enough about one-upmanship to know that accepting on the spot was poor form. Possibly, Flanigan was merely sounding him out as one of many candidates. If he sounded too hungry, he might be left with his tongue hanging out while the job went to someone else. He made it clear that a firm offer should come from the lips of the President.

A day or two later, Nixon called. "Nixon wants to give me the SEC," he told Connie Kirk. He did not look that happy, she remembered; rather, he looked like a man whose devotion had grown stale, waiting too long for the hand of the woman he adored. "I really don't want it," he told Ben Frank. "It's not what I had in mind." They still saw him as a money man. But it had been a long, dry season. Nothing else loomed on the horizon. He accepted. At least he would be the top man at the SEC, running his own show.

The appointment meant enough to him that he was willing to divest himself of businesses he had built up over the course of twenty-five years. He severed his publishing relationship with Prentice-Hall and shut down IBP. He resigned a half-dozen directorships with banks and corporations, including Capital Cities Broadcasting.

He also resigned from Hall, Casey, Dickler and Howley, a move that spread gloom over the firm. "I was concerned, to put it bluntly," Gerry Dickler recalled. "Bill was a business getter, our top income producer. He had a following. He had as clients several of his pals from the OSS, an organization which did not exactly reach down among the poor and benighted for its membership." As Casey himself put it, "I was never in a law firm where I wasn't bringing in 75 percent of the business."

He would again have to face confirmation by the Senate. In getting his papers ready for the hearings, he came across a pamphlet that sent a shudder through him. Radco was a company he had started, now run by his brother, George, that published digests of business laws. Radco had four small subsidiaries; one, called Washington Information Service, published digests of SEC decisions. Casey had personally drafted a promotional pamphlet for this company with what he thought was a catchy title, "We Have the Key to the SEC File Room"—clever then, but a disaster for the chairman-designate of the SEC. It was time to call in a due bill. He phoned Carl Paffendorf and summoned him to his Greenvale offices. "I want you to buy the whole kit and caboodle, all these little companies," he said. He had already sounded out George, who was in no position to buy out his employer. Nor, it seemed, was Paffendorf. COAP, Paffendorf explained, had hit a dry patch; there was no ready cash to acquire new businesses. "You don't need cash," Casey said. "What are the companies worth? A hundred and fifty thousand? I'll take COAP stock for them. I'll pay you the split on bid and asked." Tight as his own situation was, Paffendorf saw no way to say no to the man who had made him. "All right," he said. "I'll take care of the paperwork in a few days." "No," said Casey, "we have to do it right now." "Bill," Paffendorf complained, "I don't even have any stock certificates." Casey ignored him and started scribbling a longhand contract on a stray sheet of paper. He handed Paffendorf the pen. "I could hardly read the damned thing," Paffendorf recalled. "But I signed it. I had just bought four companies I had never heard of fifteen minutes before." But at least the owner of the firm with the disastrously titled brochure was no longer William J. Casey.

As the new owner of the companies, Paffendorf remembered Casey warning him, "You've got to take care of this guy and that guy and that guy. I was the proverbial young man in a hurry. I had never given any thought to what happens to employees when you traded companies like pieces on a Monopoly board. That was another lesson I learned from Casey. Years later, I turned down a ten-million-dollar offer for Vanguard Ventures because the guy would not give employment guarantees for my people. I would never have given that factor a thought before, except for my experience with Bill."

George Casey, however, viewed the transaction differently. He would say with a grim smile, "My brother sold me along with Radco." It was not as if George was out of a job. He was simply working for a new owner. Still, it was Bill's business-is-all attitude that hurt him. Bill Casey was in a hurry, and so, as George saw it, he had sold the business, the accounts receivable, the office furniture, and the employees, including his own brother.

On a cold day late in January of 1971, Bill and Sophia flew to Washington and checked into a suite at the Fairfax Hotel. The job at the SEC was not perfect, but the long-ago strategy had worked. After a quarter of a century, he was reentering the public arena at the top.

12.

The Cop on Wall Street

The nomination of William J. Casey as chairman of the Securities and Exchange Commission was not an instantly popular appointment, except in the investment community. "Wall Street is convinced that Bill Casey intends to give the Big Board precisely what it wants," *Business* magazine concluded. "President Nixon made a bad choice."

Nor was Casey's imminent arrival warmly received by his future employees. Nixon had promised in the campaign that he was going to get the SEC off Wall Street's back. Casey's appointment was evidently delivery on the promise. One SEC veteran remarked, "Another businessman chairman—minimum compliance, minimum enforcement. Bill Casey was the antithesis of everything we were looking for." Donald T. Regan, then heading Merrill Lynch, uttered possibly the kindest words on the Casey appointment: "I thought it was like Roosevelt's naming of Joe Kennedy to the SEC in the thirties: it takes one to catch one."

Casey appeared oblivious of the criticism. He was at his genial best as guest of honor at a party Bill Safire threw for him on his arrival in Washington. Safire was now writing speeches for Nixon and eager to welcome his friend, however belatedly, to the team. At one point, Casey lifted his drink and toasted Safire for finally becoming a true capitalist. On signing up with Nixon, Safire had sold his public relations business for a quarter of a million dollars. There was an echo of genuine admiration in Casey's gibe: Safire had displayed what Casey valued and understood—entrepreneur's blood.

Banking, Housing, and Urban Affairs was the Senate committee that would handle Casey's confirmation. He was jolted when he went down the list of members—there was his nemesis of two years before, William Proxmire. He comforted himself with the thought that though the liberal Proxmire might despise his politics, the SEC was about investments and finance. How could a fair-minded man question his expertise there?

Another threat hovered, however. The Nixon administration had just suffered two humiliating defeats in a row. Two appointees to fill a Supreme Court vacancy, G. Harrold Carswell and Clement Haynesworth, had been rejected. The media had enjoyed a muckraking field day. To Casey it was like jumping into waters already red with blood while the sharks circled hungrily, waiting for the next feeding.

He knew that the AFL-CIO had played a part in sinking the Carswell and Haynesworth nominations. But he had established a good rapport with Meany on the ABM issue. Again he dispatched Ben Frank to AFL-CIO headquarters. Frank returned with what Casey regarded as a major triumph. Meany would not support him; on the other hand, he would not oppose him.

On Wednesday morning, February 10, 1971, at nine-thirty a.m. Casey strode into room 5302 of the New Senate Office Building. Drawling John Sparkman of Alabama was chairman of the banking committee, and Proxmire the senior Democrat. The day began in the warmth of eloquent praises. Casey was enthusiastically endorsed by his home state senators, who, happily, spanned the political spectrum—liberal Jacob Javits, and James Buckley, the equally conservative brother of William F.

And then it was Bill Proxmire's turn. "Mr. Casey," Proxmire began, "I want to serve notice that I am going to take a little time in my examination of you this morning." He asked Casey, in a tone of boyish curiosity, just what he thought his qualifications were to be SEC chairman. Casey forced down his anger at the unspoken implication of Proxmire's question. He went through what he believed was his relevant experience and wrapped up brusquely, "And I don't want a job in the securities industry afterwards."

Again, with the manner of an eager but confused student just trying to understand, Proxmire raised the issue of Casey's efforts two years before to sell the ABM: "I am wondering how strict a regulator you will be, given your role in the publication of a rather controversial ad that was criticized by the members of the Foreign Relations Committee as misleading." Casey again brushed off Proxmire's insinuation. What he had done, he said, was perfectly within the bounds of rough-and-tumble politics.

The bemusement left Proxmire's face: "I am now going to raise an unpleasant subject." He then went on to inform his colleagues that the appointee before them under consideration as chairman of the SEC had been successfully sued for plagiarism nine years before in the case of *Fields* v. *Casey*. The charge seemed like a shot through the heart, but Casey shrugged it off as though he had been wearing a bullet-proof vest. To a venture capitalist, he said, getting sued was "an occupational hazard." As for the decision against him in the Fields case, he said, "The jury came in with a high verdict," and so, Casey claimed, the judge did a highly unusual thing: he called in the two opposing lawyers and told them that the verdict was not supported by the evidence. He was going to set it aside and call for a new trial unless the two parties could settle the dispute between themselves. Thereupon, Casey said, he had agreed to settle.

Proxmire noted that the trial record appeared to have been sealed, and he asked if this was not odd in a civil case. Casey was again happy to explain. "After the matter had been settled, the plaintiff asked the judge if he could get a copy of this summation that the lawyer had made. Apparently the judge didn't like this, and he said that since the case had been settled, and there would be no appeal and no need to transcribe the record, that he was ordering the record sealed."

Proxmire had rolled out his heaviest artillery and Casey appeared to have survived. The banking committee voted 15–0 to send his nomination to the Senate floor. Even Proxmire had not voted against Casey; he abstained. With virtually unanimous support in committee, Casey's confirmation by the full Senate seemed all but a formality.

The Fields revelations, however, quickened the curiosity of the press. Reporters began exhuming the past of William J. Casey. Stories started surfacing that raised the unhappy prospect in the White House of a third defeat in a row after Carswell and Haynesworth. The man Nixon had named to head the SEC had been sued not only in the Fields case but for violations of the very securities laws he was supposed to enforce. In 1963, a man named Boggs sued Casey, who was then serving as chairman of the board of Advancement Devices, Inc. Boggs claimed that the prospectus that motivated him to buy the firm's stock misrepresented a weak, failing organization as "one of America's top industries." In 1965, Casey, then chairman of the executive board of Kalvar Corporation, was sued by the company's stockholders. He and others, the complaint read, had arranged for Kalvar to buy, at an inflated price, another company which just happened to belong to friends of a Kalvar director. Other Casey suits were uncovered involving corporations Casey was associated with.

To Bill Proxmire, Casey was a barracuda being dropped into the pond to protect the minnows. The senator persuaded his colleagues that Casey's approval by the committee should be rescinded. The hearings should be reopened so that the man's fitness to protect American investors could be thoroughly investigated. The committee agreed. *Business Week* magazine ran an editorial entitled "The Wrong Man." Among its kinder words: "The part that the SEC must play in reforming Wall Street is too important to be entrusted to a man who sees nothing that needs reform. If William J. Casey does not have the good taste to withdraw at this point, then the Senate should protect the interests of the Nation by refusing to confirm him."

To Casey, his plight seemed the height of perversity. He had turned his back on an income averaging $250,000 a year to take a government job that paid $40,000. He did not mind that. He had deliberately set out to make himself financially independent so that he could become a respected public figure. Instead, when his name was finally becoming known to the public, it was as a finagler, a business buccaneer. It was all wrong. It was unfair. It was enraging.

The second round of hearings was to begin on March 9. In the meantime, Casey had gone home to Mayknoll for the weekend. Early on Sunday morning, he received a call from Len Hall. Hall's customary heartiness was muted. He told Casey that he would be coming by to pick him up and take him to Jack Wells's house in Rye, New York. They needed to discuss something important.

Jack Wells was the senior partner, with William Rogers, in the powerful and politically connected New York law firm of Rogers and Wells. Bill Rogers was off at the time serving as secretary of State in the Nixon administration. Wells was a canny, ironic, and insightful man, almost as indifferent a dresser as Casey. Wells greeted his guests at his door—Ben Frank had come along too—and took them up to an office he had built in his attic. The place was a mess, the desk and floors piled high with files, magazines, and hundreds of newspaper clippings.

The men sat around Wells's desk. Casey broke an awkward silence. "I want you fellas to know, I'm gonna fight this thing through," he said. Hall stirred uncomfortably. Wells looked away. "Bill," Hall began, "we're your friends. We want what's best for you. And, of course, we all want what's best for the President and the administration." Another awkward pause. Confusion clouded Casey's face. Hall went on. "Jack and I put together a little statement earlier." Wells took out a single sheet of paper from the drawer of his desk. He handed it to Casey. Casey read the few lines. He was innocent of any charges suggesting that he was unqualified to serve as chairman of the Securities and Exchange Commission, the statement read, but he believed wholly in the mission of President Nixon, and he was determined to do nothing that might create problems for the administration. His appointment as chairman of the Securities and Exchange Commission, however, was causing unwarranted but undeniable difficulties. Therefore, he was withdrawing his name from consideration.

Casey looked up, first to Hall and then to Wells, searching for something in their faces that would deny what he had just read. "Bill," Hall said, "believe me. It's the only way. Cut your losses."

Casey was ashen, his voice strangled as he asked, "Don't you see any other way?" The two men shook their heads. Len Hall was not a man whose judgment he could ignore, especially when aligned with the savvy Wells. Casey rose wearily and said, "Okay. Let's go home." He, Hall, and Frank returned to Long Island in total silence.

Back at Mayknoll, Casey slumped in a chair and handed Sophia the statement. She became furious. "You can't pull out, Bill. They're crazy. Everybody will believe the worst of you." Heartened by her display of fight, Ben Frank chimed in, "Tootsie's right. Nixon hasn't asked you to pull out. You don't even know if he considers it in his best interest for you to fold." Casey sat up straighter. The fog of despair seemed to lift. "I've gotta talk to John Mitchell right away," he said. "If anybody can get to Nixon on this, it's John."

He went to the kitchen phone and put a call through to the Justice Department. Casey asked Mitchell to find out how Nixon felt about his embattled appointment. Later that night, Mitchell called back and said, "The President has two questions for you. Have you misled us on anything?"

"I have not," Casey answered.

"Do you really want this job?" Mitchell wanted to know. "Are you ready to fight for it?"

"I do. I want it," Casey said.

"Okay," Mitchell said. "We'll stick by you."

Casey struggled to maintain his composure. But the pressure valves gave way in unseemly places. Connie Kirk had come to Washington to continue as his secretary. One night, before the resumed hearings, he took her and his family to the Rive Gauche in Georgetown for dinner. He began grumbling about the criticism he was taking. "I said, innocent as you please," Kirk recalled, " 'Well, you know, your investments are just another form of gambling.' Bill blew his stack. He started hollering: 'How dare you call risking capital to start new industries and create more jobs gambling! How dare you put building this country in the same class with betting on the horses!' I was cringing," Kirk recalled. "Every head in the restaurant turned around to look at him."

The second hearing before the banking committee opened, and Casey went through the charges leveled against him point by point. He explained that the Boggs suit involving Advancement Devices had been discontinued by the jury without cost to either party. The Kalvar suit had been settled out of court. His problem, he said, was that he had not sought out the calm harbor of investments in old, safe, established businesses. He was an entrepreneur, a venture capitalist. He had stuck his neck out on new products, new services, high-risk operations. As Casey saw it, if you play football you can break your neck. If you drive racing cars, you can get killed. If you are a venture capitalist, you get sued. It was part of the cost of doing business. Going before a civil court judge was no different from having a referee resolve a disputed play in a ball game. You were talking about differences of opinion, not crimes. After all, he had been a director in thirty-five corporations; the problems had involved a handful.

William Proxmire was not to be put off by capitalist pieties. The senator summoned a surprise witness, Judge J. Braxton Craven, Jr. Was it true, he asked Craven, that the judge had said at the Fields plagiarism trial that the verdict against Casey was not supported by the evidence?

Craven: "No. That is not my recollection. . . . I was not at all surprised by the jury verdict."

Proxmire than asked Craven if, as Casey claimed, he had said that he would set the verdict aside if the parties did not get together and settle.

Craven answered, "I thought that the verdict was amply supported by the evidence, and I would not have set the verdict aside."

Was it true, as Casey had claimed, that it was the judge who had raised the issue of sealing the record?

No, Casey had requested it, Craven said, and he had thereafter agreed not to have the stenographic record transcribed.

The hearing ground on for five hours, largely following party lines: Proxmire attacked; Republican members defended Casey. At the end, the committee had to decide whether or not to reverse its earlier 15–0 favorable vote to send the nomination to the Senate floor. The count this time was nine to three to forward the nomination.

Fifteen days later, on March 25, the appointment came up on the Senate floor. Proxmire was scathing: "Mr. Casey has cut corners when he considered it to be necessary to his business profit. He has wheeled and dealed his way into a personal fortune, sometimes at the expense of his clients. . . . He has made less than a complete and accurate disclosure of his activities." Proxmire was speaking to a near-empty chamber. When a voice vote was taken on the Casey appointment, Proxmire's was the only nay.

The senators, in the end, had largely accepted Casey's contention that venture capitalism involved risks, legal as well as financial. He was clearly not the kind of candidate whom Ralph Nader would have chosen to head the SEC. He had been made to appear evasive, dissembling, even lying in the Fields affair. But there was no conclusive reason to reject him. Casey had won a mixed victory—not quite Pyrrhic, not quite noble.

In trying to appease the committee's concern over his ethics, he allowed himself to be maneuvered into a position he hated. Shouldn't the chairman of the SEC put his stock portfolio into a blind trust? he was asked at the hearings. He grumbled that he was unaware that any members of the committee had blind trusts. He already had his stocks in a discretionary account with a broker named Richard Cheswick. Cheswick had complete power to buy and sell without his prior approval, Casey said. Yes, Casey admitted, he did receive monthly reports. Well, then, Proxmire pointed out, that was not really a blind trust, was it? With his integrity already at issue, Casey saw no way he could wriggle out. He grudgingly created a blind trust, with Cheswick continuing as his broker, and put his portfolio with a bank in New York. He owned shares at this point in fifty-four different companies, including by now 79,442 shares of Capital Cities Broadcasting, worth $3.38 million.

On April 14, his family and a few friends stood in the Oval Office with President Nixon as Casey was sworn in as chairman of the SEC. The moment had a certain premonitory irony. The official photograph shows Nixon smiling at the short, swarthy official brought over for the swearing-in ceremony, Federal Judge John Sirica, later to preside over the Watergate trials.

Casey was able, in the end, to laugh, although bitterly, over the confirmation ordeal. He particularly enjoyed retelling the crack that Teddy Kennedy had made at Washington's annual Gridiron Dinner. Casey's appointment, Kennedy claimed, "was the second most outrageous in the history of the SEC. The first was the appointment of my father as the commission's first chairman."

At long last, Casey was able to get on with the job. The chairman's office on North Capitol Street, with its splendid view of the Capitol, was rightfully his. He was unawed. "I have a talent for going into an operation and immediately sensing its morale and knowing how to turn it around," he said as he took charge.

The SEC was going to require considerable turning around. Wall Street had a bad odor that season. Millions of small investors had been burned in the market collapse of 1969–70. Costs were going up for brokerage houses while their profits sank. They were drowning in a paperwork backlog. In the previous two years, nearly a hundred houses had failed. And the SEC was woefully understaffed to protect investors.

Casey moved quickly. The SEC already had a budget request pending when he arrived for 230 new positions. Casey threw out that budget and asked for 560. He raided Wall Street law firms and persuaded bright young lawyers that policing the Street was more exciting than defending fat-cat clients.

In his first speech he placed himself squarely in the little guy's corner. The SEC, he said, was spending too much time investigating piddling companies and new stock issues. It ought to be examining the big firms more closely, where most Americans had their money invested. He wanted to look like the people's protector too. He wrote to Max Frankel at the *New York Times* complaining about a "terrible picture of me you're using. Let me send you a few more flattering." Soon the walnut desk in the chairman's suite looked like the desk in every other Casey office, spilling over with file folders, stacks of askew letters, books cracked open, books festooned with slips of paper—and Casey, oblivious amid the chaos, engrossed in a report while eating his lunch-hour sandwich. He liked to pop unannounced into staff offices. One such impromptu stop was to produce a key association in Casey's life.

Stanley Sporkin was the thirty-nine-year-old deputy director of the SEC's watchdog unit, the Division of Enforcement. Sporkin was the scourge of those who worked the shady side of Wall Street, a dogged Inspector Javert whose whole life was given to rooting out corruption in the stock market.

The matter of American companies operating abroad illustrated Sporkin's style. For years, it had been accepted practice for these companies to play by unwritten foreign rules, which in parts of the world meant bribery, payoffs, and kickbacks. Legitimizing these corporate expenses required considerable accounting legerdemain and the falsification of corporate records. The practice stirred Sporkin's wrath: how long could a company engage in corruption abroad before it became corrupt at home? And so he went after the perpetrators. Sporkin's zeal brought him under heavy attack from the corporations, their lobbyists on Capitol Hill, even from fellow SEC officials who found Stanley Sporkin a zealot.

Milton Gould was a New York lawyer whose clients had brought him in touch with Sporkin. He also knew Casey. Gould stopped by to see Casey and the conversation turned to Sporkin. Casey, ever the realist, sympathized with the executive doing business abroad. "How are our companies supposed to compete with foreigners if they don't play the game?" he asked. "Do you think Sporkin is going overboard?" "I know," Gould said. "Pragmatically, Stanley's wrong. But morally he's right. Bribery erodes the character of American business." They argued back and forth. "I was pleased to discover the openness of Casey's mind," Gould recalled. "He would actually listen." In the end Casey had grumbled, "All right, I'll support him."

Shortly afterward, Casey appeared unexpectedly in Sporkin's office. The man he saw had dark hair that appeared to have only a nodding acquaintance with a comb. His face was darkish and pugnacious. His eyes were also dark, with the unhealthy look of a man who works too long and too hard. His suits looked as though they had been grabbed on the run from the rack at Sears. He wore homely orthopedic shoes. His shirt collars curled skyward. He had a habit of pushing his glasses onto his forehead when not reading, and they would suddenly fall down on his nose in mid-sentence. When he became excited, his voice broke into a falsetto whine: "Whaddaya mean you can't do it?!" He suggested someone up from the streets who had made a fortune in scrap iron, or a grade-three detective working in a tough precinct. Stanley Sporkin was in fact the son of a Philadelphia judge, a Phi Beta Kappa graduate of Yale Law School—an unlikely-looking knight to whom enforcement of the securities laws was a sacred trust.

Sporkin well remembered this visit: "Casey came in, sat down, and he said, 'Stan, tell me what you need to do your job better.' I was dumbfounded. Nobody, but nobody, had ever put that question to me in all the years I was in government. I began reeling off a list of things I needed—budgets, positions, authority. And he came through with almost all of it."

For years, Sporkin had been looking for a way to put "shell operators" out of business, small-time dealers who ran up stock prices of paper companies and then unloaded at a profit. One morning he received a call from Chairman Casey. Sporkin looked at his watch. It was eight-thirty in Washington, and six-thirty in Phoenix, where

Casey was calling from. "I'm making a speech at noon to a bunch of investment bankers," Casey told him, "and I'm gonna tell them how we're gonna put shell operators out of business." "What are you going to tell them?" Sporkin wanted to know. "That's your problem," Casey said. "I'm speaking at noon. Get me something before then."

"I had been trying forever to get action against these guys," Sporkin recalled. "No chairmen would touch them before. I called my staff in for a brainstorming session. It's like a restaurant inspection—if you look hard enough, you can always find violations. We put together a crash program to yank the licenses of these guys. I phoned the plan to Casey and he announced it that noon in his speech. We eventually managed to put fifteen of sixteen of those shell outfits out of business. The only thing Casey ever said to me was, 'Stan, I don't understand you. You come up with an answer in three hours. Where the hell have you been the last three years?' That was Casey's idea of praise. You only knew you were doing well if he kept coming back to you. But he wasn't much for compliments."

Sporkin remembered how Casey went about the first reorganization of the SEC in thirty years. "He made the shifts so swiftly that most of the staff learned about them from the newspaper. Decisions didn't pile up on Bill Casey's desk. He told me once, "Stan, when you don't make a decision, that's a decision, too—it's a decision by default. But then you're not in control."

The hottest issue in the securities industry at the time was whether or not the New York Stock Exchange should abandon its tradition of fixed commissions. Donald Regan, the CEO of Merrill Lynch, came down from New York to see Casey. "I told him fixed commissions were anathema," Regan remembered. "Here we were preaching free enterprise, and the heads of a few big houses would get together and say, 'My costs are going up. How about yours?' They'd get a commission increase through the Stock Exchange board. Then they'd take it to the SEC and get it rubber-stamped. It was virtually a conspiracy in restraint of trade. It wasn't right. I talked Casey into coming around, and he subsequently went against the Street. We didn't get competitive commissions until later. But Casey was in the corner early with the good guys."

The initial suspicions began to turn. *Newsweek* magazine called him "Casey the Reformer" and went on: "He has disarmed the skeptics by coming out forcefully for more rate competition and tougher control of security firms." Myron Kandel wrote in the *Institutional Investor*: "From all signs, he could turn out to be the strongest chairman the SEC ever had."

By the summer of 1971 Casey decided to strike roots into Washington. There was at 2501 Massachusetts Avenue a French country mansion of delicate gray stone smack in the middle of Embassy Row. The home was being sold by Mrs. Robert McCormack, widow of the publisher of the *Chicago Tribune*. Mrs. McCormack wanted a quarter of a million dollars for the house. Casey agreed. Soon afterward, the Japanese embassy, across the street, put in a bid for $285,000. Mrs. McCormack called to explain to Casey that she did not see how she could refuse the Japanese government. "We already have a deal," Casey reminded her. "But I'll match their price anyway."

"But what could I possibly tell them?" Mrs. McCormack wanted to know.

"Tell 'em," Casey said, "to remember Pearl Harbor."

After nearly six months, he moved out of the Hotel Fairfax. Connie Kirk had been staying with the Caseys in the second bedroom in the suite. She took this opportunity to make a painful break. She was totally devoted to Casey; his work had been her life for fourteen years. But she was lonely removed from her Brooklyn roots. She decided to go home. "After I told him," Kirk recalled, "we were both in tears."

His honeymoon at the SEC was soon interrupted. Robert Vesco had bought from Bernard Cornfeld, another financial high flyer, control of Investors Overseas Service Ltd., a company that sold millions of dollars' worth of mutual funds overseas. Vesco and his cohorts were later accused of systematically looting subsidiaries owned by IOS for their personal profit to the tune of over $200 million. This super-scam not only had beggared thousands of small American investors but was damaging the integrity of American capital markets abroad. The SEC Enforcement Division sued Vesco and his associates to recoup the stolen money.

As the 1972 presidential election neared, Robert Vesco, while still under investigation by the SEC, contributed $200,000 in one-hundred-dollar bills to the Nixon reelection campaign. On the very day of this contribution, Casey received a call from John Mitchell. According to Casey's account, Mitchell called to complain that the SEC had sent a message to Swiss officials asking them to jail Vesco. Was that proper? Mitchell wanted to know. Wasn't the SEC exceeding its authority, behaving vindictively by harassing an American businessman who still hadn't been convicted and deserved the presumption of innocence? Casey said that he would look into the matter.

He agreed to see Vesco's lawyer, Harry Sears, but claimed later that at the time he knew nothing of Vesco's campaign contribution.

Sears came to Casey's office and complained of the damage that the SEC's drawn-out investigation was causing his client's company and its stockholders. Couldn't Casey do anything about it?

As Stanley Sporkin recalled the case, "The Vesco investigation had been dragging on and on. Casey was hearing a lot of complaints that a U.S. businessman was being prosecuted. He tended to be sympathetic." The chairman, Sporkin realized, had to be educated. He brought down a broker from Wall Street who knew the Vesco operation and who laid out before Casey a horror story: huge sums sucked out of the companies Vesco controlled; little people—servicemen and their families and retirees abroad—bilked of their life savings. "After that," Sporkin recounted, "Casey told me, 'This guy's a rotten egg. I want you to move more vigorously.' I said, 'All right. I'll file for an injunction.' 'No,' Casey told me. 'That's not enough. Come up with something tougher.' So I said, 'Okay, let's try something radical. We'll go all over the world and try to freeze Vesco's assets.' Casey said, 'Do it.' So my boss Irving Pollock and I flew to Europe. We sent another man to Canada. We managed to freeze two hundred million dollars of Vesco's funds. And we did it because Bill Casey pushed us."

Sporkin was also on the trail of $200,000 that had been spirited into the United States from the Bahamas into a Vesco account—the source of the campaign contribution? Sporkin was about to call in two Vesco secretaries for questioning who might be able to clear up the matter. The election was one week off. John W. Dean III, the White House counsel, called Casey. Couldn't the examination of these two women be put off at least until after the election? Dean asked. Why? Casey wanted to know. Because, Dean told him, the publicity could smear Nixon at the last minute. Casey said that he would have to discuss the matter with Stanley Sporkin of his Enforcement Division.

As Sporkin later recounted the conversation, "Casey asked me to postpone the examination. I asked him why, and he told me because there was a political problem. I told him that doesn't sound right to me, and I wasn't going to put off an investigation for any such reason. He tried to push me around. Casey was a political animal. His President was up for reelection in a week. He'd gotten a call from the White House for help, and he intended to help. But I had an eerie feeling, a sixth sense that something ugly could develop. I told him, 'Someday you're going to thank me if you don't go along with this.' In the end, he took my advice. He wouldn't postpone the questioning of those women. But later, the *Washington Star* ran a story that he had tried to pressure me to hold off an SEC investigation until after the election. They never mentioned the fact that in the end he backed me and that the examination was not postponed.

"As far as I'm concerned, the Vesco case was one of the SEC's finest hours. We recouped two hundred million for investors. And Bill Casey was the one who kept pushing us and driving us."

The calls from John Mitchell and John Dean in the matter of Robert Vesco, however, were like the Fields plagiarism suit—mines that would continue to bob ominously in the harbor of Casey's quest for respectability. And another mine was also being laid.

The International Telephone and Telegraph Corporation had long been under investigation by the SEC because of the questionable way in which ITT had sold stock to qualify for a merger with the Hartford Fire Insurance Company. In July of 1971, the Justice Department had settled an antitrust suit with the corporation, allowing ITT to retain Hartford in return for divesting itself of certain other companies.

Some seven months later, on February 29, 1972, columnist Jack Anderson tossed a hand grenade into the affair. Anderson published a memorandum revealing that Dita Beard, an ITT lobbyist, had written to her boss suggesting that a $400,000 pledge for the upcoming Republican National Convention in San Diego had influenced the happy resolution of the antitrust suit at Justice.

The SEC, in the meantime, had been proceeding with its own separate investigation of ITT. On May 24, 1972, the staff sent to the five members of the commission a recommendation that ITT be charged with fraud. At the commission meeting, Chairman Casey argued against the charge. As he later described his reasoning: "I thought that the facts were insufficient to sustain a fraud charge." The five commissioners voted unanimously to drop the charge. One member present that day, Hugh F. Owen, later claimed that the case for fraud was not strong, and said, "I'm inclined to think that Casey didn't ram this [vote] down our throats."

But with Nixon coming up for reelection, Democrats in Congress smelled an exploitable rat. In August, Senator Ted Kennedy, chairman of the Judiciary Subcommittee on Administrative Procedures and Practices, asked the SEC for certain documents from the ITT investigation. Casey refused to turn them over. On September 21, with the election only seven weeks off, Congressman Harley O. Staggers, chairman of a House Commerce Subcommittee, made another request for the SEC's ITT files, and Staggers sent a staff member to the SEC to get them. Casey again refused, saying that the full commission had to agree to such a request.

Casey well knew that if Staggers were to subpoena the files, he would have to turn them over. And he was aware that among the items requested was a manila envelope containing thirteen potentially explosive documents revealing ITT's attempts to influence the Nixon administration—memos and letters by ITT officials describing meetings with Vice-President Spiro Agnew, Attorney General John Mitchell, Treasury Secretary John Connally, and others.

On October 3, Casey went to the White House to discuss his problem with John Dean. Dean, Casey later claimed, told him not to turn over the files. Their next move was almost certainly suggested by Casey, a far more seasoned in-fighter than the young White House aide. Dean called Ralph E. Erickson, a deputy attorney general, and suggested that perhaps the Justice Department would be interested in taking the ITT files; they might have information of interest to the department. Though Dean did not say it in so many words, this move had the added attraction of keeping these papers out of the hands of Democratic-controlled congressional committees until after the election. Erickson said that he had no need for the files at Justice. Dean pressed him. Perhaps Erickson ought to talk the matter over with Bill Casey?

Which Erickson did on the morning of October 4. Casey began by telling Erickson that he understood Justice wanted his ITT files. Erickson corrected him: his department had no use for them. He did, however, go back to double-check with other officials at Justice, and at two-forty p.m. he called Casey to reaffirm his conclusion that there was no reason to send them the ITT files. Casey told him, "I think we'd better get together again. There seems to be some sort of misunderstanding."

But first, Casey called a meeting of the SEC for three o'clock. He asked the members to consider a request from the Justice Department to send the ITT files there instead of sending them to the Staggers committee. They had precedent on their side, Casey argued: it was an SEC tradition not to turn over the files of an ongoing case to a congressional committee. The commission voted unanimously to send the files to the Justice Department. The meeting had lasted ten minutes.

Casey then had his driver whisk him over to Justice, where, at three-thirty, he met again with Ralph Erickson. Erickson was still resisting the files when Casey pulled out his clincher. In the file boxes that he wanted to send over, there might well be evidence supporting a new charge, obstruction of justice, since ITT had initially tried to keep those thirteen sensitive documents in the manila envelope from the

SEC. This was indeed a new angle to Erickson. Casey was now talking substance. Under those conditions, Erickson said, he would certainly accept the files.

But Casey wanted one thing more. He had made his sale with his fellow commissioners by telling them that the Justice Department had initiated the request for the files. Now he needed to legitimize that request. He told Erickson to send him a letter formally asking for the files but did not mention that the commission had already voted to send them. Something did not smell right to Erickson, and he demurred. Casey choked back his annoyance and left. He had one more card to play. After returning to his office, he called Erickson to tell him that the commission had just voted to send the files to the Justice Department, *at Justice's request.*

In time-honored government tradition, both parties moved quickly to carry out standard CYA—cover your ass—procedures. A Justice Department press spokesman announced that the department was receiving these ITT files from the SEC but had not "requested" them. Casey was immediately on the phone blistering Erickson. When he had pointed out the possible obstruction-of-justice case in the files, hadn't Erickson in effect "requested" them? The next day, Casey phoned Erickson to read him a letter he was sending to accompany the delivery of the files. The letter stated flatly that the files were being sent pursuant to a request by the Justice Department. Casey also told Erickson that he had an obligation to inform Harley Staggers that Justice had requested the files, and that Casey was therefore not sending them to Staggers's committee. Erickson found himself ducking bean balls from a murderous pitcher, and Casey's own posterior now seemed amply covered. But in actuality, another mine had been slipped into a sea of future troubles.

Twenty months into the job, Casey decided that he was tired of running the SEC. "Bill had a very low threshold for boredom," Stanley Sporkin recalled. "The restlessness that made him turn the SEC upside down was the same force that drove him to look for new pastures." He had achieved what he wanted. It was time to move on.

The pasture he was moving onto was at least in the field he had desired for so long. Casey knew William Rogers, Nixon's secretary of State, through Rogers's law partner and Casey's political crony, Jack Wells. Rogers had a key vacancy tailor-made for Casey: undersecretary of State for economic affairs. Here Casey's grasp of finance and his attraction to international relations could be happily wed. The job was not at the rarefied level Casey had hoped for; at best, it was tied for third place in the State Department hierarchy. But it was in the foreign policy arena.

The appointment presented no problem for President Nixon; he was delighted to set an old gunfighter like Casey loose among the tea-and-cakes crowd he despised at State. Nixon told Bill Buckley, "I'm sending Bill Casey over there to clean up the place—to get the softies out."

Casey's departure from the SEC was as much regretted as his arrival had been deplored. The *Los Angeles Times* wrote, "Casey put more cops on the block. The staff is up from 1,400 to 1,620, with most of the new employees inspectors of broker dealers." *Finance Magazine* concluded, "The gray parade of Chairmen has been enlivened only infrequently by a dimensional person like Manuel F. Cohen in the 60s, William O. Douglas in the 30s, and the founding father himself, Joseph P. Kennedy. With due respect to all his predecessors, though, Casey may be credited with creating the modern textbook-by-example of how an activist SEC Chairman can deal with the securities industry in a time of deep trouble."

Eileen Shanahan of the *New York Times* was his most satisfying convert. No fan of the initial appointment, Shanahan now rated the Casey era: "Mr. Casey's undisputed brilliance, his industriousness, and perhaps even more, his disposition to make decisions and move on to the next thing—as soon as he felt he really had the facts—not only buoyed the old hands at the Commission, but also made of the agency once again what it has historically been: a place where some of the nation's brightest young lawyers clamor to work." But Casey relished most the irreverent accolade of the London *Economist*: "His appointment to the SEC paralleled that of Joseph P. Kennedy, who was a poacher turned into a gamekeeper by President Roosevelt. . . . Casey, a brilliant, impatient, decisive man, leaves behind an impressive record."

What his early critics had misunderstood was the motive force of the man. Because he had made his pile at venture capitalism, they reasoned, Casey at the SEC would be Wall Street's lapdog. They had confused means and ends. In Casey's catechism, the end was to excel. If the game is espionage, you penetrate Germany. If the game is business, you get rich. And if the game is regulating Wall Street, you become not a lapdog but a police dog, and best of the breed. That was the fun. The satisfaction.

In late December of 1972, virtually as Casey was cleaning out his desk for the move to State, the Associated Press reported that a federal judge had ordered a $1.5-million damage suit against directors of a company called Multiponics. The judge, Herbert W. Christenberry, said "some of the things the directors did are inconceivable to me." One of those directors, and Multiponics' former chief counsel, was the departing chairman of the Securities and Exchange Commission, William J. Casey. Once more, he was teetering on that tightrope suspended between honor and disrepute.

13.

False Sunset

Bill Casey and Bill Rogers came out of the same world—high-powered law and high-level politics. They knew the same people and moved in the same circles. They admired and liked each other. Rogers, unfortunately, was not to be at the State Department for long after Casey arrived. When Rogers learned that he was to be replaced by Henry Kissinger, he told Casey, "Things are going to be different around here. With the two of us, we've been like partners in a firm. Now you're going to be just another student in a seminar." But that was still months down the road.

The post of undersecretary of State for economic affairs had been created only the year before, and it was vacant when Casey moved to Foggy Bottom. His Senate confirmation as a member of the Arms Control Commission had been uncomfortable. The confirmation for SEC chairman had been a horror, almost fatal to his reputation. At his confirmation as undersecretary, Senator George McGovern, beaten for President the previous fall by Nixon, raised the issue of the transferred ITT files. But the matter now seemed stale after Casey's triumph at the SEC. The Multiponics problem was not raised, and he was readily confirmed. He took over his new duties on February 1, 1973, still at the salary of $40,000.

Casey's new job was to handle U.S. diplomatic negotiations that had an economic angle—to persuade NATO, for example, to buy the American-made F-114 fighter, which would pump $8 billion into the U.S. economy. He was to try to convince Western European countries to pick up more of the cost of stationing U.S. troops on their soil. He was to advise the administration on how much semistrategic equipment, such as semiconductors, the United States dared sell to Communist-bloc countries without strengthening them militarily. They were the kinds of foreign policy issues that Casey had been itching to get his hands on for years.

But first, he had to master the internal politics of the State Department. He was assigned a special assistant, Tom Dawson, a third-generation diplomat. As Dawson explained his job, "The natural reaction of career bureaucrats to a political appointee is to surround him with special assistants of their own choosing. The idea is to co-opt the appointee or render him impotent."

Dawson was only twenty-four at the time, an all-bones six-footer, jumpy with nervous energy, a nonstop talker who anticipated answers before he heard three words of a question. The Casey assignment was a career plum for him. It also turned out to be a congenial mating, since Dawson was a rare conservative Republican in the career ranks at State. He had also worked earlier as a speech writer in the Senate campaign of Robert Taft, Jr., son of a Casey hero. Young Dawson was perfect for Casey. Instead of the appointee, it was the bureaucrat who was co-opted.

Dawson found Casey by turns stimulating, puzzling, impressive, amusing, or bizarre. The man's distractedness was immediately apparent. He was rushing out one Friday for a weekend at Mayknoll, trying to cram too many papers into his attaché case. Dawson offered to loan him his. Casey returned the following Monday without the borrowed case. When Dawson politely inquired about it, Casey was sheepish but noncommittal. Dawson later learned from Casey's secretary that he had left the briefcase behind his car at home. Then, late for Sunday mass, he had rushed out of the house and backed the car over Dawson's case.

Dawson soon saw beyond the Casey foibles. "He was among the very first to recognize," Dawson recalled, "that the United States was becoming a service economy rather than a producing economy. He had spotted postindustrial America early on. And he was saying that we had to adapt our foreign trade policies accordingly or lose out. I found Bill Casey to be a man of intellectual bent, not in the academic, cloistered sense of the word but in the applied sense. He was drawn to ideas. He could be buried in all sorts of specifics and detail and connect it all together in a working hypothesis."

Dawson experienced Casey's intellectual hunger firsthand. In London, Casey decided to take a walking tour of his wartime haunts—70 Grosvenor Street, the church he had attended, the Bumpus bookstore. He entered the store with Dawson and his security detail trailing behind. He kept piling up books on the counter—a total of £76 worth. "I want to charge them," Casey told the clerk. "I'm sorry," she said, "we don't have charge accounts." I've been charging books in this place for thirty years," Casey grumbled. "Excuse me," she said, "I'll have to take this up with the manager." She returned minutes later, contrite. "I'm sorry, Mr. Casey," she said. "It seems *you* do have a charge account here."

The new job did produce a much-belated and unexpected victory. Six years before, Casey had tried to join the Council on Foreign Relations and had been rejected. He had applied again, and again he had been rejected. "It was pure snobbery," his sponsor, Milton Katz, concluded. "Bill came from a background that some people found unsuitable. He was a noisy eater, a sloppy dresser. I remember once raising the issue of Casey's application with Arthur Dean, the chairman of the membership committee. 'Yes, I know—Casey from Long Island,' he said. His tone left no doubt about Casey's chances."

Shortly after coming to State, Casey called Katz at Harvard. "I just got a letter from David Rockefeller," he told Katz. "He's chairman now, and they're inviting me to join—just like that. There's no mention of the hell they put me through. What should I do?" Katz told him, "Go to the bathroom and wipe your ass with Rockefeller's letter. Then send them a reply saying you accept their gracious invitation." "I'd rather tell them to go fuck themselves," Casey answered glumly. But in the end he joined.

For Casey, life on the slippery path of public esteem seemed to be one step up, one step down. He went on a seventeen-day trip to Latin America with Secretary Rogers and was in his hotel room in Rio de Janeiro on May 21, 1973, getting ready to make a speech when Tom Dawson knocked on his door. The traveling staff had been debating whether to show him a cable just in from the department or to wait, Dawson explained. They decided that Casey should see it right away rather than be blindsided by some reporter covering the speech. The *New York Times* had broken a front-page story implicating Casey in the Vesco and ITT cases. The lead editorial virtually called for his resignation from the State Department. "You sure know how to give a speaker a lift," Casey sighed.

The facts were old news to Casey, but as reported in the *Times* they had a fresh, biting edge. Casey was accused of deleting a charge of fraud against ITT from a recommendation of his own staff of professionals while at the SEC. And he was accused of engineering the elimination of a paragraph mentioning Robert L. Vesco's $200,000 contribution to the Nixon reelection campaign from an SEC complaint against Vesco. The *Times* editorial urged Casey to relinquish his post "until the present murky situation has been cleared."

On June 7, the *Times* ran another front-page story, headlined: CASEY TESTIMONY ON SHIFT OF ITT FILES IS DISPUTED. The Staggers committee was still investigating the ITT case and had called as a witness Ralph Erickson, the deputy attorney general who Casey claimed had "requested" the files. Erickson was now out of government, in private practice, and claiming that he had been pressured by Casey into taking the files. What Erickson was now saying was so at variance with Casey's own statements on the subject that charges—perjury, obstruction of justice, falsification of records—were being raised.

Back in the States, Casey reiterated his claim that as soon as he had informed Erickson that there might be an obstruction-of-justice charge against ITT in the SEC files, Erickson had "requested" the files. "Requested," "agreed to accept," "allowed the files to be referred"—what difference did it make? It was all a quibble to Casey. Was he being accused of obstructing justice for sending potentially criminal evidence to the U.S. Department of Justice? This was preposterous, he complained.

Still, there was nothing to do but wait out the committee's investigation. He was not, he said, going to resign to please some sanctimonious liberal writing *Times* editorials—especially since he was getting no pressure from the White House to do so. Richard Nixon, fully occupied with Watergate, had little desire to have another of his team fall from grace.

In the meantime, Casey went about his job at State. In the fall of 1973, he and George Shultz, the Treasury secretary, traveled to Moscow as members of the U.S.-USSR Commercial Commission. They brought along their wives and on the way stopped for R and R at the Soviet Black Sea resort of Sochi. On Sunday morning, Casey insisted on going to church. The KGB officer in charge of the party said that that was impossible. Casey insisted: they had passed a Russian Orthodox church on the drive in, he said. The officer relented; and, with sirens screaming, Casey and Sophia were driven to the church. The local parishioners, thinking it was a police raid, were fleeing from all exits as the Ziv limo pulled up in front. That afternoon, a KGB major posted outside of Casey's door saw his charge come bounding out of his room in a bathing suit and head for the beach. Casey moved quickly, with the major trotting behind, tearing off his clothes and following Casey into the surf in his underwear.

The Caseys and the Shultzes hit it off. On their return they had a layover in Shannon, Ireland. Casey told Helena Shultz, known as Obie for her maiden name of O'Brien, that he knew the family seat of the O'Brien clan. He organized on the spot an expedition to Drogheda. They stopped at a pub afterward and consumed several Irish whiskeys. Back at the plane, Tom Dawson watched the Irishmen, actual and honorary, come aboard and remembered, "They all seemed tipsy. Secretary Shultz was dancing in the aisle." George Shultz, a smart, tough ex-Marine of deceptive humor, was Casey's kind of guy.

In September of 1973, Henry Kissinger became secretary of State. The shift in style was immediate. Casey was informed that he was to report to a daily nine a.m. senior staff conference in the secretary's office. The morning of the first meeting, he sat fidgeting with the others until eleven, when Kissinger, fresh from business in the Oval Office, made his grand entrance. The same thing happened the next day, and the next. Casey realized that he and the other subordinates were being treated to a piece of Kissinger theater. At the fourth meeting, Casey waited for ten minutes, got up, and told one of Kissinger's aides, "If the secretary wants me, he knows where he can find me."

It was Casey's custom to invite colleagues to stop by his house for breakfast. He invited Kissinger and was under the impression that the secretary had accepted. Kissinger never showed. Indeed, Casey barely got the time of day from Kissinger. The secretary never phoned him, never invited him into the small, intimate meetings where the real policy decisions were hammered out.

William J. Casey was hardly Henry Kissinger's cup of tea. The people around Kissinger were cerebral, and conspicuously so. Kissinger remarked to an aide, "Casey may be an intelligent man, but with those marbles in his mouth, how can you tell?" Fuzzy speaking must mean fuzzy thinking. But it went deeper. Henry Kissinger was bored by economics, Casey's raison d'être in the State Department. And it went deeper still. Casey was the only Kissinger subordinate at State who had an independent relationship with Nixon, in effect, his own line into the Oval Office, one which Kissinger did not control—all the more reason to quarantine him. Moreover, Henry Kissinger thus far had managed to remain spotless amid the muck of Watergate and related Nixon scandals. And Casey had a taint about him, with the Vesco and ITT business still hanging over his head.

One morning not long after Kissinger's arrival at State, Casey had been driven to the VIP elevator in the department basement; he put his key into the elevator lock. It did not work. He tried again, without success. He fumed and went to the other end of the building and took one of the public elevators up to the seventh floor. He stormed into his office and directed Tom Dawson to find out what was going on. The locks had been changed, Dawson learned; and only one official now had a key to the VIP elevator—the secretary of State. Casey demanded an immediate appointment with the secretary. Kissinger appeared surprised. It had all been a silly misunderstanding, he explained—of course Bill Casey was supposed to have a key. Casey came back five minutes later flashing the key and shaking his head. The job was not working out.

"Kissinger doesn't know anything about economics," Casey told his old law partner, Gerry Dickler, "and he couldn't care less. I never see the guy. It's a nothing job." There was less and less for him to do. And so he filled his schedule with speeches—thirty-six of them in six months.

Bill Safire understood perfectly. Safire had left speech writing for Nixon in 1973 and had since become a columnist for the *New York Times*. He and Casey still saw each other, and Casey had confessed his unhappiness. In Safire's view, the marriage was doomed from the start. "Bill Casey had been a success outside of government," Safire observed of the situation. "So he was insufficiently awed by a Kissinger, a guy who had never made it outside of Washington, a guy who's suddenly thrust onto the world stage. Also, Henry had to be in total control of everything; and here was Bill Casey, under him, with independent lines to powerful people in Washington and New York. Henry couldn't tolerate that."

Casey told Safire, "I gotta get out of there. If I don't quit, I'll be fired."

He hatched an escape. The post of president of the Export-Import Bank was available. The title had a nice, respectable ring, and it was a job Casey could perform with his eyes shut. But there were hurdles. His name was still under a cloud because of the Staggers committee's continuing investigation into the Vesco/ITT affair. The people running the Export-Import Bank day-to-day were solid, conservative types uneager to embrace an appointee whose honesty was being examined by a congressional committee. The White House personnel people also found Casey resistible. Watergate was enough of a headache; they were not looking for another noisy confirmation brawl over an administration appointee.

Casey remained loyal to Nixon even as Watergate engulfed the President. He wrote to Nixon in May of 1973: "All of your friends, all of us who view you as a national asset with a historic mission, and the general public, want to put all the political shenanigans behind us and get on with the vital things to be done. You have more friends than you know or may think of—with experience, judgment and symbolic value—ready to do whatever needs to be done."

Early in December, he made his move. He sidestepped every obstacle by writing a note directly to Nixon saying that he wanted the

Ex-Im Bank job. He had the letter hand-delivered to Nixon's tary, Rose Mary Woods. He caught Nixon in a receptive mood a almost immediately, the President announced Casey's appointmen to head the bank. "It was," Tom Dawson remarked, "one of the shrewder end runs I've ever seen pulled on the White House personnel mill."

Casey had no illusions about what he had done. He told a friend, "I got myself kicked upstairs." But it beat being kicked out of the State Department by Henry Kissinger.

Tom Dawson would miss Casey. He found the man's mind stimulating, his gaffes entertaining, his flashes of wit amusing. He remembered a visiting foreign minister coming to Casey's office, making small talk and asking Casey if he had any children. "Yes, a daughter," Casey replied. "Is she grown up?" the minister wanted to know. "Chronologically," Casey answered, "not economically." And Dawson had arrived at a rare expertise in deciphering Casey's mumbled speech: "Over at State, they rated our foreign language skills on a scale of S-1 through S-5. I was rated S-5, bilingual, in Casey."

It was, however, by no means certain that Casey would go to the Ex-Im Bank. He had finally been touched by the spreading stain of Watergate. Just before his confirmation hearing for the Ex-Im appointment, Senator William Proxmire called Leon Jaworski, the Watergate special prosecutor. Was it true, Proxmire wanted to know, that Casey was under investigation by Jaworski? The answer was yes. The Staggers committee had asked the special prosecutor to look into three aspects of the ITT case: whether transfer of the files to the Justice Department was an illegal obstruction of justice; whether anyone had committed perjury at various hearings held on this issue; and whether the SEC had been improperly influenced to drop the fraud charge against ITT. "In all three areas," a later report of the Watergate prosecutor stated, "the principal subject of this inquiry was William J. Casey who was SEC Chairman during the relevant period."

The confirmation hearing began on December 12 at 9:37 a.m. in room 5302 of the Dirksen Senate Office Building. When Casey was questioned about Export-Import Bank loans to countries that could afford to buy without this U.S. help, he had a cogent explanation. When asked why the United States made loans to Communist countries, he spoke persuasively. When asked about loans even to Arab countries then embargoing oil to the United States, he displayed a clear grasp of the trade-offs involved. In any other climate, here was an eminently qualified candidate for president of the Export-Import Bank.

sey, the questioning quickly veered away from
. Wasn't the Watergate prosecutor investigating
d obstructed justice while serving as chairman
Proxmire asked. How could such a nominee be
to head a sensitive government agency? Prox-
t a hold on Casey's appointment and go directly
where, given this information, the nomination
would certainly be killed. The committee decided to postpone its
decision.

Casey went back to the seventh floor of the State Department a
shaken man. If this appointment failed, so would his public reputation: his brilliant tenure at the SEC overshadowed by ugly subsequent
accusations; his service at State ending with Kissinger seemingly
forcing him out; his appointment to the Ex-Im Bank denied because
he was being investigated by the same prosecutor going after John
Dean, H. R. Haldeman, John Ehrlichman, John Mitchell, Jeb Magru-
der, Gordon Liddy, Charles Colson—the whole tarnished Watergate
crowd. He would be returning to New York in disgrace. He had to
have this apopintment. It represented his vindication.

The man he chose to see was Milton Gould, whom he had dealt
with at the SEC. Gould was a partner in the leading New York law
firm of Shea and Gould. He was a well-connected Democrat, and
Casey's antagonists were Democrats. He was also one of the canniest
lawyers Casey knew. Best of all at this point, Gould knew Leon Jaworski. Casey called Gould in New York. "Milt," he said, "I need your
help."

In mid-January of 1974, Gould went to Washington and met with
Jaworski. Just because Casey had been referred to the Watergate
prosecutor for investigation didn't make him guilty, Gould argued.
It was unfair to hold up the man's appointment to the Ex-Im Bank.
"Look, Leon," Gould explained, "all we need is a letter from you to
Proxmire saying the matter's been investigated, and that there's noth-
ing to it."

Jaworski was not ready to go that far. But he called in his secretary
and dictated a letter to John Sparkman, the chairman of the Senate
banking committee. In its key passages it read: "I believe that the
deferral of the Senate's consideration of an executive nomination
merely because of the pendency of an investigation by our office may
cause substantial unfairness in the event that allegations of wrongdoing, as frequently occurs, prove unfounded. . . . As of this date,
based on the investigation already conducted, no decision to charge
Mr. Casey with any criminal violation has been made."

Gould hand-carried a copy of the letter to Proxmire, whom he also knew. It was late in the day. "Proxmire was hot as a pistol against Casey," Gould recalled. "And he wasn't pleased. He found fault with some of the language, and I had to trot back to Jaworski and get the letter rewritten. Leon's a practical guy. He removed some of the phrases that offended Proxmire. And Proxmire was finally satisfied. He withdrew his objection to Bill."

Casey was confirmed as president of the Export-Import Bank by a unanimous vote of the Senate. He assumed the post on March 14, 1974. No charges were ever made against him by the special prosecutor. The Watergate cup had come close, but it had passed his lips.

Casey brought with him to the bank a career foreign service officer, an economist named Dwight Ambach. Part of Ambach's job was to travel abroad with Casey. What he remembered most of these trips was that "Casey was so exhausting. He'd insist on doing six countries in seven days."

Ambach came to know not only the foreign economic officials they dealt with but ghosts from Casey's past. "We had a meeting in Oslo," Ambach recalled, "and that night Casey invited me to join him and his wife for dinner with some of his Norwegian friends. During dinner, they began talking about how they had carried out clandestine operations against the Nazis, parachuting OSS agents into Norway. They talked about blowing up heavy water plants where the Germans were trying to develop atomic power. It suddenly dawned on me that I was working for a man who had lived the spy stories I had only read about."

Another associate, Richard D. Crafton, vice-president for Latin America at the Ex-Im Bank, gave a vivid impression of the Casey management style to an FBI agent. The agent wrote in his report: "Casey is described [by Crafton] as a man with a brilliant mind who could see through a problem, yet inarticulate and having difficulty getting across to his staff because his 'brain was so far ahead of his mouth.' He was a 'lousy administrator' as evidenced by the numerous loose ends left upon his departure and his tendency to assign the same project to a number of people simultaneously, creating enormous duplication of effort. The appointee, recognizing his shortcomings, generally left day-to-day operation of the bank to the division heads and he himself focused on 'the broad picture.' "

In December of 1975, after more than twenty months in the post, Casey was restless again. He resigned as president of the Ex-Im Bank. He had reentered government service eager to have a long-deferred dream realized. But he left disillusioned: not only had he risked rather than embellished his reputation, but the five years in Washington had almost cost him his fortune.

While he had been in the blind trust, the stock market had gone into a tailspin. His broker, Richard Cheswick, had wanted to sell off a sizable chunk of Capital Cities stock before it headed too far south. But the bank trustee raised a technical obstacle because Casey's shares in the company were so-called insider stock. In the meantime, Capital Cities had declined from a high of 53 to 17, a nearly 70 percent drop—a paper loss of more than three million dollars for Casey. Cheswick's inability to unload the stock before the drop had cost Casey a huge potential profit. And he had taken this risk only to have his integrity impugned. No more blind trusts, he said—never again. And no more public service.

Sophia had grown fond of the house on Embassy Row. "I don't want to sell it," she told Bill. "We're getting out of here," he told her. "I've had it." Why couldn't they rent the house, she asked, in case they came back? "Because I'm going home and practice law. And we're never coming back." With that he sold the house to the government of Bangladesh for its embassy for $550,000, roughly twice what he had paid for it, and went home to New York.

He was coming back to practice law, but, much to the firm's alarm, not with Hall, Casey, Dickler and Howley. He confided to Owen Smith that he was no longer interested in meeting payrolls and handling administrative headaches as a partner. Instead, he was looking for a firm that would allow him the freedom to follow the pursuits of a public servant emeritus—writing books, making speeches, giving lectures, traveling abroad. He was going to Rogers and Wells.

The firm he chose had been in existence, under various names, for 105 years. Its offices were located on the fifty-third floor of the Pan Am building, quarters distinguished by a muted elegance, antique furniture, gently tinkling telephones, and a hushed aura that reeked of decorousness and fat fees. Rogers and Wells was a large firm; its alumni directory alone ran to forty-seven pages. And among its alums was the late Charles Evans Hughes, former governor of New York, secretary of State, presidential candidate, and Chief Justice of the Supreme Court. Bill Rogers, the senior partner, had served as Nixon's secretary of State before Kissinger replaced him.

Jack Wells was the other senior partner. At sixty-eight, he was five years older than Casey. They had known each other since the 1960 Nixon campaign. Wells still spoke with the nasal inflection of his native New York. He had a modest pot belly that spilled slightly over his belt. He was of the breed that Casey instantly took to—a cerebral man who did not look it, did not act it, and did not talk it. The dumpy figure with the plain speech was a Phi Beta Kappa from Wesleyan College and a Rhodes scholar who looked at the world, over the top of his glasses, with an owlish expression reflecting a shrewd bemusement.

Casey came aboard on January 5, 1976, after cutting his deal with Wells: he was not to be a partner, but "of counsel," which meant that he had a contractual arrangement and did not share directly in the division of the firm's profits. The arrangement gave him the free time he wanted. And all parties expected to prosper, given Casey's reputation as a rainmaker. He took over a choice corner office with floor-to-ceiling windows that laid Manhattan at his feet. Off to the east, he could see the sprawling neighborhoods of Queens, where it had all begun six decades before.

He hired an Englishwoman, Barbara Hayward, who had first come to America as a nanny ("an indentured servant," as she put it) and then made of herself a crack executive secretary. She found her new boss puzzling at first. Hayward would come into his office to find him with his feet propped on his desk, chewing on the end of his tie, staring vacantly out of the window; then, in an instant, he would be all energy. "When Mr. Casey moved," she remembered, "there was never any slightest hesitation. He always knew exactly what he wanted."

She also discovered another side to this gruff, often remote figure. Hayward had piled up heavy debts in a failed business before coming to Rogers and Wells. Her own attorney had advised her to declare bankruptcy. She found Casey surprisingly interested in her plight. He told her, "Don't declare bankruptcy. Try to settle for as little on the dollar as you can get away with. But bankruptcy? You can never tell what you might want to do with your life later. Bankruptcy could kill you." How much money did she owe? he wanted to know. She told him, and he said, "All right. I'll loan it to you. Pay me back whenever you can." She was astonished—she had just come to work for the man. She refused; "But I was deeply touched," she remembered.

Barbara Hayward soon began collecting her own Casey stories. "He was always bolting out the door, forgetting his wallet, forgetting his plane tickets. He took a cab to Newark Airport for a flight to Los Angeles. When he got to the airport, he realized he had no money. He gave the driver his name and address and said that he'd pay him later. Then he talked the cabbie into lending him twenty dollars so that he could get a cab at the other end."

And he did make rain for Rogers and Wells. In his first ten months, he brought in twenty-three new clients who were billed $300,000. He brought Capital Cities Broadcasting to his new firm and went back on the company's board of directors.

Simultaneously, he plunged back into new capital ventures. He bought an interest in a firm exporting Yugoslavian rugs to America. He and William Simon, who had served as Treasury secretary under Nixon and Gerald Ford, teamed up to form Scientific Life Systems, a chain of computerized fitness spas. Simon was then serving as treasurer of the U.S. Olympic Committee, and he and Casey offered the committee a deal: SLS would pay the Olympic Committee twenty-five dollars for every new health club member signed up; in return, SLS would have exclusive use of the Olympic logo and could use Olympic athletes as instructors. The scheme ran aground on a series of lawsuits filed by competitors. Jack Anderson later described Scientific Life Systems in his column in the language Casey seemed to dread and attract in equal measure: "He had conspired to use Olympic athletes for personal gain."

The $1.5-million Multiponics lawsuit that had surfaced at the tail end of his SEC service was still pending. The firm had gone belly up with losses of $3.2 million. Investors were suing Casey and other company directors for misleading them about the company's financial health. One of Multiponics' executives testified in court that when he told Casey and the other directors that Multiponics lacked adequate equity, "it was like informing an Eskimo that it was cold. They already knew."

Along with Carl Paffendorf, Casey invested in a midget submarine. The sub was designed for work on the ocean floor, installing and repairing offshore oil rigs. That use never worked out. The owners eventually leased the sub to Melvin A. Fisher, the sunken-treasure hunter, in return for a piece of Fisher's company. Fisher was looking for the Spanish galleon *Nuestra Señora de Atocha*, sunk off the Florida coast in 1622 burdened with gold.

The scheme that most heated Casey's blood was brought to him by the inventor he had long subsidized, George Doundoulakis. Doundoulakis had dropped out of Casey's life after Casey had severed his business connections to go to the SEC. Toward the end of Casey's tenure at the Ex-Im Bank, the inventor resurfaced. "I asked Bill if I could come to see him in Washington," Doundoulakis recalled. "We sat in this big, fancy office eating tuna fish sandwiches while I laid out my plan. I'd sworn off inventions, I told him. After all these years, I'd never made any money. But this time I knew I was on to something big. I told Bill about a new gasoline engine I was working on based on the tri-rotor principle. When I finished explaining the technology, all he said was, 'What the hell does all that mean?' I said it means a car getting thirty miles to the gallon with today's engines would get forty-five miles with my tri-rotor. It means if all the cars in America had these engines, we'd only burn 60 percent of the fuel we're burning now."

The world was still recovering from the oil price shock induced by the Arab oil embargo barely two years before. Half the international economic problems that Casey dealt with at State and the Ex-Im Bank had been caused by the steep oil price increases. Here was a way to break OPEC's stranglehold and, for intrepid investors, a chance to reap a fortune. Casey was immediately intrigued.

What Doundoulakis needed was development capital. At the time, Casey told him that he could not do anything until he returned to private life. As soon as he was back in New York, he began promoting the engine. Early in 1976, Casey wrote to Lee Iacocca, then president of Ford: "The engine is about ten times smaller and lighter than conventional piston engines of the same output." He wrote similarly to General Motors and Chrysler, Curtis Wright and Grumman. He found no takers. He gave Doundoulakis $10,400 to keep him afloat, for which Casey received a 30 percent interest in Tri-Rotor Engines, the company Doundoulakis had formed to build his invention. But, obviously, an enormous amount of money was going to be required. Reenter Carl Paffendorf and Vanguard Ventures. Paffendorf raised $1.4 million for Tri-Rotor, and Doundoulakis went to work to perfect the engine.

At this stage of his life, something possibly even more satisfying than high finance happened to Casey. He had written a book—not some manual on how to cut inheritance taxes through a Clifford will but a history of the American Revolution. Wild Bill Donovan had planted the seed in Casey's brain thirty years before, one night at his Sutton Place apartment. Donovan wanted Casey to write a book on George Washington, not only as the father of the country but also as the father of American espionage. Casey had carried on desultory research during all the intervening years. By the early seventies he was finally writing a book on the Revolution. His interest had been quickened by two developments. First, 1976, the bicentennial year, offered ideal timing for publication. Second, he saw an eerie parallel in the American Revolution and the recent American failure in Vietnam. As he wrote in one draft: "Two hundred years later, another American army commuted across an ocean and, fighting in the style of earlier European wars like the British had in 1776, was unable to cope with the irregular, guerrilla tactics of an indigenous force backed by the Soviet Union, which like France in 1776, was able to inflict defeat on its militarily stronger rival by providing supplies, money and ships, while conserving its manpower."

Here, to Casey, was history's lesson. In Vietnam, the United States had played the part the British had played in the American Revolution and the Russians had played the role of the French (and, by logical extension, the Vietcong had played the American revolutionists, though Casey had not carried his analogy quite that far). The Russians had been shrewd in Vietnam, successfully operating from behind the scenes, while America's open involvement had earned only condemnation. Casey did not, however, draw the conclusion that so many other Americans drew: no more Vietnams. Rather, he believed that in future Vietnams, America would have to learn to play more like the Soviets, by backing local forces rather than fighting their fight. In time, in spots around the world, he would have an opportunity to test his hypothesis.

Casey knew just the man to talk to about his book on the revolution. He had kept in touch with Howard Cady, now an editor at William Morrow, since their OSS years. "I really didn't want to do the book," Cady later recalled. "I didn't think much of it. But Bill was a friend. I didn't have the heart to say no, and I didn't think it could do substantial harm. I also knew he had an OSS memoir up his sleeve— and that was the book I really wanted." And so Cady arranged a contract and a five-thousand-dollar advance. *Where and How the War Was Fought: An Armchair Tour of the American Revolution* was published in July of 1976, perfectly timed for the bicentennial. Casey dedicated it "To my parents."

And then he waited. He discovered, like countless authors before him, that just because he had written a book, the earth did not move. He wrote to Cady complaining that except for King Features Syndicate, "I haven't seen a single other review since my book has been published." Some 6,300 copies of the book were printed: 2,945 were sold. "It was a mistake," Cady later concluded. "I should have killed it." Casey's pride would not allow him to have the book remaindered. He bought up all the unsold copies and stored them in the attic at Mayknoll. When Cady saw Casey again at lunch, "he behaved as though it had never happened."

In 1976 he also reentered the world of intelligence, after an absence of thirty-one years. Of all the low-profile entities of government, the President's Foreign Intelligence Advisory Board was possibly the most diffidently inconspicuous. Yet it commanded, among insiders, a certain cachet. Members at one time or another included Joseph P. Kennedy, General Maxwell Taylor, Dr. Edward Teller, Clare Boothe Luce, David Bruce, the renowned lawyer Edward Bennett Williams, even Casey's old nemesis Nelson Rockefeller.

John Bross, who had worked with Casey in London and later made a CIA career, well understood the function of "Piffyab," as the acronym was pronounced by Washington insiders. "PFIAB was full of prestigious figures seduced by the mystique of intelligence," Bross noted. "Their real function was to serve as a buffer, to protect the President from becoming the prisoner of the intelligence professionals, to give him an objective evaluation of what these people were up to. In return, PFIAB members were told virtually *everything*—all the deep, dark secrets. The members were on the inside. They never got a Xerox of anything, always a typed original. They were treated special. It could all be quite exhilarating."

Casey's friend Leo Cherne, a New Dealer in his youth, had finally gagged on George McGovern as his party's presidential candidate in 1972. He looked on McGovern as virtually a Soviet apparatchik, and so that year Cherne had headed Democrats for Nixon. For his political discernment, Cherne was named by Nixon to PFIAB in 1973. By March of 1976, he was headed for the chairmanship, and he wanted Bill Casey on board. President Ford appointed Casey to PFIAB on the day that Cherne assumed the chairmanship.

Casey was delighted. He felt like a modern-day Cincinnatus, summoned to sit among his country's other eminences and help guide the President of the Republic. But Casey's pleasure was short-lived. Jimmy Carter became President in January of 1977. Carter had little use for PFIAB or, as it was to turn out, for intelligence in general. On May 10, 1977, Casey received word that his top-secret security clearance had been yanked. He was to turn in his White House pass. PFIAB had been eliminated.

Still, it seemed to Casey that he was entering his sunset years full of the honors he had, in his modest way, hungered for. He had been a prime mover behind the creation of VOSS's Donovan Medal for public service. He had watched it bestowed on luminaries like Allen Dulles, John J. McCloy, Dwight D. Eisenhower, David Bruce, and the Earl Mountbatten of Burma. In 1974 the medal was presented to William J. Casey. In 1976, he received an honorary degree, doctor of Laws, from his alma mater, Fordham University. He joined the exclusive Creek Club on Long Island and resumed golf after a twenty-year layoff. Through his old connections with British Intelligence, he joined the Savile Club in London. In 1977, he bought a rambling

Spanish mission villa in Palm Beach, Florida, with five bedrooms, an apartment, a guest cottage, and 700 feet of beachfront near old Joe Kennedy's place. The Florida estate cost Casey $350,000. And he played golf at the Everglades.

He became a patron of the theater. The October 6, 1977, issue of *Show Business* reviewed the Actors Showcase production of Agatha Christie's *The Unexpected Guest*. "In her portrayal of the adulterous widow, Laura," the review read, "Bernadette Casey achieves a winning combination of vulnerability and ruthlessness." The play was scheduled for twelve performances at the Planting Fields Arboretum in Oyster Bay. Casey attended all twelve.

The producer of Actors Showcase Limited was Owen Smith, Casey's associate and by now Bernadette's suitor of several years' standing. Casey backed the company. But he was mystified by the appeal of a profession that required ego-bruising auditions and repeated rejection. As long as Bernadette won parts, however, he happily supported her acting career. When Bernadette glowed on stage, so did Bill Casey.

Some things never changed. He was arrested by the Florida Highway Patrol for doing seventy in a fifty-mile-an-hour zone and could not find his driver's license. He failed to appear in court and a bench warrant was issued for his arrest. He paid a Florida lawyer a stiff fee to straighten out the mess.

His first year back in New York was also a presidential election year. Carl Paffendorf had recently discovered Ronald Reagan and tried to infect Casey with his enthusiasm. But Casey's political fires were banked, almost out. He made his customary pilgrimage to the Republican National Convention, in Kansas City. He supported the incumbent, Gerald Ford, but with scant enthusiasm. When he came home, he told Paffendorf, "You know, you may be on to something. The only time there was any electricity down there was when your guy Reagan took the floor."

He discovered that he had lost his zest for the law. The years in Washington, for all the pain and disappointment, began to look, in retrospect, like high drama compared to solving the tax difficulties of the Norse Petroleum Company. Only occasionally did a case remind him of the larger world. He lobbied the departments of Treasury and State to get a tax ruling favorable to Indonesia's oil industry. He did not bother, however, to register as a foreign agent; another mine had been sown.

He quarreled with Rogers and Wells about his share of the fees. He wrote a confidential memorandum to Jack Wells: "On the Indonesia tax case, I initiated the matter with the Secretary of the Treasury [his friend Bill Simon] and the Deputy Commissioner of Internal Revenue . . . and my compensation in a six-figure fee ran to a few thousand dollars."

His old OSS friend, Henry Hyde, came over and had lunch with him in the firm's executive dining room. Casey looked conspiratorially over his shoulder and said, "I don't have the gut feeling for it any more, Henry. I could make another bundle, but what the hell—it's not as much fun as it used to be."

Instead, he enjoyed doing what men who have led full lives often enjoy doing when that life appears to be drawing to a close. He was writing his memoirs—more precisely, a memoir of his OSS years, the book that Howard Cady was eager to do. Casey, however, was still too overloaded to do the book justice. The writing habits of his IBP years died hard. He farmed chunks of the book out to ghosts. He dabbled when he had a free fifteen minutes here and there. He showed a draft to another OSS pal, who said, "It read as though it had been written in taxis between meetings."

An encounter with a writer during the late 1970s reveals something of the Casey character. The author came to interview him in 1977 for a book about the penetration of Nazi Germany by the OSS during World War II. Casey generously granted the writer several interviews. He made calls and opened doors for him to other OSS veterans. The writer then went on to publish his book and never knew until years later that Casey was writing on essentially the same subject.

Casey eventually completed a first draft of his manuscript and shopped it around to several publishers without success. Howard Cady had seen it and was disappointed. "He could write beautifully when he wanted to," Cady observed in an in-house memo, but he had produced "a horrendous mishmash, and it would continue to be until Casey was willing to give it the attention it should have. . . . He should not be encouraged to write books, except on the subject of tax law."

Casey persisted. He kept after Cady, and finally, in February of 1980, Morrow offered him an advance of $12,000 for a book tentatively entitled *The Secret War Against Hitler*. The advance was laughable to a man who estimated that, over twenty years, his desk reference books had earned over $5 million—or as Casey put it, "I earned more royalties than Ernest Hemingway." Still, this book was in his blood. He did not reject Morrow's offer out of hand. Rewriting the memoir and finding a publisher could be a pleasant project for his sunset years.

14.

The Making of a President

On a January morning in 1979, Casey buzzed his secretary. Barbara Hayward found him practically horizontal, feet on the desk, leaning back in his chair. He told her to get out the checkbook: he wanted to put some money into next year's presidential campaign. Casey instructed her to send ten thousand dollars to the Republican National Committee and one thousand to George Bush. She looked disappointed; Hayward loved Ronald Reagan. He went on: he also was contributing a thousand dollars each to John Connally, Howard Baker, and Reagan.

These scattered bets were a form of cheap insurance to him. His broker, Richard Cheswick, told Casey how much he was impressed by Connally. "Nyaah," Casey said. "Connally's dead as Kelsy's nuts." Still, Connally was worth a thousand dollars, in case lightning struck. He did have a sentimental favorite: Bill Simon, a self-made multimillionaire like himself and a former secretary of the Treasury—decisive, tough, conservative. Casey told Simon, "You're just the guy to pick up the pieces after Jimmy Carter."

Soon after sending the checks, Casey invited Cliff White, Len Hall, and George Champion, former head of the Chase Manhattan Bank, to meet him for lunch at the Sky Club. "We're going to talk presidential politics," Casey said. Champion, he knew, was also a Simon man. They were, all four of them, members of the silent fraternity of power, men whose lunchtime conversation could make or break a Republican candidate. Casey talked up Simon. Cliff White—always amiable, always civilized, always bow-tied and natty in a professorial way—began to describe the ideal candidate. He spoke of the requisite temperament, personality, and character that a winner needed. Casey frowned. "You sure don't seem to be describing Bill Simon."

No, White said genially, he was not. Simon was too abrasive, too overbearing, too cocksure. White knew people who had worked with Simon on early political forays. "These fellows called me," White said, "and they asked me, 'Do you mind if we throw this guy out of the plane over the Rockies?' "

Then who should it be? Casey wanted to know. "Ronald Reagan," White said without blinking. "The nomination is Reagan's to lose— which is quite possible if he sticks with John Sears as his campaign manager."

The lunch broke up. As they were leaving the Sky Club, Casey pulled George Champion aside. "I hope you realize," he said, "we just got about a hundred thousand dollars' worth of free political expertise."

Ronald Reagan looked and behaved like a character from a forties movie about small-town America. Even the name of his alma mater, Eureka College, sounded like the set for a Hollywood campus frolic. At age sixty-nine, he still had the aura of the most popular guy in class. And he still had the broad shoulders and bouncy step of a jock. In Hollywood, he had made a mixed bag of good and atrocious movies in a career that finally burned out and detoured him into politics. He ran for governor of California in 1966, to the scathing amusement of the intelligentsia; and to their horror, he won. Four years later, he was reelected handily. Now, Ronald Reagan was running for President.

To Reagan, the East was a foreign country. Raised on the plain geography and mores of the Midwest, believing in the virtues preached in his old movies, living a dude-ranch life on 688 acres in California's Santa Ynez mountains, he was a planet away from the old, worn, cold-winter capitals of eastern commerce and power. But in his quest for the Republican nomination, he had to run all over the country. The East would be critical.

In May of 1979, his campaign brought him to Nassau County on Long Island, where he was to speak at a Republican party dinner. Dr. William Walsh, an avid conservative who had gained a measure of fame operating a world-traveling hospital ship under Project Hope during the 1950s, knew both Reagan and Casey. Walsh thought the two men ought to get to know each other. He set up a breakfast meeting at the Colony Hill Hotel, where Reagan was staying. This breakfast marked the first substantial contact between the two men.

Reagan, with professional flair, told Casey a couple of funny Irish stories. As they warmed to each other, Casey ventured a rare compliment: "Carter would never have won if he'd gone up against you instead of Jerry Ford in '76." A long, deep conversation ensued as

Reagan voiced with force and clarity the conservative catechism that Casey could only mumble.

After the breakfast, Owen Smith buttonholed Casey in the lobby and asked excitedly, "Well, what did you think?"

Casey shrugged. "He could be President."

Four months went by. After Labor Day, Casey got a call from the Reagan staff: could he help the governor meet some of the right people in the East? "Let me put something together," Casey answered. What he arranged was a Sunday brunch with two dozen of the richest, most powerful Republicans in New York. They met in a private dining room in the Hotel Pierre. The Reagan people were duly impressed. Most significant for Casey's future, Nancy Reagan was impressed.

Early in September, Charles Wick and his wife, Mary Jane, arrived in New York. Wick was a lawyer and former bandleader who had made a fortune in California investments and had become a member of Reagan's California kitchen cabinet. Wick was running the Ground Floor Committee, staging dinners across the country to raise money for Reagan. By mid-November, Wick and his wife were to organize the first Ground Floor Dinner in New York. To Wick, it looked like a thankless assignment. Reagan had made some headway in the East, but, as Wick put it, "They were still saying that Ronald Reagan was dead in the water."

Soon after their arrival, the Wicks were joined by Michael Deaver, PR adviser and factotum for the Reagans. The three Californians went to Rogers and Wells's Park Avenue offices to see the man they hoped would run the dinner in New York and help turn Reagan's prospects around. Wick said the right thing to Casey. "I've read all your books on taxes and tax shelters," he told him. "They're impressive, especially the writing." Deaver, who was meeting Casey for the first time, recalled, "He wasn't impressive in appearance. But here was one tough old guy. And he knew all the right questions."

Shortly afterward, Cliff White got a call from Casey inviting White and his wife to the fund-raiser. What was Casey doing in so deep? White asked him. "I thought you and I agreed we're too damned old to get involved in another campaign," White said. Casey gave a sheepish laugh. "I know. I just can't keep my hands out of it."

The Ground Floor Dinner was held on November 9 at the New York Hilton. "John Connally held his dinner in the same place about ten days before us, and he drew maybe a hundred and sixty people," Wick remembered. "We had two hundred and twenty-five press alone, and over sixteen hundred guests." In one night, Casey had raised more than $800,000 for Reagan.

Ronald Reagan enjoyed the New York triumph, but he was used to being liked. It had gone that way all his life. Nancy Reagan, however, saw something deeper. Like many Californians in her set, she was secretly convinced that the real capital of class was New York. Casey was clearly a force in the Eastern Republican establishment. He could deliver. Ronnie could charm them, but Casey could produce them to be charmed.

On November 13, 1979, Ronald Reagan formally announced his candidacy.

In mid-January of 1980, a stranger was prowling around the Reagan campaign headquarters, a utilitarian office box at 9841 Airport Boulevard in Los Angeles. The man carried a certain gruff authority as he popped into offices and cubicles and muttered something about "Executive Committee . . . management audit." He wanted to know everybody's assignment. He asked about morale. He checked the books. He revealed little of his purpose, and then he left.

Shortly before, Casey had been asked to become part of the Reagan Executive Advisory Committee. Other members included most of Reagan's kitchen cabinet, Californians largely, who had counseled and financed Reagan over the years: Holmes P. Tuttle, an automobile dealer; Justin Dart, a drugstore-chain mogul; Joe Coors, the brewer; William French Smith, a prominent Los Angeles attorney; Charley Wick; and a shifting handful of others. It was this group that had bankrolled and maneuvered Reagan into the run for governor in 1966.

Casey prided himself on his ability to walk into an organization, take its pulse, and make a quick diagnosis. After his "management audit" of the Reagan headquarters, he reported back to the kitchen cabinet at Holmes Tuttle's house. "Ronald Reagan hasn't got a campaign organization," Casey told them. "He's got a civil war. There's Ed Meese and the California guys in one camp. There's John Sears and his technocrats on the other side. Between the two, the campaign's paralyzed. I also looked at the books. You're going broke." With that, he flew back to New York.

Soon after, he was having lunch with Henry Hyde. "Why are you wasting your time with these people?" Hyde asked him. "All that insane economics. This Reagan fellow doesn't seem to know anything. He's had no foreign policy experience at all. He's a second-rate actor, a jumped-up local politician."

Casey gave Hyde a tolerant smile. "Don't forget, Henry—the guys who have the brains can't get elected, and the guys who get elected don't always have the brains." He knew.

The Iowa caucus on January 21 was the first test of the 1980 presidential campaign. Ronald Reagan lost it. George Bush won, with 33 percent of the 110,000 votes to Reagan's 30 percent.

John Sears told the candidate not to worry. A handful of farmers meeting in a few scattered schoolhouses were not going to decide this campaign. Sears had a strategy and they were sticking to it. Reagan was to concentrate on the primaries in the East and wrap up the nomination early, in New Hampshire, New York, and Connecticut. The Midwest would then fall in line. And Reagan already had the West in his back pocket.

John Sears was a lawyer out of the New York Republican firm of Nixon, Mudge, Rose, Guthrie, Alexander and Mitchell, a delegate hunter in the successful 1968 Nixon campaign, a manager in the 1976 Reagan presidential effort, during which he and Michael Deaver had first met.

He had struck Deaver then as brainy, shy, self-mocking, and self-effacing. In 1979, Deaver had again sold the Reagans on Sears as campaign manager. But Sears had changed. Self-effacement had turned to arrogance, brilliance to egomania, self-mockery to aloofness, and shyness to secretiveness. He trusted nobody but a few hand-picked associates. One Californian on the staff described the impression that Sears created: "He's one of those blue-suit, silver-tie, you-dummies-out-West-couldn't-elect-a-goat-to-a-hay-party kind of Eastern smart-asses."

Sears had watched Reagan's behavior with his kitchen cabinet and had taken his cue from them. A stranger dropping in might have missed the point that the guy with the tan and the snappy patter was the *leader*. Reagan would sit amiably and let his cronies thrash out a decision. He then picked up the script and went out and performed it superbly. That was all Sears expected of him. He had so little confidence in Reagan's ability to think on his feet that he did not let the candidate take part in a debate among Republican candidates prior to the Iowa caucus. He did not laugh at Reagan's old Hollywood stories. Instead, Sears behaved like an ambitious young agent with an aging, mediocre actor for a client.

Reagan knew that he was being patronized. "I look him in the eye," he said of Sears, "and he looks me in the tie." There were days when Sears did not deign to speak to the candidate at all. Sears became a brooding, detached, chain-smoking figure in the wings at Reagan rallies. Yet Reagan stood in awe of his cerebral handler.

Sears might not speak much to his candidate, but he enjoyed giving interviews to the press, explaining how he was playing the Reagan candidacy, the effect of which was to make Reagan look like a ventriloquist's dummy in Sears's lap.

Lyn Nofziger, a veteran Reagan political organizer, called Sears a "Rasputin." Nofziger was one of the first Californians whom Sears forced out. The next victim was the scholarly Martin Anderson, Reagan's expert on domestic issues. Anderson thought he knew Sears well after ten years of working together; but, as Anderson put it, "the man who never lied to me started telling me things that were not true." Anderson left.

Mike Deaver was by now the only Californian left with a good word for Sears. But Deaver had a fatal flaw: he was close to the Reagans, and thus a threat to Sears's compulsion for total control. Deaver was maneuvered out. All that now stood between Sears and absolute power over the campaign was Edwin Meese, Jr., Reagan's longtime chief of staff, the last of the Californians.

With Deaver and the others already shot down, Ronald Reagan began to feel like a subway passenger who suddenly finds himself on a car full of menacing strangers.

Then came the defeat in Iowa.

Overnight, the Sears mystique was shattered. Arrogance might be tolerable as long as the expert from the East seemed to know something that the Californians did not know. They were already aware that he was a poor administrator. Now he was a loser, no matter how cleverly he explained the defeat. And Casey had been right about the campaign. They were operating under a $17.6-million federal spending limit. There were thirty-three primaries to go; and two-thirds of the money would be gone by the next primary, in New Hampshire, and all of it by April.

The only thing that kept Ed Meese on board, badgered by Sears and excluded from strategic decisions, was fifteen years of total devotion to Ronald Reagan. But Sears was assiduously undermining what little remained of Meese's role, telling Nancy Reagan that the man was a schemer working behind his back. The charge was true. Meese was in fact in touch with the kitchen cabinet. He arranged for a meeting at Justin Dart's house and said that if Sears remained in command, the campaign was doomed.

The public Nancy Reagan was a figure seen at political rallies, adoring eyes riveted on her husband, a smile welded to her face. The private Nancy Reagan was a Metternich in Adolfo dresses, willing to make the hard decisions that her husband let drift. Nancy Reagan decided that Sears had to go. She called Judge William Clark, Reagan's former executive secretary during the gubernatorial years, a man of judgment, good with people, totally trusted by the Reagans. But Clark liked it where he was, on the California Supreme Court bench. He enjoyed life on his nine-hundred-acre ranch—and he certainly preferred it to jumping into a snake pit. The job of electing a President required Sears-like ambition, but without John Sears. Nancy Reagan did not press the judge.

Back in January, while Casey had been in the Los Angeles headquarters carrying out his review of the campaign, Ed Meese had asked him out to dinner one night at a French restaurant on the outskirts of Bel Air. Meese brought along the exiled former campaigner Mike Deaver. Casey was relaxed, expansive. They asked his opinion of the Reagan effort. Casey went down the inventory of campaign failings: here was what they had to do to staunch the money hemorrhage; here was the reorganization needed to unsnarl staff conflicts; here were the issues that Reagan should exploit. The two Californians looked at each other as though a light had suddenly gone on.

Later, Ed Meese talked to Nancy Reagan. She quickly agreed. Sears's replacement was obvious.

Long Island at that time of year was bare, cold, and leafless. Casey liked to escape on weekends with Sophia and Bernadette to the house in Palm Beach. He had just finished a golf game there with Owen Smith and Earl E. T. Smith, Eisenhower's ambassador to Cuba, and was stretched out on the patio editing his OSS manuscript when a call came from Ronald Reagan. Reagan was all affability, warm with that gift of his for making the listener feel like the most important person in his life. "Bill, I'm thinking of some changes in my organization," Reagan began. "You don't have to give me an answer now. But I want you to think about taking over. I'm going to New Hampshire in a few days. Why don't you join me? We can talk."

Reagan's was not the first offer Casey had received. George Bush and John Connally had also tried to recruit him. His initial reaction to Reagan was cautious. "He talked about the offer while we were in Florida," Owen Smith recalled. "But he didn't jump. He thought Reagan had floundered badly so far, and he wasn't sure he wanted to jump on a sinking ship."

"For three days," Cliff White remembered, "I got calls from Bill at seven o'clock in the morning. 'What do you think I should do?' he kept asking. I told him, 'Remember, we both agreed we're at the stage of life where the only reason to do anything is if you want to do it. There's your answer.'"

Casey called his friend Paul Laxalt, a Republican senator from

Nevada. "I don't know these people, the Reagans. What are they like?" he asked. "Nancy is the strong one," Laxalt told him. "One smart, tough lady. But they're neophytes on the national scene. You won't have to worry about one thing, though. Ron will take direction."

On February 16, Casey flew the Eastern shuttle to Boston. He went to a Holiday Inn near the airport, where he met with Reagan. He would take over, he told him, if Reagan meant exactly that: he would be totally in charge. The near-fatal flaw thus far had been the internal war over ownership of the candidate. Casey wanted no part of that. Also, he had to have final say on the spending. The fact that they were talking in Boston made the point. The budget for New Hampshire was already so depleted that the primary campaign was being run by forays out of Massachusetts. Meese and the other surviving staffers present were in no position to argue. They were drowning, and Casey was the man on the dock with the life saver. Reagan accepted Casey's terms. In the meantime, he had to live with Sears, and so the decision was to be kept secret. Sears was standing on a trap door. The Reagan people had to decide when best to spring it.

A few days later, the entourage moved to the Rolling Hills Sheraton in Worcester, Massachusetts, where Casey was to meet again with Reagan. He was joined in the lobby by Dick Allen, a friend since the '68 Nixon campaign, who was now handling foreign policy for Reagan. The two men took the elevator up to Reagan's suite. A young woman got on with them and said hello to Allen. Allen felt compelled to make an introduction. "Linda," he said, "this is Frank Williams." "Aaah, c'mon," an embarrassed Casey said. He put his hand out to the young woman and said, "My name's Bill Casey." The elevator stopped and the young woman headed in the opposite direction. "Jesus, Bill," Allen whispered, "you blew your cover. She's one of Sears's people. Now he'll guess why you're here."

The New Hampshire primary was set for February 26. That afternoon, the candidate sat in his third-floor suite in the Manchester Hotel in Manchester. With him were Nancy, Ed Meese, Dick Allen, Casey, and other staff members. Three days before, an internal poll had shown that Reagan had leaped ahead in New Hampshire, sixteen points in front of his nearest rival, George Bush. He could now dump John Sears without appearing a sore loser. Still, Reagan was uneasy. The script was written, but the role of executioner was not one he enjoyed.

At three-thirty, Meese picked up the phone and asked Sears and his two chief lieutenants, Charles Black, the national political director, and James Lake, the press secretary, to come to the candidate's suite. When Sears arrived, the contented expression on Meese's bovine face instantly alerted him. Reagan managed a limp smile and handed Sears a one-page press release. The first paragraph read: "Ronald Reagan today announced that William J. Casey has been named campaign director of his presidential campaign, replacing John Sears, who has resigned to return to his law practice." Black and Lake were "returning to private business." The author of the release was Bill Casey.

Sears took it with more grace than he had shown running the campaign. By three-forty Casey was standing at the window watching the three men disappear with their bags across the parking lot. He was two weeks short of his sixty-seventh birthday—the age, he reminded Meese with a laugh, that Churchill had been when he took over the leadership of England in World War II.

By six o'clock he was standing before the traveling press corps in the hotel conference room. A reporter asked him how much authority he expected to exercise. Casey answered, "Everybody reports to me."

The press had been given a brief bio of the new director:

Dwight Eisenhower, Ronald Reagan and a lot of people in between have turned to William J. Casey when they needed decisive action. When General Eisenhower was surprised and his troops suffered heavy casualties at the Battle of the Bulge . . . Casey organized and ran an operation that put 102 two-man intelligence missions behind enemy lines. . . . Casey has demonstrated an ability to quickly take hold and direct bureaucracies in the Nixon and Ford administrations. Between World War II and the SEC, Casey pursued several careers simultaneously, building a New York and Washington law firm . . . building a publishing company . . . building Capital Cities Broadcasting Corporation, backing a dozen young innovative companies . . . working in the presidential campaigns of Eisenhower, Taft, Dewey, Nixon. . . . Ideological litmus paper doesn't work very well on Casey. If you ask him, he'll take the conservative label, yet you'll find him working with pillars of the New York liberal establishment. On his walls you can find pictures with Eisenhower, Taft, Dewey, Bill Donovan, David Bruce, Cardinal Cooke, John Connally, Admiral Zumwalt. . . . *Fortune* magazine recently proclaimed him a member of the Eastern establishment, while saying he hates to admit it. . . .

Casey had learned his lesson long ago: if your light is hidden under a basket, get rid of the basket. He had written the release.

That night the results were in. Ronald Reagan had won the New Hampshire primary with 51 percent of the vote over his nearest rival, George Bush, with 22 percent. The day after the primary, Casey flew to Los Angeles to take over the Reagan headquarters.

The man he had come to serve was mystifying, but not for any sense of mystery about him. Quite the opposite. The only mystery about Ronald Reagan was his seeming simplicity. How could so common a man hold such uncommon power over other men? The answer, at least part of it, Casey discovered, lay in the phenomenal warmth he generated. Reagan was a happy man, a secure man, a man untouched by self-doubt. He glowed with the pleasure of life. Others felt the glow and were drawn to it, wanted to bask in it. People liked Ronald Reagan; more important, he appeared to like them—an even stronger reason for liking him. Likability, a warm personality—these were qualifications to lead the Western world? As long as suffrage was universal and until ordinary folk were conditioned to elect philosopher kings, they apparently would do.

Casey began attending meetings with the candidate. He saw Reagan initiate nothing, give no orders, decide virtually nothing. In the beginning, he had been shocked. He soon learned that those closest to the man—Meese, Deaver, Nofziger—all knew what went on when the doors closed behind Ronald Reagan. It was like a family secret that no one ever mentioned. It was all summed up in what Reagan told Casey soon after he took over as campaign director: "You're the expert, Bill. Just point me in the right direction and I'll go."

Once the shock wore off, the secret did not discourage Casey. Despite the impression Reagan's style left, it was obvious that Ronald Reagan was not an unintelligent man. He had a good mind that absorbed and retained what interested him. And he possessed an inordinately high social intelligence. He knew instinctively how to treat people, what to say to court them so that they would react in the desired fashion, which was: "I want to be part of this man's circle. I want to help him to get where he wants to go."

Casey realized that the Reagan approach was 180 degrees different from his own fumbling congressional campaign of fourteen years before, when he had stuck his nose into everything. Reagan cheerily accepted being told what to say, where to say it and when. He was easily molded by stronger personalities around him. But the clay was basic conservative, and no amount of manipulation was going to change that. The ideas he held might be simplistic, the mind that held them passive, even threadbare. But with that exceptional social intelligence, the man could invest these ideas with freshness. More important, people are drawn to sincerity, and Ronald Reagan believed every word he said. Casey thought he had a winner.

The campaign itself was another matter.

Casey occupied a plain office with a rented metal desk, a chair, a couple of filing cabinets, grain-painted in a vain attempt to resemble wood. Virtually his first stop was the finance office. Darrel Trent, a finance staffer, laid out the books for him. Trent told him, "We owe two million dollars. There's no way we can avoid a financial collapse sometime next month." It was worse than Casey thought; there was not even enough money to pay for a hotel for himself. He could not pay his own hotel bill because it would be considered a campaign contribution, and he had already contributed the legal maximum. He decided to accept a standing offer to stay with Charley and Mary Jane Wick.

He had inherited a paid staff of over three hundred campaign workers. He let half of them go. Those who survived had their pay cut by 20 percent. A key handful he brought back—Nofziger, Deaver, Martin Anderson. Until now, people all over the organization had had the authority to spend; he centered the authority in the hands of a single controller and kept final approval for himself. When he ordered one field headquarters shut down, a staff lawyer warned him, "Mr. Casey, we could have legal problems if we try to break the lease." "Don't give me that legal crap," Casey shot back. "Just tell 'em we're out of money. You'll see how fast they'll find another tenant."

Ed Meese recalled Casey's initial impact: "For the first time we had a sense that somebody was in charge. You could feel the morale lift. When you sat down at a meeting with Bill, something had to come out of it—a decision, a solution, action. And it wasn't John Sears's campaign anymore. It was Ronald Reagan's. The biggest difference was in the candidate. Disharmony was an environment Ronald Reagan couldn't function in—he'd begin to suffocate. After Casey took over, you could see him breathe again. Pretty soon we started to think, maybe we could win this thing."

Soon after taking over, Casey got a phone call from a man named Max Hugel, a successful, self-made businessman whom he had met in the New Hampshire campaign. Hugel was on his way back from a trip to Japan and wanted to stop by and see Casey. He was fifty-six years old, a short, moon-faced man who wore a toupee. His grammar was as tenuous as his grasp of business was secure. He could say of an unsuccessful trip, "I never shoudda went." And his language was rough. There are in New York City—in the garment district, in the diamond business, in wholesale meat-packing—hundreds of Max

Hugels, men whose appearance, speech, and behavior totally belie the raw intelligence that produces their success. Max Hugel's net worth was estimated in the neighborhood of $7 million. This tough-talking dynamo had made almost as much money, Casey observed, as he had.

Fortunately for Hugel, there was nothing in his breed that seemed alien to Casey. Indeed, there was a strain of it in Casey himself. Hugel impressed Casey by what he had achieved in the Reagan campaign in New Hampshire. As he explained it, "I organized Nashua like a sales campaign. I broke it down by streets. I broke the streets into blocks. I found a Reagan supporter to work every block. We took nine wards we weren't supposed to win." It was old-fashioned shoe-leather-and-doorbell politics in an age of computerized demograph-ics. Casey was already suspect in the press as a man too old to un-derstand the new game of direct mail and tracking polls; but Hugel's glamourless methods had delivered the one thing that counted—votes. Casey decided to gamble on Max Hugel. He set him up in an office down the hall and told him to work up something similar to what he had done in Nashua, New Hampshire, for all of the United States.

"Whose office is this?" Hugel wanted to know.

"It's Ronald Reagan's—but he's never here," Casey told him.

Casey spent several weeks living with the Wicks. They found his ways amusing. The two Californians would breakfast at poolside in slippers and bathrobes; Casey never appeared without a coat and tie. He had brought with him what looked like a World War II duffel bag, from which he produced rolled-up suits. "Bill had shirts in five dif-ferent laundries," Wick recalled, "and he could never remember which. So he'd just go out and buy more."

The Wicks were hospitable and social. They were out almost every night, and they liked to bring Casey along. He enjoyed the Wicks, but he was carrying a crushing workload; he had little time for play. Campaign contribution limits be damned—he decided to take his own apartment. And he had just the roommate in mind: Max Hugel.

They rented a two-bedroom apartment at Marina del Rey. Hugel later described life with Casey: "Bill was up by five o'clock. No alarm, no nothing—he'd just jump out of bed and start making his East Coast calls. I was a jogger, and I'd say, 'Bill, you ought to get some exercise.' He'd look up from the phone and wiggle his little finger. All the while he was talking, he'd be shoving bananas in his mouth. We never ate regular meals. Hell, we never learned how to turn on the stove. So mostly we went out. And when Bill ate, he dripped—that's the only word for it.

"On the job, he could be rough. He was an intimidating son of a bitch. He'd tear you apart—absolutely destroy you. He never had the patience to hear you out. 'Get to the point! Get to the point!' Sometimes I used to cringe. He'd mumble, and if you asked him 'What did you say?' he'd get mad as hell. So people would walk out of meetings without having the guts to ask him what he wanted. It created a hell of a lot of confusion.

"I was always surprised at what a book guy he was. We'd go into somebody's house and the first thing Bill checked was the bookshelves. He told me you can tell a hell of a lot more about a guy by his books than his bank account—this guy's sharp, or this guy's a dummy."

Hugel was an outsider in California, a suspicious, insecure man, never certain who accepted him or who was slighting him. He took comfort in another of Casey's maxims. "Look, Max," Casey told him, "there aren't enough hours in a day to go around distrusting people. Trust 'em one time; then, if they let you down, cross 'em off. You have to do that. Otherwise, distrust can paralyze you."

Casey gave the staff a long leash. But all the leashes ultimately were held in his hand—finance, advertising, speech writing, issues, budget, polling. Geoffrey M. T. Jones, the director of the VOSS, remembered coming out to see Casey about organization business. Casey kept saying, "Be with you in a minute—gotta make a couple more calls," as Jones waited from seven o'clock to eight, to nine, to ten. They finally got to dinner at midnight. "I caught his head just as it hit the soup," Jones recalled.

Arthur Hug, a Long Island business associate, called Casey at campaign headquarters late one afternoon. "I know you're out there trying to elect a president," Hug apologized, "but we've got a problem at the bank." Casey was chairman of the executive committee at Long Island Trust, and Hug was telling him that the directors needed Casey present to oust a key executive. "Art," Casey said wearily, "it's impossible." "I know," Hug said, and waited. After a long silence, Casey sighed. "I suppose I could take the red-eye." Hug picked up a bleary-eyed Casey at the airport the next morning; by eight-thirty he was in the meeting and cast the deciding vote. By nine, he was on his way back to the airport; that afternoon, he was back in Los Angeles running the campaign. "That trip didn't put a dime in Bill's pocket," Hug observed. "But he would do something like that and it cemented you to him forever."

By early May, all of Reagan's Republican rivals had dropped out—Bush, Connally, Howard Baker, Bob Dole. Reagan had won twenty-five of twenty-nine primaries. Bush won the other four. The convention would now be Reagan's victory party. Casey had doled out the funds so prudently that by the time the nomination was locked up, the Reagan war chest showed a $500,000 surplus.

At that point, Casey made a useful decision. As Max Hugel put it, "The trouble with Republicans is they like to exclude people out. Some of those types get their kicks leaving people out. Bill knew that was how you made one friend, the guy you took in, and ten enemies, the guys you left out. Bill was an includer." Casey announced that prior to the Republican convention, Ronald Reagan would appear at five "Unity Dinners" to pay off the campaign debts of his defeated rivals.

At the same time, Casey had to fight off the politics of vengeance advocated by his fellow conservatives. He shared their philosophy, but he deplored their lack of grace or even good sense. The right-wingers considered the Republican National Committee a spoil of victory. They wanted the middle-roading national chairman, William Brock, thrown out and one of their own installed. What had a generation of struggle been all about if they won and left the party in the hands, God forbid, of *moderates?* Casey was uneasy. Primary victories might be engineered by a zealous band of the faithful, but the United States was not populated by conservative ideologues. He checked with his conservative touchstone, Cliff White, about replacing Brock. "Hell," White said, "that's just musical chairs. Bill Brock's done a fine job. He's raised money for the party. He's got organization Republicans in place and ready to go, all over the country. You dump a good man for no good reason and people resent it."

Casey and Meese worked out a plan. They would put the conservative Drew Lewis in as "deputy national chairman" under Bill Brock, "with operational control over the RNC staff." Lewis would run it, and Brock would sit on top of it, face and title saved.

In those months, Casey had come to know his candidate both better and less: better, through sheer exposure; less, in the sense that he learned that the appearance of intimacy was possible with Ronald Reagan, but not the real thing. Ronald Reagan's unfailing good nature was a layer of insulation that sealed off contact with the inner man. Casey learned that the quickest route to Reagan's mind was not a direct approach, which usually produced only amiable chitchat and no decision. The action line ran through Mike Deaver, who had Nancy Reagan's ear, and from Nancy to her husband. Nancy was the candidate's only true confidante. Casey developed toward Nancy Reagan the wary respect that one grants a porcupine. One determinedly anonymous friend commented: "Once Bill got the campaign director job, his instinct was to avoid personal contact with her. Nancy Reagan had a tendency to stick her nose in everything. And if you got on the wrong side of her, you were dead. So Casey kept some space between them. He felt safer using Deaver as his conduit and buffer."

In a rare personal comment on Reagan, Casey told a campaign aide, "If you can't give it to him in one paragraph, forget it. He doesn't absorb a hell of a lot." This aspect of Reagan still left him baffled. Casey, who read so voraciously, who had so much information stuffed inside his head, had watched a man become a candidate for President of the United States who seemingly lived by anecdotes and smiles. Casey told the same friend—defensively, it seemed—"Well, he's got terrific people instincts."

Jerry Ford posed a conundrum to the Reagan people. Ford, they assumed, harbored hard feelings toward Reagan, and with reason: he had been an incumbent Republican President running for reelection, and Reagan had challenged him within his own party. It was a stab in the back from which Ford believed he never fully recovered. In Ford's mind, one reason why he had lost to Jimmy Carter in 1976 was Ronald Reagan.

In the spring, Casey wrote Reagan a memo. "Of all the Republicans, Jerry Ford is the one who can hurt us or help us most," he said. Casey assigned himself the job of winning the help and stemming the harm. He began with a personal contribution of $5,000 to the Gerald Ford presidential library. After thus paving the way, Casey asked Ford if he could visit him at his office next to the Rancho Mirage Golf Course in Palm Springs, California. Ford agreed and was surprisingly cordial. He told Casey that he now wanted to help Reagan, to give him the benefit of his ideas on national security, foreign policy, on selecting a vice-president and the cabinet. Only one moment of discomfort intruded on the conversation. Henry Kissinger ought to be brought into the foreign policy apparatus, Ford said. Casey managed to control his enthusiasm. He guessed that Ford's resentment over his defeat was being overcome by an itch to reenter the game that had been his life for twenty-eight years.

He came back and reported to Reagan that he thought he had detected something unspoken but ever present in the Palm Springs talk: Ford might be persuaded to come onto the ticket as vice-president—a "dream ticket," as Casey described it. "But it's a trade-off," he cautioned. "If you can't get elected without him, of course, I'd say take it. Otherwise, his price may be high." At the very least, however, he said, Reagan ought to call on the former President personally, to show the public that the wound was healed. The combined staffs worked out the visit like peace negotiators meeting in the DMZ: "As Governor Reagan's car pulls up to the curb," the operations plan read, "President Ford, wearing a dark blazer and an open golf shirt, comes out to greet Governor Reagan. . . . Both will then go on foot to Ford's office."

The two men, both affable by nature and poor grudge bearers, let bygones be bygones. Reagan tested the subject of the dream ticket; Ford politely declined. Still, the meeting had been a triumph, Casey thought: the one Republican who could have hurt Reagan was now safely in camp.

The Republican convention opened on July 14 at Detroit's Joe Louis Sports Arena. The night before, Casey was having dinner at the Detroit Plaza Hotel with his family, Owen Smith, and other friends. Henry Kissinger, radiating his heavy brand of bonhomie, stopped by the table. Casey knew that Kissinger was saying the nicest things about Ronald Reagan to dubious European and Middle Eastern leaders. The old power sniffer was clearly on the scent, Casey concluded. Casey had also recently put out a directive that all convention speeches were to be cleared by him. "I have a speech, Bill," Kissinger said. "But I can't imagine you want to be bothered looking at it." Casey gave Kissinger a broad smile. "Yeah, Henry, I think you ought to drop by with it."

When Kissinger had gone, Owen Smith asked Casey, "Would Henry get a spot in the administration?"

"Over my dead body," Casey answered.

The next night, Jerry Ford delivered a rouser, a stem-winding opening speech that contained an intriguing phrase. "Elder statesmen," Ford said, "are supposed to sit quietly and smile wisely from the sidelines. I've never been much for sitting. I've never spent much time on the sidelines. . . . So when this convention fields a team for Governor Reagan, count me in."

Ronald Reagan loved the speech. And that last sentence—what could it mean but that Ford now wanted to be on the ticket? Reagan authorized Casey to meet with a Ford team led by Kissinger, to negotiate the price of a Reagan-Ford pairing. They gathered on Wednesday afternoon, July 16, in a hotel meeting room next to the conference center. Casey posted his secretary, Barbara Hayward, next to the door. She was to let no one in and to hold off all but the most urgent phone calls. And he added, "You're to forget anything you ever heard or saw in this room."

Hayward, keen and politically curious, could not, however, muffle her ears to the sounds of possible history in the making. They all seemed so imposing to her, these men in their well-cut dark suits. "The room positively reeked of power," she remembered. "The atmosphere was cordial but stiff. Henry Kissinger did most of the talking for their side, and Mr. Casey for our side. They discussed which cabinet appointments President Ford would control and what authority he would have. The more power Mr. Kissinger expected for Ford, the more annoyed I could see Mr. Casey getting."

The meeting broke up after three hours. Casey came away with an impression that if the deal were cut, Gerald Ford would be the chief operating executive of the United States, Henry Kissinger would be secretary of State, and Ronald Reagan could stroll in the Rose Garden. He went to Reagan in his hotel suite and reported: "I don't see it working. They're talking about a co-presidency."

Reagan remained noncommittal. He was a man of punctilious courtesy; and having earlier offered the vice-presidential nomination to Ford, Reagan did not feel that he could now simply walk away. He had to hope that Ford would decline and get him off the hook. Reagan called Ford that night at about nine and was friendly but uncharacteristically emphatic: he needed to speak to the former President. He had to wait nearly an hour and a half until Ford came to his suite. The two men disappeared behind closed doors. Ford clearly understood the situation—he was dealing with a suitor who had made an unwise proposal but who was too polite to retract it. He came out smiling and left Reagan's suite. After he had gone, a relieved Reagan told the staff, "His answer was no. He didn't think it was right for him or me. I'm going to call George Bush. I want to get this settled. Anyone have any objections?"

Casey had little use for George Bush. He felt that Bush's politics were too liberal and his character too soft. But the habit of inclusion was a stronger force in his reasoning. Ford had possibly cost himself the election in 1976 by not taking Reagan on the ticket. Casey saw little profit in Reagan's making the same mistake by ignoring the man apparently second-closest to Republican hearts. He agreed with Reagan's choice. The candidate made the call, and Bush accepted on the spot.

Casey had already been thinking about where to locate the headquarters for the general election campaign. The practical choices were to stay in Los Angeles or move the operation to Chicago, New York, or Washington. Casey chose Washington. "Washington's full of political expertise," he told the staff. "It's ten minutes to the airport.

It's a hell of a lot cheaper than the others. And the media run on eastern time."

He located a squat, four-story office building in the Washington suburb of Arlington across the Potomac in northern Virginia: 901 South Highland Street; rent, $8,340 per month—a bargain, Casey knew. He put his own office on the top floor. He found a furnished apartment for himself and Sophia at the nearby Skyline House for $1,067 a month.

Under the federal election law, the Reagan-Bush ticket qualified for and received $29.4 million in federal funding. Casey put all of it not immediately needed into Treasury bills. Before the campaign was over, this investment earned another $465,040. National, state, and local Republican committees could spend another $24.1 million on the campaign. Thus, the initial Reagan war chest totaled $53.5 million, slightly under Carter's $53.9 million. Casey slapped a $50,000 limit on campaign salaries and paid it to a half-dozen top staff, including himself.

The political terrain after the primaries was rather like a field after battle. Casey looked at the camps of the defeated candidates the way he had looked at POW cages in World War II, not simply as the defeated enemy but as a pool of potential talent. Among the most talented, he concluded, was James A. Baker III. Jim Baker was a Texas millionaire, forty-nine years old, the great-grandson of the founder of the old-line Houston law firm of Baker and Botts. After Princeton University, law school, and a stint in the Marine Corps, Baker had gone into the family firm and wore lightly his enrollment as a Democrat. In 1970, his life was shattered by the death of his wife, Mary, which left Baker with four sons. He had virtually been dragged into politics by his friend George Bush as a form of emotional rehabilitation. He swiftly exhibited a taste and a talent for the game in Bush's unsuccessful run for the U.S. Senate against Lloyd Bentsen that year. Baker was hooked.

In 1976, Baker ran the delegate operation that saved Jerry Ford's nomination from the Reagan assault. This year he had run the Bush campaign against Reagan—on the surface, a losing credential. But Casey remembered that it was Baker who had managed the near-fatal defeat of Reagan in Iowa. He also checked around and found out that Baker was of that rare breed of political operatives who know how to live within a campaign budget.

That summer, after the convention, Casey went to Texas to install a state chairman for Reagan-Bush. He took the opportunity to drop in on Baker at his home in Houston and offered him the job of campaign budget director. Baker turned him down. Casey did not give up; it was just a question of finding the right bait. A few weeks later he came back to Baker with a more attractive offer: senior adviser with special responsibility for preparing Ronald Reagan for presidential debates. This time, Baker accepted.

Casey installed Baker in an office near his own, where Baker displayed a sharp mind, tireless energy, and solid judgment, carried off with a charm that made it all seem effortless. Casey knew that he had recruited a star.

He was living a punishing schedule. One morning, Barbara Hayward counted seventy-two phone calls handled in an hour, including one to Frank Sinatra, whom Casey tried to enlist for Reagan. He rewrote drafts of speeches that he did not like. He persuaded Henry Kissinger to do five-minute radio spots on foreign policy. He still did not like Kissinger, but the man carried authority. He took the heat from Nancy Reagan, who was persuaded by Mike Deaver that the campaign's television commercials were dreadful. "They were concocted from outtakes of Reagan's old gubernatorial campaigns. The damned cars were '66 Cadillacs! I began to wonder if Casey knew anything about modern media," Deaver recalled. Casey stood fast. "Our guy's already branded as a Hollywood actor," he told his critics. "We have to replace the actor image with the public-figure image. Slick's our problem, not our solution. We're sticking with the commercials."

Barbara Hayward watched the telephones slamming, the troops parading in and out of his office day and night, the brutal hours, the flood of orders, the fist pounding, the wisps of hair flying as Casey ran from meeting to meeting. And she thought, "I never saw a more exhilarated human being. Here is the beast in his natural habitat."

The Reagan camp had not been spared conflict that is congenital between the traveling team and the headquarters staff in modern campaigns. Those who travel with the candidate see themselves as troops at the front. They see those left behind as rear-echelon warriors who never hear a shot fired in anger. The headquarters people see themselves as the general staff, making the strategic decisions that the grunts then carry out. Casey was a classic armchair general; he was never satisfied with what was happening at the front. He enlisted Cliff White—fellow easterner, fellow conservative, fellow political junkie, his favorite crony since Len Hall (who had died recently)— as his sidekick for the campaign. "We watched Reagan make a few goofs on the road in September," White recalled. "So we decided we had to put somebody politically astute on the plane, and Bill chose Stu Spencer."

Stuart Spencer was a short, raffish, profane, savvy political operative, half of the firm of Spencer and Roberts, the best-known political consultants in California. Spencer's gut instinct for understanding the ordinary voter was legendary. But eventually Cliff White concluded that Spencer's best game was follow-the-leader. "He reminded me of Silent Murph from Tammany Hall days," White said of Spencer. "Murph would preside over a meeting never uttering a word, until he figured out which way the wind was blowing. Then he'd make the consensus decision. That's Stu Spencer. After his first ride on the plane he came to a meeting and gave us a sketchy report until he trapped me into giving my estimate. I went on about Reagan's only problem being his lack of confidence. As soon as it was out of my mouth, Spencer leaped on it. 'That's right,' he started telling us. 'Ron is always saying, "These guys in the press think I'm a dummy." ' So after this meeting, Stu goes back on the plane and starts assuring Reagan that he's not a dummy, though I'd heard Spencer say he was."

The troops at the front had a distinct advantage: they had the ear of the traveling press. Casey, because of his appearance and manner, became the butt of staff wits on the plane. Casey stories were circulated, such as the time he summoned two key Republican chairmen from faraway states, then forgetfully left town before they arrived, which had the ring of truth. The traveling staff referred to the director as "Spacey Casey." The reporters on the plane amused themselves in idle hours by making up joke biography titles, in which Casey emerged as *The Man Who Never Was.* Lou Cannon, the *Washington Post*'s man on the Reagan campaign, was later to write, "Casey was out of his league in national politics." As Mike Deaver saw it from the traveling entourage, "Stu Spencer and I ran the campaign."

The amount of campaign authority that Casey or Spencer or Deaver carried is important only in distributing credit for victory or blame for defeat. In making this judgment, one thing was clear: who was hired, who was fired, and even who got to ride on the plane was Casey's decision. The traveling press secretary, popular, amusing James Brady (later to be crippled in the Reagan assassination attempt), often exercised his ready wit for the reporters' amusement. When he had exercised it once too often on a subject Casey judged detrimental to the campaign, Casey yanked him off the plane, and Brady had to beg his way back on.

The troops on the plane were indeed on the firing line. But it was back in the cluttered offices in Arlington, Virginia, that the strategy, the speech themes, the travel schedule, the television ads, and the financing were generated, and where, as Cliff White put it, "Casey had his finger in every pie and his hand in every decision." Those in the traveling party, beginning with the candidate, were like the actors in a movie being produced, cast, and directed by unseen figures behind the cameras. When pressed later, Mike Deaver would say, "Okay, Casey was the real boss."

During the primaries, when Teddy Kennedy had challenged Jimmy Carter for the Democratic nomination, Casey had observed something that had haunted him ever since. At that point, the fifty-two American hostages seized in Tehran had been held captive for more than six months. As Casey later described his concern: "I noticed in the last days of the Wisconsin primary that Teddy Kennedy was pulling up fast on Carter. That could be the beginning of a sweep of the industrial states. Then, on the Sunday before the election, Carter notified the networks that he expected good news on the hostages—they would be taken out of the embassy and moved to safer quarters. He got up at seven o'clock on Tuesday, election day, and announced it again as the voters were going to the polls. And he scored a tremendous victory in Wisconsin over Kennedy."

Casey's mortal fear was that Carter would make another last-minute announcement—that he had arranged for release of the hostages—and be catapulted to victory in November. Reagan was suspended on a tightrope over the hostage issue. Any faint suggestion that he did not welcome their earliest release would destroy him with the American people. Yet, if Carter did succeed in freeing the hostages, that feat would likely erase all his other sins in the voters' eyes, and they would reelect him. The fear was shorthanded in the Reagan camp as the "October Surprise."

Ugly rumors circulated that, if proven, would sink Reagan overnight—rumors that his operatives were meeting with Iranian envoys with a simple proposal: stall the release of the hostages until after the election; you'll get a better deal from our side, including the sale of weapons. Efforts by the press to uncover any dealings between the Reagan team and the Iranians turned up nothing. But the rumors persisted.

Years afterward, in 1988, as the Reagan administration was winding down, a man named Richard J. Brenneke testified before a federal judge that he had personally witnessed Casey dealing with the Iranians barely three weeks before the 1980 election, with the objective of putting off a hostage release. Brenneke made the claim at a sentencing procedure in Denver, Colorado, where he was appearing on behalf of a friend, Heinrich Rupp, recently convicted of bank fraud. In the course of his testimony, Brenneke had sought to defend Rupp's character by mentioning high-level missions that he and Rupp had been a party to as operatives of the CIA.

For his trouble, Brenneke himself was charged with five counts of making false statements to a federal judge, a charge more serious than ordinary perjury. The presumably incriminating misstatements included Brenneke's assertion that he had been a contract employee of the CIA for eighteen years and that he had taken part, in that capacity, in a meeting in Paris on the release of hostages at which Casey was present. At his trial, Brenneke maintained that in the fall of 1980 he was contacted by his CIA control officer and asked to attend this meeting. He was being sent because one of his specialties was laundering money, and a hostage-release deal would almost certainly involve the clandestine movement of funds.

Brenneke explained further that he was put up in the Waldorf Florida hotel in the Madeleine district of Paris, a few blocks from the U.S. embassy. On or about October 20, he claimed, he attended a meeting in a large room of the hotel beginning in mid-morning and lasting through the afternoon. Present at the meeting were Iranians, including a shadowy figure named Manucher Ghorbanifar; Israeli and French intermediaries; Donald Gregg, then a CIA officer attached to the Carter National Security Council; and, surprisingly, William J. Casey. Casey, Brenneke stated, had been flown to Paris by Heinrich Rupp in a privately chartered aircraft. The purpose of the meeting, as Brenneke put it, was "to work out the terms, regarding weapons deliveries and money, for releasing the hostages."

It quickly became clear to him, Brenneke recalled, that Casey was the "commanding presence" at the meeting, though he had no idea why Casey, in effect still a private citizen, should be there. "Anyone in the room could see that he was the one in charge," Brenneke observed. "It took Ghorbanifar about thirty seconds to figure it out and cozy up to Casey."

Something else startled Brenneke. As he remembered it, "The Iranians usually wanted their money up front. But it soon became clear to me that with our presidential election only about three weeks off, these people were not talking about moving money any time soon. That led me to the conclusion that something was going on I hadn't known about. I realized they were talking about a delayed hostage release, which I thought was pretty contemptible. I drew that conclusion mostly because of the time frame they were discussing for moving money."

It was this story, told to the federal judge to help his friend Rupp, that led to Brenneke's own indictment for making false statements. He was tried in Portland, Oregon, his home town. During the trial, two of Casey's former campaign secretaries testified that Casey never left the country during the period in question; indeed, they said, he barely left his office. Don Gregg, who later went on to become Vice-President George Bush's national security adviser and later still President Bush's ambassador to South Korea, was called from Seoul to testify against Brenneke and swore that he had attended no such meeting in Paris.

Yet, the jury believed Richard Brenneke. Indeed, no juror voted for a guilty finding on any of the five counts he faced. As Brenneke put it afterward, "Why in hell would I dream up a story like that, one that brought down a two-year ordeal on my head?" Brenneke's point seems well taken. And the fact is that no agreement on the fifty-two hostages was reached until after the election, and they were not freed until minutes after Ronald Reagan was sworn in on Inauguration Day, January 20, 1981.

What Casey was provably known to be doing that fall of 1980 to prepare for an October Surprise was far more prosaic. Several of the top staff were also living at Skyline House. They began meeting in the apartment of the campaign's pollster, Dick Wirthlin, at six every morning to sift through the latest hostage news and rumors—Casey, Wirthlin, Meese, Peter Daily, the campaign's advertising director, and a California public relations man and Naval Reserve admiral named Robert Garrick.

Garrick was an affable, smooth-talking Californian of colorful speech and deceptive energy. He carried the title of director of research in the campaign. As Garrick described the intelligence operation: "I bought the AP, UPI, Reuters, and New York Times wire services. Then I set up an eight-hour, around-the-clock schedule. I had a watch officer in charge of each shift, a lot of retired CIA and military types. Altogether I had about two hundred and twenty people monitoring the news day and night. Each officer produced a digest of what happened during his watch. We got this information out on printers throughout the headquarters and to the plane. Anything on the hostages was priority. For example, we learned that two hospital aircraft had landed at Heidelberg. If the hostages were being sprung, they would probably pick them up and bring them back to Heidelberg. Then Air Force One would come over and bring them back to Andrews Air Force Base, and there goes the whole enchilada."

Garrick would later be accused of, or credited with, creating a nationwide network to monitor military tip-offs of a pending hostage release. Garrick had a simpler but still ingenious explanation: "One day I'm reading the *Washington Post* and I see a photo of military equipment that the shah of Iran had bought before he was kicked out which was still in the U.S., undelivered. I figured if Carter made a hostage deal, he'd ship this stuff that was already paid for. If it was shipped, I figured, it would go in a C-5. So I tracked down the material in the picture to McGuire Air Force Base in New Jersey. Then I called a reservist I knew who lived nearby and I said, 'Could you kind of keep your eye on McGuire? If you see a bunch of C-5s go in, give me a call.' That was the whole extent of my so-called nationwide espionage operation."

Actually, it went farther, and with Casey's encouragement. Garrick may have had friends keeping a weather eye on as many as four bases. A memo from his files notes a tip from a brigadier general in the California National Guard that several military aircraft had been moved to Tinker Air Force Base in Oklahoma, "where the spare parts are." Casey gave strict instructions to Barbara Hayward: "The Garrick Iran monitoring operation is top secret," he told her. "It's never to be discussed except behind closed doors."

Casey had one last-ditch contingency plan for the hostages. He had had Pete Daily produce two hundred thousand dollars' worth of radio and television commercials; they were in the can, waiting to be released if Carter in fact pulled off an October Surprise. The theme running throughout the commercials was simple: any last-minute freeing of the hostages just before the election was a cynical manipulation of human lives for political advantage. Casey memoed Reagan that should Carter cave in to the demands the Iranians were making, "the release would be seen as a political trick anyway, and the American people would wonder why Carter hadn't done it sooner." He was not sure whether he was bucking up the candidate's spirits or his own.

Casey had installed Cliff White in the office next to his own, as his in-house guru. On the Sunday before the election, Barbara Hayward called White at his apartment and told him, "Mr. Casey looks lonely. I think it would help if you came by." White came to the headquarters. He and Casey went out to lunch, and Casey's spirits seemed to revive. "Our guys in New York think they can win this thing with another two hundred thousand dollars for television," Casey said. "What do you think?" White gave Casey his cracker-barrel sage's smile and answered, "Well, seeing it's you who goes to jail if we go over the legal limit, I say you should give it to them." Casey managed to get the money to New York through financial legerdemain, and the state later did go for Reagan.

That Sunday afternoon, as they sat talking in Casey's office, White, a Protestant, mentioned that he was going to church. Casey said, "I'll walk with you. I want to go to mass." As they were walking out of the building toward the parking lot, Casey asked White, "Why do you go to church? Is it habit or what?" White thought for a moment and responded, "I guess the answer is I think it's part of my obligation as a believer. And it makes me feel better." Casey looked off pensively. White waited several seconds to hear the roots of Casey's religious faith revealed. "Yeah," Casey finally said. "That's right." "That," said White, "was the end of my only philosophy discussion with Bill Casey."

In September, something strange had begun to happen in the Reagan campaign—something best described as uneasy good fortune. There were in the government civil servants, unhappy diplomats, Pentagon officers, even Democrats who looked on the Carter presidency as a disaster. And from such people, information began appearing in the Reagan headquarters like found money.

In mid-October, Casey was handed a confidential report on inflation that had been prepared exclusively for the Carter cabinet. A stockbroker and part-time Reagan volunteer named Daniel Jones gave his version of how the paper had made this curious journey. Jones claimed that he had been working at campaign headquarters when he was called by the security desk to come down to the main lobby. There, a man in uniform—an Air Force sergeant, Jones thought—handed him a large brown envelope, saying that he did not like the Carter military budget and he wanted to do what he could to help Ronald Reagan. In the envelope, Jones found the Carter White House inflation report along with a handwritten get-well note from President Sadat to Carter. On October 24, Jones claimed, he received a phone call from the sergeant offering to drop off more material. That evening the man gave him a memo drafted by Carter White House aides Anne Wexler and Al MacDonald dealing with Federal Reserve policy, dated that very day. This document also reportedly went to Casey.

Jones claimed he later ran into Casey in the hallway and mentioned that he was the one providing the information from the Carter camp. According to Jones, Casey told him that what they really could use was Carter's campaign schedule. The following Monday, October 27, Jones claimed he called the sergeant, who read to him an upcoming Carter schedule, which Jones took down and sent to Casey.

At about the same time, Max Hugel sent Ed Meese a three-page memorandum from the Carter-Mondale headquarters outlining the administration's campaign strategy for rural areas. Hugel's cover memo noted that the material "fell into my hands."

Tony Dolan was a recent Casey protégé who also started feeding material from a source with purported White House connections. Dolan was a burly thirty-two-year-old, glib of tongue and possessed of impeccable conservative credentials. He confessed to having fallen in love with Ronald Reagan's speeches at age thirteen. Dolan was also a passable folk singer in Irish pubs around New York. And he had picked up a Pulitzer Prize during six years as an investigative reporter for the *Stamford Advocate* in Connecticut for a series on organized crime. He came to know Casey because he had given guitar lessons to one of Bill Buckley's sons. Buckley senior urged Casey to take Dolan on and was ready to pay his campaign salary if necessary. Dolan started feeding Casey memos from a source who had information on Carter White House plans to divert personnel from government agencies to work in the campaign—a violation of Federal election laws, if true.

As these windfalls continued, Bob Garrick wrote in his notes at a staff meeting, "The director said he wanted more material from the Carter camp and he wanted it circulated."

Charles Bartlett, a former Washington columnist, called Casey and told him that there was a Democrat he should meet. Casey told Bartlett to send him over. The Democrat turned out to be Paul Corbin, a small, wizened, raffish veteran of Kennedy family campaigns, a man with a reputation for doing the kinds of jobs where you don't ask too many questions as long as the job gets done. Corbin brought with him a six-page memo written by Adam Walinsky, a lawyer and one-time aide to Robert Kennedy. Walinsky's memo contained suggested statements for Reagan to make in the upcoming debate with Jimmy Carter. The known lack of love between Senator Edward Kennedy and Carter made Corbin's offer all the more intriguing to Casey. Casey put Paul Corbin on the payroll, supposedly to do fieldwork and prepare "research reports" and to distribute campaign literature in Florida. Corbin too provided information on Carter's schedule.

Then occurred the most astonishing delivery of all. There turned up at Reagan headquarters four items, including a 249-page ring binder entitled "Presidential Debates: Foreign Policy and National

Security Issues." The first sentence read: "This briefing book is designed to assist the President in debates with Governor Reagan on foreign policy and national security issues." The second item was a forty-page summary of the above document; the third was another notebook, entitled "Debate Briefing Material: Domestic"; and the fourth, a 274-page document prepared to assist Vice-President Walter Mondale in the event of a debate with his Republican opponent, George Bush. The Reagan camp, in effect, had a complete record of the Carter debate strategy. How this trove found its way to 901 South Highland Street from the recesses of the Carter White House was a question that, like a time bomb, would not explode for another three years.

The presidential debate was expected to be decisive. The popular impressions of the two candidates made for an interesting contest: Carter with all the information and little charm; Reagan with all the charm and little information. Casey had rented a lush Virginia estate, called Wexford, for the practice sessions. Senator John Warner and his then wife, the actress Elizabeth Taylor, were the current owners. On their first arrival, the Reagan team walked into a haunting corner of the past. The house had been briefly inhabited by John F. Kennedy, and still hanging on the walls were photographs of the assassinated President and his wife and children.

Under Jim Baker's direction, the team began staging rehearsals, with Congressman David Stockman playing Carter. Casey suggested that Reagan face Washington journalists just as he would during the debate. George Will and Patrick Buchanan were asked to take part and agreed. Casey called Bill Safire and got an unexpected reaction. "I told him," Safire said, "that it didn't seem right to me—I was on the other side now. And he got mad as hell. He just couldn't make the transition. Hadn't he been a good friend to me, a good news source? Is this how I repaid him, by turning him down?"

The debate was set for October 28, the week before the election.

The polls had fluctuated since Labor Day, when the campaign got under way in earnest. At first, Carter and Reagan were virtually neck and neck, with the third-party candidate, John Anderson, trailing badly. With twenty-five days left, Reagan's pollster, Dick Wirthlin, showed the candidate with a healthy 5 to 8 percent lead. Days later, on October 14, Wirthlin found Carter coming back strong, pulling ahead 45.2 percent to Reagan's 43.4 percent. Then Reagan surged back.

The televised debate in Cleveland's Public Music Hall gave Reagan a clear boost. He seemed surprisingly well prepared, quick on the draw. One charge that the Carter briefing book had suggested using was that Reagan helped "lead the fight to defeat Medicare when it was first considered by the Congress." Carter raised the charge in the debate. Reagan seemed to be waiting for it. He had backed a different bill, he said—one that would have provided better medical care for senior citizens. When Carter's turn came to rebut, he had no answer.

Reagan rebutted some of Carter's points even before his opponent could make them. When the debate turned to energy, Reagan was shooting down Carter statistics on coal production, which had been revealed in the briefing book, before Carter had even mentioned them.

On Election Day, Tuesday, November 4, Ronald Reagan rolled over Jimmy Carter by 43.9 million votes to 35 million, 51 percent to 42 percent, 489 electoral votes to 44. Carter became the first Democratic President to be defeated for reelection in ninety-two years.

Casey went to bed that night content that he had elected a President.

But had he? Ronald Reagan might well have won regardless of who directed his campaign. He was then, and continued to remain, wildly popular, virtually impervious to the contempt of sophisticates while he captured the affection of the mass of Americans.

He was also the predictable product of the politics of the eighties, marked by the domination of the media and weakening party loyalty. Absent war or hard times, American presidential politics were increasingly becoming a straight popularity contest, scarcely different from the election of a high-school class president. In an earlier century, the likelihood that the average voter would actually see the face, hear the voice, note the gestures of a candidate and be affected in his vote by the warmth or chill of his personality was virtually nil. All that most voters of another age could do was, at best, to read about the candidate and the issues (and reading is an act of the intellect) or, at worst, to vote the way the bosses told them. But the new politics introduced a wholly new basis for choosing. Thanks to the illusion of intimacy that television created, voters could ask themselves which candidate they *liked* better. And Ronald Reagan was clearly more likable than Jimmy Carter.

As for Casey's credit in the victory, the question is not whether Reagan could have been elected without him but whether he could have been nominated without Casey. The campaign had been demoralized and near bankruptcy when he took over. And in a game where victory has a thousand fathers, key participants were ready to grant Casey paternity. Paul Laxalt, close to Reagan and honorary chairman of the campaign, said simply, "I doubt that Ronald Reagan would have been nominated if Bill hadn't come aboard." Ed Meese concluded, "I'm ready to give Bill the lion's share of the credit." Cliff White observed that though the reporters traveling on the plane might choose to ridicule the funny old guy back at headquarters, "anybody who says Bill was not running that campaign didn't understand the campaign. I can tell you this: Ronald Reagan could not have been nominated for President if he hadn't gotten rid of John Sears. Now, maybe somebody besides Casey could have stepped in. But the point is, Casey did."

And what spoils did the architect of the victory expect? He knew what he wanted and what he felt he deserved. But he assumed nothing. He was not, for all his recent authority, a Reagan insider, a member of the kitchen cabinet. They had labored in the vineyard all day. Casey had not arrived until the final hour. He remembered the old New York postcampaign button "Nice work, kid—now get lost." It shouldn't happen after the role he had just performed. But he was battle scarred in the patronage scramble. He had worked hard for Nixon and then waited two years for a decent appointment. This time, he was taking no chances. Even after running the campaign for nine exhausting months, he did not dare take time off. Instead, he told Sophia that they were staying on the scene, moving to the stately Jefferson Hotel on Fifteenth Street in Washington, kitty-corner from the Soviet embassy.

He also took nominal charge of the Reagan transition machinery, as chairman, while his now fast friend Ed Meese ran the day-to-day operations as director. They set up a transition office at 1727 M Street in downtown Washington and put the staff to work drawing up lists for the thousands of presidential appointments.

Casey knew that no major post was going to be decided in a Washington office. The coveted plums would be awarded in California in those deceptively casual gatherings of Reagan's rich friends. Casey tipped his hand to what he hoped for in the way he handled assignments at the transition offices. He was the figurehead leader of the transition team, but he made himself active head of the committee on foreign policy. Among the sixteen other members, he named ex-President Ford and Henry Kissinger. Casey was convinced that Kissinger hungered for the public stage again, and was quite prepared to let him salivate a while more with this appointment.

A transition committee on intelligence was created too, but Casey took no direct interest in it. Instead, he sent John Bross to keep his eye on the committee's recommendation. It was Bross who had long ago scrounged up the A-26s for the Joan-Eleanor missions into Germany. Bross had eventually gone back into the business, and served twenty years in key posts, including the supersensitive job of CIA station chief in West Germany. And Bross was a gentleman, the best of the WASP breed, Harvard '33 and Harvard Law '36, a quiet, unassuming man possessed of wisdom and a flinty integrity.

Within days of the election, Casey was in California with Bush, Baker, Meese, Deaver, Laxalt, Pendleton James, an executive headhunter, and the President-elect, meeting at the Reagans' home in Pacific Palisades. The subject was formation of the cabinet. They talked at length about State and Treasury. Alexander Haig had the prestige, the experience, the drive (and he looked marvelous) for secretary of State, everyone agreed. But were they handing the Democrats on the Senate confirmation committees a club to beat them over the head? Haig had virtually run the country for Nixon in the last months of the Watergate ordeal. And if Watergate had not hurt him, were they building up a competitor, since Haig was also nakedly ambitious?

Casey sat, revealing no outward discomfort as they talked about giving Haig the job he coveted. George Bush, who had said little, finally spoke: "Do what you want to. But if you pick Al Haig, I predict you'll have serious problems."

Pen James mentioned Donald T. Regan of Merrill Lynch for Treasury. "Anybody know him?" James asked. "He can handle it," Casey said, which was either generous of him or a tactic to divert attention from himself—he knew he was on the list for the Treasury job. Casey's okay sewed the appointment up for Don Regan. No other decisions were made at that time. Casey had said little. His position was awkward—a little like a beauty-pageant contestant sitting on the jury. He flew back to Washington still uncertain of his future.

The people at Pacific Palisades had been essentially a shirtsleeves crew. There was another, obscurely powerful circle of influence, the men who had bankrolled and guided Ronald Reagan's political fortunes for almost twenty years—his kitchen cabinet, men who wanted nothing for themselves but influence. They called Meese, now back in Washington. They told him to set up a meeting; they had a few thoughts on Ronnie's appointments. Meese complied and soon afterward met with them in the Los Angeles law offices of Gibson, Dunn and Crutcher. Also present were Pen James, Bill Simon, and Casey's erstwhile California host, Charles Wick. But not Casey.

The group went down the list—State, Defense, Commerce. When they reached the CIA, someone commented that Bill Casey seemed a natural. Bill Simon spoke up: "I think Bill's expecting something a little higher up." Charley Wick thought Casey deserved more elevated treatment; after all, he had directed the victory. Shouldn't he be discussing his future directly with the President-elect?

Casey, back east, had breakfast at about this time with Bill Safire at the Jefferson Hotel, just blocks from Safire's office at the *New York Times*. "The CIA would fit you like a glove," Safire observed. Casey smiled slowly. "Not a bad fallback position," he said. "What about State?" Safire asked. Casey smiled but said nothing.

He had lunch with Dick Allen, who appeared headed for the post of national security adviser. "I don't even know if I want to be in this administration," Casey told Allen. "I've got my law practice. I've got a lot cooking in New York."

Allen: "C'mon, Bill. You know you're going to be. It's just a question of where."

Casey: "Oh, well—I'd take State."

Allen wrestled with himself. Did he want to be honest or agreeable? "I thought to myself," he later recalled, " 'Bill Casey, you don't look like a secretary of State. You don't talk like a secretary of State. You only think like one.' But all I told him was, 'It's not going to happen.' "

On November 21, Owen Smith stopped by the transition headquarters. Casey was going over a letter that Barbara Hayward had just typed. The letter was to the President-elect. Casey had begun by saying that he knew he was now on the short list for State, Defense, CIA, and Commerce, and added: "Going in and out of the room while these discussions took place rather conflicted with my natural modesty, as does writing this letter." But he went on to compress in three single-spaced pages his professional life, tying what he had done to each of the four jobs. What he said about State was carefully tailored to Reagan's pet prejudices: "What the State Department needs internally is . . . a tougher minded focus on American interests rather than the needs and demands of other countries. This is something I could do quickly."

Commerce: "I have a track record in what it should be reshaped to do."

The CIA: "I know how to meet the kind of morale building it needs today."

He wasted little effort pitching himself for Defense. That slot was going to a Reagan intimate, Caspar Weinberger. Casey accepted that.

He felt compelled to remind the President-elect that Bill Casey belonged to a select company: "Only two other men in our political memory put together campaigns which drove the Democrats out, Herb Brownell for Ike and John Mitchell for Nixon. Both of them sat in on the selection of the cabinet. I would not like to be left out."

TOP LEFT: Casey's grand-parents. (COURTESY OF LAW-RENCE CASEY) ABOVE: Ca-sey's parents, Bill, Sr., and Blanche. (COURTESY OF LAW-RENCE CASEY) BOTTOM: Ca-sey, age 12, and sister, Dorothy. (COURTESY OF LAW-RENCE CASEY)

RIGHT: Casey speaks before the Research Institute of America. (COURTESY OF LAWRENCE CASEY) BELOW: Casey at a Fordham University dinner. (COURTESY OF LAWRENCE CASEY)

ABOVE: Casey arranged a trip to Vietnam for the International Rescue Committee during his 1966 congressional campaign. Refugees, he thought, were an underutilized intelligence source. (COURTESY OF LAWRENCE CASEY) LEFT: Nixon and Casey after Casey was sworn in as chairman of the Securities and Exchange Commission in 1971. (AP/WIDE WORLD PHOTOS)

ABOVE: Ronald Reaga[n] huddles with Case[y,] his campaign chai[r]man, in 1980. (AP/WI[DE] WORLD PHOTOS) LEF[T:] Reagan's chief of sta[ff,] Edwin Meese, and C[a]sey, his transition chi[ef,] in 1980. (AP/WIDE WORL[D] PHOTOS)

BELOW: Nominees for Reagan's cabinet pose for photographers in 1980. From left are Casey, director of the CIA; David Stockman, budget director; Drew Lewis, secretary of Transportation; Richard Schweiker, secretary of Health and Human Services; Malcolm Baldrige, secretary of Commerce; Caspar Weinberger, secretary of Defense; William French Smith, attorney general; and Donald Regan, Treasury secretary. (AP/WIDE WORLD PHOTOS) RIGHT: In 1981 Casey appeared before a Senate subcommittee studying terrorism. (UPI/BETTMANN NEWS-PHOTOS)

Top Left: In 1984 CIA Director William Casey and Secretary of State George Shultz briefed members of the House Foreign Relations Committee on the situation in Central America. (AP/ WIDE WORLD PHOTOS) BOTTOM LEFT: Casey with Reagan in 1984. (AP/WIDE WORLD PHOTOS) BELOW: In 1986 President Reagan met with the Tower commission, his review board that investigated secret arms dealings with Iran. From left are George Shultz, John Tower, Reagan, Edmund Muskie, and Brent Scowcroft. Seated behind Reagan is Casey. (UPI/BETTMANN NEWSPHOTOS)

Casey arrives on Capitol Hill to testify before the Senate intelligence committee on the secret arms sales to Iran, November 1986. (UPI/BETTMANN NEWSPHOTOS)

When he finished going over the letter, he looked up at Smith and said something as if to cover his pride in case his highest hopes were disappointed. "Know what this letter is?" he said. "I'm writing to Reagan. I'm asking for the CIA."

As the days dragged on and nothing materialized, Casey began to feel the same humiliating neglect that he had suffered after the Nixon '68 campaign. In truth, Casey's prospects for secretary of State had been dead at birth. His eastern connections may have looked appealing when the Reagans were hungry. But now they were running the banquet, and as one future cabinet member recalled: "I'd heard Nancy Reagan put him down. She didn't approve of his appearance, his style, the way he spoke. She didn't consider Bill Casey State Department caliber." One evening as Casey sat in his room at the Jefferson, Meese, Pen James, and Paul Laxalt were on another floor offering the State Department to Al Haig.

In the waning days of December, Ronald Reagan finally called him. Thanks to Ed Meese's briefing, Reagan was well armed. "Bill," Reagan began, "I want you in my cabinet." Casey's spirits lifted. What cabinet post did he mean? "I want you to be the director of the CIA." He paused for the appropriate dramatic effect. "I want you to know I'm giving the job cabinet rank." Still, Casey was unexpectedly cool. "If I can't have State," he said, "I guess I'll have to think about it." Reagan was confused. He thought that it had all been wired. He had just offered an overage actor the part of James Bond—and he was being stalled? "If I do take it," Casey said, "I expect to be in on policy. I'd give you the intelligence straight. I wouldn't bend it to fit the policy. But I expect to be part of the foreign policy team."

Reagan practically purred: "Bill, I wouldn't have it any other way. If it wasn't for you, you know, I wouldn't be in this hot seat."

Casey continued his work at the transition office that day. When he got back to the Jefferson Hotel that evening, he settled into a sofa. He and Sophia carried on household chitchat. He asked what Bernadette was up to. Then he let it drop casually: "Reagan's offered me the CIA. If I take it, you know, it'll swallow up my life. I've got a feeling I'd like it. What do you think?"

She sat next to him, took his hand, and said, "Bill, if you want it, that's fine with me. You take it."

"All right, I will. And I'm going to like it," he said. "I'm going to enjoy it."

As word of his pending appointment leaked out, Casey laughingly told friends, "Yeah, it's true. Reagan's trying to surround himself with younger men."

He could now take a more detached interest in other cabinet appointments. There were no blacks yet in the Reagan lineup, and so Casey suggested a former Glen Cove neighbor and lawyer to be secretary of Housing and Urban Development, Samuel Riley Pierce, Jr. On Casey's recommendation, Pierce was given the appointment, which would have a rocky, scandal-plagued finale.

Charley Wick wanted to be part of the great parade too. He had been close to the Reagans for years. But that connection was his sole visible recommendation for public office. Besides, Wick was a babe in the Washington woods. He went to Casey for help. Casey arranged for the former bandleader and financier to be named director of the U.S. Information Agency. "But what are his qualifications?" one of the transition team members wanted to know. "Reagan will take his calls," Casey answered.

He was keenly concerned with who was going to get the central job in the White House as chief of staff; that choice would affect his access to the Oval Office. Casey liked Ed Meese. He and Meese had become close. And Meese, unlike Casey, had indeed labored in the Reagan vineyard since dawn. Meese wanted and expected to be made chief of staff. But Casey had delivered the Reagan camp a jewel in Jim Baker. Nancy Reagan liked the way Baker handled the debates and noticed the smooth way the man handled himself. Mike Deaver had inserted the bug in the future First Lady's ear that Baker would make a splendid chief of staff.

Casey also threw his support behind Baker. He told Bill Safire, "Ed's too disorganized. He'll stuff everything in his briefcase. He'll take it home and lose it all." It takes one to know one, Safire thought. Casey went on: "Jim Baker's got it all together. He's super-efficient. You need a guy like that next to the President." For the second time, he had helped boost Baker to power.

He turned his attention, now with a strong personal interest, to the transition group handling intelligence. Casey had gone over a report this group had put out the month before. It read like an indictment: the CIA had failed to predict the Soviet buildup of strategic nuclear weapons, failed to assess the accuracy of these weapons, failed to spot a Soviet brigade in Cuba (a report already discredited virtually everywhere else). In the concluding paragraph, the paper used the word "failure" seven times. Most alarming of all, the transition team wanted to dismember the CIA, putting covert operations in one place, intelligence collection in another, and giving its counterintelligence branch to the FBI.

The report reminded Casey of what he had concluded long ago

about his fellow conservatives: the greatest enemies of a cause are its blindest believers. He was not about to take over an empire in order to dismantle it. He dissolved the transition intelligence committee on the spot.

Casey next turned his attention to who would run the CIA with him. Key was his choice of a deputy. The right deputy would release him from the administrative chores that bored him to death and free him for global thinking. The number-one and number-two officials at the CIA required a delicate chemistry, like a good marriage. Ideally, the deputy should be chosen freely by the director. Instead, Casey was beginning to feel like a rake being forced into a shotgun marriage with a virtuous partner.

The intended paragon was a three-star admiral who looked more like a Baptist chaplain than like a sea wolf. Bobby Ray Inman had twenty years behind him as an intelligence professional. He had been the youngest chief of naval intelligence, then the youngest director of the near-invisible but powerful National Security Agency, the NSA, the country's code-breaking and eavesdropping apparatus, the all-hearing ear capable of monitoring telephone calls and radio communications all over the world.

Bobby Ray Inman had a powerful sponsor, not as Casey's deputy but for Casey's new job. With the Republicans now in control of the Senate, Barry Goldwater was about to become chairman of the Senate Select Committee on Intelligence. When Goldwater first learned that Casey was Reagan's choice for DCI, he was alarmed. "I'd known Casey for years," he later said. "I knew he had a great record in the OSS. But I did not think experience in a war fought forty years ago qualified anybody to run a modern intelligence service." To Goldwater, Inman was "the most articulate man I ever heard on the Hill." Inman had always been totally honest with the oversight committees. He had a knack for making the members feel like partners in keeping the nation's secrets rather than like a bunch of interlopers. As an Inman colleague put it, "Bobby had a Ph.D. in congressional relations."

Goldwater went to see the President-elect and argued that one of his chief liaison problems with the Congress could be solved before it began if he named Admiral Inman as director of Central Intelligence. Goldwater later described his conversation with Reagan: "I already knew how Ron Reagan made his apointments—what did the guy do for *me?* Reagan measured everybody that way. He reminded me that we wouldn't be having this conversation if it weren't for Bill Casey. He was sending Casey to the CIA and I might as well forget it."

A best-of-both-worlds solution still remained: Casey as director, Inman as deputy director. Casey was soon being lobbied from all sides. Dick Helms, whom Casey strongly respected, checked Inman out and found him solid. Casey talked to the current incumbent in the deputy slot at the CIA, the respected Frank Carlucci. Carlucci told him that the obvious choice to replace him was Inman. Casey discussed the matter with John Bross, and, Bross recalled, "Bill made noises that led me to believe he wanted me to be his deputy." The sound was pleasant, but Bross recognized it was Casey's Gaelic schmoozing. The seventy-year-old Bross knew better. Instead, he too urged Casey to take Inman.

There was only one problem—or to Casey, possibly cause for relief. Inman did not want the job. He already ran the NSA, which, with its forty thousand employees and a far larger budget, dwarfed the CIA. And Inman was planning to retire within six months from a lifetime of military paychecks and start making real money in a second career in the private sector. He had already received handsome offers.

Word that Casey was coming out to the NSA to see him made Inman uneasy. In this first substantive contact, the two men danced around each other like cats. Casey simply sidestepped the matter of the number-two spot; he never brought it up. Instead, he used the visit to get himself briefed on the NSA's capabilities. As director of Central Intelligence, he would be the coordinator of the government's entire intelligence apparatus, including the NSA.

"The one thing he made clear to me," Inman remembered of the visit, "was that his personal interest was in the clandestine side of the business. He expected to run that himself. He'd be supportive of everything else that went on. But he didn't want to be bothered about the rest." The two men parted. The chemistry had not been bad. On the other hand, it had not been particularly good.

As 1980 drew to a close and with his appointment in the new administration settled, Casey felt confident enough to take his first break since that day in February when he had stood in a New Hampshire hotel and taken over the reins from John Sears. He went to his house in Palm Beach and stayed there until the first week in the new year.

The CIA security staff breathed a temporary sigh of relief. For more than a month, the director-designate of American intelligence had been living in an unsecured hotel suite virtually across the street from all the electronic eavesdropping wizardry in the Soviet embassy.

15.

The DCI

The man appointed director of Central Intelligence was at the time three months short of his sixty-eighth birthday. There was in his pouched, seamed face a seen-it-all, heard-it-all, done-it-all absence of innocence. The blue-gray eyes were not so much cold as guarded behind oversized glasses. A quizzical expression seemed constantly to be saying "Show me." He was, except for a few trailing wisps of white hair, bald. His lips were puckered and the cheeks, sucked in. A wattle of corded flesh hung from his chin to his Adam's apple. In certain poses, he resembled a walrus without the tusks. He was not heavy and yet not trim, but deflated-looking, like a half-empty barrage balloon. He moved with a springiness, hands and feet going off in independent timing, a picture of oddly disjointed energy. When he spoke, it was sometimes out of the side of his mouth, like an old con. On appearance alone, he could probably have had steady work as a character actor playing a big-city boss who owned a U.S. senator or two, or a mad scientist in a grade-B thriller, or even the shadowy, behind-the-scenes mastermind in a spy thriller.

He was reasonably healthy, his habits temperate except for a big appetite. He did not smoke, although he might puff a cigar at a banquet. His drink of choice was a light scotch-and-water, rarely more than two. He had high blood pressure but was controlling it with drugs.

He was a hard man professionally, yet he still remained unexpectedly soft in his personal relations. He made the transition, however, with a swiftness that stunned people. "You learned quickly," one staff member recalled, "not to go in and tell Bill Casey that your baby had walked yesterday. But if you were having trouble getting your kid into the right medical facility, he'd be on the phone in five minutes." When the son of a friend failed to turn up on his flight home from Europe, the distraught father called Casey, and the CIA had the youth tracked down in a hospital in Wiesbaden. "I could see so many similarities between him and Bill Donovan," John Bross observed. "Both of them were capable of great kindness and great ruthlessness." Dick Helms found another Donovan parallel: "They were both connivers in their own way."

One of his strongest qualities was an unapologetic certainty of manner. Casey made decisions quickly and did not soul-search out loud. He felt little need for labored defenses of his actions. He expressed his position bluntly, and that was that. The vast majority of individuals lack such assuredness and are drawn to those who possess it. Casey gave his associates a sense of security, a feeling that they were dealing with somebody who knew what he was doing. This certitude had been instilled in him in childhood, the birthright of the firstborn son who was always made to feel that he was right.

John Ranelagh, author of a book on the CIA, described Casey as a man "unhaunted by ideals." The phrase had a clever ring, and Casey's finagling style gave it the veneer of truth. But it was an inaccurate judgment. He was driven almost wholly by ideals; they happened to be the ideals of a conservative true believer as practiced by a pragmatist.

The merit of his appointment as DCI varied with the beholder. To the public it looked like a raw political payoff. "I read some of the press comment," John Bross noted, "and they seemed to react as though some guy had been named head of the CIA because he had been a World War II vet. They were completely ignorant of the sophistication of Bill's intelligence background during the war." Liberals were more concerned about a deep-dyed conservative politicizing American intelligence. But two old-line New Dealers who would ordinarily shudder at the thought of a right-wing ideologue in charge at the CIA were oddly relieved. Walter Lord and Arthur Schlesinger, Jr., both OSS London alumni, went to lunch at the Century Club soon after Casey was appointed. Lord reported of their conversation: "We knew a lot of people were ready to write Bill off as a boor. They didn't know how intellectually vigorous he was. I told Arthur that I thought the perfect man and the perfect job had found each other. We were both pleased that an old SI man had gotten the CIA. And we agreed that Bill was too smart to slip into the symbolic trenches of the Right."

At ten o'clock on the morning of January 13, Casey strode into room 318 of the Hart Senate Office Building to face the Senate Select Committee on Intelligence.

Barry Goldwater, chairman of the intelligence committee, gaveled the hearing to order and turned the floor over first to Pat Moynihan, the new Democratic vice-chairman. Moynihan had confessed to some apprehension when Reagan first named so patently a political figure as Casey as DCI. But then, he thought, Jerry Ford had named George Bush, a former Republican national chairman, to the job. Jimmy Carter had tried to appoint Jack Kennedy's speech writer and confidant, Ted Sorensen. And Moynihan "knew Casey had done a hell of a job at the SEC."

"Were there more men," Moynihan began, in his best House of Lords manner, "such as William Casey in this nation, a President would have less difficulty filling his cabinet. . . . It is the distinguished quality of this man that he has, in one form or another, served every American President since Franklin Roosevelt. His career is too well known to require any recitation from me, save to make the somewhat sad observation, what the French call *fin de ligne*. Bill Casey will surely be the last member of the OSS to direct the CIA. . . . A career so begun could only lead to the distinction that has accompanied it throughout."

Moynihan did have one question to put to Casey. It was crucial, the one on which all trust between the DCI and the committee rested: "How do you feel about telling this committee things we need to know that you would just as soon not more than two people in the world know?"

Casey: "I intend to comply fully with the spirit and the letter of the Intelligence Oversight Act. . . . There are some reservations of constitutional authority, [but] I cannot now conceive of any circumstances under which they would result in my not being able to provide this committee with the information it requires."

Moynihan: "You said *not now* conceive. And not for nothing did you go to the Fordham Law School. They taught you prudence."

Casey did not bother to correct Moynihan on his law alma mater. What mattered was that Casey had given the right answer.

Sensitive to charges that legislators were notorious leakers, Senator Joe Biden of Delaware asked Casey, "What report would you give us in keeping the secrets, in keeping the faith, so to speak? How good have we been at that?" Casey gave his lopsided grin: "I thought I'd let this committee investigate me before I undertook to investigate it." The audience laughed. Biden was leaning forward, cupping his ear to catch Casey's muffled phrases, and asked him if he would mind pulling the microphone closer.

Casey: "I have it in my lap now."

More laughter.

But he was too battle-wise to be overconfident. He had been thrice burned in previous confirmation tests; he was waiting to feel the flames. And then the question came. Moynihan looked pained, almost apologetic as he posed it. It was his duty, Moynihan said, to raise "two specific matters, that of withholding from a House committee materials concerning the ITT Corporation and passing these materials instead to the Department of Justice, and then with respect to the investigation of Mr. Vesco and the fraudulent activities in which he was involved for Investors Overseas Service."

But before Casey had a chance to fend off the old allegations, Moynihan himself snatched him from the fire. The senator had taken the liberty of getting in touch with Stanley Sporkin, now chief of the SEC's enforcement division—"a distinguished public servant by anyone's standards," Moynihan said—to get Sporkin's reading of the charges. And Moynihan was happy to report Sporkin's verdict: "Your behavior was above reproach."

A few days before the hearing, Casey had paid the customary courtesy calls on committee members, including Chairman Goldwater. Goldwater had again mentioned the great good sense in appointing Bobby Inman as deputy. Now Goldwater raised the matter in the hearing. "I think, again speaking for the committee, I do not want to see some political person sent over here to be your assistant. . . . I think Admiral Inman would be a great addition to your staff if you could see a way to put him on it."

Casey: "I hope he can see his way to come."

Moynihan felt compelled to add, "What the Chairman has said about Admiral Inman I cannot but think is the near-to-unanimous view of the committee, and certainly it would be mine."

Casey felt as though he were being beaten over the head. But the implication was clear: if he wanted a happy relationship with his oversight committee, he should take Inman.

In two hours and a half it was over. The committee sent his name to the floor with a favorable fourteen-to-nothing vote. Only Joe Biden abstained. Casey was confirmed by the full Senate, without debate, by ninety-five to nothing, and sworn in as director of Central Intelligence on January 28.

He was the thirteenth DCI, the sixth in the past seven years. He was also the oldest and the only DCI to hold cabinet rank. And he was the wealthiest. The presidential appointee forms he had been required to submit showed an average annual income over the previous four years of $286,000. His net worth was $9,652,000. He was one of ten millionaires in the Reagan cabinet. His new salary as DCI was $60,662.

Casey bowed to the inevitable. He wanted a good relationship with the oversight committees. And so he resigned himself to choosing a deputy who might well outshine him, at least on the Hill. But Inman was a hard case. He was already the head of an agency, and a large, important one. As Inman put it, "I had no desire to be anybody's number two again."

His life had been part Huck Finn and part Horatio Alger. He was the third of four children born to a father who ran a gas station in the dusty East Texas hamlet of Rhonesboro. He had been a skinny kid with glasses in high school, only five foot four, ninety-six pounds, and graduated at age fifteen. He used brain power to compensate for his size. He tutored the jocks and worked in the political campaigns of the more popular kids. "I acquired the habit of developing protectors," he said of his boyhood. He sprouted up to a bony six feet two and graduated from the University of Texas with a B.A. in history. He tried law school but dropped out after a year, and then taught grammar school for a year. When the Korean War came along, he went into the Navy as a reserve officer, expecting to serve his three-year obligation and get out. Instead, he found a home. For a non-Academy, virtually nonseagoing officer, his rise had been phenomenal: chief of naval intelligence at forty-three, director of the NSA at forty-six.

"He was a workaholic," Rob Simmons, a Senate intelligence committee staffer, observed. "If Inman had a hearing at nine o'clock in the morning, he'd be up at four prepping for it. He'd be ready to answer maybe a hundred hypothetical questions. He'd essentially memorize the answers. Then he'd go before the committee and take whatever they threw at him, without referring to a note."

His grinning, aw-shucks, country-boy façade was about a thirty-second of an inch thick. He was a driven man, and about as cool as a wire carrying a thousand volts. Years before, a rather plodding superior officer had called him in after Inman had finished a tour of duty in the Pacific. "You too rapidly dismiss the views of those whose intellect you don't admire," the officer told him. "You obviously reject the ideas of those who move at a slower pace than yourself." Thirty years later, Inman could still recite the words with the amused grin of a man who knew he had been described perfectly.

There was only one way that Casey could persuade a reluctant Bobby Inman to become his deputy. He went to Inman's new commander in chief.

Inman was in his office at the NSA when the call came from President Reagan. The President began in a mock-serious tone. "I'm not accustomed to telling admirals what to do, but I would sure appreciate it if you could help Bill Casey," Reagan said. Inman had a sense that "he had his cue cards in front of him," as the President went through the arguments, point by point, as to why Inman should take the deputy position. He apologized for not being able to give him the top job; he knew how much support he had for it. But, Reagan went on, he owed Casey this one for his role in the campaign.

A sailor in uniform was listening to his skipper as Reagan's voice turned dead earnest: "Admiral, I need you." In this situation, Bobby Ray Inman did not know how to say no. And so, he said, in effect, "Aye, aye, sir."

Inman's personal timetable had been derailed. But he exacted a fair price. He told the President that he hoped this tour would have an eighteen-month limit, two years at the most. And he managed another sweetener to get the pill down. As John Bross later recalled the arrangement: "I took the call from the White House personnel people. They said they had all the papers ready on Inman's appointment to submit to the Senate. Of course, they said, Inman would leave the NSA and revert to his rank of rear admiral. 'That won't do,' I told them. 'He expects to be a four-star.' 'Oh,' they said, 'that's not so easily done.' So I called Bill. He knew how to fix these things. And in some mysterious way, Inman got his fourth star."

Thus, Bobby Ray Inman achieved a rank few naval officers ever attain without having commanded so much as a tug. Casey got the acknowledged brightest man in intelligence to back him up. The Senate Select Committee on Intelligence had managed at least second place for its favorite son.

The CIA that Casey took over in January of 1981 suffered from a split image. To laymen, it was an omnipotent force, unseen yet everywhere, a covert government accountable to no one. To those in the know, the CIA was a patient on the convalescent ward.

The Agency's heyday had been the fifties, the Cold War era, when the ends of communism justified virtually any American means to contain it, no questions asked. But by the turbulent sixties, the CIA was just one more victim of the doubts being raised about every establishment institution in the country. Vietnam also hurt the CIA. The Agency's Phoenix operation, designed to root out Viet Cong agents in rural areas, had been branded by antiwar activists as American-initiated mass murder. The Agency had been tarred by Watergate too in both serious and silly ways, by providing disguises for Watergate figures and by having several alums among the indicted felons.

In 1974 and 1975, the Senate Select Committee to Study Governmental Operations with Respect to Intelligence, chaired by the liberal Frank Church, investigated the CIA. The committee laid bare secrets that possessed a chilling fascination. The CIA had been involved in drug research, which in one instance had led to the suicide of a civilian Army scientist who was unwittingly given LSD. The CIA had tried to assassinate foreign leaders. William Colby, unhappily in the saddle when the Church investigation struck, was shown a list that Fidel Castro had compiled of attempts on his life. Colby responded, "I looked through it and checked it off against our research and said we could account for five or six." The assassination attempts had involved botulism toxin, poison pens, bacteria planted in a diving suit Castro might use, and a poison-dart gun. And, in direct violation of the law excluding it from carrying out domestic intelligence, the CIA had been caught opening the mail of Americans.

The Church investigation in the Senate had been paralleled by an equally damning House investigation lead by Congressman Otis Pike. In 1975, President Ford was taking so much heat on the CIA that he appointed his Vice-President, Nelson Rockefeller, to conduct still another investigation.

When Jimmy Carter became President, he sent a technocrat admiral to run the CIA. Stansfield Turner was the administration's chosen instrument to rein in the Agency, which Turner did by eliminating 820 essentially clandestine positions and notifying the incumbents of their removal through a computerized form letter.

The operating budget and the manpower of the CIA were secrets scattered and buried in the federal budget. But when Casey took over, the agency had a staff of fourteen thousand and a budget hovering at $1 billion—no small staff, no mean budget. But in the view of Robert Gates, who had served as Turner's executive assistant, the CIA was in feeble condition. "With the people fired, driven out, or lured into retirement, Gates calculated that "half of our analysts had less than five years' experience. And our analysis wasn't at all sharp, forward looking, or relevant. Our paramilitary capability was clinically dead. What covert action we did carry out was super-cautious and lacked any imagination." The fearsome CIA, Gates concluded, "was hunkered down in a defensive crouch."

Casey set his first senior staff meeting for late January, a few days after he was sworn in. He was picked up that morning at the Jefferson by the CIA security detail. He was bundled into the back of a dark blue, unmarked Oldsmobile 98. One security man rode shotgun next to the driver. The windows of the car were bulletproof glass and could not be rolled down. The agents carried magnums, which they usually stuffed into the small of the back. Behind Casey's car was the backup vehicle, carrying the heavy artillery—Uzi submachine guns concealed in oversize briefcases. Ahead was the advance car. All three had radio contact with the Agency and with each other.

The motorcade escaped the heavy downtown traffic, crossing the Fourteenth Street Bridge and rolling west along the George Washington Parkway with a reassuring solidity. The extra weight in Casey's car came from the armor and a floor decked with thick antimine plating. Casey heard the security man up front report to headquarters over the radio the ETA of "Baron." He now had a code name.

There were two entrances to the CIA headquarters at Langley, Virginia, one off the parkway and another off Virginia Route 123. This morning, the driver took the parkway entrance. They approached a security checkpoint manned by a girl in a dark blue uniform and slate gray shirt that would have looked appropriate on any small-town American cop. She was occupied checking a visitor's driving license and Social Security number against a computer bank. Casey's car sped through the employees' lane, weaving around great boulders, past a huge white dish antenna on the ground, then ran along an eight-foot anchor fence topped by a V of barbed wire. Poking above the pine trees amid the rolling green terrain stood the gray-white buildings of the CIA. The setting was not picturesque enough to be a university campus nor sterile enough to be a suburban corporate office complex. It suggested, rather, a think tank with enough government contracts to afford an agreeable country setting—which, in a way, it was.

Casey intended to make a public entrance this morning, and so the car rolled to a halt in front of the main building. Nearby, the 5-K bus of the Washington Metro service was disgorging commuting employees; they looked no different than the secretaries, clerks, and bureaucrats descending that morning at Treasury or the Department of Agriculture.

A cantilevered canopy seemed to float from the front of the headquarters building. At one end of the entrance was a flagpole; at the other end stood a bronze statue of Nathan Hale, a scarf thrown around his neck, his hands tied behind his back, his feet bound at the ankles, his face set in beatific defiance. The words known to every schoolchild formed a circle around the base of the statue: "I only regret that I have but one life . . ."

The main building rose seven stories. It had been designed by Harrison and Abramovitz, the architects of the United Nations Building. The windows were long, narrow, and recessed, and those on the main floor were covered by heavy screening. Casey walked into the building and into a cavernous lobby, waving a floppy hand at people smiling at the new boss. He encountered a daunting sign planted in the middle of the floor listing the numerous items that could not be brought into the building—cameras, tape recorders, firearms, explosives.

Thirty-eight stars had been chiseled into the marble wall to his right. Over the stars were the words: "In honor of those members of the Central Intelligence Agency who gave their lives in the service of their country." Seventeen stars carried names; the rest were anonymous. Casey would later point out to visitors that the number of stars was twice the number of FBI agents killed in the line of duty. A few feet to the right of the stars was the bas-relief face of Allen Dulles, the fifth DCI. An inscription underneath read: "His monument is all around us." On the opposite wall were chiseled words from the Gospel According to Saint John: "And ye shall know the truth, and the truth shall make you free."

Directly ahead of Casey stood gateways that looked like a cross between a subway turnstile and an aiport metal detector. Employees lined up to insert plastic ID cards into a slot that opened the turnstile. Off to the right was a room where VIP visitors were waiting to be escorted to their appointments. A sign over one phone read: "This phone is for polygraph division only." A sticker on another phone read: "If you wish to contact security personnel, do not use this phone. Just knock on red door."

Casey was escorted to the left of the lobby up a short flight of stairs to a locked, key-operated private elevator that whisked him up to the seventh floor. He exited into a small, handsome sitting room where two visitors were waiting. The room was tastefully done, furnished with an Oriental rug, an abstract painting, a conventional landscape, and an end table with statuettes, including one of a man with a broad-brimmed black hat, a cloak, and a dagger.

Casey went this morning directly to the director's conference room for the first gathering of the senior staff. John Bross was already there, serving as "acting deputy" until Inman's arrival. Bross's presence comforted Casey. Bross was a living link between his intelligence past and present; the two men were virtually the last of the OSS generation at the Agency.

Just as Casey arrived and they were getting ready to sit down, a short man entered at a brisk stride and headed straight for Casey. Bross realized it was Max Hugel. During the transition period, Hugel had followed Casey to the Jefferson Hotel. Casey had become his mentor and protector. As Hugel saw it, "I got beat up in the campaign. I worked like a dog. I produced. But I got no respect. They left me out in the cold. I could have handled OMB or one of the big jobs in Defense. Instead they had me working in the transition on the Small Business Administration! I didn't want *that!* But I knew I wasn't gonna get nothing from those California guys." And so Max had gone to Casey. What he wanted, he said, was to work for the CIA.

Bross had met Hugel earlier, after Casey had mentioned over lunch one day that they had to find a place for him. "I pleaded with Bill," Bross recalled, " 'For God's sake, don't have Max Hugel at your first staff meeting!' I felt that to inject this total outsider, with no background in government, much less the CIA—a guy right out of a political campaign—would send the wrong signal throughout the agency. And here comes Max sweeping under my arm, dressed like a dandy, smelling of after-shave lotion, plopping himself down right next to Bill."

Casey opened the meeting with grace and humor. Knowing that the dust of the campaign trail was still visible on his own feet, he assured the staff, "I have taken a vow of political chastity." Their chief stock-in-trade, professional objectivity, he said, was going to be preserved. He told them how he had brought back from OSS London the first plan for a permanent American intelligence service. "I was there at the beginning," he said with a laugh. "Nobody saw me, but I was there." He spoke warmly of his gratitude to John Bross for coming back into harness for these critical opening months, which was greeted around the room by appreciative nods. He motioned briefly toward Hugel and mentioned that he was a man of vast managerial experience who would be serving as his personal assistant—news that was greeted with blank stares.

Casey then told these people what they needed and wanted to hear most. The indictment made against them during the seventies was a bum rap, he said. The specifics may have been technically accurate, but they had been wrenched out of context and grotesquely magnified to serve political ends. The ensuing bad publicity distorted and obscured the CIA's decades of patriotic service to the nation. And—almost wholly ignored by the media and public alike, Casey noted—virtually none of the sins the CIA had committed were born at Langley. They were carried out as a result of directives from above, including the wishes of American Presidents and secretaries of State, people who operated above the line while directing the dirty work to be done below it.

But the era of apology, of head hanging, hand wringing, and retrenchment, was over. The CIA was going to rebuild. It was going to be a strong, effective intelligence service again, and once more they were going to hold their heads up high.

As John Bross recalled the moment, Casey's appearance might have been unimposing, his speech hardly crystalline. But the words had been perfect. They all walked out of the room feeling good about themselves and their profession.

Most CIA officers had to be polygraphed from time to time, but not the DCI. "The box," as the lie detector was called, aroused fear even in seasoned veterans. Polygraph results, they knew, depended on the skill of the interrogator. The physiology of some people, their heart rate and blood pressure, tended to trigger the "lie" signal even when they told the truth. Casey went voluntarily to the polygraph room and donned the vest with its rows of electrical contact points. The operator slipped a large wire over his left forearm and small wired cuffs over his right index and ring fingers. The wires ran back to a box behind him, where the interrogator stood. Casey answered the standard battery of questions about drinking and drug use, past employment, police record, and a few queries tailored to his own business affairs. He passed. And he had also passed a test of comradeship with the rank and file.

Casey held the three bedrock convictions of the doctrinaire conservative: first, the world was a hostile place; secondly, the Soviet Union was virtually the root of all evil; and thirdly, that whatever is good in the world happens when America is strong, resolute, and purposeful—the bad occurs when America is weak. In Casey's world, isues were not black and white; they were red and white.

In an interview with the *American Legion* magazine shortly after becoming DCI, he named as the critical intelligence challenge of the eighties "the ever growing military power of the Soviet Union." Others might look at the globe and see countries. Casey saw a noose tightening, a rope woven of Communist victories around the globe—Cuba, Vietnam, Cambodia, Angola, Ethiopia, South Yemen, Mozambique, and, most recently, Nicaragua. The next priority, he said, was terrorism. That too was Communist inspired, when it wasn't instigated by radical states like Iran and Libya. Also, exhuming a phrase from the fifties, he was concerned about "the captive peoples under the Soviet yoke"—Poland, Czechoslovakia, Bulgaria, East Germany, Hungary, the Baltics. The present CIA was not doing enough, was not strong enough to deal with any of these threats, he said. And so the priority that tied all the others together was to make the Agency strong again.

Casey's longtime secretary, Barbara Hayward, had gone to work for Vice-President Bush; and so Casey hired Betty Murphy, a slender, attractive, gray-haired woman who had worked at the Ex-Im Bank during his tenure, as his executive secretary. Murphy was a calm, unflappable workhorse who worked best under pressure and who also knew enough to keep her mouth shut. In those early weeks, she found herself lugging in armfuls of personnel folders to him, which Casey pored over with fierce intensity. Fancy new organization charts meant nothing, Casey told Bross. That was just rearranging the furniture. Picking the right people meant everything.

He installed John Bross next door. Bross found Casey "a funny guy to work for. . . . He never gave me a direct order. He would raise an issue, a problem, some deficiency, and I'd have to assume that he expected me to do something about it."

Still, Casey's priorities were clear. Reduced to essentials, the CIA was designed to do two things: figure out what was going on in the world, and help make the right things happen covertly when open diplomacy or military action failed or were inappropriate. No matter how often the labels were changed, the old OSS distinctions still held: SI/secret intelligence, SO/secret operations. And in Casey's judgment, the CIA was doing poorly at both.

Eighty percent of the agency's activity, unsuspected by movie goers and spy-thriller readers, was the dull, indispensable collection and analysis of information. The Agency had an institutionalized procedure for producing National Intelligence Estimates. NIEs were formal forecasts representing the best collective judgment of the CIA and the rest of the intelligence community on a particular country, a foreign leader, a foreign policy issue. Next, the agency produced less formal spot estimates—quick, specific assessments of a situation, done largely in-house.

Bruce Clarke was running the part of the Agency Casey wanted to get his hands on first—the DI, the directorate handling intelligence. Casey called in Clarke and his top people. "You're sitting here on the other side of the Potomac cranking out intelligence that's not relevant to the people making policy downtown," he told them. "And you're too ingrown. There are terrific sources outside this shop. You have to start tapping them." He had been a success himself outside government; he knew how much was out there. The CIA was not exploiting the intelligence potential of corporations, think tanks, and universities.

Casey managed to lure Harry Rowan, a key figure in the Rand Corporation, to take over the National Intelligence Council, the operation that coordinated the production of NIEs. Rowan's job was to run the estimates through the dozen government agencies that made up the "intelligence community": State, Treasury, and Energy, the Defense Intelligence Agency, the National Security Agency, the military intelligence branches, and the FBI, along with the CIA.

Casey detected a downward cycle. Under Ford and Carter, the estimates had to pass through the President's national security advisers, first Henry Kissinger, then Zbigniew Brzezinski, tough, egotistical men. Few estimates from a rival source of power made it past them; fewer still were requested by them. The less the CIA's estimates were used, the less motivation the drafters had to do a good job. And the lower the quality of the estimates, the less they were used.

Casey told the analysts after looking over their output, "I hate these iffy conclusions—'If on the one hand . . . ,' 'If on the other hand . . .' We leave the damned consumer in a state of paralysis. I expect you to bring your estimates to a sharp point. I'm not looking for consensus. We don't need a bunch of analysts sitting around a table weasel-wording their way into language everybody can live with." The search for consensus was, he said, "a consumer fraud, mush passing for analysis." They were not to look for agreement; they were to look for relevance, so that after reading an estimate, decision makers could feel its sharp edge and know which way it cut. If there were disagreements, he did not want them ground into one indistinguishable lump. "Give your best judgment, and then include any dissenting opinions too. The policymakers can sort through options, but they can't consider options we don't give them. And if we don't give these people information they can put to work, then what the hell are we doing here? This isn't a graduate seminar."

He acknowledged the inherent fallibility of estimates, no matter how good the sources or how sharp the analysis. He told the DI staff, "They expect us to predict what a country is going to do when the leaders don't know themselves. We deal with the probable, not the certain. But I want all the probables."

He also wanted the walls turned down between the intelligence directorate and the operations directorate, between the people who analyzed and the people who acted. Half the time they did not even know each other. He told Bross, "I'm going to make this a place where people can take an unpopular idea, an offbeat idea, or an oddball concern. Let's hear it out before we throw it out." It was pure Donovan.

He was supposed to be passé, a man of the forties, out of step in an age in which spy satellites eighty miles above the earth could identify which newspaper a Russian was reading in Red Square. The pros argued the merits of ELINT, electronic intelligence, versus HUMINT, human intelligence. Technology was fine, Casey told them, but what did reams of computer printout reveal about *intentions?* As he put it in an early talk to a group of businessmen, "Facts can confuse. The wrong picture is not worth a thousand words." Satellites could tell you what cards the other fellow held, but a human being had to guess how he would play them.

The first White House cabinet meeting he attended dealt with terrorism. Al Haig was there, behaving, with his long White House experience, rather like the only varsity player left over from last season. They were faced with state-sponsored terrorism, and its roots, Haig argued, led indisputably back to the Soviet Union. Casey said little, though his heart was with Haig. But gut instinct was not enough— a hard case had to be made. And so when he got back to the Agency, he put his analysts to work on his first major NIE, "Soviet Support for International Terrorism."

By April, a staff draft of the estimate on the Soviets and terrorism reached his desk. He was not happy: the analysts seemed to believe that their mission was to prove Al Haig wrong. Casey lit into them. This draft represented everything that was wrong with their estimates. Yes, in a narrow, technical sense, they were right. The KGB did not car-bomb. It did not shoot up airports. And publicly, the Soviets dismissed terrorism as "leftist adventurism and simplistic ideology." Of course they would, Casey said. But the analysts had approached their task literally, without imagination. What about indirect support—money, people trained in the Soviet Union in insurrection? Why had they ignored the fact that almost all the terrorist training camps were in countries that the Soviets backed, like Cuba and Libya?

Casey knew that over in the Pentagon's Defense Intelligence Agency they were a tougher breed. Let *them* take a crack at the estimate, he thought. But the DIA's draft was unbalanced in the opposite direction: evidence had been stretched to the point of incredulity to convict the Soviets.

He had been saying all along that there was plenty of untapped wisdom beyond the Capital Beltway. So he put together a review panel headed by Lincoln Gordon, a respected academic, the former president of Johns Hopkins, a Democrat, and former U.S. ambassador to Brazil in the Kennedy-Johnson years. He would have loved it if Gordon brought in a guilty verdict against the Soviets that he could trot over to the White House. Gordon did not. But his estimate was factually solid and analytically plausible. Yes, the Soviets supported Third World wars of liberation. And from the weapons, training, and encouragement to guerrilla movements they supplied, violence and acts of terrorism inevitably resulted. But to say that a bomb tossed into a pub in Northern Ireland or a plane hijacking was orchestrated by the KGB was unprovable and unlikely. The Gorden draft underwent further bureaucratic pulling and hauling but was finally released at the end of May. Casey had passed his first test of zeal versus truth. It was not the estimate he or the administration wanted; but it was the best conclusion he had seen—and that was what he was being paid to produce.

He kept reaching out for new, fresh sources. He started inviting businessmen and academics out to Langley, giving them briefings, laying pipelines that would flow in both directions. To Casey, these people possessed priceless intelligence that some spook sitting in an embassy was not necessarily going to learn—Soviet grain purchases, Third World debt payment problems, the latest breakthroughs in computer technology in Japan.

He considered himself a student of history, and he wanted the Agency to learn from past failures. "Casey had us reinvestigate stuff going back to the Sino-Soviet split, the missile gap in the fifties, Cuba, Suez, ancient stuff," one analyst recalled. "And we did learn something. Virtually every time our estimates were off-base, it was because we'd made a single-scenario forecast. Casey got us to start saying, 'This is our best estimate. But if that's wrong, here's another way it could turn out.' "

Every morning when he was picked up at the Jefferson, the security man handed him a thick packet. The first item he reached for was printed on stiff, creamy, high-quality paper—the President's Daily Brief, the PDB, a distillation of the choisest intelligence gathered overnight and intended for the President's eyes only. But Casey thought the PDB could be more than a source of information; it could be an instrument of influence. He persuaded the President to sign an order to expand the distribution of the PDB to the Vice-President, the secretaries of State and Defense, and the national security adviser. He had a fairly senior Agency official delivering the PDB to each recipient personally. If Haig or Weinberger liked to read the PDB on the ride to work in the morning, the Agency officer would be up at four a.m. to pick up the copy, deliver it to the client's home, and discuss the contents on the drive in. That, to Casey, was the whole idea: find out what these people want, then shape the product to their needs, market-tested espionage—a relevant, usable product. By eleven a.m., Casey's high-priced deliverymen were back in his office briefing him on the reaction to the day's PDB and reporting what they had picked up about the machinations of his colleagues.

He had spent a lifetime, at the RIA, the OSS, and the IBP, shaping information for easy, instant assimilation. He wanted CIA reporting to be hard-hitting and succinct. The curse of government was the paper it generated, and nowhere more than where he now sat. "The paper flow was always a headache in this business," John Bross observed. "The amount you're expected to read is staggering. You put a bug on the minister counselor's house in some country and some poor bastard back at Langley spends days reading about the guy stopping at the store for a loaf of bread, his squabbles with his wife, that his daughter's dating a druggie. By the time the analyst has reached the part about blowing up the White House, he's fallen asleep." And so Casey pressed his drafters relentlessly for compression and relevance: "Get to the point! Get to the point!"

Some of the analytical people thought that Casey may have worked himself into a classic intelligence bind. If he followed the purist school—deliver the product to the policymaker's door, then walk away—the intelligence would be totally objective but would soon become irrelevant again. But if the DCI made himself part of the policy loop, as Casey intended, how did he treat intelligence that showed his administration's policies to be wrong, stupid, or doomed? How strong was the temptation to commit the mortal sin of intelligence, to tailor the facts to fit the policy? Casey brushed the quandary aside. Had he not shown the requisite professional detachment in the NIE on the Soviets and terrorism?

When Bobby Ray Inman had finally accepted the job at the CIA, there was talk of a ceremony to mark his installation. Vice-President Bush was a former CIA director, and he and Inman had known each other for years. Inman wanted the new Vice-President to take part in the ceremony. On virtually his first day at Langley, Inman went in to discuss the matter with his new boss. Casey's reaction stunned him: "George Bush isn't welcome out here." Inman waited for a further explanation. None followed. This was his introduction to Casey's antipathy to Bush, and to Casey's decision-making style. Inman canceled the plans for the ceremony. The marriage was off to a shaky start.

Casey soon laid out the division of labor between himself and Inman: "I'll take personal responsibility for the intelligence and operations directorates. I expect to be the President's intelligence officer. You'll handle the internal administration of this place, and science and research. You can handle all these interagency meetings too— the NSC, the cabinet. That stuff's a waste of time. Of course, you'll backstop me when I'm away." Inman's portion sounded neither flattering nor satisfying. He found himself thinking of the time limit he had given the President. Eighteen months was beginning to sound more appealing than two years.

Inman continued to maintain a close relationship with Bush. Fairly often, he went to the Vice-President's office in the old Executive Office Building next to the White House to brief Bush personally. He did not inform Casey of these visits.

Unknown to Inman, the Reagan staff had begun distributing a list of the President's and Vice-President's daily appointments to a select group. Casey was included. One morning, Inman's door flew open and Casey burst in, waving the latest appointments schedule. "Why the hell are you going downtown to see George Bush?" he demanded.

Inman struggled for the cool demeanor that he had learned to master but did not feel. "He wants me to. He's the Vice-President. He can be helpful. And I intend to keep on doing it."

Casey glared, muttered something incomprehensible, and stormed out.

Inman buried himself in his work, continuing the habits of mind that had propelled his success, trying to know everything that was going on throughout a complex new bureaucracy. In the first week of March a document came across his desk that sent him flying into Casey's office. The games that bureaucrats played never ceased to amaze Inman. Carter had come in and changed Ford's executive order covering what activities the CIA could legally carry out within the United States. So now the Reagan staff had to change Carter's order.

Most alarming to Inman, the Reagan draft lifted the current ban on CIA wiretaps and bugging inside the country. It allowed the CIA to open mail and carry out clandestine searches without first getting the approval of the attorney general. It made it easier for the CIA to keep dossiers on American citizens, to infiltrate domestic organizations, and to carry out surveillance on Americans abroad. If the draft leaked, Inman could virtually predict the headline: CIA AGAIN SEEKS TO SPY ON AMERICANS.

Inman had been aware that the draft was in the works, and he was annoyed that he had barely been consulted about it. Still, he could not stand by and watch the Agency fall on its sword. "This thing is going to give you a lot of grief," he told Casey. "What we really need are more resources, more money, more people. This order won't win you public support for any of that. In fact, it's going to cost you support. I think you ought to sit on it." Casey, who was about to leave on a trip to the Far East, said only, "I don't want you or anybody else discussing this draft outside the intelligence community until I get back."

The next day, Inman learned to his horror that Casey had allowed the draft to be sent out of Langley for review by other involved agencies and by the House and Senate oversight committees. And it had been leaked—probably by an outraged Democrat on one of the committees. The dreaded headlines quickly materialized. The March 10 *New York Times* front page read: INTELLIGENCE GROUPS SEEK POWER TO GAIN DATA ON U.S. CITIZENS. The bad old days were back.

Inman decided to take swift damage-control measures. On his own he called a press conference at Langley, a nearly unheard-of event. He tried to assure the reporters that what had leaked to the press was simply somebody's rough draft, sent out to stimulate comment. As for a return to domestic snooping, that was out of the question— not on his watch. Without consulting Casey, Inman yanked the draft executive order back.

He also wanted to calm fears within the ranks that the CIA was about to become the target of public vilification again. When he had been at the NSA, his habit was to bring the staff into his confidence by frequent reports from the chief. Now he gathered the troops at the CIA's domed auditorium. Its eight-hundred-seat capacity was filled to overflowing. Those who could not get in heard the deputy director over closed-circuit television.

John Bross watched from his office. He had heard Casey tell Inman explicitly that he did not want the executive order discussed. Ever since Inman had come over from NSA, Bross had detected another man under the tightly disciplined surface. He listened with mounting uneasiness. Inman's behavior, he thought, smacked of "mild hysteria." "All he was doing was stirring up exaggerated concern," Bross observed. "He made this speech without once mentioning the DCI. At one point he held up his sleeve with all that gold braid and said something like, 'You have to be pretty sharp to get these.' "

Bross encountered Inman in the hall the next day and told him, "That was a pretty speech. May I ask why you made it?" Inman looked uncomfortable, as Bross later described the scene. "He told me that maybe he had overshot his mark. But he was worried about a public furor over the executive order. It had far-reaching implications. And he had not really been consulted on it. Just as he was turning to leave, he surprised me. He said, 'I may not look it, but I do get rather intense.' "

Bross was convinced at this point that Casey would have fired Inman. "But he was in no position to," Bross concluded. "Inman had just come over at the personal request of the President. They were stuck with each other."

When Casey did come back, he told Inman, angrily, "I don't expect anything like that again."

The incident had been revealing. The trust was not there, not on either side. The chief and his deputy were supposed to be alter egos, not antagonists. And Casey's insensitivity toward a predictible re-action from Capitol Hill was to Inman a distant early warning of problems to come.

The Carter administration had governed in malaise and ended in humiliation. Virtually every initiative of the Carter years was suspect by the Reagan people, or disposable—save one.

In December of 1979 the Soviet Union had invaded Afghanistan to prop up a wobbly client regime in Kabul. The Carter administration, driven by its lonely hard-liner, National Security Adviser Zbigniew Brzezinski, had put a covert operation into place to support the Mu-jahedin, the Afghans opposing the Communist regime and the Soviet invaders. The CIA was piping U.S. aid primarily through Egypt to Pakistan and then into Afghanistan. The aid was running about $75 million a year.

Soon after taking over, Casey called in his covert-actions chief, John N. McMahon, the deputy director for operations, and his staff for a briefing on Afghanistan. He listened, discomfiting staffers who were in his presence for the first time by chewing the tip of his tie as they briefed him. When they finished, he said, "This is the kind of thing we should be doing—only more. I want to see one place on this globe, one spot where we can checkmate them and roll them back. We've got to make the Communists feel the heat. Otherwise we'll never get them to the negotiating table. Anyone can see what they're up to. They've pushed their way into Afghanistan, South Yemen, Ethiopia. They're surrounding the oil. They're putting themselves in a position to shut off sixty percent of the world's petroleum sources."

McMahon explained that some lawmakers on the Hill were asking tough questions about the Afghan operation. Who were the arms going to besides the Mujahedin? To drug dealers? Terrorists? To crazies in Libya and Iran? What about the risk of provoking the Russians if we pushed too hard? This time U.S.-supplied weapons were killing Russian soldiers. And some liberals in Congress questioned the morality of expending the lives of Afghan peasants and herdsmen to make points for U.S. foreign policy. Were we going to fight to the last Mujahedin?

"Aaaah." Casey dismissed the questions with a backhand wave. "We've got to make these people understand what we learned in World War II. When we supported organized resistance against Hitler, it saved lives in the long run. It's the same thing in Afghanistan. That hasn't changed."

Quite the opposite, Casey told them. "Here's the beauty of the Afghan operation. Usually it looks like the big bad Americans are beating up on the natives. Afghanistan is just the reverse. The Russians are beating up on the little guys. We don't make it our war. The Mujahedin have all the motivation they need. All we have to do is give them help, only more of it."

The Agency's own intelligence showed that the Soviet Union had some 89,000 troops in Afghanistan—not a huge force, but they were well-trained regulars backed by the resources of a world power. The United States could probably thwart them if it could help keep a force of perhaps 150,000 guerrillas in the field. Obviously, the program had to be expanded. The Saudis were already kicking in, but they were flush and they could contribute more. The Egyptians manufactured weapons going to the Mujahedin, but the quality was poor; they had to be pressured into doing a better job. The Pakistanis had to be persuaded to open more delivery routes into Afghanistan. And neutrals who were afraid to put up arms ought to be providing medicine, prosthetic devices, and other humanitarian aid. After all, Casey argued, this was not an American cause. Afghanistan was a moral cause.

He intended to take to the road himself, he said. He would see Crown Prince Fahd in Saudi Arabia. He would talk to Western European leaders. He would go to Pakistan and speak directly to President Mohammed Zia. And to China too. He was going to be the Mujahedin's chief salesman.

The meeting broke up and McMahon's people left. The experience had been rather like watching a mummy come to life. The wrinkled, gray-faced, slouching figure had slowly begun to sit up and glow with passion. They were impressed by his global grasp, the mental vigor, the raw will. The operations directorate, so long curled up in its protective shell, was being forced out into the blinding light.

"**Knowledge** Is Power," it had said in stained glass on the ceiling of Casey's high school auditorium. True, as far as it went; but in Washington, proximity was power too. The CIA was twelve miles from the White House—not good enough. An office in the White House proper was out of the question. The West Wing had space for only a dozen senior aides and their staffs. And most of the President's national security apparatus was not located there, anyway; it was housed on the third floor of that glorious French Renaissance stone heap next to the White House, the old Executive Office Building. The EOB was separated from the White House by a narrow, closed-off lane called West Exec, which contained the most prestigious parking places in the capital. Casey wanted an additional office on the third floor of the EOB, near the NSC. He told Ed Meese, now counselor to the President, and the deed was done.

Casey had managed to pierce to the center of the concentric circles of foreign policy making. He was a member of the cabinet; more exclusively still, a member of the National Security Council; even more exclusively, a member of the National Security Planning Group, which included only the President, the Vice-President, the secretaries of State and Defense, the NSC adviser, and himself. The NSPG quickly emerged in the Reagan administration as the fount of foreign policy.

The White House itself was essentially being run by a three-headed creature inevitably dubbed the Troika. Casey felt comfortable with the arrangement. Jim Baker was chief of staff, and Casey had brought Baker into Reagan's world. He had supported Baker for chief of staff. On Inauguration Day, Baker had taken Casey aside and graciously expressed his gratitude. Ed Meese and Casey were close. Meese believed that Casey had saved the campaign; and they both drank deeply from the same conservative spring. Casey did not know the third head of the Troika that well—Michael Deaver, the essentially untitled manipulator of the presidential image. But he had brought Deaver back into the Reagan campaign after John Sears had engineered him out. All Casey's power lines were good.

He held back at meetings, not pushing, rarely asserting himself, feeling no need to. Don Regan, now Treasury secretary, described Casey at the White House as looking like "a sleeping sphinx." At an early meeting of the NSPG, as Casey gave a briefing on Soviet military strength, Mike Deaver saw the President slip a note to Vice-President Bush. "I craned my neck to get a peek at this bit of private intelligence," Deaver recalled. "The President had scribbled, 'Did you understand a word he said?' I thought, here's an issue affecting the security of the United States and the only person who has this information is a guy the President can't understand. It was always a relief when Casey was traveling and his deputy would come to the White House instead. We'd actually know what was going on."

NSPG meetings were usually held in the afternoon, from one to three, and a postprandial lethargy muffled communication further. Dick Allen, the NSC adviser, learned to watch the President when Casey spoke. "Reagan was partially deaf in one ear," Allen recounted. "He'd sit there with his head cocked as Bill droned on. He'd look to me desperately and I'd break in: 'Just a minute, Bill—I'd like to emphasize what you just said.' Then I'd repeat Casey's point, and say, 'Now, Bill, I know you have more to say.' And he'd start mumbling all over again."

In one area, communication with Reagan was totally clear. "I was surprised how often Casey was on the phone with the President," Bobby Ray Inman remembered. "What astonished me was that it never had anything to do with intelligence. It was always Reagan calling Casey or Casey calling the President on politics. Who should get the deputy slot at HUD? Had the Illinois state chairman been taken care of?"

One piece of advice that Casey gave Reagan early on was that the President's Foreign Intelligence Advisory Board, which Carter had junked, should be revived. And it was, with Casey's old friend Leo Cherne appointed vice-chairman.

Casey's dedication to Reagan grew. The President remained as uninvolved as ever. But Casey, caught up in Reagan's spell, explained away the detached behavior. He told a reporter, "Reagan just won't permit himself to be bogged down in detail and minutia. He's not a yellow-pad President like Carter or Nixon. He doesn't feel compelled to scribble notes during meetings or control who gets on the White House tennis court."

Then, one afternoon, it was almost over before it had really begun. On March 30, sixty-nine days into the new administration, Casey got a call from the CIA operations center. The President had been shot coming out of the Washington Hilton. Casey rushed to the White House Situation Room, where he was immediately pelted with questions by his cabinet colleagues. Was the shooting part of an international conspiracy? Did the assailant have terrorist ties to the Soviet

Union? With Cuba, Iran, or Libya? What would the Russians do? All of which he answered through a constant flow of information passed to him by telephone from the CIA ops center.

He was in the White House Situation Room watching on an in-house TV circuit when Al Haig, the secretary of State, went on the air and told the reporters and the American people, "Constitutionally, gentlemen, you have the President, the Vice-President, and the secretary of State in that order. . . . As of now I am in control here in the White House." Casey was appalled. Al Haig might be a prettier face than he at dinners for foreign potentates, but the man did not even have the succession of power straight at a moment of national crisis. The Speaker of the House followed the Vice-President. Yes, Casey admired Haig, and they were ideological soul mates. But pressure reveals character, and the man chosen over him to become secretary of State had displayed a faintly mad zeal on the television screen. Millions of Americans thought they were watching Dr. Strangelove.

Later that evening, when it appeared that the President would survive, the knot of power in the Situation Room broke up and Casey went home. His thoughts were primarily of the abrupt turn that history had nearly taken that day. And possibly he imagined himself on that television screen, reassuring the nation, instead of Al Haig.

16.

A High-Risk Operation

With Congress, Casey was on a honeymoon. The two committees created to look over the shoulder of the CIA were in a new mood, and Casey was the beneficiary. The oversight function had swung broadly over the years. In the fifties, during the Cold War era, the Agency and the Hill had a sweetheart deal. Only the leaders—Richard Russell, chairman of the Senate Armed Services Committee; Clarence Cannon, chairman of the House Appropriations Committee; and Carl Vinson of the House Armed Services Committee—dealt with the DCI and a handful of his top staff on an old-boy basis. The Agency felt that its secrets were safe. And the committees felt scant need to meddle. The Agency's immunity had essentially continued through the sixties.

Then came the revelations of the seventies. The penance for the Agency's sins was passage of the Hughes-Ryan Act. Congressional oversight became a policing action, carried out by newly created watchdogs—the Senate Select Committee on Intelligence (SSCI) and the House Permanent Select Committee on Intelligence (HPSCI). Hughes-Ryan also required the President to make a "finding of necessity" before the CIA could carry out a covert action. The finding had to establish that a covert operation "was important to the national security of the United States." Furthermore, the oversight committees had to be notified "in a timely manner" of the operation. The very darkest secrets need be told only to the committees' chairmen and ranking members, instantly dubbed by the CIA "the Gang of Eight." Otherwise, the full committee membership had to be alerted. They had to be informed, but they had no authority to approve or disapprove.

By the late seventies, the committee members were getting uneasy: maybe the policing function had gone too far. Intelligence was part of the country's shield. Given the Carter budget slashes and hiring freezes, the Soviet invasion of Afghanistan, and the fall of the Shah, many congressmen began thinking that perhaps the shield needed to be raised, not lowered. In 1981, Republicans won control of the Senate. The new chairman of the Senate intelligence committee did not even believe in oversight. He was a seventy-two-year-old military buff, a World War II pilot who had flown the Hump over the Himalayas between Burma and China, a presidential candidate who had scared the hell out of the country as a hawk in 1964 and had since metamorphosed into a crusty, even lovable old eagle. Barry Goldwater was a technology nut who flew all kinds of aircraft, including a helicopter, and a gadgeteer, ham radio operator, and Air Force Reserve general who was completely at home with the technology of modern warfare, hot or cold. And he was a fan of the CIA.

Goldwater had, in fact, voted against the formation of the committee he now chaired. As he put it, "I don't believe in the Congress knowing too much intelligence. There's no way you can keep the secrets. There's no way you can get these congressmen to keep their mouths shut when they learn something hot. They can't wait to get to the Rotary Club back home and say, 'Now let me tell you fellows what's really going on.'"

The chairman had put his finger on a built-in contradiction in overseeing intelligence. A secret was by definition something unshared. But now, by statute, state secrets were required to be revealed to the members of the committees and, inevitably, their staffs. An intelligence secret now became known, beyond the operatives who needed to know, to dozens of people.

So far, the committees had given Casey a long leash. The Democratic vice-chairman of the SSCI, Pat Moynihan, a charter member since 1974, was sympathetic. Moynihan, whose politics fell somewhere between New Deal and neoconservative, saw almost eye-to-eye with Goldwater on intelligence. Sometimes, as Casey and his people briefed him, Moynihan recalled, "I wanted to shout at them, 'Stop! We've heard enough. No more!'"

From the outset, Casey told the committee leadership that he wanted three things from them: more money to start rebuilding the country's intelligence capability, and two pieces of legislation. One was crucial to the morale of his people: he wanted it made a crime to disclose the identity of covert operators. And next he wanted the CIA's operational files exempted from the Freedom of Information Act (FOIA). It was ridiculous, he said, that the agency that held the state's secrets had to abide by the same disclosure laws that covered the Department of Agriculture.

At one hearing he explained to the members of HPSCI the legal lunacy he faced. The CIA had done a secret survey of countries with nuclear weapons capability. The Agency thereafter received a FOIA request to have the document declassified and released. The staff struggled manfully to meet the requirements of the law, revealing what it could, blanking out whatever dealt with intelligence "sources and methods," which were exempt from disclosure. But the report had somehow slipped out with a description of Israel's nuclear capacity. The Israelis were furious, completely uncomprehending as to how something like this could be revealed by a friendly intelligence service. But, Casey explained to the committee, as long as the CIA had to service thousands of such requests, such gaffes were inevitable. "If the KGB wrote to us, and we're sure they do, under assumed names," he said, "we would have to follow the law and respond in ten days. Do we really intend to turn the CIA into the purveyor of information for the world rather than a supplier of intelligence to our policymakers?"

In the early stages, even a good liberal on the committee, Senator Pat Leahy of Vermont, was in his corner. "I saw that Casey was making significant improvements," Leahy recalled. "And I believed I could be especially useful in the needed buildup—he could muster support in the right wing of his party, and I could bring him support from the other side."

Casey won support for his plan to rebuild the CIA. He got his agent identity bill. He was making headway on the Freedom of Information bill. He was off to a splendid start.

In those early months, his only real problem on Capitol Hill was acoustical. His voice sounded as though he perpetually had phlegm clogging his throat. The CIA Division of Science and Technology came up with a meter with a dial that told him when his volume dropped to a mumble. He always forgot to turn the gadget on; he threw it out after a few weeks. The Senate committee installed an especially sensitive microphone on the witness table for him. "Every time Casey would start tapping the table for emphasis," one of the staffers remembered, "it sounded like a tom-tom."

Some of the senators thought they sensed a strategy in Casey's muffled speech. "When he testified on something he really wanted," Leahy observed, "he'd say, 'On page thirty-two-dash-B, subparagraph F, you'll see a fourteen-point-two percent increase for project X'— and he was clear as a bell. Then one of the members would say, 'Mr. Director, it appears your station chief in Rome has overstepped his authority' . . . and then all we heard was 'Mmbmbmbmbmbmb.' "

The arranged marriage of Casey and Inman was not working, and it bothered John Bross. Bross was like an old baseball scout who hung around the dugout and every once in a while whispered something valuable in the manager's ear. In the spring of 1981, Bross began looking for a way to repair the bridge between the Director and his chief deputy. And so he started telling Casey about Robert M. Gates. Casey was unhappy with his present executive assistant. With Casey, personal chemistry was all, and the chemistry between him and this aide was wrong. Bross told Casey that he had found the ideal replacement.

Unspoken was Bross's deeper motive in promoting Gates. Things had arrived at a pass where Casey's staff and Inman's staff barely communicated. Casey, in his ad hoc style, would order an NIE on, say, the Marcos regime in the Philippines, from an able staffer who happened to be in his office, while Inman would order a similar estimate through appropriate channels. Assignments were duplicated; resources were wasted. Chaos resulted.

Bob Gates, then thirty-seven, was the national intelligence officer for the Soviet Union, the priority account on the estimates side of the CIA. Bross checked around the Agency and got a uniformly positive response. Gates was brilliant. The only knock, in a way, was a plus: Bross found a certain grudging tone to some of the praise—the guy was a little too bright, too ambitious. And White House ideologues might find him tainted. Gates had worked on the Carter NSC. Worse, he had later served as Stansfield Turner's executive assistant for ten months, hardly a plus to the Republican Right. Bross, a career man himself and vaguely Republican, could not care less—nor did he expect Casey would. He spent hours talking to Gates and concluded that he had found Casey a new executive assistant.

Gates was an accidental intelligence officer. He had dropped in on an Agency recruiter while he was a graduate student at Indiana University "looking for a free trip to Washington." He was offered a job, took it, then did a stint in the Air Force and came back to the CIA. But his true ambition all along had been to become a history professor; and so, while at the Agency, he earned a Ph.D. in Russian and Soviet history at Georgetown University. He did so largely on his own time and refused any Agency aid. Gates rose swiftly in the CIA; and as time passed, his dream of a life in the halls of academe became more and more remote.

Bross moved deftly. He went to Inman and made sure that Gates was acceptable to him. Inman knew Gates and said he would be fine. Bross then went to Casey and sold Gates as the near-perfect right hand, someone who knew his way inside and outside the Agency, around the White House, the NSC, and State. Knowing the man would sell himself best, he brought Gates in to Casey. What appealed instantly to Casey was Gates's grasp of analysis, Casey's immediate priority. The deal was quickly clinched, and Gates became Casey's executive assistant.

After Gates got the job, Bross explained to him his covert mission: to make sure that Inman and Casey each knew what the other was up to. It would be nice for a change, Bross thought, to have the alter talking to the ego.

Casey liked to snatch free moments to sift through the Agency's personnel files, looking for other undiscovered gold. When he found a seeming nugget, he would test the name on Bross. But again and again he kept bringing up one name not in the files, a name that puzzled and unsettled Bross—Max Hugel.

Casey had initially given Hugel the title "special assistant" and sent him to poke around the three major directorates—operations, intelligence, and administration—and then report back. Hugel found the experience both daunting and exhilarating. As he later described it, "At first I felt inadequate. They're talking code words and a special language all their own. And these guys are trained to look you right in the eye and lie. They were so intense, so serious. I like guys who give out with a belly laugh once in a while. Not them. They had no goddamned sense of humor."

Still, Max Hugel had not risen from poverty to great wealth by being easily intimidated. He came back and told Casey that, on the whole, "you got good people. These guys are the esprit de corps."

"He was always at Casey's side," John Bross noticed, "one step to the right, one step to the rear. He was a pushy, obnoxious person, a perfumed fancy Dan, a flashy dresser, always obsequious around Casey. I did not take to him." But Casey kept selling Hugel to the perplexed Bross. In one conversation, Casey described how Hugel had organized minorities during the campaign. "Bill tried to make it sound like some super OSS operation inside an occupied country," Bross remembered. He was always hinting at Max's qualifications for something in covert operations."

Within weeks, Hugel had grown tired of serving as Casey's scout. He wanted a real job. In mid-February, Casey called Hugel into his office. He held up an organization chart and pointed to one of the top boxes. "This is the DDA," he said. "He runs half of this agency. I'm making you DDA." The DDA—the deputy director for administration—was the major managerial post at the CIA; the office controlled everything from assigning parking to buying hundreds of millions of dollars worth of intelligence hardware. The position was currently vacant, and the number-two man in the directorate had expected to be promoted to the top job.

"After Bill appointed me," Hugel remembered, "for the first time I really felt the resistance to me in the CIA, the resentment. I had to go to this other guy. 'I guess you know I'm taking over,' I told him. The guy says to me, cold as hell, 'I want you to know I'm not pleased. But I will be a good soldier.' "

It was a big job, a key job. Yet Hugel mastered it quickly. One of his responsibilities was to oversee hundreds of secret bank accounts the CIA maintained at home and all over the world. In one of his first days on the job, he asked a subordinate, "How much interest are we getting on this money?" "Interest?" the assistant said, as though a vulgar word had been uttered. "We don't get any interest." Max Hugel's voice leaped an octave. "Are you crazy! Everybody gets interest! You go to those banks and tell 'em we want interest."

The aide fidgeted and asked, "What do we do with the interest when we get it?"

"We'll use it to reduce the Agency's budget," Hugel said, as though addressing a particularly dense pupil.

"We can't. The government doesn't allow the Agency to receive income."

"For chrissakes," Hugel roared, "then we'll turn it over to the Treasury so we can reduce taxes!" Thanks to Hugel, the CIA started earning interest on its deposited millions.

Most exasperating to him was dealing with the State Department on diplomatic cover for CIA officers abroad. The CIA was constantly pushing to have more of its overseas operatives under cover as diplomats. State was constantly resisting. Even when diplomatic cover for agents was approved, it seemed to CIA officials that State Department snobbery threatened their lives. The department published a biographic register of professional-level personnel. In the register, career diplomats carried the elite designation FSO, for foreign service officer. The department chose to designate the undercover CIA people by the less prestigious FSR, foreign service reserve officer. As one covert operator put it, "You might as well put an asterisk in the book: FSR means possible CIA. That's how our people get killed." After a drawn-out struggle, the most the Agency managed was to have State classify the biographic register so that a foreign embassy could not simply obtain a copy from the U.S. Government Printing Office and pick out the likely spies. Hugel was working for the logical solution—simply to have the CIA people under cover in embassies abroad shown in the register as FSOs. But State remained stiff-necked.

Battling State was one of the livelier of Hugel's assignments. Of the rest he was increasingly bored. He had followed Casey to the CIA only to wind up doing what he had been doing for thirty years—and for a lot less money. He was not happy, and he intended to let Casey know, as soon as he could corner him, for the man was becoming the most peripatetic of DCIs.

On April 13, Casey was in Israel. But his real interest lay far to the north. While he had been running the Reagan campaign, Solidarity, the Polish trade union movement, had emerged, led by a shipyard electrician named Lech Walesa. The Agency's chief task was to interpret Soviet intentions. Would they invade Poland and snuff out this spark of democracy, as they had done in Hungary in 1956 and Czechoslovakia in 1968? The CIA's sources in the Eastern bloc were thin. The Agency had one "super source" in Warsaw—Wladyslaw Kuclinski, a colonel on the Polish general staff. But Casey wanted more, a broader picture, sources at several levels. And he was starting in Israel with the chief of the Mossad, the Israeli secret service.

The Israelis had long maintained a network that ran from the Middle East into the Balkans, through Poland, and into the Soviet Union, a collection of spies, Jewish dissidents and religious figures. The pros called it a ratline. It was this net that had spirited out to the West the historic de-Stalinization speech that Nikita Khrushchev had given at the 20th All-Union Party Congress more than two decades before. Casey wanted to know from the Mossad how much of the ratline still functioned. It was fairly active, he was told, now that more Jewish émigrés were coming out of the Soviet Union. Casey wanted in. He particularly wanted to piggyback on this network for intelligence on Solidarity and any other dissident movements inside Poland.

But with the Israelis, he found that it always had to be one for you, one for me—sometimes, one for you and two for me. The Mossad was chronically strapped for cash. They would cut the United States into this network and share the take if Casey agreed to fund the operation. He agreed instantly.

It was a delicate situation. Solidarity was a pure Polish product, born of Polish hopes and Polish desperation. Covert aid traceable to the CIA would taint the movement and leave it looking like an American front operation. And so Casey's people in Europe had to limit themselves to what they considered Mickey Mouse: paying printers and sign plasterers to put up pro-Solidarity posters in European cities; underwriting the sale of Pro-Solidarity T-shirts; influencing, with money where necessary, media support for Walesa and his workers in other countries. It was not much, and Casey felt frustrated. But in the case of Solidarity, detachment was the course of discretion.

The CIA had not been Casey's first choice. But Sophia noticed that he came home from grueling days at Langley exhilarated. The old eyes sparkled with secret satisfactions. One night she asked him, "How's it going, Bill?" And he told her with a grin, "Toots, this is the best job I ever had. I've got the best people working for me. I'm really happy." He was like a man who had pursued a tonier dame, forgetting along the way how happy he had been with his first love. Now he had returned to her, and she was the same great girl he remembered. The long-ago strategy of 1945 had worked. He had made the fortune, and it had bought him power and freedom. He had pulled a Donovan. He was, in fact, the current Donovan.

He was not a vain man, but he could not fail to be impressed by the discreet pomp that now surrounded his every move. He always moved in a motorcade. Whenever he traveled out of town, an advance team of security officers checked every aspect of the trip—the route from the airport, the hotels he would be using, the sites where he would hold meetings or give speeches, the people he would be seeing.

Protecting William J. Casey proved by turns exciting, exasperating, and exhausting. The DCI's personal security staff was soon swapping stories about the old man who was now their charge. They quickly learned that the CIA's richest director often carried no money. Betty Murphy had to institute a reimbursement system for the agents when they returned from an outing with Casey. One expense claim read, "The undersigned requests reimbursement for the following: breakfast purchased for one DCI, New York City, the Bagel Nosh, $3.13." Another read: "Request is made for $4.00 given to the DCI for the collection during mass, Sunday, August 3."

Another security agent described a typical Casey day: "We're running late for a meeting at the White House. We're barreling down the George Washington Parkway at seventy miles an hour, lights flashing, siren wailing, and Casey's barking, 'Get me Cap Weinberger.' Just as you start to dial the car phone, he barks, 'Gimme a pen.' You're reaching for the pen and trying to dial with your other hand,

and he says, 'Get me Al Haig,' on the other phone. You hand him the first phone and he yells, 'Well, where's Weinberger?' 'Sir, the phone's still ringing.' 'Goddammit, you should hang up if he hasn't answered by now! Get me Dick Allen. I don't like this lousy pen. Gimme a pencil.' In the meantime, the car's swerving, the siren's screaming, and he's mad that you aren't moving as fast as he's thinking. When you were on duty with Director Casey, you always felt too close to be safe or too far away to feel comfortable. Some of the guys would beg to ride the backup car. They just couldn't take the pressure."

They were with him around the clock—waiting outside his office during the day, watching from the wings at embassy receptions, sitting in the living room at the apartment he had moved into on Cathedral Avenue. They were on the road with him by 6:45 a.m. and usually brought him home after ten at night, since the American espionage chief was a dogged party goer, hitting six or seven events a week. Once home, he read and wrote until midnight. After he turned in, the security men would bet how long it would take for him to reappear. As one of them put it, "Around three in the morning he'd come stumbling out of the bedroom asking, 'Where'd you put that NSC folder on Libya?' "

The security detail assigned to the DCI was composed of young men and a few women, most in their twenties and thirties and all physically fit. After one early trip abroad that covered six countries in nine days, the chief of the detail came to the Agency's director of security and told him, "We can't take it. This guy is killing us." The detail was doubled. Now, when Casey came bounding out of the plane after a trip, a fresh team stepped in to relieve the returning agents.

In the early days, he had modestly insisted on using commercial airlines. But it was sticky. Security officers, moving through an airport like a flying wedge, drew attention. People came up to Casey, some to shake his hand, others to berate him for the horrible things the CIA did, which left him looking baffled and pained. He would stop and try to explain the purposes of an intelligence service in a democracy, with the security detail dragging him away. On commercial flights out of the capital, he often ran into senators and congressmen eager for a privileged peek inside his world. Finally, the security chief persuaded him to use the company plane, a Gulfstream I turbojet.

Whenever he flew abroad, the Air Force loaded what it called a VIP pack into the belly of a C-41 transport. From the outside, the pack resembled an overseas shipping container. Inside, it had a living room, a bedroom, a conference table, a bathroom, and a cubicle-size galley. False windows, with actual curtains, were painted on the walls. Casey traveled with a CIA doctor who brought along suitcases full of medical supplies, a portable electrocardiogram machine, an intravenous unit, and splints for fractures. The flying doctors found themselves treating everybody but Casey. "The man had a cast-iron constitution," one CIA physician observed. The advance team had standing instructions from Casey for all trips, foreign and domestic: wherever they went, find the best bookstore and the nearest Catholic church.

Mayknoll now seemed worlds away. But Casey tried to get home whenever he had a speech, a major dinner, or a doctor's appointment in New York. Even then the ganglia of security followed. A team arrived at Mayknoll in advance, driving up from Langley, to Long Island, bringing two metal boxes bristling with switches, which scrambled telephone calls.

No matter where the man awakened, in Washington, out of town, or abroad, he was greeted by a bulging folder, his overnight read file. Over a breakfast of black coffee, grapefruit juice, and cream cheese spread on rye toast, he plowed through the file. After years of working with printers and publishers, he was astonished by the technical capacity of the agency he headed. He would hold up top-secret, computer-engineered, enhanced color maps before Sophia and Bernadette at breakfast and exult, "Look at this—these guys are amazing!" without explaining what they were seeing.

Sophia found his new job frustrating. "I knew he was doing fascinating things," she observed, "but he never said anything about them. And I didn't dare ask. It's normal for couples to talk about what went on at the end of the day. But now Bill couldn't. I asked him once how many people worked for the CIA. 'If I knew, I couldn't tell you,' he told me. That was the end of that."

Under Stansfield Turner, the CIA executive suite had been dry. Bob Gates remembered standing outside Casey's door before he became executive assistant, chatting with Casey's secretary, Betty Murphy. Casey was inside, about to have lunch with John McCone, his predecessor as DCI during the Kennedy and Johnson years. Suddenly the door flew open. "We need two vodka martinis in here—quick!" Casey shouted, and slammed the door, while the staff stared at each other in panic. "That," said Gates, "was my first look at the new DCI."

Casey was forever pressing books on visitors: "Here, read this. You'll like it. It's important. This guy's got it right." He also wanted his subordinates to know that they were led by a man with his own literary credentials. Tom Troy, the Agency historian, recalled his dawning awareness. "We had a custom in the Agency library of displaying in a glass case books written by our own people," Troy recalled. "One day, I walked into the library, and there in the case was a magazine opened to an article Casey had written for some financial journal. Next to it were two single-spaced typewritten pages listing all his other published works: *How to Build and Preserve Executive Wealth, How to Raise Cash and Influence Bankers,* and on and on."

He intimidated the staff—not by design or tactic but by his gruff impatience. They learned too that it was far better to deal with Casey over the phone; he was easier to understand—although, as Gates put it, "he was kind of old-fashioned. He'd bellow, as though he wasn't sure the wire could carry the sound."

As he struggled to master the Agency's phones, he tested even Betty Murphy's considerable imperturbability. Casey had a red phone with a dozen buttons for internal calls; a green secure phone for outside calls, which were electronically scrambled to thwart eavesdroppers; and a white phone, his direct line to the White House. He was forever fouling up, getting disconnected, losing callers. "For chrissake," he would holler, "will somebody come in here and show me how these goddamn things work?"

Stanley Sporkin had stayed on at the Securities and Exchange Commission, rising to director of the enforcement division. Earlier he had loved working for Casey and found him the most stimulating man he knew. He had sent him a note of congratulations when Casey took over the Reagan campaign. No answer. He had invited Casey to his son's bar mitzvah. No answer.

In February, Sporkin went to the funeral in Georgetown of Raymond R. Dickey, a Washington lawyer. "I was coming out of the church," he recalled, "when two big guys took me by the arm and started steering me toward a car. I was starting to get alarmed when I saw Bill Casey in the backseat. 'C'mon,' he said, 'let's go for a ride.' He started pitching me right away. He was going on about how the CIA was an eight-cylinder car operating on four cylinders. Nobody wanted to risk anything. Everybody was afraid. Dan Silver, his general counsel, was leaving, and he wanted me to take the job."

"I know you're a man of principle," Casey said. "Maybe it's not for you. They do things over there that might make you uncomfortable."

"Like what?" Sporkin asked.

"Some of the things you fought against at the SEC," Casey answered.

"I have no problem as long as it's done legally," Sporkin said. "I don't make my own laws." With that, Casey returned him to the church and told him, "You'll be hearing from me."

After nineteen years at the SEC, Sporkin was burned out. As he put it, "I had run out of gas. I needed a new challenge. I was tired of playing cops and robbers. I wanted to work some place where everybody was pulling on the same oar."

Two weeks after the ride with Casey, the permanently disheveled Sporkin was racing around his office looking for a sewing kit to replace a missing button on his shirt, and a rag to put a faint luster on his orthopedic shoes. He had been summoned to Casey's EOB office. There, Casey formally offered him the job of general counsel to the CIA.

That night, Sporkin delivered the news to his wife and three children. His fourteen-year-old son looked at his rumpled, excitable, ever-talking father and remarked, "My idea of a spy has just gone downhill."

Sporkin took up his duties in May. After the first few days, he told Casey, "Bill, you'll never get control over this place. It'll take fifty years. You don't have that kind of time."

Casey gave him a bemused smile and said, "Stan, watch me." He was, in fact, about to give the cage its hardest rattle since he had arrived.

Casey did not like his DDI, his deputy director for intelligence. It was nothing personal. Then again, it was. Bruce Clarke was a bright, longtime veteran of the analytical end of the business. But Clarke's cautious, bureaucratic pace agitated Casey, who expressed his unhappiness to John Bross. He told Bross he wanted aggressive, harder-hitting estimates and more of them. He particularly wanted the toughest kind of estimate—predictions of the intentions of other governments. "If you don't have a conclusion about their intentions, then we have to force a conclusion. If there are differences, you put them in too. But hell," he told Bross, "Clarke's shop hasn't produced a decent estimate on the Soviet Union in five years." Clarke was dragging his feet; he had to go.

Clarke accepted his fate. He had had an honorable career; he was prepared to go quietly into the night. He was horrified, however, when Casey let it drop without warning during a staff meeting that Bruce

Clarke would be leaving. Clarke had thought he had a gentleman's agreement and that Casey would spare him so public an exit.

By pressuring Clarke to leave, and quickly, Casey set in motion the chain reaction he wanted. The job of deputy director for intelligence was now open. He also wanted to open up the deputy directorship for operations. No one, he felt, could accuse him of acting rashly: he had pored over some four hundred personnel dossiers before he set heads rolling. Now it was time.

The next move involved John McMahon, and it was going to be tricky. McMahon aroused conficting emotions in Casey. The man was a Holy Cross graduate, fifty-two years old, a thirty-year CIA veteran, a stocky, straight-shooting Irishman who exuded solidity and common sense. He had started his career as a modest GS-5 code clerk and rose inexorably to critical jobs like handling the U-2 spy pilots up to his present eminence. He occupied, just behind the director, the most sensitive job in the CIA. He was the DDO, the deputy director for operations, the man who ran the covert side of the CIA. There was an oaklike quality about John McMahon: solid appearance, solid movements, solid thinking, solid speech, earthy but not vulgar. He was the kind of man that others want in the trenches with them. And he loved the CIA. Therein lay his problem. He had taken over the operations directorate in the wake of the Agency-bashing of the seventies, and he was gun-shy of half-cocked, cowboy schemes that would bring the wrath of critics down on the CIA's head again.

Ordinarily, the chemistry between Casey and McMahon would have been ideal. But to right-wingers in the Reagan camp, and to some extent to Casey himself, McMahon's protective caution looked like timidity. On their first meeting, Casey told McMahon that his directorate was too chicken, too lacking in imagination. As much as he was drawn to McMahon, he could not have a play-it-safe operative running anything as inherently risky as covert operations. He began confiding to McMahon what he thought was wrong with the DI, the intelligence directorate, and why he thought that McMahon was just the man to take over and turn the shop around. For all the sweet talk, McMahon knew exactly what was happening. There was no way that a shift from DDO to DDI could be seen as anything but a reproach. It was at best a sideways move; after all his time in the Agency, it was as if he had hit the ceiling and could now only slide along it.

"I've got my thirty in," he told Casey. "I'm going to retire."

That was not the answer Casey wanted. He hated to lose this man. "Give me a year in the DI," he told McMahon, "just to straighten it out."

McMahon stalled. He liked Casey, and he recognized that Casey had the will and the White House clout to rebuild and restore his beloved CIA. In the end, he agreed to take over the job. Hell, he thought, he could stand on his head for one year.

Move two completed. Now, with the DDO open, Casey was ready for his master stroke.

Max Hugel had been unsatisfied with the job as deputy for administration almost from the first day. On one of his frequent drop-ins on Casey, he steered the conversation around to the DO and rendered his Hugelian judgment: "The operations directorate sucks." On another visit, he was bolder. "I can do that job as good as anybody around here."

Dick Helms was Casey's valued sounding board. The friendship reached back nearly forty years. Helms was a reasonable man, a careful listener, and his judgments had an authoritative ring. Early in May, Casey invited Helms out to Langley. Helms arrived late in the afternoon to the office he had occupied years before. He sat with thin legs crossed, with thin lips and a cool smile that seemed to be his natural expression. Casey began a familiar litany. The DO was stodgy, overcautious. You kicked it in the ass today and it felt it in the head six months later. Its operations abroad relied too much on host governments. There was not enough exploitation of the rich veins of intelligence to be tapped from business sources abroad.

"I've got a hell of a guy I want to put in," he continued, as though testing the waters. "He's got terrific background. He served in Army intelligence during the war. He made a bundle in Japan afterward. Anybody who can make profitable deals with the Japanese has already run successful operations. He's Max Hugel. I've got him running the DDA now. He's doing a helluva job there, too. But he's under-utilized. I want to shake 'em up in the DO. I want somebody who can scrape off the barnacles. I'm thinking about putting Max in."

Helms thought that Casey was straining a bit, like a used-car salesman pushing a Chevrolet with eighty thousand miles on it as if it were a new Mercedes. Helms was a judicious man, and spare of speech. The people in the operations directorate were a band of brothers, he said. He knew that from personal experience; he had been DDO. As he later explained the mystique, "They were clubby—not in the sense of the right necktie, the right salute, or the right handshake, but in the sense that they shared the common, exceedingly difficult experience of conducting espionage in foreign countries."

What Helms told Casey that afternoon was measured but firm: "Bill, I don't know anything about Max Hugel. He may be the greatest thing since Bill Donovan. But I think it would be a mistake to put him in there by force majeure and say, 'All right, you fellows get along with this guy.' I have no problem with your concept—if you want somebody to shake up the troops, that's fine. But as for Hugel, why not let him earn his spurs first, pay his dues, get his ticket punched? Then, when he's won their confidence, you might put him in at the top."

It was the same answer Casey had heard all down the line. John Bross could imagine a Max Hugel as a jewelry salesman in Toulon on the OSS payroll in '43 or as a government functionary under cover for the Agency in Budapest in the fifties. But running the DO? Bross invited Hugel out to his Virginia estate for a drink. Sure, Max ought to be in covert operations, he said. As Hugel later put it, "But he didn't mean as DDO. He meant being one of the pigeons out there— the guy who got his head knocked off."

After hearing Helms out that May afternoon, Casey told him, "Dick, you always make a lot of sense." With that, Helms, much relieved, rose to leave, believing that he had saved Casey from a blunder.

Barely a week later, on May 11, John McMahon was in Washington at an embassy reception and ran into his boss. Casey pulled him aside and said with a satisfied whisper, "Well, John, I bit the bullet. I just appointed Max Hugel DDO."

McMahon looked at him. "You didn't bite any bullet, Bill," he said. "You just fucked up."

Casey understood the concern of Bross, Helms, McMahon, and the others. They were good men, but they looked at a Max Hugel and they saw a funny little guy with bad grammar and a toupee. Casey, however, knew all about diamonds in the rough. Stan Sporkin was a diamond in the rough. Hell, Casey himself was one. He had taken a Donovanesque risk. He was throwing a hand grenade into the DO. Now he would see what happened.

Who was the man to whom Casey had just given the most sensitive job in the Central Intelligence Agency? And what of that World War II intelligence experience Casey had told Helms about? Max Hugel had a background that, by comparison, made Casey seem like a white-shoe boy. Hugel's father had died a few months before the child was born, and Max had been raised in an orphanage. As he himself described his past, "I was eighteen in 1943, going to Brooklyn College, and I knew I was going to be drafted. I said to myself, 'What the hell am I going to do in the Army? What are my prospects? I'm poor. I'm an orphan. I'm small.' So I found a Japanese-American who taught me a few words. When I filled out the Army forms where they ask about qualifications, I put down 'Speak Japanese.' "

The Army eventually found out that he could not speak the language, but they put him into a Japanese language school anyway. He wound up in Japan after the war interrogating Japanese soldiers who had been interned by the Soviet Union. After his discharge in 1947, he went back to Japan with thirty rusted-out, virtually useless prewar American cabs, sold them to a Japanese businessman sight unseen, and doubled his money. In the mid-fifties he joined up with Brother Limited, a Japanese maker of sewing machines. Brother expanded swiftly with Hugel as CEO, selling sewing machines and then typewriters all over the world. By the time he joined the Reagan campaign in 1980, Hugel had become a major figure in the Centronics Data Computer Corporation through a switch of Brother stock. Centronics became the world's largest independent manufacturer of high-speed computer printers. All of which cut little ice in the operations directorate, where Hugel's appointment was greeted like a slap in the face.

Three days after Casey announced the Hugel appointment, a syndicated column appeared in the *Washington Post* and throughout the country, entitled "Amateur Night at the CIA." Its sting was all the sharper because the column had been authored by one of the Agency's respected patricians, Cord Meyer, now retired, but with a thirty-year career in covert operations behind him. The DDO job, Meyer began,

> was once described . . . with only slight exaggeration as "the most difficult and dangerous, after the President's." The man in this position has the complex responsibility for directing all the agency's secret overseas operations from recruiting spies inside Russia, to secretly penetrating the international terrorist networks, to conducting covert political activities. Allen Dulles, Richard Helms and William Colby all held this job before subsequently becoming CIA directors. . . . The KGB chiefs in Moscow . . . are undoubtedly searching their files for Max Hugel's role as a longtime undercover agent. They will find nothing of the sort. . . . In the only other case where a CIA Director reached so far outside the ranks of the operations directorate, Allen Dulles selected a bright economist, Richard Bissel . . . the unfortunate architect of the Bay of Pigs. . . . Casey may yet prove right in having chosen an able amateur for the Agency's toughest job. But it's a breathtaking gamble for which the country will have to pay dearly if Casey has guessed wrong.

In another shot between the eyes, Cord Meyer said of Hugel that he "had an extraordinary gift for humanity which he substituted for thought."

The *New York Times* ran an editorial on the Hugel appointment entitled "The Company Mr. Casey Keeps," which virtually questioned Casey's sanity.

Pen James was heading personnel in the Reagan White House, where he had become accustomed to having Casey stop by his office in the West Wing. As James recalled, "He'd stick his head in and say, 'Why haven't you got a job for so-and-so yet? He's the guy who nailed down New Jersey.' We'd listen because he knew all the players and we respected his judgment." James was in his upstairs office when an aide alerted him to the Hugel appointment. James had known the man during the campaign. He remembered thinking, "This is absurd. There must be something wrong." He went down to Ed Meese's office. Meese called in Jim Baker. Then Meese had his secretary put him through to Casey. Meese began, courteously but firmly, "Bill, are we hearing correctly?" He listened to Casey, then pushed doggedly ahead. "I hope you've thought this one through. Pen and Jim and I are a little concerned it won't fly." Meese hung on, nodding from time to time, and then said goodbye. He hung up and shook his head. "Bill won't budge." The best they could fathom was that this appointment meant that Casey intended to run his own covert show.

At his end of the line, Casey was furious. He believed in giving people three strikes; these people did not believe in giving Max Hugel even one.

At Langley, Casey faced a near-mutiny. The stunned covert operatives went to see someone who would understand, John Bross. "They came to me," Bross said, "complaining, 'This guy's incredible. We can't live with him. How can we stop it?' " They feared that Hugel would ruin the Agency's relations with State, with Defense, with foreign intelligence services. At least three DO officers told Bross that they were thinking of quitting.

Bob Gates watched the uproar from the privileged perch as Casey's executive assistant and concluded that "the DO was going to reject this transplant. People were muttering that he was an embarrassment and that you couldn't send him up to the Hill. Which was true—you wouldn't dream of sending Max to testify."

As Billy Doswell, who headed the CIA public affairs operation, recalled, "The guys would come in on a Saturday, and there's Max in a lavender jumpsuit open to his navel, with gold chains around his neck." Some observers outside the Agency saw the resistance as pure snobbery. The excitable, hotheaded, pushy self-made millionaire was simply "not our kind."

Max Hugel bore up manfully; but, as he put it, "When I realized the opposition against me, I almost shit. I obviously had a lot of enemies. And you always like to think everybody loves you." He made the customary courtesy calls on the Hill and remembered his reception at Barry Goldwater's hands: "He gave me a couple of minutes. And he never said one word." Pat Moynihan, the committee's vice-chairman, asked, "Is this man dangerously dangerous, or is he dangerously dumb?" Moynihan was speaking not of Hugel but of Casey.

Casey stood by the appointment. And Hugel took up his duties. He did have to go to the Hill to testify. Virtually on his first appearance, he struck a reef. Hugel later described his virgin encounter on the Hill: "My staff briefed me on one covert operation. So I go over to the Hill, and they start questioning me about a second operation I never heard of. I was totally unprepared. I'm looking like an asshole. I was beaten up something terrible. I was sandbagged by my own people. So I went back and I ripped the shit out of those guys. I told them, 'I never want this to happen again—never again. I tell you this right now: I never saw a good surprise. So don't give me no more surprises.' "

Soon after Max Hugel was appointed DDO, two securities dealers, the brothers Thomas R. and Samuel F. McNell, contacted an editor at the *New York Times*. They said that they had some interesting information on Hugel. The *Times* editor referred them to a reporter, Jeff Gerth, in the paper's Washington bureau. The brothers apparently became confused and instead contacted the *Washington Post*, asking for Gerth. They were told that no one by that name worked for the *Post*. But whoever talked to them obligingly turned the McNells over to Bob Woodward, the investigative reporter of Watergate fame.

They were calling, Woodward later remembered, from a phone booth. "And they tried to play hard to get." Woodward's *Post* colleague Pat Tyler went to New York and, according to Woodward, "chased them all over town."

A month would pass before Woodward himself finally met the McNells. Evidently a busy month for them: for in those weeks, a third brother, Dennis, a business associate of Thomas and Samuel, died on June 1 under circumstances that some found suspicious; and on June 14 the two older brothers disappeared and $3.3 million in assets were found missing from the Triad Energy Corporation in New York, founded and headed by Samuel McNell and employing the two other brothers. The FBI launched a nationwide manhunt for the McNells.

The surviving McNells evidently came out of the cold long enough to turn over sixteen audio tapes to Woodward and Tyler. The tapes involved telephone conversations with Max Hugel.

In the meantime, Max Hugel was trying to master his new craft. July 10 loomed as a big day, his first trip abroad as DDO. He would be traveling with Casey—two days in Panama to meet with the Central American station chiefs. But the day before the trip, he got a call from Casey, who was at the White House. Casey told him to come over right away and see the White House counsel, Fred Fielding. What about Panama? Hugel wanted to know. Casey told him to see Fielding.

When Hugel arrived, Fielding told him that he had been alerted that the *Washington Post* had tapes that could prove damaging. "My eyes bugged," Hugel later recalled of that moment. " 'Geez,' I thought, 'it's those creeps the McNells.' "

Stanley Sporkin had been general counsel at Langley barely a week. "I had decided that I wouldn't stick my neck out right away," he later remarked. "But I began to wonder if the phone would ever ring. I had nothing to do. Nobody talked to me. Nobody showed me anything. They weren't sure they could trust me."

When his phone did ring, it rang at home. As Sporkin reconstructed the moment, "Some guy was saying, 'This is Max. I gotta see you right away.' I didn't know any Max. I asked him what his trouble was and he said, 'The boss says I gotta see you right away.' So I asked him where. 'At my place,' he said, and he gave me directions."

Sporkin hung up, a puzzled expression clouding his face. His wife, Judith, said, "Don't go—I think it's a setup." "You read too many spy stories," Sporkin told her. As he started to go out the door, his wife said, "Call me the minute you get there."

Sporkin found a highly agitated Hugel at his home, wringing his small, well-formed hands. Hugel told Sporkin that he had been involved with the McNell brothers six or seven years before in connection with their brokerage firm and Hugel's company Brother International.

Sporkin felt strangely elated as Hugel spilled out his relations with the McNells. "I'd been sitting around doing nothing. Then, hey!—my first time at bat at the CIA, it's right in my field, stocks, where I knew more than anybody else." Sporkin told Hugel that he had better get a lawyer; it was that kind of trouble. Sporkin obtained Judah Best for him, who had represented Spiro Agnew during the legal wrangles leading to Agnew's removal as Vice-President.

Sporkin knew Woodward from his days at the SEC. The next day, he called the reporter and told him that he wanted to hear the tapes. Woodward agreed, but only if Hugel was present. And so on July 10, instead of flying off to Central America with Casey, Hugel went with Sporkin to the *Post*'s offices on Fifteenth Street Northwest.

"The meeting that afternoon in the eighth-floor board room looked like a trial," Sporkin recalled, with the *Post*'s lawyers, editors, and reporters ranged around the conference table. In the center was a loaded tape recorder, now somehow ominous.

The *Post* reporters put some questions to Hugel. Had he ever provided insider information on his company to the McNells? Had he made loans to them to buy Brother stock and drive the price up? Had he ever threatened to kill their lawyer?

Hugel denied all, categorically, "one hundred percent."

Pat Tyler turned on a tape dated December 13, 1974, in which Hugel's voice was heard saying about the McNell's lawyer: "And then he had the audacity, the nerve, to threaten me with some goddamn cockamamie lawsuit, that I—it's so distasteful to me that I'm ready to throw up. . . . What the fuck kind of shit is that? . . . Let the fuck sue me. . . . That's bullshit, Sam. I've been at that cocksucker, I'll put that bastard in jail. . . . I'll kill the bastard." In another tape, Hugel was telling Tom McNell, "Get some pencil and paper, will you? What I'm giving you is strictly confidential stuff, okay?"

The *Post* was intending to go with a story based on the Hugel tapes.

On Sunday afternoon, Casey flew in from Panama and went directly to Langley. Admiral Inman and Stan Sporkin were waiting for him. "What have they got on Max?" he wanted to know. Sporkin said that he was not sure. Some of it sounded worse than it was. On one tape Hugel was heard telling his broker, "I'll cut your balls off. . . . I'll get my Korean gang after you and you won't look so good when you're hanging by the balls anyway." They went back and forth discussing what would be the smart move and yet fair to Hugel. Maybe Max should go on administrative leave until the air cleared, Inman suggested. But nothing was decided.

The *Post* was expected to run its Hugel story on Tuesday, July 14. The night before, Casey went to dinner with Arthur Burns, former chairman of the Federal Reserve Board, at the exclusive F Street Club. Sporkin, now happily putting in twelve-hour days again, was at his CIA office. He knew that an edition of the next day's *Washington Post* could be obtained as early as 10 that night in the lobby of the paper's downtown office. Sporkin sent a security man to Fifteenth Street for three copies—one for himself, one for Casey, and one for Hugel. Before Casey's dinner with Burns was over, the DCI had the paper in hand.

The story on the front page was not calculated to aid his digestion. There was a photo of Max Hugel and a headline reading: CIA SPY-MASTER IS ACCUSED OF IMPROPER STOCK PRACTICES. The story carried excerpts from the tapes, replete with Hugel's obscenities barely disguised, "f---" for "fuck," "c---------" for "cocksucker."

Casey left the F Street Club and went home visibly shaken. Sophia wanted to know what had happened. He explained glumly. Then he waved the matter aside with what had become his reflex reaction to bad press. "Aaah. It only hurts for a day."

The next day, Sporkin went to see Hugel in the latter's office. Sporkin's tone was sympathetic. "Max, I'm going to tell you something. Someday you'll realize it's the best advice anybody ever gave you. You can fight this thing if you want to. But if you try to tough it out, those committees on the Hill will murder you. They'll ask you a question. You'll say something to defend yourself and those tapes will contradict you. Then they'll get you on a perjury charge. I'm telling you, you can't win. On the other hand, if you resign, there'll be one more bad story on your resignation, and then it's all over. In a few days, everybody will forget Max Hugel. So I'm telling you, cut and run. I just gave you a million dollars' worth of free legal advice, my friend."

Hugel started to protest his innocence, the unfairness of it all. Sporkin held up his hand. Had he listened? Fairness was not the issue. By the end of the day, Max Hugel submitted his resignation.

John Bross came into Casey's office and saw him holding Hugel's letter of resignation. "The press wants a comment. What do I say?" Casey asked Bross.

"How about this?" Bross answered. " 'In the words of Fiorello La Guardia, when I make a mistake, it's a beaut.' "

Casey gave him a tired smile and said, "I always knew it was a high-risk operation."

The advice was to be one of Bross's last services to Bill Casey. He had found himself increasingly a kibitzer more than a counselor. He and Bobby Inman seemed to be stepping on each other's toes. Bross soon decided to return to retirement.

What had brought about the swift fall of Max Hugel? Was the delivery of the sixteen tapes a spontaneous idea of the McNell brothers? Hugel thought otherwise. "I was set up by the old-boy network," he later remarked. "Some guys on the inside were out to get me. Some were retired guys working from the outside."

Long after Hugel left the CIA, he visited the Agency's fabled former counterintelligence chief, James Jesus Angleton. Angleton, with close ties to people still in the Agency, told him, "Your troubles originated inside the DO." Later still, Hugel found himself in Seoul, Korea, on business and dropped in on the station chief there, John Stein. Stein had been the number two man in the DO during the trouble—in effect, Hugel's deputy—and then his successor as chief. "He admitted to me," Hugel said, "that there was a cabal in the DO out to get me."

Was it so farfetched? The DO contained professionals whose stock-in-trade was destabilizing unfriendly governments; it was all in a day's work. Knocking over a businessman from Brooklyn should not have particularly taxed their talents. When John McMahon, Hugel's predecessor as DDO, was asked if Hugel had jumped or been pushed, he laughed and said, "I don't know how those tapes got to the *Washington Post*. It might have been one of the Agency's better covert actions."

A little more than a year after the episode, Hugel brought suit against the McNell brothers in the U.S. District Court in New Hampshire for defamatory statements made to the *Washington Post*. The judge ruled that Hugel was "entitled to full compensation for all of the injuries sustained. . . . I find that the plaintiff has suffered and will continue to suffer humiliation, embarrassment, shame, and mental anguish. . . . I find further that he has suffered the loss of prestige, notoriety, and prominence as a public official." The judge made a judgment of $931,000 in favor of Max Hugel.

Bob Gates was later to observe, "Casey's approach to clandestine activity was shaped almost entirely by his experience in World War II. In that stage of American intelligence, he wasn't dealing with careerists, with people who had grown up in the business. He was remembering the guy who had been a Wall Street lawyer and a year later is doing brilliant things inside occupied Belgium. Dealing with the bureaucracy that had developed since then drove Casey crazy. So he was willing to take a chance on a tough, smart outsider like Max Hugel."

But Hugel had run head-on into a career corps that had not existed in the OSS era. "You have to understand the culture of the clandestine service," Gates noted. "It's what makes the CIA unique. They are incredibly dedicated, mission-oriented people. They are independent and self-motivated. They make tremendous sacrifices in their personal lives for a larger cause. They face risk as part of going to work in the morning. They are extraordinarily good with people. They're flexible, quick, and adaptable, sophisticated in the ways of the world. They're bright intellectually and street smart. I liken it to a priesthood. That's the positive side.

"Then there is the negative side of this culture that surfaces if it's not well guided. It's a closed fraternity. Their attitude toward outsiders is like that of local people in Maine or Cape Cod toward summer people: if you weren't born there, you're always an outsider. You haven't been through what they've been through. They've put their families through hell at times. They're not able to talk about what they do. Some may eventually wind up in London or Paris. But they start out in Third World hellholes without even a Western doctor when their kids get sick. They have a strong sense that almost no one understands them or what they do. So they feel defensive and misunderstood."

This was the closed circle that Max Hugel had been expected to crack and to lead. In the end, the smart, feisty Hugel may have said it best. Two weeks out of the job, he wrote Casey a sixteen-page, longhand letter, the cry of a broken man. At the end he said, "Bill, I did my best, but I guess I just don't fit the mold."

17.

"Not Unfit to Serve"

Casey had not taken over the CIA to carry on public squabbes over the fitness of his appointees. His purpose had been to become a key player in the conduct of U.S. foreign policy. The troubles of Max Hugel were a distraction, taking time from what he was trying to accomplish that summer.

First on his agenda was helping to get the AWACS deal through the Congress. The government of Saudi Arabia wanted to spend $8.5 billion for these "airborne warning and control systems" surveillance aircraft. The Reagan administration was eager to make the sale to cement its friendship with the Saudis. Israel was understandably unnerved by the prospect of an Arab state getting supersophisticated planes. The powerful Jewish lobbies in the United States were expected to carry the fight and likely kill the deal.

Casey went to the Middle East and met in Tel Aviv with the Israeli intelligence chief, Major General Yitzhak Hoffi, known as Haka. How could he be helpful? Casey wanted to know. Haka told him that any information the Israelis could acquire from the CIA on certain installations in the Arab world could be most useful. Any in particular? Casey asked. Yes, the Israeli told him. Ten miles outside of Baghdad in Iraq was the Osirak nuclear reactor. The reactor's core contained 26.4 pounds of weapons-grade uranium 235. The Israelis estimated that their Iraqi antagonists were within five years of producing nuclear weapons.

Casey understood Israel's concern. Of course he could help—but did Israel really need to be so worried about the AWACS sale to the Saudis? Couldn't the Jewish lobby in the States be called off? The heads of the intelligence service of the United States and of Israel managed, before Casey left, to arrive at a mutually helpful arrangement.

On Sunday, June 8, Israeli aircraft bombed the Osirak reactor. Casey was notified at home at four-fifty that afternoon. Within two hours, an American KH-11 Big Bird photo reconnaissance satellite was diverted from its customary orbit over the Soviet Union and China; and within six hours, Israeli intelligence was getting KH-11 photos direct by satellite revealing the destruction wrought on the Iraqi plant.

The Jewish lobby took a listless pro forma stand against the AWACS sale. The Israeli government barely objected. Before the year was out, Congress approved the sale to the Saudis.

During the administration's push to win approval of the AWACS deal, Casey had watched with admiration the energy of two military officers on the project. One was a young Marine Corps lieutenant colonel who was always scurrying purposefully around the third floor in the EOB, where Casey had his downtown office. His name was Oliver L. North. The second man—indeed, the point man in the AWACS campaign—was a deputy assistant secretary of Defense, Major General Richard V. Secord. Here obviously were two comers.

On the day that Max Hugel had resigned, Stan Sporkin remembered, "I had the oddest feeling that Bill's troubles weren't over." Just under its front-page story on Hugel's resignation, the *New York Times* had run another story, JUDGE ASSERTS CIA CHIEF MISLED STOCK BUYERS IN 1968. A federal judge in the Southern District of New York, Charles Stewart, had ruled that Casey, as a director and officer of the Multiponics company, along with seven other insiders, had intentionally misled investors through untrue statements in the corporation's prospectus.

Senator Moynihan, on reading the *Times*, immediately picked up his phone and put a call through to Barry Goldwater. "Barry," he told the SSCI chairman, "we have to move on this one." Goldwater was more disheartened than angry—first Casey's crazy appointment of Hugel, now this. And he had tried so hard to get Reagan to appoint the right man as DCI in the first place.

The Multiponics suit had been dragging through the courts for nine years, ever since 1972, when Casey had left the SEC. Casey had first become involved with this agribusiness in the late sixties; he invested heavily as the firm attempted to cash in on a worldwide soybean boom. Casey's law firm, Hall, Casey, Dickler and Howley, became counsel to Multiponics. Casey became an officer. But the soybean boom passed Multiponics by, and by 1971 the firm had gone bankrupt.

Goldwater called Casey and discussed the tough spot the story had put them all in. There would have to be, well, a Senate inquiry, he said. "Investigation" was too harsh a word. Casey hung up the phone and decided that he needed a lawyer. He turned immediately to his savior during the ITT crisis of 1971 and called Milton Gould.

Gould accepted, but he saw an uphill fight. The judge had already granted the plaintiffs a summary judgment against Casey and the other defendants: in effect, a federal judge had found the director of the CIA guilty of fraud. Gould moved quickly to have the motion reargued, and he won. Judge Stewart withdrew his summary judgment, and the Multiponics suit was on again.

William J. Casey was not ordinarily given to a conspiratorial view of the world. Still, there were those around him, Sporkin among them, who started to wonder. To Sporkin, the Senate "inquiry" was a retest of Casey's fitness to hold office, something that had already been determined at his confirmation. The new probe looked to Sporkin like double jeopardy, and of suspicious origin: first the Hugel torpedoing; then, on the same day as Hugel's departure, stories in the press about Judge Stewart's decision in the Multiponics case. The judge had rendered that decision two months *before*. Now it suddenly pops up alongside the Hugel story. Was Casey's fall being orchestrated?

Three days after Goldwater's call to Casey, on Thursday, July 23, the SSCI met and voted formally to carry out an inquiry into the business affairs of the director of the Central Intelligence Agency. That same afternoon, Casey and his strategy team, led by Milton Gould and Stanley Sporkin, gathered in Casey's office.

"How do you think Goldwater is going to come down?" Gould asked.

"Let's find out," Casey answered. With that, he put through a call to the chairman.

Casey was a fellow conservative. He was the appointee of a conservative Republican President. Goldwater was not looking for trouble or embarrassment for the Administration, he told Casey. Casey nodded and smiled at his end of the phone. He hung up and said, "Barry thinks it's a lot of bullshit. But he's got to keep Moynihan and the other Democrats on the committee off his back. So he's going along with this inquiry." He leaned back, lifted his feet onto the desk, and put his hands behind his head. "He says I've got nothing to worry about. He's behind me one hundred percent."

With that, the group went back to work, deciding what strategy to follow, what questions Casey must be ready to answer. Later the phone rang again. It was Billy Doswell, the Agency's press officer. Doswell had just received word that CBS News would be reporting that evening that Barry Goldwater wanted Casey to resign.

"Son of a bitch!" Casey roared. "What the hell's going on?" He immediately called Goldwater back. It was a "goddamn lie," Goldwater told him. "Don't worry, I'm going to call a press conference and straighten it out."

The Casey team worked until early evening, and then they went out to dinner. The CIA's Office of External Affairs, in the meantime, taped Goldwater's press conference. Doswell would run it for the director when he got back.

Casey and the others came back from dinner and went to Doswell's office to watch the videotape. Casey turned ashen. Goldwater had felt himself torn before the reporters. He wanted to be loyal to his party and his President, but Casey had not made it easy for him. As the press grilled him in the Senate's radio-TV gallery, he spoke as an exasperated human being rather than as a glib politician.

He was asked about Max Hugel and could not restrain himself. It was the worst thing Casey had done, he said. It was more than a bad mistake; it was dangerous. It was sufficient, "in my opinion, for either Mr. Casey to decide to retire or the President to decide to ask him to retire." Old Barry, more honest than clever, had confirmed the rumor that he had gone on the air to scotch. Casey watched in stunned silence. There was nothing more to say.

By the next day, the arithmetic was starting to look terrible. Goldwater had stated publicly that he wanted Casey out. Another presumed Republican friend on the intelligence committee, Senator William V. Roth, Jr., of Delaware, said of Casey, "He should go—now." Among the Democrats, Moynihan and Joe Biden clearly opposed Casey. Pat Leahy could be expected to go with them. There were eight Republicans and seven Democrats on the SSCI. If the Democrats voted the party line and just one Republican defected, Casey was sunk.

Senator Paul Laxalt was Casey's friend and an admirer, but not a member of the intelligence committee. It was a sad day, Laxalt observed, "when an honorable man can be driven from public office by innuendo." Laxalt started calling some of his colleagues to get a sense of the Senate and build some support for Casey. After a half-dozen calls, he quit. "They all thought Casey was a goner," he remarked. "They told me I was wasting my time."

Richard Allen and Casey were close. Allen was now in the White House running the NSC. He had hung a picture of Casey in his office. "I especially liked to have it there," Allen said, "when other people are running him down." Henry Hubbard, an Allen friend and the *Newsweek* Washington bureau chief, called Allen and asked him who would be Casey's successor. As Allen tells what happened: "I had my mind on a dozen other matters, and I carelessly answered, 'I don't know.' Hubbard taped our conversation and he played it for David Martin, a network correspondent. Martin called Casey and played the tape for him. Casey called me, furious. He said, 'What are you doing? Why are you confirming that I'm leaving?' I could have bit my tongue off for what happened. I felt I'd done a slimy thing. I'd unintentionally betrayed a friend."

More bad news arrived. Under pressure from the Democrats, Goldwater had agreed to bring in a special counsel to conduct the inquiry. Jack Blake, Goldwater's staff director on the committee, argued against the appointment; he particularly opposed the lawyer under consideration. Fred Thompson had gained national attention as chief of the Senate's Watergate investigating committee. "It's overkill," Blake told Goldwater. "Once you get a lawyer of Thompson's coloration, it looks like you're looking for felonies when we're not even sure we've got a misdemeanor." Nevertheless, Thompson was named to conduct the inquiry.

Geoffrey M. T. Jones, the executive director of the Veterans of OSS, had gone out to Long Island to visit another member and a mutual friend of his and Casey's, the oil developer John Shaheen. "Bill's in the soup this time," Jones said over drinks on Shaheen's patio. "This one is serious."

"Then we've got to do something," Shaheen said. "Somebody has got to honcho a campaign to save him. Geoff, you're the logical choice."

Jones flew to Washington immediately and arrived near midnight in a driving rain. He found Casey still up, looking morose. Jones reminded him that he had friends all over—powerful friends. Jones was going to start mobilizing them. They were going to lick this thing. Casey listened like a patient who is hearing that his doctor's opinion that he is terminal might have been a mistake. He had almost let himself be driven out of the SEC appointment in 1971, but he had fought back and won. He sat up straighter and started suggesting actions Jones might take.

Jones checked into the Madison Hotel and did not leave for four days. Except for a few snatched hours of sleep, he was on the phone constantly. He was on a mission, building a resistance movement against an enemy composed of the Congress and a hostile media. He called his old Princeton classmate George Shultz and asked Shultz to host one of two giant testimonial dinners he was planning for Casey, one at the Washington Hilton and the other at the Waldorf Astoria in New York. Shultz had warm feelings toward Casey lingering on from their Nixon years together and the trip they had taken with their wives in 1973. "I don't know anything about the charges," he told Jones, "but I'll stand up for Bill Casey." Bill Simon agreed to host the New York dinner.

Jones hired a Washington public relations firm to stage the dinners. He began recruiting the OSS power network. He called John Blatnik, an OSS alumnus who had served in Congress for twenty-eight years. Blatnik, for good measure, was also a liberal Democrat. He started working the familiar corridors, stopping to persuade old colleagues with the same message: Bill Casey was a lousy lobbyist, his own worst enemy on the Hill; but he was an honest man and a damned fine DCI.

Stan Sporkin was still a darling of the liberals for his legendary battles against Wall Street delinquents. And Multiponics was a securities problem. Casey asked Sporkin to do something visible and public for him. And he wanted Democrats seen in his corner, too. The best they could rustle up on short notice was Leonard Marks, the director of the U.S. Information Agency under Lyndon Johnson. Casey also asked Paul Laxalt to go to bat for him as proof of his powerful support among conservatives. The three men staged an impromptu Saturday-afternoon press conference at the Mayflower Hotel. The most helpful words were Sporkin's: "I know securities fraud when I see it, and I do not see it here."

A conservative senator, an inside-the-Beltway government lawyer, and a fading Johnson appointee were still not enough. Who was the most respected contemporary voice in American intelligence? Grudgingly, Casey called Bobby Ray Inman. "I was home, sick as a dog, with the flu that Saturday night," Inman remembered of Casey's call. "Bill said, 'It's going bad.' Unless somebody really influential from inside the intelligence community threw him a life ring, he might be finished. He asked if I'd be willing to go on television for him."

You don't have to love the captain of the ship, Inman knew, but you owe him the allegiance due his rank and position. Besides, as Inman put it, "for all our difficulties, I considered Casey's direct access to Ronald Reagan and his ability to get the support required to rebuild the CIA absolutely critical." Inman agreed to do whatever Casey asked. The next day he was informed that on Monday night, July 27, he would be doing a full hour on Ted Koppel's "Nightline." He told Koppel's huge and politically aware audience, "Bill Casey is the right man to continue as director." For a while afterward, Inman noticed, "Bill was so much warmer toward me. It was like a delayed honeymoon."

The SSCI staff leaned hard on Casey, demanding documents going back five, ten, even fifteen years. Sporkin became Casey's barbed and combative defender. "Why do you need that? . . . Why do you have to have that? . . . What's the relevance of that?" one Senate aide remembered as Sporkin's constant refrain. In the end, Sporkin's tactic was to drown the Senate in acquiescence. The Senate hearing was scheduled for Wednesday, July 29. On the Sunday before, every member of the SSCI received a two-feet-high stack of Casey documents.

Whatever anxiety Casey was feeling inside, his outward demeanor was a breezy nonchalance. He made one last round of visits to Capitol Hill. He told the reporters trotting behind him, "Fellas, my life is an open book. . . . The bottom of the barrel has been reached—and there's nothing there."

On the Wednesday of the hearing, Casey, Sporkin, and Gould piled into Casey's car for the ride to the Senate. Gould fixed his client with his formidable brows and said, "There'll be reporters when we get there. Anything they ask us, the answer is 'No comment.' Got it?"

The black Oldsmobile pulled under the portico at the north end of the Capitol. Cameras were whirring and mikes shoved into the three men's faces. The reporters shouted questions. Gould, in the lead, said, "No comment." Sporkin, behind him, said, "No comment." A reporter hollered to a smiling, waving Casey, "Are you worried about the committee's judgment?" "It'll be a cakewalk," Casey said. "I've been through this before."

Secret hearings of the Senate Select Committee on Intelligence were then held in a special room on the fourth floor of the Capitol. Arrivals passed first through an outer door where a security guard checked their clearances before they passed through a second door. The room had been soundproofed and secured against electronic penetration, rather like the shielding of a microwave oven. The room was an oblong. Committee members sat at one end at an elevated horseshoe. Behind them, aides moved in and out, whispering in their ears—moths circling the flames of power. Casey settled down at the witness table in front of the horseshoe with Gould and his aides. Behind him were several rows of chairs for authorized visitors.

Casey had been presented in advance with pages of questions that the committee would ask. But the main issues boiled down to two. Had he, thirteen years before, been a party to a scheme to defraud investors? And another charge had been added: how did he defend the Hugel appointment?

Pat Moynihan had been eloquent in his praises of Casey during his confirmation six months before. There were no praises this day. Moynihan was tall, lean, yet somehow soft looking. His complexion just missed being florid. The senator cut an Edwardian figure, speaking with the phrases and flourishes of another age. He gestured grandly, with sweeping movements of his arms and staccato rises of his voice, which issued through a rosebud of a mouth. He was superb at moral outrage. Under Moynihan's questioning, Casey described the mental processes that had led him to appoint Hugel. It had not been a hasty judgment, he insisted; he had considered literally hundreds of prospects. But he wanted to shatter the apathy in the operations directorate. And, as a successful businessman himself, he knew what great wells of intelligence lay out there waiting to be tapped in multinational corporations. Hugel knew that world too, better than he did. And Max Hugel was smart, aggressive, and imaginative.

Joe Biden of Delaware took up the questioning. Wasn't Hugel a political payoff? Casey denied the charge heatedly. His face turned red; he sputtered and fumed. Gould saw Casey getting himself trapped into a "pissing contest" with the young, quick-witted Biden. He slipped Casey a note: "This isn't doing you any good." Casey backed off.

The Multiponics case centered on one main issue: did Casey and the other defendants have guilty knowledge that an offering statement issued by the company contained misleading information that had induced investors to buy the company's stock and thus lose their money? The plaintiffs claimed that the offering circular had fudged the large amount of debt the company carried, and that Multiponics did not own "seven working farm units," as claimed.

Casey argued that he had had no personal role in drafting the offering circular. He had had no role in persuading investors to buy the company's stock. He was not out to hurt widows and orphans. But in the rough-and-tumble world of venture capitalism, everybody took risks and people got hurt. As far as he was concerned, the Multiponics case was a garden-variety lawsuit, almost inevitable when companies fail and investors lose money.

The hearing went on for over five hours without producing a clear-cut case against Casey. Chairman Goldwater faced a dilemma: he could not leave a suspect director running the CIA. They might as well clear him now and have done with it. Lloyd Bentsen, a Democratic member and a wealthy entrepreneur himself, understood perfectly the game Casey was describing. Hawkish Scoop Jackson believed it was far more important that Casey was rebuilding an effective CIA than that he might not be a business saint. But since the investigation had started, the press had churned up charges involving other Casey business dealings. Liberal Democrats, led by

Moynihan, wanted Casey out. Goldwater had to live with them too. The committee huddled during a recess and reached a compromise: they would give Casey an interim clearance; in the meantime, the special counsel would keep on investigating the alleged irregularities.

In drafting an interim report, the committee seesawed between two words. Milton Gould argued that Casey should be described as "fit to serve" as DCI. Moynihan preferred a British turn of phrase, "not unfit." Soon after the hearing ended, Goldwater issued a statement: "It is the unanimous judgment of the Committee that no basis has been found for concluding Mr. Casey is *unfit* to serve as DCI. The staff will follow up on points that need clarification in timely fashion."

Casey was furious. To be called not unfit was to be called barely fit.

The ordeal was not yet over. But Stan Sporkin, who had bled for him on this one, was elated. It had been a close call. After the hearing, Sporkin stopped by his favorite delicatessen and "bought every kind of salmon in the place," he said. "Scottish salmon. Irish salmon. Nova Scotia salmon. I bought lox, bagels, and pickled herring. I knew Casey loved all this stuff. I took it back to his office at the EOB and spread it out on his desk, and the three of us, Bill, Milt Gould, and I, had a victory celebration." While they devoured the impromptu buffet, Casey put through a call to Geoff Jones. He was grateful for the testimonial dinners that Jones had arranged, but he wanted them canceled. They had served their purpose.

Not quite a cakewalk; but, for the meantime, he had survived.

18.

Shakedown Cruise

In its first year in office the Reagan administration's attention in the foreign policy arena was riveted to a place most Americans could not locate with a pin and a world map. El Salvador was poor, tiny, about the size of Massachusetts, little more than an enlarged plantation inhabited by some 4.7 million *peones* and owned largely by fourteen families. Six out of one hundred Salvadoran babies failed to survive their first year. Life expectancy was under sixty years. Sixty percent of the adults were illiterate. Average annual per capita income was $650. A rough, repressive regime ruled the country. It was in El Salvador that four American Maryknoll nuns had been murdered by right-wing death squads. Here was fertile soil for the seeds of discontent. And a Communist insurgency, the Farabundo Martí National Liberation Front, was in fact waging a guerrilla war against the regime. This unhappy speck of geography hardly seemed the hinge on which the fate of Western democracy could turn. Nevertheless, the Reagan White House was obsessed with the Communist threat to El Salvador.

Central American banana republics had never been Casey's burning interest. He was essentially a man of Europe. But he remembered a long-ago warning that Bill Donovan had written him: "If Russia dominates Europe and brings her pressure on South America . . . we might be very well placed in that danger (which I have bored you to death in discussing) of being so tied down by limitations placed upon us that we couldn't fight, even if we wanted to."

The red chain that Casey spied ran from Moscow to Havana to Managua to El Salvador. Reports coming across his desk showed Nicaragua's Sandinista regime funneling arms from Cuba, the Soviet Union, and the rest of the Communist bloc, even North Vietnam, to the Farabundo Martí movement. Donovan's prescience, Casey thought, even reached from the grave.

Al Haig had found a friend and confidant in Bill Casey, and much to his pleasure, since he was beginning to feel lonely in Reagan country. His testy nature ran against the grain of the cool, nonconfrontational, image-obsessed Reagan crowd. Haig had been relieved to find in Casey a foreign policy thinker who saw beyond the next photo opportunity. But they thought differently about the part of the globe that currently consumed the administration.

At one of their regular Tuesday breakfasts, this one in Haig's smallish, stylish oak-paneled office, with its fireplace and early American originals, Haig turned up the wattage on Casey. He leaned close, his voice taking on its purring conspiratorial intimacy. The square, handsome face was ravined by deep furrows. He gestured with a thick, square hand, the wrist encircled by a heavy gold watch, complemented by a gold tie clasp, gold cuff links, and a gold bracelet on the other wrist, engraved simply in bold letters: HAIG. He was faultlessly dressed in blue serge, with a crisp, monogrammed shirt, a soldier in mufti. He interrupted his sentences with tight, mirthless smiles, a form of oral punctuation. He told Casey what he had been trying to get across to Ronald Reagan: "I've talked to Andrei Gromyko and he told me, 'Haig, all I ever hear from you is Cuba, Cuba, Cuba! From now on, Cuba is *your* problem.' "

To Haig, the Soviet foreign minister's words were an "all-clear signal." Obviously, the Russians had so many headaches of their own "that they just weren't going to rush into a confrontation with us over Cuba." Fooling around with pipsqueak countries like Nicaragua and El Salvador was a waste of time. Strike at Cuba. Quarantine Cuba. Blockade it. Put a noose around it. Cut off the head, and any other Marxist limbs in Central America would wither.

Casey was more politically attuned than the quixotic Haig. The debacle of Vietnam was less than six years old. Memories of the fifty-eight thousand American war dead, still so hard to justify, were too fresh in the American consciousness. A Caribbean Vietnam, even the • semblance of one through a blockade of Cuba, was the last thing this administration wanted. Casey felt the superiority of his judgment; still, Haig was secretary of State.

The administration may not have been ready for a frontal assault against Caribbean Communists. But Casey was ready to take a smaller bite. The Sandinistas had been in the saddle in Nicaragua since the summer of 1979, the political heirs of Augusto Sandino, a legendary peasant guerrilla who fought the U.S. Marines and the ruling Somoza family until he was killed in 1934. Before the Sandinista victory, Nicaragua had been ruled by Anastasio Somoza, a West

Point graduate who had made it into the academy through the intercession of President Franklin Delano Roosevelt, as a favor to Somoza's father.

After the Sandinistas were in and Somoza out, hopes flickered briefly for a democratic Nicaragua. But the Sandinistas quickly took a hard left turn. Umberto Ortega, brother of Daniel Ortega, the leading member of the ruling junta, openly proclaimed, "Marxist-Leninism is the scientific doctrine that guides our revolution." Casey read the intelligence out of Nicaragua with a rueful shake of his head: Cubans advising the Nicaraguan army, Cubans teaching military communications and intelligence methods; Russian, Bulgarian, East German technicians and advisers running all over Managua; and Nicaragua providing sanctuary to leftist Salvadoran rebels. How long before the Salvadoran government would fall? Then it would be Cuba, Nicaragua, El Salvador . . . and who knew what U.S. neighbor would next be colored red in the map Casey carried in his head? He told a reporter who asked about the administration's preoccupation with the Sandinistas' mischief, "If we can't stop Soviet expansionism in a place like Nicaragua, where the hell can we?"

The State Department carried on the fight above the line. The American ambassador in Managua, Lawrence Pezzullo, was dealing with Daniel Ortega, dangling $75 million in American aid before the Sandinistas, if they would back off and stop supplying the Salvadoran insurgents. But if they did not, and if American public opinion would not support open involvement in Central America, the administration was ready to go below the line.

The first step was a top secret operation that Casey presented to the NSPG in March. His proposal called for the CIA to provide covert support to pro-U.S. elements in Afghanistan, Cambodia, Cuba, Grenada, Iran, Laos, Libya, and Nicaragua. Three months into the new administration, he had sown the seed for what would not have a name for four years: the Reagan Doctrine, aid to Third World forces fending off Communist takeovers—aid to the enemies of America's enemy.

The Nicaraguan part of Casey's plan called for $19 million to support covert actions against the Sandinista regime. In order to make the operation more palatable to a wary Congress, the actions were pitched as measures to defend El Salvador against a Communist takeover. The Salvadoran rebels were presumably armed and supported by equipment delivered by the Sandinistas. Casey's proposal allowed the CIA to collect intelligence on this arms flow.

On March 9, the President signed the finding for this toe-dipping operation. Casey, as required by law, notified the two intelligence oversight committees. What he laid out did not seem the sort of activity to provoke a Hispanic Vietnam. He left with the committees' blessing. And he had his foot in the door of Nicaragua.

On April 21, Casey overnighted in Rome on his way back from a secret trip to Morocco, Israel, Cairo, Saudi Arabia, and Jordan. He had been briefed by American officials and his foreign intelligence counterparts in each country; but his keenest interest was to get a sense of his own people on the ramparts. He would take over the office of the local station chief, peppering the staff with questions. Or he would drop into their offices unexpectedly, firing off more questions, judging how they answered, how they carried themselves, always measuring and assessing. Who had brains, energy, guts, imagination? Who was in over his head? Who was underutilized? Where were the undiscovered diamonds?

For months, he had been thinking about what he wanted to do with the Rome station chief, Duane R. "Dewey" Clarridge. Casey had met Clarridge earlier in Paris, when he pulled together station chiefs from several European countries to meet the new DCI. Clarridge was then forty-nine, a graduate of Brown University, a five-foot-ten, lean, graying man. At first blush, Casey had been put off. The glib Clarridge was a flamboyant figure who favored Italian silk suits, silk shirts, silk ties, and flashy suspenders; he smoked cigars and dined in the finest restaurants. What is this, Casey had wondered, a white-shoe boy running a major station?

The judgment was short-lived. Clarridge was clearly more aggressive, more gung-ho than any of his confreres—and smart. Casey came back and told Inman, "Dewey's the only really impressive guy I met out there. He's a doer, a take-charge guy. I'm going to bring him back here for something big."

After the March 9 finding, Casey knew where he wanted Clarridge. He informed Inman that he intended to put Clarridge in charge of the Latin American division of the operations directorate. What about the incumbent, Inman asked—Nestor Sanchez, a thirty-year veteran, a good man and fluent in Spanish? Casey waved Sanchez aside. "Nyaah. Overcautious. Too long in the saddle. Besides, Frank Carlucci wants him over at the Pentagon."

But Clarridge had no background in Latin America, Inman pointed out. He did not speak Spanish. Another wave-off: "He can handle it," Casey said—end of discussion. Clarridge took over his new duties that August.

Casey was bringing a legend home to Langley. The phrases that sprang to mind when colleagues were asked to describe Dewey Clarridge were "roughrider," "cowboy," "a hip-shooter," "our General Patton." Cool analysis was not Clarridge's long suit. But as Bob Gates put it, "If you have a tough, dangerous job, critical to national security, Dewey's your man. He's talented. One of our best operations officers. Just make sure you have a good lawyer at his elbow—Dewey's not easy to control." Alan Fiers, who would eventually succeed Clarridge, spoke of the man with a certain awe: "Dewey was a storybook character. Controversial. People either loved him or hated him. The young guys on the covert side worshiped him. Their sun rose and set on Dewey Clarridge." Another colleague, Edward Juchniewicz, said of Clarridge, "He could have been a refugee from a Jesuit seminary."

The man possessed the Bondian background the layman assumes of a spy. Clarridge had served in Europe and Asia in assignments so steeped in secrecy that when the oversight committees were given his résumé it contained four blanked-out pages. Casey was convinced that he had matched the right man to the job—and the organization chart be damned. He told Clarridge to report directly to him anytime, day or night; he did not have to go through channels. Inman, as deputy, and John Stein, as Clarridge's immediate superior, were troubled at being cut out, particularly by so flammable an operative as Dewey Clarridge. What would he and Casey, huddled alone, cook up that Inman and Stein might have to defend or undo?

The duties of the director of Central Intelligence should have been job enough for any man. But the secretaries in the office and the security detail on the road were struck by the economy of time that Casey practiced, habits that had been ingrained since his graduate days at Catholic University. The minute had value. It was not to be squandered. When he had finished the last appointment, read every report, and placed every phone call, he would dig to the bottom of his attaché case and fish out a thick document held together by a rubber band and resume work on his OSS memoir.

Just before the Reagan campaign had intruded, he had received the $12,000 offer from William Morrow to write the memoir. With the Reagan victory, he temporarily shelved the project. To publish a book on intelligence while running the CIA, he told Sophia, "looks like I'm cashing in. It's too obvious. I've had enough of that kind of grief."

He had gone to a dinner that first year at the CIA and met the British publisher George Weidenfeld. "What do you think about a public official having a book published while he's in office? A little sleazy?" he asked Weidenfeld. Not in the slightest, Weidenfeld assured him. Quite the opposite: it would be a good thing for him to publish the book while he was at the CIA; it would give it a certain authority and prestige. (Not to mention—and Weidenfeld did not have to mention—the publicity now attached to Casey's name.) Weidenfeld told Casey that he would be delighted to publish his book.

Word of the conversation found its way back to the William Morrow people. Would he really consider publishing the book while at Langley? they wanted to know. Would he at least finish it, so that they could have it positioned, ready to launch, the minute he stepped off the federal payroll?

Casey seesawed back and forth: to publish or not to publish, proper or improper. In the meantime, he loved working on the book. One thing was clear to him: he was suddenly a hot literary property. Morrow could forget a $12,000 advance. He let them know that he was now thinking in terms of $100,000.

That fall, the SSCI was still probing Casey's financial affairs. Not only had Goldwater appointed Fred Thompson as special counsel, but in September, Vice-Chairman Moynihan demanded a minority counsel for the Democrats. Business associates warned Casey that committee investigators were coming up to New York, snooping around. Casey complained to Goldwater, "The approach is not to tie up loose ends but to look far and wide for anything that might be used to smear me."

He hit the ceiling when he read what Moynihan told a *New York Times* reporter: Reagan's first official mistake as President had been to appoint "the most political person in his campaign as DCI." That, Moynihan shuddered, "was unprecedented." Casey found Moynihan's charge hypocritical. He was the same man whom Moynihan had praised during his confirmation as an extraordinary appointment. "Mere home-state courtesy" was how Moynihan later explained the contradiction.

Investigative reporters, conditioned by Watergate to probe the underbelly of government, had found an irresistible target, the alleged business shenanigans of the nation's spy chief. Even before his interim clearance, fresh denunciations had popped up in the press. On July 25, the *New York Times* said that Casey had failed to report, as required by the Office of Government Ethics, a gift of a limited partnership worth $10,000 in a Carl Paffendorf company called PenVerter Partners. At about the same time, the *Washington Post* revealed that

Casey had failed to list several companies he had represented as a lawyer, as required of prospective presidential appointees. Next the *New York Times* reported that he had failed to disclose a $50,000 loan that he had made to Paffendorf while serving as SEC chairman. It was also reported that he had failed to list nine stocks he owned, worth a total of more than a quarter of a million dollars; he had not included four civil lawsuits that he had been involved in over the previous five years, and he had failed to disclose that he had represented two foreign governments, Indonesia and South Korea, while he was practicing law. The old ITT/Vesco accusations were dusted off. And it was discovered that the director of Central Intelligence, with likely the most privileged information in the country at his fingertips, did not have his stocks in a blind trust.

The papers provided the grist, and the Senate intelligence committee provided the mill. As each fresh allegation surfaced, the committee staff added it to an ever-lengthening list of perceived transgressions. By fall, five CIA lawyers were tied up virtually full-time just in meeting the SSCI's demands for more information on Casey's dealings.

The charge of failing to register as a foreign lobbyist was tricky. In 1976, Indonesia's government-owned Pertamina Oil Company had wanted to obtain a tax credit from the IRS for payments made by U.S. companies to Pertamina. Millions of dollars were at stake, and Indonesia had hired Rogers and Wells to manage its case. Casey had handled the matter while he was with the firm.

Ordinarily, a lawyer representing a foreign government before a U.S. agency in "established proceedings" did not have to register as a lobbyist. But if the lawyer tried to "persuade or in any other way influence any agency or official of the United States" to change laws or policies, then that was considered to be lobbying, and the lobbyist had to register as a foreign agent. In the Indonesian case, Casey had met with William Simon, then secretary of the Treasury, to ask Simon's help in getting the ruling Indonesia wanted from the IRS. He also contacted the Indonesian desk officer at the State Department for assistance. It looked strongly as though Casey had crossed the fine line between "established proceedings" and lobbying. Yet in his appointment forms, where asked, "Have you been an attorney for or a representative of or a registered agent for a foreign government?" Casey had answered, "Neither I nor my firm currently represent any foreign government or any foreign entity."

The exquisite morality of his critics always baffled Casey. He prepared an answer to the SSCI and shot it back. "My firm registers on other matters. If they think they have to, they do. It wasn't a requirement because the nature of the work was not involved in trying to change our laws. If we had any conception that we needed to register, we merely had to fill in a form. I would have had no objection to that. The whole thing is a triviality." And, he muttered to his own lawyers, what was the big deal? He had earned a measly $6,000 on the Indonesia case and $1,500 for the work he did for South Korea.

As for the $50,000 unreported loan, after Casey had gone to the SEC in 1971, Carl Paffendorf had come to his home one weekend, desperate. His COAP system for computerized tax returns was full of bugs. The firm was $15 million in debt, and Paffendorf could not keep it afloat. "I went to see a bankruptcy lawyer and he wants twenty-five thousand dollars up front," he told Casey. "I can't even afford to go bankrupt."

"Don't go bankrupt," Casey advised him.

"But I can't make my next payroll," Paffendorf said.

At that point, as Paffendorf recalled, Casey wrote him a check for $50,000 on the spot. COAP got back on its feet eventually, and the loan was repaid. What was the problem? Casey asked the SSCI investigators. Was there a law against an SEC chairman loaning money to a friend?

As for the other omissions in the forms, he was a busy man, he claimed. He had his fingers in a hundred pies. He was not trying to hide anything. Hadn't he willingly listed stock holdings in fifty-six other companies? "So I left out a half a dozen dead cats that don't amount to one percent of my net worth," he told the committee's lawyers. "Is that a crime? I've put money in all kinds of little companies. What's a stock worth at a dollar bid and nothing offered?" To Casey, having to remember every business he was involved in was like asking an ordinary Joe to remember every check he had ever written. And the absence of a blind trust? He still felt a shudder every time he remembered the blind trust he had created at the SEC. It had cost him millions in potential profits. He told his broker, Richard Cheswick, "I don't want another twenty-seven-year-old snot-nosed trust manager determining what I can or can't do with my own money."

He was supposed to be running the intelligence service of a great nation. How was he supposed to do it with gnats constantly nibbling at him? He tried to brush it all aside and concentrate on the global issues on his desk. With each fresh, wounding disclosure, he would tell his staff, "It only hurts for a day." But the phrase began to sound hollow.

That fall, Casey was almost heckled off the platform at Brown University. That he was there at all reflected his ambivalence about the press and public. The CIA was a secrecy-shrouded entity in an open society. The bastard child of this contradictory state was the CIA's Public Affairs Office. Was the office's mission to shield the Agency from the media or to provide the media access to the Agency—to conceal or to reveal? Its very existence, a place where journalists could call up a nation's spy service, was an anomaly. In the Soviet Union or France, Iran or Brazil, the idea would be laughable. Yet the CIA Public Affairs Office at times took up to seventy-five media calls an hour.

How were officials inside the Agency to deal with reporters? The written policy was clear: no press queries were to be taken without approval of the Public Affairs Office. But the policy was murky. Overseas, the relationship was simpler. The press and the CIA station were essentially in the same business, collecting intelligence. The only intrinsic difference was that the one reported to a mass audience and the other to a select few. Otherwise, they had much to tell each other and maintained mutually profitable contact. But when the station chief came back to Langley from Bonn or Tokyo and a reporter called, the balance shifted. Back home, the CIA had everything to give and little to get; hence the restrictions. Still, there were lunches and cocktail parties where the paths of officers and journalists inevitably crossed. Casey's frequent pen pal Richard Nixon wrote him early in the game, "The [CIA] has needed a housecleaning since World War II. A good place to start, incidentally, might be to have those so-called experts who express their views to the press either shape up or get out."

Langley contained experts on an extraordinary range of subjects, and at the time Casey arrived, the agency was making these people available to reporters for briefings on nonclassified matters. "You mean some guy from some farm magazine comes here and gets briefed on Soviet wheat production?" Casey had asked on his arrival. "Some guy from the *Wall Street Journal* wants to know what's going to happen to the yen, and we roll out an analyst? We don't have the money for that kind of stuff. We don't have the time. Shut it down," he ordered. And it was.

Still, Casey himself liked to face the public. He took on a heavy speaking schedule, thirteen speeches that first year. One of the earliest, on March 17 to the Friendly Sons of Saint Patrick in New York, revealed an unsuspected side. The Friendly Sons was a major annual event in New York, sponsored by the Catholic hierarchy and held in the Grand Ballroom of the Waldorf Astoria—a showcase for New York's politicians.

"For a spy hero, I think we can do better than Nathan Hale," Casey told his audience. "It isn't so much that Nathan Hale is of British descent. What's important is that Nathan Hale got caught. In contrast, Hercules Mulligan kept delivering secrets until the British went home. He never broke his cover to the end. Today he still lies, well covered, in Trinity Churchyard, no doubt spying on his Protestant neighbors. Hercules Mulligan, not Nathan Hale, is the example we want to emulate. I intend to speak to the grounds committee about it when I return to Langley tomorrow."

That fall, an old OSS friend, Lyman Kirkpatrick, now a professor at Brown University, invited Casey to deliver the John M. Olin Lecture at his campus. On October 16, Casey arrived at Brown's Alumni Hall on Meeting Street. He headed up the stairs with his characteristic stiff gait past a couple dozen demonstrators who were handing out leaflets protesting his presence. John M. Olin, the leaflets claimed, was the founder of the Olin-Mathieson Chemical Corporation, which produced gunpowder "for more than 90 percent of the cartridges used in Vietnam."

Inside, a crowd of over a thousand awaited the speaker. Casey took his place on the stage, was introduced to polite applause, and then plunged into his text in his customary dogged, monochrome style. The text was typed on a special large-face typewriter all in caps for easy reading. Still, Casey seemed nailed to the page, virtually never looking up. He had reached a point where he was explaining why the CIA wanted exemption from the Freedom of Information Act. Just as he was assuring his audience, "I have no desire to spy on Americans at home," protesters jumped up and started reciting Lewis Carroll's "Jabberwocky." Other students began shouting down the protesters. Amid the chaos, Casey at last looked up, beaming, as though grateful for the excitement. The battle of the catcalls went on for several minutes. When it quieted down, he thanked the protesters for providing the "entertainment."

After the speech, he took questions from the audience. An earnest student, hair long but neat, and wearing a coat and tie, rose and said: "President Reagan is speaking of cutting back on federally funded programs to aid education—for example, tuition tax credit and student loans for college students. I feel that programs such as these are far more valuable to the institution of democracy than the internal workings of the CIA within the United States. What do you say to that?"

Casey smiled and said, "I agree."

He was monitoring intelligence out of Central America closely. Since March, one thing looked good. There had been no recent evidence that the Sandinistas were continuing to infiltrate arms into El Salvador. The stoppage appeared to be the result of two factors: the Sandinistas were not eager for a total break in relations with the United States, and the Reagan administration was still dangling $75 million in aid that depended on Nicaragua's good behavior. The arms dry-up had lasted through May. But the Reagan administration choked on the thought of eventually sending millions of American dollars to a country that looked like a junior Cuba, the spitting image of a nation that had fooled liberals twenty-two years before, until Fidel Castro emerged in full Marxist feather. The administration eventually withdrew the aid offer, and the arms from Nicaragua to El Salvador began to flow again in June.

Resistance to the Sandinistas had begun almost the day the new regime took over Nicaragua. Colonel Enrique Bermúdez's saga was typical. Bermúdez was a tough guy, a former officer in the Somoza regime's National Guard. Life under Somoza had been good to Enrique Bermúdez; for one thing, it had given him a choice post as Nicaragua's military attaché in Washington. And then one day, it was all over. The National Guard was no longer feared; it was hunted. Men like Bermúdez fled into the wilds of bordering Honduras and caught their breath. Before the year was out, they had regrouped and were already beginning to strike back—just hit-and-run raids on farms along Nicaragua's northern border in the beginning, but it was the start of a counterinsurgency.

Soon after taking over his new job, Dewey Clarridge had something encouraging to report to Casey: these anti-Sandinista elements were receiving outside support—thus the United States could buy into an existing operation. The support chain stretched the full length of the continent, from Buenos Aires to Nicaragua. The rightist junta in Argentina, headed by Lieutenant General Leopoldo Galtieri, had learned that the Montonero guerrillas fighting their regime were operating out of a sympathetic Nicaragua. The Galtieri regime wanted a counterforce to the Montonero insurgents. Thus, the Argentines had reached some 3,475 miles to support a force of about a thousand men along the Nicaragua-Honduras border, anti-Sandinistas like Enrique Bermúdez. Casey shared Clarridge's information with his deputy, Bobby Ray Inman. "Bill was absolutely delighted," Inman recalled. "He knew that the Argentines' hope was to unseat the Sandinistas. And that was farther than the U.S. Congress was ready to let us go."

Casey put a proposal to Galtieri through his station chief in Buenos Aires: how would he feel about the U.S. relieving him of this far-flung burden? Galtieri, of course, was interested—a far more powerful country supporting the selfsame objective, and at no cost to Argentina. The operation would have to be covert, Casey knew. The American people, the Congress, even elements in the Reagan administration would balk at open U.S. involvement in Nicaragua. Casey thought he could probably sell this takeover of an Argentine military operation as stronger interdiction medicine, as a surer way of stopping the Sandinistas from aiding the Salvadoran rebels. "Interdiction" had the right, reasonable, limited ring.

Casey and Haig were able to trade punches like friends who could put on the gloves without getting mad—a feeling Haig shared with few others in the administration. At one of their breakfasts early in November, Casey laid out the elements of a finding of necessity he expected to put before the President. Haig repeated his belief that this approach was wrongheaded and shortsighted. "If I disagreed with Bill about anything, it was on when and how to employ covert operations," Haig later observed. "Covert operations can be ancillary to a foreign policy, but they can't be the policy. That's a cheap shot. A covert action in Central America allowed the White House people to go to bed at night saying we did something, something tough, against those terrible Marxists. And it allowed them to wake up in the morning still beloved by the American people because they hadn't dragged our boys into a war."

Casey understood this reasoning as well as Haig. But he was ready to work within the only White House he had. Furthermore, any overt U.S. involvement in the internal affairs of a Latin American government was the kiss of death. Virtually every other government south of the Rio Grande, even those that secretly applauded the move, would be compelled by domestic politics to condemn gringo intervention. Gunboat diplomacy, Yankee-dollah diplomacy, had a long and resented history in that part of the world.

Early in December, Casey rode a little-used elevator to the fourth floor of the Capitol to perform his least agreeable duty: informing the oversight committees of a covert operation. The trips to Capitol Hill had become particularly galling to Casey with the investigation of his fitness still dragging on. Even when he was testifying strictly on CIA matters, the odor of suspicion clung to him.

Sometimes the line between a covert action, which Casey was now reporting, and intelligence activities blurred. The law defined covert as "any clandestine operation or activity designed to influence foreign governments, organizations, persons, or events in support of U.S. foreign policy." As a longtime covert operator explained the distinction: "If I recruit a guy to get the Soviet order of battle in Europe, that's intelligence. If I recruit him to vote a certain way in the U.N., that's covert." The finding Casey was bringing to the Hill this day had been signed by the President on December 1. It represented the administration's second expression of the Reagan Doctrine, though the term was still to be coined, arming an anticommunist force in a Third World country. As the finding had finally been worded, the CIA was to build up, equip, and train a Nicaraguan opposition that was supposed to be both anti-Sandinista and anti-Somocista. The Somocista angle was a sop to congressional liberals and essentially meaningless, since the rebels in the Honduran wilds were heavily drawn from Somoza's old National Guard.

At the heart of the finding was $20 million to build a five-hundred-man guerrilla force. Casey thought it politic initially to play down the fact that the Argentines were bequeathing a force closer to one thousand men. The guerrillas were to operate out of hidden sanctuaries in Honduras, carrying out paramilitary operations "against Cuban presence and Cuba-Sandinista support infrastructure" and to interdict the flow of arms into El Salvador—in short, squeeze the Nicaraguan regime at home and block its machinations abroad. The finding had another feature: it was open-ended. More money could be pumped in; more troops could be added.

Casey was briefing the SSCI first and later the House committee. He took his place before the horseshoe in the secure hearing room. As the committee's press officer, Spencer Davis, remembered that day, "Casey laid out the evidence the Agency had that arms and aid were flowing to the Salvadoran insurgency. He produced intelligence to show Castro's reach into the region. He told the members that a five-man junta in Havana was masterminding the whole El Salvador war. He told us about the group's headquarters in Managua—even gave us the street address. I remember, it was a busy day in the

Senate, and a lot of other things were going on. Senators kept drifting in and out. Casey's voice was less intelligible than usual. The stenotypists were tearing their hair out trying to decipher him. I'm not sure the committee understood exactly what he was up to."

But he ran into no particular resistance. Even the Democratic vicechairman, Pat Moynihan, was favorably disposed. Asked later what he thought of the finding, Moynihan replied, "It was obvious the Sandinistas, in the best Leninist fashion, had betrayed their revolution, a revolution that outsiders, not the least being the United States, had helped them to win."

But in the more rambunctious and Democrat-controlled House intelligence committee, HPSCI, Casey ran into heavy flak. From the moment he began describing American aid, American advisers, American training, a small American-supported force, supposedly limited objectives, some congressmen smelled Vietnam. They raked him with questions: Won't the fighting escalate? What if the Sandinistas chase these guerrillas into Honduras—won't that trigger a wider war? And suppose the CIA's hand is exposed—what will that look like to the rest of Latin America? And what right does the United States have to topple a legitimate government anyway, just because we don't like it?

Nobody was talking about overthrowing anybody, Casey explained impatiently. This was a small, contained attempt to interdict weapons and to put just enough pressure on the Sandinistas to keep them from delivering their revolution wholly to communism. Throughout the hearing, he kept referring to Nica-wa-wa. One Democratic committee member whispered to a colleague, "Let's say we don't approve plans to overthrow the government of any country that Casey can't pronounce."

Casey gathered up his papers and prepared to leave. He had done his part under the law. They did not have to like what he said, just hear it. It was all still a bit vague, but the impression left on Capitol Hill was that a five-hundred-man commando strike force would be making hit-and-run raids across the border into Nicaragua, torching an ammo dump, seizing an arms cache, blowing up a bridge, cutting the supply lines into El Salvador.

Dewey Clarridge had swung into action as soon as the finding had been signed. He took a villa in the shabby Honduran capital of Tegucigalpa. He met with the ragtag anti-Sandinista forces, among them the old Somocista colonel, Enrique Bermúdez. Bermúdez had been waging his lonely struggle for two years. When he heard the news of the Reagan administration's support, "I could hear the footsteps of a giant," he said. And quickly, through Clarridge's energetic command, arms began to arrive.

The resistance movement that Bermúdez headed was formally called the FDN, the Spanish initials for the Nicaraguan Democratic Force. They stood against the Sandinista revolution in Nicaragua; they were *contrarevolucionarios*. Thus were the contras born.

The covert operation was to be coordinated among several national security elements of the Reagan administration—State, Defense, the NSC, and the CIA. The coordinating instrument was a Restricted Interagency Group, or RIG. Clarridge quickly found a soulmate on the RIG, the NSC's representative, Lieutenant Colonel Oliver L. North, who had come to Casey's favorable attention during the AWACS deal.

Just prior to Casey's appearance on Capitol Hill, Robert Ruhl Simmons, age thirty-eight, replaced Jack Blake as staff director of the SSCI. Simmons, lean, bespectacled, and pale, looked like a Bible youth fellowship leader. But he had been schooled in a harsher world—combat in Vietnam and ten years at the CIA on the covert side—before coming to work on the Hill. He looked upon himself as a Stansfield Turner casualty. "I quit the CIA," he said, "because of the way Turner was running the place. I'd served overseas, risking myself and my family in some rough spots, and was damn poorly rewarded for it. In the Turner era, every station chief was covering his own ass rather than doing the job. And people outside treated us like scum, like pariahs. I'd had it. So I quit."

Goldwater's first order to Simmons was, "I want this damned Casey investigation buttoned up. It's gone on too long." One hundred and ten people had been questioned. Tens of thousands of pages of testimony had piled up. Simmons pushed the investigation to a conclusion and produced a final report in draft form that ran over eighty pages. Too long, Goldwater said; all the nit-picking detail detracted from the seriousness of a five-month investigation. He told Simmons to boil it down to essentials.

The senators subsequently met in secure room 407 to consider a shorter version. This draft described Casey as "fit" to hold the job. But the final language that Senator Moynihan again insisted on read: "The committee reaffirms its July 29, 1981, statement that no basis has been found for concluding that Mr. Casey is unfit to hold the office of Director of Central Intelligence." The committee also cleared Casey of playing politics with the CIA in appointing Max Hugel as DDO. As for the triggering event, the Multiponics suit, the committee concluded that Casey "had no active role in the preparation or legal review of the offering circular. . . . If there was any liability it was civil rather than moral."

As for the omissions on government forms, all the dropped clients, undisclosed stock holdings, unreported lawsuits—Rob Simmons plucked a phrase from his Army experience: the committee's inquiry "showed that Mr. Casey was at minimum inattentive to detail."

In the course of the investigation, Casey had been revealed as a driver who pushed right up to the speed limit but did not exceed it. He took the curves with two wheels hanging over the edge but had managed, so far, not to plunge over. "I was as familiar with the evidence as anybody on the investigation," Simmons recalled. "Casey's ventures may have been elaborate tax dodges. But we found nothing illegal. He wasn't screwing widows or orphans. He was taking advantage of the law. I saw nothing to prove that he was corrupt or dishonest." Casey was not Caesar's wife; but then, neither was he Caligula.

In Simmons's view, Casey's biggest problem on the Hill was the man's unconcealed contempt for his overseers. "The committee kept digging," Simmons observed, "because Casey kept telling them to go fuck themselves." This view was echoed by Senator Joe Biden when the vote was taken; he concluded that, yes, "Mr. Casey has been an effective director of Central Intelligence. He has exercised decisive, imaginative leadership at the CIA's helm. . . . Mr. Casey is eminently fit to serve as director of Central Intelligence. But he has displayed a consistent pattern of omissions, misstatements, and contradictions in his dealings with this and other committees of Congress. As a consequence, Mr. Casey has lost my confidence. . . ."

Even Republicans on the committee had to swallow hard to get Casey down. David Durenberger of Minnesota, a big, assertive maverick, had gone along with what he called "an oblique endorsement." "We didn't want to kick Casey out," Durenberger said later, "because of what we had already learned about Ronald Reagan—here was a President who obviously needed all the help he could get. And as Republicans, we didn't want to saddle him with a setback."

The report was released on December 2. The headlines were predictably dreadful (the *New York Times*: FINAL REPORT FINDS CASEY INATTENTIVE BUT NOT UNFIT; the *Baltimore Sun*: CASEY FOUND NOT UNFIT TO RUN CIA; the *Christian Science Monitor*: CASEY NOT UNFIT SENATE PANEL SAYS). Herblock's cartoon in the *Washington Post* showed a potbellied Casey with a paper bag over his head that read "Not Unfit to Serve."

Casey had been given a chance to see the final report before it was issued—and he hated it. He moved quickly to repair any damage in the one place where he thought it might hurt him. He dictated a letter to his secretary, Betty Murphy. It began: "After spending a half a million dollars to have three lawyers and twelve staff members talk with over a hundred of my former clients and business associates, the report found nothing." When Casey finished, he told Murphy, "Mark it no distribution, no copies, eyes only. And I want it delivered to the President by hand."

On December 19, Casey took Inman with him to the White House for a key meeting with the NSPG in the conference room across from the Oval Office. As usual, Casey was playing everything close to the vest. He appeared to be going into the meeting empty-handed. And, as usual, even his deputy was not entirely sure what he was up to. David Stockman, now the director of the Office of Management and Budget, not ordinarily included in national security deliberations, was present. Inman describes what happened next: "Bill pulled a bunch of paper out of his breast pocket and started to outline a massive overhaul and rebuilding of American intelligence over the next decade from scribbled longhand notes. He was so laborious, so slow, so lacking in any drama. The President sat there with that pleasant expression fixed on his face. Deaver and Baker were snickering and passing notes back and forth. Bill seemed oblivious of it all and just kept plodding ahead. Weinberger and Haig were squirming.

"When Bill finished, Defense and State supported him. But the NSC people thought the time might not be right. Stockman had serious fiscal reservations. And then the President looked around the table, smiled, and said, 'I don't see how we can afford not to do it.' Bill had quite simply outflanked the budget process by winning the one vote he needed. And that's how the massive rebuilding program of American intelligence for the next ten years was born. I'd had my problems with Casey. But I give him full credit for this."

Inman's magnanimity was purchased at a high price in self-discipline. Life under Casey had become a trial. The sore point was the Hill, where Inman was still the teacher's pet and Casey the class bully. Whenever Casey was in hot water, committee members, notably Barry Goldwater, shook their heads ruefully: if only they'd given us Bobby Ray. "It was pretty hard for Bill to take," John Bross remarked. "That rough exterior concealed a sensitive guy. Bill resented playing the heavy to Inman's stainless hero." It was the old stag against the young buck; the old actor nervous over a gifted understudy in the wings; the veteran pitcher worried about the great rookie righthander coming up.

Bob Gates began to feel like the mediator between two Cold War powers. "Casey had a way of passing instructions to Inman that were kind of offensive," Gates observed. "And Inman had a way of responding that wasn't quite tactful. I'd try to smooth the communication in both directions, so that neither guy went through the ceiling."

Inman noticed that every time Casey got into trouble, a certain columnist started knocking *him*. The previous August, Inman was reading the *New York Times* op-ed page and found himself prominently and unflatteringly mentioned in Bill Safire's column. Safire had written a clever spoof in which a Russian agent, working under cover as an hors d'oeuvre specialist at a Washington catering company, is reporting back to the KGB on the meaning of Casey's problems with the intelligence committees. Safire used the satire to make the point that the persecution of Casey was "a plot by CIA bureaucracy using liberal media and befuddled Republican Senators to throw out hard-liners appointed by Reagan." Safire described a dovish clique "in the CIA that had manipulated Barry Goldwater to support Inman for DCI." Safire then zinged Inman directly, saying that while running the National Security Agency he had withheld tapes that could have embarrassed then–Secretary of State Henry Kissinger. The send-up closed with Soviet agent/caterer Boris Grishinurn warning Comrade Andropov back in Dzerzhinsky Square to "keep an eye on your own Number Two."

Inman was outraged—but at Safire, not at Casey. At this point, he had no reason to think that Casey had a hand in Safire's piece. Barely a week before, Inman had gone to bat for Casey on "Nightline," and Casey had been so much warmer afterward.

Which was why a Safire column only four days after the Boris Grishinurn piece was all the more mystifying and enraging to Inman. In it Safire described Inman as "the Admiral, who startled his aides by blabbing about sources and methods on late night TV"—a mortal sin in the intelligence trade. Inman began to wonder how spontaneous Safire's antipathy might be.

Safire and Inman had not gotten along well—not since, according to Safire, Inman had phoned and accused him of blowing sources and methods in an earlier column involving President Carter's brother Billy and the Libyans. Safire had ended that conversation by saying to Inman, "Tell me, how does a U.S. Navy admiral, the director of the National Security Agency, come off having a name like Bobby anyway?"

Late in December, Inman read in Safire's column, "If the Deputy CIA Director, Bobby Inman, had been focused on looming events in Poland instead of planting a phony story with reporters that Israel was publicizing the Libyan assassination teams in order to set up an air strike at the Libyan nuclear reactor, perhaps the Administration would not have been caught with its advisers dispersed and its leader reduced to 'warning' the Russians not to move in."

A few days after this column appeared, Inman was at a reception where he was approached by the Washington bureau chief of a major newspaper. "You'd better watch your hat and ass," the reporter warned him. "What do you mean?" Inman asked. "You don't think that column was accidental, do you?" the reporter said. "Casey and Safire are thick as thieves. Safire worked in Casey's congressional campaign. Don't you see the connection? Every time anybody puts the knock on Casey, Safire goes after you. If you don't see that, you're not as sharp as I thought you were, Admiral."

Back at Langley, Inman confronted Casey in his office. Was he feeding Safire? Inman demanded.

"Absolutely not," Casey insisted. "I don't know Safire that well. I run across him on rare occasions. I've seen him at a dinner party or two. But there's no running dialogue between me and Safire. You're letting people stir this up. Let me tell you something. In this business, you better have a thick skin."

Inman was mildly placated.

Then, soon afterward, he was working late in his office and received a call from a reporter from the *New York Times*. "He was trying to reach Casey," Inman remembered of the call. "And he wanted me to verify a number he said that Safire always used. It was Casey's unlisted home phone."

That was it for Inman. He hung up and tried to choke back his anger. As he later described his feelings, "I'd worked for people before where our personalities weren't compatible. But this was the first time I found myself working for somebody I didn't think I could trust. I was no longer comfortable that this man was being honest with me." Inman had told the President that his limit was eighteen months, two years at the most. Now he decided: eighteen months—and he was starting the countdown.

The first year had been a shakedown cruise for Casey, and a rough one. He had come close to running aground during the ethics probe. At the same time, he had accomplished all that he wanted. The CIA was coming out of its defensive coil and was going to be rebuilt with fresh millions. He was a full partner in the Reagan foreign policy apparatus. Indeed, in Afghanistan and Central America, he was defining the administration's foreign policy. He wielded influence that no other DCI, even Allen Dulles, had ever known. Bill Donovan had been his hero. It was pleasant to think he was filling his shoes.

19.

Pushing the Product

O ne day, Casey dropped in on a reception for CIA summer interns in the executive dining room. Among the interns was a tall, stunning blonde who had attracted a circle of senior officers. She was a law school student, she told them, spending her internship in the Agency's library. "I'm preparing an anthology of the trust," the young woman said—which was greeted by blank, uncomprehending stares.

At that moment, Casey found his way to the group. The intern was introduced to him, and he too asked, "What are you doing for us?" She repeated that she was working on the trust. Casey's eyes brightened. "This young lady," he said, "may be doing the most important piece of work in this building." His reaction, too, was greeted by vacant expressions. "The trust," he repeated. "Don't you guys know about it? The Moscow Municipal Trust Association. It's what Dzerzhinsky started after the revolution to trap the opposition." He went on to explain the genius of the trust, how it was secretly run by the Cheka, forerunner of the KGB. Anti-Bolshevik movements operating from England, France, and the United States funneled money into the trust, thinking they were supporting a resistance movement, when all they were actually doing was revealing the regime's enemies, who were then arrested and shot. "You fellas should know these things. That's how the opposition works," Casey said, and walked off.

From the moment he was hired, long years ago, by the Research Institute of America, Casey had been obsessed with information—getting it, digesting it, and predicting from it. He liked a particular phrase and wove it into his CIA speeches: "scouting the future." That was the business they were in. But he still was not satisfied with the scouting. Covert operations might snatch the headlines and consume the attention of the oversight committees, because, mismanaged or ill conceived, they could blow up in America's face. But they represented a fraction of what the Agency did.

After his rough grilling before the House intelligence committee on the Central American finding, Casey had stormed back to his office, livid, shouting, "They don't have any idea what the hell we do out here! I've got a bunch of geologists down in Central America right now studying the region's energy potential, the geothermal sources, the shale sources. I've got economists looking at the potential market and pricing. They don't want to hear about that. All they want to hear is 'covert, covert, covert,' like a stuck whistle!" He liked to point out to visitors that the CIA probably had the heaviest concentration of Ph.D.s per acre in the world, over five hundred of them at Langley alone. He had the phrase down pat: "Sixty separate disciplines, from acoustics to zoology."

Philip Taubman, a reporter for the *New York Times*, caught the inner tensions of the Agency accurately when he wrote, "The intelligence division, filled with scholars and researchers, looks at covert operations the same way a college faculty views varsity football teams: with a mixture of suspicion, condescension, and contempt." The covert operators returned the compliment.

John McMahon had been running the intelligence directorate since the spring of 1981. Casey pushed hard. "I want to see more estimates," he told McMahon. "We've got to get our product on the table at the White House and at the NSC and the Pentagon. That way we force the policymakers to push it aside if they don't like it. But at least they can't ignore us." And then with a pounding fist that made the phone on the desk jump, he shouted, "We're gonna be in the game when it matters! Intelligence a day late isn't worth a damn!"

He particularly wanted better HUMINT, human intelligence. In Iran, under the Shah, the United States had placed highly sophisticated telemetry and monitoring devices along the northern border to spy on the Soviet Union. But the Agency was taking little independent intelligence out of Iran itself. A National Intelligence Estimate on Iran, put out in 1978, predicted that the Shah would stay in power for another ten years at least, and if contested, he would apply whatever force was necessary to hold on to his throne. The man was the staunchest of America's friends, and he was going to be in the saddle for the foreseeable future. What more needed to be known? To Casey, that kind of blindness explained the failure of his predecessor, Stansfield Turner: trust the hardware, skimp on people. Two months after the Iran estimate had come out, the Shah folded his tent like a bedouin. Casey liked to quote Frederick the Great—the words ought to be chiseled in stone above the door to the intelligence directorate, he said—"It is pardonable to be defeated, but never to be surprised."

He was no knee-jerk worshiper of "facts." His intellectual sophistication and sense of humor saved him. The Soviet Union's Leonid Brezhnev had long been seriously ill, and handicapping his successor became a major preoccupation of the Agency's Soviet Union desk. On one day the analysts would bring Casey photographs showing the KGB chief, Yuri Vladimirovich Andropov, standing next to Brezhnev at the May Day celebration; that proved, obviously, that Andropov was the heir apparent. "I like that," Casey observed. "An intelligence chief may actually have a future." On a later occasion, the house Kremlinologists informed him that Andropov was no longer the favorite. Why? Casey wanted to know. They produced a photograph of another ceremony, with the KGB chief standing at the end of the line. Casey looked at them balefully over the top of his glasses. "Did it ever occur to you guys that maybe he got stuck in traffic?"

He was still gambling on outsiders, tossing them into the Agency's settled bureaucracies like sticks of dynamite. The very day that Max Hugel resigned, he had offered another outsider a key job. Herbert Meyer was a thirty-five-year-old associate editor at *Fortune* magazine who had written a book, *The War Against Progress*, a rebuttal of the limits-of-growth school of economics in vogue in the seventies. Thirty-six publishers had rejected Meyer's book, and so he had published it himself. After the 1980 election, Meyer got an out-of-the-blue call from Casey. They subsequently met for lunch in New York and hit it off immediately. Meyer lived up to the expectations of his book. He was an economic conservative and, to Casey's added delight, a Soviet specialist at *Fortune*.

He later brought Meyer to Langley as his special assistant—something of a staging area until he decided where to put people. Casey told Meyer, "There's no strategic thinking going on at State. The NSC is a bunch of firemen running around putting out brush fires. We're the ones who are going to fill the vacuum. We're going to do the global thinking." He let Meyer run a roving patrol through the analytical side of the Agency. Meyer had a razor-edged intellect and a matching tongue. In appearance he was slight, with reddish hair and a pale, narrow, sharp-featured face. He was arrogant, often abrasive—not a soothing figure. Meyer was soon snapping at the ankles of the careerists like a terrier, which was exactly what Casey wanted. Shake 'em up. Pester 'em.

After he had had time to look over his new colleagues, Meyer reported back to Casey. He later described what he found: "You bring these people into intelligence in their twenties. By any definition, you're not getting the best—the best go into business or to the universities. The number-one guy in Soviet studies is teaching at some place like Harvard. If he's a financial whiz, he's gone to Citicorp. Then you put these guys behind a chain-link fence out here in the Virginia countryside. When I worked at *Fortune,* I got out every day, went to lunch, bought a cigar, a pair of shoelaces. I talked to people. But these guys never leave the reservation. Overseas they're inside a different kind of a cocoon—they're sealed off by their liaison with foreign intelligence services. By the time they're in their forties, they haven't been connected to the planet Earth for twenty years. Their contemporaries have moved up in banking, the law, journalism, but they've lost touch with them. They have experts come out here for conferences who I wouldn't have bothered with for the last ten years when I was at *Fortune*—people who have nothing new to say.

"And the rule at the CIA when you go abroad is 'Don't talk to strangers.' I thought at first it was a joke. Some intelligence you can only get in a dark alley at night. But most of it you get over a white tablecloth. These guys have built a system that shuts them off from any intelligence except what you can steal. These people needed to be reconnected to reality."

If laymen wondered exactly what it was that an American spy did, Meyer had the answer: "The main function of the station chief overseas is not so much finding out what's going on in the host country. It's recruiting Soviet and Eastern-bloc agents. That's why we're always being blindsided. If you think these people are in Ouagadougou to find out what the Ougadougans are up to, you're completely wrong. They're trying to recruit the second secretary of the Soviet embassy. That's how station chiefs are rewarded and promoted—like recruiting sergeants, not on their brilliant grasp of the local political scene."

Meyer was acerbic, prickly, impatient, contemptuous. Casey liked him very much. After a few months, he gave this fire starter a key post in the analytical apparatus. He appointed Meyer vice-chairman of the National Intelligence Council. The NIC was formed of national intelligence officers, or NIOs, responsible for preparing national intelligence estimates (NIEs) by area and subject.

Meyer found his NIC colleagues unhurried, complacent, serene. "They had a phrase that drove me crazy," he recalled. "You'd raise a hypothesis and they'd answer, 'We have no evidence of that.' What do you mean, you have no evidence? Is there no evidence, or didn't you ask the right questions to get the evidence? Where did you look? 'We have no evidence' can mean you never looked at all, never asked."

To Meyer, the analysts' have-no-evidence attitude was maddeningly present in the approach to the assassination attempt on Pope John Paul II.

Back in March, Casey had received a letter from Richard Nixon. The ex-President urged him to push aside whatever else he was doing and read an article, as Nixon put it, "which appeared, to my surprise, in the *New York Times Magazine*" on March 1. "I do not know the author, Claire Sterling, but according to the article, she has written a book on terrorism which reflects two years of investigative reporting all over the world. She reaches exactly the opposite conclusion which was reported widely in the press as being the view of 'some U.S. intelligence experts, including the CIA,' to the effect that there was no hard evidence to back up Al Haig's statement that the Soviet Union was responsible directly and indirectly for a great part of international terrorism."

Not long afterward, on May 13, Mehmet Ali Agca fired a gun into the stomach of the Pope in Saint Peter's Square: a Polish Pope shot by a Turk with ties to Bulgaria, a Communist-bloc country under Soviet domination. Casey had gone along with the Lincoln Gordon NIE partially exonerating the Soviets of terrorism; but this time, there was little doubt in his mind as to who was behind the man who pulled the trigger. He wanted his analytical people to dig down to the bottom of the assassination attempt against the Pope. He pushed them mercilessly, demanding almost daily to see the latest evidence. But the analysts moved with deliberate speed, refusing to report a smoking gun until they found one.

Claire Sterling, whose ideas had been expanded in her book *The Terror Network*, had definite ideas about who was behind the assassination attempt on the Pope. The number-three man at the Agency's Rome station was present at a cocktail party where Sterling was elaborating her theory of Soviet complicity, and told her that there was no evidence to back up what she was saying. According to one witness, "That pissed her off. She climbed all over the guy."

Casey's Long Island neighbor U.S. Senator Alphonse D'Amato also visited the Rome station and bounced some of the Sterling assassination theories off the staff. The station chief told D'Amato, "Senator, I don't have a thing to substantiate those allegations." D'Amato wrote to Casey and, in the words of a CIA officer privy to the correspondence, "in effect . . . told Bill, 'Your station chief is a horse's ass. He wouldn't talk. He wouldn't share his information with me. He stonewalled me.' " Casey was not happy.

Herb Meyer asked Casey if he would like to meet Claire Sterling. Indeed he would; and so Meyer set up an appointment. According to John McMahon, who was present at the meeting, "Claire Sterling was a tough lady. She jumped all over Bill. She said, 'Your people aren't

pursuing this thing because half of them are leftist sympathizers.' "
After she was gone, Casey muttered, "God damn it. I've got a U.S.
senator impugning my station chief in Rome. I've got this woman
who's written a pretty persuasive book faulting us. And you guys say
you don't have any evidence. You're too goddamn cautious. Just because nobody heard a tree fall in the forest doesn't mean it didn't
fall."

Casey reminded the analysts of the experience of his predecessor
John McCone during the 1962 Cuban missile crisis. The intelligence
side had done an estimate predicting that the Soviet Union would
not place missiles in Cuba because it was too risky. McCone ordered
a U-2 flight over the island. No evidence of any missiles was found.
McCone ordered another flight; still nothing was found. Send another
one, McCone ordered. And, finally, photos revealed that Soviet missile
sites were indeed under construction. After the crisis, President Kennedy was supposed to have asked McCone how he knew to keep on
pressing, to which McCone reportedly replied, "If I were Khrushchev,
I'd have put them there."

"Casey kept pushing us to the limit" on the shooting of the Pope,
McMahon recalled. "He put different teams on the same job—analysts, super-analysts, insiders, outsiders. We had people who did nothing but sift through every scrap of evidence." Still Casey kept driving.
"I want more facts. Give me more facts."

Herb Meyer took up the quest like a bloodhound. The web of Soviet
complicity in terrorism was all there in Claire Sterling's book. What
did the Agency analysts have to say about her charges? "They'd tell
me. 'We don't have any evidence,' " Meyer remembered. " 'We don't
have any evidence' is a non sequitur. Bill and I would go ballistic
when they'd tell us that. Did they expect it to turn up in the mailbox?
I insisted that they go over Claire's book page by page, line by line—
is what she says true or isn't it?"

The assassination inquiry caught Casey in a bind. The case against
the Soviets made sense in theory. The Bulgarians were closely implicated in the comings and goings of the would-be assassin; and the
Bulgarians were, some would say, proxies of the Soviet Union. The
likely motive was the Soviets' belief that the Pope was responsible
for the emergence of Solidarity in Poland. This virus could spread
throughout the bloc to the USSR itself. In pre-Gorbachev Russia, that
made the Pope a dangerous man. Casey was pressing hard to convict
the Soviets. But if he pressed too hard, he risked being accused of the
cardinal sin of analysis: politicizing evidence to fit a conclusion.

The analysts continued raking over the intelligence obtainable from the Italian police investigations, from Turkey, and from every available source. One team did nothing but go through Sterling's *Terror Network*. "Our analysis showed that what she claimed often didn't stand up," John McMahon said. "It just was not true." Indeed, some of what Sterling had reported as evidence of Soviet-sponsored terrorism appeared to be "blow-back," the CIA expression for disinformation it had planted abroad itself.

Casey's gadfly was outraged. "The Agency review of Sterling's book was the filthiest, smarmiest piece of writing I ever saw in my life," Meyer later remarked. "They tried to smear Sterling, her credentials, her credibility—everything but her facts."

In the end, Casey had a final report put together and dutifully took it to the White House. It was not the conclusion he wanted, certainly not the one Ronald Reagan expected. But cooking the books negated the whole point of intelligence. He delivered his Agency's cold, professional verdict: "insufficient evidence." But he could not resist adding, "Of course, Mr. President, you and I know better."

At six a.m. on February 14, Casey's nephew, Larry, called to tell him that George Casey had died during the night. It had not been an easy relationship, with Bill incapable of abandoning the role of all-knowing big brother and too wrapped up in his pursuits to offer George much undivided friendship. And for George, there was the dispiriting prospect of never being able to keep up with this human-dynamo brother.

George was always pleased on the rare occasions when Bill included him in his lunches in the Rogers and Wells dining room. On one occasion, with several of Casey's powerful friends around the table, Bill launched into a proud recital of George's feats on the gridiron at Hofstra College. It was all very nice, but otherwise Bill seemed to pay little attention to George or to what he had to say. George was now a man in his late fifties, and to have Bill reach back more than forty years to praise him made him feel that he had not done much since. Still, beneath the poor communication, the pulls and stresses, the mutual love between the brothers remained.

Casey flew up to New York, and at the funeral home Larry Casey told him of an eerily appropriate last day in his father's life. Larry had picked up the ailing George that afternoon and had taken him on a genealogical tour: first to a public library, where they looked up a yellowed newspaper carrying George Casey's birth announcement; then to the house in Bellmore on the south shore of Queens, where the three Casey children had been raised; and finally to the burial plot of his grandfather and namesake, George Casey, the Queens fire chief. Early the next morning, George died.

Casey was not one to parade his emotions. At the end of his nephew's account, he turned to another mourner and said, "Remind me never to ask Larry to take me on a tour."

He was not much for looking back anyway; and though he occasionally played the genial Irish wit, Casey remained unsentimental about his roots. On another occasion, Larry Casey had gone to Ireland to trace the family origins. In the town of Daingean in County Offaly, he tracked down a small, sprightly Irishman who wore a fishing cap indoors and out. Jimmy Morin was his name, and when Larry explained to Morin that he was distantly related to William J. Casey, an astonished Morin asked, "Would you be meanin' the spy?" The very same, Larry Casey told him. Morin shook his head and said with a sly grin, "Do you have to tell me that, with me goin' to mass in the mornin'?"

When Larry came home from Ireland, he told the story to Uncle Bill. "Have they got any money?" Casey asked. No, Larry said. Casey stroked his chin. "Well, we'll be hearing from them."

Casey's naked disregard for the Congress would not matter except for the legislation he needed from it. He went before the Senate Subcommittee on the Constitution to get the CIA exempted from the disclosure requirements of the Freedom of Information Act, and the line of question and response suggests the Casey style and his problems:

CASEY: Our agent network is placed in jeopardy. Good agents decide they cannot entrust their careers, their lives, their reputations to work for us because they just don't have confidence that we can keep secrets.

SENATOR ORRIN HATCH: You have pinpointed some agents who have quit for that reason?

CASEY: Yes.

HATCH: How many do you have, Mr. Director?

CASEY: I don't know. We certainly don't have them all. You quit because of a variety of reasons, but we can establish that many people have signed off because they feel that everything we do—

SENATOR DENNIS DECONCINI: Can you tell us how many? Six? A dozen? Three dozen?

CASEY: I really can't tell you. I would be guessing.

DECONCINI: But you know firsthand, having talked to some?

CASEY: No, no. I get this as hearsay in the organization.

HATCH: But you are saying some of your administrative people have said that a number of agents have quit for this reason? You are definitely saying that?

CASEY: Oh, sure. Look, we have it every day.

DECONCINI: You say every day?

SENATOR PATRICK LEAHY: That is thirty a month.

DECONCINI: Thirty a month?

CASEY: It is a recurring situation. In the last couple of months we have had two instances where very productive agents in very important countries have asked to be taken out on the basis that they felt insecure.

LEAHY: Because of the Freedom of Information Act?

CASEY: Well, I can't say that. I can't say FOIA. The general atmosphere of insecurity and lack of confidence in the ability to keep secrets.

Later, DeConcini remarked, "I just don't have a lot of confidence in Casey. He's not the right man for the job. I thought he should resign back when he was in hot water last year."

To Casey, the Freedom of Information Act was democracy turned on its head. As he told the House oversight committee, "The Iranian regime, the same government that held our people hostage, has filed an FOIA request for all information in the CIA on the late Shah. This is a perfectly legal request. And we have to comply with it. This is crazy." In the end, he did win a partial exemption of the Agency from the FOIA, on the merits of his case, certainly not because he had charmed his overseers.

A 130-page book of guidelines governed covert operations. At a meeting with the DO, Casey held up the book and said, "Here's the trouble. We're too timid. The attitude is 'Don't stick your neck out. Play it safe.' This kind of crap is smothering us. You practically have to take a lawyer with you on a mission. I'm throwing this thing out." Covert actions were the foreign policy equivalent of venture capitalism— you *had* to take risks. He replaced the 130 pages with a single memorandum that said, in effect, "In conducting a covert operation, use your common sense."

Still, he had to deal with the oversight committees. And what he was doing covertly in Nicaragua made many members uneasy. Dave Durenberger was the only member of the SSCI with personal experience in that part of the world. Before entering politics he had been an executive with a Saint Paul, Minnesota, company that sold paint and plastics in Central America. Durenberger was astonished by the attention that the administration expended on these countries. Casey had said, "The stakes in Central America are huge and historic." But as Durenberger saw it, "it was inconceivable that the administration could think that the fate of the West hinged on places like El Salvador or Honduras. I'd try to explain, there isn't even as much at stake there as in Vietnam. Because there's no North Vietnam—there isn't even a Ho Chi Minh. There's mostly bananas."

Pat Moynihan, an original supporter, was growing uneasy. He did see a parallel to Vietnam. "It looked to me," he later remarked, "as though the CIA had picked up a bunch of ex-Somocistas who slipped over the border to Honduras and were being trained by the Argentine junta to restore Somoza. Casey had us putting our bet on Dien Bien Phu. If you do that, maybe you don't belong in this business."

In February of 1982, the oversight committees again called the DCI to the Hill; they wanted to know exactly what was going on in Central America. Casey brought with him his flamboyant Latin American chief, Dewey Clarridge. All went reasonably well until a member of HPSCI asked Clarridge the size of this anti-Sandinista force. Clarridge's answer brought the members up sharp. Eleven hundred men, he said. Casey had talked originally about five hundred.

Honduras lay between Nicaragua and El Salvador. One could make a logical case for covert operations in Honduras to stop the flow of arms from Nicaragua to El Salvador. But now, Clarridge and his team—the staff in Tegucigalpa had now swelled to twenty-five—were on a new tack. They were supporting an anti-Sandinista force in Costa Rica, which had no border with El Salvador. The Agency's newest asset, Eden Pastora, was based there.

Eden Pastora had been an early Sandinista, a Social Democrat who quickly became disillusioned, he claimed, by the Marxist turn of the regime. He had gone into Costa Rica, where he gathered a force to fight his erstwhile Sandinista comrades. He was a far more appealing figure than the FDN's Enrique Bermúdez. Pastora had no Somoza taint about him. He had fought against the dictatorship.

Clarridge had met Pastora at a secret rendezvous in Costa Rica and offered to help him. Pastora, with virtually no resources, agreed. But on one point he was adamant. He was a Nicaraguan patriot, he said, not a yanqui tool. The faintest trace of any association with the CIA and he was destroyed. Any CIA aid to him had to be laundered through a series of Latino intermediaries. Clarridge agreed, and took the plan back to Washington.

When John McMahon heard about the Pastora plan, he marched into Casey's office and told him that Pastora was as much a Communist as the rest of the Sandinista gang. But the ambitious Pastora had been forced out in an old-fashioned power struggle, so now he found himself on the outside looking in. "It's not as if he's a son of a bitch but at least he's *our* son of a bitch," McMahon told Casey. "He isn't even ours!"

Bobby Inman was doing a slow burn. Here he was, the director's presumed alter ego, and he had not even been privy to the Pastora gambit. He maneuvered his way into Casey's office when Clarridge was there. As he described the scene: "Bill and Dewey were pleased as could be with themselves over Pastora. But I pointed out on the map that Pastora's stamping ground was Costa Rica—and that was over two hundred miles from El Salvador. What did Pastora have to do with stopping arms going from Nicaragua to the Salvadorans?"

"Aw, you're too legalistic." Casey waved off Inman's unsolicited opinion. "Can't you see? Having a force on their southern border is how we make the Sandinistas divert their resources." And even if Pastora was a leftist, possibly a Marxist, what difference did it make if he advanced their objective? He had learned all this nearly forty years ago, from Donovan, when they recruited Communists to parachute into Nazi Germany.

And so the enlistment of Eden Pastora and his followers was approved. But one thing Inman knew; Casey was going to have a hard time convincing Congress that a force in Costa Rica was there to block arms going to El Salvador. He began to wonder if maybe Casey had a larger, unspoken objective.

Casey's senior deputies at Langley were starting to resemble a logjam on a river. He wanted to break it up. But it was not going to be easy; some of the logs had been put in place by Congress, and if he tried to move them, the deluge could sweep him away too. The principal obstacle was next door—Admiral Bobby Ray Inman.

Casey loved young Bob Gates. And in the Casey style, he expressed his approval not by praise but by piling more work on him, until by 1982, Gates was holding down four jobs. As executive assistant, he ran Casey's personal staff. Casey had been reluctant to put anybody in Gates's old slot as national intelligence officer for the Soviet Union, and so he still wore that hat. He was also director of the Office of Policy and Plans and chairman of the Executive Career Service. And Gates was getting the kind of fat offers from the private sector that lure people from public service. A new hotshot company providing intelligence to U.S. corporations on overseas developments was ready to double Gates's salary and pay him big bonuses. He had made up his mind to take the job. He talked to Casey, who said sure, but why didn't he bring the head of the company out to Langley for a chat? Gates did so. Afterward, Casey told him, "This is a bad move for you. The timing's not right."

Gates had found Casey "rough to work for. He'd buzz you to come to his office. You'd be putting on your jacket and the phone would ring again and he'd be asking where the hell were you. At meetings his hands were in constant motion, bending the paper clip, making notes on a yellow pad, stuffing them first into one pocket, then in another. I don't think he'd recognize the Agency organization chart if it fell on him. An idea would flash in his mind and then a face, and he'd hit a button on the phone console and hand out the assignment. Afterward, we'd try to sort out who really should be doing what. Sometimes you'd see him drifting off, eyes closed, so you'd stop talking, thinking he had fallen asleep. As soon as you did, he'd hit you with a question. On the other hand, he could be staring at you intently as you spoke. Minutes would go by. You'd stop and he wouldn't even notice you weren't talking. You had his eyes, but his mind was a million miles away." Once, when Gates commented on the clutter that surrounded him, Casey answered, "My mind's organized, not my desk."

Gates was torn by the corporate job offer. Casey had his faults, but he was clearly committed to rebuilding the Agency. And Gates also felt a strong personal pull. He had worked for two other foreign policy stars at the NSC, Henry Kissinger and Zbigniew Brzezinski. He later described a major difference: "Henry and Zbig knew all the answers to all the questions in the world already. There was nothing you could tell them. But Casey was always learning, questioning, listening. If somebody caught his attention with something new, the schedule went out the window. He'd sit and listen all day if necessary. He taught me to listen too, even to some of the goofy people who find their way in here. You listen, you extract the two percent that's good, and you throw out the garbage. I also admired that Casey had the intelligent man's capacity to change his mind.

"I never met anybody who read as widely. If there was a journal with three subscribers in the world, Bill Casey was one of them. He'd show me something in some obscure review and say, 'What do you think of that?' What I'd be thinking was, 'How the hell did you come by this?' Intellectually he was the most stimulating man I ever met."

And so, on the eve of the day that he was about to sign the contract with his new employer, with a thousand crisp new business cards on his desk, Bob Gates pulled out. One year later, the firm went out of business.

Casey saw a way to start breaking up the personnel logjam. He had managed to hold on to John McMahon by putting him in the DDI slot. McMahon was a Casey favorite, but reflective analysis was not his long suit. What Casey needed was an activist-intellectual as DDI. He reactivated a long-dormant slot, executive director of the CIA, and put McMahon in it. The job description—day-to-day internal management of the Agency—seemed to cut turf away from Inman. As far as Casey was concerned, so what if it did?

The larger effect of the move was to open up the DDI position for the man he wanted in it. And so, on January 4, 1982, he jumped young Bob Gates over sixty other senior candidates and gave him the job. And he took advantage of the occasion to untangle a bureaucratic knot. Previously, the intelligence directorate and the NIC, the National Intelligence Council, had been separate, one essentially churning out the intelligence, the other preparing estimates from this ore. Duplication and confusion had been inevitable. The DI people were in the classic job hell of trying to serve two masters, the DDI and the chairman of the NIC. And so Casey gave both jobs to Bob Gates. Through this arrangement, Gates would also be better able to control the NIC's vice-chairman, Casey's personal cattle prod, Herb Meyer. "Herb captivated Casey," John McMahon recalled. "But mostly the guy was disliked, especially for injecting his politics into the analytic process. Without the Casey umbilical he was just an *auslander*."

Gates, a scholar himself, recognized the value of intellectual cattle prods. "Some kids," as he put it, "don't play well with the other kids in the sandbox. Herb stirred up a lot of hostility, and I frequently had to move in and pull the players apart. But you need people who push, who ask the hard questions. He served this purpose, and so I protected him."

Casey now had the machinery in place. He called in the senior analysts and told them a parable about General Walter Bedell Smith. Smith had just been named Harry Truman's DCI. Truman was leaving the next day for his historic confrontation with General MacArthur on Wake Island. Truman wanted to take with him estimates on seven different nations. Smith had still not moved from his office in the Pentagon when he got the order. He called the analysts at the Agency and told them to get over right away. He parceled out the subjects and said that he expected the estimates on his desk by seven o'clock the next morning. Casey surveyed the faces arrayed before him. "And Harry Truman had them when he flew to Wake," he said. "I'm a Bedell Smith fan."

Because Casey was an ideologue, he was constantly suspected on the Hill of trimming the estimates to fit his conservative cloth. But the pleasure of intellectual combat, nourished in the fireplace debates at the Research Institute of America more than forty years before, had never waned. He reveled in dissent; it heated his blood agreeably. He encouraged his analysts to take conflicting, unpopular stands.

The Soviet Union was building a gas pipeline from Siberia to Europe, and Western allies of the United States were aiding the Soviets by selling them supplies and equipment. The response from the American Right, from Casey's confreres, was swift: impose a boycott on these ingrates. Casey initially agreed. A boycott should kill the pipeline. Nevertheless, he ordered up a spot estimate from his staff on the likely effect of a boycott. The answer came back that it would have little impact. We would cut off our own nose and the Russians would complete the pipeline anyway, the analysts had concluded. Casey took the unwelcome estimate to the White House, and the proposed boycott was killed.

Casey and his number-two man on the National Intelligence Council, Herb Meyer, made an odd pairing: Casey, old, crusty, a word masher; Meyer, young, delicate looking, shrilly articulate. To Meyer, it often seemed as though it was him and the director against the world— two outsiders battling the bureaucrats. To Meyer, the best part of the job was sitting alone with Casey, after the regular work day, and letting their minds rove. One night Casey started talking about arms control. He was looking for a fresh angle, something that went beyond the stale weapon-for-weapon formulas that dominated the disarmament dialogue.

The Soviet economy was a mess, Casey pointed out. The Russians had suffered crop failures three years in a row. Their economic growth rate was under 2 percent a year. Alcoholism was rampant, corruption the rule. The Soviet Union was now the only industrialized nation where life expectancy for men had fallen. "They're not providing any quality life for their people," he observed. Maybe that was the disarmament angle, he told Meyer. Instead of comparing head-to-head reductions in classes of weapons, maybe they should be looking at disarmament in a whole new way. Maybe they could persuade the Russians to cut back on weaponry that would give their civilian economy its biggest boost.

Meyer agreed. Disarmament talk always centered on nuclear weapons. The truth was that the whole nuclear arsenal represented only about 15 percent of the U.S. defense budget, and the Soviet Union figure was comparable. If you looked at the economics of nuclear disarmament, the incentives were not great. "Herb," Casey said, "take a look at disarmament from the economic angle. Do a paper on it."

"Can the Soviet Union Stand Down Militarily?" was the result. Meyer and his fellow analysts found that cutbacks in the production of Soviet tanks could produce huge savings, far in excess of nuclear arms reduction. Fewer tanks offered another incentive. The steel saved could be diverted to the production of locomotives and rolling stock to break up the transportation bottlenecks that were holding down the Soviet standard of living.

Casey was delighted. He brought copies of the assessment to the White House. His agency was always being pictured as an insidious force for fomenting cold wars, hot wars, secret wars; but he had been arguing all along that intelligence could be an instrument for promoting peace. Here was the proof.

Toward the end of March 1982, Bobby Ray Inman submitted his resignation. Cut out of major initiatives like the Clarridge Central American operation, his authority chipped away by the new assignment to McMahon, distrusted by White House purists because his knee did not jerk at every proposed right-wing covert caper, zapped in the press by Casey's friend Safire, fat private job offers awaiting him, he felt that he owed the Reagan administration nothing more.

Capitol Hill mythology had it that every time Casey supposedly fudged the facts before the oversight committees, Bobby Inman would tug on his sock to alert the members. It was not quite true. But as Inman explained, "I'm not a poker face. I hiss the villains and cheer the heroes, and it shows. When I hear things that make me uncomfortable, I tend to squirm; I crane my neck. I pull at my pants— maybe my socks too."

The sock-pulling story got back to Casey, who confronted Inman. Inman vehemently denied it. "No, it's true," Casey growled. "You sit there fidgeting all the while I'm testifying." Casey was right. While Inman later admitted that he had never heard Casey actually lie to the Congress, "What I heard him do was not tell the full story."

For Casey, the prospect of Inman's departure presented a dilemma. They had started out as a man who did not want a job working for a man who did not want him in the job. It had gone downhill from there. Still, Inman remained Casey's badge of respectability on Capitol Hill, part of an unspoken pact that had sealed his own confirmation. He was ambivalent about seeing the man go. And so he sat on Inman's letter of resignation.

After two weeks, Inman told Casey he might as well accept it; he was going. When word of his departure reached Congress, Senator Joe Biden told a reporter, "I'll tell you one thing—the wrong guy is leaving." Senator Richard Lugar, an SSCI member and a Republican, called reporters to his office and said, "We voted for Casey and Inman as a package. The President had better replace Inman with another career professional to back up Casey," Lugar warned.

The warning was timely, because Casey had quite the opposite intention. Again, he was thinking of bringing in an outsider as his chief deputy. Among those on his list was a successful businessman and friend named Henry Greenberg, a smart, hard-driving, more suitable Max Hugel. Inman started to think that maybe Casey was a slow learner. Soon after Casey made this admission to Inman, the DCI coincidentally started getting warning calls from the Hill. The members wanted another intelligence pro—was that clear? In fact, they knew just the man they wanted: solid, reliable John McMahon. Casey was not pleased about being forced into another shotgun marriage. But at least this time he liked the bride.

John McMahon had a distinct advantage over Casey in dealing with Congress. As he expressed it, "I belived in oversight. It's the greatest protection, not only for the CIA but for the individual officer." He liked the idea that the President had to sign off with a finding of necessity on covert operations and that the operations had to be reported to the oversight committees. "Otherwise, when the operation falls on its face," said McMahon, "the Congress and the press jump all over the CIA. They don't condemn the administration that put you up to it."

In his courtesy calls on the Hill prior to his confirmation, McMahon was shocked to learn of Casey's standing. "They all drilled me on Bill," McMahon recalled. "They didn't trust him. They couldn't have an open, honest dialogue with him. One member complained if they didn't ask him exactly the right question, they didn't get the right answer." A HPSCI member, Norman Mineta, a California Democrat, told McMahon, "He treats us like mushrooms—he keeps us in the dark and feeds us manure." Barry Goldwater told McMahon, with a wry smile, "If you ever think things aren't going right up here, could you lean over and pull up your socks?"

June 10 was set for the formal changing of the guard. Inman left and McMahon became deputy director of the CIA. Paul Conrad, of the Los Angeles Times Syndicate, noted the event with a cartoon showing Diogenes with a lamp knocking on a door labeled "CIA." Casey is poking his head out and says, "Sorry, Bobby Inman isn't here anymore."

After he had gone, Inman looked back on the man he had served and concluded, "Bill Casey was a free-lance buccaneer." And he had another judgment, perhaps prophetic for the years that lay ahead: "If I had to sum the man up in one sentence, I'd put it this way. If it's not specifically prohibited by the law, then it's okay. Do it."

The Caseys moved that summer. The situation at the Cathedral Avenue apartment had become impossible; the family and the security people were constantly tripping over each other. It was also the season of death threats, real or hyperbolic, against the President, Vice-President Bush, the secretaries of State and Defense, allegedly by Libya's mercurial strongman, Muammar Qaddafi. Casey had also made the hit list, and security in an apartment house was awkward and difficult. He began looking into kidnap insurance.

The Caseys bought a home at 4500 Foxhall Crescent, a posh Northwest complex. The $300,000-and-up homes had been built on the twenty-six-acre Washington estate of Casey's least favorite Republican, the late Nelson Rockefeller. While Sophia had been house hunting, a saleswoman showed her one home and told her, "You mustn't tell a soul it's on the market." "Bill won't tell me what he does all day," she said, "and I'm not supposed to mention this house. It's going to be a very quiet night."

"You ought to take a look at black Africa," Al Haig advised Casey at one of their regular Tuesday breakfasts. "Stan Turner dried everything up there. We've got nothing left. We're at the mercy of the Brits and the French."

Casey had taken the warning to heart and reopened stations in key black African states. In September of 1982, he decided to see for himself how the reconnected pipelines were working; and so he set off for a swing through Senegal, the Ivory Coast, Kenya, Nigeria, Zaire,

Zambia, Zimbabwe, and South Africa, taking Herb Meyer with him.

Casey had visited South Africa thirty-three years before as a director of the Intercontinental Hotels Corporation. On his return, he had written an article for the Research Institute of America's newsletter. "The native has little education, will or inclination for our world," he wrote. "Those living in the primitive tribal state seem happier than those in the city. . . . The [white] South African is much like the American. . . . With the invigorating climate, energetic stock, vast natural resources and free institutions, the future of South Africa is a good bet. . . . Their future will depend on the extent to which they take in the populations which Europe can no longer support and the speed with which the native is educated, trained and fitted into their society."

The massive infusion of European whites had not occurred. Instead, the blacks had streamed to the cities, and the problem was no longer the docility of the natives but their strivings. That was not Casey's immediate concern on his return in September of 1982. What he was looking for were friends to support America's involvements in Central America and in Afghanistan. The ruling party in South Africa should be receptive; after all, the Reagan administration was not leaning overly hard on them to curb apartheid. Casey did find the South African government receptive to helping the contras.

He went on to Lagos. Meyer came down to join him for breakfast in the sweltering, fly-ridden dining room of the hotel where they were staying. He found the DCI tearing into a grapefruit. Casey looked up, lecturing with his spoon. "Herb," he said, "this is the best grapefruit I've ever had in my life. Remember the lousy grapefruit we had in the last country? But they had great cattle. If these people could arrange an export loan, and if they could . . ." The entrepreneurial virus was a hardy strain, Meyer concluded.

Back home, Casey's racial behavior was pragmatic. He pushed the operations directorate to hire more blacks, more Hispanics, and more Arab-Americans. "It wasn't exactly the equal-opportunity mentality," Bob Gates noted. "Bill wanted our personnel to match the range of people we deal with. He wanted people who could move in and out of Tehran, Tripoli, Kinshasa, or Tegucigalpa, who didn't look like they'd just stepped out of Harvard."

Casey's relations on the Hill were bad; his image in the press was no better. Billy Doswell handled both Casey's congressional relations and the press. Doswell was a likable, courtly Virginian, an ex-lobbyist in Congress and in the Virginia legislature. He had had no government experience, much less intelligence experience, when Casey brought him in as part of his new-blood crusade. The ordinarily able Doswell had been a whiz at getting bills passed for optometrists in the state capital, but Casey's problem was getting covert operations by Congress. And he was coming around to believe that only someone steeped in the game, someone who had the built-in mental filter for knowing what could be divulged and what must be concealed, could do the job. Doswell was burned out anyway: the twelve-hour days, the unremitting pressure, Casey's middle-of-the-night phone calls had exacted their toll. Billy Doswell was out of his job as head of the Office of External Affairs that summer of 1982. Casey eased his exit with a one-year undercover assignment in Cental America.

Casey then reinvented the wheel. He went back to the arrangement that had prevailed when he took over the CIA, a separate lobbyist for the Hill and a separate Office of Public Affairs for the media. For both of these highly visible jobs he turned to men of unlikely background.

George V. Lauder had put in thirty-two years at the Agency, most of it under cover in the Middle East. Lauder was in his late fifties, just under six feet, starting to thicken around the middle. He had a big, expressive face and was that rarity, a passionate WASP, a man who spoke with a vigorous voice punctuated by bursts of laughter and choppy gestures. As a youth he had played tennis with George Bush. He had gone to Yale, then took a law degree "just for the intellectual discipline." He rejected the State Department as too anemic and had gone to work for the CIA. He was serving as deputy inspector general and getting tired of the job when he suddenly was summoned to the DCI's office.

What Casey wanted him to do struck Lauder as bizarre. "I'd spent my entire career running away from reporters, and now he wanted me to be the Agency's press officer," Lauder remembered of their conversation. It was like pulling a bat into the sunlight. "Why me?" Lauder asked Casey. "What do I know about dealing with reporters?"

Casey answered, "Do you know what Roosevelt told Bill Douglas when he brought him to Washington and Douglas asked him what he was supposed to do? 'If I knew, I'd have done it myself'—that's what FDR told him."

"Those are my marching orders?" a dubious Lauder asked.

"Right," Casey answered, and ended the interview.

"I left thinking," Lauder recalled, "here I am the only director of public affairs for any intelligence service in the world. I'm an Ivy

League type working for this tough old Irishman who calls us white-shoe boys. Is this going to work?"

The man Casey picked to take over congressional relations also came out of the covert world. Clair George had put in twenty-seven years at the Agency. He seemed an unlikely spy, which made him an even better one. George was effervescent, amusing, a ready wit. A colleague described him as "smart, smart, smart. Clair was fun to be around. And he had that marvelous gift of never seeming to work hard, no matter how hard he was working."

George resisted becoming the CIA's lobbyist. Do it for a year, Casey urged. The tradition in the DO was to respond to a challenge with "Yes, sir"; and, in the end, George said it. When the committees were informed of Casey's choice, Rob Simmons, staff director of the SSCI, remembered thinking, "Billy Doswell was open and above-board. I knew George only as an outstanding clandestine operator. I figured Casey put him in Doswell's job to stem the flow of information to us."

Iran had been lost to the United States for three years, and was unlikely to be accessible as long as it was ruled by Ayatollah Ruhollah Khomeini, a zealot who had branded the United States "the Great Satan." Still, the country was much on Casey's mind. The estrangement bothered him. Iran stood at the center of a crescent that embraced much of the world's oil. Iran bordered the Soviet Union. The country was easy prey to Soviet penetration, especially now that it was so far removed from American influence.

Vladimir Kuzichkin was a senior KGB officer posted to the Russian embassy in Tehran. In the fall of 1982, Kuzichkin defected to the British. The CIA had a sharing arrangement with MI-6, British intelligence, and thus became privy to the contents of two trunks full of documents that Kuzichkin had spirited out with him. From these documents, the CIA was able to put together a list of more than one hundred people, mostly Iranians, working as secret agents in Iran for the Soviet Union.

Iran had kept fifty-two Americans hostage for more than a year. But geopolitics was a cold, unsentimental game; and Casey was prepared to play whatever cards fell into his hand to break the U.S. isolation from Iran. And so he allowed the list of the Soviet agents to be turned over to the Khomeini regime—a good turn might soften up the Ayatollah. The agents were subsequently rounded up and executed.

That fall, the covert operation in Central America struck a reef. Every time Casey briefed the oversight committees, it seemed he was reporting a bigger contra force. By late summer, the contras numbered fifteen hundred. The disturbing question to the oversight committees was, just what was the United States trying to accomplish? The interdiction argument rang ever more hollow. Nicaraguan rebels were unlikely to give up their lives to block weapons from going to El Salvador. No songs of glory were going to be lifted to the theme of interdiction. The CIA's support of Eden Pastora in Costa Rica did not even fit the interdiction rationale. The contras, however, would risk their lives to topple a Marxist regime in Managua. The suspicion was growing on Capitol Hill that the United States, by backing the contras, was provoking a Latin Vietnam.

The chairman of the House intelligence committee was Edward Boland, a mild, well-liked Democrat from Springfield, Massachusetts, and no enemy of sound covert operations. But if the Reagan administration meant what Casey was telling his committee—interdiction and nothing more—then let's put the limit in writing, Boland argued. And so in August of 1982, he introduced an amendment to the Intelligence Act that barred the CIA or the Defense Department from taking any action "for the purpose of overthrowing the government of Nicaragua." Casey was in a box. If he was bluffing about interdiction and had a wider objective, then Eddie Boland had called his bluff. If he was sincere, then how could he object to the restrictive language? The bill passed both houses. In December, the President reluctantly signed it.

Part of Casey's problem was that the contras had an unappealing taint. Eden Pastora's attitude was not helping any. The charismatic "Comandante Zero" refused to be allied with Enrique Bermúdez's FDN, which he referred to as "Somocistas and criminal mummies." CIA operatives began combing the exile communities in Miami, Honduras, and Costa Rica for more palatable Nicaraguan leaders. In a one-week crash effort in December, they were able to assemble and unveil a new "directorate" at a Miami press conference. The members included a new propaganda chief with impressive credentials, Edgar Chamorro, who had a master's degree from Harvard and had been a dean of the University of Central America in Managua; Indalecio Rodríguez, a former Jesuit; and a new chairman for the FDN, Adolfo Calero, once the head of Coca-Cola of Nicaragua, a man who had done time in Nicaraguan jails for opposing Somoza. Enrique Bermúdez remained as military chief. Clarridge and his staff stressed one thing to the new leadership: whatever they felt in their hearts, they were never openly to call for the overthrow of the Sandinistas. That would kill them with a wary U.S. Congress.

Casey continued to travel the world, evaluating his people abroad, becoming known to kings, presidents, and prime ministers. In his first two years he visited twenty-three stations, eleven in one two-week burst. Ted Atkeson, his NIO for foreign military assessments, recalled traveling with him that November to West Germany. "The schedule ran from seven in the morning to ten-thirty at night," Atkeson noted, "working breakfasts, working lunches, working dinners, until everybody's tail was dragging except his."

At eleven-thirty at the end of a bruising day in West Berlin, Casey's entourage was driving back to the hotel, eager to collapse in their beds, when Casey suddenly turned to Atkeson and said, "Where's the action in this town?" The half-asleep Atkeson mumbled, "What?"

"Action," Casey said. "A little fun."

A German interpreter in their party suggested the name of one of the livelier *Bierstuben*. "We pulled off our ties," Atkeson said, "to look a little less like a bunch of CIA types, and headed for it."

They arrived just as a leftist street demonstration was breaking up. Casey and his party followed the demonstrators, who were trailing their placards and banners, into the beer hall. The chief of the security detail tried to form his men into an inconspicuous shield to get Casey through the crowd. They managed to find a stand-up counter, corraled a barmaid, and ordered beer all around. The music was ear-splitting. The security chief, fearing that Casey might be recognized by a mob of German labor radicals, kept the party in a living stockade around Casey. Casey appeared oblivious, banging his stein on the counter with everyone else and singing along with the music.

After an hour of reveling, Casey turned to Atkeson and said, "Okay, what's next?"

Casey's determination to improve analysis produced one satisfying victory. On November 12, 1983, Leonid Brezhnev, after a long illness, died. "The CIA buried Chairman Mao twenty times before he died," Casey told a visiting group of businessmen. "That's an indication of the hazards of prediction."

Divining the successor to Brezhnev had long been a challenge to the Soviet division's handicappers. Getting it right was important, and not only for the fact itself. Here was one of the few situations where an Agency assessment could be objectively measured—either it was right or it was wrong. Months before Brezhnev's death, the White House had requested a succession estimate. A thick report wound up on Casey's desk. Casey looked at the pile with the revulsion of someone eyeing a dead rat. He announced to his secretary, "I'm gonna boil this one down myself." The end product was a short letter to Reagan that closed, "Chernenko peaked too soon. Kirilenko faded in the stretch. Grishin is a dark horse. But if I had to bet money, I'd say Andropov on the nose and Gorbachev across the board." This was intelligence that Reagan could savor—especially when, two days after Brezhnev's death, Yuri Andropov became the leader of the Soviet Union.

During Casey's second year at Langley he lost two allies. Already by January, Dick Allen had been forced to resign as national security adviser because of charges, which Allen vehemently contested, that he had accepted two watches from a Japanese friend and one thousand dollars as a gift for obtaining an interview with Nancy Reagan for a Japanese women's magazine. The loss to Casey had not been great in the power structure; Allen had never been allowed the role a Henry Kissinger performed. Casey wanted Jeane Kirkpatrick, the administration's ambassador to the U.N., to replace Allen.

They had met briefly during the 1980 campaign, when Kirkpatrick came to Casey's office to discuss how to woo Democrats like herself to Ronald Reagan. Jeane Kirkpatrick was a neoconservative academic, a Georgetown University political scientist who had seduced the Right with a single article in *Commentary* magazine, "Dictatorships and Double Standards," in which she had managed to locate a moral distinction between "authoritarian" regimes and "totalitarian" regimes—or more simply, good dictatorships and bad dictatorships, the good ones being those friendly to the United States.

She was then in her mid-fifties. She dressed plainly but attractively, and her hair appeared to have had a duty brushing in the morning. She resembled the high-school history teacher that everyone remembered, the one whom the kids liked but feared a little too. In person, she was a softer, more appealing woman than the hard-edged intellectual that her public pose projected.

She and Casey quickly gravitated to each other at White House meetings. "You could put the two of us in a room of ten to a thousand people," Kirkpatrick recalled, "in the Roosevelt Room, in the cabinet, a cocktail party or reception, and within fifteen minutes we'd be huddled in a corner talking about Central America. Bill was more intellectually sophisticated and he had greater analytical skills than the other people I was meeting in the Reagan administration. Bill was a heavyweight." Some of their colleagues got the impression that Kirkpatrick regarded herself and Casey as the only intellectuals in the administration.

"He treated me as an equal," Kirkpatrick also recalled. "That's the ultimate test of male chauvinism—do they take you seriously? You sense that very quickly. Bill was more interested in my views on Nicaragua than my sex." Still, John McMahon concluded, "Casey didn't think much of most women in positions of power. He didn't enjoy dealing with Ann Armstrong, who the President named chairman of PFIAB. Jeane Kirkpatrick? That was another issue. Bill thought she had balls."

Casey lost the campaign to promote Kirkpatrick to NSC adviser in a White House power contest. He lost to Deaver and Baker, who had another candidate. Reagan's old stalwart, Judge Bill Clark, who earlier had been drafted into the Reagan State Department, took over the NSC on January 2. Clark's knowledge of foreign affairs was virginal; but he was a devout anticommunist, and Casey could live with him.

The departure of Al Haig from State later in 1982 had been a greater loss. Haig was smart, tough, and deeply experienced in foreign affairs. But there were those Strangelovean quirks—the power twitch the day of the Reagan shooting, the naked ambition. Haig made the Reagan team uncomfortable. Casey was the one colleague with whom he could be comfortable. He poured out his frustrations to Casey at their regular breakfasts. "I'm being shut out by the palace guard," he told him once. "I've got horrendous problems, and I can never be alone with the President. I'm not in his office for thirty seconds before Meese or Baker or Deaver or all three are in there telling the President he's got a photo opportunity." But alone or in company, it did not make that much difference, Haig concluded. "With that habitual good cheer, I can't tell if Ronald Reagan is agreeing or disagreeing with anything I say."

Casey rarely said anything directly disparaging of the President. But Haig observed, "Bill and I both recognized that his span of attention and his interests were terribly narrow. We would commiserate over it. Ronald Reagan knew little about foreign policy and cared less."

After his departure from State, Al Haig reflected, "I don't blame Ronald Reagan. I blame his kitchen cabinet, those men who believed that the man was qualified to be President of the United States. They thought they could run him. But some sharpies around the President took over, and they ran him instead. With Ronald Reagan, you were dealing with an amorphous mass that had no substance, no opinion. I know that Bill Casey's frustrations were as great as mine. He told me so after I left."

Casey and Haig may have commiserated about the frustrations of working for Ronald Reagan, but Casey was not Haig. His access to the President was unobstructed, and he was philosophical and illusion-free about Reagan. His old secretary Connie Kirk saw Casey during one of his visits to New York and she told him, "I'll bet you put in more time at the CIA than Reagan does in the White House." "Are you kidding?" Casey said. "He barely works at the job."

There was another odd wrinkle to Haig's departure. He had won the title that Casey had coveted. Yet, by virtually authoring what would become the Reagan Doctrine and by assuming the policy-making lead, especially in Afghanistan and Central America, Casey had captured much of the substance of the job. The essential difference between them was that Haig was a skilled bureaucrat who had never mastered politics, while Casey had become a politician who maneuvered skillfully around the bureaucracy.

Martin Anderson, conservative thinker and Reagan policy aide, grasped the unusual nature of the influence Casey had gathered to himself. Casey's intelligence estimates "drove the defense budget," Anderson later wrote; "the defense budget drove fiscal policy, and fiscal policy had enormous impact on all other national policies."

Haig, out of office, questioned that power. An intelligence chief should be simply a purveyor of facts, Haig believed; he should not even be in the cabinet. "When Dick Helms was DCI," Haig recalled, "he'd make his briefing and leave. That's proper in theory. But knowing Bill, I knew he wasn't going to be content unless he was in the thick of it."

Casey was happy enough with Haig's replacement—George Shultz, an ally from the Nixon administration, a man with whom Casey felt a kinship, a reliable, practical man, yet possessed of a keen intellect, like himself. They ought to get along fine.

That December, strange things began to happen, all too close for coincidence. On December 17, Casey's clipping folder included a story by the *New York Post*'s White House correspondent, Niles Lathem, headlined, CIA BOSS CASEY FACES STRIKE THREE. According to Lathem, the covert war against Nicaragua, Casey's scars from the SSCI investigation, and his alleged demands for CIA domestic spying had conspired to make Casey "the first casualty of a reshuffle of Cabinet members." Lathem referred to Casey as an "outsider" in the Reagan administration and said his job was "a political reward." In the unkindest cut of all, Lathem added nine years to Casey's age, saying he was seventy-eight. At about the same time, *Newsweek*'s "Periscope" and a Capitol gossip columnist ran similar end-of-Casey items.

One bad story was always possible; but three in swift succession suggested an orchestrated assault. Casey found a clue to the source of the speculation on his departure in the last line of the Lathem story: "[Jim] Baker is known to covet the top CIA job."

Baker was a man of enormous personal charm. That fact plus the adroit use of his position had given him a prized possession in Washington—a good press. Baker understood that good press relations came from nourishing reporters. As Meese described his colleague-adversary, "Jim Baker was a terrible leaker, and it drove me and Bill Casey up the wall." Al Haig had found Baker "an opportunist of unparalleled skill." "Baker," he said, "usually used agents to do his leaking—Dick Darman or Dave Gergen," the former Baker's deputy, the latter the White House communications director. A secretary in the White House, who observed the Baker operation, concluded, "We all knew Mr. Baker was leaking. He was very good at it. He had a leak network. Whenever his assistant, Margaret Tutwiler, closed her door, you knew she was leaking to the *Washington Post*, or *Time*, or *Newsweek*."

Casey flipped angrily through the stories of his imminent departure and told his press officer, George Lauder, "I'm going to see the President." He met with Reagan alone in the Oval Office. He showed him the stories and said, "Somebody's making a run for my job." Ronald Reagan went through the now familiar litany: if it weren't for Casey, he would not be in this chair. Bill Casey's job was safe, as long as he wanted it. But Casey wanted more. He told the President that he wanted to see the obvious author of his torment called to account. The President was his customary agreeable and affable self. Casey left with no idea of what, if anything, Reagan would do about Jim Baker.

Ed Meese told Casey what the President was going to do—nothing. He had learned something in eighteen years of devoted service: Ronald Reagan shrank from confrontation. And Casey learned something that was painful for him to accept: he was the one who had first brought Baker into the Reagan camp. He had helped place a Judas in the White House, one who was likely to stay there.

Still, nothing shook his affection for Ronald Reagan. When the President dithered over hard decisions or seemed not to grasp the complexities of foreign policy, Casey might grumble and shake his head; but it was the forgiving exasperation of a teacher for a likable, if not too gifted, student. Soon after the confrontation in the Oval Office, a Christmas present arrived at Casey's office, an "Executive Weekly Minder," a cowhide-covered notebook with a daily calendar, date book, and pages for phone numbers. It was not particularly impressive. On the cover the presidential seal had been messily stamped in gold leaf. The inside cover bore the scrawled inscription "To WJC from RWR." Casey cherished his present from his President.

20.

The Case of the Pilfered Papers

Bill Safire wanted to understand Afghanistan better, what it all meant to the United States. As a conservative, he preferred to believe that American support of anybody fighting the Soviets had to be, on the face of it, worthy; but there must be more to it than bloodying the nose of the Russian bear. Early in 1983, he called Casey and asked him what was significant about this distant struggle. "Where are you?" Casey wanted to know. Safire told him he was at home. "I'll be right over," Casey answered and hung up.

As Safire described the visit: "Bill pulled up, bounded out of the car, ran into the house, and said, 'Gimme a map of Afghanistan,' as though that's what every home has, maps of the remotest parts of the earth. We found one in the atlas of my Encyclopaedia Britannica. Casey immediately cracked the book open and broke the spine. And then he started. 'Here's the Persian Gulf and the oil. Here's Iran, which is now out of our orbit. Here's Afghanistan, next to Iran. Here's where the Russians are in Afghanistan.' He gave me, on the spot, a twenty-minute analysis of the Soviet stake in Afghanistan and how it finally tied into control of the gulf region and the oil. He had all the history at his fingertips, going back to the Soviet attempts to control Iran in World War II, and what Roosevelt and Truman did to stop that. He went through how the CIA put the Shah on the throne." Casey also believed that Afghanistan fit another ancient Russian dream, not just of the Communists but of the czars: a warm-water port on the Indian Ocean. Afghanistan put that goal a tantalizing 325 miles away.

"He traced all these threads up to the present," Safire recalled. "It was a brilliant analysis, and it was all in his head. I didn't get the sense that the behavior of the Ayatollah and all the human rights violations bothered him all that much. It was the geopolitical significance, the oil—that was the stake. And Afghanistan was part of it."

If Casey had a favorite among his covert children, it was the contras; but the Afghan Mujahedin were close behind. If the Soviet invasion of Afghanistan was wrong, if it was in fact a geostrategic threat to the West, why did the United States need to conceal its role? The far deeper American commitment in Vietnam, with no stronger rationale, had been completely open.

Edward Juchniewicz became assistant DDO under McMahon in 1983 and worked on the Afghan operation. "We had to have plausible deniability," Juchniewicz observed of the covert pose. "Of course, the Russians knew we were involved. But they didn't know how far. We had a sophisticated system of support, and they had no sure way to know where the aid was coming from. We also went covert because Afghanistan was different from our other operations. This time, our effort was resulting in the direct death of Soviet boys. And we needed to rob the Russians of the ability to point a finger at the President of the United States."

The aid program was full of the ironies of clandestine warfare. "A lot of the weapons we were getting to the Mujahedin were either Soviet or Eastern-bloc makes," Juchniewicz noted. "Communist-bloc weapons offered us a nice advantage. A lot of the Mujahedin were armed with machine guns, rifles, and mortars taken from Soviet dead and prisoners. So the Soviets might think that even the arms we supplied had been stripped from their own casualties. And the Soviet ammunition the Mujahedin captured from the enemy fit these weapons."

Was buying Eastern-bloc weapons difficult for the CIA? "Our people used private middlemen who'd go and buy them in the international arms bazaar," Juchniewicz recalled. "Or they'd buy them direct from the factories right in the Communist countries."

Casey and his people roved all over Europe and beyond promoting the rebels' cause. He had had little trouble in Saudi Arabia. In May Casey had gone to the desert retreat of King Khalid. The king, a mild man of delicate health, insisted that Casey see his dairy herd. The cows were tended by an Irish family that Khalid had brought to the desert. Next the king put Casey aboard a Land-Rover to visit the herds of royal camels. Khalid pressed a warm, thick glass of camel's milk on Casey, which he politely resisted. Khalid brought Casey back to his own quarters amid the tents, which was an air-conditioned Winnebago motor home, where he regaled Casey with the story of his dynasty. His brother, Ibn Saud, had founded the kingdom forty-eight years before by marrying seventeen daughters of various tribal leaders. Ibn Saud had sired twenty-three sons and eighteen daughters, each of whom had been given a palace. Five of the founder's brothers, Khalid told him, including himself and Crown Prince Fahd, still survived. It was Fahd whom Casey had really come to see; for while the gentle Khalid raised his cows, Fahd ran Saudi Arabia.

They flew back to Riyadh for a dinner at the royal palace, where Casey sat next to the crown prince. In his smooth, polite style, Fahd expressed his unhappiness. He trusted Casey, he said; Casey had fought for the AWACS deal for Saudi Arabia. But Fahd said he must be frank. His previous American visitors had been the Senate majority leader, Howard Baker, and a half-dozen other senators. "They conducted an inquisition of me," Fahd complained. And, he gathered, tiny Israel exercised virtual veto power over the foreign policy of the great United States in the Middle East. Why should this be? Fahd wanted to know. Casey walked the Israeli-Saudi tightrope with enough agility to convince Fahd that he still had a friend in America. It was important not to upset these people, for one key item on Casey's agenda was to keep the aid flowing from the Saudis to the U.S.-backed rebels in Afghanistan. The nurturing of Fahd was time well invested. In June, Khalid died, and Fahd became king in name as well as in power. The Saudis stepped up help to their Arab brothers who were keeping the Russians far from their oil fields.

Casey also won support from Israel for the Afghan rebels. Even Communist China provided arms. Sweden and Switzerland balked at giving lethal aid, but CIA operatives managed to pressure them to provide medical supplies. The Agency had a smooth but expensive arrangement with Anwar Sadat to ship supplies bound for Afghanistan through Egypt. After Sadat was assassinated in October of 1981, Casey had to renegotiate the deal with Sadat's successor, Hosni Mubarak.

Casey took full advantage of a psychological edge. Congress was giving him a hard time on the Nicaraguan operation. The goals there were foggy, the risks more certain than the rewards. If the contras seemed a shaky bet, the members could still prove their anticommunism by giving Casey what he wanted for the Mujahedin. They virtually lined up to double covert aid for the Afghan operation.

Afghan students, teachers, and workers living in Europe found themselves invited to lunch by a visiting American professor, a clergyman, maybe a businessman. They were drawn into conversation about the struggle back home. Their hosts were all working under cover for the CIA. If any of these expatriates revealed pro-rebel sentiments, the CIA later approached and attempted to recruit them. More than a hundred Afghans were thus trained by the CIA in the exotica of international shipping. By the spring of 1982, the graduates were being dispatched to work for private companies that shipped cargo to Asia. Soon, in vessels docking at Karachi, Pakistan, among the crates of computers, color television sets, and sewing machines were concealed shipments of arms and ammunition. The author of this entire initiative had been William J. Casey.

There were still 325 miles of Pakistan that the arms had to cross after arriving in Karachi before reaching Afghanistan. These routes were the rebels' arteries. The key to keeping them open was the Pakistani president, Mohammed Zia Ul-Haq. Zia was in a difficult position: his cooperation was vital, but it had to be carried out without bringing the Russians down around his own neck. As Casey instructed his people, "Keep Zia's hands clean." To make sure, he usually dealt directly with the Pakistani strongman himself.

Casey was in Islamabad, the capital, toward the end of March 1983. Zia sat him down in a heavy gilt chair at an ivory-inlaid table and offered cups of a hot, sweet drink. Casey faced a taciturn man of ramrod bearing. Casey had no pleasure in small talk, and Zia had no gift for it, though he spoke flawless English. They went immediately to the agenda. Casey began by briefing Zia on the latest intelligence gathered by U.S. spy satellites. Zia nodded in appreciation, particularly at what Casey told him of the military movements of Zia's arch-foe, India. Zia then complained of the Afghan refugee burden, a flow into his country that was fast approaching three million. Pakistan was already poor. How was he to feed and clothe and house these people? Casey assured him that the United States would help pay.

The Afghan rebels wanted American SA-7 Stingers, portable, heat-seeking surface-to-air missiles. As Juchniewicz put it, "With this weapon, a nearsighted, illiterate Afghan could bring down a few million dollars' worth of Soviet aircraft." Yes, Zia told Casey, he would allow these Stingers to be delivered through Pakistan—after he received the first one hundred for himself. After all, what about the day when the Soviets might send their bombers against Pakistan?

The sessions ran from ten in the morning until one in the afternoon. And the last item was always the same: Zia would bring the subject around to the real enemy, not the Communist regime in Kabul, not the Soviet Union, but India. The Indians were encroaching on his borders, he said. That should concern Casey as much as him. The Soviets might well provoke an Indian invasion of Pakistan just to distract the Pakistanis from helping the Afghans. And so, if he was to keep taking in the refugees and keep the routes open, he needed more weapons to defend Pakistan against India. And Casey agreed.

The arms to the Mujahedin flowed so profusely that Casey dispatched McMahon months later to get to the bottom of ugly rumors. He had received reports that the rebels were selling some of the arms. The oversight committees heard the rumors too, and the Mujahedin were starting to look less noble. And so McMahon traveled to Peshawar, to training camps at the top of the world along the Afghan border.

"I went out and I met with the people who ran the supply operation," McMahon recalled of his mission. "The Mujahedin were divided into eight tribes, and they were running eight different wars. I said I had to see the chiefs of all of them. I went over their plans and tried to get them to work together, which wasn't easy. Finally, I brought up our main concern. We'd given them enough land mines to mine the whole goddamn country. So I just laid it out. I said, 'We have a feeling that all the weapons we're giving you aren't showing up on the battlefield. What's going on? Are you cashing them in?' "

The answer stunned McMahon. A tribal chief named Khalis said, "Yes, we are. We do sell some of your weapons. We are doing it for the day when your country decides to abandon us, just as you abandoned Vietnam and everyone else you deal with." Zia had voiced a similar fear to Casey. Being a friend of the United States, Zia had told him, was like living on the banks of a great river. "The soil is wonderfully fertile, but every four or eight years the river changes course, and you may find yourself alone in a desert."

On Casey's flight back from Pakistan he faced a moment of stark terror: there was nothing left to read. He had gone through all his paperwork. He had finished a book by P. T. Bauer, a British economist, whom he called "my rabbi on the developing world." He had polished off Leonard Mosley's 524-page biography of General Marshall in an hour and a half. He had extracted the meat from the book, he was sure, because of his reading method. He took out a legal pad and wrote across the top, "How to Read a Book." He was going to share the secrets that enabled him to go through a dozen volumes a week. "Start reading at the back," he wrote, "going through the source notes. Who has the author talked to? What research has he done? Then you know if there is anything new for you. Then use the notes as a guide to start dipping." If the book has no notes? "Go to the index to see who or what triggers your interest." No index? "The book is probably not worth reading, but at least check the table of contents. The idea is to find a way into the heart of the matter quickly. Never feel that you have to read a book through. The author isn't there. He won't feel insulted."

Herb Meyer once took note of the books Casey was reading at a given moment: Paul Johnson's *Modern Times*, Jane Jacobs's *Cities and the Wealth of Nations*, Edward Crankshaw's *Shadow of the Winter Palace*, Norman Davies's *Heart of Europe*. Casey had recently dashed off a letter to a friend capsule-reviewing books he had just read: *Yankees at the Court* by Susan Mary Alsop: "how covert assistance from France enabled George Washington, with a few thousand Contras, to defeat the strongest army in the world"; *Street of Joy* by Dominique LaPierre: "tale of how folks in the depths of Calcutta sustain each other with love and hope"; *Red Storm Rising:* "Tom Clancy throws back the Soviet army, navy and air force—just barely—in 650 pages." The thriller was unusual on his list. As Herb Meyer recalled, "Whenever anybody at the office suggested a spy novel to Bill, he'd say, 'I've got better things to read, and so do you.'"

He made it a point to visit the Strand bookstore in lower Manhattan two or three times a year. He enjoyed roaming among the narrow aisles, along the creaking wooden floors amid books piled to menacing heights. On one occasion he put a call through to the President from the Strand's rare-book room. The Strand, he thought, was "the best bookstore in the world."

On the flight back from Pakistan, as soon as he finished his draft of "How to Read a Book," he called a secretary into the living room of the VIP pack and gave the scribbled pages to her to type up. Thousands of man-hours were wasted by people at Langley who did not know the right way to read, he told her. He wanted her to run his advice off and circulate it to the staff.

One of the first people Casey had talked to when he took over the Agency was Robert C. Ames, chief Middle East analyst. Ames was something of a legend; he had worked both covert operations and analysis. Casey wanted Ames to tell him how it all worked in the Middle East—what spawned America's enemies in the Arab world, the radicals and terrorists. Ames gave Casey a real-life parable. He told him how, fifteen years before, he had been stationed in Aden in South Yemen and befriended a young revolutionary named Abd' Al Fatah Ismail. Fatah felt a curious ease with Ames and told him about his political odyssey. The Russians had entered him in their school in Moscow for training young revolutionaries from the non-Communist world. According to Fatah, his teachers schooled him in the art of control through informers, block committees, and the secret police. They told him that he would have to infiltrate the educational system in South Yemen and destroy the country's traditional religious values. Most of all, the Soviets counseled patience. Fatah should be prepared to spend twenty years, if necessary, in building his revolution.

Fatah ran well ahead of his timetable. He became president of South Yemen, subverting a legitimate war of liberation into a Marxist conquest. And his regime began fomenting subversion among South Yemen's neighbors.

Bob Ames's saga of Abd' Al Fatah moved Casey deeply. It supported his gut belief: most mischief in the world was traceable to the Soviet Union.

Two years after this conversation, Casey stood in a hangar at Andrews Air Force Base while a cold rain fell outside. The interior of the hangar was decorated with flags. A small dais had been set up draped with red, white, and blue bunting and black crepe. In front of the dais were seventeen flag-covered coffins. On April 18, a vehicle full of explosives had blown up in front of the U.S. embassy on Beirut's waterfront, collapsing the center like a house of cards. The toll was sixty-three dead, including the seventeen Americans in the coffins. Seven of them bore the bodies of CIA employees, among them Bob Ames. Ames had been walking down a corridor, checking into his office on his first day in town. The explosion had sucked the air out of the hallway, killing him instantly without leaving a mark on his body.

Casey was visibly shaken. The bombing was his first major experience with the deadliness of the game since his OSS days in World War II. Eleven days later, he stood in the CIA auditorium and read from Romans 14. His speech was slow, careful, still not particularly audible. He described the victims, the anonymous people who manned CIA stations in far-off posts: Ken Haas, the Beirut chief of station, who had just gotten married; James Lewis, the deputy chief, and his wife, Monique, who had started working as a CIA secretary four hours before the blast; Phyllis Faraci, another secretary; and Bob Ames, whom Casey described as "the closest thing to an irreplaceable man." "Their deaths," he said, "cannot be robbed of meaning. For the great use of a life is to spend it on something that outlasts it." He cited the lines carved into the rocks at Thermopylae in 480 B.C. after the Greeks stood off the Persians: "Go, passerby, and to Sparta tell / That we in faithful service fell." Seven more stars were chiseled into the lobby at headquarters.

To Casey, the enraging part of the attack was the difficulty of striking back. "Terrorist targets had shifted," John McMahon observed. "At one time, we had a PLO that was big enough to penetrate. But what we were getting now in places like Lebanon were small mom-and-pop operations. Unless you're practically a member of the family, you don't get in. These organizations are almost impossible to infiltrate."

The odds also worked in favor of terrorists. As the provisional IRA was to say later in a public statement after a 1984 attempt to blow up British Prime Minister Margaret Thatcher, "This time you were lucky. But you have to be lucky all the time. We only have to be lucky once."

Who blew up the American embassy in Beirut? The United States spent billions to keep satellites in the sky that could intercept virtually every international cable, radio signal, and phone call. The NSA operated powerful code-breaking computers. Technically, every cable coming out of the Middle East could be intercepted. But economically this total capture was unfeasible. Consequently, the electronic ears were programmed to pick out certain watchwords in messages. When these watchwords occurred, the computer intercepted the full message for analysts to evaluate. Computers could also be programmed to pick out the beep-tone patterns heard after long-distance calls are placed. The pattern reveals who is calling whom, and the computer could be programmed to start recording predetermined callers.

Just prior to the Beirut embassy bombing, this listening apparatus had intercepted traffic from the Iranian foreign office to Iranian embassies in Beirut and Damascus, hinting that something was in the wind. The best that could be puzzled out was a likely conspiracy between Iran and Syria to strike an American installation somewhere at some time. On later reflection, the analysis concluded that the Beirut embassy bombing was the target of these transmissions. The explosion occurred less than six months after Casey had made the ingratiating gesture of revealing to the Ayatollah Khomeini a hundred Soviet spies operating in his midst.

The CIA station in Beirut was a shambles, with the number-one and -two officers and other key people dead. Casey needed to get somebody in there quickly, somebody well grounded in terrorism. In nosing through Agency personnel records, he had been intrigued by the file on a man named William Buckley. As a young Army officer,

Buckley had won a Silver Star in Korea for destroying an enemy machine-gun nest. Afterward, Buckley strode among the enemy dead like a latter-day Patton. He had gone to work for the CIA in the Golden Age of the fifties. Later, he served under cover as the political officer at the American embassy in Damascus, but he was unmasked—"burned," in Agency jargon. He had then been posted to Egypt, where he acquired a dubious credit: he was among those who trained the Egyptian bodyguards who deserted Anwar Sadat at the moment of his assassination. When Moslem fundamentalists stormed the American embassy in Islamabad, Pakistan, where Buckley next served, he managed a dramatic escape via the British embassy. In his long career, he had become the Agency's foremost expert on terrorism and was now posted back at Langley. Like Dewey Clarridge and a handful of others, Buckley had developed a close personal rapport with Casey. He traveled with him, particularly on his trips to the Middle East.

In the wake of the Beirut disaster, Casey called Buckley up to his office. He told Buckley that he wanted him to take the place of the murdered Ames. The man he was talking to was now fifty-five, tall, saturnine, with hooded eyes, and dark, lank hair that fell over his brow. His face had the world-weary expression of someone who had clocked a million miles. He was a bachelor with few outside interests. If he was married, it was to the CIA.

The gung-ho Buckley was uncharacteristically quiet on hearing Casey's request. He raised a point. Company rules said that an agent who had been burned in a particular area was not to return there for at least five years. Even before such a return, the Agency had a team assess the danger of such an assignment. It had been less than four years since Buckley was revealed as a CIA operative in Syria. Now Casey was talking about making him the station chief next door in Lebanon.

Casey did not insist. If anything, he seemed uncomfortable over what he was asking of Buckley. He was not ordering, he said—just suggesting. But the job demanded somebody who understood the terrorists.

Buckley answered the call—not eagerly, but loyally, like an old fire-horse hearing the bell in the night. He went off to Beirut under cover as political officer at the U.S. embassy. Casey had just dispatched one man to one post in his far-flung empire. But Buckley's assignment was to prove one of his most fateful decisions.

He had to make another personnel switch that season. There was a loose cog clanging around in the machinery, and it had to be removed.

Hiring Constantine Menges had seemed a splendid idea back in May of 1981, when Casey was determined to jolt the bureaucracy. Menges was of that contemporary breed of intellectuals who move easily between think tanks and government. His track record had impressed Casey. In an article entitled "Echoes of Cuba in Nicaragua," Menges had called the Marxist turn in Nicaragua even before the Sandinistas overthrew Somoza. He predicted that if the Communists took over Central America, Mexico would fall next. He referred to Mexico as "the Iran next door." That was good talk, Casey's kind of talk, geostrategic, conceptual. Casey invited Menges over to Langley to have a look at him.

On his first visit, Menges carried a letter that he hoped Casey could get in front of Ronald Reagan. As Casey started to read it, he said brusquely, "I don't want the taxpayers to lose fifteen minutes of your time sitting here while I read." With that, he shoved a stack of reports at Menges and said, "Here, you read this while I read this." After one more meeting, Casey hired Menges as his NIO for Latin America.

But Menges had not meshed well with the machinery already in place. Some of his CIA colleagues found this supremely serene man who spoke in orotund tones a trifle pompous. One critic described him as a "right-wing crank." The charge was not entirely fair. In his early twenties, Menges had worked in Martin Luther King, Jr.'s voting rights education project. In his writings on Latin America, he favored the promotion of democracy rather than reliance on right-wing dictatorships. But he was also peddling Star Wars long before the Reagan administration adopted the scheme, when it was still known as Strategic Defense.

Menges was a memo pusher, always promoting his papers, trying to maneuver them in front of the right people. He had written one memo before the Reagan administration began that laid out a strategy for Central America and Cuba. In his new job, he pressed the memo on Casey. "This is the third time I've received this document," Casey said annoyedly. "Once from Leo Cherne—then you gave it to me when you discussed coming to work here. Now you want me to give it to Bill Clark?"

John McMahon found Constantine Menges—his pushing, his pontificating—hard to take. The man seemed somehow thick-skinned and thin-skinned at the same time. As one Menges watcher put it, "Constantine was always eager to be helpful by trying to show others where they were wrong. And he was hurt when they resented his help."

Menges was increasingly being cut out of the loop because some Agency analysts feared he was committing the mortal sin of favoring data that fed his conservative political biases. By the spring of 1983, Casey accepted that Menges's usefulness was at an end. At virtually the same time, Bill Clark asked Menges to come over to the NSC as his man on Latin America. Casey did not stand in his way.

Finding the right replacement for Menges was critical because, to Casey, Central America was critical. Some of the professionals who had been down on Menges talked up a man named John Horton. Horton was a member of the club in good standing—or, rather, an ex-member, since he had been retired from the Agency for almost eight years. His life was now far removed from the clandestine world he had inhabited for nearly three decades. He was now sixty-two years old, operating his own vineyard in Maryland and growing hybrid grapes for table wine. To Casey, Horton had an appealing mix of experience: deputy chief of the Latin American division and chief of the Soviet division in the DO—ideal for grappling with the Nicaraguan situation.

He was a trim, lively man with a puckish humor. He wore steel-rimmed glasses and dressed in khakis and tweeds that suggested a teacher in a private boys' school. And he was a registered Democrat. When he mentioned to a friend that he had been asked to go back to the Agency, she said, "But, John, you can't work for those people— for Ronald Reagan!"

"Look," Horton found himself saying, "you don't understand. I'm not going to work for *those people*. It's not political. I'm an intelligence professional."

In late May, Horton left his vineyard for an interview with Casey. He later described the encounter: "Casey had my file in front of him. He got up to shake my hand and I was surprised at how big he was and somewhat intimidating."

Casey told Horton, "I know your background's been in operations, but I want you to take over as NIO for Latin America. That's the kind of thinking I want in there—people who've been out on the street." The deal was sealed, and Horton came aboard.

Horton was supposed to cover all of Latin America, but he quickly understood that to Casey the heart of the region had moved to Central America. Why did Casey, and the administration he served, invest so much of the attention of a great world power in countries as obscure as Nicaragua? In speech after speech Casey revealed his thinking: "Creeping Soviet imperialism has, in my view, two primary targets, the oil fields of the Middle East and the isthmus between North and South America." He told an audience of businessmen the year before in Hot Springs, Virginia, "It is no coincidence that today the eleven insurgencies under way throughout the world supported by Russia, Cuba, Libya, and South Yemen happen to be close to the natural resources and the choke points . . . on which the United States and its allies must rely." What was the Panama Canal but a choke point on America's throat. Communist interest in Nicaragua, just 250 miles from the canal, was no coincidence to Casey. It was part of the grand Soviet design.

Even people in the State Department, he feared, failed to grasp the strategic prize in this small package. On the eve of a key vote on aid for the Nicaraguan resistance, Casey started getting calls from friendly Republicans on the Hill asking for ammunition to support the program. Casey was furious: the State Department was already supposed to have provided this material. Supporting the contras was not a CIA show; it was administration policy—and State was supposed to be a full partner. He had been happy with George Shultz's appointment as secretary, and so far Shultz had backed the covert operation. But, he concluded, State Department careerists were trying to emasculate another secretary of State.

"State," Casey told his new NIO, "is no goddamn good. If they were, they'd have won us some support in the rest of Latin America for what we're trying to do in Nicaragua."

But exactly what was the administration trying to do? On May 23, George Lauder brought Casey a front-page story from the *New York Times*. The *Times* had reported that Casey and Thomas O. Enders, the assistant secretary of State for Latin America, had "predicted that American supported Nicaraguan rebels have a good chance of overthrowing the Sandinista regime by the end of the year. . . . They told the [intelligence] committees that anti-government forces in Nicaragua were planning a steady increase in fighting this summer culminating later in the year in a pincer assault on Managua, the capital." Casey and Enders supposedly had made these disclosures in secret testimony. One source the article cited was an unidentified Democratic congressman on the House intelligence committee.

To Casey, here was the worst possible story at the worst possible time, just what liberals in Congress, the press, and the public were aching to hear—something that stripped away the administration's claim that the operation was simply intended to interdict arms. Casey immediately issued a denial. "There is nothing in the record of congressional briefings which remotely resembles the story in the *New York Times,*" he said.

The reporter who had written the story went back to his source. At first the legislator stood his ground. The reporter pressed him hard. Well, maybe Casey and Enders hadn't made the prediction in actual testimony; maybe it was in informal chitchat before or after the actual testimony. But hadn't the member said he heard it in secret testimony? The reporter talked to HPSCI member Lee Hamilton, who said he had never heard Casey or anyone else make the statement. Norman Mineta, another member and a frequent Casey critic, never heard it either.

To its credit, the *Times* ran another front-page story the next day, leading with Casey's denial and reporting the string of witnesses who supported him. To Casey, the experience made unmistakably clear the futility of congressional oversight. Secrets obviously could not be kept; they could not even be kept straight. What was said in briefings was not only leaked but deliberately twisted to sabotage the administration. And he had to share classified information with these people! To Casey, secrets and Congress were a contradiction in terms.

The contra force continued to grow; it could now rightfully claim to be more than the last refuge of Somocista scoundrels. Thousands of peasants, angry at the Sandinistas for expropriating their pig or collectivizing their potato patch, began to swell the ranks. The *Washington Post's* Christopher Dickey, living with the contras in their camps, reported the motive of these people, and interdiction clearly was not it. "We are fighting to liberate Nicaragua," one contra told him. "The people who are fighting, they are not fighting to stop the weapons."

There was something farcical in calling the contra support operation "covert." Congressional deliberations on the program were reported openly in the media. The covert pretense produced bizarre effects. A contra team stormed over the Honduran border to attack a guardhouse thirty yards inside Nicaragua. The Sandinistas counterattacked. The contras fled back over the border, and their commander ran to a pay phone at a bar, where he placed a long-distance call to his control officer at the CIA in Langley. "We need mortars," the commander pleaded. The startled officer at the other end asked, "Where are you calling from?" "Honduras. We're under attack right now." "And you're calling me on an open line? Are you out of your mind?"

Casey could holler at McMahon and McMahon could holler back

without permanent damage to either party. "I told Casey right out that what we were attempting in Central America was all wrong," McMahon later remarked. "The size of the operation was getting out of hand. When a covert action become publicly known, it's not the CIA's bag anymore. We should send in the Marines." The CIA, McMahon pointed out, was directing more troops in combat in Central America than the combined U.S. Army, Navy, and Air Force in that part of the world.

McMahon went on a trip to South Africa, and while at the U.S. embassy he received a secret cable from Casey. Casey wanted him to see the country's defense chief. The South African army had recently captured a huge cache of weapons from Cuban forces fighting in Angola. McMahon was to try to get them for the contras.

He came back empty-handed. Casey demanded to know why. "The guy was out," McMahon answered. Casey was furious; McMahon's effort had obviously been halfhearted. "It was a goddamn stupid idea," McMahon concluded—didn't the Agency already have enough trouble with Congress over Nicaragua without making arms deals with a racist government?

This bastard public-covert operation in Central America was going to cost the CIA dearly in the end, he was sure. The public did not understand that covert action was merely the secret part of foreign policy—not the CIA's foreign policy but the *administration's* foreign policy. It was the underside of the same garment. Foreign policy in the Reagan White House was made by the NSPG: the President, the Vice-President, the secretaries of State and Defense, the national security adviser, and, in this administration, the DCI. But it would have made no difference if Casey had been a traditional, staff-style DCI with no policy input. The President could still sign the findings of necessity, and the CIA would still be assigned to carry out covert administration policy. That was the CIA's job; that was what spies were paid to do. The IRS collects the taxes, but the administration develops the country's tax policies. The Department of Agriculture pays out farm subsidies, but the administration makes subsidy policies. The State Department carried out the overt part of the foreign policy, and it was not reviled. If the Marines were sent into Nicaragua in an open assault, the Marine Corps would not be reviled. But when the CIA carried out the covert part that it was assigned to do, it was reviled as the author of the act rather than as the implementer. That, in McMahon's phrase, "was pure bullshit."

What McMahon needed was a little religion on Central America, Casey told him. He was planning a quick, secret trip down there in

June and told McMahon, "I just want you to see what Dewey Clarridge is accomplishing." It was unusual for the number-one man and the number-two man to be out of the country at the same time; but if it meant that much to Casey, McMahon was willing. Casey also wanted John Horton to come along, and Robert Magee, the expert who provided the hardware and logistical support for covert ops, and, of course, Clarridge, the founding father of the contras.

The party flew out of Andrews Air Force Base in a white-topped twelve-seater Air Force plane kept ready for special VIP missions. They flew first to Tegucigalpa in Honduras. As soon as they landed, Casey began a round of meetings. It was Horton's first exposure to Casey on the road, and he was astonished by the man's vitality. They drove out to the Agency's safe house in Tegucigalpa, the nerve center for the contra support operations. Dewey Clarridge was absorbed in the mechanics of support, getting enough arms to enough men in the right places. The contras were begging for heavier weapons, small aircraft, more secure supply routes. Casey liked Clarridge's can-do drive and his capacity to motivate people. But he also saw the man's limitations. It was not enough to put a gun in a guerrilla's hands. Casey had heard reports that too many contras were on a soldier-of-fortune kick; they lacked political direction, any meaning behind their fighting. Casey's talk made Clarridge uneasy. He was a covert operative, a superb one, maybe the Agency's best. Give him a shipment of arms and he would walk through hell to get it delivered. But he was not a political cheerleader.

Casey, the man who had made a fortune with desk reference books, described his confidence in the power of the written word. What these men needed, he said, was political indoctrination. Somebody ought to be writing a manual that would lay out in simple, forceful language what they were fighting for and how they should go about it. Here was something that Clarridge could deal with: a superior telling him to get something done. Produce a manual. He took note of it.

The next day, they flew to El Salvador's capital, San Salvador. The trip to Honduras had been an inspection, and a psychological booster, encouragement for the troops. In El Salvador, Casey had a more pointed objective. The previous fall, he had been stung by a HPSCI report on El Salvador. The House report maintained that, yes, the CIA had produced a mountain of information about the terrible leftist guerrillas in El Salvador, but it produced next to no information about the terrorism of the Right. According to HPSCI, the CIA had "not considered the subject of Salvadoran rightist violation as a target for collection." The Agency seemed content to accept the promises of Salvadoran military leaders that they had reduced the number of atrocities committed by death squads operating in their own ranks.

The death squads had murdered four American missionary nuns, a Salvadoran bishop, and thousands of their own people. Here it was again, the HPSCI majority members believed—further evidence supporting the impression that the United States was willing to get into bed with any bastards as long as they were anticommunist bastards. More damaging were suspicions that the CIA not only had turned a blind eye to right-wing terrorism but may have colluded in it. Senator Edward Kennedy requested that the SSCI also investigate these allegations. The committee's staff carried out an intensive two-month inquiry which cleared the CIA of involvement in the machinations of the death squads. Still, Casey was concerned. In his practical mind, the real problem was that political murder played directly into the hands of the Salvadoran leftists. Few motives to join the rebels were more powerful than the murder of an innocent father, a brother, a son or daughter by right-wing killers.

Casey had a grudging admiration for the sophisticated methods of the Farabundo Martí National Liberation Movement, the Salvadoran guerrillas. Any damn fool could blow up a power line; but, as Casey told a reporter in a wide-ranging interview, the rebels would also threaten to shoot any pilot who dusted crops. "Now that's smart," Casey said, wagging a finger. "That could cut the agricultural output thirty percent in a country that's already on the ropes." Or the insurgents would firebomb a storekeeper. "The owner's insurance goes up," Casey observed. "He has a forty-five-day line of credit with a bank in Florida, and, boom, in one day he is out of business." That was how you broke the back of the middle class. He had the admiration for these tactics of one street fighter for another.

He spent the day at the American embassy talking first with the U.S. ambassador, Dean Hinton, then opened his door to anyone who had anything to tell him, including Salvadorans in descending rank, until one embassy official announced, "The ones coming in next won't have any necks." He attended a dinner that night given by the acting Salvadoran president, Alvaro Magana. After dinner, Casey pulled Magana aside and wasted no words. "Stop the death squads," he warned. "I'm not going to lecture you about morality—you can worry about your own souls. But I'm telling you this: if you expect the United States to save you from a Salvadoran Castro, cut it out."

Within forty-eight hours, Casey was back in Washington. No one was supposed to have known that he was even gone. Less than a week later, a story in the *New York Post* began, "CIA Director William Casey made a secret trip to war torn Central America. . . ." He shook his head. He was supposed to be working in a leak-proof compartment; it seemed more like a sieve.

As for the effect of the trip on John McMahon, he returned saying, "I didn't learn anything I didn't already know." And he had not changed his mind that in running the contra operations the CIA held a losing hand.

Back in October of 1980, on the day the Carter-Reagan presidential debate was to take place, a boyish twenty-nine-year-old congressman from Michigan's Fourth District was making a speech before some sixty members of the Optimists Club of Cassopolis, Michigan. The youthful, bespectacled lawmaker was David Stockman, who had the air of a likable but smart-alecky kid, the kind who cuts up in class all semester and still winds up on the honor roll. Admirers found Stockman brilliant; detractors called him a wise-ass. "I'm glad to see there are so many optimists left in Cassopolis County," Stockman began his speech. "I thought you might have dwindled down to three or four after four years of Carter."

He went on for a half-hour, and at the end of his speech, Stockman yielded to an impulse to let the folks back home know that they were hearing a local boy who had made the big time. "I spent the weekend as Carter," he said, enjoying the quizzical expression on the Optimists' faces. "That's why I'm so confused and disoriented." He went on to explain that in preparation for the presidential debate they were all waiting to hear that night, Stockman had played Carter in the Reagan practice sessions. He could not repress the urge to titillate further: Reagan had been briefed for the debate using "a pilfered copy of the briefing book he [Carter] was going to use."

Reporters for the *Dowagiac Daily News* and the *Elkhart Truth* went back to their papers and wrote their stories of the speech. They included Stockman's startling disclosure.

There the matter appeared to have died until three years later. In 1983, the incident was reported as "a dirty trick played against Carter" in a newly published book, *Gambling with History*, by Laurence I. Barrett of *Time* magazine. On June 9 brief stories of the anecdote, citing Barrett's book, appeared in the *New York Times* and the *Washington Post*. Three days later, Carter's former press secretary, Jody Powell, called the "pilfered" notebook story "skullduggery" and asked for an FBI investigation.

Soon afterward, Casey received a call from the White House counsel, Fred Fielding. They had a problem, Fielding said. It was true, debate material prepared for President Carter had found its way into the Reagan campaign. Jim Baker seemed to think he had received it from Casey. "All of this," Casey told Fielding, "is a surprise to me."

Casey then called Barbara Hayward, who had been his secretary during the campaign. Hayward, quite coincidentally, had gone to work three months earlier for Jim Baker as an administrative assistant. As she recalled the conversation with her old boss: "Mr. Casey asked me if I recalled any Carter briefing papers during the campaign. I believe I saw everything that came in for Mr. Casey. I told him I had no recollection of any Carter briefing papers. We were so wrapped up in what we were doing that I think something out of the Carter campaign would practically be hot in my hands."

No sooner had she talked to Casey than Baker asked her what she remembered of the papers. "I told him," she recalled, "that I'd just had this conversation with Mr. Casey. And he asked me what I told him. I said that I'd never seen the papers and I didn't think that Mr. Casey had, either. Mr. Baker didn't say anything. He just looked unhappy and walked away." In the weeks that followed, Barbara Hayward began to feel increasingly excluded from the confidences of her new boss; eventually she decided that she had been frozen out and left Baker's employ.

Casey later maintained that in addition to Hayward, he put the same question in calls to all his close campaign associates, including Cliff White, Ed Meese, Bill Timmons, Dick Wirthlin, and Bob Gray, and their responses all had been the same: they knew nothing of any Carter briefing papers.

A few days later, Casey received a letter from a congressman he had never heard of before. Donald J. Albosta was a fifty-seven-year-old Democratic representative from Michigan, a beet farmer by occupation. Albosta chaired the barely visible Human Resources Subcommittee of the House Post Office and Civil Service Committee. The subcommittee appeared remote from Casey's line of work, except that it had jurisdiction over the Ethics in Government Act. The obscure congressman, perhaps hearing the resonances of another Watergate, quite possibly egged on by ambitious staff aides, or maybe just plain outraged, had written Casey asking for his explanation of the reputedly stolen Carter papers. Albosta sent similar letters to Baker, David Gergen, and David Stockman, who had sown the original story three years before. Casey wrote back to Albosta that he had "no recollection" of the documents "as described in Mr. Barrett's account."

Jim Baker answered Albosta that he remembered getting "a large looseleaf bound book (I believe in a black binder) that was thought to have been given to the Reagan camp by someone in the Carter campaign." Further, it was Baker's "best recollection" that Casey had given him the book, "with the suggestion that it might be of use to the [Reagan] Debate Briefing Team."

The press sniffed raw meat. With the allegations of political theft, the possibility of a rigged presidential debate, the prospect of a fight between two major Reagan officials, this could be as good as Watergate. Inevitably, headline writers dubbed the affair "Debategate" as it moved from the back to the front pages.

On June 25, just days after their split versions became public, Baker called Casey, all affability, and in a tone of sweet reasonableness he invited Casey to stop by his office the next day to discuss forming a compatible account of the affair, before their differences caused the administration serious embarrassment. The next day, a Sunday, after his driver had taken him and Sophia to mass, Casey had himself let off at the West Wing of the White House and went to Baker's office. There on a table was a set of the Carter papers, which had turned up in the Reagan campaign files. Baker invited Casey to look the material over; it might help jog his memory. Casey was as wary as a fox poking around a trap. Baker also delivered another sharp prod to Casey's memory. Did Casey remember the name Paul Corbin, the old Robert Kennedy aide whom Casey had put on the campaign payroll in 1980? Casey did. Baker told him that Corbin was claiming that he had obtained a Carter briefing book and had given it to Casey.

Baker had been alerted to the Corbin story by Dick Cheney, then a Wyoming congressman and chairman of the Republican Policy Committee. Cheney had been told by Tim Wyngaard, executive director of his committee, that Corbin, an old family friend, had telephoned him some six weeks *before* the Debategate affair became public. During that conversation, Corbin let drop that he had obtained a Carter briefing book and had given it to Casey. He also claimed that during the campaign, he arranged for Adam Walinsky, a former Robert Kennedy aide, to write a speech for Reagan. What Corbin had actually delivered from Walinsky to Casey was a six-page memorandum describing positions Reagan might take in the debate with Carter.

Casey tracked down Corbin, who was vacationing in Aruba. After their conversation, both Casey and Corbin made public statements that the only information that passed from Corbin to Casey was the Walinsky memo. But if Wyngaard's account was correct—and there seemed no profit in his inventing the story—how had Corbin known about the Carter debate material well *before* the story broke in Barrett's book?

Two days later, on June 28, President Reagan held a press conference, and reporters peppered him with questions on the budding scandal. Reagan dismissed the affair airily; it was "much ado about nothing." This answer, too reminiscent of Nixon's initial dismissal of Watergate as "a third-rate burglary," only whetted the press's curiosity.

The next day, Congressman Albosta announced that his subcommittee was going to conduct a full investigation of the affair. The day after, the FBI announced that it would carry out a criminal investigation.

In a later profile of Jim Baker in *The New Republic*, Fred Barnes was to write, "It's practically impossible to resist the guy. I don't know of a single reporter who dislikes him. The result is that Baker's been transformed into the Teflon adviser, the fellow to whom no blame sticks." The phenomenon was evident in Debategate. Given a choice of whom to believe, that crafty old conniver William J. Casey or the universally liked James Baker, the answer was obvious. Casey was now muttering to friends, "Baker's setting me up again. The son of a bitch wants my job!"

On July 5, Casey called his most powerful friend in the media, Bill Safire at the *New York Times*, and invited him to the EOB for lunch. The chemistry still worked. They were two men alike in their obliviousness toward external appearances and in their intellectual energy. Safire could often be found in shapeless khakis, shod in Wallabys, wearing a dress shirt and no tie. His triangular face was usually set in a small, bemused smile. The eyes looked tired yet alert— the eyes of a man who works hard and rarely stops thinking. His voice was soft but unmistakably New York.

That day, Casey asked his secretary to bring in sandwiches as he began to pour out his frustrations to Safire. "I'm being made the heavy," he told him. "Baker's dumping it all on me. I tell you. I'm not the source of those briefing books."

Safire heard Casey out and finally said, "Why are you telling me all this? I'm a columnist. This is a news story. You should be talking to the reporters—it's their stories that have been hurting you. Come on back with me. I'll set you up with them."

A fair shake for him from the *Times?* Casey was dubious. "I've got better things to do," he answered.

Safire went back to his office. As he walked through the door, Casey was already on the phone. "I'm coming right down," he said. He had thought it over. How much worse could his press get?

Facing the *Times* staff, Casey was forceful, emphatic, and unusually intelligible, Safire thought. He was ready to undergo a lie detector test, Casey said, if Baker was willing to do the same. He had no fears. He also told the reporters, "It would be totally uncharacteristic and quite incredible that I would hand anybody a book I knew to be from the Carter campaign and say this might be helpful to the debate. I wouldn't tolerate it. After being involved in seven presidential campaigns, I know that's dynamite. I wouldn't touch it with a ten-foot pole. . . . I think the debate team was remiss in not bringing to me and to the campaign strategy group the fact that they were using Carter material."

To the reporters, righteous claims of ten-foot poles did not ring like true Casey. This was the SEC chairman who had hustled the ITT papers out of the reach of Congress, the man who had been investigated by the SSCI for presumably defrauding investors, the DCI who refused to put his stocks in a blind trust. Still, the old boy had been persuasive, Safire thought. On the way out, one reporter said to Safire, "Where'd all that stuff about mumbling come from? He couldn't have been clearer."

Also on the way out, Safire took Casey aside and said, "That business about being polygraphed—you'd better be careful." Casey gave him a dismissive wave and a laugh: "Ahh, I know how to handle those things." Did Casey mean that he would have no trouble because the truth was on his side? "No," Safire was to conclude later. "What he meant was he knew how to beat the machine."

There was around the polygraph a certain insider's lore. The machine did not literally detect lies; it recorded minute changes in blood pressure, heart rate, and skin temperature—physiological clues that someone *might* be lying. Nerveless types, especially those skeptical of the machine, might beat it. Pathological liars might beat it. And supposedly there were tricks to beat it. One rumor had it that by tightening the anal sphincter on a question, one could induce changes in blood pressure that would confuse and mislead the machine. Casey, who read virtually everything and possessed insatiable curiosity, doubtless knew all this.

The story the *Times* carried on July 6 did get out Casey's side of the story. But by going public, pitting his word against Baker's, he seemed to be hanging the Reagan administration's dirty linen in front of the White House. Days later, in his column, Safire wrote, metaphorically, that Casey and Baker were not speaking. Casey was instantly on the phone. "He started beating up on me," Safire remembered. "He got very rough. Bill could push very hard. All of a sudden, I was no longer his friend of twenty years' standing. I was a journalist he could intimidate. Casey, in a position of power, was not to be crossed. I was stunned by his behavior."

Robert Garrick, who had run the news-monitoring operation in the 1980 campaign to spot any October surprise, was summoned to Washington to testify before the Albosta committee. Garrick checked into the White House first and there ran into Casey. They greeted each other warmly. Casey motioned Garrick into a nearby men's room. He started to question him about his expected testimony, then suddenly stopped and put a finger to his lips. An astonished Garrick watched Casey get down on his hands and knees. "There was the director of Central Intelligence checking out the crapper stalls in the White House," Garrick recalled.

Under questioning on the Hill, Garrick quickly caught the drift of the investigation. The Albosta staff was deeply suspicious because the day-to-day operation of Garrick's monitoring center was under Robert A. Gambino, a retired CIA security specialist. Three more ex-CIA men had worked under Gambino. Weren't these people pros at collecting information through clandestine means? Wouldn't stealing opposition briefing books be all in a day's work?

The actual Carter material found in the Reagan campaign files and turned over to the Albosta committee included the 249-page document entitled *Debates: Foreign Policy and National Security Issues* and a 274-page collection untitled but called "the Mondale papers" because it had been prepared for a debate that never came off between Vice-President Walter Mondale and the Republican vice-presidential candidate, George Bush. Though it never turned up, several Reagan staffers also remembered having seen another major Carter document, entitled *Debate Briefing Material: Domestic*.

Was the delivery of the Carter debate material merely the act of disgruntled insiders—a Reagan windfall? Or was it a deliberate penetration? That was the issue facing the Albosta committee. Theodore White, chronicler of presidential campaigns, put it another way. All campaigns are conducted unethically, White said; but was this one conducted illegally?

Casey was questioned by the FBI on three occasions. And on November 8, he spent two and a half hours on Capitol Hill answering the questions of the Albosta committee lawyers.

During this period, Casey stopped by the office of Tony Dolan, a

Casey protégé during the campaign, now a White House speech writer. Dolan had a nose for conspiracies. He had won a Pulitzer for investigative reporting. Casey was inclined to listen to him. Dolan warned Casey that Richard Darman was lobbying on Baker's behalf to have the investigating committee sandbag Casey. Soon after, something happened that convinced Casey that Dolan was right. The CIA public affairs staff spotted a story in the September 26 *Richmond News Leader* in which Albosta was quoted as saying of Jim Baker: "I term him a friend. I'd feel badly if anything came up that reflected badly on Jim Baker. If it does, it's a loss to the country. As for the others, I don't take any positions." What kind of a referee was this? Casey wondered.

He had pointed out to the Albosta committee several arguments in his favor. The FBI had found Baker's fingerprints and those of Frank Hodsoll and David Gergen, Baker's campaign assistants, on the Carter papers. But they found no prints of Casey's or his immediate staff.

Gergen was a forty-one-year-old veteran of the political communications wars, having served on the Nixon and Ford White House staffs. After the Reagan victory, he had returned to the White House as assistant to the President for communications. Gergen too was queried by the Albosta committee, and on June 28 he wrote Albosta, "I do not recall ever receiving or seeing a 'Carter debate book' or any other notebook from the Carter campaign. Had that occurred, I believe that I would remember it." But days later, Gergen was writing Albosta, "I have found that I made a mistake, and I want to correct the record. . . . I wrote that letter before completing a thorough search of my files."

What Gergen found was a copy of the Carter foreign policy briefing book. Gergen also had something to say about how the Carter papers may have entered the Reagan camp. He said that he vaguely recollected standing in front of the campaign headquarters with other Reagan aides on a rainy Saturday morning, probably October 25, 1980, the day before the debate rehearsals were to start, and seeing someone in "a taxi delivering a big box . . . to the door and taking it in." The box might have contained Carter material, Gergen recalled. A young woman named Jackie Tillman, who worked for Gergen at the time, told the Albosta committee that she also remembered that "in a discussion with David Gergen . . . he mentioned something about someone coming over from the Carter campaign in a taxi bringing Carter campaign materials related to the debate preparation."

The most that Casey himself would admit about his culpability was that conceivably, just possibly, the documents may have crossed his desk, since so much paper did, and that he might have passed them on to Baker without remembering them. But he doubted that anything so startling would have escaped his notice. To Ben Frank, Casey said, "If I got those papers, I'd say so. What's the big deal? I didn't steal them. I didn't have them stolen. If they'd come into my hands, I wouldn't have shouted it from the rooftops. But if anybody asked, I'd tell the truth." Here was a different tune than he sang to Safire and the *New York Times* reporters, when he had said he would not touch the stuff with a ten-foot pole.

The Albosta inquiry and the FBI investigation ground on, with witnesses questioned beginning to approach three hundred. Casey could only wait out their verdict, in that now familiar posture, with a cloud hanging over his head.

The worry in the White House was how to end a family feud between Baker and Casey. Cliff White stopped by to see the President and had a solution: send Baker to the CIA and make Bill Casey ambassador to Ireland. White's remarks got back to Casey. He called White, sputtering with rage. "What the hell do you mean, giving my job away?" The courtly White tried to assuage his old friend. "Didn't you and I agree that the important thing was to get Jim Baker out of the White House?" "Not that way, you don't!" Casey said. "The next time you get any bright ideas, check with me first!"

Of that period, Mike Deaver recalled, "Of course, we thought it would be better if Casey left. But we never actively did anything to get him out because it wouldn't work. The President wouldn't dump him."

21.

"A Drop in Casey's Stock"

By the spring of 1983, John McMahon was warning Casey, "We've lost our credibility on the Hill on the contras. The way I read the tea leaves, if you don't make some changes in our people who talk with the committees, we're going to be legislated out of business."

Dewey Clarridge, virtually the creator of the contra army, had a particularly grating effect on people on the Hill. Rob Simmons, the SSCI staff director, commented, "I looked at Dewey's flashy dress, the silk suits and the like, as a kind of costume, a way of thumbing his nose at Congress." Senator Moynihan, no sartorial drab himself, sat watching one day while Clarridge, leaning back, jacket wide open, thumbs hooked under red suspenders, testified. Suddenly, Moynihan pulled himself forward and in the tone of a headmaster addressing a cocky upperclassman, said, "Mr. Clarridge, you are *snapping* your suspenders. You are engaging in chitchat with people behind you. Need I remind you, this is an official body?"

Clair George, the congressional relations officer, was not working out, either. George and Simmons were the day-to-day contact points where the CIA and the Senate met. "I respected Clair as a clandestine operator," Simmons said, "but he was all wrong for the Hill. His mind-set was the same as Casey's—suspicious, minimal notification. That's fine at a station overseas, but it doesn't work in a democratic forum." Another congressional staffer found Clair George "argumentative, nonresponsive, and snide."

"Clair never wanted the job," Bob Gates recalled. "He never pretended to be good at it. But Casey was the one who insisted. Once Clair got there, he reinforced all of Casey's worst instincts. Their attitude toward the Hill was screw 'em. And that attitude communicated itself throughout the operations directorate—don't tell Congress anything unless you're driven to the wall."

"It was kind of fun to watch the old walrus snap back with so little concern for the august solons," John Horton recalled of his trips to Congress with Casey. "He took no guff from any of them." His security detail, observing the DCI's behavior from close up, began referring to Casey as the "Duke of Disdain." "I have to deal with guys on those committees," Casey told Cliff White, "who couldn't get a security clearance for a job in a post office." Another aide, sitting next to Casey at a HPSCI hearing, watched as the members quarreled among themselves. Casey turned to his man and said quietly, "Sometimes I fear for the republic." His mike was live; and for once, Casey's words reverberated around the hearing room with total clarity.

The unconcealed quality of Casey's scorn amazed David Durenberger, the ranking Republican on the SSCI. "We used to carry around what we called the 'Quotations of Chairman Casey,' " Durenberger recalled. "My favorite was, 'Tell them everything you think they ought to know.' He actually said that one time when we complained that his people were not giving us the full story on the contra operation. He looked straight at us and said, 'I've encouraged everybody in the Agency to tell you everything we think you ought to know.' The irony sailed right over Casey's head."

He was seventy years old. He went before members some of whom were still children and some not yet born when he was parachuting men into hell and could only hope they might come back. In Casey's mind, his generation had fought and won the Good War, a war that had allowed these wet-behind-the-ears know-it-alls to sit here hassling him. He should be awed? Deferential?

Dick Helms had known what it was like to have old DCIs peering over his shoulder. He swore that he would give his advice only if asked. But as he watched Casey squander the good he was doing at Langley by the bad he was doing on Capitol Hill, Helms felt compelled to say something. He got Casey to invite him to lunch at the Agency. Helms told him it was a mistake to be so blatant, to deny the committees even the illusion of cooperation. "I see trouble coming," Helms warned. "You can tell the people on the committees just about anything and they'll cooperate—but only if you're aboveboard and you tell them. You'll find the only thing you can't tell them are operations you shouldn't be in in the first place, like the Bay of Pigs."

On July 19, Congress demonstrated the depth of its distrust. For only the third time in a hundred and fifty years, the full House of Representatives met in secret session. The press gallery was cleared.

A tight security force guarded all entrances. Representative Edward Boland rose to speak. Boland was quiet, even-keeled, an unlikely boat rocker. He had spent thirty years in the House, scarcely making a wave or a headline. So secure was Boland's Springfield, Massachusetts, seat that he had spent forty-seven dollars on one recent reelection campaign. He was so circumspect that the joke around the House was that Eddie Boland wouldn't tell his left hand what his right hand was doing. On national security, Boland was moderate, even conservative.

However self-effacing and nearly faceless, Boland was a member of the House inner circle. For years he had been the Washington roommate of the Speaker, Tip O'Neill. And since it was created seven years before, Boland had chaired the House Permanent Subcommittee on Intelligence.

The contra operation had long since begun to strain even Boland's forbearance. He found the administration's rationale impossible to swallow. The year before, he had engineered passage of the first "Boland Amendment," forbidding the use of U.S. funds to overthrow the Sandinista regime. Spurred on by young liberals on the committee, he was now prepared to go further.

Using maps of Nicaragua and Honduras, Boland and other Democratic opponents tore apart the contra operation. Casey had sold them on a plan for a small, limited, commando-type force to block the flow of arms to the Salvadoran rebels. What had emerged was neither small nor limited. Casey had also assured them that the only other U.S. objective was to force the Sandinistas to "look inward" and moderate their Marxism. To Boland and the others, it looked as though the goal was to overthrow the government of a sovereign country because the United States opposed it. Congress had seen virtually no evidence that the contras had captured or destroyed any large caches of smuggled weapons. Instead, they were attacking targets like ranches and granaries. And, eerily reminiscent of Vietnam, as soon as the United States began backing the contras, the Soviet Union escalated its aid to the Sandinistas.

Eddie Boland now called for a complete cutoff of military aid to the Nicaraguan rebels. And nine days later, the House, by a vote of 228 to 195, approved.

Casey's only hope now lay with the Senate. He would need every friend he could muster there. His relationship with the SSCI chairman, Barry Goldwater, was a sometime thing. Goldwater loved to regale the members with his Casey imitation. He would flap his arms and do a raspberry spray in all directions, aping Casey's speech. Still, he usually backed Casey on Central America. Pat Moynihan, the vice-chairman, was harder to handicap. In the spring of 1983, Moynihan decided to have a firsthand look at the region. On his arrival in El Salvador, he arranged to have breakfast with the rector and the provost of the Jesuit university, who was a graduate of the University of Chicago. He and Moynihan had mutual friends. The provost confided to Moynihan that probably half the Salvadoran rebels out in the hills were his former students. Moynihan put his question to his hosts squarely: "How many of their arms do they get from Nicaragua, through the Sandinistas?" The rector gave him a tolerant smile. "Almost none," he said. "You Americans have supplied our little country with all the arms both sides could possibly use. Our army keeps maybe a third; another third, the guerrillas capture or buy under the table." The other third? The rector turned up his hands and shrugged. "Who knows where they go?"

Later, in Nicaragua and with a nose for ground truth that would have done credit to an Agency analyst, Moynihan wandered through the farmers' market in Managua. "I saw almost no food," he recalled. "I was also invited to lunch by the regime's minister of the interior, Tomás Borge." Borge assured Moynihan that the Sandinistas would behave if only the United States would stop trying to overturn their revolution. As Borge spoke, Moynihan contemplated his meal—odd by Latin standards, he thought. "They served tureens of Stroganoff and Pepsi-Cola, the drink of choice in Marxist countries." Moynihan asked if he might have any of those Latin staples, rice and beans. Borge averted his eyes and confessed sheepishly, "We have no rice and beans."

The journey confirmed what Moynihan had long since concluded. As he put it, "The Marxist ethos was disappearing into a black hole, beginning in Moscow and spreading to Eastern Europe." The only people who apparently had not yet gotten the word were Third World countries like Cuba and Nicaragua—and the Reagan administration. "I also learned down there that the contras hadn't interdicted a shotgun. That's when I began to think that the administration's real intention was to overthrow the Sandinistas' regime."

That June, Barry Goldwater and the senator's old pal Bill Quinn, now an SSCI consultant, made a trip through Europe and Asia, inspecting U.S. installations and talking to CIA station chiefs. Goldwater was much surprised. Whenever he talked to the people in the trenches, the reports on Casey were always glowing. As Goldwater described the experience, "They'd tell me, the director's great. He backs us. He's not afraid to give you your head. He's one hundred percent in our corner." On the Air Force plane flying back to Washington, Goldwater sipped his drink and told Quinn, "Bill, I don't care what we think of Casey on the Hill. Here's one commanding officer whose got the troops behind him. That counts for a hell of a lot more in his game than having a bunch of us sticking our noses, frankly, where I don't think we have much business."

When Goldwater got back, he gave Casey a call and told him what he had heard. The old lawyer asked if Goldwater would put it in writing, which Goldwater did, in a letter that Casey carefully filed.

That fall, Goldwater held his Republicans in line and brought around enough Democrats to stop the latest Boland initiative in the Senate. The contras were voted $24 million to stay alive another year. "There's no problem," one contra leader told a United Press reporter. "We'll be in Managua by Christmas anyway."

Debategate was still hanging over Casey's head when another cloud darkened his sky. This one had been growing from the day he had been sworn in. Now it was about to burst.

Before his appointment as DCI, he had filled out the financial disclosure forms required of prospective presidential appointees. Question 12 asked, "Explain how you will resolve any potential conflict of interest regarding stock ownership." Casey had answered, "By disposing of assets or establishing a blind trust, if necessary." Two and a half years into the job, he had done neither. At the time he had gone to the CIA, his holdings were considerable. He owned stock in over sixty companies—IBM, Philip Morris, 3M, E.I. Du Pont, Johnson & Johnson, Exxon, Deere & Co., and ALCOA among them. His current 68,000 shares of Capital Cities alone were worth $4.7 million. His total portfolio was valued at well over $6 million. To observers, to legislators, even to well-disposed friends, his refusal to start a blind trust seemed obtuse. He had left himself open to charges that he was using the CIA as his own private investment-research arm.

From the beginning, Casey had handled the ethics of the matter in classic Casey fashion. He checked the law to see what, minimally, he was required to do. Yes, disclosure was required, and there must be no conflict of interest. But the Ethics in Government Act did not *require* cabinet officials to put their holdings in a blind trust. As his counsel reported back in a written opinion that Casey asked for, "There are no considerations dictated by your position as DCI which would bear on your decision whether or not to place your holding under some kind of trust."

He owned stock in companies—IBM, 3M, Du Pont, Johnson & Johnson—that did business with the CIA. But his counsel also informed him in another secret memorandum that "decisions relating to the choice, acquisition and use of these types of materials and services are not within the primary responsibility of the Director." In other words, no conflict of interest; no need to divest.

His two immediate predecessors as DCI, George Bush and Stansfield Turner, had both created blind trusts. In the cabinet, Al Haig and later George Shultz at State, Don Regan at Treasury, Cap Weinberger at Defense, Vice-President Bush, and President Reagan were all in blind trusts. But that was their business, Casey reasoned. He had complied with the law. If the law permitted behavior that some people found unethical, then change the law. Don't try to change him. Trying to put a somewhat more respectable face on his resistance, he told one of his lawyers, "I have a right to keep up with inflation."

He still had Richard Cheswick as his broker, and Cheswick had full discretion to buy and sell without consulting Casey, an arrangement that had been in place since the sixties. When asked, Casey would say, "My financial adviser makes all my decisions about stocks. I haven't talked to a broker in twenty years." It was not quite true. His telephone logs show five phone calls each year from his office to Cheswick in 1981, 1982, and 1983. Cheswick maintained that the calls occurred only when Betty Murphy phoned to let him know that Casey needed cash.

There was one exception. On August 24, 1982, Casey called Cheswick from Chicago, where he had gone to make a speech before the American Legion. Capital Cities had had a nice run up to eighty dollars a share, an all-time high. Casey instructed Cheswick to sell 30,000 shares. Cheswick had already sold 20,000 shares of Capital Cities the year before. Casey said he wanted to reduce his holdings even further. Cheswick told him that he thought the move was a mistake, that he ought to hold on. But Casey insisted, and the sale netted almost $2.4 million.

As pressure mounted from Congress and the media, Casey put in place something instead of a blind trust, something curious if not bizarre: he adopted a "screening arrangement." A dozen of the highest CIA officials received a list of Casey's stocks. As they went about their duties, they were to check the particular matter that they were handling against the list to determine if it might involve any of Casey's stocks. If so, the deputy director and Stanley Sporkin, as counsel, would decide if a possible conflict of interest existed. Was it appropriate, for example, for Casey to become involved in a decision to launch a covert operation in Kuwait if Casey owned stock in an oil company doing business there? If a potential conflict did exist, then McMahon and Sporkin went to Casey with two choices: he could keep the stock but stay out of the issue, in which case McMahon would act in his place; or he could sell the stock and become involved.

As Cheswick bought and sold stocks for Casey's account, the list had to be updated. Thus, notices went out from the DCI to the people who ran America's intelligence service: "Add Wendy's. Delete Burger King."

Members of the intelligence committees found the screening arrangement ludicrous: hours of the nation's intelligence chiefs spent keeping the director out of trouble; the director of Central Intelligence potentially staying out of a major decision because he held stock in a particular company. The whole arrangement was "a dodge to cover Casey's ass," as one member put it. "It did not make any sense."

Barry Goldwater was the soul of tolerance where the CIA was concerned. But Casey was trying his soul. The summer before, he had written Casey:

Bill, just a piece of advice. Why don't you take all of your funds and put them in a blind trust? That is going to eliminate any question about what you do or don't do. . . . Anytime this group says anything about your background on money, someone on the intelligence committee is going to demand a hearing which I am going to have to grant and you are going to be subjected to the same old routine you went through before. You and I aren't exactly children anymore. . . . As the saying goes, you can't take it with you, so why don't you put it in a blind trust?

Casey's response was to have an aide find out how many of the 535 members of Congress had blind trusts. The list totaled ten, and he did not see Goldwater's name on it. He was polite enough to omit that fact in his reply to Goldwater, but he did say, "I agree that we can't take it with us. You will agree that, if I were concerned about taking it with me or piling it up, there are other ways I could spend my time to greater effect."

Every spring, Casey was required to update his financial-holdings statement. The statement covering 1981 revealed that he sold six hundred thousand dollars' worth of oil stocks that year. The report was released in May of 1982, and an Associated Press story on it began, "CIA Director William J. Casey, who has access to secret government oil supply estimates . . ." and went on to describe what sounded like the most inside of insider trading. The CIA did have analysts whose job was to monitor the world oil market. These people had produced an estimate that the Soviet Union was not about to become an importer and would be self-sufficient for at least the next four years—news calculated to drive world oil prices down. Such information was not unknown to outside market analysts. But how much of a head start did Casey have? .

A former intelligence officer was quoted in another AP story saying, "The CIA director will know almost before anyone else when an oil fire shuts down a major field in the Persian Gulf; whether the Chinese have to buy wheat . . . when a foreign government is planning to expropriate an American firm. . . . Casey is one of a half dozen people who have got it all."

Richard Cheswick read the press allegations with alarm. "I saw news stories where I was supposedly getting calls from Casey that he had seen satellite photographs showing tankers riding low in the water, which meant a worldwide oil glut and falling prices," Cheswick recalled. "So Casey was supposedly telling me to sell. The truth is that I began to liquidate his holdings out of my own belief that oil prices were threatening to come down. I sold oil stocks for all my clients, not just Casey. I never got the faintest whiff of information from the CIA. I wrote to the *Washington Post* saying so. But nothing was going to change the appearance that Bill Casey was making megabucks off of CIA intelligence."

Michael Sniffen, an AP reporter, called Stanley Sporkin and grilled him hard about the oil stock sales. As Sporkin defended Casey point by point, the reporters said, "Yes, but we wouldn't have to take Casey's word on all this if he just went into a blind trust." "Oh yeah?" Sporkin answered. "In a blind trust the public wouldn't have any idea of his transactions. Besides, if Casey's a crook, he can be a crook just as easily under a blind trust."

Sporkin was a lawyer, a smart one with all the answers, and a scrapper, utterly loyal to Casey. Still, Casey was getting harder and harder to defend. Why the hell didn't he go into a blind trust, Sporkin wondered, and end this damaging suspicion? Casey's behavior may have been legal, but it was "stupid," a fellow millionaire in the cabinet observed.

The only beneficiary in the present situation seemed to be Richard Cheswick. As the flood of stories identified the man who had so skillfully managed Casey's portfolio, Cheswick found himself deluged by would-be clients.

On June 2, the *Washington Post* ran another front-page story, headlined, CASEY TRADED HEAVILY IN STOCKS. Some $1.5 million had been bought for his account in a recent twenty-six-day period. His latest financial disclosure report revealed that, all told, Casey had made seventy-five stock transactions, totaling millions of dollars, over the past year. Outraged Americans wrote to their congressmen and wanted to know how they could let Casey "thumb his nose at ethics in government."

President Reagan received a letter from Senator Carl Levin of Michigan, the ranking minority member of the Subcommittee on Oversight and Government Management, warning the President to get Casey into a blind trust. Levin, a man of formidable rectitude, added a kicker: "In the absence of such an arrangement, I will seek legislation requiring that a blind trust be established."

Levin was gentleman enough to speak directly to Casey about his intentions. Casey argued that members of Congress were also privy to inside information. That was not the same at all, Levin retorted. Congress customarily operated in the open. And people knew how the members voted; if the public did not like it, they could vote a congressman out of office. "But if I go to a blind trust now," Casey said, "it'll look like I'm admitting guilt."

"If we have to pass a bill forcing you to," Levin said, "you'll look a hell of a lot guiltier."

Casey asked for time to think it over.

Casey buckled and told Levin that he would create a blind trust. The matter seemed ended—but not quite. Casey's largest single holding, the remaining shares of Capital Cities Broadcasting stock, were kept out of the trust. Casey said it was his understanding that the Office of Government Ethics would not allow him to include in the trust a stock that comprised more than 20 percent of his total portfolio, as Capital Cities did.

Casey was a man who gave the external appearance of having the hide of an alligator. John McMahon read him better. Despite the airy wave-offs, despite the claims that "it only hurts for a day," the lack of public esteem pained Casey. That October, in Casey's absence, McMahon was chairing a meeting of the senior staff. He looked around the room in his most commanding pose, chin jutting out, eyes narrow and measuring. He proposed something that had never been done before at the CIA. "I don't have to tell you people what Bill Casey's done for this place," he said. "Here's a guy who needs a bucker-up." McMahon proposed that Casey be awarded the Agency's highest honor, the Distinguished Intelligence Medal. The decoration had been given to DCIs and senior officials before, but always at the end of their service. As George Lauder remembered the moment, "Hell, if Stan Turner had stood in the window of the seventh floor and said 'Follow me,' we'd have pushed him out. If Casey had said it, we'd jump with him."

On October 6, the CIA auditorium was crowded to overflowing. Sophia and Bernadette were there. John McMahon made the presentation. Casey was being honored, McMahon said, for "restoring the credibility of the Agency and pumping life back into it." As McMahon slipped the medal over Casey's head, he saw a tear run down the old man's cheek. Casey had the medal framed and hung on his wall—the only personal memento there other than his swearing-in photos.

The glow was indeed warm. But its warmth could not last. In November, another spate of damaging stories erupted. The *Washington Post*, the *New York Times*, the *Wall Street Journal*, the wire services, the major networks all carried stories that thirteen companies in which Casey held stock were doing business with the CIA. Casey tried to put out the fire. He issued a statement saying yes, he did own these stocks, and one of the companies did have a CIA contract in excess of $1 million. But four of the companies had contracts under $3,000, and one for $12.49. He had not, he said, been involved in negotiating any of the contracts. Furthermore, the Office of Government Ethics had "scrutinized every one of my holdings . . . and determined that not a single one of them was related to my primary area of responsibility."

The inside might be sensitive, but the alligator hide had again failed to sense that everything legal was not necessarily admirable. The media did not miss the distinction. Editorial indignation ran hot (the *Louisville Times:* "CIA Chief Still Doesn't Get the Point"; the *St. Louis Post Dispatch:* "Mr. Casey's Dubious Ethics"; the *Chicago Sun Times:* "Come Clean, Casey"; the *Tampa Tribune:* "Casey Should Put Himself Above Suspicion or Quit"). The press fallout washed away any trace of goodwill that his creation of a blind trust had earned.

Jack Anderson was hardly an admirer of Bill Casey, yet in his *Washington Newsletter* the columnist wrote:

Casey was disturbingly slow about placing his holdings in a blind trust. The CIA happens to be a clearinghouse for the most sensitive intelligence the United States gathers, including financial transactions that would be an investor's dream. . . . CIA sources came to me with whispered reports that Casey used his secret financial information for his personal profit. I conducted a painstaking investigation and could find absolutely no evidence of wrongdoing.

On the contrary, I concluded that the accusations not only were false, but that the accusers were CIA careerists who want to get rid of Casey. They don't like his tendency to ignore proper channels and to promote derring-do covert operations.

Bill Casey was not a stupid man. So why the bullheadedness? Why did he resist not only pressure from without but the advice of those whose judgment he prized, men like Sporkin and McMahon? In part, it was simply that, bullheadedness. As he told Sporkin, "I'm not gonna let the press push me around. I didn't do anything wrong. Fuck 'em." Partly it was the habit, ingrained over a lifetime, of skating to the very edge of the abyss and safely gliding away. At bottom, it was a deep-seated fear of something far worse than what a bad press could do to him. He had had a close call with a blind trust during his government service in the seventies. He was haunted by a specter that the painfully constructed foundation of wealth that had lifted him up to power might suddenly disappear and send him back to oblivion.

22.

October Surprises

The CIA had been eavesdropping on telephone conversations of Soviet officials between cars as they drove around Moscow, until a nationally syndicated U.S. columnist wrote about it. Then the Soviets took countermeasures; the source went dead. Leaks enraged Casey. Ninety-nine percent of them would dry up tomorrow, he believed, if only people on the Hill, and yes, in the White House, kept their mouths shut. If no one else was going to do anything about it, then he would take on the responsibility himself. He had his security office put together a dog-and-pony show which he took to State and Defense, where he lectured senior officials and brought home with horrifying examples the cost of loose talk.

On June 21, 1983, he took his show to the White House. Some thirty senior officials gathered in the Roosevelt Room. The doors were closed and Secret Service agents posted outside. Those remaining inside were informed that the session they were about to take a part in was confidential. Much of what they would hear was classified and must be treated as such. Casey then went on to describe the damage to American policy and the danger to American lives when those entrusted with keeping the nation's secrets leaked.

The secret White House meeting on leaking leaked. Within days, Lou Cannon had the story in the *Washington Post*.

Hopping mad, Casey went to see the President. But Ronald Reagan was so genial, so cordial, that he made one feel like a boor for spoiling his day; the hard edge of Casey's anger was dulled by the softness of the material it struck. Still, Casey said what had to be said. The leak of the meeting in the Roosevelt Room obviously had come from someone in the room that day. The leaker should not be hard to trace. Casey had a suggestion: why shouldn't everyone who was present be polygraphed? Casey did it all the time with his people at the CIA, he explained. "You've got to do something to give your staff some signal other than words that passing confidential information out of this building is no longer a risk-free enterprise," he told Reagan.

The President was appalled. To Reagan, the leaks were breaches of patriotism and acts of personal disloyalty to him. But polygraph his friends—people he trusted and who worked alongside him day after day? Casey left not knowing what the President would do. Only time would tell. And time usually told him that the President would do nothing.

Back at Langley, Casey poured out his exasperation to John McMahon. "I know a surefire way to find out who's leaking," McMahon said. "What's that?" Casey asked. "Who's benefiting, who's getting the good press," McMahon answered.

"Yeah," Casey said. "Jim Baker rushes to mind."

A few days later, on Sunday, Casey had just returned home from mass when Bill Clark phoned. The national security adviser told him to come to the Situation Room in the White House right away for an NSPG meeting. Lending the moment urgency was the fact that the President would be there on a Sunday morning.

Sixteen people in the room awaited the President's arrival, among them George Shultz, Cap Weinberger, Jeane Kirkpatrick, Jim Baker, Clark, and several high-level officials from State, Defense, and the NSC. Reagan entered, glowing and sinfully vigorous for a man his age. He was dressed in slacks, a checked sport jacket, and an open-collared shirt, as though he had just been called in from a country-club barbecue. Everyone rose; he asked them to sit down, with that good-natured humility that said all the fuss was unnecessary. He smiled at Bill Clark, seated at his right, and said, "Bill, take it away." Clark, by contrast, was baggy-eyed, unhealthily pale, a man worn down by constant crisis management and the unrelieved infighting among the national security players.

They had been called together because of a cable that had come in that morning from Clark's deputy, a former Marine lieutenant colonel named Robert C. "Bud" McFarlane, who was on a sensitive mission to Beirut. Some fifteen hundred U.S. Marines had been sent into Beirut the previous October to help maintain peace during a period hazardous even by Middle East standards. Israel had invaded Lebanon in June of 1982 to drive out PLO terrorists. Syria, occupying Lebanon's Bekaa Valley, was objecting to this upset of the precarious balance of power in the region. The United States was now attempting to arrange the withdrawal of all foreign forces from Lebanon. The Marines had taken up positions around the Beirut airport as a symbol that behind America's diplomatic efforts lay American muscle. Other than that symbolic value, no one, including the administration and doubtless the Marines themselves, was sure what they were doing there. And they were terribly vulnerable.

The substance of McFarlane's cable was that the Marines should be authorized to call in air strikes to defend themselves from forces that were occasionally lobbing shells at them. In short, McFarlane was calling for escalation. President Reagan approved. All communications on the matter, including McFarlane's cable, had been classified "secret/sensitive."

Two days after the Situation Room meeting, the lead story in the *Washington Post* began: "President Reagan has authorized Marines in Beirut to call in air strikes against forces shelling their positions, serving notice that the United States is ready to escalate its fire power." The story went on to explain that the decision had been based on the recommendations of Robert C. McFarlane. The byliners, Lou Cannon and George Wilson, cited unnamed sources in their essentially accurate, at times verbatim account.

Casey was horrified. Recently, in the same country, Bashir Gemayel, the president-elect of Lebanon, had been blown up nine days before he was to be inaugurated. Two days after that, Gemayel's armed supporters had gone into two Palestinian refugee camps in Beirut and butchered nearly eight hundred people, including women and children. To Casey, whoever had revealed McFarlane's activities in this powder keg not only had jeopardized U.S. policy but had endangered the life of an associate. The leaker had to be one of eighteen people in the Situation Room that Sunday. There was no doubt in Casey's mind: the leaker must be Jim Baker or someone on his staff, what Casey called "the White House whispering apparatus."

Casey called Bill Clark as soon as he finished the *Post* story and poured his fury into a sympathetic ear. The two men agreed on a plan. Two days later, Casey received formal approval of it in a secret/sensitive letter from the President. Referring to the Situation Room meeting, Reagan wrote:

> Bill, as much as I regret the necessity of this, I ask you to interview the above named people to determine if any one of them spoke with any of the [*Post's*] authors . . . or to any other unauthorized person concerning the subject matter reported, particularly relating to Bud McFarlane. I ask that you use all legitimate means in your interviews, including use of the polygraph. As I have said before, if you determine in your personal judgment, that reasonable cause exists for believing anyone in my Administration has breached his

duty of confidentiality or anyone fails or refuses to cooperate with you in the interview, I will expect that person to resign.

Some officials agreed to be polygraphed; some did not. Casey wrote a letter to Baker that read, "As you know, letting that information get out of the room that day put Bud McFarlane's life in immediate danger and undermined him as a diplomatic emissary. You have fiercely resisted the use of the polygraph to determine how this happened." But it was George Shultz's reaction that killed the polygraph as a weapon in the investigation. Shultz said yes, he would agree to be polygraphed, once—and then he would resign.

The investigation into the McFarlane leak sputtered out inconclusively. Casey felt like the prosecutor who knows in his gut who did it but lacks hard evidence that will stand up in court. He also knew that Ronald Reagan was not going to dump Jim Baker any more than he was going to dump Bill Casey.

To Casey, leaks from the White House were unforgivable. But Congress, in his judgment, remained the prime offender. "Come off it, Bill," Senator Pat Leahy told him after one of Casey's blistering phone calls. "I get calls from your people that they've got something hot. They tell me they have to see me right away. I turn on CNN and there it is on the news before your guy gets here. It happens again and again. Why don't you just take the *New York Times* and the *Washington Post*, stamp them top secret, and have them delivered here. Look at the advantages. We'll get the intelligence faster than waiting for your people to level. We'll get more details. And we'll get a crossword puzzle."

Casey was not amused.

CIA employees below grade sixteen ate in the main cafeteria, with one section screened off so that visitors could not see people who worked in covert operations. Senior officers dined in the executive dining room, where they tended to cluster, DO people at one table, DI people at another, administrative types at still another. One day, John Horton had taken a seat among the NIOs. They were joined by a colleague, Charles Waterman, a senior analyst on the National Intelligence Council—a slight, anxious man. "I've got a problem," Waterman said quietly, looking especially frazzled. "I didn't do too well on the box." His colleagues instantly understood his concern.

Casey was about to face a personal test of his determination to punish leakers. The NSA's global listening devices had twice intercepted transmissions from the Japanese Mitsubishi company's Washington offices to Tokyo containing information lifted whole from the National Intelligence Daily, a top-secret summary that went supposedly to only 150 cleared U.S. officials. The NSA had brought the FBI into the case. And the FBI had traced the leak to Waterman.

According to the FBI investigation, Mitsubishi had obtained the information, part of which dealt with Iranian and Iraqi border troop movements, from a Washington consulting firm. The firm had received the information, it said, from someone in the intelligence community. Waterman denied that he was the source. He admitted only to having had a conversation with a member of the consulting firm, admittedly on the Iran-Iraq war. But he had not leaked verbatim chunks of the NID, he insisted. Unfortunately, he had flunked both the FBI and CIA polygraphs, because, according to Waterman, he was so agitated.

Casey had wanted the President's chief of staff fired for leaking. Now he had an alleged leaker in his own house. He called for Waterman's file and found twenty years of blameless, indeed outstanding, service, most of it on the covert side, much of it in rough Middle East stations.

Part of the mystique of the U.S. Marine Corps was that it did not abandon its wounded. Should the CIA do less? What kind of message would jettisoning Waterman send throughout the Agency? On the other hand, suppose it looked as if Casey practiced a double standard on leakers, one for his own staff and another for everybody else? His own security office made the choice easy for him. The in-house recommendation was to fire Waterman. That was also what the FBI wanted.

Casey had devoted two and a half years to restoring the morale and self-esteem of the people in this building. He was not going to throw it away by sacrificing one lamb for the satisfaction of outside critics. What if Waterman had talked with outside sources? That was precisely what Casey had urged his analysts to do—to break out of the mold, to reach out to untapped private founts of information. Besides, the man had said he was innocent. Casey slapped Waterman's wrist. He docked him two weeks' pay.

The FBI was not satisfied. It upgraded the Waterman case to one of criminal espionage. Casey felt the increased pressure and put Waterman on administrative leave. Still, he refused to fire him.

Was Casey himself a leaker? Herb Meyer had prepared a secret assessment on the Soviet Union. In it he produced evidence that the

Russians could not continue indefinitely on their present disastrous economic course. Something had to give. He had proudly dispatched a draft to Casey. He thought the piece represented the kind of fresh thinking that the director wanted from his NIOs. He was shocked to find the assessment surface in the syndicated column of Rowland Evans and Robert Novak. The morning it appeared, Meyer drove into the garage under the CIA headquarters just ahead of the director's motorcade. As they rode up in the elevator, Casey said, deadpan, "Interesting reading in Evans and Novak."

"Well, I didn't leak it," Meyer answered.

"I never said you did," Casey replied. "Anyway, don't worry about it. Maybe somebody's just trying to make us look good for a change." He gave Meyer a mischievous smile. It was true, Meyer thought. He had written a good piece, and it did make the Agency's assessment capability shine. Maybe the good or evil of leaking depended on who leaked, and for what reason.

Casey had grown close to Jeane Kirkpatrick. It was not simply the shared conservatism; the Reagan administration was filled with true believers. Rather, it was the sophistication of the conservatism they shared. So many of the others were primitives mouthing thirdhand Tory platitudes. But to Casey, a woman like Jeane Kirkpatrick gave conservatism intellectual respectability. Her convictions were grounded in serious reading, thinking, and scholarship. Casey and Kirkpatrick did not have to explain to each other who Russell Kirk was, or the defects in Keynesian economics.

Kirkpatrick was one person with whom Casey felt that he could level about the President, because they shared a common frustration. They both liked the man; they even admired him; he had good instincts and good judgment, they thought. But as Casey told her at one cocktail tête-à-tête, "I just wish the guy would get a deeper handle on things." What they particularly lamented was that the President was so manipulable. To Kirkpatrick, the Reagan circle could be divided between "the pro-manipulators and the anti-manipulators." She and Casey were obviously in the latter category.

Casey was convinced that Jeane Kirkpatrick's mind and strengths went well beyond the heavily ceremonial demands of ambassador to the United Nations. "He started talking to me about running for President," Kirkpatrick recalled. "He was quite serious. He brought it up again and again. He said that when the time came, he would run my campaign. He kept telling me, 'You can do it. You can win.'

Which told me he didn't think much of George Bush, who everybody assumed would follow the President as the next Republican candidate."

On October 13, an opportunity arose to elevate Kirkpatrick to something Casey thought equal to her talents. The President suddenly announced that Bill Clark would be leaving the NSC to become secretary of the Interior. Casey was not surprised. Clark's strength was his stability and his dogged loyalty to Ronald Reagan, not his grasp of global affairs. The man had been exhausted by twelve-hour days, seven-day weeks, carried out amid constant sniping, not from outsiders but by colleagues—namely, Jim Baker and Michael Deaver.

Casey feared that Clark's deputy, Bud McFarlane, might be elevated to the post. To Casey, McFarlane was a born subordinate, one of the faceless, always standing to one side and behind the principal—a spot McFarlane by now had occupied on the Senate Armed Services Committee, Henry Kissinger's NSC staff, and, most recently, Bill Clark's. McFarlane's elevation to the top job, in Casey's judgment, would represent a double setback: not only would the administration get a plodder but it would likely lose a star, Jeane Kirkpatrick. Rumor had it that if the NSC job opened up again and she did not get it, Kirkpatrick intended to leave government. True or not, Casey was not above using this argument to promote the move he had in mind. The morning after Clark's departure announcement, Casey closed his door and started jotting down notes for the NSPG meeting scheduled for that afternoon:

- McFarlane, competent, knowledgeable. But not for National Security Adviser.
- Perceived moderate. Sends wrong signal to Hill and Moscow.
- Result in loss of major asset, Jeane Kirkpatrick.
- Be perceived as putting foreign policy totally in hands of State Department.
- Cause loss of confidence and anguish among conservatives.
- Appointing Kirkpatrick would galvanize conservatives, give us articulate public spokesman.

What he left off the list was his fear that McFarlane would be captured by Baker. Then where would Casey be? He would not be able to get a message through to the President that the White House was burning. Bill Clark might not have been Talleyrand, but he was at least an ally.

As the NSPG meeting opened, Casey had his notes stuffed in his inside breast pocket. Ordinarily, Kirkpatrick would be present. He was just as glad that she was not (she was at home with the flu): his pitch would be less awkward without her in the room. But before he could pull out the notes, Clark, still aboard for his closing days, was passing around a note of his own.

When the note came to Casey, he read it with disbelief. McFarlane's appointment would have been unfortunate; what Clark reported was a catastrophe. The pro-manipulators had pulled off a stunner: the President had already agreed that very day to make Jim Baker the new national security adviser and Michael Deaver the new White House chief of staff.

The move apparently had been born in Baker's agile mind. He had told Deaver that the chief of staff job had lost its savor for him. Foreign policy was his real interest. He was not going to be able to bump Shultz, Weinberger, or Casey; the next best thing was the NSC. "Look," he told Deaver, "we've always made a great team. We still will." Deaver was uneasy about his gifts to hold down the second-most-powerful office in the White House. "But," he later confided, "Jim Baker talked me into it." They had gone to the President, who had agreed to the switch as easily as if they had suggested changing seats in the White House mess. A statement announcing the changes had already been prepared for release to the press.

When Clark's note completed the circuit, Casey glanced around the room at the likeliest allies, Meese and Weinberger. They could virtually read each other's eyes. "How the hell can you put the worst leaker in the administration in charge of the NSC?" Casey muttered to Ed Meese. And as for Deaver, Casey went on, he was "a lightweight, a fly speck." This crazy development was exactly what Casey found so troubling about the President. Couldn't he see these things? It was, he said, shaking his head, "mindless, just mindless."

As soon as Clark could decently bring the meeting to a close, he, Casey, Meese, and Weinberger corralled the President. They argued strenuously against the switch. Reagan listened with the bewildered expression of a man who, gosh, was trying so hard to please and had wound up pleasing nobody. In the end, they carried the day. The plan was scrapped and the announcement torn up. Reagan said he would rethink Clark's replacement.

Casey went to see Jeane Kirkpatrick at home. He found her bundled in a bathrobe, hacking, wheezing, her nose rubbed raw. Casey told her that he was fighting hard to get her the NSC post. As he left, he said with a laugh that if the NSC gambit did not work, they had a fallback position—the presidency.

On October 17, the President announced the compromise choice for national security adviser: Robert C. McFarlane. After the close call of almost having Baker in the job, even McFarlane was looking good to Casey.

Long before McFarlane's warning about the U.S. Marine contingent in Beirut, the NIO for the region had already produced a top-secret estimate entitled "Prospects for Lebanon." Part of this paper dealt with the role of the Marines encamped around the airport, who had been deployed to keep a lid on an explosive situation until the contending Lebanese factions could be brought together. The estimate concluded that these rivals were still far apart. In the second-to-last paragraph, in italics, the paper warned that the Marines were perilously exposed and highly vulnerable to a terrorist attack.

Herb Meyer had been heavily involved in the preparation of the estimate. He recalled the day Casey returned from the regular Friday breakfast he had begun with George Shultz. "He called Bob Gates and me into his office," Meyer said, "and he told us Shultz didn't approve of the estimate—it was too harsh, too pessimistic. He told us we had to rewrite it. I said, 'Christ, Bill, the ink's not even dry! What Shultz is saying is he doesn't like our conclusions. That doesn't mean we're wrong.' "

Casey was apologetic. "I know, I know," he said. "But you know how hard I've had to work to get George to take our stuff. I've finally got him coming around. And I hate like hell to say no the first time he asks me for something. Look, we *could* be wrong. Take another crack at it." Meyer wailed, and Gates said of course they could.

The estimate was recirculated through the analytical system, and to Meyer's delight and Casey's annoyance it came out more vehement: the conclusion now reached was that the prospects for the Lebanese factions coming together were nil. Gates and Meyer braced themselves to take the rewrite back to the DCI. Casey went through it at his usual lightning pace, then looked up coolly and said, "Never use words like 'nil' in intelligence reporting. Nothing is ever one hundred percent. You guys are just trying to ram this down Shultz's throat." Gates and Meyer eyed each other uneasily. "Make it 'bleak' instead of 'nil' and release it," Casey said. They burst out laughing.

On October 23, Casey was in Oslo. He had just completed a tour of obscure Norwegian towns—Tromsø, Vardø, Vadsø—parts of the eavesdropping apparatus that encircled the Soviet Union. It was a Sunday morning. He had spent the night at the residence of the American ambassador and had just finished breakfast when his secretary, Betty Murphy, informed him that his Norwegian chief of station was there and needed to speak to him urgently. The station chief informed him that a truck, apparently loaded with TNT, had sped past the sentries and plowed into a building at the Beirut airport housing men of the Eighth Marine Battalion. The building had been reduced to rubble. The casualties were heavy: 241 dead and 80 wounded.

Just before departing for the Norway trip, Casey had had a conversation about another part of the globe with his erstwhile aide Constantine Menges, now handling Latin America for the NSC. An anthill island in the West Indies was much on Menges's mind. Grenada, population 110,000, area 120 squares miles, had fallen under the rule of a magnetic young Marxist named Maurice Bishop. Tiny Grenada was building a runway to accommodate the largest jets. That fact in itself might not be remarkable on an island where the principal industries were coconuts, nutmeg, and tourism. But the nine-thousand-foot runway was being constructed with Cuban aid, and when it was done, the Soviet Union had permission to use it. Cuban ships were also tying up in Grenada's port. To Constantine Menges, referred to in his CIA days as "Constant Menace," the Soviets were clearly intent on establishing a new foothold in the Caribbean.

On October 19, Maurice Bishop was assassinated, and chaos followed. Nearly a thousand Americans, mostly medical students, lived on the island, and their safety appeared in jeopardy. Menges had caught Casey just before his departure to Norway and briefed him on a plan that he had put into the national security mill for protecting these American citizens.

By the time Casey returned to Washington on Monday night, October 24, the Menges plan had grown to a full-scale American invasion of Grenada, which was launched the next day. The American force encountered unexpectedly stiff resistance from Grenadians and Cubans, but the tide soon yielded to overwhelming U.S. superiority in numbers and firepower. Concern persisted, however, that Grenadian troops and Cuban auxiliaries had withdrawn to the hills around the capital of Saint George to carry on the fight. U.S. transports lay off the island waiting to see if reinforcements were going to be needed.

John Horton, as NIO for Latin America, was to coordinate a spot assessment. The report concluded that, between Grenadians and Cubans killed or captured, all but a few had been accounted for. Castro was not going to reinforce the island. This little war was over.

Herb Meyer saw the assessment first and virtually flung it back at Horton, saying, "It stinks." Horton felt his stomach knot. If Meyer said the report stank, Casey would say it stank, and an unpleasant time lay ahead for Horton. Indeed, as it turned out, Casey did not like the assessment. He called Horton to his office and grumbled, "This thing lacks imagination."

"What do you mean?" Horton asked, puzzled.

Casey complained that Horton had described the Cuban military aid in defensive terms. "He wanted the assessment to say that a catch-all collection of old weapons that the Cubans had given to the Grenadians were intended for spreading subversion throughout the Caribbean," Horton recalled of their conversation. "I felt that my professional integrity was being squeezed, if not twisted." For Horton, plucked from the peace of his southern Maryland vineyard, it was like being plunged back into the Cold War. Casey was getting harder and harder to serve. He found the man impossible to satisfy, "an intellectual bully."

A cache of documents seized in Grenada had been brought back to Langley. "It was pathetic stuff," Horton remembered. "Here were these poor, barely educated blacks, trying to cope with dialectic materialism and the rest of Marxism. Some of the writing, like the material on the New Jewel movement down there, was juvenile. The reports of meetings were comical in a sad sort of way. And the result of the stuff was innocuous—an agreement for setting up a Bulgarian fish hatchery, for example."

Horton was again called to Casey's office, where he found the director plunging his hands into a box of the documents as though scooping gems from a treasure chest. "This time we've got the goods," he told Horton. "We've caught 'em red-handed. We have here the proof of a Soviet-Cuban plot against the peoples of the Caribbean."

Horton was perplexed. "Why are we speaking of a Soviet-Cuban plot? Maurice Bishop was Castro's man. And now, this guy Bernard Coard is in charge. Coard is the Soviets' fair-haired boy. He's just back from Moscow. And it looks like he was in on the Bishop killing. The Cubans have to be suspicious when their guy, Bishop, gets knocked off and the Russians' boy takes over. But you're talking about Soviet-Cuban collaboration. If we can't stir up some dissension between the Russians and the Cubans on this one, maybe we don't belong in this game."

Casey thought for a long time, then said, "Yeah, you're right. The Cuban-Soviet stuff is just what Jeane Kirkpatrick is peddling at the U.N. That's the propaganda line." Still, he dipped his hands into the pile of paper again. "Anyway," Casey exulted, "this stuff is better than what the Germans seized from the Communists at Smolensk in '41."

On September 28, Casey, the scourge of leakers, a man who could say "We probably lose more information through the media by leaks than we do to foreign spies," granted an exclusive interview to the nation's premier investigative journalist, Bob Woodward of the *Washington Post*. So far, Casey had followed a zigzag course in his dealings with the media. In the early stages at Langley, he had simply avoided most reporters. In the first year, Mike Wallace had pleaded with him to do a television profile for "60 Minutes." Casey turned him down. He would lose face and trust in the intelligence community, he said, if he were seen as a publicity hound. Still, insulating himself went against Casey's natural grain. He thought of himself as a word man. He liked writers and reporters; he enjoyed fencing with them.

As his image in the press darkened, George Lauder, his current public affairs officer, occasionally hazarded having him see a reporter. To Lauder, Casey was a brilliant man doing a good job of rebuilding the country's intelligence service. Some of that ought to seep through in direct encounters with the press. But the prospect of an interview with Woodward made Lauder nervous.

According to Tony Dolan, the presidential speech writer, Woodward's request to see Casey had begun when Woodward first called him. "We'd known each other as fellow investigative reporters," Dolan recalled. "Bob asked me about seeing Bill on Debategate. So I called Casey and I told him I thought he should, because the *Washington Post* was going to drive him crazy on this story. 'You ought to sit down with Woodward to forestall exaggerated speculation,' I said. 'If you level with the guy, he's not going to waste his time following a bogus story.'"

Casey laid down his own ground rules. The interview was strictly for background. "If I talk to Woodward, I never want to see anything in print from that session," he warned Lauder. According to Woodward, the interview took place on September 28 at Casey's office in the old EOB. Barely two weeks after the first encounter, Casey told Lauder, "Woodward wants to talk to me again. I'm going to have him over for dinner. Do you want to come?" Lauder was surprised, and what looked like a developing pattern made him uneasy. He declined the invitation and said, "Just give me a blow-by-blow afterwards."

Casey had Woodward over to his new home in Foxhall Crescent. Sophia was in Florida, and so Bernadette served as hostess. Casey invited the reporter into the den for a drink. They talked about the big stories that week—the bombing of the Marine barracks, the invasion of Grenada. Casey parted the curtain on Grenada and gave Woodward a peek. The Cuban penetration had been far deeper than feared, he said. The Cubans passed off as "construction workers" on the island were real fighters, he said. He described the cache of captured documents, some of which he claimed had been booby-trapped. John Horton would have winced.

Over the lamb chop dinner that Bernadette prepared, Casey described a huge Soviet investment in the Caribbean region, $4 billion. But he was unable to support the figure when Woodward pressed him on it. He did, however, make one intriguing revelation as to why he gave such high priority to obscure countries like Nicaragua and El Salvador. Casey told Woodward that the Soviet penetration of the area was a feint, an attempt to distract America from the arena of serious consequence, the world's oil aorta, the Middle East. The feint was not going to work, Casey said. The United States was going to thwart the Soviets in both places.

President Reagan was to speak to the nation that night on television about Grenada and the bombing in Beirut. Casey invited Woodward to stay and watch with him. They retired again to the den. In weaving a tapestry of Soviet international conspiracy, the President had pulled in Korean Air Lines flight 007, shot down over Soviet territory on September 1 with the loss of 269 civilian lives. This was no accident, the President said. "It was an act of barbarism born of a society which wantonly disregards individual rights and the value of human life."

Casey knew better. He had written to Richard Nixon on the subject shortly before, telling him, "Our intelligence assessment was that the downing was an accident, a case of mistaken identity. We believe they were not going to let any plane overfly that much of the Soviet Union and get away." This assessment was also known to the White House, though so far it had been kept under wraps. In the meantime, the President went on righteously flagellating the Soviets. Casey virtually beamed as the President flailed away.

Bernadette, other than playing the gracious hostess, had said little.

But as the door closed behind Bob Woodward, she told her father, "That's the smoothest guy I ever saw in my life. You'd better watch out, Dad."

Casey continued to give Woodward time over the next several months, at formal interviews, in phone calls, and during casual encounters at social events. Why did a man so sensitive about protecting secrets risk these encounters with a reporter extraordinarily skilled at unearthing them? The explanation contained a mixture of Churchill's dictum about good reasons and real reasons. Casey's good reasons were good enough. As Dick Helms saw it, "Woodward was going to write anyway, and Bill didn't want his point of view missing." But there was more to it. Casey's friend Cliff White, thinking back on the Woodward-Casey relationship, probably struck closest to the real reason: "I think Bill thought he had the candlepower to brainwash Bob Woodward." Seeing if he could best the vaunted journalist was an intellectual duel, a game, a challenge.

During his dinner with Bob Woodward, Casey had given the reporter a copy of a speech he was to deliver on October 29 at Westminster College in Fulton, Missouri, where Churchill had delivered the fabled Iron Curtain speech thirty-seven years before. His arrival on the campus was greeted by protesters carrying signs that read, "Hey, Hey, Uncle Sam, We Remember Vietnam," and "U.S. Troops Out of Grenada."

But Clare Boothe Luce, who shared the podium with him, loved the speech, a standard attack on Soviet troublemaking in Third World countries. As they were leaving the platform, she took his hand and said, "Bill you must give me a copy of your speech so I can crib and quote from it. You know, the older I get the fewer isms I have. Catholicism and plagiarism are about all that's left." Casey understood perfectly. He lived by the one, and he had been sued over the other.

He was a tough old bird. The soul-searching of his youth was far behind him. He had made his way as a gambler, a risk taker, in the law, in business, in espionage. He chalked up his victories, shrugged off his defeats, and moved on to the next game. In those final months of his third year at the Agency's helm, he was feeling good about himself and the job. He occupied a seat at the highest councils of power. He woke up in the morning knowing that a multimillion-dollar, worldwide intelligence apparatus awaited his orders, and that he virtually directed an invisible foreign policy. In Central America, starting at ground zero, he had created a force that was checkmating Soviet moves in the hemisphere. He made speeches in places where Winston Churchill spoke. The embarrassing investigations of his business affairs appeared to be behind him. And as his Agency medal proved, the troops understood the old man. Only the Debategate verdict hung over his head.

He felt good physically too, alive and vital from the moment he got out of bed at dawn. The energy level he maintained throughout twelve- and fourteen-hour days amazed those who had to keep up with him. His blood pressure was high, hitting 160 over 105, but he had medicine to control it, when he remembered to take it. An Agency physician who treated him, Arvel Tharp, commented, "His compliance was what we in medicine call spotty." In Casey's presence, Tharp felt half fascinated, half intimidated. "When I'd go into his office to take his blood pressure," Tharp recalled, "I never had a sense that he knew I was there. He might talk to me; he might ignore me."

Tharp wanted to come up with some way to make sure that Casey remembered to take the blood pressure pills. He took the problem to the Agency's Division of Science and Technology. He and the CIA experts engineered a pill box that was round and flat, easy to carry, with a dated dial that released a pill when it was turned. Tharp thought the pill box might be marketable. But he had a problem: the idea had been developed on company time, with company materials, by company personnel. Who owned it? "I figured I needed a lawyer who was an expert in this area," Tharp recalled. "So I went and asked Director Casey." Would he owe anything to the Agency if he went ahead—any royalties? Could he patent the idea in his own name? Casey looked at the doctor with new respect for a fellow entrepreneur. "Never mind a patent and the Agency," Casey said. "Just market it."

He still disdained regular exercise, though when he was home, he could do twenty laps in his pool at Mayknoll. Golf was now his sport. He occasionally played in a threesome with the Treasury secretary, Donald T. Regan, and the FBI director, William Webster. As one of Casey's security detail described this scene: "We formed a small army. Besides the players and the caddies, Casey had his security team, Regan had his, and Webster had his. You'd see all these guys trying to look inconspicuous along the edge of the fairway, talking into their sleeves." On one occasion, as they passed sweating joggers running near the course, Casey announced, "Look at that—working their asses off just to be as old as we already are."

He had been pleased to be admitted to exclusive Burning Tree in suburban Washington. On his first day at the club, he arrived, as usual, without any money; his security man paid the greens fee. Casey was being driven back into town after the game when he asked the security officer, "What did you tip the caddy?"

"Tip the caddy?" the man asked uneasily.

"You didn't tip the caddy?" Casey bellowed. "My first day as a member of Burning Tree, and I'm made to look like a cheap son of a bitch!"

At Langley, he inspired a curious blend of affection, respect, exasperation, and fear. The staff understood that because of him, they were experiencing a literal golden age. The Agency's funding was up almost 50 percent. Casey had inherited approximately 13,900 people; classified records reveal that the staff now numbered 16,400 and was still growing. When Casey brought corporate executives out to visit the Agency, he had a standard line for them: "This country's intelligence community, judged by the money it spends and the number of employees, would rank in the top five percent of the Fortune 500."

During the turmoil of the late sixties and early seventies, the CIA had been a red flag on college campuses, the very presence of Agency recruiters a cause for riots. Casey started inviting college presidents to Langley. They were given a one-day top-secret clearance as Casey and the staff gave them briefings spiced with noncritical secrets. Billy Doswell recalled that during his tenure, "Casey had loads of them down here, heads of big colleges and small. We had Bart Giamatti from Yale. We had the presidents of Boston College, Texas A & M, all colors, creeds, and sizes."

Casey had the staff develop a three-day orientation session for college placement directors. "I'm sure some of you came here thinking you were entering the devil's den," he would say in his opening remarks. "I hope you'll leave agreeing that intelligence work is an honorable profession." The approach apparently succeeded. Professional-level job inquiries ran more than 150,000 a year. From these, 23,000 people were interviewed. Of these, 1,500 were hired.

As an employer, the CIA rated high. People went there and stayed. The Agency had one of the lowest turnover rates in government. *Washingtonian* magazine surveyed the federal job scene and concluded, "The CIA is one of the ten best places to work in Washington." Why people went into this life might surprise those who looked askance at the CIA. Ed Juchniewicz, a thirty-year veteran, grappling for his own motivation, concluded, "The exciting thing about the work was that you could make good things happen in the world."

The eastern elite that had ruled the CIA's parent, the OSS, had long since been displaced. The change had begun during the fifties as recruits came increasingly from the Midwest and the West, from state universities and Catholic colleges. The demand for technical experts grew as spying became a game of hardware more than of people. The white-shoe boys, the old school tie counted for less. American espionage, in a little over one generation, had been democratized.

The Agency also had to change the rules of the priesthood if it was going to keep its seminarians in a new age. Social drinking had always been acceptable, but now the CIA had to deal with the reality that a huge proportion of Americans had at least experimented with drugs. The Agency established a contemporary personnel standard: it would hire someone who had previously used marijuana but would not take on present, habitual users. More serious drug use remained taboo. Known homosexuals were still unhireable. "Bill Casey," Leo Cherne observed, "even had trouble uttering the word. Once I asked him about bringing Bayard Rustin, the civil rights leader, onto the International Rescue Committee's board, and Bill said, 'Bayard's fine. But he's . . . you know, he's . . . uh . . . uh . . . uh . . .' "

Was the CIA good at its job? A modern intelligence service had to be judged in three broad categories: SIGINT, signal intelligence, embracing all forms of communication; IMINT, imagery, such as radar, photo intelligence, and other visual methods; and HUMINT, human intelligence, which ranged from secret agents operating in hostile lands to analysts sitting at desks at Langley. As Casey began to round out his third year, intelligence scholars judged the United States number one in SIGINT and IMINT, but no better than the top ten in HUMINT, well behind the Israelis, the Soviets, the Poles, and Britain.

The American character presumably explained both the strengths and weaknesses: a love of, indeed a faith in, gadgetry, an ignorance of history, and a fear of foreign languages. As one congressional critic put it, "We can read the numbers on a license plate in Moscow from one hundred miles up, but we don't know what the guy inside the car is thinking, and we don't have somebody in the car pool working for us." Casey recognized the deficiency. As he told an Israeli colleague, "My friend, in the end, all life is HUMINT."

David Halevy, from *Time* magazine, intrigued Casey with his slant on the intelligence services of various countries. Halevy began with a conviction that its intelligence service mirrored the nation. The French: "Always cynical and dubious, therefore always fucking up." The British: "Penetrated like a swiss cheese because of their public school homosexuality and thirties communism." The Israelis: "What the Jews have always had to resort to to survive in a hostile world, trading, including trading in intelligence." The Soviets: "Ironically elitist because their service is dominated by White Russians." The Americans: "Very square. Give me an order and I'll do it. Give me some hardware, and I'll do it better."

For all the distrust Casey had aroused on the Hill, the committee members, including Democrats of liberal bent, granted that Casey's CIA was a stronger CIA. Most would concur in the conclusion drawn by Morton Kondracke in *The New Republic* that year: "Three years into this Republican Administration, the United States certainly has a better intelligence capability than it did in 1980—it could hardly fail in that."

It was a highly subjective enterprise, judging intelligence success. Those engaged in the game preferred to keep their victories secret, and even more so their failures. Rating their performance was rather like judging a play where the curtain never goes up. The failures, however, had a way of seeping out. As Herb Meyer saw it, "We were in a game where your home runs are never printed and your strikeouts are the lead story on the sports page."

On April 13, 1983, in a speech at Georgetown University, Casey had hauled out a rhetorical relic from the Cold War. He referred to the contras as "freedom fighters." The phrase had first come into vogue twenty-seven years before, when the Hungarians had revolted against communism only to be crushed by Soviet tanks. Casey dusted off the phrase and happily put it on like a pair of comfortable old shoes. He was quickly paid the highest compliment of imitation. Ronald Reagan was soon referring to the contras in his speeches as freedom fighters.

Casey may have wished that Ronald Reagan had "a deeper handle on things," particularly the foreign policy of his own administration. But at least the man clung tenaciously to a few simple axioms, one being that the spread of communism must be stopped, which left Casey enviable leeway for implementation. If the means Casey proposed would promote the end, the President uncomplainingly signed on. As one CIA wit put it, "Reagan is the Will Rogers of intelligence— he never met a covert operation he didn't like." Dewey Clarridge, through his tireless pushing, stretching, and driving, had already created a 10,000-man contra force, twenty times the plan originally sold to Congress. What Reagan approved of that August was a revised finding to increase the contra force to 15,000.

Casey went up to the Hill and confronted incredulous faces. There was nothing to worry about, he told the members: even at that size, the contras did not have the punch to be more than a harassing force. They did not have the money, the armaments, the training to take on a real army, like the Sandinistas, who could field a combined regular army and militia of 75,000 men. The United States was not slipping into a Latin Vietnam. All the contras could do was raid, annoy, keep up the pressure.

The President also approved a secret project in preparation for the all-too-likely day when Congress might cut off aid to the contras entirely. The operation was called Elephant Herd. It had been concocted by Dewey Clarridge and Lieutenant Colonel Oliver L. North, now the NSC's assistant deputy director for political military affairs.

Casey loved Elephant Herd. It distilled his wisdom of a lifetime. If you are making a deal and run up against a legal wall, you look for a crack in it—and you slip through. If the military declared equipment "surplus to requirements," it then had no value. Consequently, this equipment could be given to the contras without being counted as part of congressional limits on aid. Clarridge told Casey that they were going to shoot for $32 million worth of this surplus hardware, actually more than the current level of appropriated aid. They had so far managed to get $12 million.

Casey took other precautions for the day the well might run dry. Earlier in the year, the Israelis had captured tons of PLO weapons in their invasion of southern Lebanon. Casey managed to persuade them to give a share to the contras. He was quietly planting a principle in the Reagan administration: the contras were going to be kept alive, with or without the support of Congress.

The precautions were taken none too soon. Congress was increasingly uncomfortable with the Nicaraguan operation. A growing number of members were ready to bail out. There was little political profit in this venture. Polls showed that Americans opposed aid to the contras by 60 and 70 percent. The House had by now voted not once but twice to shut off aid. Only the Republican edge in the Senate saved the contras. When Senate and House conferees got together this year, they compromised on a $24-million package. To Casey it was ridiculous. The Pentagon, he said, "spills that much on the way to a defense contractor." Still, the money was important even if inadequate; it kept the imprimatur of congressional approval on the operation.

What Casey found most infuriating in the threatened Boland cutoff was how completely the Congress had misread him. He knew that he was seen, particularly by younger members of the oversight committees, as an old coot bent on reliving his OSS days, a rash, impetuous adventurer, eager to win the sobriquet as well as the mantle of his idol, Wild Bill Donovan—Wild Bill Casey. They were blind, Casey believed. They did not know their own country's history. One thing that he and Donovan had in common was not foolhardiness but historical perspective. That fall he had made one of his happier appearances before the SSCI, testifying on a resolution to build an intelligence museum. "I claim that my first predecessor as director of Central Intelligence," Casey said, "was not Admiral Sidney Sours, who was appointed DCI by President Truman, but George Washington, who appointed himself. How did Washington's ragtag army, some 6,000 or 8,000 men for most of the war, defeat what was then the most powerful nation in the world? Second only to Washington's qualities as a leader in this achievement was his natural aptitude as a director of covert operations. . . ." Hardly a senator had turned up for that testimony.

Casey also liked to tell how Jefferson had been aided in writing the Declaration of Independence by intelligence smuggled in from London to Philadelphia. That was how Jefferson got the information that allowed him to write that George III "is at this time transporting armies of foreign mercenaries to complete the works of death, desolation, and tyranny."

How, Casey wondered, could his congressional critics fail to see the historical parallels? And in the old days, Congress helped keep the secrets, he liked to point out. Keeping quiet about covert operations was not undemocratic, Casey argued; it was as American as Yankee Doodle. He had a group of committee members over for breakfast and at one point asked if they knew the story of Tom Paine and the French leak. None did. In one of his columns, Casey related, Paine had unwisely revealed intelligence that he had obtained from his post on the Foreign Affairs Committee: France, he disclosed, was covertly aiding the American rebels. The Continental Congress thereafter passed a false resolution refuting Paine, thus covering up his blunder. "Those were the good old days," Casey told his guests.

When his conservative friends argued that the United States ought to hit a pipsqueak like Daniel Ortega with its full power, Casey liked to whip out chapters from his OSS manuscript. Sure, you could send vast armadas of B-17s over Schweinfurt, and maybe if enough planes dropped enough bombs and you were willing to take the 10 percent losses in men and aircraft, you might hit the German ball-bearing plants. But how much more effective and cheaper in lives and money it was to put in a team of saboteurs to blow up the plants. That was what he was trying to help the contras do in Nicaragua.

That August, Casey called in John Horton. The chemistry between the two men was all wrong. Some perverse force seemed to distort their strengths into failings; Casey's efforts to motivate turned to bully-ragging; Horton's independence became petulance. Still, Casey recognized that Horton remained highly respected in the Agency. He did not want to lose the man.

He told Horton, who sat looking into the soles of Casey's shoes propped on the desk, "I want a paper, a Sandinista vulnerability study. Hell, maybe our contras *could* knock off Ortega and his guys." He withdrew his feet and walked to the thick plate glass overlooking the rolling Virginia countryside. "I want you to look at something else too. Maybe we can squeeze the bastards a little harder economically." Horton reminded Casey that the United States had already cut off the shipment of spare parts to Nicaragua and had cut the country's sugar quota by 90 percent. Casey turned toward him. "It's not enough. We gotta stick it to them," he said. "Take a look at what a total boycott will do."

Horton went back to his office and quickly set the machinery in motion. He knew that Casey was likely to ask for a paper in days that would have been in the works for months in the past. He soon turned in a draft assessment, and then waited, always an anxious time for him. With Casey, the writing was never good enough, the organization sloppy, the research thin. If the writing *and* the substance failed to please, Horton was in for a rough afternoon.

Horton received a call to come to the seventh floor. He went to Casey's office, where the DCI was sitting with the "vulnerability study" in hand. "Dewey doesn't like it," Casey announced. "He says it's a reflection on him. And he's doing a helluva job down there."

Horton sat down, feeling a tension in his scalp. "It's no reflection on Dewey. We're just saying that the Sandinistas aren't going to fall. The contras aren't going to beat them. That's the judgment of the intelligence community. Do you want to change it?" Of course not, Casey snapped, as though somebody had asked him if he wanted to lie. They turned to the blockade proposal.

"Won't work," Horton said.

"Why not?"

"We've looked it over carefully. Anything we stop buying or selling, they can buy or sell somewhere else."

Casey punched his fist into his hand. "We gotta punish these sons of bitches, make 'em hurt."

"That may be true," Horton said. "But don't expect us to supply evidence of things that aren't there." This skinny kid on the beach was not about to have sand kicked in his face.

Casey was interested in the economic infrastructure of adversary countries. That's how you choke off their windpipes, he told his people. He had been involved in this tactic long before the CIA, even before the OSS, when he worked for the Board of Economic Warfare. As he had said then, "My job was pinpointing Hitler's economic jugular and investigating how it could be squeezed." How could Danny Ortega's jugular be squeezed? he now wanted to know. Maybe John Horton did not have any answers, but Dewey Clarridge did.

Corinto was a steamy town of 13,800 on Nicaragua's Pacific coast. It was the country's major port, its docks piled high with the coffee, sugar, hides, and hardwoods that were the country's chief exports. There, also, were huge storage tanks, holding Nicaragua's most vital import, oil.

Just before dawn on October 10, unmarked speedboats attacked the Corinto tanks. Commandos pumped mortar and cannon fire into the depot, setting five tanks ablaze. The jugular had been given a hard squeeze. The month before, a similar raid had been made on another Nicaraguan port, Puerto Sandino. The attacks were totally indefensible as arms interdiction; but, as Casey told congressional critics who suspected the Agency's hand in them, once you put a guerrilla army in the field, you can't control its every act, especially with men who want to free their country. The contra high command faithfully claimed responsibility. But the attacks had in fact not been mounted by the contras. The speedboats were manned by Latin Americans contracted, trained, and paid by the CIA. The boats had been launched by American vessels standing offshore.

Clarridge could walk through Casey's door any time he wanted. The DCI always welcomed the visits, like an indulgent uncle, secretly delighted to learn what pranks Peck's bad boy was up to now. Ed Juchniewicz watched Clarridge's easy entree from the vantage point of the operation's directorate and observed, "I'm sure Dewey didn't tell even Casey everything he was up to. He had his own agenda. He figured he could pretty much do what he wanted, and Ollie North would protect his ass at the White House. He'd ride to the top on Ollie's coattails. I know how they pictured themselves: Ollie and Dewey leading a ticker tape victory parade down Managua's main street."

In the latter part of 1983, Clarridge hatched his boldest gamble so far. The earlier raids on the Nicaraguan ports had reflected quintessential Casey behavior: keep testing the limits—see what you can get away with, how far you can push before anyone stops you. Casey listened to Clarridge's latest proposal, smiled contentedly, and told Clarridge to get moving, to work it out with the Restricted Agency Group on Central America, with Ollie North, the State Department people, and the others involved. If this one worked, it would be a real stranglehold on the Sandinistas' windpipe.

23.

The Director Strikes Back

In February of 1984, Bill Casey left on a secret thirteen-country journey that took him around the globe. All the bumps were removed in advance; he had only to appear. As the chief of his personal security detail put it, "We do the best advance job in the U.S. government in the CIA—better than the White House Secret Service. Director Casey never even knew if he owned a passport. We took care of everything."

He headed westward this time. On the first stop, in Honolulu, he was registered as "Mr. X. Smith," a name whose falsity seemed to jump off the hotel register. At the next stop, Tokyo, he was registered as "Mr. Kashi."

The next stop was Beijing. He loved China, and he was something of an expert on it, at least on the Christian missionary movements there—not a subject of particular interest to his present hosts. More intriguing to him was the irony of China's geopolitical position: the largest Communist country on earth, yet a thorn in the Soviet Union's side, the country that shared the longest border with the Soviets, a border tense, uneasy, bristling, and a border that offered infinite opportunities for peeping.

And yet he had had a hard time making the White House crew understand the value of courting Beijing. Reagan and his Californians had brought to Washington the Taiwan mentality: mainland China was Communist; Taiwan was anticommunist, an Oriental showcase of capitalism, a springboard for romantic fantasies about an invasion, someday, that would wrest China from the Reds. The Reagan people had inherited from the Carter administration a pending deal to give the Chinese a twenty-year-old computer system to carry out a national census. Diehards in the administration had managed to kill the deal. The pragmatist Casey saw Communist China for what it was: an enormous counterweight to be played against the real enemy, the Soviet Union; and a superb listening post.

Earlier, Al Haig had described to Casey the groundwork he had done during the historic Nixon visit of 1972 to get the Chinese to allow the United States to monitor the Soviet Union from the Chinese border. Casey had continued to build on that arrangement. In return, he carried back to Washington and argued for China's appeals for Western technology and for training more Chinese students in the United States.

On this trip, he was pushing another product. The Chinese foreign minister threw a private dinner for him in Beijing. The minister sat on Casey's right, the chief of Chinese intelligence on his left. Across from Casey was his station chief in Beijing, Ted Price. Casey attacked the dinner with a zest suggesting that it was the main reason why he had traveled 12,000 miles. After several courses, he began to talk about what was on his mind. The Chinese listened politely, leaning forward to catch his words. But Price sensed an increasing bafflement in their faces. Finally, the foreign minister whispered to Price, "But what country is Mr. Casey talking about? Surely not China?"

No, Price explained—Afghanistan.

"Ah, *that*," the minister said, relaxing visibly. "Let him talk. We have already agreed on the details, haven't we?"

The next stop was Islamabad, where Casey bucked up President Zia, promising more aid for the Afghan refugees still pouring in and more arms to protect him from the nasty Indians, as long as Zia kept those delivery routes open to the Mujahedin. And Casey happily reported to Zia that in China he had sold a new aid package for the Afghans.

He spent two days in Tel Aviv, talking to, among others, the chief of the Mossad and his lieutenants. Casey was uncomfortable. Three years into the administration and he still had virtually no human assets in Iran. He was at the mercy of the Israelis to tell him what was going on there. The Mossad was good, but he had nothing against which to check its reports. Israel was not the United States; it had its own objectives. He constantly had to ask himself why they were telling him what they were telling him about Iran. What was their angle?

President Reagan wondered if something could not be done to overthrow Ayatollah Khomeini. The best that Casey had been able to come up with was a finding permitting the CIA to support Iranian exile groups who opposed the Ayatollah. Under the finding, Casey's people in Turkey established a chain of covert sanctuaries for anti-Khomeini exiles in towns along the Iranian border. But it was low-level stuff, Casey knew, not at all the answer to Iran's hostility toward and isolation from the United States.

In the spring of 1983, George Shultz had pushed successfully for Operation Staunch, a worldwide campaign to persuade other countries not to sell arms to Iran. With Iran at war with Iraq, the success of this operation could prove fatal to the Ayatollah. The boycott was operated largely by State, but the CIA conducted the underside of Staunch.

Ed Juchniewicz, as assistant DDO, had a piece of the effort. Juchniewicz, a big, affable, earnest officer out of Jersey City, New Jersey, got along fine with the director. He represented the new wave who had succeeded the elitist old guard in the CIA. He loved sitting in Casey's office and talking about the fine points of Jesuit education. "They made us systematic, methodical, logical, and penetrating in our thinking," Juchniewicz recalled. "The Jesuits gave us the intellectual weapons to tackle the world. They let us know who we were. People like Bill Casey and me were comfortable with ourselves and what we were doing with our lives."

From time to time, Juchniewicz reported to Casey on the state of the boycott. "We were always figuring out how we could do more— not only to cut off weapons but how to keep everything else from getting through," Juchniewicz remembered. "First we'd identify the channels used, then we'd go to the countries involved to try to block them. We'd explain, say, to the Swiss or the West Germans, 'It's not to your advantage in the long run to trade with the Iranians.' It was not an easy pitch. Iran could pay whatever the traffic would bear. The Swiss were selling them aircraft parts. The Germans were selling them naval equipment. The Japanese were buying their oil. A Japanese company like Mitsumi had $3.5 billion invested in a petrochemical plant in Iran. And we're trying to get them to drop these good deals. Every government official we'd talk to would say, 'Look, we're in the same boat you are. We can't dictate to our private companies. Do you want us to violate our laws?' "

Then had come the bombing of the U.S. embassy and the Marine barracks in Beirut. The intelligence collected led to the inescapable conclusion that the acts had been perpetrated by militant Lebanese Shiites loyal to and financed by Iran. There was enough evidence in hand for the administration to place Iran, on January 18, 1984, on the official list of "terrorist states." As Casey was now saying regularly in his speeches, "Iran is the most dangerous state sponsor of terrorism in the world." The President's line was that the United States would never make concessions to terrorists. The response of the terrorists was to start kidnapping Americans in Lebanon.

Casey was unhappy. Sanctions against Iran obviously did not work. American attempts to quarantine the country did not work. The United States was doing nothing subtle, nothing imaginative to break the stalemate. Casey began pressing his people to start thinking about fresh approaches to Iran.

William Buckley had been in Beirut for almost a year, ever since Casey had sent him there as station chief, the Agency's authority on counterterrorism in the terrorism capital. On March 16, he was seized by three masked men at gunpoint and whisked into the labyrinthine ruins of Beirut.

Casey, upon getting the news, summoned McMahon, Gates, the head of the Agency's security office, and the Middle East chiefs for operations and intelligence. He seemed reasonably calm, stoic, Bob Gates remembered. He wanted Lebanon turned upside down until Buckley was found, he said. Partly it was the cold, hard intelligence loss if Buckley talked, if he spilled his unrivaled knowledge of the Agency's assets in the Middle East. But it went far deeper than the peril of the moment. As Dick Helms, one of Casey's predecessors, later observed of the Buckley episode, "Your people don't think much of you as an intelligence chief if you let them rot. One of the great distinctions the KGB has had over time is that they are relentless at getting their people back. If Buckley was the Russians' man, they'd tear Beirut apart. Sadly, we don't have that reputation."

Casey was in no position to order the demolition of Beirut, but he did act with speed and energy. The NSA was directed to take high-resolution photographs of likely hideouts in Beirut. Lebanese agents working for the CIA were sent into Shiite neighborhoods. Casey called FBI director William Webster and had him send a team of agents to scour the region. The U.S. Army's specially trained covert unit, the Intelligence Support Activity, put its people into Beirut's alleys.

It all produced nothing. As the weeks passed and the search burned out, Casey grew fatalistic. One of the people involved reported the latest failure and Casey in a subdued voice said only, "Rough game. People get hurt. People get killed."

But Betty Murphy noticed that the mask fell after the pros left the office. "He was more openly shaken by what happened to Mr. Buckley in front of us secretaries than he ever let himself be in front of the men," she recalled.

Even in his moment of peril, possibly even of his death, William Buckley had to remain part of an institutional lie. The Agency to which he had devoted his life could not acknowledge him. As far as America knew, a William Buckley, a State Department political officer in Beirut, had been kidnapped.

Edgar Chamorro was one of the good ones, one of the contra directorate brought in in November of 1982 to brighten the image and diminish the Somocista taint. The CIA was paying him $2,000 a month, plus expenses—less than a good executive secretary earned in Washington, but a comfortable living for someone operating out of poverty-mired Honduras. On January 6, 1984, Chamorro was sound asleep in his house in the capital city, Tegucigalpa, when a pounding on the door woke him. His caller, an American whom he knew only as George, actually the CIA deputy chief of station in Honduras, stepped in. "Get over to the radio station and get this out, now," George told Chamorro. Chamorro read the single sheet of paper handed to him. It was a press release, in Spanish, stating that the contras took full responsibility for mining three harbors in Nicaragua. Chamorro had never heard of the operation, but he dutifully dressed and went to the clandestine radio station beamed into Nicaragua. And by six a.m. the mining story was on the air.

This middle-of-the-night maneuver had been prompted by a timing problem confronting the Agency. Three days before, the Sandinista regime had publicly complained that Nicaragua's harbors had been mined. It was important, for reasons that would emerge soon enough, to get contra fingerprints on the operation.

Eighteen years before, when he was running for Congress, Casey had opposed mining the North Vietnamese harbor of Haiphong; it was, he said, "a reckless action that would risk escalation into a big land war in Asia." What had changed since then? Why was mining a risky escalation in Vietnam but a risk worth taking in Central America?

What Casey admired about Dewey Clarridge was the man's imagination. Clarridge's mind virtually popped with ideas. So what if four out of five were bad? Some people, Casey well knew, never had an idea in their lives. One out of five was not bad—about the same ratio as Wild Bill Donovan's, Casey recalled.

Beginning in the fall of 1983, as a natural progression of the raids on the Nicaraguan oil storage tanks, Clarridge had begun talking to the Restricted Interagency Group about mining Nicaragua's harbors.

He quickly won the support of Anthony Motley, State's present assistant secretary for Latin America. And Ollie North was already eager.

Casey, the inveterate reader and scholar, particularly admired that Clarridge had done his history homework this time. During the 1904–05 war between Russia and Japan, the Japanese had mined Russia's Pacific ports and paralyzed the czar's fleet. The flagship of the Russian naval commander had struck one of the mines and had gone down, with the commander. Japan won that war.

Casey was not quite ready to go that far, to blow up ships, possibly the ships of allies who might find themselves in Nicaraguan ports. That was not necessary, Clarridge explained. The *fear* of mining would be enough to choke off Nicaragua's vital sea trade. Clarridge also had done his operations homework. They would not use real mines. The Navy could supply old sewer pipes and fuses. Clarridge's people could pack the pipes with C-4 explosive, just enough to make a hell of a bang.

The contras did not know anything about mining harbors, so the Agency would have to run the show itself. They would put a mother ship carrying these giant aquatic firecrackers off the Nicaraguan Atlantic and Pacific coasts, at least twelve miles out, safely in international waters. They would run the mines in, in the dark of night, on speedboats—what they called cigarette boats, the kind used for smuggling. Americans would only be on the mother ship. The small boats would be manned by specially trained Latinos. No, they were not contras; but if caught, they would be assumed to be contras. As Clarridge explained the strategy, once these loud but supposedly harmless mines popped under a few hulls, "Lloyds of London pulls the insurance from ships going into Nicaragua, and that's it. They don't get any oil." The Sandinista regime would wither.

It was brilliant, Casey thought—the kind of economic strangulation he had preached in London in '43. Mining was more subtle and effective than blowing up oil storage tanks. The plan also had the virtue of making the contras look formidable. It was victory at bargain prices—a few paid Latino operatives and some phony mines.

Others were not as easily persuaded. John Horton attended a meeting of CIA, Defense, NSC, and State people at the Pentagon for a briefing on Central America where Clarridge described his scheme. As Horton recalled, "We were aghast—even the diehards. 'You're crazy,' they were all telling Dewey. 'You can't pull something like that.' In the meantime, Dewey's going on blithely about these teams pretending to be Nicaraguan contras."

Casey did not even bother to ask Bob Gates and his analysts for an assessment, for the usual, careful weighing of risks versus return. He took the mining operation directly to the NSPG and won the President's approval.

He still had to inform the intelligence committees. This did not mean that he had to go in with a brass band and loudspeakers. Minimum information, minimal compliance. Meet the law, don't overdo it. On March 8, Casey faced the SSCI for the first full-scale briefing since September of 1983, nearly six months before. He had a long agenda to cover that day. Casey briefed the members for two and a half hours. Tucked away in his opening statement was one sentence that read: "Magnetic mines have been placed in the Pacific harbor of Corinto and the Atlantic harbor of El Bluff as well as the oil terminal of Puerto Sandino." Twenty-five words—and they had been nestled in a list of actions that the contras, not the CIA, were carrying out.

It was a hectic time for the committee. As Rob Simmons, the staff director, remembered, "Our attention was on the floor fight over funding for the whole contra operation. Teddy Kennedy was going to attack the funding, and we were gearing up for the debate." Thus, Casey was asked plenty of questions during the briefing, but none about the mining. A few days later, Casey incorporated essentially the same sentence in a second briefing of the Senate committee.

The briefings had followed a somewhat different course before the House. For one thing, Casey's staff had informed HPSCI of the mining much earlier, on January 31. And the operation had been questioned. One disbelieving House member asked, "Now the CIA is mining harbors in Nicaragua?" Well, no, not exactly, the Agency witness explained; not mining harbors. Then what were they talking about? They were not mining harbors, the official said lamely; they were mining *anchorages*. It was an answer worthy of the boss, a Casey answer—one that qualified as true by a quibble. The joke around the House committee was that if your coat was on fire, before Bill Casey would tell you, you had to ask him, "Is my coat on fire?"

Between March 7 and March 27, seven vessels struck the mines, among them a Japanese freighter loaded with cotton and the *Lugansk*, a Soviet oil tanker. George Shultz had initially gone along with the plan. Now, he and others at State were getting nervous. As one of Clarridge's coarchitects of the scheme put it, after the first few mines exploded, "We never dreamed that merchant captains would keep sailing in."

Steven Ward, a staff member who reviewed covert operations for the SSCI, had been alerted by a counterpart on the HPSCI staff that the CIA was far more involved in the mining of the harbors than Casey's 25-word sentence suggested. Late in the evening of April 5, Barry Goldwater was on the Senate floor plugging for another $21 million to replenish the near-bankrupt contras. Ward had typed up what he had learned about the mining and took it to Senator Moynihan, also then in the Senate chamber. The memo explained that the mining had been carried out not by the contras, but by the CIA, using Latinos on the Agency's payroll. Moynihan told Wade to show the paper to Joe Biden, a sharp Casey critic. An astonished Biden could not even recall being briefed on such an operation. He took the paper to William S. Cohen, a Maine Republican also serving on the intelligence committee.

Cohen spotted Rob Simmons in the chamber and summoned him. "What's this all about?" Cohen demanded. Simmons was embarrassed; the Senate intelligence committee maintained a professional staff precisely to catch such developments. "I don't know what the hell it's about," Simmons confessed. Cohen decided to go directly to the chairman. He took the note to Goldwater, who had resumed his seat after making his appeal for the contras. Goldwater had retained a quality rare in septuagenarians, impetuosity. He was red-faced and furious. He asked to retake the floor, and in a tone of would-you-believe-this, he started to read to the full Senate what he had just seen.

Rob Simmons was startled. Goldwater was reading into the Senate record a raw piece of unverified intelligence about a top-secret operation, claiming that the President had authorized mining the ports of a country with whom the United States was not at war. He rushed to Cohen and said, "You've got to stop this." Cohen went quickly up to Goldwater and whispered in his ear. Goldwater stopped and slumped back into his seat, the paper dangling from his hand.

Simmons and his staff had to move swiftly to block Goldwater's words from being printed in the next day's *Congressional Record*. But an alert reporter for the *Wall Street Journal*, David Rogers, was already off and running with the story, which appeared the next day under the headline U.S. ROLE IN MINING NICARAGUAN HARBORS REPORTEDLY IS LARGER THAN FIRST THOUGHT. Goldwater was outraged. Never in thirty years in the Senate had words of his had to be expunged from the record. He dispatched Simmons to Langley to see Casey and find out what was going on.

Casey was not about to be cross-examined by some Senate employee who would be lucky to be a Grade 16 if he had stayed with the CIA. Instead, he had John McMahon speak to Simmons. Yes, it was true: the administration had approved the mining operation and the CIA had executed it. But, God damn it, McMahon said, *the committees had been informed*—and he could prove it.

Simmons reported back to Goldwater. It was a Friday afternoon. Goldwater was alone in a half-darkened room, brooding. Was Casey saying that a single sentence buried in a report of things the *contras* were doing—one sentence in eighty pages—*that* was keeping Congress fully informed? Goldwater inventoried all the things he had done for this DCI. He had backed the rebuilding of the CIA, gotten the Agency exempted from parts of the Freedom of Information Act. "I've pulled Casey's nuts out of the fire on so many occasions," he said. "I feel like such a fool. I feel betrayed."

That weekend the senator went off to his friend Bill Quinn's place on the Maryland shore. Quinn was Casey's friend too. They went back almost forty years, to the time when Casey had come to Washington to save that OSS remnant the Strategic Services Unit, then run by Quinn. Over the weekend, Goldwater and Quinn pondered the imponderable behavior of William J. Casey.

Monday, when Goldwater got back to his office, he called in his press aide and did something totally uncharacteristic. There was no other way to get through to Casey, he concluded. He had written a letter, and he was going to give copies of it to the press. The letter began: "Dear Bill . . . I've been trying to figure out how I can most easily tell you my feelings about the President having approved mining some of the harbors of Central America. It gets down to one, little, simple, phrase. I am pissed off."

By now the ships of six countries, including the USSR, had struck the mines. Casey was like a city under siege. He had managed to alienate Barry Goldwater, a prointelligence, conservative senator who ordinarily would have walked through barbed wire for the CIA. Teddy Kennedy got a resolution through the Senate—a Republican-controlled Senate—condemning the mining by a vote of 84–12. Prime Minister Margaret Thatcher, the administration's staunchest ally, condemned the mining. Casey's pal Jeane Kirkpatrick thought the mining was "dumb"; she told Casey that she had to go through all kinds of legalistic acrobatics ("As article so-and-so of the U.N. charter reads . . .") to defend the mining in the United Nations. Nicaragua announced that it was taking the case to the World Court at the Hague. Casey had handed Jim Baker another club to beat him with at the White House—there he goes again, humiliating the administration by his antics. Even at the CIA, people were asking, is this old

schemer going to drag us back into the gutter of hostility and suspicion we went through during the seventies?

Casey had lunch with an old OSS friend and gave his side of the
story. Of course he had notified the committees, he said. Maybe Barry
Goldwater had not gotten the word; but then, Barry was getting on,
he took all that medicine for his hip pain. What was he going to do,
Casey asked, get up and say publicly that Barry Goldwater couldn't
cut it anymore? "I don't want to embarrass him," Casey concluded.
And other members of the intelligence committee, he pointed out,
admitted that they knew what was happening.

Goldwater was not going to be the immediate problem. Four days
after the instantly legendary "pissed off" letter, he left for a trip to
the Far East, and Pat Moynihan became temporary chairman of the
Senate intelligence committee.

Moynihan had supported the $21 million in contra funding on April
5. In explaining why he still stuck with the operation, he paid the
CIA a high compliment: "In Nicaragua, you had the army, a bunch
of hideous Marxists, and three social democrats in between. We, as
usual, were trying to support the three social democrats. People don't
realize that for thirty years, the CIA has been trying to get the good
guys to win. But in most of these countries, there just aren't enough
good guys."

John McMahon suggested to Casey that he had better go courting.
Casey agreed and told Betty Murphy to phone Moynihan's office to
say that he was coming over to pay a call. He and McMahon were
kept waiting for fifteen minutes in Moynihan's outer office while
Casey grumbled. Suddenly, the door opened and Moynihan came out,
along with David Brinkley and an ABC television crew.

Moynihan greeted Casey cordially and ushered him and McMahon
into his office. He got quickly to his concern. He had supported rebuilding the CIA; he had even voted for the money for the contras
the very day that this whole affair had exploded. Was concealing the
mining any way to treat a friend?

But, Casey asked, wasn't it true that Moynihan had been briefed
on the details of the mining by a member of his own staff? McMahon
fished out the proof. Gary J. Schmitt, minority staff director for the
SSCI, was supposed to have briefed Moynihan. Is that what you call
"timely" notification, asked Moynihan, his voice rising in righteous
dudgeon—an explanation in April for an operation that had been
under way for months? "If this action was significant enough for the
President to approve it in December, it was significant enough for
the committee to have been informed in December. "I think that's a

rather good definition of 'significant,' don't you?" Moynihan said. "If the President of the United States has to sign something, it's significant."

Casey did not enjoy being lectured on the fine points of the English language. When he felt he had done enough penance, he signaled McMahon that it was time to go. Moynihan's theatrical righteousness turned Casey off. But the man *was* a friend of the intelligence community; and in making this visit, Casey believed that he had eaten just enough crow to placate the vice-chairman.

But not quite enough, he soon found out. The talk with Moynihan had been on Friday, April 13. That Sunday, the interview that Moynihan had been filming with David Brinkley was broadcast. In it, Moynihan said that he was resigning as vice-chairman of the Senate Select Committee on Intelligence to protest the poor way in which the CIA had informed the committee. Casey was outraged. So that was what Moynihan had been telling Brinkley, while he was outside cooling his heels! Moynihan had not mentioned a word about resigning during their discussion that day.

Casey already had put the CIA public relations apparatus to work on a credibility offensive, inside and outside the Agency. The day before seeing Moynihan, he issued a bulletin to all CIA employees, headed "Recent Press Articles." Besides his mentioning the mining in three formal hearings, he said, Agency officials had also briefed individual senators and SSCI staff. He assured his people that their organization had "not only complied with the letter of the law in our briefings, but with the spirit of the law as well." He also approved a public statement that said, "Since the first of the year, the subject of mining Nicaraguan ports has been discussed with either members or staffers of the committees and other members of the Congress eleven times."

Moynihan had a word for all this effort. "Casey was running a disinformation operation against our committee. In a way it was rather successful. It put us in an awkward position. If we didn't know, we should have known. I lost a lot of skin on this one." But all Casey's assertions ignored an elemental fact, Moynihan claimed. "Yes, he made that statement about mining. But the implication was that it had been done by the contras. What we did not know was that it had been carried out by the United States. Casey's habit of deception has mutated into a policy of deceit." To Moynihan, Casey revealed information the way a squid releases ink.

How much of Casey's defense was strictly smoke? The reference to the mining, however cursory, had been made. And certain members had been individually briefed. Senator Pat Leahy, often a Casey critic, admitted that he received a fairly detailed briefing after being out of town because of his father's death. Leahy opposed the mining, but he did know about it. HPSCI members, whatever they thought of the policy, had not complained about the timing or depth of their notification. Another Casey critic on the SSCI, David Durenberger, concluded, "It was an unfair knock to put the whole mining business on Casey. I had begged Barry for months to get Casey in to find out just what the hell the administration was doing under that finding on Nicaragua. As I recall, we hadn't had him before us since the previous fall when we should have had him in monthly." In short, Durenberger believed, Chairman Goldwater had not been on top of the situation.

Still, Casey lost the public opinion contest. That mining was an act of war was evident to anyone not in a coma. And the fact that a U.S. senator was giving up a powerful committee post because, he said, the CIA had misled him was a devastating charge.

Casey, pushed by McMahon, counseled by valued old OSS comrades, accepted the inevitable: he would have to try to woo Moynihan back. Better the devil you know. Moynihan's replacement as vice-chairman would likely be Leahy.

On April 25, Casey went to Capitol Hill to ask Moynihan's forgiveness and urge the senator to withdraw his resignation. Moynihan listened. Yes, he would stay on, Moynihan finally agreed, but only if in the future notification of the SSCI was full and timely. One more thing: it might be useful if Casey also made a formal apology to the full committee, and soon—tomorrow, in fact. Casey agreed with the alacrity of a man consenting to be hanged in the morning.

The next day, he faced the Senate intelligence committee. His mistake, he said, was that "the committee had not been informed in a timely manner. And for that, I apologize profoundly." As Dave Durenberger observed, "He mouthed the words. But true contrition was not in his vocabulary." And Casey's intelligence chief, Bob Gates, observed, "When Bill made that apology, his tongue turned black and fell out."

Moynihan was still not satisfied. He put the staff to work on an instrument to avoid any possible repetition of the mining fiasco. The final product, entitled "Procedures Governing Reporting to the SSCI on Covert Action," seemed to plug any escape from full and timely disclosure. Paragraph 3 read: "Notification . . . will be provided to the SSCI as soon as practicable and prior to the implementation of the actual activity." The accord was signed on June 6 by Goldwater,

Moynihan, and Casey. As Goldwater described the moment, after Casey signed, "he dropped the pen, as if it had been poisoned."

Besides the dented hulls on several merchant ships, there were two more casualties of the Nicaraguan mining affair. Clair George had been less than a success as the point man for congressional relations, as he would be among the first to admit. A man who had spent a career as a clandestine-operations officer had been forced into a job that ran against every instinct that he had honed for twenty-seven years. It was Casey who had miscast him. In the wake of the mining affair, Clair George had to go. He was replaced by the Agency's inspector general, Charles Briggs. George subsequently returned to a more congenial world as DDO, the head of the operations directorate.

The Dewey Clarridge comet also burned out over the harbors of Nicaragua. One SSCI member reported, "He came up here and told us, 'I dreamed up the mining'! And he did it without even apologizing!" Clarridge had already used up much of his credit long before. On another occasion, when Casey was making a point before the House committee, Clarridge interrupted and whispered in his ear. Congressman Wyche Fowler, Jr., a Georgia Democrat, observed wryly, "Your Iago, Mr. Director, says differently." "It got to a point where I wouldn't believe a word Dewey Clarridge said," Congressman Norman Mineta remarked. Clarridge fell, but gently. Casey later returned him to Europe as chief of covert operations there.

In May, Clarridge bade farewell to the contras, standing before them at a Honduran sanctuary, wearing an immaculate safari jacket and polished boots. He spoke in short staccato bursts that were translated into English by Edgar Chamorro. Next to him as he spoke was a recruiting-poster U.S. Marine Corps officer in battle fatigues.

Chamorro recalled Clarridge's magnetic effect: "He spoke with great conviction, and all his CIA aides treated him with deference, like an emperor." What Clarridge told them was, yes, he was aware of the possibility that the U.S. Congress might shut off their aid. But this would not be the end. He pointed to the Marine. "And to assure you of that, I have brought Colonel Oliver North. You will never be abandoned. Colonel North will take charge, if necessary. He will provide all the support you will need."

The contras, riding the seesaw of congressional backing, were much relieved. As Chamorro observed, he knew that "Dewey Maroni [Clarridge's code name] spoke to President Reagan himself two or three times a week. The President had told him that he loved to hear what we were doing." And now Dewey Maroni was promising that this fine-looking officer would see that they were never deserted.

John McMahon had been out of the country when Casey made his apology on the mining debacle. When he came back, Casey told him, "I sure as hell didn't want to do it. I gagged on it. But I don't have to tell you, the Nicaraguan operation was on the ropes. I only apologized to save the contras."

24.

Verdict on Debategate

On March 2, 1984, Casey had been interrogated by the Albosta committee over "the unauthorized transfers of non-public information during the 1980 presidential campaign." He told the committee that he had never known at the time that Carter briefing papers had even come into the Reagan campaign. He repeated that he had checked around with everybody who worked closely with him, and none of them knew about any Carter campaign briefing books. He denied that he had presided over a meeting during the campaign in which he was quoted as wanting "more material from the Carter camp." "I might have said something like 'We need faster information on Carter's statements and appearances'" was all that he would concede to the committee.

Don Albosta was a folksy, down-home beet farmer from Michigan with fundamental ideas about right and wrong. He was, as one associate put it, "no rocket scientist," but he possessed a certain earthy shrewdness. As Casey's memory seemed to fail on point after point, Albosta steered the questioning to other aspects of the 1980 campaign. "All of a sudden," Albosta said, "his memory would become razor sharp. But when we'd go back to Carter's briefing papers, he got amnesia again."

One member of the committee staff described Casey as a witness: "He was tough—no pushover. He had a well-developed sense of self-protection."

On May 27, the committee's final report was released to the public. After ten months of investigation, the testimony of more than three hundred persons, the expenditure of more than half a million dollars, and a twenty-four-hundred-page report, the Albosta panel had essentially come up dry: "It is difficult to reach definitive conclusions as to how the Carter debate briefing materials entered the Reagan/Bush campaign and to determine who had access to them." Nevertheless, the committee was willing to hazard a guess at the culprit: "The better evidence indicates that Carter debate materials—probably the big book and the Mondale papers—entered the Reagan campaign through its director, Casey."

The investigation had largely pitted Casey's word against Jim Baker's. As a member of the committee later commented privately, "Baker struck the investigators as credible." Donald Albosta put it more baldly: "Casey did not come before the committee to tell the truth."

One of the most damaging aspects for Casey was his relationship with Paul Corbin, the apostate from the Kennedy Democratic camp. Tim Wyngaard had testified that Corbin had told him that "he had obtained briefing material for the debate with Governor Reagan and provided these materials to William J. Casey." Corbin was a character around Washington—a small, thin, weasel-like man, whom one friend described as "pure Damon Runyon, an odd-job sort of guy and a great heaver of the bull." Under questioning by the Albosta committee, Corbin denied having made such a statement to Wyngaard.

The hardest thing for the committee to swallow was why Casey had put Corbin on the 1980 Reagan campaign payroll. Corbin claimed he had been hired to pass out campaign literature in Palm Beach. The idea of the national director of a presidential campaign hiring someone to go to Florida to stuff leaflets into condo mailboxes strained the committee's credulity. Don Albosta had a private opinion. "I think Paul Corbin was a courier. He probably delivered some of the Carter papers."

After the report came out, Casey summoned his faithful fireman, Ben Frank. Frank came to Casey's office and remembered, "Bill was cursing Baker, kicking things. He was more profane than I ever remember." Casey told Frank that he was going to sue Baker. He asked Stanley Sporkin to rate his chances of a successful suit. "I plowed through the Albosta report," Sporkin told him, "and as far as I can tell, you're innocent." But if Casey wanted to take on Baker, Sporkin warned, "I think you're going to need a private lawyer." Casey engaged an attorney named Alan Levenson.

Casey prepared a "white paper," a gauntlet he intended to throw down before Baker. He attacked on several fronts. Fact: The FBI had found Baker's fingerprints and those of some of Baker's aides on the Carter documents, but none of Casey's. Morality: "However you got those papers, what was unquestionably wrong was what you let people do with them." Tactics: "Some of your colleagues have been heard to brag about their success in lobbying the Albosta report to go against me." Prejudice: Casey quoted the story from the *Richmond News Leader* in which Congressman Albosta had said, virtually nine months before his committee had completed its work, that he would feel bad if his friend Jim Baker was hurt by the investigation.

Privately, Casey railed at the unfairness of it all. He was blunt, gruff, often rude, and consequently he had not been believed. Jim Baker was the soul of charm, wit, and affability; therefore, he had been believed. But, as Logan Pearsall Smith had once observed, and as Casey liked to quote, "Charming people live up to the edge of their charm and behave as outrageously as the world will let them." Casey had bridled at this white-shoe-boy advantage all his life.

Sporkin looked over Casey's white paper and suggested, "Maybe I ought to go over and have a talk with Fred Fielding at the White House before you do anything rash." Casey harumphed but agreed. Sporkin came back with news that Casey did not want to hear—or possibly he did, since there was nothing of the kamikaze pilot in his makeup. "Bill, if you keep pushing this thing," Sporkin warned him, "there's gonna be civil war in the administration. I know Baker intends to hit back. You'll wind up trading punches. In the end, you'll leave the President only one choice—to drop both of you. The President will lose, the administration will lose, the CIA will lose. And you'll lose. There won't be any winners except your enemies. Drop it."

Casey, feet on the desk, hands folded across his lap, stared at his belt buckle for a seeming eternity, then said, "Yeah. I'll save it for my memoirs."

How to reconcile the conflicting stories: Baker claiming Casey had given him the Carter papers, Casey denying that he had ever seen them? The fingerprints of Baker and his people found on the documents, and no fingerprints of Casey or his immediate staff? And who had taken these documents out of the White House in the first place?

Two points provide the keys to the contradictions. First, the Carter briefing papers were prepared in two distinct areas of the White House, in the NSC offices and the domestic policy offices. Second, only the foreign policy material prepared by the NSC actually turned up, with fingerprints, in the Reagan files; the domestic briefing book was never found, though several Reagan people admitted to seeing it. The material came out of the White House from two different channels, one for the foreign policy briefing book and another for the domestic book.

People assigned to the National Security Council staff are ordinarily career professionals, often on loan from State, Defense, the military, and the CIA. Many of them in the Carter administration were disenchanted with Carter's defense and foreign policies; a half-dozen of these had easy access to the foreign policy debate book and the Mondale book. One of them survived the Carter-Reagan transition and went on to an unusually swift rise from middle-level bureaucrat to a fairly high-level Reagan appointment. This unnamed official, certain members of the Albosta committee and staff concluded informally, was the source of the foreign policy debate material.

David Gergen, who had worked for Baker on the debates, told the investigators that he remembered standing in front of the campaign headquarters with other staffers on a rainy Saturday morning shortly before the debate when a taxi pulled up and delivered what he thought might have been the Carter foreign policy book. What is most likely is that Gergen and the others had been tipped off to wait for a delivery that dreary morning. Does this suggest that they knew who dispatched this material from the NSC, or knew what it was? Possibly, though not certainly. The NSC was laced with people familiar with covert operations. A pro-Reagan NSC staffer takes a copy of the foreign policy briefing papers from the office; at some point he alerts the Reagan camp; he hails a cab and tells the driver to deliver a package to an address in a northern Virginia suburb. The anonymous taxi driver provides a perfect cutout. The result: a clean, near untraceable drop. Good spycraft.

The delivery might have been a windfall—or it might have been worked out between accessories in both camps. This side of the story remains unknown, because the Albosta committee failed to reach conclusive answers. This failure is perhaps understandable, since a congressional committee is not a detective agency. But the FBI also failed—and here questions of the will to succeed arise. As an ex-FBI official who was involved in the investigation put it, "The Bureau ran scared of the White House"; and for the Reagan White House, there was no profit in an exhaustive, conclusive FBI investigation as to how a rival's presidential debate briefing books came into Reagan hands.

The path from the NSC to a cab to the Baker staff explains how Casey could protest his innocence. Indeed, none of his fingerprints had been found on the filched foreign policy papers. But what about Carter's domestic briefing book? Paul Corbin apparently claimed *before* Debategate became public (and later denied) that he had gotten hold of this briefing book and had given it to Casey. This feat, however, was not beyond a man of Corbin's wide contacts. The task would have been eased by the fact that there were people in the Carter White House, especially on the secretarial and clerical staff, who had access to these papers and who had revealed pro-Reagan sentiments.

Such a second channel, White House to Corbin to Casey to Baker, explains Baker's claim that he received Carter debate documents from Casey. There would be no Casey fingerprints found because the domestic briefing book was never found in the Reagan files. Yet, the Reagan staff remembered having it during the campaign.

The Department of Justice decided that Debategate offered no evidence of criminality. No one was going to be tried; no one was going to jail. Don Albosta lost his potential Watergate—in fact, he lost his seat in Congress later that fall when his Republican opponent managed to hang the charge on him that he had squandered public funds trying to embarrass the President.

Casey had survived again, albeit a bit tarnished. Soon after the Albosta report came out, President Reagan made a high-profile gesture of support. The President went to Langley for the ground breaking of an addition to the main CIA headquarters building. It was a rare, even unsettling experience for old Agency hands, to have reporters roving the grounds, photographers, and people with tape recorders. Before appearing at the outdoor ceremony, the President went indoors, where no press was permitted, and talked to the covert operations staff. He turned to the wall where the stars were chiseled and noted that six new stars had been added since his last visit two years before.

Outside, Agency employees had been told to remove their ID badges, and the press office warned photographers not to take any close-ups of employees. Casey and Reagan threw a few spadesful of earth, and then the President put his arm around Casey and lauded him as the rebuilder of the Agency and "the eyes and ears of the free world." Jim Baker ordinarily accompanied the President on these ceremonials. This day he was busy elsewhere.

William Casey was like the successful father whose sons never quite measure up. He had done it all long ago, at the Research Institute of America, in the OSS. He had taken mountains of shapeless facts and pounded them into a report with a cutting edge. Analysts who brought the fruits of their labors before him hardened themselves for a common reaction: "I could have done this myself in half the time—and better!" As John Horton noted, "He knew exactly what he wanted from us. And he never explained it."

Even one of Casey's favorites, Herb Meyer, found that "if you went to Bill complaining that people weren't going through channels, he didn't know what you were talking about. You were just a whining bureaucrat. And he hated that."

Horton was particularly exposed to the Casey flame thrower, because, as he noted, "I had a special account, Latin America, which was of intense interest to Casey." He had been dragged out of retirement, and now found himself being badgered like a junior associate in a Casey law firm. During a congressional debate on contra aid, Horton was called into Casey's office to brief a Republican congressional staffer who had been sent over to get ammunition supporting the appropriation bill. Horton sat for a time listening to Casey and the aide, thinking, "I'm a professional intelligence officer. I'm not supposed to be taking sides in a political debate. What am I doing here?" He got up and left, to Casey's annoyance.

Horton divided the CIA senior staff into those who knew how to play Casey and those who did not. He placed himself squarely in the latter category. In the former category was Herb Meyer, who, as vice-chairman of the National Intelligence Council, was Horton's superior. Two men could scarcely have been more unalike: Horton, old, courtly, reasonable; Meyer, young, brash, opinionated. Horton was willing to admit Meyer's considerable brainpower; but he found Meyer's naked contempt for career professionals like himself harder to take than the man's reflexive conservatism.

Casey occasionally took Horton with him to National Security Council meetings at the White House when Latin America was on the agenda. "I went as Casey's horse holder," Horton recalled. These were the only times that he had observed his hard-driving chief perform in the presence of *his* superior, President Reagan. On one occasion, when it came time for Casey's briefing on the Americas, he sent Horton, "feeling like an idiot," to a map with a pointer. After Casey's presentation, Horton recalled, "I noticed that the President was looking around the room and smiling. He started telling a story about a letter he'd gotten from a little girl in South America. Instantly, all the other people fixed their eyes on the table. But I was the new kid, and he'd caught me looking at him. So he started smiling and telling the story to *me*. On those occasions when I was in the White House, I had a sense of no one being at the center, that the President was out to lunch, that nobody was really in charge."

"Destabilizing Mexico is a fundamental objective of the Soviet Union," Casey told Horton. What proof did he have? Horton asked. "The hardest thing to prove is something that's self-evident," Casey repeated from his intelligence catechism. What he had to go on thus far was gut instinct. He had talked to an American who ran a successful executive search firm in Mexico City. "The guy's flooded with résumés from Mexicans," Casey told Herb Meyer. "They all want to get out. They want to get their money out. That tells you what's coming." He came back from a White House meeting with another tidbit. Another American executive based in Mexico City kept his company jet at the airport, ready for takeoff at a moment's notice. Obviously, Mexico, with its crushing $80-billion foreign debt, with inflation shoving the middle class down into the poor class, with its long-simmering anti-Americanism, could be the next Iran. He wanted to hear what the analysts had to say. Casey told Horton to arrange an oral briefing on Mexico.

Horton had the Mexican desk of the intelligence directorate come to Casey's office. Horton described the briefing: "They were all a little nervous. Casey could have that effect on people. He sat there picking his teeth with the paper clip, groaning whenever somebody made a point he didn't like. Herb Meyer was there too, feet on the desk, like a second-string Casey. I'll admit, from the theatrical standpoint, the briefing lacked fire. But it was balanced and factual—certainly respectable."

As soon as the briefers left, Meyer swung his legs off the desk and said to Horton, "What a goddamned bunch of crap! That's our Mexican desk?"

Casey threw Horton an accusing stare. "What's going on?" he wanted to know. "That country's going to hell in a handcart and you're not getting the right stuff out. You're not talking to the right people. What's wrong?" He repeated the anecdotes about the flood of résumés from anxious Mexicans, the plane revved for a quick departure.

"I was thinking all the while," Horton remembered, " 'going to hell in a handcart'—how do you put that into a professional intelligence assessment? The story about the plane on the runway was a year old. Was the motor still running?" Horton had been the station chief in Mexico City. The dissatisfactions coming out of Mexico now were no different from what he had heard when he served there. It was a chronically troubled nation, but relatively stable. They had not had a full-blown National Intelligence Estimate on Mexico in years, Casey concluded. And he wanted one now.

Horton knew that there was more to Casey's concern about Mexico than the fate of the Mexicans. The main purpose of the Soviet embassy in Mexico was to run spy operations into the United States. The embassy staff was bloated. Filed in the CIA's counterintelligence operation were mug shots of all the Soviet diplomats in Mexico City with their histories; "KGB" and "GRU"—the Soviet military intelligence group—appeared after an alarming number of faces. Mexico's border was perfect for penetrating the United States. For a while, U.S. airlines had supplied the CIA station chief in Mexico City with manifests for flights between Mexico and the States. But checking the thousands of passengers' names became overwhelming. "Hell, getting in and out was a breeze," Horton noted. "There was one U.S. Air Force sergeant who went from Washington, made his drop at the Soviet embassy in Mexico City, and was back home the same day. For all his friends knew, he'd gone fishing."

The National Intelligence Estimate that Horton had been directed to produce, entitled "Mexico Under [President] de la Madrid," led to a brawl. Horton had assigned the first draft to a subordinate who described a Mexico on the brink of revolution. Horton found the piece alarmist and the conclusion unsubstantiated. Horton rewrote it. Herb Meyer brought both versions to Casey, and said, "You want to have some fun? Take a look at these."

Casey was furious. Horton's subordinate had produced a crisp, hard-hitting scenario of Mexico as indeed the next Iran. Casey loved it. Horton, in Casey's judgment, had gutted a fine piece of work. Casey leaned hard on Horton to salvage some of the sharp language of the original draft. Horton resisted; it would produce a distorted picture of Mexico, he said. Casey pushed hard, but he did not dictate. His friend John Bross had always preached, "Manipulation or distortion of an estimate is a sin against the Holy Ghost of intelligence." Casey knew it. If you start playing with objective reality, you might as well close up shop. But was there nothing between a partisan polemic and mush?

He found the deceptively mild-looking Horton nearly impossible to move, flinty beneath the courtly surface. The draft kept bouncing back and forth among various components of the analytical apparatus. "Paragraphs kept creeping back in that weren't supported by evidence, and I kept cutting them out," Horton happily reported. After all this churning, the final product that went out into the intelligence community was, in Horton's judgment, "a mess." But in his eyes, he had won a small victory. The mess was at least untainted by political bias.

The Mexico estimate, however, had been the last straw. When Horton had first been asked to come back to the CIA, his friend had said, "How can you work for those people?" In the end, he concluded that he could not. "I'd go to meetings with Tony Motley, Dewey Clarridge, and Ollie North," Horton recalled, "and it was just awful. Ollie would sit there making these stale gibes about the cookie pushers at State. He was always plotting end runs around established procedures, some of which had been established for damned good reasons. And everything these fellows uttered was 'Fuck this' and 'Fuck that.' I'd spent six years in the Navy and I knew all the naughty words. They sounded like a bunch of adolescents trying to prove how macho they were. And Ollie North? God, the man could speak a blue haze of bullshit. At times, I was convinced he was mad." Worst of all, Horton found that he was beginning to feel disloyal. "I started writing memos to Casey, telling him where his policy was wrong. I had no business doing that—although I must say my criticisms bounced off him like darts off armor plating."

His contract was up for renewal in May. "I wrote Casey a letter," Horton recalled, "and I said that obviously he had no confidence in me. Then I said, 'I think one of us ought to leave. And since it doesn't look like you are leaving, I'd better go.' " He sat on the letter for a few days, then sent it up to the seventh floor. Almost instantly, Casey was pushing Horton's button on his telephone console, telling him to come up right away. As Horton came in, Casey was holding the letter like a contaminated object. All that he said was "You're right." Thus ended John Horton's second career at the Central Intelligence Agency.

Word got back to the Democrat-controlled House intelligence committee that Casey had been trying to politicize the Mexico estimate. The HPSCI staff was instructed to trace the history of the document. The conclusion reached in the committee's official report read, "We examined the earlier drafts and the final version of that particular NIE and found that dissenting views were printed at the very beginning of the study, a practice the Committee applauds."

While at the CIA, Bobby Ray Inman had had little love for Bill Casey. His brilliant career had been capped, thanks to Casey, by nearly two years of frustration, friction, and distrust. But Inman had been in a good position to watch Casey's handling of estimates. "Casey put a lot of heat on people to make them justify their conclusions, especially if he didn't like them," Inman observed. "And he was always attacking the writing style—this wasn't punchy, this was too evasive, this didn't come down anywhere. His constant criticism made the analysts uncomfortable and made them feel pressured. But the charge that he twisted intelligence reports to fit his politics or the administration policy is pure bunk. He was not guilty of that."

Barely had Debategate died when Casey was back in hot water, this time in the U.S. Tax Court. The Internal Revenue Service claimed that he owed between $100,000 and $200,000 in back taxes.

In 1976, his longtime partner and protégé, Carl Paffendorf, had given Casey a 1 percent interest in PenVerter for a nominal $95 payment. (The PenVerter technology, when developed, was supposed to allow computers to read handwriting.) The IRS was challenging business deductions that Casey had taken on his investment. The company had generated huge paper losses of nearly $6 million. Casey, as a 1 percent owner, had deducted his share of these losses, which came to an average, between 1977 and 1980, of $52,500 a year. These losses saved him about $14,000 a year on his income taxes, or a total of approximately $56,000 on a $95 investment.

On the stand in the Tax Court, the lawyer for the IRS suggested that PenVerter was really "in the business of selling tax deductions." Casey was incensed. "I would like to take exception to any notion that I purchased a tax deduction. . . . To say I purchased tax deductions is an outrageous distortion." What he was doing, he said, was investing in America's future, the kind of bold entrepreneurship that had made the United States the technological wonder of the world. He could not, however, resist a little outrageousness himself. Of course, he admitted to the court, he was the author of the book *Tax Sheltered Investments*. "I invented the whole thing," he said with an impish grin. "Then, when I became chairman of the SEC, I redeemed my sins."

The IRS ruled that the $6 million in losses existed only on paper. And the Tax Court ruled against Casey, hitting him with taxes due, plus stiff penalties.

Three months after William Buckley had been kidnapped without a trace, an American journalist in Beirut awoke to find a videotape on his doorstep. The journalist turned the tape over to Lebanese officials, who sent it by secret emissary to the U.S. State Department. State sent a copy to Langley, where Casey viewed it. On the tape were seen three American captives of the Hizbollah, the radical Shiite group: Jeremy Levin, the Reverend Benjamin Weir, and William Buckley. They were pleading with their government to help obtain the release of seventeen Moslem terrorists being held in Kuwait for blowing up the French and American embassies the previous fall. The Americans looked terrible, especially Buckley, who was emaciated, dazed, and stared out at the camera from haunted eyes. "Look, his nose is broken," one covert operator said. "They must have tortured him." As the tape ended, Casey said, "I'm taking this to the White House"—which he did. Ronald Reagan was moved to tears.

From what the CIA had been able to learn, Buckley apparently had been spirited out of Beirut after his capture and held in the terrorists' Abdullah barracks in the Syrian-controlled Bekaa Valley of Lebanon. Then he had been shipped to Syria for interrogation, likely under torture. Later reports had it that Buckley had broken and gave his captors a four-hundred-page confession that included the names of numerous U.S. agents in the Middle East.

But all that was known with any certainty at this point was that Buckley was likely still alive: in the videotape he had held up close to the camera a newspaper with a recent date visible.

The conflict in Nicaragua provided a commentary on modern guer-rilla warfare: both sides had hired American PR firms. Casey, an old hand at engineering full-page political ads in the *New York Times,* was a firm believer in the power of propaganda. He arranged the hiring of a Miami-based firm, Woody Kepner Associates, at $300,000 for a six-month contract, to win worldwide support for the contras. Daniel Ortega, the strongman in the Sandinista junta, hired an ex–Maryknoll priest now doing public relations in New York to woo the hearts and minds of Americans to his position. Casey was going to need all the goodwill he could muster. The House, which was making a habit of rejecting contra aid, was headed for another vote in August. After the outrage over the harbor mining, Casey was not sure this time that he could save the contra operation in the Senate.

In his speeches, he began painting the bleakest possible portrait of Central America. If the threat of another Marxist neighbor was not enough, he began advancing another argument—old-fashioned self-interest. He began talking about "feet people," hordes of refugees who would be fleeing Communist takeovers in Latin America, stream-ing where else but to the United States. He had his own pipeline into the White House speech apparatus through Tony Dolan. Thus, by the summer of 1984, President Reagan's speeches also raised the specter of "one hundred million people, from Panama to our southern border, under the control of pro-Soviet dictatorships. Violence and a human wave of refugees will then cross into the United States." Here was a new twist on the old Yellow Peril scare of the nineteenth century, a wetback invasion on an alarming scale.

A reporter for *U.S. News and World Report* asked Casey how he reacted to congressional threats to cut off aid to El Salvador if the death squads were not stopped. "What we're talking about," he an-swered, "is whether our primary purpose is to establish a better society in El Salvador, which isn't likely to happen under present circumstances, or to protect the security interests of the United States." The security interests of the United States—that, to Casey, was the prism through which every global issue had to be seen. The political turmoil in countries like El Salvador, Nicaragua, and Guatemala grew out of deep-dyed poverty caused largely by maldistribution of wealth. This was the condition the Communists exploited. To Casey, if poverty fostered communism, communism had to be defeated first, because it threatened priority number one, U.S. security. Then, when communism was rooted out, the United States could get around to dealing with economic injustice.

In August, the House passed the latest version of the Boland Amendment, a total cutoff of military aid to the contras. Eddie Boland thought the intent of his bill was crystalline: "It clearly ends U.S. support for the war in Nicaragua." There were no exceptions to the prohibition, he told the House. Bob Gates remembered being in Casey's office when word of the House vote came. "He gnashed his teeth," Gates said. "Casey literally gnashed his teeth. You could hear it." Now Boland had only to see his amendment passed by a Senate still seething over Casey's behavior on the mining affair.

The *Washington Times* was the latest attempt to float an afternoon paper in the capital. The *Times,* staked by the Korean evangelist the Reverend Sun Myung Moon, head of the Unification Church, had plenty of money. The paper was conservative, pro-Reagan, and had excellent pipelines into the administration. One summer day just before noon, Casey's press officer, George Lauder, came in with the early edition. "Does the *Washington Times* know something we don't know?" Lauder asked.

"Lemme see that," Casey said.

The story Lauder showed him read:

The Reagan White House has begun assembling a list of possible successors for Central Intelligence Agency director William J. Casey who reportedly has made known his intention to leave government service in January. Well-placed administration officials said there are at least five names on the informal list of individuals who will be considered for the cabinet-rank CIA post if Mr. Casey makes a final decision to return to private life. Three of those being considered to take over the CIA are White House chief of staff James A. Baker III; national security advisor to the president, Robert C.

McFarlane; and Laurence Silberman, former Justice Department official. . . .

Five days later, an article appeared in the *New York Post* headlined: CIA BOSS TURNING IN HIS CLOAK AND DAGGER. This account was not even speculative. It flatly reported: "CIA Director William Casey has informed senior White House officials that he plans to step down at the end of the year—even if his close friend, Ronald Reagan, wins re-election. . . . His reasons for leaving are simply that he wants to return to private life."

To Casey, there was not the slightest doubt as to who was responsible for these stories. Jim Baker was after his scalp and his job again. He had to come up with a counterstrategy. He wrote to the President the day the *Post* story came out. "I write this note in the hope that the circulation of fake representations can be curtailed." He included copies of the offending stories.

Casey hoped that he still had a firm purchase on the President's loyalty, because he evidently had lost the other Reagan, the First Lady. His friend Ed Meese noted, "Baker and Deaver were constantly undermining Bill with Nancy Reagan, telling her that he was an old fossil hurting the President's image by his antics on the Hill."

Stan Sporkin stopped by Casey's office during the latest tempest. "Bill, why don't you resign?" Sporkin asked. "Hell, you're no kid. You don't need this."

"Stan, what would I do?" Casey answered. "Go back to New York and practice law? Go to Florida and play golf?"

What about the two of them practicing law together? Sporkin suggested. He had never made any real money. Here was a chance.

"That's a bore," Casey said. And with that Casey turned to something else, the discussion over.

Just days after Casey sent Reagan the note and the news clips, the white phone rang in his office. It was the President. "Bill," Reagan said, "as long as I'm safe in this office, you're safe in that office."

Casey had read Ronald Reagan well. As a New York friend of his observed, "Casey's not really Reagan's pal. Reagan just thinks Casey is a smart guy who got him elected. It's the way an actor feels about his agent. As long as he gets good parts, he's got to believe the agent's good."

His letter to the President had turned a knock into a boost. Casey was, as far as he could tell, the only Reagan cabinet officer reappointed for the second term—and the election had not yet been held.

25.

Ollie and Uncle Bill

He was to become one day a hero, a burning patriot to millions, a zealot, a misguided missile to others, but an undeniable American phenomenon. In the spring of 1984, however, Lieutenant Colonel Oliver L. North was known only to a small fraternity of national security specialists in State, Defense, the military, the NSC, and the CIA.

His roots were as American as Andy Hardy's. Oliver Lawrence North was born in 1943, during World War II, in San Antonio, Texas, while his father, a winner of the Silver Star for gallantry, was serving as an Army colonel. Ultimately, North senior abandoned his military career to go back into the family business, a wool-combing mill in Philmont, New York, where young "Larry," as he then was known, was raised. His mother was a schoolteacher. His father also wound up teaching after polyester killed off the wool business.

Philmont is small and rural but not picturesque, a rough-edged blue-collar town actually, one of many once-thriving communities along the Hudson River valley that time has passed by. There, Larry North enjoyed a comfortable if strict upbringing with his three younger siblings in the family home on Maple Street. His first taste of the military occurred when his family enrolled him as a day student at the Christian Brothers Academy in Albany, a three-hour round-trip commute. It was a school where students went through rigorous daily inspections, with demerits handed out for unpolished brass and unshined shoes, where a wisecrack in class could earn a slap in the face. The commuting was too much; and after a year, North returned to the local public school. Like Bill Casey, he continued to serve as an altar boy, at Sacred Heart Church, until he graduated from high school. He was a diligent if unspectacular student. In his yearbook, he was voted "best looking" and "most courteous."

In 1961, young North entered the State University of New York at Brockport, where physical education and grade school teachers were trained. At Brockport, North enrolled in the Marine ROTC unit; and that summer, the Marines sent him to Camp LeJeune in North Carolina. North was hooked. After two years at Brockport, he won an appointment to the U.S. Naval Academy. There the distinctive North persona began to take shape.

At Annapolis, he was involved in an automobile accident in which a fellow midshipman was killed. North, by now called Ollie, suffered a serious leg injury; doctors feared he might never walk again. Ordinarily, that should have finished off a military career. But North managed to remain at the academy and adopted his own rehabilitation program—overcompensation. If the drill instructor called for fifty push-ups, Midshipman North did sixty-five. If his class ran three miles, North, in a knee brace, ran four. He took up boxing and became brigade middleweight champion, fighting with a leg that literally had to be held together with tape and substituting furious bludgeoning for finesse.

But along with the doggedness, the will to succeed, there also emerged a darker side, a willingness to trifle with the facts. His years at an obscure teachers college somehow metamorphosed into two years of pre-med. To make sure that his knee problem could not bar his dream of a Marine Corps career after Annapolis, one classmate claimed, North managed to strip any harmful information from his medical records.

He graduated in 1968, at the height of the Vietnam War, and took a commission in the Marines. By the end of the year, he was in Vietnam commanding a platoon. And six months later, he matched his father's feat. A nearby platoon was pinned down by enemy guns. North led his men into a hail of machine-gun fire and managed to rescue the trapped unit. On May 25, 1969, he was awarded the Silver Star.

There was a fierce, manic quality to North's dedication. A fellow officer observed, "We're not talking tunnel vision, we're talking needlepoint vision. Ollie was bore-sighted." An enlisted man commented on the compulsive mother-henning North exercised over his men. "If you took a piss," the Marine said, "Lieutenant North would critique you on how you held your dick."

Back in the States with his tour up, he volunteered to return to Vietnam to testify as a witness for one of his former men, who was being court-martialed for murdering sixteen women and children in a My Lai–type incident at a village called Son Thang. Shortly thereafter, North won his first national exposure when he wrote a letter to William F. Buckley defending the military after the My Lai massacre, in which 347 unarmed civilian women and children had been shot by American soldiers. Buckley was so impressed by the passion of the letter that he invited North onto his television program, "Firing Line," to discuss the incident.

After Vietnam, North spent essentially ten garrison years. One moment stands out from that period. Late in 1974, North, by then married with children and living in a northern Virginia suburb of Washington, was reported to be wandering around the house, naked, brandishing a .45 pistol, saying he was going to kill himself. Thereafter, he spent a brief period in the psychiatric ward of Bethesda Naval Hospital. It was later said that he managed to have the record of this confinement removed from his file.

The real breakthrough from obscurity began for Ollie North when he was selected for the Naval War College at Rhode Island. There, he caught the eye of the secretary of the Navy, John Lehman. Lehman recommended North to Richard V. Allen, Casey's old friend, who took over as the Reagan administration's national security adviser in 1981. North came to the NSC as a member of the defense policy staff. It was not an exalted post. As Allen described it, North's job was "to set up easels and carry charts."

North had two attributes that are rarer even than intelligence: he was indefatigable and he was ambitious. He was capable of putting in an eighteen-hour day, sleeping for three hours, and going back to work. His NSC assignments grew to encompass two of Casey's hottest interests, antiterrorism and Latin America. As a colleague on the NSC described Ollie North in action: "Some of his ideas and plans will be based on a great deal of knowledge and will be really smart things to do. Others will be based on no knowledge and will be really dumb things to do. But you won't be able to tell the difference by listening to him, because they will both sound the same."

John Horton, before his exit from the CIA, often worked with North, and spotted a talented player. "Ollie learned quickly how you get from here to there in the bureaucracy," Horton observed. "He knew how to use paper, how to call a meeting, who to bring in, who to cut out. He was a skillful bureaucratic predator."

The early weakness for embellishing the truth continued. North liked to tell how he had taken a map into the Oval Office to "the old man" and persuaded President Reagan to carry off the invasion of Grenada. North and his intimate sessions with the President became a staple of his well-told tales. But Ollie North was never, ever alone with the President.

Constantine Menges, as the NSC's deputy for Latin America, also worked with North and came away half mesmerized, half appalled.

Menges once listened to North tell him in great detail about a dinner he had had the previous weekend with Jeane Kirkpatrick, then the U.N. ambassador. When Menges saw Kirkpatrick, he questioned her about it. "I've never had dinner with Oliver North," she answered.

On another occasion, Menges came into North's office while North was on the phone. North was telling the caller that Henry Kissinger was with him and that he would have to call him back because he and Kissinger were going to be busy writing a report on Central America. Menges at first thought that North was kidding. "Ya, Ollie, we haf got to finish dis discussion," Menges said in his best Kissinger imitation. But as the phone conversation went on, he could see that North was conning the caller.

Chance made North and Casey EOB neighbors. Casey had a choice corner office that looked out over Pennsylvania Avenue and Seventeenth Street NW. The room was high-ceilinged, Victorian, and full of the feel of history. Casey loved it. There, the phones rang less than at Langley. The visitors were fewer. He had time to think. North's office was just seconds away, down a black-and-white-tiled corridor in room 302. Along the way were the offices of the President's Foreign Intelligence Advisory Board, PFIAB (re-created at Casey's insistence after President Carter had killed it), the Intelligence Oversight Board, and a string of other NSC offices in what was called Spook Alley.

The relationship that grew between the seventy-one-year-old Casey and the forty-one-year-old North is best described by North: "Bill Casey was, for me, a man of immense proportions and a man whose advice I admired greatly. . . . I know who my superiors are and I know the chain of command. And he wasn't a boss so much as he was a personal friend and an adviser, and a person with whom I could consult and get good advice."

The man Casey came to know was no intellectual. But he had worked hard at the Naval War College and had good retention of what he read. But all the knowledge he assimilated went to buttress his primal convictions rather than to enlarge his mind.

The legendary chief of the German general staff, Alfred, Graf von Schlieffen, was said to have divided his officers into four categories: Schlieffen I, bright and ambitious, an able officer, possibly dangerous politically; Schlieffen II, stupid and lazy, a harmless officer all around; Schlieffen III, bright and lazy, the best officer because he will find the easiest way to do the job and yet create no political problems; Schlieffen IV, stupid and ambitious, the most dangerous officer of all. Where North fit is an open question, except that he was clearly not II or III.

That spring, the fortunes of the contras had reached a low ebb. The latest $24-million appropriation was virtually spent. The writing on the wall stood out in bold italics as Casey's handling of the mining affair shrank congressional support. The likelihood was that the Senate would follow the House, approve the Boland Amendment, and cut off aid completely. Without support, the contras could be expected to collapse within six to ten months. The grim joke around the Agency was that the only territory the contras would then control was part of Miami.

While the press and Congress were raking Casey over the coals for going too far in Nicaragua, he was meeting secretly with the President and Bud McFarlane, now the national security adviser, to prepare for the day when the money was shut off and the CIA was legally shut out. The President's wishes were clear. As word was relayed down the line, he wanted the contras kept alive as a viable fighting force.

The pending Boland Amendment read: "None of the funds appropriated for the Central Intelligence Agency or any other department, agency, or entity of the United States involved in intelligence activities may be obligated or expended for the purpose or which would have the effect of supporting, directly or indirectly, military or paramilitary operations in Nicaragua by any nation, group, organization, movement or individual." In short, no U.S. military aid for the contras.

But in a manner that had by now become as instinctual to him as breathing, Casey read this language not for what it prohibited but for what it missed, and he saw a crack the contras could slip through. The amendment barred government agencies "involved in intelligence activities" from aiding the contras. That clearly meant the CIA, and State, Defense, and the FBI for that matter. But what about the NSC? The statute creating the NSC read: "The function of the council shall be to advise the President with respect to the integration of domestic, foreign and military policies relating to the national security, as to enable the military services and other departments and agencies of the government to cooperate more effectively in matters involving the national security." Nothing about "intelligence activities" there. If pushed to the wall, the administration could always get a legal opinion from Casey's next-door neighbor in the EOB, the Intelligence Oversight Board. This small, three-member body, appointed by the President, was charged with keeping intelligence agencies honest by reporting to the President any improper or illegal activities.

In all this, Casey played two roles. The first was as director of Central Intelligence. His responsibility here was to see that the CIA was never again maneuvered, as it had been in the 1970s, into questionable, even illegal, and ultimately destructive activities foisted on it by the White House. He had worked hard to rebuild the battered intelligence service that he had inherited. Nothing must reverse the gains made.

But there was another Bill Casey. This Casey was a member of the Reagan cabinet, a shaper of Reagan foreign policy, a trusted confidant of the President of the United States who was going to do all in his power to serve that man's ends. Could he play both roles? Inevitably they must collide. But he had spent his life skirting the edge of the abyss. He was nimble, agile, sure of foot. Why should it be different now?

At this point, with Boland still pending, the CIA still had legal authority to help the contras. But the point was academic, since there was virtually no money left. And Congress refused to ante up a supplemental appropriation. To wait while a blind, obstinate Congress let the contras starve was foolish. The time to act was now. But if the Boland Amendment was passed, the CIA's skirts must be kept clean. Who, then, should carry out the President's wishes to keep the contras together as a fighting force at all costs? To Casey, the choice was obvious. That spring, he told the President that the man was Oliver North. The President accepted Casey's judgment.

The chain of command, however, was to be scrupulously observed. North still worked for McFarlane, and it was McFarlane who actually handed North the assignment. As North later described his situation, "Mr. McFarlane tasked me to be the person who was the principal action officer." And McFarlane passed along to him the President's order: "Your mission is to hold the resistance together body and soul." Nothing was put in writing. No finding was made. North nevertheless understood that he was to carry out covert operations from the NSC, in cooperation with the CIA for the time being, but without the Agency, should Boland become law.

Thus it was that in May of 1984, North had found himself standing next to Dewey Clarridge at a base in Honduras, as Clarridge explained to the contras that this was the man who would never let them down.

To Casey, the great human failing was lack of imagination, the inability to see the larger possibilities. All the money in the world was not in the purse of Congress. Plenty more could be found in the coffers of countries that wanted to help—indeed, that owed help to this administration. Casey started to tap alternate sources of aid for the contras. As early as March 27, Casey and McFarlane talked about making a pitch to the Israelis. Casey urged McFarlane to try other countries too. One rumor had it that Casey met secretly to put the arm on King Fahd aboard the royal Saudi yacht off the French Riviera. Not true: they met in the royal palace in Riyadh. Fahd had been receptive. Ultimately, a deal was cut whereby the Saudis provided $1 million a month to the contras.

That spring, Casey made another bid for the huge cache of Cuban arms captured in Angola by the South Africans. The chief of staff of the South African armed forces was in town, and Casey had him out to Langley for lunch. The two men had gotten along well during Casey's visit to South Africa. The South African was eager to please. His country was becoming a global pariah; and the antiapartheid pressure coming out of America was a strong contributor to South Africa's image problems. Helping the Reagan administration in Central America might, he reasoned, ease at least some of the pressure.

Casey practically salivated over the arms South Africa was willing to part with. But a CIA analyst on the South African desk spotted potential disaster. Congressman Louis Stokes of Ohio, a black, an articulate, respected man, was a member of HPSCI. The administration was already being accused of being soft on apartheid. Imagine, on the heels of the Nicaraguan mining debacle, to have the next headlines read that the Reagan administration was in bed with the South African military!

The administration's attempts to tap third countries for aid for the contras inevitably leaked. Exactly one week after apologizing to the committees for the mining affair, Casey had been back on the griddle at the House intelligence committee. The *Washington Post* and other news media had gotten wind that lethal assistance for the contras was being sought from Israel and South Africa. Congressman Wyche Fowler, Jr., the sharp-tongued Georgia Democrat, asked Casey point-blank, "Is any element of our government approaching another element of another government to obtain aid for the contras?" Casey answered: "We have not been involved in that at all. No, not to my knowledge."

Casey did not like to lie; his preference was to control the truth by omission. But occasionally one had to lie to protect an operation. No, "lie" was a harsh word. A lie was a deliberate falsehood told to advance one's selfish interests, possibly at the expense of an innocent party. What he had done was protect a national security secret. There was, in his mind, a clear distinction. Still, he did not enjoy it, because lies were like dry rot: exposed, they undermined support by destroying confidence. These third-country appeals were going to require some law to lean on.

And so Casey arranged with McFarlane to have third-country aid for the contras placed on the agenda for an NSPG meeting set for June 25. Both the President and the Vice-President were present. The meeting opened with George Shultz and Cap Weinberger discussing the prospects for a negotiated peace in the region. Casey's reaction was quiet scorn. The President said the sort of thing that endeared him to Casey: "That's too farfetched to imagine, that a Communist government like that would make any reasonable deal with us." What the President preferred, he repeated, was to keep the anti-Sandinistas in the fight. Casey saw his opening and suggested that the way to do it was to get third countries to kick in.

Shultz bristled visibly. "You can't do indirectly what you can't do directly," he said. The U.S. government could only raise and spend money through congressional appropriations. They were getting into deep water. Shultz mentioned the horrible of horribles: they might be talking about "impeachable offenses." All eyes were averted from his.

They were not talking about the United States spending other countries' money, Casey argued. Let the third countries give aid to the contras directly. That, under the current finding, was legal.

Shultz was unpersuaded. "I think we need an opinion from the attorney general."

Ed Meese came to Casey's rescue. Meese recalled that the attorney general, William French Smith, had made a recent ruling on the subject. Meese understood that third-country solicitations were legal.

McFarlane recognized that they were playing with rocket fuel, and as the meeting broke up he said, "I certainly hope none of this will be made public in any way." The President agreed. "If such a story gets out, we'll all be hanging by our thumbs in front of the White House until we find out who did it." And then he spoiled the threat with his good-guy smile.

The meeting ended with neither McFarlane nor Casey mentioning one fact: both of them already had made third-country solicitations. He needed a legal leg to stand on in the future, Casey told Sporkin when he got back to Langley. The next day, he and Sporkin went to the Department of Justice and talked to the attorney general. William French Smith confirmed what Meese had said: it was perfectly appropriate to ask a third country to help the Nicaraguan resistance, provided that country expected no form of repayment from the United States for its help. Good, Casey said. He would have this opinion in his back pocket the next time Congress pressed him.

The press office made Xerox copies of all articles from major papers that mentioned the director. In the batch dropped on Casey's desk one March morning, he found he had made columnist Joe Kraft's sleaze list. Ed Meese had just moved from the White House to the post of attorney general, and Kraft had bitterly criticized the appointment in a column entitled "Meese and the Appearance of Justice." In the last paragraph, Kraft wrote, "The Meese case is not an isolated example of hanky-panky in high places. President Reagan keeps at the Central Intelligence Agency a director who was in and out of the stock market while serving at the CIA. . . . The appointment of a pol to the Justice Department is only one more blot on a long record of sleaziness."

"It's a one-day story"; "It only hurts for a day"—these were Casey's reflex defenses. Inside he raged.

A few nights later, Casey was at a dinner given at the Decatur House by Arnaud de Borchgrave, a columnist and former *Newsweek* chief correspondent. There Casey ran into Dick Allen, now back in his own consulting firm. Allen had also been zinged by Kraft in the same column as "a national security adviser who took watches from Japanese businessmen." Allen mentioned the Kraft piece. It was unspeakable, Allen said—yellow journalism hiding behind a respected byline.

"Yeah," Casey said. "But what can you do about it?"

"Plenty," Allen said. "I don't take that shit anymore. Sure, you're tempted to ignore a deliberate distortion, a slur on your character like that, because they wear you down after a while. But God damn it, Bill, you've got to fight back. Because every time this stuff comes out, it gets burned a little bit deeper into the public's brain cells."

Allen had been forced to resign as national security adviser because he allegedly had taken $1,000 to arrange an interview with Nancy Reagan. His defense: "I intercepted somebody trying to give the money to the First Lady and I took the fall."

"What do you do?" Casey wanted to know.

"I force retractions," Allen said. "I'll send you a batch of them tomorrow."

Casey was impressed. He had never considered that approach.

"Don't just stand there and take it, Bill. Fight back," Allen urged.

The next day, Casey wrote Kraft and accused him of publishing insidious and unsubstantiated charges. He demanded a retraction. He got back a brief "Dear Bill" note from Kraft that said, "I'm glad you're beginning to take this business seriously." The Allen defense had failed.

"You gotta be nuts to put up with this garbage," Max Hugel told him. "I've got me a hell of a lawyer. He's brilliant—he's tough. He's the guy that won my defamation suit against those McNell bastards. You ought to see Paul Perito. He's right here in Washington."

Casey had a battery of his own lawyers in the Agency. He had Stanley Sporkin, as smart and as tough as they come. But he did not want to reveal his bruised ego to the troops. It only hurt for a day—that was what he told them. And so, without informing Sporkin, he saw Paul Perito. What he wanted to know from Perito was whether or not he had grounds to bring a defamation suit against any of his media detractors.

Perito's staff spent a month reviewing the unflattering heap of press comment that Casey had amassed since his appointment as DCI. And in a lawyer's measured prose (which cost Casey $6,990) Perito concluded: "Our review . . . of your alleged improprieties leads to the conclusion that you would probably not prevail in a libel action in an appropriate Federal district court. First, a few of the allegations about you are, in fact, true, although incomplete and misleading. Second, to the extent material omissions or misrepresentations have occurred, there is no evidence that the critical element of constitutional malice is present." In short, Perito said, Casey was a "public personage, subject to what the courts would likely interpret as fair comment" about him. He had courted fame; he would have to take the heat that went along with the bright lights.

Ollie North had little idea how he was to run a foreign guerrilla army from two thousand miles away without any U.S. funds. And he was self-aware enough to know that he was in over his head. But he knew where he could get smart fast: he had only to walk around the corner from his room in the EOB, number 302, to Casey's corner office at 345.

McFarlane already had directed North to set up an offshore account. They needed a place, insulated from the United States, McFarlane told him, where they could park money coming in for the contras from third countries. According to North, Casey told him how to set up an operational account offshore. And as North was later to testify when the Iran-contra affair came under investigation, "All of the transactions were recorded on a ledger that Director Casey gave me for this purpose." North cleared the offshore arrangement with McFarlane and directed Adolfo Calero, the contras' political director, to set up an account in the Caribbean into which, according to North, "shortly thereafter, money began to flow."

Casey also proposed the enlistment of Major General Richard V. Secord in the contra-aid operation. Secord had been deputy assistant secretary of Defense for the Near East and South Asia. He had been the administration's point man in the successful fight for sale of the AWACS aircraft to Saudi Arabia. Later, the man had allegedly been linked to business deals with Edwin Wilson, the former CIA agent who eventually went to prison for life for illegal arms traffic with Libya's Muammar Qaddafi. After that suspicion surfaced, Secord's career stalled. In May of 1983, a bitter Dick Secord resigned from the Air Force. To Casey, Secord had been poorly used by his country.

Secord knew his way around the Pentagon; he knew his way around covert operations; he knew his way around the international arms market. Secord was, in fact, in private business now, selling arms and security devices. Should North have any qualms over the old Secord-Wilson association, Casey showed him a document, North later recalled, a determination by a judge in the U.S. District Court establishing Secord's innocence. The guy had been screwed, Casey said. He was perfectly honest. Secord was a patriotic American, and tailor-made to help North in his new assignment.

North took Casey's suggestion back to his boss, McFarlane. As North later explained, "I don't want either of my previous superiors to think that I was working for Director Casey. I know who I worked for." As far as Casey was concerned, it was just as well. Guiding this eager-beaver Marine served both Casey roles: the President's wishes regarding the contras would be carried out, and at the same time there would be no CIA fingerprints on North's contra supply operation.

Shortly thereafter, North gave Secord his first assignment. Secord was to start buying guns for the contras from the money coming into the private offshore account. They had a name for the operation. They called it the Enterprise.

On July 31, Casey took North with him on a quiet trip to a secret rendezvous in Central America, where they met with CIA station chiefs and embassy people in the region. Casey also took North to meet Panama's virtual dictator, General Manuel Noriega. Noriega, a longtime CIA asset, was well placed to help North bring arms into the region and ultimately into the hands of the contras.

North, with a life lived almost wholly in the military, held Casey's vast experience virtually in awe. Casey was a shrewd lawyer, and it was a comfort to have him available as they navigated treacherous shoals. The Enterprise was so legally fragile that, as North was to phrase it later, "I guess that Director Casey was the one who pointed out that there would come a time when there would need to be, if these activities were exposed, somebody to stand up and take the heat for it." Being the "fall guy" was one way of putting it; but that had a criminal ring. What North understood better was the Marine who throws himself on the hand grenade to save his buddies. And North understood one other thing: Casey wanted to know as little as possible of the specifics of North's activities to supply the contras.

Stanley Sporkin and Casey meshed beautifully. As Sporkin saw their relationship, "We reached a point where we communicated by not communicating. Nothing needed to be said. I'd say to my guys, 'Start drafting an amendment to the Freedom of Information Act.' And they'd say, 'Why? Nobody asked for it.' I'd say, 'Because Casey is going to ask for it.' Since he always wanted everything done yesterday, it was the only way I could stay ahead of him. Nine times out of ten, he would ask for the thing I'd already put in the pipeline." Sporkin's chief appeal to Casey was that Stan viewed the law creatively. "Don't tell me it can't be done legally" was Casey's constant refrain. "Find me a legal way to do it." And Sporkin would start digging.

On September 19 and 20, ABC's "World News Tonight" broadcast a two-part story about a businessman in Hawaii named Ronald Ray Rewald. Rewald faced federal criminal charges for fraud, tax evasion, and perjury growing out of a failed business. In his defense, Rewald claimed that his business was a CIA front and that the CIA had hired a killer to silence him.

Casey was alarmed. Since the intelligence investigations of the seventies, political assassination had been expressly barred by law. The ABC story about a CIA plot to liquidate a used-up business asset would confirm the critics' worst suspicions about the Agency. Casey summoned Sporkin, who found him roaring, "How the hell do we stop this crap?"

"We can't sue," Sporkin said, "because an agency of the government can't be libeled."

"Well, come up with something," Casey ordered.

"I've been thinking about it," Sporkin answered. "It's a long shot. It's never been done by anybody before."

"Get to the point," Casey said.

"In a situation like this," Sporkin explained, "a private citizen or a private organization could go before the Federal Communications Commission and file a complaint. They could demand equal time under the fairness doctrine. So we go to the FCC and we demand time to present our side of the story. If nothing else, at least we'll get some press mileage out of it. We'll get a public hearing."

"I like it," Casey said. "Give it a try."

"I called up ABC's lawyer that same day," Sporkin later recalled. "I told him, 'We're bringing an action unless you retract.' They didn't believe me. They never heard of such a thing from a federal agency. I told the guy, 'Okay, that's the last call you get from me. The next thing will be the complaint papers'—which I got over to the FCC before the day was over."

ABC subsequently retracted. The network reported that it had "no reason to doubt the CIA's denials," and subsequently, the FCC issued a landmark ruling. Based on Sporkin's complaint, the FCC ruled that henceforth federal agencies, along with private parties, could file complaints against broadcasters under the fairness doctrine just as an ordinary citizen could.

"That was the thing about Casey," Sporkin remembered of the affair. "He pushed me to greatness."

It appeared, however, that Casey was about to lose Sporkin. It began with a lunch that Casey had in his office with Milton Gould and Sporkin. Casey momentarily left the room, and Gould said, "What are you going do, Stan, be a bureaucrat forever? You've got to get out of here."

Gould had touched an unspoken yearning. Stanley Sporkin's dream had long been to follow in his father's footsteps and go on the bench. Sporkin senior had been a county court judge in Philadelphia.

"Just tell Bill," Gould said.

"I don't like to ask him for anything," Sporkin replied.

Later, Gould caught Casey alone and told him about the conversation with Sporkin. "I knew Bill well enough," Gould later observed, "that if you were in his corner, he'd go the limit for you. He wouldn't stand in your way."

Casey went to Ronald Reagan, and shortly thereafter, in June, the President nominated Sporkin to the U.S. District Court for the District of Columbia.

Sporkin waited for approval by the Senate Judiciary Committee.

But Stanley Sporkin, the people's watchdog at the SEC, winner of the Federal Civilian Service award, the nation's highest honor for a government official, had never encountered right-wing zealotry. A chief objective of the Reagan administration was to put conservative judges on the federal bench. Sporkin had won the President's blessing only because Bill Casey had interceded personally and directly. But the right wing was furious.

As Sporkin saw it, Senator Jeremiah Denton, an Alabama conservative, a prisoner of the North Vietnamese for nearly eight years, a member of the Judiciary Committee, blocked his judgeship. At the SEC, Sporkin had been in the little guy's corner against the corporations. "I had done things there to make conservatives unhappy," Sporkin claimed. "I taught law courses at a liberal college like Antioch, and at Howard here in Washington, a black university." The Judiciary Committee stalled. By the end of the year, time ran out; the appointment expired. "I was," Sporkin said, "devastated." Casey, a longtime acquaintance of bruised feelings, assured Sporkin it was not over. They would be back.

On October 12, both houses of Congress passed Public Law 98-473, which appropriated funds for the continuing operation of the government. Attached to the bill was the second Boland Amendment. The President would have no choice: since 98-473 was an omnibus spending bill, he would have to sign it, the Boland Amendment included. The United States had finally cut off all military aid to the contras.

Ironically, Casey had invited members of the two oversight committees and their staffs out to the Agency for a reception that very afternoon. His press officer, George Lauder, had warned Casey earlier, in his hammering, unflinching style, "Bill, those guys don't believe a word you ever say." Lauder told him that his distrustful and disdainful manner, epitomized by the mining affair, probably had provoked approval of the Boland Amendment. Casey had been his own worst lobbyist.

As Lauder pointed out, when the committees found his requests reasonable and open, they bent over backward to please. They recently had given Casey a bill he had been fighting for for nearly four years. The Freedom of Information Act that he had inherited had driven Casey to something approaching apoplexy. On one of his impromptu tours through the Agency, he had stumbled onto the Freedom of Information compliance office. There he watched CIA professionals spending thousands of man-hours going over documents, line by line, fulfilling Freedom of Information requests, blacking out, with felt-tipped pens, information that could not be released, laboriously appending the reasons, as required by law, why a particular item could not be released. In some instances, page after page was blanked out, with only an "and" or a "the" escaping the censor's pen. One of the compliance officers told him, "Some of these requests are filed by people paid by the Ayatollah to use the Act to get this stuff out of us." Casey shook his head.

That spring, the Agency had had to handle one of its stickiest Freedom of Information cases. The request involved one of the darker secrets exposed in the seventies, the Agency's earlier experimentation with the effects of drugs. Most damaging had been the case of a civilian scientist unwittingly given LSD in the course of a research project called MK-Ultra. The man subsequently committed suicide. A private citizen named Simms had asked, under the Freedom of Information Act, for the names of the scientists and universities with whom the CIA had contracted to carry out MK-Ultra. The CIA refused, and Simms went to court.

The whole MK-Ultra affair had been so shabby that the Agency's argument that it had to protect the identity of these individuals and institutions had a bad odor. But Casey saw a larger principle at stake: if someone could come in off the street and demand the names of people who did things for the CIA, sometimes unpalatable things, how could you get anybody to do them in the future?

He had turned over the problem to Sporkin, who took the position that however tragically this particular incident had turned out, the people involved were "sources," and sources and methods had to be protected. That was the cardinal rule of intelligence. Sporkin forced *Simms* v. *Central Intelligence Agency* all the way up to the Supreme Court, and the Agency eventually won.

But the CIA could not fight every individual request in court. Casey had wanted the law changed. And so he had gone to Congress for an amendment to the Freedom of Information Act. If the CIA carried out a covert operation, he wanted those files exempted.

In effect, the committees had said: "Come to us with a loony idea, like mining the harbors of a country we are not at war with, and we say no; ask us to protect the people and the methods by which this country must carry out its intelligence function, and we say yes." That October, Congress approved the exemption he wanted. And so Lauder had advised Casey to show his gratitude. Hence the invitation to the oversight committees to come out to the Agency for a reception on the day that Congress approved Boland.

The Casey the congressmen saw in a social setting on his own turf was another man. Absent was the why-do-I-have-to-be-here? contempt. He circulated easily among the knots of guests, telling stories and revealing a phenomenal memory for incidents, names, and faces. If he felt any resentment over passage of the Boland Amendment, he kept it to himself.

Alan Fiers was approaching twenty years of service. He had come to the director's attention during Casey's frequent trips to the Middle East, where Fiers was working under cover as chief of the Saudi peninsula. In the summer of 1984, Fiers was back at Langley, awaiting his next Middle East assignment. Casey had other plans for him. He needed someone to fill the Dewey Clarridge vacuum in Central America; he needed somebody to take over what he called the Central American Task Force. But he did not need a Dewey Clarridge clone. With the passage of Boland, the Agency was out of the derring-do business in Nicaragua—that was now Oliver North's turf.

The first time Fiers had met Casey, he left thinking, "I've met this guy before." Then it dawned on him: Casey was another Woody Hayes, Fiers's old football coach at Ohio State. "Woody Hayes had been a powerful influence in my life," Fiers observed. "Woody sized people up quickly. He drove them. He was a student of literature and history. And he could swear up a storm. He was an intellectual and an activist. He stretched people. Now I was working for another one. I came to the conclusion that this breed was produced by a particular era—the Depression and the war. I don't think we have that kind of a crucible anymore."

Fiers was something of an unusual amalgam himself. He had an open, pleasant face, a receding hairline, and wore glasses; he appeared mild and soft-spoken on first meeting. Yet the intensity would build as he warmed to a subject, the subsurface mental and physical energy breaking through. Fiers once had received an efficiency report that was perfect in every category except one, where he received an "excellent" instead of an "outstanding." He had gone to his superiors with a formal written protest. "All drive and zeal" was how one colleague described Fiers.

Fiers was puzzled when Casey offered him the job of running the Central American Task Force. He knew nothing about the area. He spoke no Spanish. "I didn't even know that British Honduras had become Belize," he confessed. Still, Casey was ready to take the gamble. Dealing with Panama, Honduras, and Guatemala were fairly conventional. In El Salvador, Fiers was supposed to try to help maintain the fragile democracy that had begun with the election that year of José Napoleón Duarte as president. But Nicaragua? The contras? "It was never made clear to me," he recalled, "exactly what I was supposed to do. I suppose it was, in the jargon, to retard the consolidation of a Marxist-Leninist government. But I had to do everything looking over my shoulder at Boland. We could give the contras intelligence; we could try to support anti-Sandinista elements politically inside Nicaragua. But no rough stuff. I began walking a tightrope from day one."

Within days he came to know someone who seemed to be running merrily along the tightrope while Fiers teetered. He met Ollie North.

Casey had moved quickly to put the CIA into a safe post-Boland posture. He had Sporkin draft what he called a "compliance code," the rules of engagement under Boland. It read: "Field stations are to cease and desist with actions that can be construed to be providing any type of support, either direct or indirect, to the various entities with whom we dealt under the program. All future contact with those parties are, until further notice, to be *solely*, repeat *solely*, for the purpose of collecting positive and counter-intelligence information of interest to the United States."

The CIA was officially out of the war. Fiers was to live by the compliance code. Yet Casey kept pressing him to do everything short of breaking the law to aid the contras. Stanley Sporkin offered what Fiers called "the best advice anyone ever gave me. He told me to put a lawyer on the Central American Task Force, somebody who could test everything I was doing against the law. I had this guy at my right arm as we tried to figure out what we could and couldn't do. We made up lists of dos and don'ts. The big don't if you were CIA was 'Don't cross the Nicaraguan border.'"

But the line was fine. Fiers tried to play it safe by going to the oversight committees on close calls, in effect making them a party to his decisions. On one trip to the Hill he asked, could his people give the contras intelligence that they were walking into a trap? Yes, the House committee staff advised him. Could they give the contras weapons to fight their way out? No. It seemed to Fiers a weird way to run a railroad.

What Ronald Reagan had told the NSPG was unequivocal, Boland Amendment or not: "I don't want to pull out our support for the contras for any reason. This would be an unacceptable option." And so the administration, through the NSC and North, supplanted the CIA and began to run the Nicaraguan resistance. The NSC was acting in a legal limbo, which was its advantage. Unlike the CIA, it had no legal obligation to obtain findings for conducting covert operations. It was not required to notify Congress of its activities. It did not have to defend a covert-operations budget to Congress. It escaped these controls simply because nobody expected this paper-processing outfit to be carrying out guerrilla warfare.

Casey remembered a legendary agent from World War II named Freddy, an American Jew who always volunteered for the most hazardous missions, who offered to parachute into a concentration camp and lead a breakout, who had jumped into Germany and actually passed as a Wehrmacht officer. Freddy's fear nerve was dead, his OSS friends liked to say. But after the war, the impetuous Freddy had been unable to stay on with the CIA. It was a different era. Sheer nerve had to be tempered by sound judgment.

Casey thought of Freddy when he learned of Ollie North's latest stunt. Casey was in his office in the EOB and immediately marched down Spook Alley to the office of Admiral John Poindexter. Poindexter was McFarlane's deputy in the NSC and thus North's immediate superior.

Since taking over the contra support operation, North's talent for self-invention had flourished. He liked to give the impression around the White House that Sandinista sympathizers had threatened his life. A bullet-proof vest hung on his wall—it was for his trips abroad and when he testified before congressional committees, North said. Even his sunglasses were supposed to be bullet proof. To Alan Fiers, "The only guy who could put more spin on the ball than Ollie North was Hoyt Wilhelm."

Under Boland, the CIA was to deal only in "defensive" intelligence. Yet North had come over to the CIA and had managed to wheedle information from the Central American Task Force on where the Sandinistas had deployed their newly acquired HIND-D helicopters, and he had passed this information to the contras for a planned attack. North had very likely involved the CIA in a violation of the Boland Amendment. Casey was furious.

North was good—goddamned good, Casey told Poindexter. But he was indiscreet, a blabbermouth, a show-off. He had committed a serious intelligence goof. "You've got to keep the lid on Ollie—tell him to button up," Casey warned Poindexter. The contras' battles were no longer the CIA's account. The Agency was going to play by the Boland rules. Poindexter—a pipe-puffing, imperturbable naval officer whose bald head, round face, and bland features suggested a WASP Buddha—heard Casey out but said nothing.

North perhaps had reason for the breezy confidence he was feeling these days. He had prepared a memo describing how the guerrilla army would be funded by third-country aid and appeals to private donors. Later, he entered this notation in the log he kept on his contra activities: "Call from RCM [McFarlane]: Pres. has approved funding plan."

Betty Murphy was sitting at her desk outside Casey's office when she heard a volcanic roar. A representative of the State Department had been sent over to inform the director that the secretary of State was in Managua. Casey told his secretary to get him Constantine Menges at the NSC, right away. Menges would know what this was all about. Casey heard Menges's explanation and instantly understood what had happened. Ronald Reagan's agreeable nature had betrayed him again. He had let George Shultz talk him into promoting a peace plan for Central America that Shultz had been talking up for months. Shultz was obviously in Managua peddling his plan at the other end. They had to get together instantly, all the foreign policy reliables, Casey told Menges.

The next day, October 13, a Saturday, Casey was driven into the basement of the State Department. He took the elevator up to the office that Jeane Kirkpatrick used when she was in town. Casey's rapid footsteps echoed down the empty corridors. When he got to the office, Kirkpatrick and Menges were already there, sitting on a sofa, sipping coffee.

"Okay, Constantine," Casey said, settling into an armchair, "let's see what you got." Menges fished from his briefcase two copies of Shultz's proposal, which he described as "a plot against the President's policy in Central America."

Casey flipped noisily through the sixty-page document. What he read would make his three years of effort to build up an anti-Sandinista army a farce. Casey began to tear the proposal apart before Kirkpatrick had a chance to finish reading her copy. The image boys, Jim Baker and Mike Deaver, were obviously attempting to pull off a public relations coup on the eve of the presidential election. The polls had shown repeatedly that the American people disapproved of aid to the contras. The Shultz peace plan called for having a treaty signed by the end of October, one week before the election. Ronald Reagan could go before the voters as a peacemaker, the man who ended an unpopular, dirty little war.

The only problem, as Casey, Kirkpatrick, and Menges agreed, was that the Shultz plan sold out the contras. It was a pact between Ortega, the United States, and the other Central American governments. No demands were made of Ortega and his junta to deal with the contras, to ensure their participation in democratic elections. Yes, Shultz's idea would bring peace, but a Munich-style peace, with the contras playing the Czechs. All the pressure would be off the Sandinistas. Instead of stopping the consolidation of a Marxist regime, this document would, the three agreed, confirm it.

It looked to Casey as if Shultz had let himself be brainwashed by the career apologists in his own department. Had Shultz forgotten what Tomás Borge, the Sandinista minister, had said: "Rivers would reverse their direction before any contra leaders walked the streets of Managua." To the Sandinistas, the contras were a contemptible American invention. Another senior Sandinista official warned that his government would never negotiate with the contras, only with the United States: "We want to talk to the owners of the circus, not the clowns."

"This has got to be stopped," Casey said. "I'll get to the President over the weekend."

"Let Reagan be Reagan" had become the conservatives' cry. In their view, softies at State, even his own secretary of State, were undermining Ronald Reagan's bone-marrow anticommunism. "Let Reagan be Reagan"—it was a cry that seemed to say that the President of the United States did not have the power to impose his will on his own subordinates.

On Sunday morning, Casey tracked down Reagan in Des Moines, where he was campaigning. Casey was gentle. He recognized that the President was busy, he said, especially now in the final weeks before the election. It was understandable if the impact of George Shultz's peace plan had not exactly leaped off the page. But this treaty would kill the contras.

After he hung up, Casey got a call from Menges, who wanted to know how it had gone. He had convinced the President, Casey said. They had derailed George Shultz. How had he managed it? an admiring Menges wanted to know. "Oh, that was easy," Casey answered. "I told him we'd get a better deal out of the Sandinistas after the election, if they knew they'd face four more years of us."

The victory was crucial to Casey, but it was purchased at a high price in his relations with George Shultz. To Shultz, here was an unpardonable invasion of his territory by a man who had no business being there. The secretary of State negotiates peace initiatives on behalf of the President. DCIs collect intelligence and run covert operations to help carry out foreign policy. Casey did not belong in the policy loop. What likelihood was there that he would report intelligence that went against his positions? As Shultz saw it, "It's a common observation that when someone gives you change, they rarely give you too much."

Casey had been having a regular Friday lunch with the secretary ever since Shultz had replaced Haig. But now Betty Murphy seemed to find that the secretary of State always had a conflict when she called to confirm the date. Eventually, the weekly lunch withered and then died. George Shultz did not intend to be shortchanged again.

Just before the election, Casey called North and told him to keep open the night of October 31. "We're going to a Halloween party," he said. Casey was taking North and Herb Meyer as his guests to an annual conservative rite, the dinner of the Pumpkin Papers Irregulars. William F. Buckley, a member, described the Irregulars affair as "half comic, half serious, a way to kick up our heels." The name derived from the Alger Hiss trial of 1950 when Whittaker Chambers, former Soviet spy, had produced secret State Department documents from a hollowed-out pumpkin on his Maryland farm to prove that Alger Hiss had been a Soviet agent while at State.

Casey and his guests entered the International Club on the corner of Eighteenth and K streets, a coolly modern setting favored for social gatherings by the intelligence, national security, military, and diplomatic communities. During the reception, Casey circulated among the guests, conservatives old and neo-: Sidney Hook; Michael Novak; Eugene Rostow; Norman Podhoretz, the editor of *Commentary* magazine; Priscilla Buckley, William F.'s sister and a member of the *National Review* staff. After dinner, Xerox copies of lyrics were passed out and one of the Irregulars led them in song. Casey stumbled manfully through parodies such as "Chiquita Havana," sung to the melody of "Chiquita Banana" ("I'm Anthony Lewis and I'm here to say / Revolutions have to ripen in a certain way"). Then they sang, to the melody of "Hills of Shiloh," "Have you heard from Abram Tertz, off in Far Siberia . . ."

Then Laurence Silberman, a tough-talking, forty-eight-year-old vet-

eran of the departments of Justice and Labor, introduced the evening's speaker, the director of Central Intelligence, William J. Casey.

Elements of the Pumpkin Papers Irregulars celebration were silly,
even infantile. But Casey was deadly serious. He was not mumbling
his way through a hearing before a bunch of congressional skeptics.
He was speaking to a brotherhood, people who understood his brand
of patriotism. As he retold the familiar saga of the Hiss trial, it was
as if the Irregulars were hearing a well-loved bedtime story:

> Alger Hiss did steal and pass along through Colonel Bykov, his
> Soviet handler in New York, information about Japanese troop
> movements to Manchuria, French military supplies to Rumania,
> and such things in the late thirties. Hiss was at the side of President
> Roosevelt at Yalta and, as secretary general, welcomed President
> Truman to the first convocation of the United Nations in San Fran-
> cisco. How the NKVD [predecessor of the KGB] must have preened
> itself at the photos of a smiling Alger Hiss standing behind Roo-
> sevelt, Stalin, and Churchill at Yalta and welcoming Harry Truman
> to the podium for the first address of an American President to the
> U.N. . . . I have often marveled at how Hiss deftly moved from the
> office of Secretary of State Stettinius to the side of John Foster
> Dulles. How lucky or possibly how shrewd a move, as the long reign
> of the Democratic administration entered its final stages, to posi-
> tion oneself near the ear of the prospective Republican secretary
> of State.

Then Casey warmed to his real message:

> We haven't improved. In our lifetime, Soviet agents have succeeded
> in getting hold of detailed data on everything from the nuclear
> bomb to the MX, including a real sidewinder missile, stealth
> bomber technology, vast amounts of computer methodology, and
> buckets of information about our satellites. . . . After all, they roam
> freely among us, read uncensored technical publications, use a legal
> right to request documents from our files, profit from a flood of
> leaks used as weapons in policy struggles, and attend the debates,
> which we conduct in public and they conduct among a handful of
> men behind closed doors.

He mentioned Jimmy Carter and had to stop to let the audience
enjoy a rousing boo. Then he went on: "Carter had sold our European
allies on deployment of the enhanced radiation weapon, the nuclear

weapon that killed people and left the buildings standing. Then the Soviets went to work. When they had managed to raise world opinion against the weapon, Carter reversed himself. We figure the Soviets spent on the order of one hundred million dollars to pull that off."

The goodness and decency of Western democracies was always being manipulated, Casey said. "They criticize us for supporting a massive defense buildup. But look at the way the defense contractors of the thirties were vilified. The Nye Committee branded them 'merchants of death.' And who was the counsel to the Nye Committee? Why, it was Alger Hiss!"

Herb Meyer later remarked, "These people had come to the dinner for fun and games. But when Bill finished, there was a stunned silence. They sat there spellbound. And then there was an explosion of applause. Norm Podhoretz looked at me incredulously, and he said, 'That's terrific—who wrote it for him?' I informed him that Bill Casey had written every word of it."

At the end of his speech, the Pumpkin Papers Irregulars presented Casey with a first-edition *Life of Nathan Hale* by George Dudley Seymour. On the flyleaf Ronald Reagan had penned an inscription, citing a lesser-known quote of Hale's: "Every kind of service to the public good becomes honorable by being necessary." That, Casey concluded, was about as good a definition of this strange craft of espionage as anything he had ever seen.

26.

Four More Years

"The man must be a tropical fish," a congressman observed of Casey. "He has an absolute passion for hot water." Barely six months after the mining affair, Casey was back in the docket on Capitol Hill.

It had begun the year before, the summer of 1983, with what Casey thought had been the best of intentions. He had taken McMahon and others to Central America. He had observed Dewey Clarridge's progress in building the contras. But, Casey had warned, they also had to build an army with moral authority. He had suggested a manual, something that would give the contras political direction and lay out in clear terms what they were fighting for.

Dewey Clarridge subsequently had contracted with a "psychological warfare expert" who was hired under the pseudonym John Kirkpatrick to write the manual. The objective, Kirkpatrick was instructed, was to teach the contras to carry out their operations in a way that would win popular support, particularly among the Nicaraguan peasantry and small villagers, and thus give them a psychological edge over the Sandinistas. Kirkpatrick had found something to go on, a similar 1968 manual prepared for the Vietnam War. What ultimately emerged, through various editions, was a ninety-page primer in Spanish, entitled *Psychological Operations in Guerrilla Warfare*. The putative author was "Tayacan," a fabled Central American Indian warrior. Clarridge had not read it. He could not, since it was in Spanish.

In the summer of 1984, a year after Casey first had planted this seed, Edgar Chamorro, now a disillusioned former spokesman for the contras, leaked a copy of the booklet to the press. Its existence was subsequently reported in the *New York Times* under the headline CIA PRIMER TELLS NICARAGUAN REBELS HOW TO KILL. The little book was instantly titled, in reporter's shorthand, "the assassination manual."

The word "assassination" did not actually appear in it, but the manual did discuss "neutralizing" Nicaraguan officials and creating "martyrs." It spoke of blackmailing civilians to work for the contras and of inciting violence at demonstrations. It dealt with shooting people trying to leave a captured town and "implicit and explicit terror." One early edition contained the sentence: "If possible, professional criminals will be hired to carry out selective jobs." And the manual spoke openly of overthrowing the Sandinistas. Casey had never seen the manual. It barely had made it to the middle level of the bureaucracy before it was cleared and sent out to the field.

The manual threw the oversight committees into an uproar. Overthrow the Sandinistas? Here was a clear breach of the Boland Amendment. "Neutralization" of officials? What was that but a violation of the President's Executive Order 12333 banning assassination? The Speaker of the House, Tip O'Neill, said, "Casey owes the American people an explanation. I want him out of there." HPSCI launched an investigation.

On December 5, Casey was driven to the House side of the Capitol and took the elevator to the now all-too-familiar secure hearing room of the House intelligence committee. The grilling lasted two and a half hours.

He could not defend the manual, so he tried to defend the motive behind it. Yes, it had been poorly supervised; his people had not exercised due care. But damn it, the original point had been to train the contras to win over their own people. No "assassination manual" had ever been intended. The implementation, not the idea, had been a monumental screw-up.

The language of the committee's final report was harsh. The manual "was a violation of the Boland Amendment." It "has caused embarrassment to the United States and should never have been released in any of its various forms. Specific actions it describes are repugnant to American values." But the committee took no action beyond its words. In effect, it accepted Casey's defense: "Negligence, not intent to violate the law, marked the manual's history." He and the CIA had been guilty of stupidity, not evil.

Still, Casey had to take punitive action. Six middle-ranking members of Clarridge's staff received written reprimands, black marks that would cost them a year or two of promotion. "John Kirkpatrick" lost his contract. But Dewey Clarridge went unscathed. He was by now in his post in Europe, heading covert operations.

By the end of 1984, Casey had lost another ally—even more, a friend. Jeane Kirkpatrick had hoped for a White House portfolio in foreign policy. But George Shultz blocked her. Casey understood Kirkpatrick's frustration. Under the President's light touch, there was no real center of authority, just competing fiefdoms. She decided not to get embroiled. Her husband was not well. It was time to leave the U.N., to come home to what she considered "academic heaven," her chair at Georgetown University. Casey's last words as she left the administration were, "Don't forget, I'm completely serious about running you for President."

As Christmas approached, he received a strange request: he was asked to play Santa Claus at the White House Christmas Party. It was not the dignified image that he wanted to project, but he sportingly put on the red suit and the white beard and handed out the gifts to the children and grandchildren of the White House staff.

On the last day of the old year, as he was leaving CIA headquarters, he swung by a corridor gallery where the portraits of past DCIs were hung. He wanted to see the latest addition. He had been a terrible sitter, driving the artist, Everett Raymond Kintsler, to distraction with his fidgeting. But he was delighted with the result. He cut a fine figure in the painting, trim-looking in boardroom blue. The wisps of hair looked thicker and lay neatly in place. He was up there with the legendary Allen Dulles. If Bill Donovan had headed the CIA instead of the OSS, he would be there too. It was tempting to pack it in now and go home. But he was going to be the first DCI ever to survive from one full presidential term into the next. And there was so much more he wanted to do.

On November 7, Ronald Reagan had crushed Walter Mondale by 54.5 million to 37.6 million votes in the popular election and by 525 to 13 in the electoral college. For the first time in more than twenty years, Casey had been legally barred from participating in a presidential election. The CIA chief was limited to giving a briefing to the opposition candidate. The Mondale staff, however, had declined Casey's briefing. They did not trust him.

With the election won, he thought he would try a new tack with Jim Baker. He was still bristling from Baker's last attempt to torpedo him. But Casey was a realist. They were both going to be around for the foreseeable future. And so a few days after the election, he put on his most affable face and stopped by Baker's office in the West Wing.

What were Baker's plans for the second term? Casey asked. "I'm thinking of staying put, at least through the second honeymoon," Baker answered. Nah, Casey told him—poor move. He knew what Baker wanted. Baker wanted foreign policy experience and he wanted visibility. These White House staff jobs, even the chief of staff, were backbreakers, and anonymous to boot. Casey understood all that. Sure, the CIA looks good at first blush. He understood why Baker had wanted to take his job—no point being coy about it. But the CIA was a mistake. "You get mussed up there. You have to keep your mouth shut. It's a lousy base for a political career."

Now, take the U.N. There was an excellent launch pad. "Look at Henry Cabot Lodge . . . Pat Moynihan, Jeane Kirkpatrick. They all won international reputations at the U.N. They became household words."

Yes, Baker agreed. But his wife did not think New York was a good place to raise children.

"Hell," Casey said. "Jeane didn't move to New York. She kept her home and family here in Washington. You go up once or twice a week. It's even easier than commuting from Long Island every day, I can tell you that."

He left thinking he had lit a small, promising fire. But he was taking no chances. He sat at his desk, wrote out a longhand letter to the President, and had Betty Murphy type it. It came back six single-spaced pages. He could never get Reagan to read anything that long. He cut and pruned. He got the letter down to two and a half pages. And then he told Murphy to get him an appointment with the President. That was never a problem. He used his credit with Reagan sparingly, never squandering it on anything less than what he called "Supreme Court cases."

The next day, he took the letter with him to the White House. He asked Reagan to read it in his presence. It was the only way, like pinning a butterfly to a board. "It is an open secret," the letter began, "in fact a scandal, that the White House staff regularly gives information to the media . . . to open up jobs they covet and to cut down colleagues seen as rivals." He quoted a *Washington Post* editorial that revealed that the most damaging sources of information on Cap Weinberger, Bill Casey, Richard Allen, Al Haig, and Ed Meese were not the opposition but other "high Administration officials." He was not going to pussyfoot any longer. The chief orchestrator of these leaks was Jim Baker. "Jim could not escape responsibility for a process which always runs in one direction and which has continued unabated under his wing for three years." Get him out, Casey said. "The proper thing is for him to move on and pursue his ambitions at the U.N." Yes, leaking was intolerable, Reagan agreed; he just could not understand it. Still, the President seemed distressed by the visit. He liked Jim Baker. He depended on him. Casey left feeling that he had ruined the boss's day.

In February of 1985 Casey did something he had not done for forty years, not since he had been an employee at the Research Institute of America: he asked for a raise. He had taken advantage of what he regarded as a splendid change in the White House staff. Jim Baker was gone at last. Soon after the second term began, Baker and the Treasury secretary, Donald T. Regan, had simply switched jobs. They had gone to the President with the idea, and, to their astonishment, the President had agreed without so much as asking a single question—not even why.

Casey was now earning $75,000 a year. He wanted the status of the full cabinet-level salary of $86,000. The idea of asking Jim Baker for a raise had been unthinkable. But Don Regan was a friend going back to Casey's days at the SEC. It was Casey's recommendation that originally had brought Regan into the cabinet.

Regan barely had settled into his new office in the West Wing when Casey hit him for the raise. There was about the man a tough geniality. He spoke with a metallic Boston accent. Don Regan could have passed for a prosecutor with an unbroken string of convictions. "Hell, Bill," Regan replied to Casey's request, "I'm not getting a cabinet-level salary myself, and I'm chief of staff. I took a pay cut to come over here. Besides, there's no money in the budget."

Casey persisted. "I'll tell you what," Regan said. "I'll play poker with you, double or nothing."

"Aaah!" Casey said, and walked out with his dismissive wave.

"But he kept coming back at me," Regan recalled. Salary was like the stars on an officer's epaulets. It signified rank. Regan, who had pulled his way up from trainee to the top of Merrill Lynch, understood these games. In the end, Casey got his raise. They were off to a good start. As Casey now saw the White House staff, it was a friend in, a viper out. He appeared to have forgotten that Baker too had once been his protégé.

Casey also faced a new lineup on Capitol Hill this season. But there the changes were less welcome. His relations with Goldwater had swung like a pendulum, but always at least on the right side of the spectrum. Now Goldwater was gone. He had served the maximum eight years allowed members on the SSCI. On leaving, he sent Casey a letter in pure Goldwaterese: "I think you've done a heck of a good job and you've certainly brought the intelligence group a long way up the road that the Church committee darn near destroyed you on. I appreciate it as an American citizen. Not just as a United States Senator."

Early in the new year, Casey sat in his office with *USA Today* spread out on his desk, reading an interview given by Goldwater's successor as chairman of the SSCI, David Durenberger. The more Casey read, the angrier he became. The new chairman had torn into Central America. The administration had backed and filled all over the lot on Nicaragua, Durenberger claimed. The only shred of a policy was "aiding the contras," which was no policy at all. "I have this nagging fear that if you asked the key 12 actors in the Reagan Administration for a one sentence explanation of U.S. policy in Nicaragua you would get twelve different answers," he said. He closed the interview with words possessing a prophetic irony: "The thing that keeps boggling my mind is why the Administration can't see that whichever way they go, they have to go through the Congress—there's only one way to get to Nicaragua and that's through Capitol Hill."

Durenberger had earlier told a *New York Times* reporter his number-one priority in dealing with the CIA: "We've got to get the trust back on both sides." He complained to another reporter, "Casey's a used-car salesman. He tells you what he needs to tell you to sell the car. If you don't ask if there's an engine under the hood, he won't bring it up." Durenberger was also the senator who when asked to rate Casey had given him a two on a scale of ten. Mutual trust was going to be a tall order.

Durenberger was a complicated personality, a strictly reared Catholic whose liberal, intellectual bent put him on a collision course with his religion. At the time he took over the chairmanship, he was separated from his wife and living in a Christian fellowship house on the banks of the Potomac called the Cedars, trying to sort out his life. To some Senate observers, the new SSCI chairman was "a flake."

Casey needed friends on the committee. And so, after reading *USA Today*'s interview of Durenberger, he picked up the phone and called his sometime supporter, sometime critic Pat Moynihan. He wanted Moynihan to come out to Langley. He wanted to award him the Seal Medallion, one of the CIA's highest honors.

The House committee, HPSCI, had a new chairman too: Lee H. Hamilton, an Indiana Democrat with twenty years' experience on the Foreign Affairs Committee. He replaced Eddie Boland, who had left the committee, though his amendment lived on. Hamilton was reasonable and a nonleaker, Casey believed.

Casey's war against the White House leakers might have been less convincing if his own contact with the press—more precisely, with one member of the press—had been known. The previous fall, George Lauder had been invited by Bob Woodward to join him for lunch. To

Lauder, it still took some getting used to: spending much of his life concealing what he did, living under pseudonyms, ducking people's questions, and now, suddenly, having a job where he was expected to talk to the most daunting investigative journalist in the country.

The man Lauder lunched with was then forty-one years old. He had been born Robert Upshur Woodward in Geneva, Illinois; but he went by "Bob" even in his byline. He had graduated from Yale in 1965 and started his Washington journalism career reporting for a Maryland suburban weekly, the *Montgomery County Sentinel*. By now, he was assistant managing editor of the *Washington Post*, with a twelve-person investigative team under him and with President Nixon's scalp dangling from his belt. He was, at bottom and incorrigibly, still a shoe-leather reporter.

He was twice divorced, the father of an eight-year-old daughter, a man who made stabs at living the life of luxury that his success permitted. He owned an elegant six-bedroom Georgetown town house and for a time had a forty-five-foot yacht. But at heart he was a workaholic. Why did he stay in day-to-day journalism? he was once asked. And he answered: "Casey had venture capitalism in his bloodstream. I had the newspaper in mine."

There was something trustworthy and sympathetic in his low-key manner. Bob Woodward spoke with the voice of a young priest in the confessional who had adopted a tolerance for the failings of his flock: just tell him—he would understand. It was only when he himself talked at length, surmising whirls and whorls of conspiracy, that the soft brown eyes began to narrow and harden; the lips curled in almost diabolic pleasure at the skulduggery he suspected. The smooth face started tightening when he heard objections to his views or sensed a hostile listener. But then the young priest quickly returned. The favorite expletive of this man, who in his books was prone to put four-letter words in the mouths of others, appeared to be "gee." The nodding, unthreatening "I certainly understand" manner was capable of seducing the wariest of interviewees.

And now, Woodward was working his charm on George Lauder.

He was going to write a series of articles on national security, Woodward said. Was national security better under Reagan than it had been before? It was a home-run pitch, and Lauder went for it, starting to tick off the Casey successes in reinvigorating the CIA. Yes, that was the sort of thing he needed to know in order to draw a comparison between the Turner CIA and the Casey CIA, Woodward said. Could he talk to some of the people in the Agency? He was not so much interested in the unmentionables, the covert stuff, as in the analytical business, the improvements in the estimates. Again, Woodward had rung the right bell. Improved estimates were the source of Casey's greatest pride.

George Lauder was no pushover. Once out from under the benign Woodward spell, his defenses resurfaced. And he remained dubious about any profit in Casey's seeing Woodward again. Still, he reported the conversation to Casey; and to Lauder's discomfort, Casey said yes, they would cooperate with Woodward on his articles.

One of the first people that Woodward wanted to talk to was Bob Gates, the deputy for intelligence and chairman of the NIC. To Casey, it was a reassuring choice, since Gates was his number-one man on the analytical side.

"I gave Woodward over an hour and a half," Gates later recalled. "I tried to help him understand how our analytical and estimating process worked. His manner was so vulnerable and nonintimidating: 'Gee, I don't understand that. Could you please go over it again?' He had no hard-edged agenda. We just roamed. He would have made a great case officer. He never used anything I said in any articles about national security. And when his book on covert operations came out, I barely recognized a word from our conversation. I assume talking to me was the price he figured he had to pay to get to others."

Woodward tracked down John Bross. "He was such a plausible guy," Bross said of his interviewer. "You talk to Bob Woodward and you start to believe he's on your side even when you have to know he'll hang you by the balls."

George Lauder had to admire the reporter's shrewdness. Word soon spread that Woodward was talking to Casey and his people. "When that got around," Lauder noted, "it softened the resistance of others in the national security business." Jeane Kirkpatrick called Casey and told him that Woodward wanted to talk to her about his articles. "Yeah, go ahead," Casey told her. "You can handle him."

Toward the end of December 1984, Casey urged his deputy, John McMahon, to see Woodward. McMahon balked. "Bill," McMahon told him during a ride to the White House, "this guy's a snake. He's gonna stick it to you. No way. I'm not talking to Woodward."

"You don't understand how the media works," Casey told him. "He's gonna write whether we talk to him or not. At least this way we get to shape some of it. He only wants to talk about the analysis side of the Agency anyway," Casey assured him.

"Okay, I'll do it," McMahon said. "But I want a witness sitting with me."

The day of the interview McMahon was nervous. Woodward was

believed to have sources not only among the oversight committees but within the State Department's intelligence apparatus, in the NSC, even in the CIA itself, certainly among Agency retirees. Part of the local lore had it that Woodward once showed an Agency official the entire transcript of a secret briefing carried out in one of the most secure hearing rooms on Capitol Hill.

McMahon started by describing to Woodward the Agency's intelligence collection capabilities. Woodward steered the conversation to covert operations. McMahon went back to analysis. Woodward again veered to covert ops. And then, with that hardening of the features, the narrowing of the eyes, Woodward started asking McMahon knowing questions about a top-secret covert operation aimed at a leading terrorist in the Middle East, an operation McMahon regarded as fraught with risks. "Jesus Christ," McMahon thought, "the bastard is on to us!" And he ended the interview.

Casey and Woodward fascinated each other. As George Lauder watched the interaction over several months, he concluded, "I could see that Bill looked forward to this gladiatorial combat. He thought he could beat Woodward." For his part, Woodward discovered in the gruff old pragmatist an unexpected quality. "Casey was passionate," Woodward observed. "He got passionate about the contras, passionate about the Soviets, passionate about winning one back from them; passionate about changing the flow of history. These matters were alive to him. They engaged his whole soul and his mind."

Woodward also found that Casey possessed his own powers of persuasiveness. As Woodward related one experience, "I let him talk me out of a story for a year. I knew William Buckley was not the political officer in Beirut when they nabbed him. I knew he was the station chief. I told Casey I wanted to run the story. Casey said, 'Don't do it. We still think he's alive. His captors might kill him if they found out.' We went back and forth. We didn't print the story for over another year."

Woodward himself wondered why Casey had given him access. And he concluded, "Partly it was curiosity. He liked writers. And he liked fencing with them. Partly it was defensive. I was writing about his Agency, and he wanted to get his side in. And part of it, frankly, was because he knew it was dangerous. He knew I was writing about him, and he liked to court danger. His seeing me was totally explainable in terms of Casey's character."

Casey also made a friendly overture to the columnist Jack Anderson, from whom he had no reason to expect much love. Anderson, along with CBS News, had broken the story in 1983 that the United States was intercepting Iranian communications; and it was this leak, Casey believed, that had tipped off the Iranians and led them to shut off the source. "But he called me, cordially enough," Anderson recalled. "He said we ought to get together once in a while, have a closer relationship. You see, a person like Casey just loves conspiracy. He liked the idea of talking to a reporter without his own people knowing it, conspiracies within conspiracies. So I wasn't surprised when I found out he was talking to Bob Woodward."

Anderson further told the readers of his *Washington Newsletter*, "Though Casey is personally a rock-ribbed Conservative, he's intellectually honest enough to entertain views that go against his otherwise hard line. Casey also gives prominent play to competing analyses of an event or situation in the appraisals sent to the White House." Casey liked the comment. It was "like the frog being kissed by the princess," he said.

George Lauder was getting edgy. He picked up from the Washington press grapevine that it was not a series of articles on national security that Woodward intended but a book on Casey and covert operations at the CIA. "I got word," Lauder said, "that it was going to be a black hat–white hat book, with Casey as the black hat and Stan Turner as the white hat—the moralist versus the schemer." Lauder took his concerns to Casey one day, just as·Casey was flying out of the office. "I think we'd better break it off," Lauder warned. "You know goddamn well it's going to be a hatchet job."

Casey answered in a way that betrayed that he already knew what Woodward intended. Besides, he was tired of a bunch of bureaucrats thinking that a reporter could get the better of him. "He's gonna write the book anyway, isn't he?" he growled as he marched past Lauder. "Well, I want *me* responding about *me*. Not somebody else."

On the first Saturday morning it happened, the archivist at the National Archives thought it was some kind of joke. The old fellow had come in wearing a baggy pair of golf pants and a rumpled blazer. He stood in line with the other weekend scholars filling out a call slip. It was only when the archivist looked at the signature on the slip, a request for some old declassified OSS documents, that he realized his client was the director of Central Intelligence.

Whenever he could, Casey liked to get up early on a Saturday and, after plowing through his read file and having breakfast, head down to that splendid old structure on a triangle of land at Pennsylvania and Eighth Street and disappear into the world of scholarship. He loved sifting through the boxes of yellowed carbon copies, the primitive mimeographed records of old operations and after-action reports from that long-ago war. He took down on his ever-present yellow legal pad the data that he intended to use in his constantly revised memoir of the OSS in Europe.

To the amazement of the aides he was running ragged, he was also working on another book—the one he and Bill Donovan had discussed long ago, espionage during the American Revolution. He found a scholar and writer and, in his customary fashion, hired the man to put the espionage manuscript in final shape. Previously, his collaborator had known Casey only socially, as a family friend, affable, story-telling, and charming in his blunt way. In their preliminary discussions, the writer (who chose not to be identified) recalled, "I was amazed at his grasp of history—not just the American Revolution but the whole panoply. And a strange thing struck me. The further back we went in history, the clearer his speech became. I don't know what a psychiatrist would make of that."

His collaborator worked hard for several months over Casey's sprawling manuscript and turned it in with his bill. The letter he got back was like a sock in the jaw. "It would not be fair to you to let you think that what you turned in was worth that much," Casey wrote. "There are no more than 60 pages of fresh writing, which comes out to over 50 cents a word."

Thereafter, Casey began to pressure the writer to take less money. He was astounded to discover this unsuspected Casey. "Here was this multimillionaire," he recalled, "he's running the intelligence apparatus of the United States, and he's fighting me over a few thousand lousy dollars as though he was settling a case with Exxon. He obviously didn't need the money. He was playing a game. Winning was what counted. Winning meant everything to him. Bill saw money and power as a zero-sum game. There always had to be a winner and a loser. As long as the game was going on, he was one tough son of a bitch, hard as nails. When the game was over, he forgot it immediately—especially if he won. This was the same guy I could go to for a favor the next day, and he'd say yes. There was no bitter carryover. Friendship was one thing, business another."

For Casey, his books were something of a psychological parachute. If the endless tensions, the criticism, the pressures at Langley became too much, he could always bail out. He had something to do, a place to land.

27.

Death in Bir al-Abed

The covert Middle East operation that John McMahon had feared Bob Woodward was on to had its roots in a tragedy that occurred on September 20, 1984. On that date, a van loaded with explosives snaked its way around concrete barriers and blew up in front of the U.S. embassy annex in Beirut. Underneath the rubble lay twenty-four dead, including two U.S. servicemen, and ninety wounded, including Reginald Bartholomew, the American ambassador. First the U.S. embassy, then the Marine barracks, now the embassy annex.

Ollie North's bailiwick at the NSC by now included antiterrorism. And McMahon was all too familiar with North's approach. North had drafted an eye-for-an-eye finding that called for CIA-trained hit teams to take out terrorists. A key target was to be Sheikh Mohammed Hussein Fadlallah, chief of the Hizbollah, the Party of God movement, the radical Shiite group believed to be implicated in all three of the Beirut bombings.

The North proposal sparked a sharp intramural debate. Casey liked the idea. But his frequent ally Cap Weinberger was reluctant. "We'd thrash out the proposal in meetings," Weinberger recalled. "Bill was always more eager than I was to apply force." Weinberger wanted precision in any countermeasures, assurances that the eye you were extracting was the eye of the enemy. "I was more concerned," he later recalled, "with collateral damage—that's the current euphemism for killing women and children."

Casey argued, "If you wait until you're absolutely sure the people you're hitting are the people who hit you, you're not going to do anything. The deterrent effect lies in the act of retaliation."

Others argued that the North-Casey approach would run afoul of the country's legal prohibition on assassination. President Reagan himself had reaffirmed the policy, Executive Order 12333. "We're arming the Afghans, right?" Casey said. "Every time a Mujahedin rebel kills a Soviet rifleman, are we engaged in assassination? This is a rough business. If we're afraid to hit the terrorists because some-body's going to yell 'assassination,' it'll never stop. The terrorists will own the world. They'll know nobody's going to raise a finger against them."

Subsequently, Casey put the assiduous Stan Sporkin on the case, and Sporkin found Casey a loophole. Striking at terrorists planning to strike at you was not assassination, it was "preemptive self-defense."

Apart from the director's enthusiasm, the North proposal ran into heavy weather at the CIA. "I thought the idea of training Lebanese intelligence groups in counterterrorism was a lousy idea from the first," John McMahon commented. "Do you know what intelligence means to these people?" he asked Casey. "It's tossing a bomb. It's blowing up people."

This was the side of McMahon that Casey did not like—the crippling caution. He took North's draft finding to Reagan at an NSPG meeting and sold it. As Casey left with the signed document, the President put his arm around his shoulder and said, "Bill, we've got to build a world where an American can walk down a street and be safe—the way you and I grew up."

John McMahon had given Casey his customary unsweetened opin-ion of the finding. "You better go back and tell those cowboys they can't have it both ways," he said when they were alone in the DCI's office. "If the President lifts the executive order banning assassina-tion, we'll knock off terrorists. But if he keeps that one on the books, and we're bumping people off, do you know what happens when the shit hits the fan? It's the CIA's ass. To the rest of the world, it's not administration policy, it's not an NSC idea—it's those crazy bastards at the CIA." Casey listened and said nothing. McMahon had long since learned to read his silences. The deputy obviously had not made a sale.

Among purists of the Right, the conviction was growing that Casey had a weak sister as second in command. McMahon began to feel their pressure. "I had stopped a lot of foolishness from coming out of the NSC," McMahon observed. "Bud McFarlane thought I was practically a Soviet agent. So the right wing cooked up a hate cam-paign to get me out as Casey's deputy. First they began working on Bill. But he told them to shove it. Then their mouthpiece, the *Wash-ington Times*, started after me. The paper would print anything the right wing said against me."

One day a piece of junk mail came across McMahon's desk. He, probably along with the entire intelligence community, had wound up on the mailing list of a newsletter called *Free the Eagle*. An article in the newsletter claimed that John McMahon, deputy director of the CIA, was sabotaging the Afghan aid program. McMahon did not know whether to laugh or cry. "Sabotage it?" he reacted in disbelief. "I'm the guy who invented it! I'm the guy who first got the Mujahedin their surface-to-air missiles!" The newsletter contained a cutout coupon urging readers to donate $10, or $100, or $1,000 to the campaign to get John McMahon out of the CIA, contributions payable by VISA or MasterCard.

He took the newsletter into Casey's office and tossed it on his desk. Casey glanced at it and told McMahon, "They're just a bunch of jerks. Don't worry about it." And, McMahon observed, "Bill Casey stuck by me all the way on that one."

On March 8, 1985, the duty officer in the ops center tore off a wire service story on the Middle East and brought it up to Casey's office. The story had an almost prosaic horror about it. Another car bomb had gone off in a Beirut suburb called Bir al-Abed, killing eighty people outright and wounding more than two hundred others.

Casey called in McMahon and Ed Juchniewicz from the operations directorate. "He was visibly shaken," Juchniewicz remembered, as they gave Casey more details. The vehicle, packed with high explosives, had gone off fifty yards from the home of Sheikh Mohammed Hussein Fadlallah, the chief target of the recent CIA counterterrorism operation in Lebanon. A crater of destruction had been blasted in the residential area, with buildings blown apart, fires started, and people cooked in their cars. What McMahon feared most had happened. The immediate appearance was that the CIA had botched an assassination attempt, killing eighty people while missing the target, since Sheikh Fadlallah was not among the victims.

"I'll have to call the President," Casey said, "and tell him we have to rescind the finding and shut down the operation. In the meantime, let's find out what the hell happened."

McMahon managed to walk out of Casey's office without saying 'I told you so.' Still, Juchniewicz remembered, "John was shaking his head as he left."

Someone else was also determined to find out what had happened in Bir al-Abed. The *Washington Post*'s Bob Woodward started digging into the story.

Sometime in the spring of 1985, Congress would again be voting on whether to uphold the Boland ban or to turn the arms stream back on for the contras. Casey already had begun his own campaign to open the eyes of the country to the nature of the Sandinista regime. He spoke to the Union League in New York City in January. What did the liberals think Nicaragua was under Daniel Ortega, he asked— a tropical Switzerland? The Sandinistas had forcibly relocated nearly 15,000 Indians and destroyed their villages. They had thrown more than two hundred members of the non-Marxist Democratic Conservative party in jail. Dissenting newspapers and broadcasters were censored or shut down. The political opposition was harassed and forbidden to leave the country. Neighborhoods had been organized with informers on each block, a leaf taken right out of Castro's Cuba.

Bill Casey was not going to sway public opinion, as he was the first to recognize. Ronald Reagan was the acknowledged Great Communicator. If Congress could not understand what was at stake in Nicaragua, Casey believed, then the President should go over its head directly to the people. And so that January, Casey had left his third-floor office in the EOB and gone down to the first-floor corner where the White House speech writers labored. There, Casey cued Tony Dolan and his colleagues to the requisite themes. The lessons for Central America had to be drawn from history. The contras were the Latino equivalent of those ragged heroes at Valley Forge. The contras were today's resistance fighters, like the French, the Dutch, the Belgians in World War II, trying to drive a hateful regime from their homeland. Ronald Reagan had to make the American people understand this.

By early February, President Reagan was telling the Conservative Political Action Conference, in a widely reported speech, "[The contras] are our brothers, and we owe them our help. They are the moral equivalent of our Founding Fathers and the brave men and women of the French Resistance. We cannot turn away from them, for the struggle here is not Right versus Left but right versus wrong."

His critics heard the President's remarks, thought of the heavy Somocista element among the contras, the reports of corruption, and wondered if the comparison with the Founding Fathers and the Resistance was particularly flattering to Washington, Jefferson, and Adams, or the French Maquis.

By April, Congress was headed for the vote. On April 17, Casey went before the SSCI to testify. The members were puzzled and concerned, they told him. U.S. aid had by now been shut off for six months. Yet the contras appeared to be thriving. The force was now up to 16,000 men. The committee staff estimated that they needed from $18 million to $24 million to operate at their current level. It was as if the oxygen had been turned off on a respirator, yet the patient had gone on breathing lustily. Where was the support coming from? Rumors were circulating that the contras were being kept afloat by indirect means, likely in violation of the Boland Amendment. And the members wanted answers.

Casey sat at the witness table totally at ease. The CIA was clean, he said. "We strictly honored in practice and in spirit the congressionally mandated restrictions on military aid to the contras." In fact, he had put compliance officers right in the operations directorate to make sure his people never stepped over the line.

But, one member asked him, how was it possible that the contras were still operating? They had gone out and raised money, Casey explained. "They've gone into the international arms market. But we don't have any idea as to the quantity, or what they've got in the pipeline."

"That's all I wanted to establish," Chairman Durenberger said, apparently satisfied.

If, in his answer, Casey's "we" referred to the CIA, then he was telling the truth. But the White House Casey knew better. For starters, the contras were assured of a floor intake of $1 million per month. Casey had won that commitment from Saudi Arabia during the first year of Boland. And Bud McFarlane had managed to arrange a meeting between President Reagan and King Fahd in February. The king, flush with oil billions, not only agreed to continue the $1-million-a-month contribution; he volunteered another $24 million.

Dewey Clarridge was now running covert operations in Europe. But an entry in Ollie North's log of contra operations suggests that Clarridge had not abandoned his old *compadres*. An entry for January 5, 1985, reads, "Call from Clarridge: 200 T of arms en route from South Africa to C.R." "C.R." was Costa Rica, whence the weapons would pass to the contras. The entry is significant. The shipment occurred post-Boland. It involved the subordinate with whom Casey had had a special and direct relationship. It suggests that Casey was making exceptions in his policy of keeping the CIA clear of Boland, or that North had private arrangements with certain CIA officials. When ABC News reported that Casey was running a "vest pocket" aid operation between South Africa and the Nicaraguan rebels, the CIA issued a denial—possibly sincere from an institutional standpoint. But Casey knew better.

In dealings with outsiders, Casey was inclined to be scrupulous. When Joe Coors, the beer baron, came to see him at the EOB, asking,

"What can I do to help the contras?," Casey sent him away. "I can't do anything for you, Joe," Casey told Coors; his hands were tied by Boland. Casey sent him down the hall, explaining, "Ollie North's the guy to see."

It would be a poor American intelligence service that would not know of arms shipments to the contras. And as John McMahon admitted, "Sure, we *suspected* that the Israelis, the Saudis, the North Koreans, and even both Chinas were helping them. But we did not go out of our way to find out. When Congress asked us, we said truthfully that, under Boland, we didn't want to know." Indeed, one of North's log entries read, "The CIA will not be told of the source for their [the contras'] funds."

The National Security Council was an unlikely outfit to be directing a secret war. The staff consisted of some 135 people supposedly writing options papers for the President and the foreign policy apparatus. In its new role, the NSC had found a slim reed of law to lean on. On Spook Alley was the obscure, three-member Intelligence Oversight Board, which advised the President on the legality of intelligence activities. North, most likely at Casey's recommendation, had asked the IOB to determine if the NSC was covered by the Boland Amendment. The IOB happily obliged. Boland barred only agencies engaged in intelligence from militarily aiding the contras. North had in his files an opinion from the IOB that "the NSC is not governed by the prohibition, because it was not involved in intelligence." Therefore, the NSC could direct a covert war against the Sandinistas. It was preposterous reasoning. By the same logic, the National Park Service or the National Endowment for the Arts could have run the contra operation too. But the President, and certainly Bill Casey, were not concerned with logic. They were looking for a loophole to keep the contras alive.

North's detailed logs show fairly frequent contact between the Marine and Casey, averaging perhaps a phone call or a visit per week. Casey was playing the avuncular role shrewdly, advising, warning, but always with his hands in his pockets.

The vote on contra aid was set for Tuesday, April 23, at five p.m. in both the Senate and House. Durenberger, by then, had hired his own SSCI staff director, Bernard McMahon—no relation to Casey's deputy, John McMahon. Bernie McMahon was an ex–Navy captain with formidable intelligence credentials. He had been with the CIA in Vietnam, served as executive assistant to Stansfield Turner at the CIA for three years, and had most recently come off the Joint Chiefs of Staff, where he was the Latin American expert.

An intense, tough-minded man, Bernie McMahon had a keen sense of what Casey and his people were up to in Congress. "Casey ran congressional liaison," McMahon observed, "as if Congress was a hard-target country and his people were penetrating a denied area. He had more covert operations people over here than he had in any Eastern-bloc country. One day they'd try to curry favor with us. The next day they'd be working behind our backs: 'Let's get this piece of intelligence against Senator So-and-So and let's play it against Senator What's-His-Name'; 'Let's plant stories that discredit the oversight process and prove Congress can't be trusted.' "

The only reason that the oversight function worked at all, McMahon believed, was that "the committee members overlooked Casey's disdain. Larger matters were at stake, and they recognized, however he treated them, that he was a damned good chief of the intelligence community."

McMahon read his own staff colleagues equally well; all the trouble was not on Casey's side. "A lot of our staff people liked to play little senator," he recalled. "They loved sitting in the committee room when a member was absent, and they could get to question the CIA witnesses. I could just see how it looked to Casey. Here was a guy that nobody in the Reagan administration dared to second-guess, and he comes over here and a bunch of horses' asses are telling him, 'We don't think that's such a hot idea.' Guys who never saw a covert operation in their lives, never risked their necks, are telling him his accounting procedures are too sloppy on some two-bit operation." McMahon recognized, in this antagonistic environment, that the director of Central Intelligence faced a hot fight in getting Boland lifted.

Casey sat watching C-Span on his office television set the day of the contra vote. He was grim-faced as the aid program went down again by the narrowest possible margin, 213–215. Days later, Daniel Ortega flew from Managua to Moscow to sign new aid agreements with the Soviet Union. When informed of the trip, Casey remarked, "Cocky little bastard." But then, Casey said, who could blame him? The U.S. Congress had just given Ortega a green light.

On May 8, Casey was in the Philippines paying a secret visit to President Ferdinand E. Marcos at the Malacanang Palace. The islands were the major fortification on America's Pacific flank; they held the huge Subic Bay Naval Base and Clark Air Force Base. Ordinarily, Casey would have been in Marcos's corner—indeed, for a long time he had been. Marcos was a dictator, ruling for the past ten years through martial law. The scale of the man's corruption was stupendous. But, to Casey, a greater threat than a larcenous Filipino leader was the Communist insurgency breeding in the country's backlands. His analysts told him that possibly 40 percent of the Philippines was influenced by the Communists. Consequently, Marcos had been assigned to that pragmatic category a son of a bitch but *our* son of a bitch.

This time, Casey was delivering the Philippine ruler a hard message. Marcos ought to be thinking about allowing an election before his term was up. An honest election would ease the tensions mounting in the country. It could avoid a possible violent overthrow of the regime. The next thing you knew, the Communists would be marching into downtown Manila. Marcos told Casey that he had a solution. Why not install his wife, Imelda, as his vice-president? He would resign, and she could succeed him. Casey left wondering how long it would be before the lid blew off the Philippines.

Casey was still in the Far East when George Lauder got a call at home on a Saturday from Bob Woodward. Woodward was calling to tell Lauder that the *Washington Post* would be running a story the following day on the failed Sheikh Fadlallah car bombing that had resulted in the deaths of eighty people. The reporter had managed to discover the existence of the finding that authorized the CIA training of Lebanese units for preemptive attacks on terrorists. Woodward told Lauder that his newspaper saw no reason to withhold the story, since the operation had failed and the finding had subsequently been rescinded. The *Post* was willing to concede that the bombing was a runaway mission by one of three units the CIA had trained, a unit that had acted without CIA authorization, and that this group had hired mercenaries who actually pulled off the bombing. But Lauder knew that these fine distinctions would not offset the broader impression that the CIA had trained the Lebanese to hit terrorists and the result had been the deaths of innocent people.

Now it was Lauder's turn to say "I told you so." He had opposed Casey's meetings with Woodward all along; Casey's accessibility was never going to spare the Agency Woodward's relentless probing. But Casey had been unmoved. Just the month before, on April 17, when Casey was going up to Massachusetts to make a speech at Tufts University, Woodward had asked if he could fly with him in the Agency plane. Lauder had blocked the request, but Woodward had shown up at Tufts anyway.

After the speech, Casey agreed to give Woodward a lift back to Washington, thus providing the reporter with a couple of uninterrupted, exclusive hours with the director of Central Intelligence. And here was the payoff, Lauder thought: Woodward's paper was about to produce a story that made the Agency look guilty, at the very least, of mass negligent homicide.

"I must have been on the phone in my kitchen five times that Saturday with Woodward," Lauder recalled. "I was trying to get him to spike the story." Lauder argued that running the story was "an invitation to murder." To tie the CIA publicly to the car-bombing operation was certain to incite retaliation, he said.

The following Sunday morning, May 12, the story appeared under the headline ANTI-TERRORIST PLAN RESCINDED AFTER UNAUTHORIZED BOMBING. On Wednesday, May 15, Casey was back at Langley trying to pick up the pieces.

One of Casey's earliest acts at the Agency had been to establish a counterterrorism center. The center was tracking more than one hundred terrorist organizations worldwide. As John McMahon described this operation, "We'd find out about a car full of explosives heading over a border and alert the local gendarmes. We'd learn that some American journalist was on some outfit's hit list and warn the guy in time for him to get out of the country. Hell, in nine months, we frustrated 163 terrorist acts. But a lot of this is done by infiltration. And you can't crow about your successes without exposing your sources." Casey felt himself caught in a classic intelligence trap. Blunders like Bir al-Abed made headlines. But who would ever know about their successes in blocking terrorism?

One day that spring, Herb Meyer passed Casey in the hall. "Hey, Bill," he said, "I understand Sam Donaldson's working for you now."

Meyer's jibe struck a sore point. Casey was back in hot water. Capital Cities Broadcasting, now called Capital Cities Communications, was in the process of taking over the American Broadcasting Company in a $3.5-billion merger deal. The company that Casey had helped build from one radio station in Albany, New York, now owned seven television stations, more than twenty radio stations, and eight newspapers. It was big enough to swallow up one of the three major national networks.

The press had made an intriguing discovery: though Casey had been virtually bludgeoned into a blind trust in the summer of 1983, his shares of Capital Cities had been omitted from the trust. The implication was that the director of Central Intelligence was soon to be a substantial shareholder in one of the country's major forums of free expression, with wondrous opportunity for managing the news.

Casey claimed that he had been advised by the Office of Government Ethics that his block of Capital Cities stock, since it comprised more than 20 percent of his portfolio, was too large to leave in a trust; it should be out where the public would know what was being done with it. But now, with reporters on their necks, the government ethics lawyers were saying, "Well, yes, but he *could* have applied for an exception." As the bad press poured in, Casey complained, "Son of a bitch! Following the law isn't enough. Now I'm supposed to be asking for exceptions!"

It was Stanley Sporkin's habit, born of long experience, to anticipate Casey's needs. Toward the end of March, Sporkin came into Casey's office with forms that would simply move the Capital Cities stock into the blind trust. "You didn't do anything wrong," Sporkin said, putting the papers in front of Casey. "But let's cut our losses short." He waited for Casey to sign.

Instead, the lower lip protruded. "I'm not gonna sign."

"Whaddaya mean, you're not gonna sign it? You've *got* to sign it," Sporkin said.

"Like hell I do. I'm not going to let a bunch of chicken-shit bureaucrats push me around," Casey growled. "I'm not letting the press scare me. Now get out of here. I'm busy."

For Sporkin, it was the last straw. He had stood by Casey through the SSCI investigation, through the battle over the blind trust, through every other attack on the man's ethics. "Bill," he said, his voice choking with anger, "why do you let these things drag on and on? Why don't you just end it? Who do you think is the loser? Right now, you're the only loser."

"No!" Casey banged his fist. "I didn't do anything wrong, and I don't have to sign."

They were jaw to jaw. Sporkin was having difficulty comprehending such stupid behavior from so intelligent a man. "You either sign this paper or you fire me."

Casey glared for a seeming eternity. Then he snatched his pen and signed.

By the summer of 1985, the resupply of the contras, Boland or not, was running smoothly. Ollie North was a gutsy soldier, however, but no businessman. Fortunately, Casey's candidate for handling the arms procurement, former Major General Richard V. Secord, was something of both; and so Secord essentially ran the operation that they had christened the Enterprise. What Secord did not know about the international arms bazaar, his partner did. Secord had brought into the venture with him Albert Hakim, an Iranian-born business-man who previously had made a fortune brokering arms deals with the Shah before that monarch fell. Hakim was knowledgeable in the financial acrobatics of that world.

On May 4, Secord and Hakim arranged for the charter of a company in Panama and set up a Swiss bank account for it. They called the company Lake Resources. When North wanted weapons, or planes, or ammunition for the contras, Secord bought them from Taiwan, Communist China, North Korea, Israel, or Taiwan, whoever was will-ing, paid out of the Lake Resources account, and he and Hakim took their cut.

It was an unusual arrangement: a Marine lieutenant colonel sitting in a White House office, directing the actions of two private busi-nessmen to carry out an administration foreign policy that Congress thought it had banned.

Early in July, Casey received a phone call from Ollie North. There was a journalist he just had to meet, North told him. The man already had been turned down by George Lauder, but Casey should see him anyway. He had just come back from Nicaragua and had lived with the troops on both sides. His name was David Halevy, of *Time* mag-azine.

Casey hated being a captive of his own bureaucracy. However hon-estly intended, the company line was still the company line. Thus, shortly after the North conversation, Halevy got a call at the *Time* Washington bureau offices on Connecticut Avenue. As he described the conversation, "I heard this growling voice telling me, 'David? Bill Casey here. Come on out this afternoon.' "

Halevy was then forty-four years old, a Jerusalem-born Israeli who had been with the magazine since 1968. He was also a combat veteran of the Arab wars, a paratrooper with seventy-four jumps to his credit, and an alumnus of Israeli military intelligence. Halevy was a student of power as well, and had wanted to interview Casey, because, he said, "I looked the administration over and I concluded that William J. Casey was the second most important man in town."

It was Casey who started firing off the questions. Halevy was thrown off stride; *he* was the one who was supposed to be doing the interviewing. But he found something not to be denied in Casey's manner. And so he began to tell about the two weeks he had spent with the contras. He did not have a high opinion of the military commander. Colonel Enrique Bermúdez, he said, was a shrewd self-promoter but not much of a field commander. In fact, Halevy found relations generally unhealthy between the officers and men. Discipline was stiff and artificial. Halevy saw none of the camaraderie one expects in a guerrilla army. "You've got peasants who joined up because the Sandinistas took their chickens, or wouldn't let them sell their cornmeal on the free market, or they conscripted their brother. They join and they're fed nothing but rice and beans. Yet I went into one tent and there are two contra orderlies serving the chief of logistics, an ex–Somocista major. He's got candles on the table and a nice white napkin. He's eating meat. What are these peasants fighting for—to serve dinner to this Somocista?"

Casey was visibly uncomfortable. He got up and began pacing. He asked Halevy about the contras' fighting prowess. They were brave enough, Halevy said. But he had gone with them on a raid from their Honduran sanctuary into Nicaragua, across the Rio Coco, and had been appalled. They had crossed the border with 850 men—"far too large for a guerrilla operation," he said. "Within a week, they're down to fifty men. They keep drifting off to see the wife and kids, to work the land for a few days, to shoot the breeze with their friends in the village. So, as far as the contras' guerrilla capacity, I would rate it low."

"There has to be something good about them," Casey said annoyedly.

"Get rid of the Somocistas, get rid of that top-down leadership, and they'll fight better," Halevy said.

"You couldn't dodge him," Halevy remembered of the visit. "Casey kept questioning, questioning, always pushing me for more. I felt like I was handling a sharp knife."

He then described his two weeks with Sandinistas. He was blunt, telling Casey: "They're better fighting men, no doubt about it. I was with a counterinsurgency unit. They used the Russian doctrine, which was maybe too rigid for what they were doing. Otherwise I found their troops well trained, and morale was high. The men in the ranks were better material, mostly middle class and working class."

At long last, Halevy told Casey something he wanted to hear. He had spent some time in Managua after being in the field. He had remembered a joyous, fun-loving people from earlier visits. But now the human landscape was bleak, the Nicaraguans as unsmiling, cowed, and listless as any populace in the Eastern bloc. "Of course," Casey said. "That's because you were seeing the true face of communism."

"I came away with the impression that he was an open-minded man," Halevy recalled of the visit. "I hadn't brought him much good news. But he wasn't going to kill the messenger."

28.

The Boy Scouts and the Rug Merchants

On June 14, 1985, 153 passengers boarded TWA flight 847 for the short flight from Athens to Rome. Among them were thirty-nine Americans. Soon after takeoff, two gunmen took over the plane and ordered the pilot to land at Beirut International Airport. On the ground, the hijackers threatened to execute the Americans unless nearly seven hundred prisoners, mainly Shiite radicals, were released from prison in Israel. In case their threat might not be taken seriously, the gunmen shot to death a twenty-three-year-old U.S. Navy diver named Robert Dean Stethem and threw his body onto the tarmac. Over the radio circuit between the plane and the central tower, a voice rebuked the hijackers for the cold-blooded killing. One terrorist shouted back, "We have not forgotten the massacre of Bir al-Abed!"

The hijackers were members of the militant Shiite band connected to Sheikh Fadlallah. To Casey, what was happening was instantly clear. The March 8, 1985, car bombing that had killed eighty people in the Beirut suburb of Bir al-Abed had been aimed at Fadlallah. The *Washington Post* story of May 12 had revealed a link between the CIA and the Lebanese team involved in the attempt on Fadlallah's life. Fadlallah's people were taking their revenge against America. Woodward had been warned by George Lauder not to run the story precisely because it could provoke vengeance. As Casey saw it, there was blood on the reporter's hands.

But Woodward was to have the last say on what had led to Bir al-Abed. After Casey's death, Woodward presented in his book *Veil: The Secret Wars of the CIA 1981–1987* an extraordinary explanation of how the failed Fadlallah assassination had come about, an account that, if accepted, bloodied Casey's hands. According to Woodward, the DCI had grown impatient because "Casey's own CIA people began slowing down. No one inside the agency wanted to step out front on terrorism," even with the hit-team finding approved by the President. Consequently, Casey was supposed to have gone to his ally King Fahd of Saudi Arabia to instigate bolder action, and the king agreed to help in the form of $3 million.

Woodward then described how Casey met with the Saudi Arabian ambassador to the United States, Prince Bandar bin Sultan, and, in Woodward's phrase, slipped into his "operational mode."

Prince Bandar was a sleek, charming man, a former pilot in the Royal Saudi Air Force and the son of the minister of defense. He and Casey had lunch early in 1985 at Bandar's palatial weekend retreat in northern Virginia, not far from the CIA. After lunch, in Woodward's telling, they left their wives and wandered out alone into the garden. There, Casey allegedly gave the ambassador a card with the hand-written number of a bank account in Geneva, Switzerland. Bandar was to deposit the $3 million into the account. The money was to be used to finance the killing of Sheikh Fadlallah. "Later it was decided to give effective operational control to the Saudis," Woodward wrote, "particularly as the CIA bureaucracy grew more and more resistant to active anti-terrorist measures." The Saudis took over the operation, Woodward went on, and hired an English mercenary who worked out the plot. A Lebanese intelligence service hired the assassins. And a car loaded with the explosives was thus detonated near Fadlallah's high-rise.

Is this account true? Had Casey completely bypassed the 16,000-man clandestine organization at his disposal, acted contrary to the explicit policy of the United States prohibiting assassinations, and, by himself, initiated with a foreign country a clumsily executed scheme that left scores of innocent dead?

Woodward's account contains certain puzzling features. He reported that Casey first went to the Saudis for help because his own bureaucrats were too gun-shy to arrange a hit of a major terrorist. But even after the Saudis presumably kicked in the $3 million, the operation was still inexplicably placed in the hands of the supposedly timid CIA. Only later, Woodward says, was it "decided to give effective operational control to the Saudis, particularly as the CIA bureaucracy grew more and more resistant to active anti-terrorist measures." Thus, we have Casey going to the Saudis to get money for an operation that he doesn't want to entrust to the CIA, which is then turned over to the CIA. Further, if the mission was initially entrusted to the CIA, why did Casey need to go to Saudi Arabia for money? The CIA had its own millions for such purposes. Casey also had a presidential finding authorizing operations against terrorists. Which raises the final puzzlement: what exactly was Casey's role in this affair? It was Saudi money that financed it, and Saudi operatives who took it over, according to Woodward. Casey's role comes down to his giving Prince Bandar the number of a Swiss bank account. Did Saudi oil sheikhs need the CIA to tell them how to put money into a bank in Switzerland?

Subsequently, both oversight committees investigated the bombing. The HPSCI report concluded: "No U.S. government complicity, direct or indirect, can be established with respect to the March 8 bombing in Beirut." Bernie McMahon, who ran a Senate inquiry, concluded: "The SSCI could not trace a line from Casey to the Fadlallah bombing, and we had a hell of a lot more capability to look into it than Bob Woodward."

McMahon, a hard-bitten intelligence veteran, had witnessed other colossal foul-ups in a thirty-year career and had possibly the fairest explanation of what happened at Bir al-Abed. As he later put it: "Did the CIA participate in the bombing? No. Did they create a mechanism which ultimately got out of control and led to the bombing? Yes. Was training antiterrorist hit teams an acceptable risk for them to undertake in that environment in the first place? That's what the CIA does for a living."

Woodward neglected to mention in his book the reports of the oversight committees that cleared the CIA of blame in the Bir al-Abed tragedy. But then, Woodward had not said the CIA was to blame. He had said William J. Casey was to blame. Bandar, predictably, denied any involvement, and as Woodward later said himself, "Casey's death provided unexpected protection of my sources." Of the two participants in the alleged transaction in the garden, one denied it happened, and the other, by the time Woodward's book came out, was dead.

Robert C. McFarlane now occupied the office once held by Henry Kissinger. That position had launched Kissinger into history, made of him a statesman to rank with Metternich and Talleyrand. As an NSC official, Bud McFarlane had been an eyewitness to Kissinger's elevation. Now McFarlane was national security adviser to the President. And why, from the same launch pad, should he not aspire to greatness? Of course, they were different men: Kissinger, a man of brilliant intellect, a conceptualizer, a figure of authority; McFarlane, a smallish, forgettable-looking man of plain, earnest aspect, suggesting a computer-hardware salesman. The most dashing thing about Bud McFarlane was the burgundy Jaguar he drove.

He was now forty-eight, the son of a conservative Texas congressman and, like Ollie North, a graduate of the Naval Academy who had gone into the Marine Corps and then into national security posts. McFarlane had been the compromise candidate to succeed Judge William Clark as national security adviser—everybody's second or third choice.

He did not act, look, or speak with the weight of a Henry Kissinger. Yet he burned with quiet ambition. And he understood the key to Kissinger's rise—conceptual audacity. The Soviet Union was the heavy on the international stage; yet Kissinger, with President Nixon, had dared a new policy of reduced tension through cooperation with the Soviet Union, the policy of détente. Communist China had been blacklisted by the United States for a generation; yet Kissinger had opened a new door to China. Act boldly; break through conventional thinking: that is what wins one's place in history.

And so Bud McFarlane began thinking the unthinkable. If there was a world figure that the American people had been conditioned to hate, it was the Ayatollah Ruhollah Khomeini. Khomeini had humiliated the United States by holding fifty-two Americans hostage for 444 days. His regime was connected to Shiite terrorists behind the U.S. embassy bombing, the embassy annex bombing, and the Marine barracks bombings in Beirut. Rapprochement with the Iran of Khomeini? What could be bolder?

From the beginning, Casey had hungered to have the administration's foreign policy apparatus make use of his National Intelligence Estimates. He wanted State, Defense, and the NSC to have his people's best judgment as they shaped policy. Relevance and involvement were the marks of a successful intelligence service. Anything less, he felt, was bureaucratic masturbation.

To Casey's delight, Bud McFarlane asked for a new assessment of the situation in Iran. The task was assigned to Graham Fuller, the NIO for the Middle East. By May 17, 1985, Fuller's think piece was in final shape, and he sent it for review to the DCI. "The Khomeini regime was faltering," Fuller wrote. "We will soon see a struggle for succession. The U.S. has almost no cards to play. The USSR has many. Iran has obviously concluded that whether they like communism, the USSR is the country to come to terms with. . . . Iran has in fact now begun moving toward some accommodation with the USSR." Here was Casey's nightmare threatening to materialize: the Soviet Union in league with Iran, in a position to choke off 60 percent of the West's oil supply.

Fuller's memo listed several options. The one he recommended certainly had to be credited with daring. He favored "inserting Western allies and friends into Tehran quickly through the arms door." However understated, Fuller's recommendation was a bombshell. Only the month before, in his speech at Tufts, Casey had said, "Probably more blood has been shed by Iranian-sponsored terrorists during the last few years than by all other terrorists combined." Operation Staunch, being pursued by the State Department and the CIA, was pressuring other nations not to trade at all with Iran. Now Casey's NIO was calling for arms sales to Iran.

McFarlane seized on Fuller's recommendation. Here was his détente, his opening to China, his chance for a place in history's sun. He had Fuller's ideas refashioned as a formal National Security Decision Directive that proposed scrapping the policy toward Iran in place since 1979. Under that policy, the United States had prohibited the shipment of American arms whose ultimate destination was Iran. McFarlane's NSDD proposed that America's European allies, along with Israel, Japan, Turkey, and Pakistan, be allowed to sell arms to the Khomeini regime.

The first piece in a mosaic of disaster had been set in place.

At the Pentagon, Caspar Weinberger thought he was reading a joke in poor taste. Across the top of his copy of the NSDD, Weinberger scrawled, "This is too absurd to comment on." George Shultz at State responded that sending Western arms to Iran was "contrary to our interests both in containing Khomeinism and in ending the excesses of this regime." McFarlane had to wonder, was this how Kissinger's bold new thinking had been greeted? Still, he enlisted one powerful ally. To Casey, the only thing more abhorrent than a Khomeini who hated the United States was a Khomeini in cahoots with the Soviet Union. He supported McFarlane's National Security Decision Directive.

Most Americans saw Israel as a tiny island of democracy awash in a sea of Arab hostility. It was true, with one exception. Iran was not Arabic; it was even anti-Arab. In the days of the Shah, an Iran allied to the United States had been a source of comfort to the Israelis. Now, however, they were uneasey. Khomeini hated them too.

Iran had been at war with Iraq since 1980. Iraq was rabidly anti-Israel. And by 1985 Iraq was winning that war. An Iraqi victory would be a disaster, totally fulfilling the specter of an Israel engulfed by Arab power. Consequently, the prospect of arms shipments tilting the war in favor of Iran, plus the prospect of the United States once again involved in Iran, had a comforting ring in Tel Aviv. Israel would do what it could to promote this end.

The second piece of the mosaic of disaster was in place.

The Iranians were desperate for weapons. Their cities lay naked to Iraqi air strikes. Their armor on the battlefront was inferior. And the weapons they wanted most were those denied to them: American Hawk missiles to down Iraqi bombers, and TOWs, tube-launched, optically tracked, wire-guided missiles. The TOW was the most fearsome antitank weapon in the world, capable of penetrating thick armor from a distance of two miles and ricocheting a tank crew to shreds. Khomeini may have considered America the Great Satan, but he was prepared to traffic with the devil to avoid a threatened military defeat.

Another piece of the disaster was in place.

The United States had a secretary of State. It had ambassadors throughout the Middle East to carry out the administration's foreign policy. But Bud McFarlane chose to send, on his own hook, a private consultant on terrorism to sound out the possibilities of a new opening to Iran. The consultant was Michael Ledeen, a forty-four-year-old academic with a beard like an Old Testament prophet's. One colleague described Ledeen as "a combination of academic ability and political ambition." Ledeen had good connections in Israel. He made several trips there, meeting with Prime Minister Shimon Peres and other top officials. And he brought back encouraging news to McFarlane: the situation in Iran was more fluid than anyone had imagined. There were even moderates to be cultivated. These elements might be persuaded to arrange the release of seven American hostages currently held by the Shiites: William Buckley; the Reverend Benjamin Weir; Peter Kilburn, a librarian at the American University in Beirut; the Reverend Lawrence Martin Jenco, a Catholic priest; Terry Anderson, the Associated Press's chief Middle East correspondent; David Jacobsen, director of the American University Hospital in Beirut; and Thomas Sutherland, dean of agriculture at the university— all kidnapped over the preceding fifteen months. Arms for Iran were the key to their freedom.

The Israelis had also put Ledeen in contact with a gem, an Iranian who appeared to have remarkable contacts inside Iran. His name was Manucher Ghorbanifar. Ghorbanifar was the one who claimed to be in contact with Iranian moderates. He also reported that William

Buckley was alive but was being tortured. And if there was any question about Ghorbanifar's bona fides, the man, in Ledeen's presence, put through a call from Israel straight to the prime minister's office in Tehran and talked to the deputy prime minister, Mohsen Kangarlou, about arms deals and the possible freeing of the hostages.

Ghorbanifar, Ledeen was later to say, seemed "too good to be true. . . . He was exactly the thing we were looking for. If we could have prepared a wish list, there he was, and he had it all." There was only one condition that Ghorbanifar set for his cooperation. He would be happy to work with the NSC. But he wanted nothing to do with the CIA.

Manucher Ghorbanifar was a portly, black-bearded, black-haired, balding man, with a hawklike nose and eyes of smoldering intensity. He had been born in Tehran in 1945, or in 1938, or in 1944, depending on what document he was using at any given moment, since he carried Iranian, Portuguese, and Greek passports. He also used six aliases. He lived in Paris, dressed elegantly, went first class, and seemed at home anywhere in the world. He spoke broken but glib English. By his own admission, he had been a wheeler-dealer since his twenties. His survivability is perhaps best demonstrated by the fact that Ghorbanifar had been a paid informer for the Shah's intelligence apparatus, SAVAK, and was still able to move among the leading circles in the Khomeini regime. He had won the Ayatollah's affection, reportedly, because he had informed on a group of Iranian Air Force officers plotting against Khomeini. Some 160 of the plotters were said to have been executed.

Ghorbanifar had been in the pay of the CIA in 1980, but so much of his reporting was bum dope that the Agency dropped him in September of 1981. According to one CIA operative who worked with him, "Manucher Ghorbanifar was an expert at predicting things that had already happened." He approached the CIA in July of 1984, this time with his hook well baited: he said that he knew who had kidnapped Bill Buckley; he also knew of an Iranian plot to assassinate President Reagan and his Democratic opponent that year, Walter Mondale. The CIA strapped him to the polygraph and he flunked resoundingly.

Yet Ghorbanifar was back the following month peddling a new line: he could set up secret talks with a key Iranian leader, he claimed. He was polygraphed again, and again failed. Knowing that Ghorbanifar might well insinuate himself into stations abroad, the CIA put out a worldwide "burn notice," a formal warning that he was "an intelligence fabricator and a nuisance." Ghorbanifar did, in fact, make an approach to the American ambassador in London, who sent a cable back to Washington describing him as "a sleazebag of dubious repute." Thus, Ghorbanifar's desire not to have anything to do with the CIA was understandable.

But what chance did Ghorbanifar, the Israelis, Khomeini, or McFarlane have of advancing a new U.S. initiative with Iran? The President of the United States had made unmistakable his stand against dealing with terrorists. His administration had formally branded Iran a "terrorist state." The month before Michael Ledeen was so entranced by Ghorbanifar, the President told the American Bar Association: "Let me make it plain to the assassins in Beirut and their accomplices that America will never make concessions to terrorists; to do so would only invite more terrorism. Once we head down that path, there would be no end to it, no end to the suffering of innocent people, no end to the bloody ransom all civilized nations must pay."

But luck was with the arms sale's supporters. At the moment the President made that speech, the thirty-nine Americans of the hijacked TWA flight 847 were being held under threat of death. Twelve days later, thirty-eight were freed. And their freedom had been won in part by the intercession of Hojatolislam Hashemi Rafsanjani, the speaker of the Iranian Parliament.

Ronald Reagan could sign an abstract piece of legislation that would cut federal programs for tens of thousands of the poor or sick or homeless without losing sleep. But he felt an overwhelming compassion when faced with flesh-and-blood suffering. And it was precisely this kind of immediate, palpable tragedy that the hostage situation presented. Wherever he went—the White House, or on the road—families of the hostages pleaded to see him, and he could not turn them down. They begged him to do something to bring their loved ones home. He shared their pain, genuinely and deeply.

Rafsanjani's role in freeing the TWA passengers had obviously been the act of a moderate, reasonable man. It confirmed the signals that McFarlane had been getting. It stirred Ronald Reagan's hopes that maybe this terrible ordeal of imprisoned Americans might at last be lifted from his shoulders. McFarlane had been present and had seen the eyes mist over when the President met with the hostages' families. The President was willing to consider trading guns for a fresh opening to Tehran and possible freedom for the American captives.

That summer of 1985, Casey was getting independent information that the Iranian foreign ministry was ready to cut a deal, hostages for arms. His source was John Shaheen. Casey and Shaheen had both been in the OSS, though they had not met until after the war. Shaheen was two years younger than Casey, born on a farm in Illinois, though he looked anything but a midwestern sodbuster. Dark, small, of Middle Eastern antecedents, Shaheen could have passed more easily in Beirut than in his native Lee County.

Shaheen, too, had had a good war. He came out of the OSS with the Silver Star. He became a lone-ranger oil developer, eager to tilt against the Seven Sisters who dominated the business. He had met Casey at lunch at General Donovan's Sutton Place apartment. The rapport had been instantaneous; for Shaheen, too, was a dynamo, a man perpetually exploding with schemes. He had sent Casey $3,000 for his 1966 congressional race, and Casey was deeply touched. Casey was constantly giving Shaheen legal advice, until Rogers and Wells complained that the oil man owed the firm $30,000. Casey told Jack Wells to back off: "He won't be able to pay anything unless his deal comes through. So let me help him make his deal work." Shaheen was indeed going to need help. He had launched the Newfoundland Refining Company in a place called Come By Chance. Shaheen expected to pump 100,000 barrels of oil a day. Instead, the venture failed, and Shaheen scored the largest bankruptcy in Canadian history.

Some time in June of 1985, Shaheen called Casey to tell him that a mutual friend named Roy Furmark had stumbled into something hot. Furmark was an operator himself, always on the brink of great things; he had worked for Shaheen on the Come By Chance project. Shaheen had brought Furmark to VOSS dinners, where he came to know Casey. Furmark subsequently had become involved with a Saudi Arabian business associate, Adnan Khashoggi, who made the flamboyant Shaheen seem comparatively lackluster. The tabloids proclaimed Khashoggi "the richest man in the world."

Early that year, on January 5, 1985, Furmark had gone to Hamburg to work out a crude-oil contract with Iranian businessmen. Among them was Manucher Ghorbanifar. The negotiations involved a half-dozen lunches and dinners, where Ghorbanifar and Furmark warmed to each other. "We had good chemistry," Furmark was later to say. "He's a very considerate person, always asking about your family, the kids."

Along with oil deals, Furmark was also negotiating a plan to get Caterpillar, the American heavy-equipment company, back into Iran, where it had enjoyed a lucrative business before the fall of the Shah. Big money was going to be required, and so Furmark brought in Adnan Khashoggi.

On June 12, Furmark and Khashoggi were in Hamburg to work with Iranian trade officials on the Caterpillar deal, which by now involved a billion-dollar contract. While they were there, Furmark introduced Khashoggi to Ghorbanifar. As Furmark recalled, the two men "hit it off."

Khashoggi would later tell a touching story of these two new acquaintances lamenting the terrible waste of blood of their Middle Eastern brothers in the war between Iran and Iraq. The solution, they agreed, was a new relationship between Iran and the United States, and that, Ghorbanifar said, could be accomplished by an arms deal.

Furmark had a less sentimental recollection of that conversation. As he later put it, "In Adnan's mind was the idea if we could get Iran closer to the West—and Ghorbanifar was the person to do it—we could then go to a ten-billion- or twenty-billion-dollar contract. That was the ultimate in Khashoggi's mind." Caterpillar's $1 billion was starting to look like peanuts.

Ghorbanifar was the key, because, as Khashoggi later recalled, "he represented himself as the head of intelligence for the prime minister of Iran." A world-class manipulator like Khashoggi knew enough to deflate at least part of the claim. Still, Ghorbanifar obviously had connections in Tehran. Over a good dinner at a restaurant favored by the Iranian community in Hamburg, they discussed the billions in arms sales through which they could bring peace to their troubled corner of the world.

Another piece of the disaster was in place.

Khashoggi assured Ghorbanifar that he had highly placed connections in the United States. Ghorbanifar was uneasy; he had had bad experiences with the CIA, he explained. "They want to treat us like Kleenex—use us, then throw us away. They are unreasonable and unprofessional. If you check with them, they will say I am unreasonable and undisciplined." If Khashoggi meant to cooperate with the CIA, the deal was off. Khashoggi assured him that he had enough other American connections to work around the CIA.

Israel was going to be critical to any arms deal, and Adnan Khashoggi was the rare Arab with friendly ties to Israel, including Prime Minister Shimon Peres. Within days after the conversation with Ghorbanifar, Khashoggi put his new associate in touch with the Israelis.

Thus it was that, one month later, on July 6, Michael Ledeen was introduced in Tel Aviv to Manucher Ghorbanifar, the man who was "too good to be true."

At Ghorbanifar's insistence, the CIA was supposed to be cut out, but Casey quickly learned, through John Shaheen, that Roy Furmark was working on a hostage release deal with a well-connected Iranian intelligence officer named Manucher Ghorbanifar.

Ed Juchniewicz, as assistant DDO, received a request from Casey. "Whenever he came across an interesting lead," Juchniewicz said, "he'd say, 'I want you to trace so-and-so. This time he mentioned Ghorbanifar. I told Bill that we'd already dropped him once before— that he'd flunked the polygraph twice. I told him, 'This one's a bum.' Bill was flipping through the man's file all the while. I thought I'd convinced him. But he looked up at me in that noncommittal way, and all he said was, 'Yeah. Sure. Thanks.' " Casey had already met Ghorbanifar, if the assertions of Richard J. Brenneke were true. Brenneke was the man who later swore that he had seen Casey in Paris with Ghorbanifar and other Iranians working to stall the release of the fifty-two American hostages held in Tehran until after the 1980 presidential election.

Casey never wanted to be wholly dependent on his own Agency's sources. He was enormously impressed by Israeli intelligence, and the Israelis were chanting the praises of Manucher Ghorbanifar. As Dick Helms later read Casey's behavior: "Bill thought you had to be ten feet tall to work for the Mossad. He wasn't taking sufficiently into account that the Israelis had their own agenda. They wanted the United States back in Iran."

At this point, the United States was almost wholly dependent on Israel for intelligence out of Iran. And Israel's best source was now Ghorbanifar, a man saying exactly what Israel and the United States wanted to hear: there were Iranian moderates with whom they could do business.

If a rapprochement with Iran was possible, if it helped check any Soviet move toward the Persian Gulf, if the hostages, particularly William Buckley, could be released, Casey concluded, why not give it a try?

Another piece of the disaster was in place.

On July 18, McFarlane went to see the President in the hospital, where he was recuperating from minor cancer surgery. McFarlane laid out his scheme for opening a dialogue with Iranian moderates. It would require having the Israelis provide a small amount of American-made defensive arms to Iran. But the Israelis were uneasy about drawing down their own inventories of Hawks and TOWs; and so the United States would have to agree to replenish Israel for any weapons sold to Iran. The initiative should produce a release of the hostages,

McFarlane explained. Reagan's eyes brightened at the thought of bringing these Americans home. "Gee," he said, "that sounds pretty good."

By August 8, McFarlane briefed the NSPG. Cap Weinberger was disbelieving. "This would undercut everything we were going to do in the Middle East," he said. Casey went instinctively for the loophole. "I think we're forgetting something here. It isn't the United States that's acting. It's our support of an Israeli action." More objections were raised. What about the Arms Export Control Act, which outlawed even the Israelis forwarding American arms to third parties without clearance? What about the fact that the United States had formally designated Iran a terrorist state? What about Operation Staunch, which at that very moment was being pushed to pressure other nations *not* to sell arms to Iran? All those obstacles could be worked out, Casey said; besides, "if the President determines it's his policy, then under the National Security Act, he can do it legally." The President was convinced. As McFarlane later put it, "President Reagan was foursquare behind the shipment."

The key piece of the disaster was in place.

Different eyes looked at the identical act and saw different possibilities. Bud McFarlane wanted to be a statesman. Shimon Peres wanted the United States back in Iran. The Ayatollah wanted arms for his war. Ronald Reagan wanted the hostages freed. Bill Casey wanted to checkmate the Soviets in the Persian Gulf. And all their lofty objectives were abetted by two men, Manucher Ghorbanifar and Adnan Khashoggi, with a much simpler motive: they wanted to make money. Thus the rug merchants and the Boy Scouts joined forces.

To conduct covert operations was a major reason why the CIA existed. Yet McFarlane was given operational responsibility for the secret arms-hostages deals. He managed to take possession because the plungers on the NSC found the CIA, except for Casey and a few others, too cautious—people like John McMahon. George Lauder recalled a conversation with Ollie North over a leaked news story on the contras. "How did they find out?" North had wanted to know. "We briefed the Congress," Lauder said, "and they must have leaked it." "Why the hell did you brief them?" North demanded. "Because," Lauder explained, "it's the law, Ollie." "God damn it," North said, "those people are preventing the President from carrying out his foreign policy! Maybe we should stop telling you guys and do everything ourselves."

As McMahon saw the situation, "It looked to the NSC as if we hadn't even been able to secure our own station chief in that part of the world. So they grabbed the hostage operation."

The sly old fox did not feel affronted at all. Yes, Casey favored the operation; but he knew it was fraught with peril. If McFarlane wanted to lead the charge across a mine field, so be it. Casey, the baseball fan of yore, had never forgotten the wisdom of Henry J. "Zeke" Bonura, the old first baseman of the Chicago White Sox: you can't be charged with an error unless you touch the ball. Consequently, Bonura usually had the highest fielding average in the league.

No finding was thought necessary for this most covert of covert operations. The NSC, unlike the CIA, did not have to obtain findings. Nor was Congress informed. The NSC, unlike the CIA, did not have to notify Congress.

All the elements of disaster were complete.

29.

"The Most Valuable Defector in Fifty Years"

That summer of 1985, another appointment had to be shoe-horned into Casey's schedule. During a routine annual physical, the Agency medical office found that he had cancer of the prostate. Casey opted for radiation. And so, every afternoon at five, he went to Georgetown Hospital for treatment. He was annoyed at the hour. "It's in the middle of the work day," he grumbled to Arvel Tharp, his CIA physician. As one member of the director's security detail remarked, "At least for one month we got home at a decent hour." As for Casey's reaction to cancer, "He brushed it off," Tharp said, "like a common cold." He also kept the circle of those aware of the disease small, applying the classic need-to-know rule of intelligence. The medical office and security detail necessarily knew, but almost no others.

In the course of his treatment, Casey had invited Alan Fiers in for lunch for an update on the contra situation. Fiers found Casey hopping mad. "Alan," he said, "somebody's started a rumor that I'm dying of cancer. Tell the truth—do I look like a guy who's got cancer? Just tell me!" Fiers examined his feisty chief and answered, "Of course not. You obviously don't have cancer." "I tell you, it's outrageous," Casey said. Long afterward, when Casey was denying knowledge of his involvement in certain delicate operations, Fiers was to remember the convincing quality of Casey's denial.

Casey was more concerned, or at least more self-conscious, about the condition of his voice. He tried to laugh off the constant cracks about his now legendary mumbling. He was invited to speak at the golden anniversary dinner of the SEC and told the audience, "Mumbling is more in the mind of the listener than in the mouth of the speaker." He granted an interview to a *Newsday* reporter named David Kahn. Afterward, Kahn offered to let Casey hear the tapes.

Casey said no, he would rather see a transcript. That was not *News-day*'s policy, the reporter told him. "To hell with your policy," Casey said. "Send me the transcripts." A puzzled Kahn took his problem to George Lauder. "Oh, it's nothing," Lauder told him. "He just doesn't like to hear the sound of his own voice."

Evidently, Lauder did not like the sound either. The producers of CBS's "60 Minutes" had been trying for months to land Casey. Lauder repeatedly turned them down. "What's the matter?" Casey grumbled to Lauder. "Don't you think I'm presentable?" As Lauder later put it to the producer, "If you had a guy who talks like Bill Casey, would you put him on television?"

Stuart Jackson had first met Bill Casey when he was fresh out of Harvard Law School and had gone to work at Rogers and Wells. He came to look upon the older man as a mentor. Jackson ultimately went into practice on his own and, not long after Casey went to the CIA, called Casey and asked to see him.

As Jackson described his visit to Langley, "I told Bill I was representing a client who handled the interests of several American companies doing business in the Soviet Union. I went there often myself. I saw a lot of sensitive people—government department heads and academics." Jackson offered to be useful.

Exploiting intelligence through international business sources had been a constant Casey refrain. He told Jackson the kind of information that would be particularly helpful. He wanted the Soviets' shopping list—what they were buying, what sources they had for blacklisted American products. He was interested in general economic and social conditions in the country, too. But the CIA's number-one objective in the Soviet Union, far and away, he explained, was to obtain the manuals for Soviet strategic weapons. Of course, Casey said, he doubted that Jackson's contacts were *that* good.

Still, Jackson said, he was well positioned to help. He was often invited out to the dachas of prominent officials, handsome old places converted from the long-ago-confiscated estates of Russian aristocrats. "I spoke a little Russian," he recalled, "and sometimes I'd pass myself off as an East German or a Yugoslav, especially when I was invited into people's homes. The vodka would flow and their tongues would loosen. I'd get a sense of daily life." As for Casey's key interest, Jackson found that the Soviets' shopping list was always topped by sophisticated computer hardware, especially computers capable of designing the manufacture of other equipment.

Thereafter, on his return from the Soviet Union, Jackson would write out his report. When he finished, he called a telephone number that Casey had given him. "I'd say, 'I have something for the director.' Then a courier would come up to my office, seal the report in my presence, and take it somewhere, I don't know where. But afterward, I'd get a brief, nonspecific thank-you note from Casey, and occasionally an invitation to come down and visit him."

Where Jackson's intelligence went was to a CIA operation called the National Collection Division. The division had offices in thirty major American cities. Its agents contacted corporations doing business abroad. They would ask if they might question employees returning from business trips or extended tours overseas. "Before we started the National Collection Division," John McMahon observed, "we used to deal with these business types randomly. If somebody knew somebody who was going into a target area, we might ask them to look into something specific. But these damn fools always wanted to go out and play cloak-and-dagger. They were always taking more risks than they were worth. So we institutionalized the process by creating the National Collection Division."

Casey loved inviting business executives out to Langley. Few of them could resist an opportunity to set foot inside the CIA. Between 1984 and 1985, nearly three hundred major American business leaders came to the Agency's executive seminar. Mainly, they were briefed on the world economy, plus just enough intelligence not likely to be found in the *Wall Street Journal* to create the desired aura of intrigue. Then Casey would shift into his "dangerous world we live in" speech. When he had properly persuaded his audience that it was a jungle out there, he made his pitch. He was fairly blatant: "Corporate executives and experts returning from overseas trips have been invaluable not only in providing information but in giving us leads to people willing to make available information which may be critical to our national interests." And then he assured his audience, "You have my personal promise of confidentiality."

The Mars candy company asked the CIA for information about the chocolate industry in the Soviet Union and Eastern-bloc countries— an odd expenditure of CIA time, the staff thought, and were prepared to turn the request down. Casey told his people to get cracking: you could never tell what Mars employees might someday be bringing out of the Soviet Union.

These silent business partners paid off, as one of the secret monthly reports of the National Collection Division to Casey makes clear. From it he learned:

- An engineer with a firm doing business in the Soviet Union had spotted titanium-alloy scrap in a trash pile at a Soviet metallurgical plant, a tip-off that the plant was producing parts there for Soviet nuclear submarines.
- A high-ranking Libyan diplomat serving in Europe was susceptible to CIA recruitment because he was eager to get his diabetic child into an American hospital.
- An American construction firm that was building a $50-million communications system for a Middle Eastern government was offering to bug the place while building it.

It was a businessman who tipped Casey off early to the likely next leader of the Soviet Union. Yuri Andropov had succeeded Leonid Brezhnev as general secretary of the Communist party in October of 1982 only to die himself sixteen months later. His successor, Konstantin Chernenko, was also known to be seriously ill, and the succession sweepstakes were on again.

The president of World Health Technologies, Harry M. Hament, had a meeting with Georgiy Arbatov, director of the Institute of the United States of America and Canada, the Soviet think tank that studied North America. On May 30, 1984, after the Arbatov meeting, Hament wrote Casey that Mikhail Gorbachev would succeed Chernenko. "Gorbachev will be a real moderate compared to recent leaders," Hament added. Thirteen months later, Gorbachev took power. Casey loved to flaunt the private personal intelligence that he gathered before his own analysts.

Bob Gates acknowledged the value of Casey's contacts in the international business community. But, said Gates, "for every guy who said Gorbachev was going to take over, there was another one assuring him that Marshal Ustinov was going to pull off a coup. Casey had us listening to some smart people, and just as many kooks."

Still, to Casey, what American business people were bringing out of the Soviet Union sounded like amateur night compared with what the Soviets were obtaining, by means fair or foul, from the West. He took a perverse pleasure in shocking business audiences at Langley with Soviet technological coups. As he said in one confidential briefing:

Soviet trucks rolled into Afghanistan from the Kama truck plant outfitted with sophisticated U.S. and European machinery.
The high-precision gyros in Soviet ICBMs were designed in the USA.
The radar in the new Soviet AWACS is ours.

The Soviets got the plans to our C-5A transport before we could test-fly the plane.

The Soviet space shuttle is a clone of ours down to the imperfections.

There could be no doubt, he told this audience: the priority objective of the KGB and the GRU, Soviet military intelligence, "is the clandestine acquisition of Western technology. Where do they get it? The CIA has spotted three hundred dummy companies operating in thirty countries with one assignment: acquire our technology." What they did not steal, they could buy. He particularly enjoyed quoting Lenin: "The capitalists will sell us the rope we need to hang them."

On the morning of July 29, 1985, Casey briefed the editorial staff of the *Wall Street Journal* in New York. Afterward, he was driven to the Links Club at 36 East Sixty-second Street. There, he was to meet in secret with the American members of the U.S.-USSR Trade and Economic Council and two dozen other American CEOs. As he approached the third-floor dining room, Casey was greeted by the council's co-chairman, Dwayne Andreas, head of the giant Archer-Daniels-Midland grain empire, who escorted him to the head of a U-shaped table. Among those around the table were Edgar Bronfman of Seagram; George Champion of the Chase Manhattan Bank; Martin S. Davis of Gulf and Western; Donald M. Kendall of Pepsico; Laurance Rockefeller and Happy Rockefeller, the widow of Laurance's brother Nelson; Rawleigh Warner of Mobil; and Daniel Ludwig of National Bulk Carriers, one of the world's wealthiest businessmen.

After lunch, Andreas rose and gave Casey an enthusiastic introduction. In the room there was something of the excitement of grown-ups playing at spies; Andreas, in fact, had been assigned a code name for his secret reporting to the Agency's National Collection Division. A secret/sensitive document prepared for Casey by his staff prior to the meeting revealed that among the CEOs were several whose co-operation with the CIA went back to the sixties. At this point, 165 U.S. firms were providing cover for CIA operatives at home or abroad—a key Casey objective.

Casey thanked Andreas for the introduction. "I can only guess," he said with a grin, "that somewhere in Moscow my opposite number on the KGB, Viktor Chebrikov, is breaking bread with your opposite numbers on the U.S.-USSR Trade and Economic Council."

Casey then went on to share his reading of Mikhail Gorbachev, now nearly four months in office. Among these worldly fellow entrepreneurs, Casey was freed from the knee-jerk anticommunist rhetoric he reserved for conservative audiences. Gorbachev, he told them, would try to repair the failing Soviet economy; he was not going to be bent on Soviet imperial expansion, at least not until he had the patient back on his feet. The key question, Casey said, was how far Gorbachev would be willing to reduce the Soviet Union's military establishment and pull back its destabilizing probes around the world.

Then he got to his major message: intelligence was too important to be left strictly to intelligence officers. "I look to you for clues as to what's happening in the Soviet Union. In fact, I rely on you. You members of the Trade and Economic Council are in a privileged position to take the pulse of the Soviet economy—and give us the heart rate." Here was how the U.S. representatives on the Trade and Economic Council could best help, he said:

They'll use you to send up trial balloons. They'll use you to pass along messages not in accord with the Politburo party line. You may be our earliest source of factionalism and internal dissent in the Kremlin. These are hard subjects for us to get a handle on. And what you can help us with best is passing along whatever you have on the new players on their side.

And lest you think that valuable information on the latest Soviet military technology is beyond your reach, I will share with you the following: it was U.S. industry that provided my analysts with some of the best and most detailed information on the Soviet directed energy program—the Soviet equivalent of our "Star Wars" program. The information included specific locations of Soviet ground-based laser systems, technical details of various laser systems and R and D programs, and assessments of Soviet capabilities in these areas.

At the end, his audience gave him an ovation. It had been revealing. It had been exciting. For people to whom the power of money had lost its novelty, here was a taste of another form of power—and they savored it.

For the past year, Casey had also been pondering another use of the world business community. He had gone to the Far East the year before. In Tokyo, he was briefed by an Agency officer with an obvious flair for extracting intelligence from American businessmen working in Japan. An idea clicked in his mind.

When he got back to Langley, he immediately called in John McMahon. "The guy's bright, he's sharp," he told McMahon. "I've got just the job for him, something I've been thinking about for a long time—sleepers."

"Sleepers?" To McMahon it had a quaint ring. And indeed, Casey had first learned about sleeper operations back in World War II. Agents were recruited in foreign businesses or in government ministries. They were to lay low and go about their regular jobs. But if their country was overrun, the sleepers were activated. The Allies would thus have spies in place.

"Look what happened in Iran," Casey said. "The Shah falls, the Ayatollah takes over, and what have we got? Zilch. I know guys who are doing business all over the world. I want to place sleepers with their firms now, in nonofficial cover. That way, when an Ethiopia or a Vietnam falls, we've got something offshore, on the shelf, ready to put in place."

"He told me that day," McMahon later recalled, "that he wanted this bright guy in Japan to organize and manage the sleeper operation. And he told me, 'John, you and I will run him ourselves. The less people who know about it, the more secure it'll be.' I said, 'Bill, we haven't got time to run agents ourselves. We've got too much on our plates already.' But he was determined to put these sleepers in place so that no matter what happened to the official U.S. apparatus in a country, even if they kicked out all our people and shut down the embassy, we'd still have eyes and ears. His idea was, no more Irans."

Increasingly, Ollie North would round the corner with his quick, purposeful stride and pop in at Casey's EOB office. He relied on Casey's advice now that he had taken over the contra supply operation from the CIA and was becoming involved too in McFarlane's Iranian initiative. North was a thirsty pupil, and often the conversation drifted to other areas of expertise in the old man's repertory. Casey told North about the sleepers, how they would act like a backup generator when the power was cut to your official sources. He told North how these operations could be kept almost totally secret, entirely in private hands, so that their security was not threatened even when the U.S. government was out of the picture.

North found the scheme exciting: an offshore, free-standing, self-sustaining, private intelligence network, not even known to the government—rather similar to what he was developing to supply the contras, only better; a private CIA, no longer accountable to interfering congressional committees and overcautious, civil-service intelligence bureaucrats.

Not quite, Casey cautioned. But that was Ollie, picking up an idea and taking flight on the wings of his own heated imagination. Casey admired the sheer bravado of the man, though he recognized that his enthusiasms had to be controlled by cooler heads.

To Casey, McMahon was just the opposite, having to be dragged into uncharted oceans, always seeing icebergs in the sea lane, land mines on the path. Yet his deputy occasionally had saved him from his own excess of zeal. As Casey pressed for the sleeper program, McMahon told him, "Sure, it's a fine idea. And the guy in the Tokyo station is right for it. But that's how we get in trouble, by having people run off on their own. You're bending the organization out of shape unnecessarily. Do the sleepers. But do it on the chart. Institutionalize it. It belongs in the National Collection Division. We've already got all the machinery in place." Casey grudgingly agreed.

In July of 1985, a high-ranking KGB security officer received a plum assignment. A Soviet nuclear scientist, Vladimir Alexandrov, had disappeared while attending a conference in Western Europe, and the security officer was sent to Rome to look for him.

July 28 was a hot, muggy morning in the Italian capital. The security man and two other Soviet officials were returning to the embassy. He told his companions that he wanted to visit the Vatican Museum, which was just a few minutes away on the via delle Fornaci. He would be back soon. At the museum, he walked up to one of the medieval-clad Swiss Guards and identified himself as Colonel Vitaly Yurchenko of the KGB. He wanted asylum.

Vitaly Yurchenko was first turned over to the Italian police. He proved his bona fides to the Italians in a long meeting with foreign minister Giulio Andreotti, in which he exposed several KGB agents and operations in Italy. But Italy was just the vestibule to the West. Yurchenko gave the Italians the name of the CIA's Rome station chief, with whom he wanted to be put in touch.

Soon afterward, a group of senior officials gathered for cocktails and lunch outside of Director Casey's dining room. Among them was Gus Hathaway, chief of counterintelligence. On Casey's arrival, Hathaway took him aside and announced excitedly, "Yurchenko's come over." By the end of August, Yurchenko had arrived in the United States under the attorney general's parole powers for emergency immigration.

Vitaly Yurchenko was then forty-nine, the son of a Russian factory worker who had died in the siege of Leningrad during World War II. Yurchenko had begun his career as a lieutenant in the Soviet submarine service, then switched to intelligence. He was married, had a daughter, age twenty-four, and an adopted son, age sixteen.

He was no stranger to Washington. Yurchenko had been posted to the Soviet embassy in 1975 as KGB officer in charge of security. He was, in effect, the counterintelligence officer, a watchdog over his countrymen. He enjoyed the good life, cut something of a figure around Washington, and was on a first-name basis with the bartenders at the better watering holes. He had picked up an American woman in a bar and initiated an affair with her before he was eventually reassigned to Moscow.

Casey was overjoyed at the catch. Yurchenko was the security officer for Soviet agents conducting operations in North America. The very nature of his work in counterintelligence meant that he had a wealth of knowledge of the holiest of holies, Soviet sources and methods. As a British intelligence officer said when he learned that the Americans had him, "One Yurchenko is worth twenty thousand seduced West German secretaries."

Such a high-level KGB defector raised the too-good-to-be-true specter. Was Yurchenko a mole, a deliberate plant, worming his way inside the American espionage apparatus? If he was, even the way the American's interrogated him, what they were trying to pump from him, could be revealing to the Soviets. Whether the man was a true defector or a mole would depend on the quality of the information he gave, chicken feed or valuable Soviet secrets.

What Yurchenko revealed appeared convincing. For months, the Agency had been troubled by the loss of its most precious assets, spies recruited directly inside the Soviet Union. In February, a prize agent, A. G. Tolkachev, an aviation electronics authority, a man deeply knowledgeable about Soviet electronic countermeasures, radar, and radar-evading technologies, was arrested and believed to have been executed. Tolkachev was just one of five American assets arrested over a short period. The CIA's painfully constructed Soviet network had virtually been destroyed overnight. And the Americans could not figure out what had gone wrong. But Vitaly Yurchenko knew: it was Robert. Robert, he told his CIA interrogators, was the only name he had for a KGB informant, a former CIA officer who had been slated for assignment to Moscow and then pulled off before he could complete his training.

That was all Yurchenko knew, but it was enough. With that lead, CIA counterintelligence officers were able to go to the Agency's Soviet covert operations desk and quickly pinpoint Robert. He had to be Edward Lee Howard.

Howard had presented the CIA with a classic espionage dilemma. He had indeed been in training in the early 1980s for the most delicate of assignments, a posting to Moscow, where he was to help run clandestine operations in the Soviet Union and Eastern Europe. But after Howard had learned the complex procedures for making contact with the network—indeed, after he learned the members of the network— the CIA developed doubts about Edward Lee Howard. The man had a drinking problem. Further investigation revealed that Howard had used marijuana, hashish, cocaine, LSD, and Quaaludes. He had committed petty thievery. The CIA now faced a head cracker: fire him and risk having a disgruntled former employee spill everything he knew, or keep him in a nonsensitive position and have a clear security risk working inside the pale. The CIA chose to fire Howard. And he did spill. He sold his secrets to the Soviet Union.

After Yurchenko's tip revealed Howard's betrayal, the CIA informed the FBI. In 1985, the FBI located the man in New Mexico and kept him under surveillance while they built a case against him. Howard, however, managed to give the bureau's agents the slip, using tricks he had learned at Langley. He escaped to Moscow and became the first defector in the CIA's history.

Thanks to Yurchenko, the CIA at least had been able to solve the mystery of its blown network inside the Soviet Union. He also tipped off the Agency to another traitor, Ronald Pelton, an ex–NSA employee who had sold the Soviets code-breaking secrets at the time Yurchenko was serving at the Russian embassy in Washington. Pelton was arrested by the FBI and faced prosecution for espionage.

Yurchenko was also full of KGB trade craft, which he happily compromised. He revealed, for instance, how the KGB tracked foreign diplomats in Moscow by dusting their cars, rooms, and door handles with a radioactive powder. As one of his handlers remarked, "The guy seemed to know everything. He was twenty-four-carat gold."

Just days after Yurchenko arrived in the United States, Casey invited four senators from the SSCI and the staff director, Bernie McMahon, out to Langley for breakfast. Yurchenko, he told them, was far more valuable than some frustrated Soviet nuclear physicist skipping the country. Vitaly Yurchenko was *sources and methods*. Equally important, he knew what the other side knew about us. Furthermore, the defection of a high-ranking official enjoying cushy perks demonstrated the erosion of morale in the Soviet Union. For an intelligence professional, Bernie McMahon remembered thinking, "this was spine-tingling stuff." Casey told the new SSCI chairman, Dave Durenberger, "Let me tell you, Senator, I'm damned glad I'm not my counterpart in the Kremlin this morning."

Vitaly Yurchenko enjoyed the VIP treatment. The agency put him up at a safe house within an easy commute to Langley, a modern colonial in a secluded, sparsely developed Virginia development called Coventry, about forty-two miles southwest of Washington. He had lunch with the director of Central Intelligence in his private dining room. Yurchenko, aware of the fine dining Washington offered, was unimpressed by Casey's table. But he was voluble, speaking a breezy broken English with a thick Slavic accent. "What's Gorbachev like?" Casey wanted to know. The man was very smart, very shrewd politically, Yurchenko told him. He favored good Western tailoring. He was full of charm and magnetism. And underneath, he was as hard as a Siberian winter. Casey had Yurchenko as his dinner guest on two more occasions.

The defector began negotiating his deal with the United States. Yurchenko was in a good bargaining position: he had lived in America; he understood the economics of daily life. How long would it take before he was self-sufficient? Would he have a new family to support? What standard of living was he abandoning back in Russia? And ever present, how valuable was what he was selling? The talks resembled a new CEO working out his salary and stock options with the board of directors. In the end, it was agreed that he was to get, right off, enough to buy a house, a car, and home furnishings. And so the CIA agreed to a package of $1 million up front and $62,000 per year for life. Yurchenko was also promised one of the ten annual instant-American-citizenship slots reserved for key defectors, a piece of legislation that Casey had successfully lobbied.

For an ordinary American struggling to make ends meet, this payoff to a Communist traitor might seem excessive. But as one CIA operative saw it, "Suppose he tips you off to just one billion-dollar Soviet weapons system? Yurchenko was worth every penny. In fact, he wasn't all that thrilled with the package."

And as the weeks passed, Vitaly Yurchenko was no longer quite so thrilled with America. He quickly descended from dinner conversations with the DCI to daily grillings by Grade 12 bureaucrats. He was stricken with bouts of depression. John McMahon was assigned to keep an eye on Yurchenko and saw trouble brewing. "He was a pro," McMahon observed, "and he was very sensitive about status."

Yurchenko began drinking heavily, even during his interrogations. His handlers tried to ease his homesickness by setting up little parties with Soviet refugees, people who spoke colloquial Russian. A fellow defector assured him that he could look forward to a comfortable job on an American college faculty. But Yurchenko was clear-eyed. He may have been a diamond to the CIA, but of the roughest cut. He was intelligent yet coarse, not deeply educated, and had a not particularly endearing brashness about him. Vitaly Yurchenko could expect few offers from academia.

He had not been motivated by ideology. Few defectors are. He had sought freedom, mainly the personal freedom to have a good time fueled by plenty of cash. And he had wanted to escape an unhappy marriage. He told his handlers that he would probably feel better if they could bring him his old American girlfriend. They managed to track her down and had to bring him the bad news: she had no interest in seeing Vitaly ever again.

He confessed that he had had a heavy affair with the wife of a Soviet diplomat now serving at the embassy in Ottawa, Canada. After constant beseeching, two agents flew with him to Ottawa and took him to his old mistress's apartment during the day, while her husband was at the embassy. A smiling Yurchenko announced that he had defected and he wanted her to come away with him. She slammed the door in his face.

He began drinking more. He was surly to the security people, whom he scorned as mere guards and unfit company for a man of his rank. "I decided the guy needed some R and R," John McMahon finally concluded. Yurchenko had said that the one American mecca he wanted to visit was Las Vegas. And so his handlers took him on a three-week vacation through New Mexico and Arizona.

One morning, Yurchenko and his Agency companions went for breakfast to a fast-food joint. The waitress flipped her pad and asked, "What do you want?" Yurchenko ordered. She could not understand him. He tried again, and again failed to be understood. He slammed his fist on the table and covered his eyes with his hand: he could not even successfully order ham and eggs in this alien land. As they waited in brittle silence, Yurchenko finally spoke. His voice was cold and menacing. He knew a Soviet journalist who had defected to the British, he said. The defector had not been treated with dignity. He had not been able to adjust to life in London. And so he had gone home to the Soviet Union.

In mid-September, Casey attended a meeting of the National Security Council run by Bud McFarlane. Afterward, McFarlane asked if he might have a word with Casey privately. They stepped into Mc-

Farlane's West Wing office, where the NSC adviser appeared uneasy as he started to speak. McFarlane told Casey that Colonel North would soon be sending the CIA a request for surveillance of any arms movement between Israel and Iran. He further told Casey that the surveillance reports were to go only to North and the service chiefs at the Pentagon, not to Shultz or Weinberger.

Casey drove back to Langley with McMahon and told his deputy what he had just heard. When they got back, Casey also informed Clair George, now the chief of covert operations. "I wonder what the hell they're up to," Casey said. His bafflement, however, could not have been total. From his attendance at the NSPG debates over the arms initiatives with Iran, Casey knew that Shultz and Weinberger were opposed. Obviously, McFarlane was cutting them out.

But what neither Casey nor his organization knew at this point was that McFarlane already had arranged the first shipment of TOWs from Israel's stocks to Iran. At the time, Ghorbanifar had assured McFarlane that the hostages would be released when Iran received the antitank weapons. The first hostage that McFarlane wanted out, he said, was William Buckley. Ghorbanifar had agreed.

The original deal called for shipping 508 TOWs, which the United States would then replenish. But the Israelis were nervous: a drawdown of that many weapons would dangerously deplete their own arsenal. And so they agreed initially to send only ninety-six TOWs to Iran. Even that shipment had been delayed by mutual distrust. The Israelis said they would not deliver any arms until they were paid, and the Iranians would not pay for the arms until they were delivered. Ghorbanifar knew where to go to solve the dilemma. Toward the end of July, he had boarded the yacht of Adnan Khashoggi, anchored off Marbella in Spain.

Ghorbanifar announced to Khashoggi that he had worked out the first arms deal, but he had the problem of the Israelis and Iranians not trusting each other. He needed a bridge loan of $1 million to cover the sale of the ninety-six TOWs. What did a TOW missile cost? Khashoggi wanted to know. About $3,500, Ghorbanifar answered, and he was going to sell them to the Iranians for $10,000 apiece. Khashoggi nodded appreciatively—a 185 percent profit. Khashoggi was only too willing to help. He gave Ghorbanifar the $1 million. In return, Ghorbanifar gave him a postdated check. Ghorbanifar was to pay the government of Israel for the weapons; Israel would then deliver them to Iran. Iran would pay Ghorbanifar for the weapons. Ghorbanifar would then deposit the payment in his account. And Khashoggi could collect his $1 million by cashing the check against Ghorbanifar's account.

The arrangement worked perfectly. Khashoggi made the bridge loan on August 7. On August 22, the TOWs were loaded onto a chartered DC-8. Ghorbanifar boarded the plane and accompanied the weapons to Iran. And on August 29, Khashoggi got his money back.

The deal had gone perfectly for everybody—everybody, that is, but Bud McFarlane. No hostages were released. McFarlane had taken terrible risks, and so far he had nothing to show for it. He complained to Ghorbanifar. What did he expect for a partial shipment, Ghorbanifar responded, "an arm and a leg of Buckley?"

McFarlane believed he had no choice but to push ahead, deliver the rest of the TOWs, and hope to get the hostages out. It was at this point that he went to both Casey and the NSA asking for surveillance so that he could oversee a second delivery. Subsequently, on September 14, another 408 TOWs were loaded aboard the same DC-8 and flown to Iran.

On September 15, a thin, haggard American was dumped in front of the bombed-out U.S. embassy in Beirut and gazed up at the dazzling blue sky for the first time in a year. The man was Benjamin Weir, the Presbyterian missionary, the only one of the seven hostages released. Ghorbanifar explained to McFarlane that Buckley was too ill to be moved and that the other hostages could not be freed quite yet. The month before, Charles Allen, the Agency's chief of counterterrorism, had reported to Casey that all evidence indicated that Buckley was probably already dead of sickness and maltreatment— something that Ghorbanifar would certainly have known. Between the American McFarlane and the Persian Ghorbanifar, it was as if a child born yesterday were dealing with a man five thousand years old.

Vitaly Yurchenko stood amid the material splendor of a suburban Washington shopping center. He was soon to be a modestly rich man. But he was feeling poor in spirit, cut off from his roots, an object of interest only for the salable memories in his head. What human kindness he was shown—manufactured visits by Russian countrymen, shopping sprees with his CIA handlers, sessions with an Agency psychologist—had all the warmth and spontaneity of institutional charity. Nobody, he was convinced, cared about Vitaly Yurchenko. He had been accompanied this day by one lone security man and asked to be excused to go to find a men's room. Before he came back, he managed to locate a pay phone and call the Soviet embassy.

On October 31, his Agency psychologist thought it might be fun to take him to Georgetown to watch the Halloween parade. Two nights later, a Saturday, Yurchenko mentioned to the security chief on duty at the safe house that he had seen an interesting restaurant on his recent outing to Georgetown; he wondered if he might go there for dinner. He had been malleable, if morose, of late, and so the chief agreed and sent him off with one of the junior officers.

The night was drizzly and cold, with intimations of winter in the air. The restaurant that Yurchenko had spotted turned out to be the Pied du Cochon, the Pig's Foot, an all-night French bistro on Wisconsin Avenue. Nearby stood the hulking, ugly yellow-brick mass of the new Soviet embassy.

Yurchenko and his companion took a window table. "What you do if I take a walk?" Yurchenko asked. "You shoot me?"

"We don't treat defectors that way," the young officer answered.

Yurchenko got up. "I come back in fifteen, twenty minutes," he said. "If I don't come back, not your fault."

The next time anybody from the CIA saw Vitaly Yurchenko was on television. On Monday, November 4, he appeared at a televised press conference emanating from the Soviet embassy.

Casey had boasted of snagging Yurchenko to the White House and on the Hill. He had described Yurchenko as "the most valuable defector in fifty years." Now he watched his prize catch on the television set in his office. His press man, George Lauder, was with him, along with McMahon, other top staff, and Betty Murphy. Casey was slumped low in his chair, legs crossed, his hand stroking his chin.

Yurchenko glowed in the limelight. He had not defected, he said; he had been drugged and kidnapped by the CIA. Thereafter, he had been tortured and interrogated. The drugs had turned his skin green, and his handlers had dragged him out and made him play golf to give him some decent color. The brash manner, the rough wit, the fractured English suggested a Russian stand-up comic.

Nobody had spoken Russian among his handlers, he complained. Nobody paid any attention to his problems. "Even if I try to commit suicide, they won't give me such chance to escape," he said, "because twenty-four hours, even when I was sleeping, they prohibited even to close the door." As Yurchenko continued his tale, he smiled devilishly and said, "If I make some mistakes, please ask Mr. Casey to verify it." He described Casey as an "old man," with his fly unzipped at one of their dinners.

George Lauder stole a glance at Casey, who seemed to have sunk even lower into his chair. "The staff guys," Lauder remembered, "were making a running commentary like, 'That's a bunch of crap! . . . We never did that! . . . That's a goddamn lie!' Casey said not a word. He was in his 'I'm hurting but I'm not gonna show it' mood."

Yurchenko finished his performance and closed the press conference with a genial "Bye-bye."

The redefection had been a calamity. Immediate speculation centered on whether Yurchenko was a legitimate defector or a plant. Either way, the Agency lost. If he was legitimate, he obviously had been mishandled. The man seemed to have added a new phrase to the lexicon of American social ills: defector abuse. If he was a plant, how had the CIA been so totally bamboozled? President Reagan took a middle course. He told reporters that Yurchenko was a legitimate defector, but what he had given the CIA was insignificant, "not anything new or sensational." That did not help much. If so, what had all the fuss been about?

Among the intelligence pros, a tactical debate went on: should Yurchenko have been allowed simply to walk away? "I'd have said, 'You leave this restaurant and you won't last long,' " George Lauder observed. "If it had been me," John McMahon told members of the SSCI, "I'd have driven Yurchenko to the Soviet embassy. I've worked all my life to keep this a free country. This man was a defector, not a criminal."

Chairman Durenberger and other senior SSCI members called Casey on the carpet. If this man was the prize Casey had boasted of, how could his defection have been so bungled? Durenberger said he intended to conduct an investigation. Casey was half livid, half contrite. He squirmed in his armchair. "I'm the last guy in this town you have to convince of what a dumb thing this is," he said. "I'm totally aware we screwed up. We as a family know what we've done. And we'll fix it. I've already got an investigation going, and we'll overhaul the defector program. What purpose do you think a long, drawn-out public investigation is going to serve? We're supposed to be trying to rebuild the intelligence services in this country. Your meddling isn't going to help. Let us handle it ourselves."

And, he asked, what about the CIA's overall record compared with the KGB's? In the past three years, more than two hundred Soviet secret operatives had defected or had been arrested and expelled from countries all over the world. That meant two hundred highly trained assets essentially lost for any further covert use. Nothing remotely comparable had ever happened to U.S. intelligence. Yet because of security considerations, the CIA could not reveal to the American public how it had helped provoke this Soviet intelligence hemorrhage. As he was leaving, Casey said, "Remember what Eisenhower said about this business? Success can't be advertised. Failure can't be blamed." Durenberger finally agreed to let the CIA clean its own house.

Still, the debate went on over Yurchenko's intentions. In the end, the evidence was overwhelming: Yurchenko had been a legitimate defector. He had blown good Soviet operations in Italy even before he came to America. His revelations here, those that had been made public, had exposed valuable Soviet secrets. His unpublicized revelations to the CIA included "pearls," according to John McMahon. If the defection had been a brilliantly contrived penetration, then his redefection within three months, virtually empty-handed, made no sense. The one small satisfaction left the CIA was that Vitaly Yurchenko had changed his mind before he got his million dollars.

Within days he was back in Moscow. The conventional wisdom had it that Yurchenko would be executed. One rumor had him shot by a firing squad; another had him plunging from a fourteenth-story window. But a West German television crew saw him on the street, and he told them he was writing a book about his torture and drugging at the hands of the CIA. He was evidently going to live—an early beneficiary of the new Soviet Union that Mikhail Gorbachev was creating.

30.

A Finding After the Fact

On November 20, Casey was in Beijing, renewing with Chinese officials his arrangements for surveillance into the Soviet Union. He was shaving in the American embassy complex when the chief of his security detail brought him a cable. The officer stood by, waiting for Casey to finish reading it, since the cable carried special instructions: it was marked "Top Secret—Flash Beijing—Eyes Only." Only Casey was to see it. After that, it was to be destroyed, and the operations center back in Langley was to be notified of its destruction. The message read: "Possibly can settle your share Multiponics suit $100,000–$125,000. Strongly recommend your approval." The cable had been relayed from Casey's attorney, Milton Gould.

The Multiponics case had dragged through the courts for more than twelve years. Gould finally had managed to work out a tentative settlement for under half a million dollars with the Multiponics plaintiffs. He was pleased at getting out so cheaply, particularly since the eight other defendants feared that, as Gould put it, "Casey would be willing to pay any amount to avoid the publicity of a trial." "If Casey wasn't the director of Central Intelligence," Gould also said, "I would have fought this case to the last ditch and won." Instead, Gould advised Casey to end what he regarded as a "nuisance" suit.

Casey sent word back, agreeing. Ultimately, his share of the settlement cost him $117,000. By agreeing to pay the plaintiffs, he risked being seen as guilty of what was essentially an action for fraud. But in Gould's skilled hands, the case ended with no media publicity.

Another Casey investment turned out more successfully that year. He managed to turn what had seemed a dead loss into a rather colorful gain. The mini-sub that he had invested in nine years before had long since been leased to the sunken-treasure hunter Mel Fisher for a share of recovered treasure. After a sixteen-year search, Fisher had found the Spanish galleon *Nuestra Señora de Atocha* and was bringing up the richest haul in the history of underwater salvage— gold coins, silver ingots, and emeralds worth an estimated $400 million. Casey's estate would ultimately receive 2,200 gold pieces of eight and an exquisite emerald that had lain at the bottom of the ocean for 333 years.

A jet-lagged Casey was back from his trip to China and in his office by Tuesday, November 26. Virtually his first caller was Stanley Sporkin. Sporkin handed him a one-page draft of a presidential finding of necessity. The finding stated that efforts were being made by private parties "to obtain the release of Americans held hostage in the Middle East." The President was hereby authorizing the CIA to assist these private parties by "the provision of transportation, communications, and other necessary support." Further, "As part of these efforts, certain foreign materials and munitions may be provided to the government of Iran which is taking steps to facilitate the release of the American hostages. I direct the Director of Central Intelligence not to brief the Congress of the United States. . . ." For the first time, however vaguely, the concept of arms for hostages had been set forth in cold print. And for the first time, a draft finding proposed to have the CIA ignore Congress regarding a covert action.

Behind this draft lay a tangled weekend.

After the TOW deliveries of August and September, Ghorbanifar had added American-made Hawk antiaircraft missiles to his shopping list. Iraq was pounding Tehran almost nightly from high-altitude Soviet Bear bombers. The Iranians were desperate for the highly effective Hawks. The "moderates" in Iran were begging for these weapons, Ghorbanifar told Bud McFarlane. After his previous dealings with the man, McFarlane was leery; still, he agreed to another indirect transaction, in which Israel would provide 120 Hawks and the United States would replenish Israel. For their part, the Iranians were to deliver the remaining American hostages still held by the Shiite radicals. McFarlane's hope was to have the hostages home by Thanksgiving.

This time, however, there was no expectation that William Buckley would be among them. On October 15, the Islamic Jihad, an umbrella name for numerous Arab radical groups, announced that Buckley had been executed in retaliation for the bombing of Tunis by Israeli aircraft on October 1. More likely, according to the Agency's best intelligence, his captors were squeezing propaganda mileage out of a man dead months before.

Part of the legend that later would form around the Iran arms affair was that it had been triggered by Casey's anguish over Buckley's fate and his determination to free the man. He had, in fact, been badly shaken at the time of Buckley's capture. But it was not in Casey's nature to let emotion shape policy. "Sometimes we wondered, 'Is this the kind of guy who gets emotionally involved in anything?'" Ed Juchniewicz later observed. What disturbed Casey was that one of his station chiefs had been nabbed. "How could we let something like that happen?" he kept asking. "Sure, Casey cared," Bob Gates noted. "But Buckley was a casualty of war as far as Casey was concerned."

On November 18, Bud McFarlane was with the President in Geneva at the summit conference with Mikhail Gorbachev. McFarlane checked once more to get the President's approval for still another Iranian arms deal. The President told him to go ahead. McFarlane also informed Secretary of State Shultz, who denounced the deal as a craven arms-for-hostages swap. But McFarlane had the President's support, and Shultz backed off.

With McFarlane tied up at the summit, he turned over management of the shipment to Ollie North. A diversionary plan, complete with cover story, was worked out with the Israelis. The Hawks were first to be flown in an Israeli El Al 707 to Lisbon, then reloaded onto another aircraft for the flight to Iran. The cargo was described as oil-drilling parts. The cover story might fly; the Iranian wells on Kharg Island recently had been taking a pasting from Iraqi bombers.

North brought in Richard Secord from the contra operation to help him. Secord flew to Lisbon to work out the logistics. And there he ran into a snag: the Portuguese refused to grant the Israeli aircraft landing rights unless what was aboard the aircraft was disclosed in writing. This, North knew, he dared not do. He needed help. He had little faith in the CIA as an institution; but he had faith in individuals: the director and that "can do" operator who was now conveniently the deputy for European covert action, Dewey Clarridge.

On Saturday, November 23, North went out to Clarridge's office at Langley. He wanted U.S. embassy officials in Lisbon, including the CIA station chief, to exert their influence with Portuguese officials to get landing rights for the Israeli plane. But without something in writing, the Portuguese still refused to budge. The 707 was turned away.

North's back was to the wall. Ghorbanifar was presumably some-where in Iran awaiting the shipment and arranging for the release of the hostages. And a piece of paper, a technicality, was blocking the mission.

An Israeli plane could not fly openly into Iran loaded with American-made arms. What North needed was an unobtrusive aircraft. He explained the problem to Clarridge. It also appears that he leveled with Clarridge as to the true identity of the cargo. As North was later to say, "I did at some point confirm to Clarridge that that's what was taking place." Clarridge later insisted that North told him only that the cargo was drilling equipment. But Secord, in Lisbon, had admitted to the Lisbon station chief what was in the crates. And the station chief had cabled Clarridge, eyes only, that the plane held Hawk missiles intended to secure the release of the hostages.

North asked Clarridge to help him find a private air carrier operating in Europe that could discreetly deliver the arms. What North was asking would amount to the CIA's involvement, for the first time, in the arms-hostages scheme. And Clarridge came through. He gave North the name of Saint Lucia Airways, a CIA proprietary—that is, a private company secretly controlled by the CIA. North subsequently made arrangements for the first batch of Hawks to be flown, by a circuitous route, from Israel, over Turkey, and finally to Iran. The charter company was to be paid $127,000.

With Casey out of the country, John McMahon was in charge at Langley. By seven-fifteen a.m. on Monday, November 25, he was in the ops center, where he ran into Ed Juchniewicz. Juchniewicz was agitated. "Do you know what our guys did?" he said. "What?" McMahon asked. Juchniewicz explained how North and Clarridge had spent much of Saturday and Sunday trying to get embassy officials and the station chief in Lisbon to obtain landing rights for an Israeli aircraft. Then Clarridge had helped North find an Agency proprietary that could fly oil-drilling equipment to Iran.

As McMahon later described his reaction, "I hit the goddamned overhead! I called Sporkin. I told him to get to work on a finding right away. We couldn't be involved in influencing foreign officials or flying equipment into Iran without a finding. And I told Sporkin he damn well better make it retroactive." Then McMahon called Oliver North. Juchniewicz remembered overhearing the conversation: "John told Ollie, 'You know what you are? You're pure bullshit. You're dangerous. You're a disaster!'"

Stanley Sporkin spent a feverish day on the finding with North and people in the operations directorate privy to the weekend transactions. North kept insisting that the operation had to be kept from the oversight committees: they were at a delicate stage in obtaining release of the hostages; a leak could cost their lives. As Sporkin and the others worked, Saint Lucia Airways 707 J6SLF touched down in Tehran with a load of Hawk missiles. North's butt was now on the line. Ghorbanifar had promised the remaining American hostages. And McFarlane had instructed North, no hostages, no weapons.

North's insistence that the oversight committees be cut out troubled the CIA people. But the adroit Sporkin found a loophole. The President was required to inform the oversight committees of a covert action presumably in advance of the action, *except* when the urgency of the situation required that notification be delayed. The Agency thereafter was to make disclosure on a timely basis, which customarily meant within forty-eight hours. The draft finding that Sporkin put before Casey that Tuesday morning read only that notification was not to take place until the President directed.

Though the finding made only scant reference to "munitions," and though North was still saying the cargo shipped was oil-drilling equipment, Casey knew better. He had been a party to the decision to sell arms for hostages; even more, he had become an ardent advocate. He was lucky, however, during his absence, to have on hand the sensible McMahon, who instantly recognized that the Agency had been tainted by involvement in an unauthorized covert scheme, and pushed through the retroactive finding. It was rather like back-dating a contract. It might not be quite kosher; but as Casey had learned from his father long ago, "You don't lie, Bill, but sometimes you have to bend the truth."

Members of the congressional oversight committees would be outraged if they knew of the nonnotification clause. To Casey, that only proved they did not understand their own history, which he could spout chapter and verse. During the Revolutionary War, a courier had brought word that France would provide covert arms and money to the American rebels. Benjamin Franklin and Robert Morris wrote at the time, "We agree in the opinion that it is our indispensable duty to keep it a secret, even from Congress. We find, by fatal experience, the Congress consists of too many members to keep secrets." Even the Founding Fathers knew that Congress leaked.

Before okaying the draft finding, Casey put a call through to Don Regan, the White House chief of staff. He wanted assurance that this last delivery was approved by the President. He then called McFarlane and told him he was sending the finding over for the President's signature.

Usually, the CIA got back from the White House signed copies of findings to prove that it had the President's blessing for covert operations. Days passed, and McMahon grew uneasy. He began badgering Casey to call the White House to see if the finding had been signed yet. Charlie Allen, the counterterrorist expert, was seeing Ollie North, and McMahon also told him to check up on the status of the finding. Allen reported back that Ollie North told him that as of December 5, the finding had been signed and was in North's safe. McMahon would have preferred to have the copy in hand, given North's reputation for veracity. But he was partially relieved: the CIA appeared covered.

After delivery of the Hawk missiles, not a single hostage was released. The wrath of the Iranians had first been aroused, McFarlane learned, because the crates containing the missiles were covered with markings in Hebrew and half of the Hawks were stamped with the star of David. The Iranians also test-fired one Hawk at an Iraqi bomber flying over Kharg Island. The missile came nowhere near close; it was an obsolete model and lacked altitude. The Iranians shipped the other Hawks back. So far, McFarlane's bold opening to Iran was suspended somewhere between tragedy and farce.

Godfrey Sperling's breakfasts at the Sheraton-Carlton Hotel were a Washington institution, a leisurely opportunity for reporters to question public figures over eggs and bacon. In mid-November, the *Christian Science Monitor* columnist invited David Durenberger, chairman of the Senate intelligence committee, as his guest. Much of the questioning was about Casey. To any dispassionate observer, Durenberger was fair, praising Casey as much as knocking him. Balance, however, was not the flavor of the story that came out in the *Washington Post* the next day. A fair-minded reader would likely come away with the impression that Durenberger had had Casey for breakfast along with the bacon and eggs.

George Lauder barged into Casey's office waving the *Post* story. "We can't let this one go by," Lauder warned. Casey read it, and the anger rolled across his bald pate like a crimson wave. He flung the paper aside. " 'Failure to understand the Soviet Union'! That's the first goddamn time Durenberger ever mentioned that!" he exclaimed. "We don't look at brewing crises? We missed the Philippines? The rise of Muslim fundamentalism? What the hell's he talking about? Henry Kissinger told me there's better analysis coming out of this place than any time he was in government. The son of a bitch's files are bulging with our reports—why doesn't Durenberger read them before he starts pissing all over me in public? And what the hell is the chairman of the Senate intelligence committee doing blabbing in front of a room full of reporters? I'm going to send that guy a letter that will burn his hands. And I'm going to send a copy to the *Washington Post*. Just watch—Durenberger will say he was quoted out of context."

Casey's letter to Durenberger began: "When Congressional oversight of the intelligence community is conducted off-the-cuff through the news media and involves the repeated compromise of sensitive intelligence sources and methods, not to mention unsubstantiated appraisals of performance, it is time to acknowledge that the process has gone seriously awry."

Bernie McMahon, the SSCI staff director, learned that Casey's letter was in the mill. All McMahon could foresee was a public brawl with no winners. He believed that the *Washington Post* story was indeed unbalanced. Its headline said that Durenberger had criticized Casey, while other newspaper headlines said that Durenberger had praised him. "I caught Casey on his car phone while he was riding home," McMahon recalled. "I told him that my boss had been misquoted. I pleaded with him not to send his letter. He told me, 'If I don't do something, it will look like I rolled over at the Agency. I'll look like a wimp.' "

The *Post* ran Casey's letter and a rebuttal by Durenberger side by side on the November 17 op-ed page. "In Casey's view," Durenberger wrote, "the public has no right to know how effectively the CIA does its job. . . . The head of the U.S. intelligence community does not feel that the intelligence agencies should be accountable to the American people." All Casey's counteroffensive had done was provoke another public criticism.

Casey was further upset by what he saw as Durenberger's loose control over the intelligence committee's staff. The week before the Sperling breakfast, wags on the SSCI staff had decided to have a little fun at Casey's expense over the Yurchenko affair. They drafted a mock press release headlined "Casey the Defector." The release had Durenberger supposedly saying, "Mr. Casey's defection to Moscow would have 'mixed' effects on American intelligence operations." And, the spoof went on, "Mr. Casey was repeatedly subjected to such torture and abuse at the hands of U.S. authorities as being repeatedly required to appear before the Senate Select Committee on Intelligence." Word leaked to the *New York Times*, which printed the release, making clear that it was a gag. Casey did not find it funny.

He had shaken his head over the stories swirling around Durenberger—that he had left his wife and was having an affair with his secretary, that his children had drug problems, that the guy lived in some sort of monastery. The month before, a story had made the rounds in Washington of a public fracas between Durenberger and his mistress at Washington National Airport. According to an account in the *St. Paul Pioneer Press and Dispatch*, "Durenberger was preparing to board a flight to Minnesota when the woman loudly accosted him. . . . She accused Durenberger of ruining her life, and the contents of her purse were scattered after she swung it or threw it at the Senator."

To Casey, it was insane. This man was not merely on the committee to which he was supposed to reveal the state's deepest secrets; he was the chairman! Casey had signed a pact with the SSCI the year before, after the mining fiasco. He had agreed, at Pat Moynihan's insistence, that "notification . . . will be provided to the SSCI as soon as practicable and *prior* to the implementation of the actual [covert] activity."

Durenberger's behavior made it easier for him to go along with not notifying Congress of a covert action. It was shortly after his public flap with the chairman that Casey approved the draft presidential finding Sporkin put in front of him on arms for Iran. Besides, he had a loophole for seemingly breaking his word. He had signed the agreement with Moynihan and Goldwater—and by now, they were both gone from the SSCI.

In November 1985, General Manuel Noriega visited Casey at the old Executive Office Building. Though Noriega held no civilian title, he ran Panama from his post as head of the Panamanian Defense Force.

Noriega had made his way up through the intelligence side of the army, the real power in Panama. He had been spotted early by the CIA. By now, his association with the Agency went back nearly twenty-five years, through seven presidential administrations and even more DCIs. He had taken CIA money when Vice-President George Bush was director of Central Intelligence. Reportedly, he was on the payroll for $110,000 a year. But it was nothing so clumsy. As one CIA officer described the arrangement, "Money would be paid by the Agency, let's say, 'to train Panamanian army officers in counterintelligence,' and Noriega would put it in his pocket."

The meeting this November was at least Casey's third encounter with Noriega. He had met him first in Panama on the trip with North in 1984 and later at Foxhall Crescent during a Noriega trip to Washington. During dinner that evening, Casey remarked that they were sitting on land once owned by Nelson Rockefeller. As true a friend as Latin America ever had, Noriega commented, to which Casey's response was total silence.

During that visit, Noriega said he wanted to pick up some presents for his family. Casey placed him in the hands of Dewey Clarridge, and since Clarridge spoke no Spanish, John Horton had gone along. Horton, a published novelist, studied the visitor with a practiced eye. "Dewey and I took him to an Italian restaurant in the Arlington Towers in northern Virginia that afforded a magnificent view of the Potomac," Horton recalled. "Noriega looked to me to have black, white, and Indian blood, a cruel-looking man, but unctuous and servile around people more powerful than himself, like Casey. Afterward, we helped him finish his shopping, which consisted mostly of a load of VCRs and stereos."

Three months before this latest November 1985 visit, Noriega had shoved aside Nicolás Ardita Barletta, the first democratically elected Panamanian president in sixteen years, and had installed the vice-president in his place. "You make it tough to have a good relationship with you when you just sweep aside democracy," Casey warned. "It's hard to defend dealing with you."

According to those present, however, Casey did not discuss Noriega and drug trafficking, for which the United States would later invade Panama and bring the dictator back to stand trial. Casey was, of course, thoroughly aware of Noriega's involvement in drugs. But as John McMahon put it, "Not all our sources are people you'd take home to meet mother. You have to use them anyway."

And Casey also knew full well that Noriega was working both sides of the street—indeed, the curbs and the center stripe as well, since he had profitable intelligence arrangements with the United States, Cuba, the Sandinistas, Palestine, Libya, and Syria. "He'd come and tell us what Castro was doing," Horton recalled. "Then he'd reverse course and tell Castro about us." The CIA also knew that Noriega was letting both Nicaragua and Cuba use Panamanian banks to evade U.S. trade embargoes. At the same time, he was allowing the United States to use Howard Air Force Base in Panama to send spy planes over Nicaragua, a violation of the canal treaties. The Agency also had reports that Noriega had allowed the KGB to set up a station in Panama City. Still, Casey had concluded the intelligence that the man gave the United States had dollar value. "You couldn't buy Noriega," John McMahon observed, "but you could rent him."

As for Noriega's involvement in drugs, it was not so much a question of the CIA turning a blind eye. As Bernie McMahon of the SSCI described Noriega's methods, "This guy isn't standing in front of a high school dealing coke. Big drug money comes into Panama to be laundered. Some bank puts the money in an account. Maybe Noriega, or his cousin, or his brother-in-law owns a piece of the bank. The money is fungible. It mixes with the rest of the bank's money. How do you prove that the money Noriega or his brother-in-law take out is drug money?" Whatever the arrangement, the profits were staggering. A money launderer for the Colombian drug cartel claimed that Noriega was making as much as $4 million a month from bank-skimming operations.

As Noriega left Casey's office that fall, Casey remarked to his staff, "This guy presents a serious management problem."

Nothing stirred the wrath of CIA officials more than allegations that the Agency not only looked the other way at the drug trade but used drug operations as an instrument of clandestine policy. "That's enraging," one official responded hotly on being asked. "We've got kids too. Do you think we're stupid enough to think we can isolate the impact of multimillion-dollar drug deals so they don't touch us and our families?"

Beyond dispute, drug money was aiding the contras. General Paul Gorman served until 1985 as the chief of the U.S. Southern Command, based in Panama. When Gorman was asked directly if the contras benefited from drug money, he answered, "The most ready source of money, big money, easy money, sure money, is the narcotics racket . . . particularly if they [the contras] had been on somebody's payroll and had their funds cut off. It would be the natural recourse of these people."

And the motive of the drug dealers? Generosity? Hatred of communism? The advancement of free enterprise? Felix Rodriguez was a former CIA official involved in the contra supply operation with North. Rodriguez was suspected of obtaining drug money for the contras. Vice-President Bush had known Rodriguez for years, going back to Bush's leadership of the CIA. Rodriguez was said to have had frequent contact with Bush's staff, and three meetings with Bush himself, after he became Vice-President. And so if the lords of the drug cartel dealt with a man like Felix Rodriguez, they drew the conclusion that they were buying goodwill for themselves from the Reagan administration—maybe even immunity. The money they gave the contras was an insurance policy, and cheap insurance at that.

The official policy of the CIA, as Alan Fiers put it, was: "We do not work with people involved in the drug trade. We don't hire them. We don't condone their activities. And when drug trafficking comes to our attention, we report it to law-enforcement officials."

But it was not that simple. People who were adept at bringing intelligence out of Iran or Afghanistan were often the same people who knew how to bring narcotics out. Terrorist groups also formed marriages of convenience with drug dealers. They could be useful to each other: the terrorists needed the dealers' money; the dealers needed the terrorists' routes. And so the CIA, in seeking to penetrate terrorist organizations, at times found itself dealing with drug traffickers. As the Justice Department or the Drug Enforcement Agency closed in on a suspect, they were occasionally waved off—the suspect turned out to be a CIA asset. As so often, the Agency operated in a swamp of moral ambiguity. What were the priorities when the choice was to thwart a car bombing or turn in a drug peddler?

"It's tricky," Bernie McMahon concluded. "Over at the committee, we knew that the CIA had to deal with drug people to get information and to penetrate terrorist organizations, or to recruit informers. But we did not believe that the CIA was acquiescing or cooperating in the drug trade." McMahon's predecessor, Rob Simmons, a CIA covert operations veteran, concluded: "The CIA is not in the business of running drugs. Which is not to say that they don't deal with some awful people who are."

Members of the oversight committees like Joe Biden and Pat Leahy were the foes in Casey's eyes. Eddie Boland, author of the hateful amendment, might well expect to be numbered among them. Boland had previously chaired HPSCI for seven years, but he was now off the committee. Casey was reminded at a senior staff meeting that the custom was to honor a chairman and key members with an Agency medal when their service ended. Yes, the Massachusetts Democrat had pushed his amendment relentlessly for three years, had finally won and thrown the stoutest roadblock of all against Casey's hopes for the contras. But that was not the whole of Eddie Boland. The man had also fought against Jimmy Carter's efforts to emasculate the CIA. He had pumped money into most other covert operations. And, as Casey gratefully recognized, Eddie Boland was not a leaker; furthermore, he did not publicly dump on Bill Casey. "Give him the Seal Medallion," Casey ordered. Casey personally presented the medal to Boland at a ceremony at Langley that December.

———

On December 10, Casey was summoned to an NSPG meeting in the Oval Office. A major change was brewing in the Iran-arms-hostage situation. Casey arrived to find the President, Cap Weinberger, Don Regan, Vice-Admiral John Poindexter, and Bud McFarlane present. Secretary of State Shultz was off to Europe. McFarlane was there in an anomalous position: he had resigned as national security adviser on November 30, and Poindexter had been appointed his successor on December 4.

The expressionless admiral was no more physically prepossessing than his predecessor. Still, Poindexter possessed the seeming credentials of brilliance and leadership. As an Annapolis midshipman, he had scored a rare triumph: he graduated first academically in a class of more than nine hundred and was also the midshipman brigade commander. The only other military academy graduate ever to have taken such double honors was Douglas MacArthur at West Point. Poindexter subsequently earned a Ph.D. in nuclear physics and commanded a destroyer squadron. For the past fifteen years, however, he had been a political sailor, assigned to policy posts that eventually brought him to the NSC in 1981.

He was a precise, orderly man who seemed misplaced amid the machinations of the White House. He also seemed unsuited for the glare of publicity in his new post. He loathed the press and disliked dealing with Congress. His passions were solitary: he liked to close his office door and reprogram his computer; at home, he liked to make furniture and tinker with his car.

Tony Dolan remembered stopping by Casey's office a few days before Poindexter's appointment. Casey was just hanging up the phone and told Dolan, "That was the President. He told me he's going to name John Poindexter NSC adviser. I'm not happy, but it's a done deal. The guy just hasn't got the weight."

But the admiral's loyalty to his President was incandescent. On the morning of December 5, his second day on the job, Poindexter had gone in to see Reagan for the regular nine-thirty national security briefing. He had with him the retroactive finding covering the November 25 arms shipment, the one John McMahon was so eager to have signed. The President signed the finding on the spot with no questions asked. But afterward, Poindexter studied the single page with growing uneasiness. Its language, he concluded, was "too narrow, too colloquial." The finding was a flat arms-for-hostages arrangement. It had not tied the risky deal to the loftier strategic purpose of improved relations with Iran. If this crude piece of paper ever became public, Poindexter reasoned, it could badly embarrass the President. No copy of this finding was leaving the office, he decided, not even for the CIA.

Five days later, the NSPG gathered in the Oval Office so that McFarlane could report on presumably one of his last duties for his government. He had just returned from a meeting in London with Manucher Ghorbanifar and other Iranian and Israeli figures. McFarlane seemed subdued, humbled. His resignation had been prompted in part by the failure of his Iranian initiative. He had reached out boldly for national security stardom and found himself instead face down in the mud. As one colleague described him at this point, "Bud went through what people in the old days called a nervous breakdown."

McFarlane had gone to London to deliver a message to the Iranians and Israelis: the deal was off; the United States would no longer engage in transactions to sell arms for hostages. Now he was back to report on that meeting. Casey said little but was scribbling notes as McFarlane spoke. As for Ghorbanifar, McFarlane said, "this is a person of no integrity, and I would not do any more business with him. He is not trustworthy and has a different agenda from our own. He is not a satisfactory intermediary. I recommend that you have nothing further to do with this person or with these arms transfers."

With that disclosure, the genial mien of Ronald Reagan darkened. He spoke mildly, not pushing his view but hoping against hope. Couldn't they just let the Israelis go ahead without the United States getting involved, except to agree to replenish? Someone pointed out gently that this was what they had been doing. The President went on: "That means another Christmas with the hostages in captivity. It sure makes me look powerless and inept." What about the opening to Iranian moderates that McFarlane had spoken of so brightly just months before? the President asked.

"The only moderates in Iran," Cap Weinberger commented, "are in the cemetery." The meeting ended with most participants assuming that the arms-for-hostages deal was dead.

But Casey had become an astute reader of Ronald Reagan. When he got back to Langley, he had Betty Murphy type up his notes of the meeting. He had written: "As the meeting broke up, I had the idea that the President had not entirely given up on encouraging the Israelis to carry on with the Iranians. I suspect he would be willing to run the risk and take the heat in the future if this will lead to springing the hostages."

On December 19, Michael Ledeen, the NSC consultant whose trips to Israel had helped sow the seed of the Iranian initiative, visited Casey. Ledeen told Casey that the administration should be seeking geopolitical objectives, particularly rapprochement with Iran—once this happened, release of the hostages would follow naturally.

Casey listened to this bearded academic with a knowing smile. He suffered from the disease of intellectuals, rationality. Yes, Casey said, it was chiefly a political matter. But you have to understand Ronald Reagan. The average American did not give a hoot in hell about geopolitical chess and "openings to moderates." But a brother, a father, a husband held in captivity was something people could grasp; and their release was something that would move Americans. Ronald Reagan understood this because he felt that way himself. The President recently had met again with families of the hostages and had to tell them that their loved onces would not be free this Christmas. The experience had left him emotionally drained. Reagan also understood that the hostage crisis of 1979–80 had destroyed the Carter presidency. You had to work with the President you had, Casey told Ledeen. You had to respect his priorities. That meant, get the hostages out first, and then move on to the high-level stuff.

After getting the lecture in realpolitik, Ledeen mentioned something that could buttress the President's lingering hopes. Maybe McFarlane was disillusioned with Ghorbanifar, Ledeen said, but he still had faith. "You don't just walk away from such a useful character," Ledeen concluded. Would Ghorbanifar take another lie detector test? Casey wanted to know. Ledeen said that he would ask.

After Michael Ledeen left, Casey told a stunned Clair George to take another look at Manucher Ghorbanifar.

For Stanley Sporkin, his failure to get a federal judgeship the year before was as though a dream had been snatched from him just as it grazed his fingertips. Without any prompting, Casey had gone back to the President and persuaded him to nominate Sporkin again in April of 1985. This time Sporkin's appointment was getting flak from both right and left. The conservatives branded him a hot-eyed New Deal Democrat, when in fact he had been a Republican committeeman in his native Philadelphia. From the left, Senator Joe Biden, serving on the Judiciary Committee as well as the SSCI, reportedly had stalled Sporkin's confirmation because the man was so close to Casey.

Casey launched an all-out offensive. He called Senator Edward M.

Kennedy, the liberal power on the Judiciary Committee. He emphasized Sporkin's brilliant enforcement career at the SEC, the very SEC where Teddy Kennedy's father had trailblazed as the first chairman. Ollie North, doubtless with Casey's guidance, reportedly was working the conservative side of the committee, making the difficult case that "Stanley Sporkin is one of us" and crediting him with performing legal miracles in crafting findings for covert operations.

On December 16, Sporkin was confirmed by the Senate as a Federal District Court judge for the District of Columbia.

Afterward, two of his friends, Larry King, the radio and television talk show host, and Herbert Cohen, who had written a book entitled *You Can Negotiate Anything*, decided to take Sporkin to lunch to celebrate. They were delighted when Casey agreed to join them at Washington's Palm restaurant.

King later described the lunch: "All of us were city boys who had pulled our way up—Herb Cohen and me from Brooklyn, Stanley from Philadelphia, and Casey from Queens. It was warm, nostalgic, a lot of laughs about big-city playgrounds and sitting on stoops on hot summer nights. Casey was the quintessential New Yorker. His eating habits were like my eating habits—you heard us eat. And the voice! If you closed your eyes, it was the voice of a Teamsters official or a guy delivering a package. I had trouble picturing Casey having lunch in Palm Springs with William French Smith."

King could not suppress the interviewer in him and peppered Casey with questions. What did he think of George Bush? "He's a namby-pamby," Casey said. "I don't know where the guy stands on anything." What about a presidential contest between Bush and New York's governor, Mario Cuomo, in 1988? "Cuomo would murder Bush," Casey answered. "He'd wipe him out." "You like Cuomo?" King asked, surprised. "Mario Cuomo is my kind of guy," Casey admitted. "Maybe I don't agree with him on everything, but I could back him." "But you're a Republican," King interjected. "Don't forget I'm an American first," Casey answered. "He'd be the right man to follow Ronald Reagan."

And what about Ronald Reagan? King wanted to know. "The President has one big weakness," Casey said with his mouth full. "He's incapable of firing anybody. He can't dress anybody down. He never blows up over a failure. Call somebody into the office and give him a chewing out? He just can't do it. It's beyond him. Do you remember that Bill Grieder story on David Stockman in the *Atlantic* magazine? His own budget director made the President look like a fool. If he asked me, I would have told Ronald Reagan, 'This guy is a son of a bitch. He's a prick. Bury him.' Instead, do you know what Reagan did? He called Stockman into the office, and as soon as he walked in, Reagan said to him, 'They quoted you out of context, right, Dave? They didn't print the whole thing. What you gave them was good and bad in balance and all they printed was the bad, right? I know the way they work, Dave.' Reagan let Stockman off the hook. He never put the fear of God in him. Instead, they wound up having a nice, relaxed visit." And then the man with the delivery man's voice quoted Machiavelli's *The Prince* on the place of intimidation in the makeup of a successful leader.

Casey lost his cattle prod that December: Herb Meyer told him it was time to go. Meyer had made enemies among the career bureaucrats, and they were waiting in ambush for him. "When I told Bill I wanted to resign," Meyer recalled, "he said all the right things, how he couldn't get along without me. But he agreed with me." To Casey, this particular hair shirt had served its purpose, and he was ready to take it off the backs of his analytical staff. Casey gave Meyer a final word of advice plucked from his own life: "Go out and do what you want to do. Get to the top. And then you can come back at the top."

There was also a departure from the Casey household that December. Bernadette, the apple of his eye, married her longtime companion and Casey's protégé, Owen Smith. Casey was deeply content. He had given the hand of his daughter to a trusted friend. The couple were married on Saturday, December 7, in Old Westbury, Long Island. Casey retained his old speech coach, Betty Cashman, to coach him for the wedding toast. Bernadette and Owen had dated for fifteen years. Casey had grown impatient over the marathon courtship. At one point, the staunch old Catholic had advised his surprised daughter, "Go ahead, get married. You'll like it. And if you don't, you can always get out of it."

31.

"Qaddafi Belongs Dead"

In January of 1986, as Bill Casey began his sixth year in office, he was approaching his seventy-third birthday. His staff noticed no diminution in his pace. He liked to boast that as DCI, he had visited every country on the globe that cooperated with the United States. He was also a fixture on the Washington social scene. "Bill never turned down dinner at a foreign embassy," Sophia remembered. "We went to several receptions a week, and he would work the room like a candidate." The Caseys also held weekly dinner parties, usually for a dozen or so people. "We would hobnob one night, and then the next day he'd show up at the house with some old high-school friend," Sophia recalled. He belonged to twelve social and country clubs. He was certainly the most visible spy master in the world.

The month before, while Bud McFarlane was telling the Israelis and the Iranians that the arms deal was off, Ollie North had been talking it up. He told Israeli officials that he had in mind a deserving beneficiary for the profits that had been made on the sales thus far: the freedom fighters in the Honduran wilds, cut off from support by a short-sighted U.S. Congress. Later, North was to credit Manucher Ghorbanifar with the idea of shuttling profits from the Iranian arms sales to the contras. But the idea had first popped into his own febrile imagination, as he later admitted. North's attitude was critical, since, with McFarlane gone, Poindexter had assigned Ollie as his man on the apparently moribund account.

One of the early visitors to the White House in the new year was Amiram Nir, adviser on counterterrorism to Israel's prime minister, Shimon Peres. Nir had been involved in the arms-for-hostages transactions from the beginning. As far as Israel knew, the initiative now looked dead. And so Peres had dispatched Amiram Nir to breathe life into a corpse. On January 2, Nir met secretly with Poindexter and North. Nir's message was compelling. Iran was losing its war with Iraq. Iran's defeat would mean further radicalization of the country. Iran would become even more vulnerable to Soviet penetration, which would put Moscow closer to the Gulf oil states. However, Nir's argument ran, U.S. arms could still tip the scales against Iraq. America should not give up so soon.

The argument was full of holes. It could equally be argued that the defeat of Iran by Iraq would be desirable because it would likely bring down Khomeini, and the country might again turn to the West. In fact, the best intelligence that Casey's analysts were coming up with at this point was the opposite of Nir's message. An NIE then in the works showed that Iran now held the upper hand in the Gulf war, with Iraq suffering serious military and morale setbacks.

At one point, Nir suggested that they could overcharge for the weapons and pass the profits along to the contras. It was like North talking to himself. As for Poindexter, he knew the President's priority: get the hostages back. Nir had been preaching to the converted. Poindexter decided to put the plan to the President again.

The CIA, particularly John McMahon, would demand a finding to cover the CIA's involvement in any renewed arms shipments. And so North immediately contacted Stanley Sporkin, who was still at the Agency waiting to assume his judgeship. He needed a new finding drafted, North explained.

The two men met that evening at eight. North looked haggard; he was getting by on two and three hours' sleep a night. He had roughed out a finding for Sporkin to check. Sporkin immediately spotted two troubling features. Like the previous finding, this one also directed the DCI not to inform Congress. Further, the finding mentioned nothing about the release of hostages. Its stated objective was the opening of relations with Iranian moderates. Why had the hostages been left out? Sporkin wanted to know. The State Department thought it degraded the higher purposes of the operation, North told him. It was late. Both men had put in a long day. They decided to take up the matter again the next day.

Sporkin reworked North's draft to include two options, notification or nonnotification of Congress. The President ought to be the one deciding which route to go, Sporkin reasoned. As North had requested, Sporkin also left out any mention of hostages. Sporkin then arranged for himself and North to clear the finding with Casey, who had just returned from a short vacation at his home in Palm Beach.

They met in a downstairs study at Casey's home in Foxhall Crescent. The DCI had virtually just come in the door, and Sporkin was much relieved to share the responsibility. He was uneasy about the finding. North had brought along another draft that left out the options Sporkin had included for the President to choose from; it simply directed that Congress *not* be informed. The antennae in Sporkin, the old securities cop, were still quivering over the other omission. As Sporkin described his wariness, "A finding was analogous to an offering statement in the securities business—you want to put everything in it like an insurance policy, so you're protected all around. But this policy had a glaring omission. Hostages were a key part of the deal, but the finding said nothing about them."

Casey, however, seemed untroubled. He handed the draft back to North and said, "Okay, get the President to look at it."

North and Sporkin got up to leave. They had reached the front door when Sporkin could not stand it any longer. "Tell me again," he said to North, "why aren't we putting in the hostages?" North repeated the alleged State Department objections—unconvincingly, Sporkin thought. "Wait a minute, I want to talk to Bill," Sporkin said, and went back to Casey. "You know," he told him, "this may be the most sensitive finding we'll ever deal with. Bad enough it says you're not supposed to notify Congress. On top of that, it leaves out what I think is the most important element—the hostages. That ought to be in there." Casey was impatient, eager to get on with other matters. "All right. Go ahead—put it in," he said gruffly.

Sporkin had rendered his last substantial service to Casey. Soon afterward, he left Langley and was sworn in as a federal judge.

On January 6, Poindexter went in to see the President for the regular nine-thirty briefing. Among his papers was the latest version of the finding, which now, at Sporkin's insistence, mentioned the release of American hostages along with the pursuit of Iranian moderates. The document was still in draft form as Poindexter set it in front of the President. He started to brief him on it when Reagan took out his pen and signed the draft unread.

On Saturday, January 11, an annoyed Manucher Ghorbanifar reported to a room at the new Four Seasons Hotel in Georgetown. He was to be polygraphed for the third time. He was hoping for an older, sympathetic operator who would understand that he was a special case. His hopes sank when he entered the room to find a young operator who seemed totally unaware of his importance. He left five hours later and went to Scott's restaurant in Georgetown to meet

Roy Furmark, Michael Ledeen, and a girlfriend of the Iranian. Ledeen described Ghorbanifar as "a basket case."

On Monday morning, Clair George brought Casey the polygraph results. Ghorbanifar had been questioned in fifteen areas. He showed deception in thirteen (he got his name and nationality right). He lied about his connections inside Iran. He lied about his knowledge of terrorist organizations. Most damning, the polygraph indicated that he had known in advance that no hostages would be released as a result of the Hawk deliveries the previous November. As Clair George explained, "Guys lined up outside of my office, fighting to get in to tell what a crook Ghorbanifar was." "Bill," George told Casey, "the guy's no good."

At the eleventh hour, however, the wily Ghorbanifar managed to throw himself a life line. He had earlier sent Casey a batch of photographs. Casey put down the polygraph results and studied the pictures. "They looked like group shots of the annual Elks convention of terrorists," Clair George recalled. "We could not imagine how Ghorbanifar came by them. Casey was impressed." He wanted Manucher Ghorbanifar kept in the game.

On January 7, Casey went to the White House for a meeting of the NSPG in the residential part of the White House. Present were the President, Poindexter, Shultz, Weinberger, Regan, and Bush. The main item up for discussion was the resumption of arms sales to Iran. The President already had signed the finding that Poindexter had put in front of him a few days before. But the Admiral was a prudent man and realized that not much thought—indeed, none—had gone into the President's reflexive approval. The issue should still be thrashed out.

Poindexter described the Israelis' willingness, even eagerness, to keep shipping arms as long as they were replenished. Next, Casey spoke up for the proposal. The meticulous Poindexter watched with genteel distaste as Casey spoke from a fistful of scribbled notes. "There are risks," Casey warned, "particularly if this thing blows"; but the risks were worth taking. He went into his briefcase and extracted photographs of the very apartment buildings in Beirut where the hostages were reportedly held. If the CIA's information was that precise, the President wanted to know, why couldn't a detachment of Marines or Green Berets storm these buildings and free the prisoners? Cap Weinberger looked pained. How long, he asked, would it take for a platoon of Green Berets to be spotted on the streets of Beirut and for the hostages to be murdered in consequence? As one difficulty after another was raised in liberating just five men, the irony dawned on them that all of America's military might was virtually useless against a handful of fanatics.

There were legal obstacles too. The Arms Export Control Act required that countries, such as Israel, who ship arms to a third country, such as Iran, had to report these transactions to the U.S. government. Once that word reached the bureaucracy, there would be no keeping it secret. So far, that problem had been avoided by keeping the earlier shipments small enough to be exempt from the reporting requirement. But Poindexter was now talking of larger deliveries. Casey had the answer, another crack in the law: the CIA could purchase arms from the Department of Defense and sell them to other countries under something called the Economy Act. These sales did not have to be reported. In that instant, the debate took a crucial turn. Until now, the shipments had involved arms sold by Israel to Iran. Now they were talking, for the first time, about the United States selling arms directly to Iran.

George Shultz hated the plan. America had virtually shouted to the world its policy of no truck with terrorists. The United States had initiated an embargo on arms trade with Iran. Shultz's people, and Casey's for that matter, were out there right now pressuring countries all around the world *not* to sell arms to Iran. If the administration continued on this course and was found out, the repercussions for the United States were going to be dreadful.

Admiral Poindexter explained that they were talking about a covert operation. If anything did go wrong, the President would of course have a cover story. He would be protected by plausible deniability. "Plausible deniability is nonsense," Shultz said, and slumped back in his chair, a man who knew he was right but also beaten.

The President had been listening with a frown, his fingers in constant motion, drumming them on the table, doodling little faces on his talking-point cards. He had said little thus far, but now he spoke. They wouldn't really be selling arms to the Iranians for hostages, would they? The hostages were actually held by Lebanese Shiite groups. It was thin reasoning. But then this was the same man who could say of a cancer operation, "I didn't have cancer. I had something inside of me that had cancer, and it was removed."

The issue of not notifying Congress came up again. Poindexter pointed out that the law required "timely" notification. The shipments could be completed over the next thirty to sixty days. Once the hostages were safely home, Congress could be let in on the secret.

One more item had to be covered. Before the Iranians would resume the deal, they wanted intelligence from U.S. spy satellites to help them in their war with Iraq. Formally, the United States had taken a position of neutrality. In fact, it had been covertly providing limited intelligence to the *other* side, to the Iraqis, out of fear of the consequences of a victory for the Ayatollah Khomeini.

Casey was perfectly aware of a revised NIE then being prepared in his own agency showing that Iran was currently winning the war. He said nothing of it and instead let stand the assumption that Iran was losing. He had no problem with providing the intelligence the Iranians wanted.

Ten days later, on January 17, the President signed an updated finding authorizing the direct shipment of arms from the United States to Iran, superseding the finding of January 5. The deal was for phased shipment of four thousand TOWs. And Congress was still not to be informed.

Months before, Dick Helms had advised Casey, "The only thing you can't tell Congress about are operations you shouldn't be doing in the first place." That advice was far from Casey's mind at this point. He was ready to run the risks. He liked a saying of David Lloyd George, "You can't cross a great canyon in two small jumps."

Soon afterward, Casey was traveling in the Middle East. While he was in Riyadh, the station chief brought him a secret, high-priority message from McMahon. "We have been asked to provide a map depicting the order of battle on the Iran/Iraq border showing units, troops, tanks and what have you," McMahon had cabled. "Everyone here at Headquarters advises against this operation." He mentioned that he had pointed out to Poindexter that "providing defensive missiles was one thing but when we provide intelligence on the order of battle we are giving the Iranians the wherewithal for offensive action." He feared that the United States was crossing a dangerous line, "tilting in a direction which could cause the Iranians to have a successful offense against the Iraqis with cataclysmic results." McMahon added at the end of the cable to Casey that he was complying with the request, against his better judgment. That was what Casey admired about McMahon; in the end, he was a good soldier.

The man was loyal, but crafty too. When North came to Langley on a Saturday morning to collect the intelligence, he encountered both McMahon and Gates. They had spread out astonishingly detailed photos of the Iran-Iraq front taken by spy satellites. They persuaded North to take only pictures of a segment of the front that the Iranians probably knew about. Not for nothing had McMahon observed Casey's doctrine of minimum compliance.

Casey was back in Washington by January 27 and immediately under pressure from McMahon. All they had was North's word that the President had signed the old finding for the November 25 shipment. And now there was another finding, the one the President had signed January 17, for which they also had no signed copy. How was the CIA going to prove it was acting on orders from higher authority? Casey said that he would look into it.

In February, Casey began mobilizing for the next vote on contra aid, hoping to break the Boland blockade. He arranged to have the Republican congressional leadership invited to the White House for a briefing. They met in the Cabinet Room, a dozen top lawmakers, a handful of White House aides, and Casey. He passed around unmarked brown envelopes and described the contents as documents obtained from Nicaragua that proved the Sandinistas were involved in drug dealing, that they were torn by factionalism, and that they were waging a disinformation campaign to smear the contras as Somocistas. This was the nature of the enemy, as proven, Casey explained, in their own words.

Dave Durenberger turned and whispered to Senator Mark Hatfield, "Is this déjà vu? It sounds like Vietnam all over again—captured documents, the whole bit."

Durenberger started cross-examining Casey. Casey was abrupt. Maybe some people did not understand Marxist expansionism, he observed. Durenberger turned angry; that was stale Cold War scare talk, with even a touch of McCarthyism thrown in. "I think it's outrageous, Mr. Director," Durenberger said, "to portray every senator and congressman who votes against lethal aid for the contras as a stooge of communism."

Casey's staff, the front-line troops who would have to lobby the contra-aid package through Congress, left the White House depressed. Casey the lobbyist still needed work. The campaign was off to a shaky start.

The current deal with Iran called for the CIA to buy arms from the Department of Defense and sell them to Iran, an arrangement that, if revealed, could have a more devastating effect on the CIA than the exposures of the seventies. What Casey needed was a cutout to provide his own plausible deniability.

He summoned Dick Secord again. For present purposes, the man had interesting credentials: Secord had served four tours in Iran, the last one selling U.S. arms to the Shah's air force.

Secord had made a soft landing after he left the Air Force. Thirteen days before his retirement became official, he had gone into business with Albert Hakim, who ran a company called Stanford Technology Trade Group International. Hakim was Iranian born, now an American citizen who had gotten out of Iran two steps ahead of the Shah. Hakim was fifty years old, with the pleasant manner of a low-key car salesman. He had continued to prosper selling arms and security systems all over the world. One of his customers had been the U.S. Congress, which bought equipment from Hakim to secure its hearing rooms.

Hakim was now working with Secord buying arms, ammunition, and equipment for the contras. He had no illusions about his motivation. He told North and Secord, "You're soldiers. You get the medals. I get the money."

Casey had come up with an arrangement that would shield the CIA in the Iran initiative. The Agency would buy arms from the Pentagon, but instead of selling them directly to Iran it would pass them to a private broker. The private broker would work through intermediaries in Israel to get the arms delivered to Iran. Hence, a double cutout for the CIA. Now he needed a broker. The obvious choice was Dick Secord.

Ollie North was willing to undertake bold enterprises, even to shift money from one covert operation to another, halfway around the world. But after a lifetime in the military, he was also part bureaucrat. Bureaucrats went through channels and obtained authority from superiors. And so he drafted a memo to the President proposing that profits from the sale of arms to Iran be diverted to help the Nicaraguan resistance. At the bottom, in the White House style, he had included a place for the President to check "approve" or "disapprove." North turned the memorandum over to Poindexter, who he assumed would buck it up to the President.

On February 15, the first thousand of a planned four thousand TOWs were delivered to Iran. By February 23, the five remaining American hostages were to be released. The CIA had obtained the TOWs from the Pentagon for approximately $3,500 apiece. Again, Ghorbanifar had managed to extract $10,000 for each of them from the Iranians. Mutual distrust still prevailed between buyer and seller, and so Adnan Khashoggi again had come through with a bridge loan, this time $10 million. The Pentagon was paid $3.5 million. The remaining $6.5-million profit raised a key question. If U.S. government–owned weapons were sold at a profit, to whom did the profits belong? There was no doubt in the minds of Secord and Hakim. They put the money into the same Lake Resources account in which the contra funds were kept, the account that Secord controlled.

After the delivery, the Iranians complained that they were not expecting TOWs; they had been told they would be getting a highly sophisticated American air-to-air missile, the Phoenix—that was what Ghorbanifar had told them to expect. And he probably had, as he led both sides around by the nose. No hostages were released by Iran.

In supporting the scheme, Poindexter had assured skeptics on the NSPG that if it did not work after the first thousand TOWs, they would quit. But the initiative had acquired a life of its own. Even a sale that produced no hostages was not a total loss from North's standpoint: there were the profits to be diverted to the contras. The middlemen were taking their cut. Adnan Khashoggi did not do badly, either. His $10 million was out for exactly two months, on which he took back $2 million in interest.

The good soldier had had it. Toward the end of February, John McMahon went into Casey's office and announced that he was going to resign. Casey sat back, and crossed his feet on the desk as though sighting McMahon between his shoes. "I suppose you're going off to some aerospace industry," Casey said.

McMahon had put in thirty-four years with the CIA; and in fact, he did have an attractive offer from Lockheed. He was also tired of providing target practice for the right wing. Campaigns by super-patriot organizations like Free the Eagle and the Federation for American Afghan Action had generated over ten thousand letters to the White House demanding McMahon's resignation. Reflecting later on his decision, McMahon observed, "I didn't like McFarlane. I didn't like Poindexter or North. I fought off as many of their schemes as I went along with. If you're CIA and you can't get along with the NSC, it's goddamned uncomfortable." He was fifty-five years old. It was unlikely that he would ever make DCI, though Casey had thrown out enticing hints. If he wanted a second career, he had better get moving.

John McMahon had served as Casey's conscience, nag, and worry wart. They had fought over Nicaragua and a dozen other operations, most recently over intelligence for Iran. Yet, as Ed Juchniewicz observed, "Of all the people at the Agency, the one who came as close to being a friend as Casey allowed was John. You could see it in the rough way they dealt with each other, in the way John talked back to Casey in front of other people, most of whom Casey scared the hell out of."

Casey accepted the decision, but he had plans for McMahon. "Forget that corporate stuff," he told him. "You're too smart. You belong in investment banking, or broadcasting—maybe publishing. I'll tell you what: if you'll give it a try, I'll stake you a million bucks on a handshake." McMahon knew he meant it.

When word went out that he was leaving the Agency, McMahon suddenly found himself the darling of the liberals. Pat Moynihan asked in great umbrage, "I'd like to know why John McMahon was forced out of the government." McMahon found it all uncomfortable, particularly the idea that he had been a voice in the intelligence wilderness crying out against the machinations of a rogue director of Central Intelligence. When asked later what he thought of Casey, McMahon answered, "He was a mental giant in my judgment. He never looked at an event in isolation. He looked at causes and consequences. Everything was part of a continuum of what would follow and what had gone before. Sure, he was an ideologue. But I found him open-minded. In over thirty years in this business, I can tell you, I didn't meet many people who could hold a candle to him."

McMahon's place was taken by the fleetest figure in the Agency fast track, Bob Gates, then forty-three. Casey's choice of Gates was greeted with relief on Capitol Hill, a pro succeeding a pro. Bernie McMahon, the SSCI staff chief, concluded, "Bob wasn't going to talk to the boss the way John did. He's not the kind of guy who's going to say to Casey, 'That's a stupid idea, and if you go through with it, I'm walking out that door.' But he was smart, a good man, a wise choice."

Bobby Ray Inman commented, "Bob Gates is unpopular with some of the people out there because he makes them read and think and work. But I think he's just the best intelligence officer of this generation." High praise, since many in the fraternity thought that distinction belonged to Inman.

———

Two terrorist attacks had occurred the previous December. Two days after Christmas 1985, television screens were filled with scenes of carnage at the Rome and Vienna airports, where terrorists slaughtered nineteen people, including five Americans, one a girl of eleven. Casey suspected that Libya was involved. A notorious terrorist, Abu Nidal, was thought to have masterminded the attacks. And Nidal was known to be in Libya at the time they happened.

Early in 1986, Casey had invited the Washington chapter of the Howard Law School Alumni out to Langley and explained to them how, in his judgment, Qaddafi was virtually the godfather of Middle East terrorism: "As soon as Qaddafi took over, he started looking for a kindred spirit. He found it in the PLO. The PLO was Muslim, revolutionary, anti-imperialist, and fighting Israel. He opened his doors and treasury to the Palestinians. Libya runs twenty-five terrorist training camps. It's their second-largest export, after oil." Casey agreed with another high-ranking national security official, who said of Qaddafi, "He belonged dead."

On April 5, 1986, a powerful bomb went off in La Belle, a West Berlin discotheque frequented by black American GIs, killing an American sergeant outright and a young Turkish woman. Fifty more American servicemen were among the total of 230 injured.

Two messages intercepted by the NSA appeared to leave no doubt as to the perpetrators. A message sent on March 25 from Tripoli, the Libyan capital, to several "People's Bureaus" (the Libyan term for embassies) in Europe, reads, "Prepare to carry out the plan." One of these bureaus was in East Berlin. On the eve of the bombing, two more messages were intercepted from the East Berlin People's Bureau to Tripoli. The first reported, "We have something planned that will make you happy." The second message, arriving virtually as the La Belle bomb went off, read, "An event occurred. You will be pleased with the result."

The Reagan administration had its provocation. The national security team wanted to lash back but faced the President's own order barring political assassination. Ironically, bombers raining death from thirty thousand feet smacked less of assassination than a gunman firing a revolver at point-blank range. The administration seized on this paradox. And so, in retaliation for the discotheque bombing, an air strike was set in motion to hit targets inside Libya, including the compound where Qaddafi lived and worked.

The NSC became the designated planning agency, and its point man was to be the NSC's terrorism chief, Oliver North. Casey's responsibility was IFO, intelligence for operations. People conducting presumably surgical strikes need highly specific information: the exact location of buildings; how many tons of explosives are required; where the antiaircraft batteries are located; their range; which people occupy particular buildings; what their movements are. Casey had few lines into Libya—an officer assigned to the Italian naval mission in Tripoli and one Libyan dissident under cover, hardly enough for the demands of this job. And so he again went to the Israelis, leading experts on intelligence for operations. The Mossad managed to penetrate the intended targets with its own people, and soon the necessary intelligence started flowing back to Langley. Qaddafi and his family occupied a two-story stucco house inside the El Azziya military compound in Tripoli. He spent much of his time working in a nearby camouflaged tent, sometimes well into the night. Qaddafi's movements were charted hour by hour.

The strike was originally set for Thursday, April 11; but the Mossad asked for a delay, since it had not yet been able to extricate all its agents. The following Monday, April 14, late in the afternoon, the leaders of Congress were summoned to a secret meeting in a secure room in the EOB. The air was electric with tension. The President arrived, trailed by Shultz, Weinberger, Casey, Poindexter, and staff aides. Reagan was uncharacteristically subdued, as though assigned a heavier role than he was accustomed to playing. Each administration member had a part. Poindexter described the overall mission. Weinberger briefed on the nuts and bolts—how many aircraft, what bomb load they carried, where they would fly from, how they would refuel. The White House counsel, Peter Wallison, explained the President's authority to act under the War Powers Act. And then it was Casey's turn, as he laid out the justifying intelligence, the record of Qaddafi's involvement in terrorism, the monitoring of communications that seemed to point an unerring finger of guilt at Libya for the discotheque bombing. "He had these notes scribbled on a yellow pad," Wallison recalled. "He got it all out, but in a disorganized fashion." After the briefing, the meeting was opened to questions. A Senate leader asked Casey, "Is Qaddafi in that tent?"

"We don't know," Casey answered. "He might be. He might not be."

During the entire briefing, the word "assassination" was never uttered. The lawmakers were finally released after six p.m. The timing was deliberate; it was too late for any dangerous leaking. Eighteen Air Force F-111s and twelve Navy A-6s were already aloft and would be hitting targets in Libya within the hour.

The Israelis had managed to park a Boeing 707 reconnaissance aircraft at a Tripoli airfield to relay last-minute intelligence. The plane flew out just forty minutes before the first F-111s arrived, reporting that, as of that moment, Qaddafi was working in his tent.

The bombers struck targets in Tripoli and Benghazi, including the El Azziya base. Nine F-111s went against Qaddafi's compound. After-action infrared photography revealed a line of craters running right past the Libyan leader's house and tent. Shortly after the attack, one of Casey's two assets inside Tripoli reported that all eight of Qaddafi's children and his wife had been hospitalized from shock and injuries. A fifteen-month-old child, described as his adopted daughter, had died. But Qaddafi himself had survived, shaken but untouched. One F-111 mistakenly had bombed a residential neighborhood, killing more than one hundred people.

Shortly after the raid, David Halevy of *Time* magazine invited Casey to join him as his guest at the White House correspondents' dinner. Halevy ribbed Casey about trying to "knock off" Qaddafi. Casey became serious. "There was no decision to kill Qaddafi," he insisted. "But if it happened, I was ready to take all the heat you guys could dish out." What was the point of the raid, another reporter at the table asked, if not to get Qaddafi? "There are dissident elements inside Libya," Casey said. "They might have seen their chance to rise up and launch a coup. I'm sorry that didn't happen."

Another reporter asked Casey if, with Qaddafi spared, no major military destruction done, no coup occurring, and a hundred pointless deaths, the raid had not been a failure. West German authorities even disputed the authenticity of the messages between Libya and East Berlin that had triggered the attack. "It'll go down like Grenada," Casey answered coolly. What did that mean? a puzzled reporter asked. "It means," he said, "like Castro and Ortega got the message when we hit Grenada, this attack will scare the hell out of Qaddafi." In the cold-blooded calculus of terrorism and counterterrorism, he could have been right. In the two years following the raid on Libya, no further terrorist attacks on Americans were traced to Qaddafi.

The fate of Joseph F. Fernandez epitomized the confusion created for the CIA by the dual Casey roles. Fernandez had started his professional life as a cop, then made detective sergeant, then began a late-blooming career with the CIA. He had suffered a modest setback when he was among those officially reprimanded for his role in the preparation of the embarrassing "assassination manual" in 1984. Nevertheless, Fernandez, under the pseudonym Tomás Castillo, later was named station chief for Costa Rica. In the pre-Boland era, he had worked with Dewey Clarridge in building the contras. Subsequently, he had received, along with other station chiefs, the Agency's stay-clear guidelines.

But it was not that simple. On a trip back to Washington, Fernandez had had a few beers with Ollie North. Later, North drove him back to his motel; and there, sitting in the parking lot, North started telling Fernandez how William Buckley had been tortured to death. Fernandez had known Buckley. North started to cry; Fernandez found himself crying too. The two men parted, knowing that one true believer had met another.

Early in 1986, North contacted Fernandez: he was arranging for the delivery of privately funded arms to contra forces operating out of Costa Rica; he needed Fernandez's help in passing information for an airdrop. Was that legal? Fernandez wanted to know. "Yes, of course," North assured him. "All you're doing is passing information." As Fernandez later described his reaction, "I didn't ask Clair George. I didn't ask anybody. I made the decision on my own." Clair George doubtless expressed Fernandez's feelings as well as his own when he explained how people in the CIA reacted in such situations: "I suffer from the bureaucrat's disease. When people call me and say, 'I'm calling from the White House,' or the National Security Council, I am inclined to snap to." North subsequently gave Fernandez a KL-43 radio, which allowed them to communicate directly over a secure system without going through CIA communications. What Fernandez appears not to have known is that North had made a similar request for help from the station chief in El Salvador, who, citing Boland, turned him down cold.

On April 23, Joe Fernandez found himself, with Poindexter and North, in the Oval Office with the President of the United States. He had with him the Costa Rican head of security and the man's wife. They had their picture taken with the President. No one from the CIA was present. Fernandez thereafter reportedly served as North's channel to the contras another six times while Boland was in force.

The absence of CIA people in the Oval Office that day, the back-channel communication with North, the refusal of a neighboring station chief to cooperate all raise interesting questions. Was Fernandez acting on his own in violation of CIA guidelines for obeying the Boland Amendment? Had he been conned by North? North later was to claim that Casey had given him the green light to approach Fernandez for help with the airdrops. Possibly true, though by doing so, Casey would have seriously violated his intention of holding the CIA blameless. It is just as easy to believe that North, on his own, had gone directly to Fernandez, as on previous occasions he had gone directly to Dewey Clarridge.

Either way, any qualms Fernandez might have felt doubtless were soothed by what had happened the month before his White House visit. On March 27, in a close 53-to-47 vote, the Senate had approved $100 million in contra aid, including $70 million for lethal support. The House would still have to act. But the first crack in Boland had developed.

On May 15, Poindexter warned North in a message sent over the NSC's PROF (professional office communications) computer system: "I am afraid you are letting your operational role become too public. From now on, I don't want you to talk with anybody else, including Casey, except me about any of your operational roles." "The CIA are really bunglers," Poindexter told North, and he did not trust Casey all that much, either. Poindexter particularly said that he did not want Casey to know about the scheme for diverting a share of the Iranian arms payments to the contras. As he later explained why: "I did not want to put him or anybody else in a position of being evasive in terms of answering [Congress's] questions."

The day after Poindexter sent North the note, on May 16, the President met with the National Security Council. When it was his turn to speak, Casey delivered what he called the "bad news" about Central America. The contras were down to their last $2 million of nonmilitary aid that Congress had allowed. Poindexter was present as Casey spoke. That very day, however, North had written Poindexter a memo happily reporting that $5 million had come in from the Iranian arms sales, which meant that "the resistance support organization now has more than six million available for immediate disbursement." As Casey told the President about the contras' desperate condition, Poindexter said nothing about the infusion of new funds.

Was Casey privy to this information about diverted funds? If he was, would he have given a briefing to the President misleading him about the actual condition of the contras? Mislead the Congress? Quite possibly. But mislead the President, who had said he wanted everything possible done to keep the contras alive? There seemed to be little motive for Casey to do so. Few people choose to bring bad news to the boss, particularly bad news that is not true.

A few days later, Secord and North stopped by Casey's EOB office. North had long since moved from his earlier office. He now commanded a five-room suite in the EOB with a splendid view of the

Ellipse and the Washington Monument—the same view the President had. The three men plunged instantly into the plight of the contras. They were short of everything, North said, including food. And private contributions were drying up. They speculated on the chances of the $100-million package getting through Congress now that the Senate had approved. That had been the easy part, Casey said; the Senate was Republican controlled. The House would be a bitch. They broke up. Again, no mention had been made to him of the new money available to the contras.

In the last week of May, Casey had a special visitor. He closed the door and told Betty Murphy he wanted no interruptions—no phone calls, no pop-ins.

The visitor was George Cave. Casey had brought Cave into the Iran operation a few months before because he spoke fluent Farsi and Mullah and understood most other Iranian dialects. Cave had also been the Agency's station chief in Tehran. Ollie North, whatever his other virtues, was not a linguist. Consequently, in their dealings with Iranians the Americans had become totally dependent on the interpreting of Manucher Ghorbanifar. Cave not only gave North linguistic support but gave Casey a front-row seat on the conduct of the Iranian initiative. Cave's view was especially important to Casey now, because the rashest gamble of all was about to take place.

Thus far, the operation had been a colossal flop. But Ghorbanifar was now assuring North that he could arrange meetings with people at the very top—the Iranian president, the speaker of the parliament, possibly Khomeini's own son. And so a meeting had been arranged for the Americans in Tehran. Casey admired North's nerve; he had less confidence in his judgment. He wanted George Cave along on so delicate a mission. Apart from the participants themselves, only the President, the Vice-President, Don Regan, Poindexter, and Casey knew of the journey to Tehran. Casey told Cave, "George, it has to be your decision. You know better than anybody what the risks are. I could still call up the President and cancel it."

Casey was asking Cave to reenter a city where fifty-two American hostages had been held captive for more than a year, where the plots to bomb the American embassy and Marine Corps barracks and to seize William Buckley had been abetted, possibly even hatched. To Casey, the mission evoked the atmosphere of London forty years before—putting men into the enemy heartland. "I don't think anything will happen to us," Cave said. Casey was filled with admiration.

Poindexter believed that on delivery of the next shipment, the Iranians would turn over all five hostages and the remains of William Buckley. But Cave himself was more cautious. "We may get two or three out," he said. "But they'll never let them all go until there's more movement on the Dawa 17." The Dawa 17 were members of an extremist Muslim group, Al Dawa (the Call), convicted of the truck bombing of the U.S. embassy in Kuwait. The United States had been firmly behind Kuwait in its refusal to release these terrorists.

Cave left Casey's office and went home. He told his wife that he would be gone for a few days on a business trip but did not tell her where.

Casey also talked to Ollie North on the eve of the mission. North's account of his visit rings rather more dramatically then Cave's. "Director Casey raised another issue," North later recalled. "The government might disavow the entire thing." And so, Casey reportedly told him, "I am not going to let you go unless you are prepared to deal with the issue of torture." According to North, "Director Casey told me that he would not concur in my going on the advance trip unless I took with me the means by which I could take my own life. I did not tell my wife and children that."

On Sunday, May 25, George Cave, with North, McFarlane, Howard Teicher (the NSC's Near East specialist), Amiram Nir (Israel's man on counterterrorism), and a communications technician, boarded a white, unmarked Israeli 707 and flew out of Tel Aviv, headed for Tehran. McFarlane was by now a private citizen in a consultant status, yet somehow the leader of the mission. North and McFarlane got along well, better than North and Poindexter. McFarlane kept a computer terminal in his home linked to the NSC. He and North talked about North's leaving the government so that they could form a private covert operations company. Iran might be one of their accounts. It would be "off the shelf," "stand alone"—phrases that North had picked up from Casey.

The party all had pseudonyms and carried fake documents. North was "William Goode" and used an Irish passport. Cave had grown a mustache as a thin disguise; his passport identified him as "Sam O'Neill," an even thinner cover, since it was so close to the name of the actor, Sam Neill, who had played the title role in the television series "Reilly, Ace of Spies."

The tightly restricted knowledge of the mission betrayed a split in the administration. Not long before the group embarked, Casey, Poindexter, and Shultz had flown together in an Air Force jet for a meeting of NATO officials in London. Shultz, as an opponent, had not been informed that the Iranian initiative was still very much alive. But he kept hearing bits and pieces, and so he put the question to them point-blank: was the arms deal on? "This operation has been told to stand down," Poindexter told him. Casey did not blink. The chief proponent of foreign policy in the U.S. government, on a vital matter directly within his jurisdiction, had just been told a bald-faced lie.

By May 30, Cave was back in Casey's office. Casey wanted to hear every detail of the mission.

Cave told him that before leaving, North had dreamed up presents to bring: a gift-wrapped brace of .357 Colt pistols and a chocolate layer cake decorated with a brass-colored ring to symbolize an opening between Iran and America. As far as Cave knew, North had not brought along any suicide pills. Loaded aboard the plane was a pallet of Hawk missile parts. Three more loaded pallets had been left behind to be sent as soon as the hostages were released.

North fully expected that the hotel where they were to stay would be bugged. And so during the flight, he had Cave rehearse with him a phony conversation that they would have once they got into their rooms. They would start talking about how sorry they were that they would not be able to reveal to the Iranians the source of their intelligence on the Soviet invasion plan for their country. And he was such a good source, "Vladimir"—a major general who already had taken part in two Soviet war games on Iran. That conversation, North said, should scare the Iranians right into the Americans' arms.

They landed in the morning at Tehran's Mehrabad Airport. No sooner were the passengers off the plane than an Iranian cargo crew boarded and unloaded the Hawk spare parts. No hostages had yet been released, and some of the leverage was already gone.

The deposed Shah had built a U.S.-style arterial expressway from the airport into town. But Ghorbanifar had warned them that radical elements knew of their coming, and so they came into the capital via a maze of back alleys. They were finally delivered to the Istaqlal hotel, the Independence, known in palmier days as the Tehran Hilton. They were taken to rooms on the fifteenth floor. And there they cooled their heels. None of Ghorbanifar's promised luminaries came to meet them.

Ghorbanifar and the Iranian delegation finally arrived that afternoon. It included no high-level people. The Iranians were, Cave said, hostile, negative, and rude, particularly the spokesman. He complained that the Americans had delivered used Hawk parts. It fell to Cave, as the interpreter, to point out that they were not supposed to take the parts anyway, not until the hostages were released. To which the Iranian replied that their release depended on the delivery of all the parts, including those left behind.

From there, the discussion deteriorated. The Iranians reported that the Shiites who actually held the hostages had upped their demands. Before the Americans could be freed, they wanted the seventeen Dawa prisoners from Kuwait. They wanted Israel to withdraw from the Golan Heights and southern Lebanon. They wanted, George Cave began to understand, the impossible.

The negotiating dragged on, hour after hour. Cave found himself hoarse from interpreting and let Ghorbanifar spell him; but, exhausted as he was, he had to keep interrupting. Ghorbanifar was not translating—he was telling the Iranians whatever served his purposes.

At one point, Ghorbanifar took Cave aside. "I want to talk to you out in the hall," he whispered. In the hallway, he revealed that he had told the Iranians that the price for all the Hawk spare parts was $24.5 million. "Tell them that is the right figure," he told Cave. Cave was staggered. According to Pentagon price lists, the parts were worth about $6.5 million. The markup was exorbitant. Cave went to North with this information. "What the hell is going on?" he asked. North seemed as unwitting as Cave. He asked the Israeli, Amiram Nir, about the stiff markup. Nir told them to relax; the price was fine. It included a lot of expenses, other moneys that were owed to Ghorbanifar. The explanation was all double-talk to Cave. He did not understand it, and he doubted if North did. But North did not object.

The haggling ground on, with the Iranians now saying that they would arrange for the release of only two hostages, and only after they had all the spare parts. This was too much for the chief of the mission. McFarlane told the Iranians that the United States had been duped for the last time. He wanted all the hostages or the deal was off. The Iranians stiffened at any suggestion of bad faith on their part. They pulled out lists of equipment they had been told to expect, none of which the Americans had brought. Where had they gotten that list? the Americans wanted to know. Why, from Manucher Ghorbanifar.

They broke up late that night, with nothing resolved, and planned to meet again the next morning.

But the next day none of the Iranians showed, including Ghorbanifar. The Americans killed time for one more day, and by the morning of May 28, McFarlane had made his decision: they were going home.

The mission to Tehran had made three things unmistakable to George Cave. First, the Iranians were not necessarily in a position to deliver the hostages. They could only hope to exert leverage on the Shiite captors. Second, Ghorbanifar was promising the moon to the Iranians and the sun to the Americans—anything to keep the profitable deal alive. And finally, Ollie North had not the foggiest idea about what was going on with the money.

As the plane touched down at Ben Gurion Airport in Israel, North could see that McFarlane was depressed by the failure of yet another mission. McFarlane should not take it too hard, North said. "The bright spot," he confided to him, "is that we're using part of the money in the transactions for Central America"—except that North had no knowledge of how much was going to the contras and how much into the pockets of the middlemen.

If there was anyone in the Reagan administration equipped to spot a bum business proposition, it was William J. Casey. Why, after still another dismal failure, did he stick with a demonstrated loser, a stock that Casey the investor would have dumped in a second? The answer seems to lie in the selfsame pragmatism that had made him a business success. This measuring of things by their practical outcome had coarsened his judgment over the years. So what if these Iranian arms deals did not work? The initiative was cheap—a few million bucks' worth of equipment in a world where even Iran spent billions on a war. If the gamble paid off, they would all be men of vision, saviors of the hostages, initiators of a new era in the vital Gulf region; and if they failed, the United States was out some military hardware. Costs not measurable in dollars—the improper bypassing of Congress, the damage thus done to a government of laws, the betrayal of public promises concerning deals with terrorists—were by now beyond his sensitivity.

Earlier, back in March, a week after their actual wedding date, Bill and Sophia celebrated their forty-fifth anniversary. Bernadette had thrown an elegant black-tie bash for them at the Watergate Hotel. The guest list included the humble and the mighty from the Caseys' past, from old college pals to two former secretaries of State, Al Haig and Henry Kissinger, the latter no doubt invited to ratify Casey's ultimate social arrival.

The embattled Casey still felt his spirits recharged by the warmth and security of his home life. Even when he traveled abroad, he liked to bring the family along, his portable cocoon. Sophia and Bernadette were often in the VIP pack as he moved around the world. From these journeys, they brought back an array of gifts: a Rolex watch from

Hassan II, king of Morocco, value $3,250; a leopard skin from the Sudan, value $50; a rug from the chief of the Pakistani intelligence service, value $7,217.50; a porcelain plate from Manuel Noriega, value $2. Sophia enjoyed sorting through the gifts before turning most of them over to the government. By law, only a gift appraised below $165 could be kept. Casey told Sophia that he was taking no chances; he wanted her to give back anything worth over $100.

Two months after their anniversary party, on May 29, the Caseys had gone to a Veterans of the OSS dinner at the Washington Hilton. Casey had personally picked the recipient of this year's Donovan Medal: Ronald Reagan, who had made training films in Hollywood for the Army Air Corps during World War II. The ballroom was filled with tuxes and organza gowns; the faces of the guests were seamed, their war now forty-one years behind them. They watched an ancient print of an OSS propaganda film that brought tears to their eyes. Ronald Reagan spoke from underneath a huge, sepia-tinted blow-up of Wild Bill Donovan. Reagan was gracious and amusing, telling how he had asked Casey where the dinner was going to be held, "and Bill said, 'Go to the corner of Seventeenth and K and wait for the phone to ring.' . . . I asked if the dinner was going to be black tie. 'No,' he said, 'trench coat.' "

Sophia was eating her dinner when a piece of meat lodged in her throat. As she later described her terror: "I thought I was going to sit there and die before anybody realized what was happening." A woman nearby, Jane Dudley, caught on and said to Casey, "Do you know how to do the Heimlich maneuver?" A dazed Casey shook his head no. The diminutive woman virtually shoved him aside and seized Sophia around the waist from the back. Casey stood by, watching helplessly, his face frozen in disbelief. By now, one of his bodyguards had run to Sophia. The Dudley woman lacked the strength for the maneuver; the security man took over, and the piece of meat popped out of Sophia's mouth like a cork.

The white-hot romanticism of his youth was long years behind him, a casualty of life's unpoetic erosion. Still, his wife remained his ultimate anchorage. Bill had copied a passage from the Bible that he always kept: "I pleaded and the spirit of Sophia came to me. I preferred her to sceptre and throne and deemed riches nothing in comparison with her. . . ." Whenever the priest read these words at mass, Sophia recalled, Bill would nudge her affectionately.

And he had almost lost her.

32.

The Public's Right to Know

O ne of the more startling revelations Vitaly Yurchenko had made to the CIA before he went home explained why a brilliant U.S. SIGINT operation had somehow gone bad. Yurchenko told the CIA that during the mid-seventies, while he was serving in Washington, he had received a telephone call from an American who said he had something useful to offer. The caller was a bright, erratic loser by the name of Ronald Pelton, a former employee of the National Security Agency. Pelton had quit his NSA job, drank, took drugs, failed at a number of pie-in-the-sky business ventures, and finally decided to cash in his knowledge of his country's secret surveillance operations to the Soviet Union. The Soviets bought Ronald Pelton for $35,000. The value of what they got in return was incalculable.

Given Yurchenko's tip, the FBI was able to track down Pelton, who was arrested and charged with espionage. Among the secrets Pelton had sold to the Soviets was his knowledge of a U.S. operation called Ivy Bells. In the Sea of Okhotsk, that huge bay between the Kamchatka Peninsula and the Asian mainland, the Soviets had laid an underwater cable linking various military and civilian installations. The cable was used, among other things, to pass messages dealing with Soviet ballistic missile tests in the Sea of Okhotsk. Through an ingenious technological triumph, the United States was reading these messages. A Navy submarine had managed to lower a pod that fit over this cable at the bottom of the sea. The pod recorded all transmissions. Ivy Bells had worked beautifully for years until, in 1981, a U.S. sub tried to bring up the pod to retrieve the latest batch of recorded messages, and the pod was gone. The Soviets had been alerted to Ivy Bells by Ronald Pelton.

By April of 1986, with the trial of Pelton coming up, the *Washington Post* learned of the blown Ivy Bells operation and was preparing a story on it. The director of the NSA, Lieutenant General William Odom, was deeply distressed. He tried to dissuade the *Post*, particularly the executive editor, Ben Bradlee, and the managing editor, Leonard Downie Jr., to kill the article. Odom was not having much success.

One of Casey's victories as DCI had been to win the allegiance of the entire intelligence community. He was director of Central Intelligence, and the CIA was just one piece of that community, the piece directly under his control. But he was also responsible for coordinating the activities and budgets of a dozen other agencies that made up the full U.S. intelligence apparatus. Casey had assiduously cultivated these fiefdoms, calling on their various chiefs, bringing them out to Langley, soliciting their opinions, hearing their gripes, fighting for their budgets. And so, unlike several of his predecessors, most notably the ill-starred Stansfield Turner, Casey was accepted as the de facto head of the intelligence family.

And so General Odom, fearing damage to his NSA if the *Post* printed the Ivy Bells story, went to Bill Casey. Casey listened to Odom and said he had an idea, a new way to deal with leakers. Still on the books was an old espionage statute passed in 1917 and updated in 1950. Section 798 of Title 18 of the U.S. Criminal Code prohibited "knowingly and wilfully communicating, furnishing, transmitting or publishing any classified information concerning communication activities." The worst leaks usually involved communications, and the old law sounded tailor-made for Ivy Bells.

On May 2, Casey was alerted that the *Washington Post* planned to run the Ivy Bells story two days later, on Sunday. He had thereafter gone to the Justice Department, where he talked to the head of the Criminal Division, D. Lowell Jensen. He wanted Jensen to consider going after three newspapers, including the *Post*, and two magazines that he considered in violation of Section 798.

After the meeting, he told his security man to get him Ben Bradlee on the car phone. He invited Bradlee to discuss the Ivy Bells story. They could meet, he suggested, at four p.m. in the bar of the University Club, which was near the *Post* and, coincidentally, next door to the old downtown Soviet embassy.

Bradlee agreed and brought Downie with him. They could publish what they wanted to, Casey said without any particular menace. But he had to warn them that he would recommend prosecution of the *Post* to the Justice Department under the old espionage law.

To the newsmen, Casey clearly was infringing on freedom of the press. Their argument, first with Odom, and now with him, was that the public had a right to know. The Soviet Union knew about Ivy Bells; the Soviets had discovered the pod and killed the operation. What danger was there in informing the American public about some intelligence ploy that had been compromised five years before?

But Casey saw it far differently. The term "Soviet Union" was amorphous. The Soviet government, like the United States government, was a composite of hundreds, even thousands, of subunits. It was not a flawless monolith but an aggregation of millions of flawed human beings. Exactly who in the Soviet Union knew about Ivy Bells? Quite possibly, the part of the Soviet government that had been spied on by this operation had not revealed to any other element of the government that it had been penetrated. Bureaucrats in the Soviet Union, just as anywhere else, do not trumpet their failures. The story the *Post* was planning would shove the failure in the Soviets' face. The whole country would know that it had been taken by the Americans. The entire Soviet national security apparatus would be alerted, become more vigilant, checking any other possible breaches of security, and therefore would likely discover other ongoing U.S. penetrations. Is this what the *Washington Post* wanted? Casey asked. Was that what their vaunted "people's right to know" was all about?

The threat of prosecution had the desired short-term effect: the *Post*'s editors decided not to go with the story that Sunday.

Ben Bradlee was a responsible man. He pushed Bob Woodward and other reporters working on Ivy Bells to defend why the paper *should* publish this story. What redeeming virtue was there in publication? Woodward had worked up a rationale. For one thing, he said, "the story would show how easy it was to walk into the Soviet embassy here and sell American secrets." Furthermore, by running aggressive operations like Ivy Bells right off the Soviet coast, the United States might be pushing too hard, scaring the Soviets with our technological superiority and thus increasing tension between the superpowers. Still, Bradlee was uneasy about running the story.

The previous April, Casey had been invited to speak before the American Society of Newspaper Editors. Beforehand, he had asked his staff to pull together security violations horror stories. In his longhand draft of the speech, he explained that during the hijacking of TWA flight 847 the year before, while the hostages were being held in Beirut, one of the Shiites in the room was a CIA agent. The agent managed to get to Cyprus and provide a detailed report of what the captors were up to. But, Casey charged, within two days David Martin, a CBS correspondent, put this report on the air. "Our agent's life was put at risk," Casey wrote. "When he learned what happened, he was unlikely to take such a risk again." Another example: The *Washington Post* had run a story headlined, SOVIETS FILL CRATERS, DIG NEW ONES TO FOOL U.S. ON MISSILE ACCURACY. That story, Casey said, tipped off the Soviets to the accuracy of U.S. satellite photography, which would make them more careful and make the job of judging the precision of Soviet missiles harder in the future. This compulsion to print leaked secrets was costing the American people billions of tax dollars in blown technology and operations. "Even a brand-new method of intelligence collection that will cost a billion dollars and which can not be deployed for some years," he wrote, "has already been damaged by the publicaton of unauthorized disclosures."

George Lauder had tried to convince Casey not to speak before the editors. "Bill," he said, "you say anything about that new collection method, and the press will just start trying to track it down." Casey pruned the speech, but he did address the editors. He wanted them to think about the implications of "the public's right to know" in a new light.

The phrase had a sacred ring. It had the sound of making Americans better citizens by making them better informed. But how, Casey argued, was the individual American's citizenship improved by knowing that an American spy had managed to get into a room with Arab terrorists, or that the United States could measure the accuracy of Soviet missiles by measuring craters, or by knowing that a U.S. device had recorded Soviet military messages on the ocean floor? To Casey, the public's right to know had to be balanced against the nation's right to be secure. Everything published could not be dignified by arguing that it served public enlightenment. What Casey saw at work was a different right being exercised by the media—call it a right to astonish, to feed on the public's understandable curiosity, to shock, to entertain. Divulging intelligence operations, Casey believed, allowed the reader to say, "Wow, would you look at that!" before flipping to the sports page. Maybe the media did possess a right to publish for all these purposes. But to Casey's way of thinking, the disclosures should not habitually be clothed in the holier robes of "the public's right to know."

The *Post* was still mulling over the Ivy Bells story when, on May 7, it published a front-page article on Casey's meeting with Bradlee and Downie headlined, U.S. WEIGHS PROSECUTING PRESS LEAKS. Casey felt deceived; he had thought he was having a private conversation with these people. The *Post* story reported his stated intention of moving against publishers of leaks under the old espionage statute. And the story provoked a predictable furor among the news media.

Bill Safire read of Casey's latest maneuver with dismay. "What this story suggested to me," he observed, "was that Bill had lost his bearings. The great good judgment that was the trademark of Bill Casey seemed to have fled him." The once warm friendship and mutual respect dropped another notch. The previous December, Safire had run into Casey at a Christmas party for more than one thousand guests at one of the federal auditoriums. "I'm standing there with a shrimp in my hand," Safire remembered, "and Casey comes over and starts hollering at me in front of all these people. This was because I had referred to him as a source in my column." Stephen Engelberg, also of the *Times*, was standing next to the startled Safire. As Casey stomped off, Engelberg remarked. "That's a friend of yours?"

Shortly after the story broke about Casey threatening to prosecute the press, Safire heard something curious from a man he would describe only as "a friend in law enforcement." As Safire recalled the conversation: "He told me, 'Your friend Casey is talking about sending reporters to jail for leaks. But we understand he's been seeing Bob Woodward, alone, at his home and at the office.' "

With this tip, Safire called Casey. "I hear you've been seeing Bob Woodward," he said. "How could you be doing that and denouncing reporters, threatening them with jail in the same breath?" "Casey told me," Safire said, "that he hadn't seen Woodward for eighteen months." It was not true. Just four months before, Woodward had been to Casey's home for breakfast. According to George Lauder, who was present, Woodward had shrewdly baited his request by saying he was interested in Casey's book about the OSS. "But when he got there," Lauder observed, "he kept trying to turn the conversation to Afghanistan and the contras, not the Battle of the Bulge."

On May 19, to Ben Bradlee's understandable annoyance, NBC's "Today" show carried a news story on the Pelton trial, including the statement that the spy had alerted the Soviets to Ivy Bells, "believed to be a top secret underwater eavesdropping operation by American submarines inside Soviet harbors." Because of the less-than-subtle pressures exerted by Odom and Casey, the *Post* had been scooped on a story it had sat on for weeks. Bradlee called Casey. What was he going to do about NBC? Bradlee wanted to know. That afternoon, Casey issued a statement saying that he was going to refer the network's broadcast to the Justice Department for possible prosecution.

But in the end, nobody was going to be prosecuted. The old espionage law was never applied in Casey's time. He grudgingly came around to the conclusion that in a democracy the press would usually have the last word. For all practical purposes, it was immune.

As for his own treatment at the hands of the media, he became equally convinced that he could never get a fair shake. As he told another *Washington Post* reporter, Jim Conaway, "The way the media works, they put a label on you. In my case, it's a false label." And it was not a flattering label. *Washingtonian* magazine recently had published a satirical piece entitled "Where Have All the Rogues Gone?" The article drew a distinction between political rogues and political buffoons, defining rogues as people "charmingly outrageous." "The leading buffoon right now," the piece went on, "is CIA Director William Casey, who surely must be clowning by the way he runs those 'covert' operations in Central America."

Actually, his image, as projected in the press, was more villain-buffoon. In Casey's view, whatever confirmed that image was page one; whatever contradicted it was page 36. Casey's inventor friend, George Doundoulakis, remembered getting a call from a reporter on a major newspaper while Casey was at the CIA. "He said he wanted to give me the chance to tell how Bill Casey dealt unfairly with me, how he had cheated me in our financial dealings," Doundoulakis remembered. "But Bill never did. Bill was an honorable man in all my experience with him."

For two years, the President, Casey, the NSC, the State Department—indeed, the entire national security apparatus—had been unable to convince Congress that the Nicaraguan resistance movement deserved support. The proponents, however, had not counted on a surprise ally, Daniel Ortega, the president of Nicaragua. Ortega had been the victor in November of 1984 in an election that American observers found lacking in certain democratic niceties. Ortega subsequently failed to restore basic political freedoms and began to make Nicaragua into what seemed the westernmost outpost of the Communist bloc.

The Senate already had passed a $100-million aid package for the contras. Republicans and conservative Democrats in the House were not about to appear soft on communism, particularly toward another Marxist regime in the Western Hemisphere. And so, on June 25, by a narrow 221-to-209 vote, the House passed its own $100-million contra-aid package. Differences in the two bills would have to be harmonized in conference; but, barring an unlikely reversal, the United States would be back funding the contras by October.

But it was still June. In the meantime, the contras were reportedly in desperate shape. In the past two years, tin-cup financing from private donors had produced $2.5 million and third countries had given $34 million. That was gone. Congress had permitted $27 million in humanitarian aid. That was gone. The contras were reportedly $2.5 million in debt. Yet, while they verged on destitution, some $8.5 million in profits from the arms sales to Iran—profits that were supposed to aid the contras—were unaccounted for.

Bob Gates was troubled. By the end of June, over seven months had passed since the finding covering the November 25 arms shipment to Iran had been made. Five months had passed since the January 17 finding. Both findings contained the discomforting clause directing the CIA not to notify Congress of the arms deals. Gates expressed his uneasiness to Casey. The law said that findings were to be reported to Congress in a "timely" manner. Forty-eight hours had been considered timely in the past. But seven months? The policy itself, Gates noted—trading arms for hostages—was explosive enough; but not to report it to Congress bordered on the suicidal. Casey did not seem to share his anxiety. During those months, he had gone before the oversight committees on a dozen top secret matters, brazenly concealing the hottest secret of all.

Gates faced the classic dilemma of the public official: go along or get out. He had invested his professional life in the CIA. His rise had been phenomenal. Casey had hinted that Gates would be his successor, the youngest DCI in history. People well above him—the President of the United States, his own CIA director, the whole foreign policy team—were all willing to leave Congress in the dark. As Casey had put it, there was nothing to worry about: "Who's gonna condemn the President of the United States for trying to save a bunch of Americans held hostage by those bastards?" Bob Gates reluctantly decided to go along.

On July 26, a dust-caked automobile pulled to a stop on a road near a village in Lebanon's Bekaa valley. The driver got out and helped a bound and blindfolded man out of the trunk. He untied the man and removed the blindfold. For the first time in eighteen months, the Reverend Lawrence Martin Jenco was free.

Jenco owed his freedom to the fears of Manucher Ghorbanifar. After the McFarlane-North mission to Tehran had aborted, Ghorbanifar found himself in desperate shape. By now, Adnan Khashoggi had put up $15 million in bridge loans payable at 20 percent interest, which came to $18 million that he was owed. Ghorbanifar had given him postdated checks to cover the outlay. But until Ghorbanifar had his money from the Iranians, Khashoggi's checks were just pieces of paper. And the Iranians would not pay up until the deliveries resumed. Ghorbanifar was in actual physical pain, sick with worry, constantly popping pills, his blood pressure dangerously high. He checked briefly into a hospital in London.

Khashoggi ordered his man Roy Furmark to "stay on top of Ghorbanifar, push him." And it seemed to Ghorbanifar that wherever he went, there was the large, looming presence of Furmark. Ghorbanifar had heard that Khashoggi had taken another precaution to make sure he was not stiffed: Khashoggi had reportedly taken out a $22-million insurance policy on Ghorbanifar's life, a development that did not reduce the Iranian's anxiety. He had to get the arms deal back on the track. He therefore had assured the Iranians that the Americans would deliver the rest of the Hawk spare parts if he could deliver a hostage. With that leverage he had been able to engineer the release of Father Jenco.

Poindexter was still leery of Ghorbanifar. But Casey wrote him: "I believe that we should consider what we may be prepared to do to meet [Iran's] minimum requirements that would lead to the release of the rest of the hostages." Casey was also prepared to use Ghorbanifar's scare tactics, since he told Poindexter, "It is entirely possible that Iran and/or the Hizbollah could resort to the murder of one or more of the remaining hostages." Here he had touched the right pressure point to move the President. Reagan was, as ever, eager to press on. The deal, to Ghorbanifar's infinite relief, was back on track.

On August 4, the remaining Hawk spare parts were delivered to Iran. This was the very shipment that McFarlane had refused to release in May because the Iranians had offered only two hostages instead of all five. Now the United States was turning it over for one hostage, already released. The Boy Scouts and the rug merchants had cut another deal.

Former Major General Richard V. Secord was still the cutout, taking arms that the CIA bought from the Defense Department and getting them to Iran through other middlemen. But Secord was having problems. People at the CIA did not trust him. They bad-mouthed him. They threw roadblocks across his path, would not come up with air transport where and when he needed it. The shadow of the notorious Edwin Wilson still followed Secord, and it made CIA people nervous.

Secord complained to North, who complained to Poindexter, who went to Casey. Couldn't the DCI do something about this obstructionism in his own shop? Poindexter wanted to know. Casey, he of the many scrapes, was sympathetic toward Secord, whom he saw as suffering from guilt by association. Casey's own judgment was on the line as well, since he was the one who had nominated Secord as the agent for both the contra and the Iranian arms deliveries. He put out the word in his organization: Dick Secord was to be helped, not thwarted.

How worthy was this man of Casey's and North's and Poindexter's solicitude? The money that Iran paid went eventually into the Lake Resources account, which Secord controlled. The CIA was reimbursed from this same account for the arms it obtained from the Pentagon. But nobody in the U.S. government had any idea of what was in the account, because North had no idea what Secord and Hakim charged for the weapons they sold the Iranians, or how much they kept for themselves, or how much they presumably passed along to the contras. Later, when the whole affair was investigated by Congress, North admitted, "I still do not know how much money was under [Secord's] control and where it was. I simply relied on the fact that I had a relationship of trust between myself and General Secord."

And so, while North was pleading poverty for his contras, shortages of ammunition, boots, even food, he assumed that Secord was easing their condition. One transaction serves to illustrate how Secord and Hakim provided that help. They bought arms in the international market for $2.1 million and sold them to the contras for $2.96 million, a 41 percent profit. North was totally unaware of the size of this profit. Adolfo Calero, the political chief of the contras, later said that he was unaware that Secord was even charging a profit. He assumed Secord was selling to the contras at cost. The issue is probably best summed up by the fact that North liked to refer to his contra aid efforts as "Project Democracy," while Secord and company preferred "the Enterprise."

Casey was suffering from gingivitis, a gum disease, and some of his teeth were getting loose. The problem was not helping his diction. He trusted only his dentist in New York and began going up to see him as often as possible. On one trip in September he called his attorney, Milton Gould, and made a date for lunch at the Sky Club in the Pan-Am building. Unlike most of Casey's social friends, Gould did not tiptoe around Casey's job. They were at a quiet table, and so

Gould, as was his habit, plunged in. How, Gould wanted to know, could Casey be a party to so many bonehead plays, like the so-called covert operation against Nicaragua? Didn't Casey understand that covert operations by the United States were hopeless? "We're never going to be equal to the Russians in that game," he said. "There are always going to be leaks. You're required to tell Congress. You're going to be scrutinized by the press. The press is liberal. It's hostile to your aims. So the only stories you'll ever get are when you're caught making a mistake."

"This isn't bean bag," Casey answered. "The other side plays rough. We have to play rough too."

Gould felt that he had to get his feelings about Ronald Reagan off his chest. "Look, Bill," he said, "you've done some historical writing. So have I. We've both got a sense of history. This guy Reagan never read a serious book in his life. How can you entrust the fate of the American people to a man who rejects the substance of human experience because he doesn't know about it? He's an ignorant man by the standards of guys like you and me. Jack Kennedy wasn't ignorant. Even Jimmy Carter wasn't ignorant. Ronald Reagan is ignorant."

Gould waited for Casey's response. There was none, save for a bemused, tolerant smile.

Gould later described the conversation: "You couldn't get Bill to criticize Reagan. But I understood. It's like when I go before a judge who's a shithead: you won't ever hear me say it—it could get back to him. And I can't afford to alienate the bench." That, Gould concluded, was Casey's posture.

Casey had little cause for complaint that season as the fall of 1986 approached. He was riding a wave. The anemic, cowering agency he had inherited five years before was now hale and robust. Its secret budget was approaching $3 billion, nearly tripling under his rule. Manpower was up from under fourteen thousand to over seventeen thousand.

Congress finally had come around again to support the contras. As of October 1, the Boland ban would be over, and $100 million would be available for the resistance fighters, by far the largest appropriation yet. The back-street, handout financing could be ended. The legal mine field the CIA had been threading its way through would be cleared. The tiny contra force of a thousand of five years before now numbered sixteen thousand—Adolfo Calero even hinted at twenty-two thousand. And soon the CIA could support it legitimately.

Casey was even getting some unaccustomed good press. *U.S. News and World Report* had published a scorecard that summer. In the

Philippines, the magazine noted, "the CIA foresaw the rise of Communist rebels, erosion of Marcos' support, unrest in the military, and Marcos' vote fraud. The result: Reagan dumped Marcos, helping usher in the Aquino government." To Casey, that had been the whole point: to have his intelligence estimates drive policy. "Bill Casey," the magazine concluded, "has become the most influential director of the CIA since Allen Dulles. . . . There is no doubt that morale is shooting up within the ranks of 'The Company.' "

There were still nearly two and a half years left in the second Reagan term. Sophia had never liked the house built on Nelson Rockefeller's old estate at Foxhall Crescent. Bill told her to find a place she did like; they were going to stick around. In September, she found one in McLean, in northern Virginia, five minutes from his office. There was plenty of land, a pool, and an entire lower floor where they could keep the security detail out of their hair. Casey took the precaution of checking the tax advantage of moving from the District of Columbia to Virginia and then paid $450,000 for what became his third home.

In his current mood, Casey's thoughts could turn to historical reflection. He always had been displeased that the only statue at the Agency was of Nathan Hale. He wanted a statue of General Donovan there too. He called the executive director of the Veterans of OSS, Geoff Jones. Jones's mother had been a sculptor, and he wanted Jones to come down to Langley and give him some advice. "Hell," he told Jones, "is Hale the spy we want for a model—a guy who got caught and strung up?"

He finally gave a commission for a statue of Donovan to a retired CIA official who also sculpted. Later that fall, he invited Jones, Leo Cherne (an accomplished sculptor himself), Dick Helms, other old OSS hands, and the sculptor for the unveiling of the model. As Jones described the moment, "We were sitting in a conference room and the model was under a sheet. The sculptor did the unveiling, and there was one body and three heads to choose from. Unfortunately, the body was shaped like Gregory Peck, while Donovan was roly-poly. Casey sent the sculptor out of the room, and he said, 'Well, what do you fellas think?' We all said it was lousy—all three heads." Later, Casey relied on Leo Cherne's guidance and commissioned Laurence Ludtke, a sculptor in the heroic tradition, whose bronze Donovan stands to the left of the headquarters lobby today.

Casey was in good enough spirits that fall to agree to appear on a panel discussion held by the Washington chapter of Sigma Delta Chi, the journalists' society. His copanelists were Senator David Durenberger, James Polk of NBC-TV News, and Bob Woodward.

Casey started out genially enough, telling Woodward, "I'm not tapping any journalists' phones, including yours."

"My daughter will feel much better now," Woodward observed.

"Ask him about senators' phones," Durenberger quipped.

Casey then went to the heart of the matter, telling his reporter audience, "When you publish leaks, you're handing our intelligence to our adversaries on a silver platter." He turned to Polk, who had broadcast the Ivy Bells story over NBC, the story that the *Washington Post* had held back. That was why he had asked the Justice Department to prosecute Polk last May, he said—for handing intelligence to the opposition. Polk was ready. He had broadcast an almost identical story five months before, he pointed out. In fact, stories of U.S. subs gathering intelligence in Soviet waters had appeared in *U.S. News and World Report* five years before, in the *Washington Post* eleven years before, in the *New York Times* twelve years before. Ivy Bells was more ancient history than news.

Durenberger chimed in. "If you're going to prosecute leakers, you'd better start at home." The administration had wanted to build support for the air strike on Libya, and so it released intercepted Libyan messages *before* the Berlin discotheque bombing, thus compromising one of its own methods. The administration had leaked word that it had spies operating inside the Sandinista government. As a result, their cover was blown and three Nicaraguan officials were arrested. Casey's hands were not clean, either. "You yourself came out of a White House meeting a few weeks ago," Durenberger pointed out, "and you revealed that Soviet pilots were flying reconnaissance aircraft in Nicaragua."

Casey was like a bomber pilot encountering heavy flak, starting to wonder why he had volunteered for this mission. He went on the offensive and asked Woodward point-blank, "What would you do if somebody offered you a document stamped top secret?" Woodward answered that he would read it first, then authenticate it, and if it bore on some important public issue, he would "find some way to publish it." "But aren't you dealing in stolen goods?" Casey asked. "No, sir," Woodward answered without elaboration. Casey stared at the reporter quizzically, as though presented with some alien species. He shook his head. "Okay," he said. "I just wanted to confirm that." Afterward, driving back in his car, speaking to no one in particular, he remarked, "These people will never understand."

————

After more than thirteen months of American arms deals with Iran, only two hostages had been freed. Indeed, in September 1986, after the delivery of the Hawk spare parts, two more Americans had been seized by radical Shiites. The Reagan administration was back where it had started. The worst fears of those who condemned dealing with terrorists had been confirmed. Hostages were no longer simply unfortunate pawns but pure gold. The new kidnappings meant the terrorists obviously were replenishing their inventory.

Still, Ollie North was not discouraged, though by now even this congenital optimist had become disillusioned with Ghorbanifar. He simply moved in a different direction. With Poindexter's approval, he shut down what was called the "first channel," the dealings through Ghorbanifar. Secord's partner, the Iranian-born Albert Hakim, had opened a "second channel." Hakim produced Ali Hashemi Bahremani, a rising young Iranian official, well educated, and supposedly the favorite nephew of Hojatolislam Hashemi Rafsanjani, the speaker of the Iranian parliament. Future arms deals were to be worked through Bahremani. The young Iranian was brought to Washington and treated royally. Before his arrival, North sent one of his staff to the Globe bookstore to buy a Bible. He copied out a passage from Saint Paul's Epistle to the Galatians, paper-clipped it to the Bible, and had the President pen the words on the flyleaf and sign the page. North presented Bahremani with the Bible. He took him on a private tour of the White House and peeked into the empty Oval Office. They passed a painting of a group of dogs. That, he told his visitor, was the American cabinet. "The one who's sleeping," he said, "is Bill Casey." His oft-professed reverence for his mentor was apparently not total.

Shortly afterward, North again met with Bahremani, in Frankfurt, to commence business through the new second channel. There he received a severe jolt—two jolts really. With Bahremani were other Iranians who had come to negotiate the arms deals. But they were the same old faces, people whom North had dealt with before through Ghorbanifar. Worse still, North learned that there were no Iranian moderates operating separate from the Ayatollah Khomeini. These people whom they had been seeing all along were Khomeini's agents.

Ghorbanifar, however, had been cut out, and he was getting panicky. Khashoggi had been paid $8 million of the $18 million he was owed in bridge loans, but he was hounding Ghorbanifar for the remaining $10 million. Ghorbanifar seized at one last hope. Khashoggi should stop bugging him about the money and start putting some pressure on the U.S. government through Roy Furmark's friend William J. Casey.

That fall of 1986, an incident in Moscow further strained Casey's relations with George Shultz. Since August 30, Nicholas Daniloff, the Moscow correspondent for *U.S. News and World Report*, had been under arrest by the KGB. The governments of the respective countries made the predictable noises. The United States charged that Daniloff had been framed. The Soviets claimed that the reporter was engaged in espionage. Why the KGB had reached that conclusion was understandable. The year before, a man who identified himself as "Father Roman," a priest, had contacted Daniloff in Moscow and told him that he was going to leave him some material on religion in the Soviet Union. A few days later, Daniloff found an envelope outside his apartment addressed to the American embassy.

He took the envelope to the embassy, where it was opened and found to contain other envelopes, one addressed to Casey. A letter in the packet also contained information on Soviet military rockets. Daniloff was asked by embassy officials how Father Roman could be reached, and he provided the information. Soon afterward, a member of the Moscow CIA station telephoned the priest over an open line and also wrote to him, saying he was a friend of "Nikolai" and that he had received "your package from your journalist friend." The KGB intercepted these communications, suspected that Daniloff had served as a courier, and arrested him.

In retaliation for the arrest of Daniloff, the United States threatened to expel twenty-five members of the Soviet U.N. mission in New York. On the list were Valery Sarchenko, believed to be the KGB station chief at the U.N., and Vladislav Skvortysov, identified as the top official in New York of the GRU, the Soviet military intelligence agency. Casey was delighted—until he heard that George Shultz was considering allowing the Russians to substitute two relatively innocuous diplomats in place of the Soviet spy chiefs on the expulsion list. Casey immediately flew to New York and headed for a room in the U.N. Plaza Hotel, where the negotiations were taking place. He managed to stall the substitution.

In the end, Daniloff came home under another deal. The week earlier, the FBI had arrested Gennady Zakharov, another Soviet U.N.

official, for espionage. Indeed, Daniloff was likely arrested by the KGB as a bargaining chip to obtain Zakharov's release. Daniloff was exchanged for Zakharov.

But relations between Casey and Shultz continued their downhill slide. Casey began to wonder if George Shultz was tough enough for this business.

Two weeks after the Daniloff affair, Casey met in secret in New York with a group of American financial titans. He was concerned about a highly subtle form of potential Soviet subversion. Could the Soviet Union's operatives throw sand in the financial gears that drove Western economies? Could they, by currency manipulation, disinformation, even computer tampering, engineer an economic collapse? He wanted their opinion.

That fear was farfetched, they told him. But on another point, in assessing the challenge before Mikhail Gorbachev, Casey appeared more prophetic. "To compete in the world of tomorrow," Casey told the financiers, "the Soviets are going to have to make great use of the computer and modern telecommunications. Yet the degree to which they do that will force them to relax the political grip on their people, and will create the kind of pressures for spreading information that they have always resisted before." He then posed the dilemma that the United States faced in dealing with Gorbachev: "Should we foster this process in the hope of opening up their society, or should we resist it to maintain our technological and economic lead?" His audience hung on his answer. Casey smiled and said only, "Maybe we can't influence the situation all that much."

On October 5, 1986, a Sunday, a Sandinista patrol operating near the southern Nicaraguan border heard the drone of a C-123K cargo aircraft above. One of the soldiers armed his surface-to-air missile and took aim.

Piloting the plane was William J. Cooper, who worked for a company called Southern Air Tranport, which once had been a CIA property and was long since supposed to have been sold to private owners. The contras had bought the plane with money provided by Saudi Arabia. This day, it carried several tons of weapons. In the back, near a hatch, stood Eugene Hasenfus, something of a cargo soldier of fortune. Hasenfus was a "kicker," whose job was to parachute the crates out of the hatch, a task he had done before in Vietnam, Cambodia, and Thailand.

The Sandinistas' missile scored a direct hit. Hasenfus was soon in the Sandinistas' hands, the only survivor of the downed aircraft.

A *Newsday* reporter went to the house in San Salvador where the ill-fated crew had been staying and found several phone records and numbers revealing calls to North and Secord and one that led to the Costa Rican station chief, Joe Fernandez. If Fernandez was involved, then was not the CIA involved? And did this operation likely originate during the Boland ban? Casey was informed to have some answers ready for Congress.

Casey geared up for the latest crisis, but he was not feeling all that well that fall. A year had passed since he had finished the radiation treatment for the prostate cancer. In October he went back to Georgetown University Hospital to test for any recurrence. He was X-rayed and given an MRI, a magnetic resonance imaging; prostate cancer could spread to the bones. The MRI showed him free of the disease.

He wrote his physician Bill Foley about a friend of his who had similarly suffered from cancer of the prostate: "His doctor prescribed a medicine available only in Canada, which he had difficulty getting," Casey wrote Foley. "I was able to get it out of Canada for him and it seems to have done the job." There were, evidently, even medical benefits in running a worldwide clandestine service.

As for himself, he was relieved to have the clean bill of health. Still, something was not quite right.

Charles Allen had one of the more challenging accounts in the Agency. Officially, he was national intelligence officer for counterterrorism. Along the way he had become, in effect, Manucher Ghorbanifar's control officer, which was rather like controlling an eel.

As a key NIO, Allen had access to the messages and photographs snatched from the air by the NSA bearing on his bailiwick. What he had been seeing for the past several months made Charlie Allen uneasy. All the evidence indicated that the Iranians were being grossly overcharged for the U.S. weapons. And there was something even more disturbing. Allen knew that Secord and Hakim, who were initially involved only in the contra supply operation, were now middlemen in the Iranian arms deals. Allen began doing what analysts are paid to do: he started putting two and two together. He found the answer alarming. It was time to bring his suspicions somewhere, and he began with Casey's deputy, Bob Gates.

He went to see Gates on October 1. They sat down in the office next to the DCI's, where an anxious Allen poured out his concern. "I have no faith in this second channel," he said. "For one thing, the first channel is very unhappy. Ghorbanifar is in hock for millions. This thing looks like it's going off the rails. It's going to be a disaster."

Of course, Gates responded—that was because they were dealing with a pack of liars and cheats.

But there was more, Allen said. He detailed what he knew about the Iran hostage arrangements—the amounts paid, the channels used, all available to him through intelligence surveillance. Allen finally got to what was really on his mind. Something just did not smell right. He cited the involvement of Secord and Hakim in two supposedly unrelated covert actions. And then he blurted it out. "I can't prove it, but I've come to an analyst's judgment. Money is being diverted to the contras." Allen went on to describe the high markups, Secord's and Hakim's access to funds from the two operations.

Gates was alarmed—you did not commingle funds from separate operations. But it was more than poor trade craft. If Allen's suspicions were right, the law had been broken. If a government agency sold anything for a profit, Gates knew, the proceeds could not legally be plowed back into other agency operations; they had to be turned in to the U.S. Treasury. Any money made on the sale of U.S. arms did not belong to the contras. And it certainly did not belong to Dick Secord and Albert Hakim.

"This has gone too far," Gates told Allen. "You're going to have to go in and tell Casey what you told me."

33.

Patriotic Lies

E ver since the Shah had been driven out, the government
of the Ayatollah Khomeini had constantly hammered
home the message: the former American ally was an immoral nation
ruled by evil men. There could be no truck with these international
gangsters. And yet here were members of the very Shiite organization
that had seized the American hostages seven years before, standing
on street corners in Tehran handing out leaflets revealing that certain
opportunists had done the unthinkable: they had trafficked in arms
with agents of the United States, right here in the capital.

The leaflets appeared on October 15. Soon the story spread to the
Bekaa valley, citadel of Arab radicalism. News of the McFarlane mission to Tehran next appeared in a tiny Shiite radical newspaper. Two
Iranian leftists carried the story to Hassan Sabra, editor of a small
magazine, *Al Shiraa*, published in Beirut. Hassan wrote an article
describing how high-ranking advisers to President Ronald Reagan
had come to Tehran the previous month to negotiate a deal to release
hostages for arms. Hassan played the story as evidence of rifts and
intrigue inside the Khomeini regime. He had his facts right except
that the McFarlane party had been in Tehran in May, not September.

By November 1, *Al Shiraa* was on Beirut's newsstands. For the first
time, reporters from the West learned of the arrangement with Iran.

The shock of the average Iranian was matched, if not exceeded,
when the news reached heartland America. To the Caseys, the Mc-
Farlanes, the Ledeens, the Poindexters, and the Norths, the scheme
may have seemed the ultimate in realpolitik. To millions of Americans, it was sickening. Still fresh in their minds were images of howl-
ing mobs outside the U.S. embassy in Tehran, hot-eyed fanatics
holding fifty-two American prisoners inside, a religious zealot who
dripped hatred for America ruling the country, and convincing evidence that these people were implicated in the deaths of 241 Marines
and the car bombings of the American embassy and embassy annex
in Beirut. On November 4, the day before the story broke, the Reagan

administration had put out still another statement insisting that "as long as Iran advocates the use of terrorism, the U.S. arms embargo will continue." Yet the government was secretly selling arms to these people? The hypocrisy was numbing.

The news hit the two intelligence oversight committees like a bombshell. Had the administration dared to carry out the most covert of operations, yet flagrantly ignore Congress? "I learned about the arms deals at the same time the guy in the street did," observed David Durenberger. Ultimately it was disclosed that even the Soviets knew about deliveries, and that as of mid-October, any Iranian reading a leaflet on a street corner had known what the chairman of the Senate Select Committee on Intelligence did not know.

The SSCI's staff director went to Langley to find out from Clair George what was going on. "How can you do this without showing us a finding?" Bernie McMahon wanted to know. The Iran initiative was a White House operation, George told him. The CIA had provided only logistic support to the NSC. When McMahon reported this back to Durenberger, the senator was more baffled than ever. "I thought the NSC was supposed to do Kissinger-style conceptualizing, like the breakthrough to China," Durenberger remarked, "not stuff planes full of arms for the Ayatollah."

Even within the administration shock waves were felt. When the story broke, George Shultz was still vigorously pushing Operation Staunch, the arms embargo against Iran, assuring foreign leaders that the United States meant business. And CIA operatives, like Ed Juchniewicz, were working the underside of Staunch.

Ronald Reagan began flailing like a nonswimmer in a sea of contradictions. On November 6, the day after the story broke, Reagan had reporters in for the ceremonial signing of an immigration bill. One reporter asked him about stories of McFarlane going to Tehran to work out an arms deal. The President replied, "That story has no foundation." Actually, two more shipments of arms had been made four days before the President's denial. Recently, the President had also told the American Bar Association that Iran was part of "a new international version of Murder Incorporated." But within days of the speech, the Iranians apparently underwent a miraculous conversion. Reagan was now saying, "There's been no evidence of Iranian government complicity in acts of terrorism in eighteen months."

The unraveling of the operation had not come entirely as a shock to Bill Casey. The month before, his secretary had informed him that a Mr. Roy Furmark was calling for an appointment. Casey had not seen Furmark since the VOSS dinner that summer, for which Furmark had bought a table. Casey okayed the appointment, and Furmark flew to Washington and saw Casey on October 7.

They met alone in the DCI's office in the EOB. Furmark was a big man, in his mid-fifties, with a salt-and-pepper beard. His background did not respond to easy categorization. Neither his name nor his company's was to be found on the frosted glass door to his office on lower Broadway in Manhattan. Furmark told Casey that he was currently working for Adnan Khashoggi. And Khashoggi was very worried. He had put up the bridge financing to cover the arms-hostages deals; at this point, he was out $10 million in unpaid loans. Khashoggi was further claiming that he had borrowed this money from two Canadians, Donald Fraser and Ernest Miller—tough customers, Furmark explained. The loans were overdue—and these boys were putting the heat on Adnan Khashoggi. The bridge loan, Furmark said, had initially been paid into the account of an outfit called Lake Resources.

It did not sound like one of the CIA's accounts, Casey told Furmark. In fact, this arms-for-hostages business was not his operation, he maintained. It sounded like an Israeli operation.

He doubted that, Furmark said, because the whole business seemed to be run by a Marine named Oliver North.

"Ah, yes," Casey said. "Let me get Admiral Poindexter over here." North was Poindexter's man, Casey explained. Poindexter, however, was not in.

What he was really hoping for, for all their sakes, Furmark explained, was that Casey could straighten out the problem, because a very disgruntled party named Manucher Ghorbanifar could make trouble.

Yes, Casey admitted, he knew of Ghorbanifar.

The whole mess could be resolved easily enough, Furmark went on, if the United States would just continue to make the arms shipments through Ghorbanifar. Ghorbanifar would then be paid by the Iranians and could use the money to repay Khashoggi. But, Furmark explained, North and his pals Secord and Hakim had cut Ghorbanifar out. That was the heart of the problem.

Casey repeated that he would see what he could do.

He certainly hoped something could be done, Furmark said, because Ghorbanifar was threatening to reveal the secret operation to three U.S. senators not all that enamored of Casey—Leahy, Moynihan, and Alan Cranston of California.

Furmark got up to leave. Casey looked pensive. "Roy, I want you to do one more thing for me," he said. "Will you sit down with one of my people at some point and tell him everything you know about this business?"

"Sure, Bill," Furmark said. He left to return to New York, relieved that Casey seemed receptive. Casey was a powerful man. Khashoggi was a powerful man. In undertaking this mission for Khashoggi, Furmark had felt rather like a thumb thrust between two millstones.

Later that same day, Bob Gates brought Charlie Allen in to relate to Casey the suspicions Allen had expressed to Gates one week before. Casey and Allen had a standing joke. Allen had been assigned to the Pentagon for three years before he came back to Langley as Casey's NIO for counterterrorism. "Defense kidnapped you," Casey liked to say. "I liberated you."

Allen repeated his concern that the security of the arms-for-hostages deals was coming apart, "spinning out of control," he said—not exactly news to Casey after the Furmark visit. He then went on to say that he had no proof, just the gut sense of an analyst, that some of the Iranian money had been diverted to the contras. As Allen later recalled the moment, Casey seemed genuinely surprised. He claimed that this was the first time he had ever heard of such a diversion. Casey told Allen to write a memorandum for him and to put down everything he knew or suspected. He wanted to send it to Poindexter.

Two days later, October 9, Casey brought North out to Langley for lunch and an update on the badly wobbling arms-for-hostages situation. Gates had not been invited. He would, however, be going with Casey afterward to the Hill, where the director had to testify on the matter of the C-123K downed over Nicaragua. As Gates saw it, North was the go-between with the contras; he wanted to know what North could tell them about the plane. Gates had another nagging concern. The CIA had still not yet received any signed copies of the presidential findings authorizing the arms deals with Iran. Gates simply poked his head into Casey's office and invited himself to the lunch.

North had recently come back from a trip to Europe, where he had been working out the details of still another delivery to Iran. North seemed oblivious of his lunch as he described the latest gambit with his usual enthusiasm. Casey interrupted. He had something urgent on his mind, he said. He had recently had a conversation with an old friend named Roy Furmark who worked with Adnan Khashoggi. The people from the old first channel thought they were being stiffed. Their unhappiness increased the possibility of the whole Iranian operation blowing sky-high.

And then, as Gates recalled the conversation, Casey told North, "You'd better get this cleaned up." The words were important, because North was later to report similar words in a far different context.

Gates seized the opportunity to inject his concerns. "Maybe I read too many spy novels," he told North, "but we still don't have a copy of the January 17 finding. We ought to have it. Otherwise, we have no basis for what we did." He seemed to be warning Casey as much as North. "If you think it's that sensitive," Gates went on, "we can put it in the director's personal safe. But we need our copy."

Casey nodded his support. North said that he would talk to Admiral Poindexter. And soon after, the Agency did get a copy of the finding. Still, the CIA had no copy of the previous finding covering the November 25, 1985, delivery. The Agency was still vulnerable.

Gates had another concern. Eugene Hasenfus, the cargo kicker who had survived the crash of the C-123K, was now in the hands of the Sandinistas. They had put Hasenfus on television that very day, and he had said he was under the impression he worked for the CIA. "Do you know of any contact of any kind, of any use of our people in the operation to supply the contras through the private benefactors?" Gates asked. North did not hesitate. No, he said, the CIA had been kept absolutely clean. Gates sat back relieved.

That afternoon, Casey went before the two oversight committees, maintaining that the CIA had nothing to do with the supplying of the contras during the Boland ban or with the doomed aircraft that was obviously part of the effort. Yes, he knew something was going on. He showed the members a CIA computer printout describing the planes, trucks, even burros, bringing aid to the contras. In the Senate, David Durenberger asked Casey who was carrying out this supply operation. Casey told an incredulous Durenberger, "Our role under Boland was only to gather information, not to get involved in the actual effort. We did not know who was giving what to whom. We deliberately stayed out of that."

After the hearing, as the senators were leaving, Durenberger said to one of the other members, "Did you believe that?" His colleague answered no. "Well, I do," Durenberger went on. "I believe that the director of Central Intelligence has just told us what the CIA knows. But I'll bet you Bill Casey knows everything about it." To Durenberger, the second Casey was coming into focus.

On October 17, Charlie Allen brought Casey an eyes-only, seven-page assessment of the arms-hostage machinations. Allen tiptoed around the ticking time bomb with a practiced bureaucrat's delicacy. In the key passage, he wrote, "The government of the United States, along with the government of Israel, acquired substantial profit from these transactions, some of which profit was redistributed to other projects of the U.S. and of Israel."

Casey finished the memo and put a call through to John Poindexter; he needed to see him right away. Poindexter put Casey off for a day.

The next day, Casey brought Gates with him to the White House, where they met the pipe-puffing admiral in his customary state of Buddha-like imperturbability. Casey gave Poindexter the Allen memo. The admiral went through it without comment.

Maybe Poindexter did not get the point, Casey suggested. The memo raised serious questions of impropriety, even illegality. Casey's advice to Poindexter was to bring in the White House counsel, Peter Wallison, right away. Casey had faith in Wallison, a younger fellow alumnus of Rogers and Wells whom he had warmly recommended that Don Regan hire.

And another thing, Casey said, they had better not paint themselves into a Watergate-style corner. The initiative with the Iranians could not be hidden much longer. "The worst thing is for it to come out in dribs and drabs," Casey warned. What was he suggesting? Poindexter wanted to know. That they go public, Casey said. The President should explain to the American people what he had been trying to do; they were not going to hang him for trying to save American lives. The admiral looked faintly horrified but did not commit himself.

Casey next asked Furmark to come back to Washington and tell his story to Charlie Allen. Furmark came and repeated Khashoggi's plight to Allen, this time with a new twist: the Canadian creditors, Miller and Fraser, were going to sue Khashoggi, and when that happened, Khashoggi intended to sue the United States. All the dirty linen would then be on the line.

Casey was flying back to New York that evening and offered Furmark a lift in the CIA plane. As soon as they were strapped in, Furmark said, "Look, Bill, I see this as a straight commercial transaction. Somebody prepays for a thousand items. You only deliver five hundred. Okay, maybe you can't deliver the whole five hundred. Can't you make a partial delivery?" And, he repeated, it would have to be done through Ghorbanifar. The new guys, this second channel, did not owe Khashoggi anything. Unless the deal was wired through Ghorbanifar, Khashoggi would still be out in the cold.

Casey was thoughtful for a moment. "I'm a businessman," he said sympathetically, "and I can see, even for a guy like Adnan Khashoggi, ten million dollars is a chunk of change." Did that mean Casey would help? "Give me some time," Casey said.

And then Casey changed the subject. Knowing that Furmark had long been involved in energy enterprises, Casey started grilling him on the cogeneration of electrical power. The questioning was exhaustive. This was the old Casey that Furmark remembered.

Charlie Allen had still another meeting with Roy Furmark on October 22 in New York. They met at Christ Cella, a steak house. Khashoggi was not getting his money, Furmark said, because it was being diverted to the contras. How did Furmark know that? Allen wanted to know. Because Ghorbanifar had told him. Allen was furiously scribbling notes on a hotel notepad. This was crucial—the first confirmation by a participant of what Allen had suspected all along. As soon as he was back in Washington, he wrote a memo to Casey of what he had learned.

Casey again went to Poindexter and urged him to bring in the White House lawyer. But Poindexter said he distrusted Wallison, because, he complained, "he talks to the press." And the admiral already had his own lawyer on the NSC staff, Commander Paul B. Thompson, a fellow naval officer to boot.

Late in October, Ollie North came to see Casey. He badly needed counsel. The Furmark disclosures about diverted funds, the Khashoggi threats of going public, the shootdown of the private contra supply aircraft all made one point clear: the web of deception was fast unraveling. Only North's version of this conversation with Casey exists. North later claimed that Casey told him, "Things ought to be cleaned up." He should "get rid of things. Get rid of that book, because that book has in it the names of everybody, the addresses of everybody. Just get rid of it and clean things up."

North, never one to underplay a role, also claimed he told Casey that the time had come for someone "to take the hit or the fall." North was now ready to throw himself on the hand grenade. Casey reportedly responded that a Marine lieutenant colonel was not heavy enough. The fall guy might have to be someone higher up, maybe Poindexter. Casey also gave North one more piece of advice, which left him shaken. North ought to get himself a lawyer.

It was soon after this conversation, North claimed, that he started shredding all documents dealing with the arms deals and the contra operations. The "book" that Casey reportedly had told him to destroy was the spiral ledger that he said Casey had given him in 1984 to keep track of money given to the contras by private contributors.

November 4 was Election Day. Casey had his eye on a particular Senate race. He was still a political animal, unable to master the neutral, serve-all-masters tradition of the intelligence professional. He wanted Patrick J. Leahy of Vermont defeated. Casey was convinced the man was a notorious leaker and that he had always been an enemy of the administration's war-by-proxy against Nicaragua. Leahy made no secret of the latter. "The Senator has been outspoken in his opposition to covert action in Central America," his official Senate biography read.

Leahy had succeeded Pat Moynihan as vice-chairman of the SSCI; if the Democrats won control of the Senate in this off-year election, he could well become chairman. Casey believed that Leahy had committed the mortal sin of leaking intelligence that compromised sources and methods. It supposedly had happened the year before, when an Italian vessel, the *Achille Lauro*, was hijacked by PLO terrorists. Leon Klinghoffer, a sixty-nine-year-old passenger confined to a wheelchair, had been killed and thrown overboard by the hijackers, apparently because he had a Jewish name. Intercepted telephone conversations of Egyptian President Hosni Mubarak had helped the United States capture the hijackers. Afterward, Leahy said something on television that made clear that the United States was listening in on Mubarak's most private conversations. Casey blew up. Leahy tried to explain to him that he had learned of the intercepts from the morning news and that the network's source had been Oliver North. Casey was unforgiving. Leahy was still a leaker—deliberately or carelessly, it did not matter. He was a threat to national security.

And so Casey took a step that fell somewhere between a CIA destabilization operation and his own hardball politics of yore. He drafted a letter to Leahy that spelled out Leahy's alleged security breach of the year before regarding the *Achille Lauro*. As Leahy's campaign approached for his third term in the Senate, Casey had copies of the letter leaked to opinion molders and the press in Vermont.

On election day, Casey watched the election returns with the sinking sensation of a gambler who has put the rent money on the wrong horse. Leahy was reelected by a whopping 30 percent margin. And he was furious over what he regarded as Casey's unconscionable interference in domestic politics.

Soon after the election, Casey took the opportunity of offering Leahy a lift after a White House briefing. As they got into the car, Casey was all geniality. "We Irishmen have got to get along," he said with a grin. The remark went back to an old joke from happier times. Casey had kidded Leahy before about the Irish getting along until Leahy twitted him that Casey was only half an Irishman. "Well, so are you," Casey said, pointing out that Leahy's mother was of Italian descent. "But," Casey said, "I can forgive that because of your wife." Leahy's wife, born Marcelle Pomerleau, was, like Casey's mother, French Canadian.

Leahy was headed for Georgetown. On the ride over, Casey apologized for trying to defeat him. It was wrong, he admitted. True enough, Leahy told him; a DCI had no business sticking his nose in a Senate race. The car bogged down in the chronic congestion of Georgetown's M Street. Leahy said he was close enough to his destination to walk. But Casey kept on talking as traffic backed up and horns honked. Leahy finally got out. Casey trotted after him. "We've got to bury the hatchet," he pleaded. "We're both good Americans. We can find common ground."

Leahy found himself, grudgingly, falling under the man's spell. In spite of himself, he liked Bill Casey. He did not agree with him, but he liked the man. As he later described his ambivalence, "I could enjoy sitting down, having a drink, swapping stories with Bill. He was a charmer at a dinner party. But he was also a riverboat gambler. When you started to play with Casey, you made damn sure he cut the cards."

As Leahy reached his destination, he said, "All right, we're going into a new year. Let's put it all behind us."

Casey had gotten a clean bill of health from the doctors in October. Still, he did not feel quite right. Instead of slowing down, however, he drove himself harder; there was so much to be done. With Boland out of the way, the Agency had to be reinserted into the contra fight. As of November 5, with the Iran initiative now out of the bag, the committees on the Hill were clamoring for hearings. As Betty Murphy recalled those days, "Director Casey started coming into the office earlier and earlier. And he left later and later." His pace did not let up, but the spirit began to falter. Art Hug, his old friend and business associate from Casey's days as a director of Long Island Trust, came to town. Hug dragged Casey to a Georgetown club where, for the first time, he heard him speak of his life as DCI. Of the fire storm the arms deal had ignited, Casey said wearily, "I'm just astonished at the viciousness. You know I'm no pansy. But this is rough, really rough." "I'd known Bill Casey for twenty-five years," Hug observed. "And this was the first time I ever heard him complain about taking the heat. I had never really seen a discouraged Bill Casey."

John Bross called him that November. Bross had long since left

Casey's service, but he was always there when Casey needed him. Bross recently had recovered from cancer and subsequently had become involved in a cancer research organization. "I called Bill to get him to kick in some money," Bross recalled. "It was the first time in all the years I had known him that Bill Casey did not have time for me. He was rude. 'Don't bother me,' he said. 'I've got important things to worry about.' " "What I'm calling about is more important than anything you're doing," Bross shot back, and hung up, puzzled and hurt.

Around this time, Casey's old friend John Shaheen died after a protracted struggle with cancer. Casey's nephew Larry described his uncle at Shaheen's funeral. "He was ashen. He looked beat throughout the service. Shaheen was so much like him, so vital, so alive. And now that irrepressible spirit had been stilled. Johnny's death had been like watching himself die."

Still, Casey kept driving himself. He had been itching to get back to Central America. Three times in the past eighteen months Alan Fiers had persuaded him to cancel scheduled trips. It would have been unseemly and suspicious, Fiers argued, to have the DCI down there at a time when his agency was contorting itself into a pretzel trying to conform to the Boland Amendment.

But since October 1, Boland had been lifted. Cap Weinberger at the Pentagon was still holding Nicaragua at arm's length, like a poisonous snake. The U.S. military had already had its Vietnam. Casey's people would have to go back in and manage the war. The director wanted to witness the situation firsthand, after a two-year layoff. And he wanted to show the flag, to let the contras know that Uncle Sam was officially back in their corner. And so he went to El Salvador, Costa Rica, and Honduras, during which time he made the visit to the contra camp within the sound of the guns.

It was in the course of that trip that Alan Fiers first began to wonder about Casey's condition, as he observed the man's sluggishness in meetings, the absence of the old curiosity, the spring missing from Casey's step. When he took Casey back to the airstrip, the man veered off course like a ship with a broken rudder. Fiers literally had to steer him onto the plane.

While Casey was in Central America, Poindexter called him on a secure line and persuaded him to come back a day early so that when they were questioned by the oversight committees on the Iran-contra affair they would be singing in the same key.

Casey returned to Washington on November 19 to pandemonium. Before leaving, he had given Gates instructions about the material he wanted ready for his appearance before the oversight committees, now set for November 21. The staff had gone a step beyond and drafted an opening statement. Gates had told the people working on the draft to bear one point uppermost in their minds: Casey was testifying as director of the CIA, not as a cabinet member. The statement must be seen not as a defense of administration policy but as an explanation of the CIA's part. If Casey chose to play defender of the administration, that was a separate role, and his decision.

The sticky issue was going to be the November 25, 1985, shipment, the first to involve the CIA and one that had been papered over by an after-the-fact finding, a signed copy of which the CIA still did not have.

The following morning, Casey's secretaries were putting the finishing touches on the testimony. He seemed distracted and unsteady. He peered anxiously over the shoulder of a secretary with long hair who was typing at a word processor. He suddenly stood up and had started to walk away when the secretary let out a yell. His coat button had snagged in her hair, and she had virtually been yanked out of her chair.

By one-thirty p.m. he was in Poindexter's office in the West Wing of the White House. Also present, besides Poindexter, were North, Attorney General Ed Meese, and members of their respective staffs. Casey had brought copies of his draft and passed it around. On the most sensitive point, concerning who knew what, and when was it known, the CIA draft read, "In late November 1985, a CIA proprietary airline was chartered to carry cargo to Iran at the NSC's request. The cargo was described to us as oil drilling parts." Ollie North, who could spot a cover-your-ass maneuver as quickly as the next bureaucrat, jumped on this passage. "Look," he said, "you've got to stop calling this an NSC activity. The NSC is not a government unto itself, it's an organ of the U.S. government."

Another crucial sentence in the CIA draft read, "We in the CIA did not find out that our airline had hauled Hawk missiles." Again, North swooped down. The CIA was saying it did not know what was on that plane. Why didn't they change the text to read, "No one in the U.S. government found out" what the actual cargo was? The CIA's version at least had the virtue of technical truth, since the Agency, as an institution, at the time of the shipment, did not officially know what the plane carried. What North was proposing was a bald-faced lie. Still, Casey, Poindexter, and the others wrote North's suggested alteration onto their copies.

Over at State, Abraham Sofaer, the department's legal adviser, was also reading a copy of Casey's draft. When he reached the part about the CIA believing the cargo to be oil drilling equipment, an alarm went off in Sofaer's head. Secretary Shultz had spoken of a conversation with Bud McFarlane in Geneva at the time of the shipment, in which McFarlane specifically spoke of a shipment of Hawk missiles from Israel to Iran. Sofaer believed he was looking at false testimony. He began calling officials of the White House, the Justice Department, and the CIA—the upshot of which was that the offending portion of the testimony was simply deleted. Nothing would be volunteered to the committees about what was or was not on the plane that November day.

A groggy Casey left Poindexter's office only to enter another meeting at the CIA, where some twenty staffers were gathered around the table in the senior conference room to help pound his draft into final shape. Casey's face was the color and texture of rubble as he collapsed into his chair. But as they began to work over the testimony, line by line, the old Casey, the impossible-to-please editor, stirred to life. He did not like the opening. He did not like the closing. He did not like much that was in between, or the way it was organized, or the language. As Bob Gates remembered the day, "It was a madhouse. Everybody was running around looking for this cable or that document. Everybody was talking at once. People kept running in and out. Casey was scribbling on his yellow pad. Inserts were going in and passages coming out. Papers were flying around the room. And the facts were getting foggier and foggier as more and more qualifications were heaped on to make the damned statement correct. If I wanted to define the word 'chaos,' it was that room that day."

Casey was not out of the office and back home until nearly midnight. By seven-thirty the next morning he was back at his desk, looking like a man who had slept on a train. At eight a.m., a deputy attorney general, Charles J. Cooper, showed up at the office to make sure that the delicate language about who knew what was on the aircraft had been deleted. Casey was impatient and annoyed: now Ed Meese's boys were checking up on him?

By nine-thirty, he was at the HPSCI secure hearing room facing 100 percent attendance from the fifteen members. Casey labored through his prepared statement. As soon as he was finished, the chairman, Lee Hamilton, took off after him. Poindexter had only now, *after* the arms-hostages deal had been exposed, sent copies of the January 17 finding to the oversight committees. Hamilton wanted to know if Casey considered a ten-month delay "timely" notification. No, Casey admitted, he could not defend the delay; but that, he said, was not the real issue. The Constitution placed the power to conduct foreign policy in the President's hands. At stake was a question of constitutional prerogative.

Sensationalized media treatment, he said, had blown the issue out of all proportion. The administration had attempted laudable goals—freedom for the hostages, rapprochement with a key Middle Eastern state—and for a relatively small price. What was all the fuss about? At most, $12 million in weapons from the U.S. arsenal. Iran and Iraq were already spending $20 billion on their bloody war.

The members pressed him to say who was really responsible for this misguided policy. They were all in it, Casey said, but "I think it was the President."

The House committee was not through with him. But time was running out, and Casey had an eleven a.m. date with the SSCI. He agreed to return to the House by one-thirty.

By the time he arrived at the Senate, Poindexter already had testified there. Having their stories match was going to be critical. Casey read his prepared statement again. He admitted that in November of 1985, the CIA had been asked to recommend a proprietary aircraft to ship what he described only as "bulky cargo." Senator Leahy, so recently wooed by Casey, fired right between his eyes. "Did the CIA know what was on that aircraft?" he asked.

Casey: "There is some question about that. I was told yesterday that the CIA didn't know until later on."

It was a vintage Casey answer, technically correct. The CIA, at the exact moment of the flight, as an institution, did not officially have knowledge that arms were being shipped. Casey had also spoken of the CIA impersonally, as though it were something separate from himself, as if there were a CIA Casey who did not know what the White House Casey knew.

Leahy pressed on: " 'Did not know until later on'?"

Casey answered, again omitting personal pronouns: "Did not know until the Iranians told them some time in January [1986]."

This time, the old fox, who had always trod the line so cautiously, stepped over it. In sticking to the cover story that Poindexter had also peddled to the Senate that morning, Casey lied outright. During the flurry of activity at the time of the shipment, Charlie Allen had seen strong evidence that the cargo was arms. He had shown the evidence to Dewey Clarridge. In Lisbon, Secord had told the CIA station chief the cargo was arms, and he in turn told Clarridge. The retroactive finding that Sporkin drafted covering the November 25 delivery spoke of the sale of "munitions." The eavesdropping and photographic capacity of U.S. intelligence alone could have produced photos of the weapons being uncrated and tapes of the principals haggling over price. And Casey had been a party to the decision to sell arms for hostages from the beginning.

He was twenty minutes late getting back to the House committee. In this second round he played DCI Casey to the hilt, protecting his cub, the CIA, like a lioness. The NSC had the operational role in this Iran business, the same way they had in Central America during the Boland period, he said. He agreed, it was poor policy for the NSC to be running actual operations.

Finally, late in the afternoon, it was over. It had been a grueling day, but not a total loss—perhaps only a semidisaster that might easily have been worse. Bernie McMahon remembered thinking after the Senate session, "Casey was not great, but we came out believing the CIA had acted only in a support role at the direction of the White House." The lioness had saved her cub.

CIA officials were accustomed to the perils of testifying before Congress about top secret operations that they might have been involved in two years ago, when they were having trouble remembering what they had for breakfast. And so they had developed a series of qualifiers to save themselves from perjury. As one frequent witness put it, "You start out saying 'to my best recollection,' then you back down to 'to my best current recollection,' then you retreat even further to 'to my best current and refreshed recollection.' " But Casey had gone this day beyond qualifiers into untruth. In that supple and sinuous mind, however, he was able to draw the line between lies and cover stories. A cover story might be described as a falsehood that advances national security, almost an obligation on the teller. The captured spy in wartime lies about what he knows. He tells what can be described as patriotic lies. That was what Casey had cut his teeth on forty years before in the OSS. But now it was peacetime, and he was being grilled by the U.S. Congress, not the Gestapo. One lesson he seemed not to have absorbed from that long-ago conflict was Hitler's dictum: "The greatest strength of the totalitarian state is that it will force those who fear it to imitate it."

That same morning, the President had agreed to let Attorney General Meese begin an inquiry into the Iranian affair. One of Meese's first phone calls was to Admiral Poindexter asking him to start pulling together all relevant documents. Poindexter's NSC counsel, Commander Paul Thompson, brought in the first batch, including three findings: the first covering the November 1985 shipment; the second, the draft that Reagan had carelessly signed on January 6; and the third, the official finding of January 17. Poindexter had decided months before that the first one could hurt the President, speaking as it did only of a crass swap of hostages for arms and saying nothing of grand strategic openings to moderates in Iran. The finding had virtually been forced on the White House by John McMahon to protect the CIA. Poindexter solved the problem neatly. He tore up the finding and stuffed it into his burn bag with the rest of the classified trash to be incinerated. Now, the CIA would never have its protective copy.

As for the two earliest shipments, of August and September 1985, Poindexter had told the oversight committees that these were Israeli operations discovered after the fact and not at all to President Reagan's liking.

The next day, November 22, a Saturday morning, two of Meese's subordinates, William Bradford Reynolds and John Richardson, were in North's office going through documents. They came across a manila folder, the tab stamped in red "W. H." for White House. Inside was an undated memorandum to the President. The drafter was Oliver North. It described one of the upcoming arms deals with the Iranians. One sentence practically jumped from the page: "The residual funds from this transaction are allocated as follows: $12 million will be used to purchase critically needed supplies for the Nicaraguan Democratic Resistance Forces." It was one of Ollie North's grander slips. In the shredding of documents that he continued to carry on, even under the noses of these lawyers from the Justice Department, he had missed one of the five memoranda he had sent the President requesting approval of the diversion scheme.

Reynolds and Richardson met their boss, Ed Meese, for lunch at the Old Ebbitt Grill, just a short walk from the EOB. They told Meese what they had found.

Afterward, back at his office, Meese got a call from Casey. "I've got something we have to talk about," Casey said. He was by now living in his new home on Old Dominion Road in McLean. It was on Meese's way home. Meese told Casey that he would stop by as soon as he had things wrapped up.

Meese pulled into the steep, winding drive to Casey's place just before six. They went into a room off the kitchen that Casey used as a study. Now that the President had Meese looking into this mess, Casey said, there were things he ought to know. A guy he knew named Furmark was saying that the United States owed some Canadian investors $10 million over this Iran arms business. They were threatening to go public. "They might even claim," Casey said, "that the money that should have gone to them was used for other United States and Israeli projects." That could be devastating for the administration. But, Casey said, he had gone to see Poindexter that very afternoon about Furmark's claim that funds had been diverted, and the admiral told him there was nothing to it.

Meese later insisted that he did not mention to Casey what his people had found in North's files just hours before because the evidence was then too conjectural. In light of what Casey had just told him about a possible diversion, his alleged silence on this point seems bizarre. It was as though Meese were carrying on a conversation while pretending there was not an elephant in the room.

Messe was again in his office on Sunday. He had an appointment to question Ollie North. North arrived at two-fifteen. Meese raised the matter of North's diversion memo. Yes, North admitted, funds had been diverted. He was not sure how much; he had heard an estimate of between $3 million and $4 million.

The profits on the arms deals had amounted to $16.1 million. Thus, if the contras received even $4 million, at least another $12.1 million was out there somewhere, unaccounted for. North did not have the faintest idea where the money had gone because he had left everything up to Secord. It later was established that Secord and his partners had taken at least $6.6 million in profits and commissions, while North's contras, whom the profits were supposed to benefit, got $3.8 million. If there had been a diversion, most of it had gone into the pockets of the people North trusted.

Meese asked North who in the government knew about the diversion. Only three people, North said: himself, Poindexter, and Bud McFarlane, in whom he had confided after the failed Tehran mission. He also had assumed all along that the President knew, since he had sent five memos to Poindexter to pass on to the President explaining the diversion. But Poindexter, the day he came back from testifying on the Hill, had a shocker for North: he told him that the President did not know. As Poindexter later explained, "It would cause a ruckus if it were exposed. And so I decided to insulate the President from the decision and give him some deniability."

Bill Casey and George Shultz had become like two engineers working for the same railroad. Plying different tracks, they might have given a friendly wave as one passed the other. But Casey's position as a DCI who had won foreign policy influence put their two engines on the same track, with the inevitable result. Casey had made of himself a clandestine secretary of State. His involvements in Afghanistan,

China, the Philippines, Iran, and Central America had not been simply those of a spy chief but those of a covert foreign minister. The two men had collided on Central America, with Shultz pushing his plan for a negotiated peace while Casey pursued a secret war. And Casey had won out. They had also fought over the handling of leaks in this leak-plagued administration. Casey had pushed for the hard-nosed solution: polygraph everybody. Shultz had said that he would resign after being polygraphed once. Shultz had taken that round. Casey's lie-detector campaign had to be scrapped.

Since the revelations about arms and Iran, Shultz, in Casey's eyes, had committed the team player's mortal sin. An unspoken code prevailed at the core of power: say whatever you want behind closed doors, object as vigorously as your conscience dictates; but once a policy is adopted, if you still find it distasteful, keep your mouth shut—go along or get out. In Casey's eyes, Shultz had done neither. Instead, he had made clear publicly that he had fought the policy of arms for hostages. He was putting moral distance between himself and his teammates. Casey was further enraged over stories seeping into the press that it was Shultz's people who presumably had blocked Casey from going before the oversight committees with lies in his prepared statement.

For Shultz's part, he observed Casey's behavior the way one watches a once-respected friend succumb to drink. "I no longer had much use for the kinds of things he was doing," Shultz remarked. "This was not the Bill Casey I knew." What Shultz had discovered was the crevasse of philosophy yawning between two seemingly similar men. Blunt, practical, conservative they might both be. But to Shultz, principles, statutes, the Constitution were not quite the flexible materials they were in Casey's hands.

Casey went to see the second most powerful man in the White House, his friend Don Regan. "The son of a bitch is trying to save his own skin," Casey charged of Shultz. "Sure, we all stuck our necks out. We took the kind of risks you have to take. But you tell me what George Shultz ever did as secretary of State to bring those poor hostages home? When he stands up in public and says 'I'm innocent,' he's saying Ronald Reagan is guilty. And if that's the way he feels, he ought to be canned."

"If you feel that strongly," Regan told him, "put it in writing."

"I just might," Casey said as he left.

That Sunday, at home, he began writing a letter to the President. "Last week," he began, "I spent over five hours discussing and answering questions for the House and Senate intelligence committees on our efforts to develop a relationship with important elements in Iran. . . . The public pouting of George Shultz and the failure of the State Department to support what we did inflated the uproar on this matter." He and the President were both sports fans. He wanted his message unmistakable. "Mr. President," the letter ended, "we need a new pitcher at State."

The next morning, Casey took the longhand draft from his briefcase and gave it to Betty Murphy to type. "Put it on my personal stationery," he said. She wondered, why on earth does he bother? She had been through Casey's epistolary catharsis before. He would write virtual poison-pen letters—several to Jim Baker—and then, with the poison out of his system, throw them away.

Murphy brought back the typed letter. Casey read it and told her, "Mark it 'For the President's eyes only,' and have it hand-carried to the White House." He already had Shultz's successor picked: Jeane Kirkpatrick.

That Monday morning, November 24, Casey got another phone call from Roy Furmark. Furmark had just read the newspapers and thought he had spotted a fast shuffle. "I see where the government got paid like $12.2 million for the arms," he said. "You people have got all your numbers wrong. The Iranians paid a hell of a lot more than that."

"You better get down here with everything you've got," Casey told him.

Furmark was on the next available New York–to–Washington shuttle and met with Casey that afternoon at Langley. Furmark said he knew that the Iranians had paid some $30 million for the arms. And the middlemen had paid back the U.S. government $12.2 million. So where was the rest? Incredibly, after the massive Iranian payments, only $30,000 was left in the Lake Resources account, which Dick Secord controlled—the account from which Khashoggi expected to be paid his $10 million.

Casey listened. Then he put through a call to the chief of staff. Don Regan was not in. He then called Ollie North. "There's a guy in my office who says you owe him $10 million," he said. The conversation was brief. Casey hung up and looked blankly at Furmark. "He says the Iranians or the Israelis owe you that money. Would you like to talk it over with Ed Meese, the attorney general?"

Furmark answered wearily, "Bill, as far as I'm concerned, you're the government. I'm dealing with you."

"Roy," Casey shrugged, "I don't know where the money is."

That day, Casey also attended an NSPG meeting. With the exposure of the arms-for-hostages deal dominating the media like no story since Watergate, with the equally jarring discovery within the administration of the diversion, the subject of the meeting, surprisingly, was whether or not they should continue to deal with the Iranians. More astonishing still, the decision was yes. Poindexter argued for it. Casey argued for it. And Reagan wanted the hostages home. As the President saw it, the new second channel appeared to work: it had freed one more hostage, David Jacobsen, just as the *Al Shiraa* story broke. Overlooked was the fact that the snatch of new hostages left the score where it had been when the negotiations began, with seven Americans still in captivity. Iran, in the meantime, had obtained millions of dollars' worth of U.S. weapons.

There was one more development that busy Monday: Admiral Poindexter appeared ready to unload Ollie North. If they somehow survived all this, Poindexter said in a PROF note to North, "what would you think about going to the CIA and being a special assistant to Bill?" He had not consulted Casey yet. He just wanted North to consider the idea.

Sophia knew that her husband was driving himself furiously. Here he was this morning of November 25, already up, dressed and on the phone at six-thirty. He was talking to Ed Meese, telling him that they had to get together again before Meese went to the office. The day before, Meese had gone to the President with the evidence of a diversion. Casey knew that this afternoon Meese was going to go public with the news. In Casey's judgment, it was time for preventive medicine.

By seven Meese had parked in the side entrance of Casey's house and strode past the swimming pool into Sophia's bright kitchen. Casey, Sophia, and their son-in-law, Owen Smith, were having breakfast. Casey offered Meese coffee and again took him into the study off the kitchen and closed the door.

According to Meese's later accounts of what happened in that room, Casey told him that he should be aware of certain points: his own lack of knowledge of the diversion while it was going on, and the blamelessness of the CIA.

Bernadette remembered coming into the kitchen just as Meese was leaving. She watched her father walk him to his car. Casey was bent, lost in thought, she recalled, as he came back into the house. He said to no one in particular, "There's a lot about this I didn't know."

Casey saw Meese again later that morning at another meeting of the NSPG in the Situation Room. Before the meeting got under way, Casey watched the President take Shultz aside and say something that brought a contented smile to the secretary's usually impassive face.

The meeting began. The President opened it by telling his foreign policy team that negotiations with Iran would continue, but the NSC was now out of it. The CIA was out. He was turning over the account to Secretary Shultz and the State Department. The President was not replacing the pitcher; he had just made him team captain. Casey, head lowered, said nothing.

At noon, the President and Meese held a televised press conference. Reagan announced that Admiral Poindexter had resigned his post at the NSC and that Colonel North had been relieved of his duties. Meese followed the President. He informed the country, regarding the arms sales, of "the hint of a possibility that there was some monies being made available for some other purpose." The reporters quickly knifed through the circumlocutions and homed in on the diversion. Had Colonel North committed a crime? Meese was asked. "We are presently looking into the legal aspects of it as to whether there's any criminality involved," he answered.

Another reporter asked him about the CIA's involvement in the diversion. "I know for a fact," Meese said, "that Bill Casey did not know anything about it. And beyond that, the CIA, from what we know at the present time, had nothing to do with the transfer of funds to Central America." The preventive medicine had worked.

North had been fired. But later that day he received a phone call from the President. As for the diversion of money to the contras, the President said, "I just didn't know." Then Reagan added, "Ollie, you're a national hero. . . . This is going to make a great movie one day."

The President's words were agreeable music to the Marine's ears. But North also had heard Meese's words at the press conference. And at the mention of "criminality," Ollie North, the man once willing to take the hit, decided it was time to roll off the hand grenade.

The following day, the President yielded to mounting public outrage over Iran and the diversion and created an investigative commission, to be chaired by former senator John G. Tower of Texas. Tower's committee was supposedly looking into only "the proper role of the National Security Council." The hard digging, to determine if anyone should be criminally indicted, went to a special prosecutor, a distinguished attorney, Lawrence Walsh. And the House and the Senate soon began to organize their own secret and public hearings on the Iran-contra affair.

Casey was in constant motion. Sophia feared that he would drop from exhaustion. She gave him an order: they were going to the Palm Beach house over Thanksgiving. There, on Thanksgiving day, he went out and played golf, but he tired quickly and came back home. He put through a call to Milton Gould. "I feel lousy," he told Gould. "I couldn't even finish nine holes." Gould wanted to know what was happening. "The shit's hit the fan," Casey said. "I might need you. You may have to represent me. Are you going to be around?" Yes, Gould assured him. He would be in New York.

Casey spent part of the time in Florida trying to relax with the latest draft of his OSS memoir. He had had in hand for over a year an unsigned $100,000 contract from William Morrow, arranged by his friend Howard Cady. The advance had shot up as the publishing house counted on Casey's celebrity to boost sales. Cady had told his superiors at Morrow, "What do you give a guy who already had at least eight million dollars several years ago, and since then his stocks have doubled?" Cady was right: the money was not important. As far as Casey was concerned, they could plow most of it back into promotion. He wanted the big advance so that his book, as he put it, "would be treated importantly." But in his present state, he was having trouble concentrating on writing.

By Monday, December 1, he was back in the office, his desk groaning under a backlog of accumulated work. As he started attacking the piles of paper, one of his aides noticed that his right hand was trembling badly.

Casey was a hot item on Capitol Hill. Previously, his testimony had been restricted largely to the intelligence committees. On Monday, December 8, he was summoned before the House Defense Appropriations Subcommittee. The members wanted to know if any Iranian payments had been diverted to Afghanistan. On Wednesday, he went to room 2118 in the Rayburn Building to face the House Foreign Relations Committee. The Duke of Disdain was nowhere to be seen this day; Casey looked vulnerable and confused. He waded through a brief opening statement and braced himself for the interrogation.

When had he first learned of the diversion? a member asked him. Casey clung feebly to the claim that he had first learned of it from

Meese after Meese's aides had discovered the diversion memo. That was not going to wash; the committee had already heard Roy Furmark say that he had told Casey the month before that he was sure funds had been diverted. That was pure speculation, Casey said—Meese had found hard evidence. The members were not appeased.

Another member asked Casey if North had not lied to the CIA when he claimed that the November 1985 shipment contained oil drilling parts. "Maybe he got confused," Casey answered lamely. They grilled Casey for five and a half hours. When it was over, he walked out, hunched and listless, wading through the reporters, brushing aside their questions. Peter Kostmayer, a Pennsylvania Democrat present at the hearing, told the press. "The man seemed befuddled." Another member remarked that "questioning Bill Casey was like punching a pillow." Another commented, "He didn't seem to know what was going on in his own agency."

The next day, Thursday, December 11, Casey did three hours more before the House intelligence committee. His voice barely carried as he pulled the microphone closer and closer. Alan Fiers was with him and watched from one row behind. He was shocked. "The guy had lost his stuff," Fiers later remarked. "He stumbled and fumbled. At times, it seemed he couldn't talk. He had to be carried. He'd start to answer and wave to one of us to take over when his words or his facts failed him."

Casey finished late in the afternoon and raced to the airport to make a speaking engagement in Philadelphia. He was bone tired, but he could not pass this one up. La Salle College was staging a memorial dinner for Robert Ames, the Middle East analyst who had died in the bombing of the Beirut embassy three years before. Ames was a La Salle alumnus. Casey had been invited as the main speaker.

At the airport, he headed for the CIA plane and walked into a baggage cart before one of the security men could catch him. On board, he settled into his seat and started to go over his speech notes. Almost instantly he was in a deep sleep. As the plane touched down in Philadelphia, the chief of the detail gently woke him. Casey looked around, dazed. "Where am I?" he asked.

On his arrival at La Salle, he was escorted to a seat at the head table in the huge dining hall of the College Union Building. Dick Helms was seated nearby. He came over, shook Casey's hand, and then resumed his seat. The master of ceremonies asked the guests to rise for the invocation. "I noticed that Bill didn't get up, " Helms recalled. "One of his security people had to come over and tap him on the shoulder. After everybody sat down, Bill was still standing, and the guy had to sit him down."

Finally, Casey was introduced. As he made his way toward the lectern, Helms noticed that one foot was dragging. Helms wondered if the man had been drinking. He looked at Casey's wine glass. It was untouched.

Casey began in a low, muffled voice, telling the audience about the wall at the CIA where stars were chiseled and that one of them was for Bob Ames. He recalled how Ames had been a star on La Salle's championship basketball team. Then he went on to describe Ames's distinguished career at the Agency. He closed with the lines: "They shall not grow old as we that are left grow old; age shall not weary them, nor years condemn them. At the going down of the sun and in the morning, we will remember them." He was barely audible.

Afterward, Helms came over to chat again, and Casey offered him a ride back to Washington. Aboard the plane, the steward took drink orders, and Casey asked for a scotch-and-soda. They were conversing when Helms noticed that Casey's glass was at a precarious angle. He appeared oblivious as the liquid spilled out, down his sleeve and onto the floor. The steward came by, straightened the glass, and wiped him off. The plane landed. Casey preceded Helms, who watched him walk straight into the hatchway and hit his head.

When he got into the office the following Friday morning, Casey called Owen Smith and told him he was coming up to Mayknoll for the weekend. He wanted to see Dr. Foley, and he needed to visit an eye doctor, too. "I can't see," he said.

He had promised an exclusive interview to *Time* magazine that Friday. George Lauder brought in the magazine's assistant managing editor, Henry Muller, and a correspondent, Bruce Van Voorst. Casey had before him a dope sheet which the staff had prepared, supporting the points he wanted to make. He particularly wanted to get across that in six years he had pulled the CIA out of its lassitude, won budget increases of 15 to 20 percent every year and similar personnel increases. He also wanted the *Time* people to understand the sharp improvement in the Agency's analytical product. The CIA had called the shots on Andropov, on Gorbachev, on the fall of Marcos, on the danger to the Marines in Lebanon. One note read, "Six years and no surprises. CIA ahead of policy curve."

But the newsmen wanted to talk about Iran-contra. What did he know about the diversion of funds? they asked. "I don't know anything about the diversion of funds," Casey said sullenly. "We were barred from being involved with the contras, and we kept it that way." Did he regret the arms deals? How much was the President to blame? The questions kept coming. Lauder was getting worried. Casey sat slouched, with his mouth hanging open, his eyes glazed. Thirty interminable seconds would pass after a question, and Casey still would not have answered. After one such wait, Muller said, "Mr. Casey, can we assume that's your answer?" Casey stirred himself as from a trance and answered, "Uh . . . no."

He managed to get through the rest of the day's schedule. He had to prepare for still another hearing the following week, on Tuesday, December 16, before the Senate intelligence committee. But he desperately needed to get away for the weekend, he told the staff. That night, he flew to Long Island.

The next morning, he went into Manhattan to see Bill Foley. Foley had good news: he thought he knew what was bothering his patient. Even with Dr. Tharp's gadget, Casey was terrible at remembering to take his pills for his high blood pressure. Consequently, he had been put on a new drug that only had to be taken once in the morning. Casey had started feeling poorly at the same time that he had started the new medication. Foley took him off of it. Casey also told Foley about his vision problem, that he had been bumping into things, Foley got him an appointment with an ophthalmologist later that day.

On Sunday, unable to relax, Casey put through a call to Bill Safire. He had learned that Safire was doing a piece on his role in Iran-contra. They had once been such good friends; then the shouting, the recriminations, the suspicions and loss of candor had poisoned the friendship. "I'm glad you called," Safire said. "We haven't spoken for a long time." "Yeah," Casey said. "You froze me out." Safire felt that the charge was unfair. But he was not looking for an argument; he was genuinely glad to hear from Casey. As they talked, the stiffness dissolved and some of the old warmth came back.

Casey had been insisting all along that he had not seen Roy Furmark for years before that fateful call last October. Safire knew this was not true. He recently had persuaded Furmark to have breakfast with him, and Furmark had told Safire that he had probably seen Casey a half-dozen times in recent years. But on one point Furmark was adamant: Casey had nothing to do with the financing of the arms deals involving Khashoggi and Ghorbanifar. The first serious contact he had had with Casey was, he said, the visit of October 7, when he tried to put the arm on Casey on Khashoggi's behalf.

Casey told Safire that he ought to get hold of the transcript of Barbara Walters's interview with Khashoggi and Ghorbanifar from the previous Thursday on ABC's "20/20." That was the true story. There the conversation ended. But within minutes Casey called back. Safire should read the Walters interview on ABC with Khashoggi and Ghorbanifar, he said. He called still a third time, with the same message. It was strange, this seeming mental confusion—so unlike Casey, Safire thought.

On Sunday night, Casey left Mayknoll and flew back to Washington. He was up the next morning at seven. He told Sophia that he had had a good night's sleep. She happily watched him down a breakfast of coffee and rye toast spread with generous slabs of cream cheese. He was feeling much better, he said. Obviously, it was that damned morning pill for his high blood pressure that had been affecting him. He finished his breakfast and was off to the office.

34.

Failure Is an Orphan

Visitors were stacked, as usual, outside the office waiting to see the DCI. Jeane Kirkpatrick was in the VIP waiting room, one of the appointments Casey was looking forward to this Monday morning. He also had to finish his testimony for still another grilling the next day before the SSCI.

Betty Murphy took a call from Dr. Tharp. The CIA physician had talked to Dr. Foley over the weekend and was concerned when he learned that Casey had gone off his high-blood-pressure medication. Tharp asked Murphy to squeeze him in for a few minutes with Casey that morning. Yes, she said, that was a good idea; the director had been looking terribly tired lately.

Tharp was in Casey's office by 10:05 a.m. Tharp was a mild-mannered, conscientious physician, a graduate of Indiana University who had been recruited by the CIA while serving at a mission hospital in India. He never knew what to expect when he entered Casey's office. Sometimes when he went in to take Casey's blood pressure, the director would stand up without a greeting, keep his eyes riveted on what he was reading, let his jacket slip off, roll up his sleeve, and hold out his arm. Tharp would take the blood pressure and be on his way, with Casey still reading—and not a word exchanged.

When Tharp finished taking his blood pressure this morning, Casey leaned back in his chair. "Doctor, that other medicine was doing me in. I'm already feeling . . ." he started to say, when he could not get the words out. A sickly grimace spread over his face. His eyes mirrored panic. He began tugging at his collar.

"Are you having chest pains?" Tharp asked. Casey could still not speak when, suddenly, his right arm and leg began jerking violently. The motor centers of the brain were sending irrational messages to the limbs. He was suffering a seizure. Tharp threw open the door and shouted to Betty Murphy, "Get the emergency medical team up here right away!" They had rehearsed this moment a dozen times before, while Casey was out of the office, using a dummy.

The spasms became so violent that Casey almost fell out of his chair. Tharp gripped the man's legs and held them still. The right arm still kept flapping. Tharp went to his medical bag, drew out a hypodermic needle, and gave Casey an intravenous shot of Valium. Casey calmed down and asked in a terrified voice, "What's happening to me?"

"I'm not sure," Tharp said.

The emergency team, two nurses and two paramedics, arrived in two minutes. Tharp decided that he had to get Casey to a hospital. Georgetown University Hospital looked like the best bet, a good teaching institution, with several physicians on the CIA's approved list, and just a quick ride over the Potomac from Langley.

Tharp got on the phone. He was obviously having some difficulty getting the director of Central Intelligence admitted. Bob Gates, Casey's deputy, arrived on the scene. What was the trouble? he asked. "They haven't got any beds," Tharp replied. "Give me that phone," Gates said. He was courteous but steely. Casey got a bed.

As the ambulance of the Fairfax County Fire and Rescue Squad arrived, Tharp called Sophia Casey. She immediately started complaining to him that her husband was not getting proper treatment. Tharp broke in gently and asked her to go immediately to Georgetown University Hospital.

As the ambulance sped off, George Lauder sat down with Gates to figure out what to give out to the press. What Lauder told reporters was that the DCI had suffered a seizure "as a reaction to a medication he had been on that didn't agree with him." In a hopeless attempt at anonymity, Casey was admitted to the hospital as "William J. Lacey."

Lauder went to visit Casey that night. As he approached the room, he was relieved to see Casey cheerily waving him in. The man seemed almost chipper. Sophia, Bernadette, and Owen Smith were in the room. "Dave Durenberger's going to think I pulled this to duck his hearing tomorrow," Casey said, laughing. Lauder stayed and chatted for a time and left as the nurses began getting Casey ready for computerized axial tomography, a CAT scan.

By one a.m. the scan had been read. Casey had a large, as yet unidentifiable mass on the left side of the brain.

The next morning, further tests were conducted. That afternoon, a neurological team headed by Dr. Thomas Auth, a neurologist, and Dr. Alfred J. Luessenhop, a neurosurgeon, discussed the results with Casey. Owen Smith had watched all day as Casey shifted from total lucidity to a dazed torpor. But as the medical team gave its judgment,

Casey's mind was clear. They informed him that he probably had a brain tumor; they could not tell what kind. Dr. Tharp, who was present, remembered Casey grilling the doctors the way he would his analysts. What were the various possible tumors? What were the effects of each kind? What treatments were recommended for each? What were the side effects, the downside risks of each treatment? What was the worst-case scenario? He asked if the tumor might have spread from his prostate cancer. That, the doctors said, was unlikely. It was the first time that Smith learned that his father-in-law had had cancer of the prostate. Finally, Casey asked, "If you were in my shoes, what would you do?" The physicians virtually chorused that they would opt for surgery. When did they want to operate? he asked. Right away, he was told. The hard-edged confidence vanished. "Why don't we wait a week or so, consider the options?" Casey pleaded. "A week is too long," Luessenhop told him.

As Owen Smith recalled the moment, "It was the only time in over twenty years of association with this man that I ever saw Bill Casey indecisive and wavering. It was really the first time I ever saw him shaken up."

Casey entered the operating room at seven-forty the morning of December 18.

At one time, the CIA had insisted on having one of its people present, wearing surgical "greens" if necessary, when an officer underwent anesthesia: suppose the chief of the Soviet desk blurted out the name of the Agency's mole in the Kremlin while on the operating table? But an expert study had been commissioned, and the conclusion reached was that the risk of anyone disclosing secrets while anesthetized was virtually zero.

Dr. Luessenhop led the surgical team. Casey first underwent a craniotomy, the removal of a piece of his skull with a bone saw so that the brain could be reached. With the skull open, a piece of the exposed tumor was excised and sent to the lab for a biopsy.

The likeliest diagnosis was a primary brain tumor—that is, cancer of the actual brain cells. But when the report of the biopsy came back, the mass in Casey's head proved to be a lymphoma, a rare form of cancer that had spread from the lining of the brain. The tumor was large, jellylike, with numerous fingers protruding into the brain tissue. This growth presented the neurosurgeon with a dilemma. Try to remove too much and you start cutting into the brain cells that control movement, the senses, and speech. Remove too little and the pressure continues to damage the brain as the cancer continues to grow. It was a devilish business, determining where malignant tissue left off and healthy tissue began.

Luessenhop removed as much of the tumor as he dared, particularly to relieve the swelling. What was left, the protruding fingers, would have to be killed off by radiation. The surgical wound to the head was closed and the patient moved to intensive care. The operation had lasted over five hours.

That the chief spy of the Western world suddenly required brain surgery in the midst of a constitutional crisis in which he was deeply involved sparked the deepest cynicism and wildest speculations. It was as if Americans were expected to swallow reports that the head of the KGB had gone into a coma from natural causes just after an aborted Kremlin coup. Obviously, one school of rumors ran, the CIA or the NSC or the White House had arranged to have a piece of the brain removed from the man who knew the secrets. One White House reporter, on hearing of Casey's surgery, quoted Metternich upon learning a crafty Russian ambassador had died: "I wonder what he did that for?"

As Casey began to come around, the family was shocked. The right half of his face and his right arm and leg were paralyzed, as if he had undergone a massive stroke. Equally alarming, he could not speak. He could only make struggling, strangling sounds. Occasionally an intelligible word came through, but he could not put phrases together.

If, instead of surgery, Casey had undergone only radiation, might his full faculties have continued unimpaired for a while longer? Might he have been able to undergo deeper questioning about his knowledge of the arms deal and the diversion? Might the still-cloudy areas of Iran-contra finally have been cleared up? Radiation would have been the likely treatment for a lymphoma. But Dr. Luessenhop maintained that he had to remove surgically what he could of the tumor to relieve the destructive swelling and pressure on Casey's brain. After Casey came out of the operating room, his days as a witness were over.

Still, the doctors spoke optimistically to Sophia and told her the operation had been a success. It would only be a matter of time, she believed, before Bill recovered. She was also a shrewd woman and knew that what would speed his recovery was having a purpose for living, the belief that one day he would be back on the job. In the meantime, it was important that the world not see him in his present condition. And so she put out the word to the security detail that had set up around-the-clock surveillance over Casey's room: there were to be no visitors without her permission.

A few days after the surgery, Nancy Reagan called to express her sympathy. Just before Christmas, the White House staff alerted the Caseys on two more occasions to expect further calls from the First Lady. They waited all day, but the calls never came. Nor did the President ever call.

Progress, such as it was, came slowly. It wasn't until twenty days later, on January 6, that Casey was released from intensive care to a private room.

In her conversations with Agency staff, Sophia maintained an unshakable optimism. George Lauder reported to the press that Casey was asking for his briefing materials. The papers were in fact sent, but they went unread. The director could not focus his attention. The security team eyed each other uneasily as they listened to Sophia's unbridled hope. The director, they thought, looked terrible.

With Casey incapacitated, Bob Gates became, by law, acting director of the CIA. Gates had been led to believe that Casey would make it back to the Agency, at least long enough to defend himself in the Iran-contra affair. But Gates was becoming alarmed. The press was filled with speculation, some emanating from the White House, that Casey was soon to be replaced. And Sophia would not allow Gates to see the man.

Late in January, Gates went to see Frank Carlucci, who had replaced Poindexter as national security adviser. He told Carlucci that he thought Don Regan might be behind a movement for Casey's removal. No, Carlucci told him; both he and Regan were willing to let the situation drift awhile out of consideration for the stricken man. But, Carlucci added cryptically, "there are higher powers involved." Gates left not knowing whom Carlucci meant.

Don Regan told Gates that he had no problem with a delay; he was comfortable with Gates running the CIA. Furthermore, almost immediately after Casey was taken to the hospital, Regan had talked to the President, and Ronald Reagan had not appeared eager to dump Casey. Nevertheless, Don Regan also hinted that there was a far tougher White House figure that he had to contend with.

Yes, Nancy Reagan had called Sophia, solicitous about Bill's condition. But, Don Regan reported, she had also told him that her stepbrother, a neurosurgeon, had talked to Casey's doctors, and they had admitted that Casey would be incapacitated for the foreseeable future. She began hounding Regan, her message always coming down to "Get rid of him." Regan reminded her that her husband was President thanks in no small measure to Bill Casey. But in the wake of Iran-contra, the President's approval rating in the polls had, for the first time, dropped to under 50 percent. "Casey's an embarrassment to Ronnie," Nancy told Regan. "He should be out."

Regan wanted to see Casey to get a firsthand sense of his condition. But Sophia repeatedly put him off. "She was always telling me that Bill was fine, and he'd be back soon," Regan remembered. "But I had known friends with similar conditions. I didn't have the heart to tell her that no one recovered from that kind of operation." "Look, Sophia," he told her in one conversation, "I'm the chief of staff to the President of the United States. I should be able to come out and see how Bill is."

"Well, I'm sorry, you can't," Sophia told him. "If the President has something to say to Bill, he can come over here himself. He's Bill's boss."

"She may not look it," Bob Gates told Regan, "but Mrs. Casey is a very tough lady." Regan looked at him gloomily. "Tell me about it. I've got that problem in spades," he said. But he agreed with Gates about Sophia. She had shrewdly figured out, he knew, that Ronald Reagan could not fire anybody.

"Nancy Reagan was looking for somebody to throw off the sled to save the administration," Regan later observed. "But I kept thinking of Sophia going to mass every morning, and about my friend Bill, and I was damned if I was going to be the one who pushed him over the side. I'm tenderhearted. People don't believe that about me, but I am. I knew that Bill had to go eventually. I just wanted to find the decent way to do it."

Casey was suffering from "expressive aphasia." His ability to understand and to conceptualize was fairly well preserved. His thought processes were intact. The problem lay in translating his thoughts into words. What came out was either slurred, garbled, or gibberish. As a neurologist described Casey's condition, he was like a computer with a malfunctioning printer.

Sophia was learning, by signs and by asking questions to which Casey would nod or shake his head, how to understand him on an elemental level. He would indicate displeasure by scrunching up his face and feebly slashing away with his good left hand. He could utter a comprehensible "yeah" or "no." In this way, she finally deciphered the message that most dashed her hopes. She understood him to be saying that he wanted to resign as director. And he wanted to see Bob Gates appointed as his successor.

On January 28, Sophia finally agreed to let Gates visit her husband. He arrived at Georgetown University Hospital at five p.m. and was pleased to see the security detail in place, one man in a room designated as the command post near the elevators, another in the hallway opening onto the ward, and another at the door to Casey's room, number C6316.

The director was seated by a window, wearing a blue bathrobe. It was the first time that Gates had seen him since the day of the seizure some six weeks before. He was shocked. Casey's head was hairless, his face lifeless on one side. There was a small patch of blue ink behind his ear, marking the site where he was being radiated. His eyes lit up at seeing Gates. He raised his hand weakly and waved.

From Sophia's interpretations and a few comprehensible words, Gates believed he could understand Casey and that Casey was indeed saying he wanted to resign. After the visit, Gates went back to the White House to see Don Regan and report on his visit. Finally, a solution was in sight. Regan decided that he and Casey's trusted friend Ed Meese must see Casey the next day.

Regan went to the White House counsel, Peter Wallison, and asked him to draft a letter of resignation from Casey to President Reagan. Wallison noticed that Regan, the man with the reputation as the administration's ogre, seemed genuinely upset. The next morning, Regan looked over the letter. He was uneasy. Casey's wife had been so fiercely protective in Regan's dealings with her that he was not sure she would let Bill resign. At the same time, he had Nancy Reagan on his back. Regan therefore rewrote the Wallison draft, turning it completely around. It was now a letter from Ronald Reagan to Casey. In it, the President thanked Casey for his service to the nation but noted his incapacity and relieved him as director of Central Intelligence. To take the sting out of the message, Regan had included an offer by the President to make Casey "counselor to the President" as soon as he was on his feet again. Regan had the President sign the letter, put it in a manila folder, picked up a spy novel, *The Red President*, as a present for Casey, and went to meet Ed Meese.

The two men arrived at the hospital at eleven-thirty on the morning of January 29. Regan later described the visit: "Bill was sitting up in a chair. He greeted us with tears in his eyes. He was terribly frail. He looked awful. I asked him how he was feeling. And all I got were noises and waving of his hand. Sophia tried to interpret the noises for us. I took her aside and asked her if we could talk to her husband now about his job. She agreed. So I went back to Bill and told him I wanted to talk about the Agency and himself. All I got was more 'argh, argh, argh.' And Sophia was saying to him, 'Bill, what you mean is "Get the best man you can," right?' I seized on this and I said, 'Bill, what you're saying is you want us to replace you, right?'

I got more noises. So I said, 'That's very generous and probably in everybody's best interest. But I'll accept your resignation only on one condition. You have to agree to come back to the White House when you're well and take Ed's old job as counselor to the President. You understand that, old buddy?' I saw the tears well up in his eyes and I gripped his hand. It was done. But there had been no real communication."

Regan put the spy novel on Casey's nightstand, and he and Meese left. He was relieved: it had not been necessary to take the letter of dismissal out of the folder.

As soon as Regan was back at the White House, his phone rang. It was Nancy Reagan. "What's the news on Casey?" she demanded. He told her that the man had agreed to be relieved of his duties. "Good," she said.

She was evidently not alone in her satisfaction. As Michael Deaver reported, "When it was learned that Bill Casey was probably dying, some staffers—and I won't name them—could scarcely contain their relief. Casey was the logical candidate to be fingered as the evil genius behind Iran-contra. The secrets would be buried with him. And the President would be protected."

That evening at six, Gates was back at the hospital. He had in his breast pocket a letter he had dictated earlier that read simply, "Dear Mr. President, I herewith submit my resignation as Director of Central Intelligence effective this date, January 29, 1987. It has been a great honor serving you."

Casey was now back in bed. Gates took out the letter and showed it to Sophia. She read it, choked with emotion. They went to the bed and let the prostrate man see the letter. Gates and Sophia tried for several minutes to maneuver Casey into a position where he could sign it with his left hand. Casey was getting increasingly impatient and gestured for Sophia to sign for him. He slumped back and Gates thought he heard him say, "That's the end of a career." Gates now felt himself overcome with feeling and said, "It was never supposed to happen this way."

The next day, Ronald Reagan appointed Robert Gates director of Central Intelligence. At forty-three, he was the youngest appointee ever.

Don Regan's frustration in attempting to communicate with Casey had been the norm. Casey's old OSS pal Bert Jolis also came for a visit after the operation. "Bill was totally unintelligible," Jolis recalled. "Bernadette would keep repeating, 'Dad, say it again. Say it again.' But I was not able to understand a single word he uttered."

Two days after Jolis's visit, Casey's secretary, Betty Murphy, came to the hospital. "Bernadette, I'm sure, was putting words in his mouth," she concluded. "Mr. Casey could no more communicate than the man in the moon." Owen Smith was frequently in Casey's room and, recalling Casey's arm-waving and a repeated "Yeah, yeah, yeah," said, "I got the impression he agreed with anything you said." Arthur Hug, Stanley Sporkin, Dr. Tharp, and Leo Cherne all visited and reported that they could understanding nothing. As Tharp put it, "The man had severe aphasia. I never heard him make a coherent verbal response."

The one person who claimed to have understood snatches of Casey's speech was Bob Gates. Gates later wondered, "Was I reading words into Casey's noises? But I'll bet nobody had spent more time than I had with the man over the previous six years. I could decipher him at the Agency when no one else could."

Whether or not anyone could understand Bill Casey in the wake of his operation is important only as it relates to what happened several months after his death. In the fall of 1987, Bob Woodward published his book *Veil*. In the last two pages of the book, Woodward reported that he had managed to slip undetected into Casey's room and extract from the stricken man a confession that he had known all along of the diversion.

Woodward wrote that he went to Casey's room, found the door open, and went in. He asked Casey how he was feeling and Casey answered, "Okay . . . better . . . no." Then Casey is reported to have asked, "You finished yet?" referring to Woodward's book on the CIA. After a few more desultory comments, Woodward wrote: "You knew, didn't you, I said. The contra diversion had to be the first question: you knew all along."

To this, Casey was said to have nodded.

"Why?" Woodward asked.

Casey: "I believed."

Woodward: "What?"

Casey: "I believed."

With that, he said, Casey fell asleep and Woodward left, again unidentified by anyone.

Woodward's account is intriguing because, of all the elements of the Iran-contra affair, the diversion was the most egregious, the most flagrant, one that the joint congressional investigation clearly branded as illegal. And Woodward was claiming that Casey had admitted to guilty knowledge of it.

His report of a near-deathbed confession raised a storm of controversy and protest, beginning with Casey's family and the CIA security detail, all of whom vociferously denied that Woodward could have gained entrance to Casey's room unnoticed. And even if he did, friends and colleagues who visited Casey in the hospital found it unbelievable that anyone, particularly popping into the room for what Woodward said was at most five minutes, could have had any sort of meaningful conversation with the man.

In his book, Woodward did not give the date or time of day of his visit. But he suggests that it was in early February, shortly after Casey's resignation. CIA officials had decided to continue protecting Casey, and therefore the security detail assigned to him was still in place. One person was always to be at the command post next to the sixth-floor elevators, and one person always at Casey's door, in rotating shifts, around the clock. The chief of the hospital's security force, Ferdinand Frank, had assigned his own people to watch Casey's room, one for each eight-hour shift. "We did this for all VIP patients," Frank said, "even if they had their own security." In addition, Sophia and Bernadette had worked out a system so that Casey would rarely be left alone: Sophia would stay overnight; Bernadette would arrive in the morning at about nine and stay all day until her mother came back. Thus, at any given moment, there was likely to be a CIA guard and a hospital guard on the door and a member of the family in the room.

On one occasion, the security detail refused to admit a new doctor on the case before checking out his credentials with the hospital. On another occasion, Bud McFarlane was reported to have shown up at Casey's door, accompanied by a journalist. Both were turned away because the visit had not been cleared by Sophia.

Woodward admitted that he himself already had been turned away once before the famous visit. According to the security detail, it was January 22, exactly a week before Casey's resignation, that a man appeared on the corridor and headed toward Casey's room. The security officer on door duty blocked his path, asking what he wanted. The man identified himself as an old friend of Casey's and kept pressing ahead. The security man back-pedaled, insisting that the new arrival could not see Casey without his wife's permission. The man kept up a stream of reassuring patter, saying that Casey had sent for him. By now, nearly abreast of Casey's door, the visitor reportedly said, "Just let me put my head through a crack in the door. As soon as he sees me, he'll know me."

At this point, the security man's patience ran out and, he later reported, "I was ready to deck this guy if he didn't back off." Then the visitor identified himself as Bob Woodward of the *Washington Post*. He was turned away. Casey's room had a large picture window facing the ward. It is entirely possible that, having reached that far, Woodward may have glimpsed Casey in bed or sitting in his blue bathrobe by the window.

Woodward, in his book, claimed that it was several days after this ejection that he managed to get in and have his conversation with Casey. Stansfield Turner, Casey's predecessor, talked to Woodward about the encounter. Turner said that the reporter told him that he had arrived in the morning and that "there was just nobody in the corridor of the hospital, and he walked down, got to Casey's room, and Casey waved to him to come in." If so, his timing was exquisite, since it meant that at this point, the CIA security officer had left his post, the hospital security guard had left his, and neither Sophia nor Bernadette was in the room. It also meant that, having gained entry unseen, he was able, in a few minutes, to communicate with a man who most of his closest associates said never uttered an intelligible word in their presence after his operation. He would have had to have left as invisibly as he arrived.

Questioned at length by this author about the hospital visit, Woodward, in sum, said that he was not going to reveal on what date, at what hour, or how he got into Casey's room, except to say that someone helped him and that he was not alone. Asked if he found himself in a court of law, what evidence he could produce to prove he had made the visit, Woodward closed the discussion with, "I'm not in a court of law."*

Comments from some of Woodward's fellow journalists over the incident ring with a certain disappointment at the course taken by a much-admired colleague. Thomas Powers, a respected writer on intelligence, reviewed *Veil* in the *New York Review of Books* and wrote: "Woodward's publication of this 'interview' is a literary misjudgment of heroic proportions. . . . Woodward never should have published this flimsy story as the climax of his book." Bill Safire, agreeing that *Veil* was one of the most important books written on the CIA, nevertheless concluded: "The melodramatic scene, foolishly added to show enterprise and to squeeze a controversial news lead into the book, contributes nothing to our understanding of our most activist DCI."

Others preferred the judgment of Casey's old friend Leo Cherne,

---

*The complete conversation between this author and Woodward on the hospital visit appears in the appendix.

who had visited Casey in the hospital and understood nothing. Said Cherne, "I think Woodward is full of shit."

What was Casey's awareness of, involvement in, contribution toward, and blame for those intersecting fiascos that came to be known as Iran-contra? He was perfectly cast as the heavy by a lifelong reputation for wheeling and dealing. He looked the part, the cagey manipulator, plotting conspiracies within conspiracies. After it was all over, the same speculation was heard from ordinary observers and insiders alike: "Of course Casey was behind it all." Given the man, it fit so neatly, it seemed so obvious, so plausible.

In determining Casey's true role, what must be borne in mind is that Iran-contra was two entirely separate operations that intersect, albeit critically, at only one point: when the profits from the arms sales are diverted to the contras. Thus, to be clearly understood, Casey's role must be examined in both of these operations separately.

Taking the Iran-arms half of the affair first: who bears the heaviest responsibility for its birth? That credit belongs to Robert C. Mc-Farlane. Among the Reagan administration's foreign policy team, it was McFarlane who first sought a change of strategy toward Iran, McFarlane who was persuaded by the Israelis of the wisdom of the plan, and McFarlane who brought it before the President and the National Security Planning Group.

Ultimately, however, responsibility for the decision must rest with the President. The plan was presented to Ronald Reagan. He approved it again and again over the course of fourteen months. He signed the findings. He was willing not to inform Congress. And he could have killed the operation at any time. He chose not to.

Was Casey blameless? Hardly. But the man deserves the right kind of blame. No evidence exists that he was the mastermind, putting McFarlane up to the arms deal in the first place; or, as has been speculated, that Casey put an old friend, Roy Furmark, together with the billionaire Khashoggi to finance the scheme. Furmark always stuck by his account that he had gone to Casey only after Khashoggi ordered him. For both McFarlane and Furmark, the most effective defense of their actions would have been that they were acting at the behest of the director of Central Intelligence. Neither of them ever used that defense. Neither of them claimed that Casey invented the arms-hostages deal.

Casey may not have been the mastermind, but he bears heavy responsibility. He was an early and enthusiastic convert to what even his loyal friend William F. Buckley described as "a hare-brained scheme." Casey's support was so unwavering at points when the enterprise looked dead that he deserves billing as co-architect. His greatest sin, however, was his willingness to leave Congress in the dark, a clear violation of his lawful responsibility as DCI regarding covert operations. Had Casey insisted, at any point, that he would not touch a finding that ordered him *not* to notify Congress, the whole idea would likely have collapsed on the spot. Instead, he embraced the evasion.

The legal fate of the rest of the Iran-contra cast of characters raises the inevitable question: had Casey not undergone brain surgery and died subsequently, would he also have faced criminal charges? Of the major figures who were charged, McFarlane, North, Secord, Hakim, and Poindexter, Casey's situation was most similar to that of the admiral. Three of the five counts on which Poindexter was ultimately found guilty related to statements he made to the Senate and House intelligence committees on November 21, 1986: namely, that he made "false, fictitious and fraudulent" statements in claiming that he did not know of the November 1985 shipment of Hawk missiles to Iran until January of 1986.

Casey also testified before both committees the same day, his and Poindexter's statements having been essentially coordinated the day before when the Iran-arms chronology was worked out. While the questioning and testimony of the two witnesses was obviously not identical, Casey had carried a message similar to Poindexter's to the Hill: that the CIA was not made aware of the November 1985 shipment of arms to Iran until January of 1986. Not true. Norman Gardner, as special assistant to the DDO, had helped Casey prepare his testimony for the congressional hearings, and was later called as a witness in Poindexter's trial. There he was asked by the prosecution: "And while you were there listening to Director Casey speak to the Senate on November 21, 1986, didn't you hear him say to the senators almost exactly the same thing that Admiral Poindexter had told the Senate and the House about that shipment earlier that morning?" Gardner answered, "Yes. As I recall there wasn't any significant difference." He was then asked if it was not true that Poindexter and Casey were both misleading the Senate and House committees, and Gardner answered, "That's correct." Thus, a strong case can be made that Casey would have faced charges similar to those for which Poindexter was convicted.

Would Casey therefore have been convicted as well? At the congressional hearings, Poindexter was in full possession of his faculties. Casey was already displaying the effects of the brain tumor that ultimately led to his death. Absent that condition, would the usually astute old fox have responded so carelessly to Congress? Further, even in his impaired condition, Casey drew a careful line; he spoke of what the CIA as an institution supposedly was told of the arms shipment, not what he, as an individual, knew. Further, a Casey trial would have involved different counsel, different defense strategies, a different jury. Thus, a fair-minded conclusion is that he would likely have faced charges; but the likelihood of his conviction is too conjectural.

As for Casey's agency, what institutional blame did the CIA bear for the arms deal? So long as it was operating under a finding in providing logistical support to the NSC for the arms deliveries, the CIA was legal. The DCI and his organization were clean. But Casey the presidential adviser was not.

What Casey and the rest of the supporting Reagan cast were all guilty of was monumental gullibility. Through failure after failure, the Americans seemed never to have grasped the role that greed played in keeping the enterprise alive. Just before suffering his seizure, Casey had called Bill Safire three times in one afternoon, pleading with the columnist to read what Adnan Khashoggi had said about the arms deal in a December interview with Barbara Walters. Khashoggi had said nothing remarkable then. But what he said later was extraordinary. On March 8, 1987, Khashoggi summoned the press to his sumptuous Paris apartment. The whole affair apparently had been something of a billionaire's lark. Khashoggi had been playing "games within games," he confessed. He had fabricated the story about the two Canadians, Miller and Fraser, putting the heat on him if he did not come up with the $10 million. The men were in fact Khashoggi associates and doing his bidding. The bridge loans had actually been put up, Khashoggi claimed, by an unidentified Saudi. One guesses that the Saudi's name was Adnan Khashoggi. He had concocted the story of these two "tough guys" threatening to go public and then planted it on Roy Furmark because Furmark knew Casey personally. He then sicced Furmark on Casey.

As for the contra half of Iran-contra, if Casey were materially implicated in the diversion, it would be the worst blot of all on his name. On the technical level, to take profits from the sale of U.S. arms and to channel these profits into a private account was most surely a crime. It would make no difference if the money had been diverted to the Boy Scouts of America. Such monies are required by law to be returned to the U.S. Treasury. That no one was charged with a crime for the diversion has more to do with protecting classified information (or concealing official stupidity) than with the participants' innocence.

Far more serious than malfeasance, the diversion flouted the constitutional safeguards that make the United States a democracy. Congress, exercising its right, had cut off military support of the contras. The administration did not come back with an alternative bill or a veto; it simply bypassed Congress. The NSC's conduct of a privately funded war in Central America, including the diverted money, was in open violation of the Boland Amendment. To say that the law barred only "intelligence agencies" from helping the contras and that the NSC was not an intelligence agency was flagrant hypocrisy. If democratically elected representatives enact a law and leaders in the executive branch simply circumvent it, there is no democracy.

And who was the author of the diversion? In the speculation that the affair nourished, Casey's name comes up again and again as the mastermind behind it all. But that credit, at least among the Americans, belongs to Oliver L. North. The idea first occurred to North in the fall of 1985, by his own admission. The scheme was seized upon by Ghorbanifar, Khashoggi, Secord, Hakim, and the Israelis as a way of turning North's determination to stick by the contras to their own ends. North sold the scheme to Poindexter, drafted the memoranda seeking the President's approval, and gave Secord complete control over the profits. The only thing North did *not* do was make sure that the diversion benefited his contras more than the sharks.

Still, the impression created by North, in his testimony before the Iran-contra committee and at his later trial, was that his actions were guided by a gray eminence working behind the scene, William J. Casey. North claimed that he first mentioned the possibility of a diversion to Casey soon after Ghorbanifar and the Israelis had discussed the steep markups in January of 1986. He further said that at some point he showed Casey a memorandum asking for the President's approval. And he stated that once the diversion was in motion, he informed Casey of the fact. Casey, he reported, reacted enthusiastically, calling the diversion "the ultimate irony"—the Ayatollah's money used for the contras' arms. North, however, made none of these assertions until Casey was dead. While Casey still possessed the ability to defend himself, North told Attorney General Meese that Casey was not one of those privy to the diversion.

In the spring of 1986, at an NSC meeting, Casey had alerted the President that the contras were in bad shape, down to their last $2 million in U.S. humanitarian aid. North and Poindexter knew that on that very day another $5 million from Iranian arms sales had come in, presumably available for the contras. Casey was either lying to the President or did not know about the diverted $5 million. General Secord testified that a few days afterward, he and North dropped in at Casey's EOB office and discussed the desperate condition of the contras. No mention of the diversion was made. And just before these events, Poindexter had warned North not to tell Casey "about any of your operational roles." He specifically mentioned the diversion.

Only one other person, Lieutenant Colonel Robert Earl, a fellow Marine also assigned to the NSC, ever heard North say that Casey had knowledge of the diversion. But Earl was not sure when North told him this; it might have been any time between May and November of 1986. The latter date would have been well after the scheme was in motion. During the Iran-contra investigation, when North was pressed to answer whether Casey approved of the diversion, North backed down. "I don't know if 'approved' is the right word," he said.

Casey's behavior, even before the Iran-contra affair became public, was not that of a man who appeared to be trying to hide something. At his first meeting with Furmark alone, he told Furmark to repeat the story to one of his staff. Casey urged Poindexter on two occasions to bring in the White House counsel, Peter Wallison, and to go public with the story. "I've always had my doubts about North's statements concerning Casey's involvement in the diversion," Wallison later commented. "After all, Casey did tell Poindexter to bring me in to investigate the suspicions about a diversion. I would have questioned Poindexter and Poindexter would have said, 'Who's Casey trying to kid? He knows all about this.' Casey took a risk going that route, unless he honestly wasn't involved."

When Furmark last saw Casey on November 24, Casey offered to put Furmark in touch with the Justice Department—not the move of someone seeking to evade the law.

It is entirely possible, indeed likely, that North did discuss the diversion with Casey. But what cannot be known is the context or how Casey reacted. Did North bring up the diversion with his customary gusher of ideas, the good indiscriminately with the bad? Did he spell out to Casey what specifically was being done, even ask for his advice? Did Casey in fact exult to North that the diversion was the "ultimate irony"? Did he encourage North to go ahead? Or did he listen impassively, happy to see something done for the contras without getting his or his agency's feet wet? Casey's half of their private conversations went with him to the grave, and only North's versions are left.

What is most damaging to Casey, however, regarding the diversion is that he had nominated a reckless romantic, Oliver North, to run the covert contra operation in the first place. And then it was Casey who suggested that North use Secord for both the contra supply operation and as the middleman in the arms sales to Iran. Secord, however, never claimed that Casey was behind the diversion, though it would also have benefited his defense.

Assessing President's Reagan's responsibility for the diversion is tricky. On the only occasion in which Reagan was questioned formally, by the Tower commission, he denied any direct knowledge. Quite possibly he was, in a narrow sense, telling the truth. Poindexter testified that he had deliberately *not* informed the President, to save Reagan from political damage in case the story blew. Shakespeare understood these games. In *Antony and Cleopatra*, Menas, an ally of Pompey, explains that he has a plan for eliminating Marc Antony, Octavius Caesar, and Lepidus so that Pompey can become emperor of Rome. Says Menas: "These three world-sharers, these competitors, / Are in thy vessel. Let me cut the cable; / and when we are put off, fall to their throats. / All there is thine." To which Pompey replies: "Ah, this thou shouldst have done / And not have spoke on't. In me 'tis villainy, / In thee't had been good service."

A Pompey, a king, a President does not say, "I want profits from the sale of arms used to buy the contras a thousand AK-47s." These are means, and chiefs of state deal in ends. What the President told his foreign policy team at the time the Boland ban went into effect was, "I don't want to pull out our support for the contras. This would be an unacceptable option." Under that generous grant of authority, the zealous subordinate will always figure out how to do the king's bidding. Indeed, while Reagan denied knowledge of specific help provided to the contras during the Boland Amendment, he admitted to the Tower commission, "It wasn't contrary to policy." In North, it had been good service.

Supreme Court Justice Robert Jackson probably summed up the Iran-contra affair best thirty-six years before it happened when he wrote, "Security is like liberty in that many crimes are committed in its name."

More spectacular than the diversion is North's claim that Casey had cooked up a scheme for a private CIA, supranational and accountable to no government. Or as North put it: "Director Casey had in mind, as I understood it, an overseas entity that was capable of conducting operations or activities of assistance to the U.S. foreign policy that was stand-alone, self-financing, independent of appropriated monies and capable of conducting activities similar to the ones we had conducted here [the arms sales and diversion]." Or as North put it at another point in his testimony, "Director Casey said, you want something you can pull off the shelf and use on a moment's notice."

It all sounded so like Casey—the unseen intriguer, the covert adventurer. And it made great copy. But when pressed by Arthur Liman, the Senate Iran-contra committee's counsel, North again backed down. Liman reminded the witness that Casey had an entire directorate of covert operations to carry out secret, dirty tricks.

Liman: "As I understand your testimony, Director Casey was proposing to you a CIA outside of the CIA be created. Fair?"

"No," North said, and allowed that his conversations with Casey had been hypothetical.

John McMahon, who spent hours listening to Casey spin his schemes, later pondered what North might have been talking about. McMahon had heard Casey's pet refrains over and over. Casey was forever urging that they make more use of overseas companies for agent cover. He also wanted to install "sleepers," agents who would become active whenever the U.S. government was frozen out of a country, such as Iran. "Bill knew all these international tycoons," McMahon observed. "He knew where the private power was, the money, and how to get at it. I'm sure Bill talked to North about these things too." In McMahon's judgment, North's active imagination had taken Casey's idea and catapulted it to the "off-the-shelf," "self-sustaining," "stand-alone" private CIA outside the CIA.

Casey's friend Bill Safire probably had the best explanation. "The Bill Casey I knew would certainly go outside of channels," Safire said, "but inside government." Theodore Draper, writing in the *New York Review of Books* on North's claim that Casey supported a supranational CIA, was blunter: "It was feather brained and no one has ever accused Casey of that particular imperfection."

North also claimed, again not until Casey's death, that it was Casey who told him to "get rid of things, clean things up," after which he started destroying documents. This assertion strongly supports a conclusion that Casey was the evil genius, deciding to pull the plug on Iran-contra. But Bob Gates remembered hearing the words in quite another context at the October 9 meeting between Casey, North, and Gates. They had been discussing Roy Furmark and the supposedly unhappy Canadian investors, and Casey had advised North, "You'd better clean this up."

North also spoke of a ledger that Casey had given him for keeping track of all the private funds coming in and going out for the contras. The NSC had its own computerized PROF system for written communications and record keeping. The Iran-contra hearings are replete with references to these "PROF notes." North could just as easily have kept his contra account in this system. And he could have eliminated it with the press of the "delete" button. Instead, he said, he kept these records in a spiral ledger which Casey gave him and later told him to destroy.

On hearing the account of the spiral ledger, Bob Gates observed, "What did Casey do, pad down to the local Dart drugstore to buy Ollie North a notebook? Did he call the CIA supply room and say, 'Send up one spiral ledger'? And then he trots over to the EOB to deliver it? It just doesn't ring true."

To demands for proof of Casey's complicity, North had an unassailable answer. Casey had instructed him never to take any notes of their meetings. And he had destroyed the spiral ledger Casey gave him. The trail was erased.

Was North working for Casey? That question too was put to North during the investigation by Counsel Liman.

Liman: "Did you look upon him in a way as a boss?"

North: "He wasn't a boss so much as a personal friend."

And at another point, when asked whether he went to Casey "for direction," North answered, "I don't want either of my previous superiors to think that I was working for Director Casey. I know who I worked for."

North's reputation for veracity was never his strong point. Ollie stories took on something of a Baron Münchhausen quality within the national security community. Bob Gates described North as "the only person in my twenty-two years in government who I know lied to me flat-out." North admitted to the Iran-contra committee, "I will tell you right now, Counsel, and all the members here gathered, that I misled the Congress. . . ."

Curiously, the joint investigating committees chose to believe North when he incriminated the deceased Casey. The committees' final report concluded:

We believe that the late Director of Central Intelligence, William Casey, encouraged North, gave him direction and promoted the concept of an extra-legal covert organization. . . . Casey's passion for covert operations—dating back to his World War II intelligence days—was well known. . . . Further, it was Casey who brought

Richard Secord into the secret operation, and it was Secord who with Albert Hakim organized the Enterprise. These facts provide strong reasons to believe that Casey was involved both with the diversion and with the plans for an "off-the-shelf" covert capacity. . . . The Committees are mindful, however, of the fact that the evidence concerning Casey's role comes almost solely from North; that this evidence, albeit under oath, was used by North to exculpate himself; and that Casey could not respond.

In the matter of Iran, the arms, and the hostages, Casey did not invent the policy. But he did embrace it, becoming along the way more Catholic than the Pope. In the case of the diversion, apart from North's statements, and as much as it stretches credulity, the weight of evidence favors a conclusion that Casey was not materially involved. If he knew, it was certainly not as the guiding hand. Yet, three years after Casey's death, Hugh Sidey, the *Time* magazine columnist, reflected a still popular perception. ". . . there is still the acknowledgment," Sidey wrote, "that the man who really put the grand plot together has left the scene. That is Bill Casey." History, however, is not served by pronouncing Casey the archvillain, the mastermind, the evil genius, simply because he seems so beautifully cast—though it certainly would make a better movie.

In the end, Casey's role in the twin disasters must be judged by the knowable record, not by preconceptions of his character. Casey did advocate the Iran-arms deal, and enthusiastically. He willingly connived in excluding Congress from knowledge of it. He favored keeping the war going in Nicaragua in spite of the Boland Amendment, which created the climate in which a diversion could happen. These acts constituted a serious menace to a government of laws. That is guilt enough.

Ironically, the behavior of White House Casey hurt the chief objective of CIA Casey, to rehabilitate the Agency. The public, hearing of clandestine shenanigans, hearing Casey's name invoked again and again, did not draw fine distinctions between the NSC, the CIA, and who was responsible for what. Bob Gates, for one, felt the fallout. Appointed to succeed Casey as director of Central Intelligence, Gates went through two grueling days of confirmation hearings before the Senate intelligence committee in March of 1987. The brilliant analyst, the man whom Admiral Inman called "the greatest intelligence officer of this generation," analyzed his own fate with customary insight: he had been too close to Casey. With Casey incapacitated, he was now the surrogate target for an outraged Congress. Gates withdrew his appointment before it could be defeated. Judge William Webster, director of the FBI, was subsequently named DCI.

Joseph Fernandez, the Costa Rica station chief, maintained to the end that his superiors knew that he was helping Ollie North supply the contras. Fernandez had lost his way in that twilight zone between the CIA's official hands-off posture and the administration's clandestine support during the Boland ban. He became the only CIA officer to be indicted in the Iran-contra affair. The case against Fernandez was ultimately dropped for security reasons, but his career lay in ruins.

In the end, Casey's embrace of the policies of folly diminished the genuine good he achieved. He had been colossally successful in pumping money and manpower into the Agency's rebirth. He had rejuvenated the listless and demoralized organization he had inherited. Yet the Iran-contra affair sent the CIA back into a defensive crouch to escape the shell fire its chief had drawn.

Casey had a tumor on his brain. It is thus logical to ask what effect this condition had on his judgment. During his confinement, Georgetown University Hospital put out a statement on the possible effects of a lymphoma: "Depending on location, they can cause everything from major language disturbances to memory disturbances and can affect abstract thinking." Dr. Nicholas Zervas, chief of neurosurgery at Massachusetts General Hospital, told reporters that Casey's type of lymphoma was particularly insidious because it grows like a network within brain tissue rather than in a ball or a lump. As a result, the tumor could induce gradual, subtle changes in personality or mental functioning. Bill Safire was later to write, "The desperate mind that led the Reagan Administration over the cliff in his final years at the CIA was not the old Bill Casey. The Big Bill we knew was an enthusiast, not a zealot, warm-hearted, not thin-skinned, loyally discreet, not secrecy obsessed."

The best judgment of his attending physicians, however, was that Casey's lymphoma was probably only about three months old at the time of his seizure. As one of them observed, "Pure speculation based on how fast such tumors grow and the type of cell suggests that Casey's tumor probably started in September or October." His support of the arms-hostages initiative, his support for the contras in the face of a congressional ban, however, predate this period considerably. Casey advocated these policies when he still possessed his full faculties.

His visible decline began in the fall of 1986, when it is believed the tumor began. It was then that he became fogged with fatigue on the trip to Central America. It was that fall that he made his abysmal appearances in the congressional hearings and had the puzzling phone conversations that Safire reported just before his seizure. It was also during this period that Casey lied in congressional testimony. Evasions, omissions, obfuscations before? Yes. Outright falsehoods? Rarely. Not until this time, when likely his judgment was affected by what was happening inside his skull.

After Casey died, William F. Buckley spent an evening with President and Mrs. Reagan. They fell to talking about Casey's illness. "My problem with Bill," the President said, "was that I didn't understand him at meetings. Now, you can ask a person to repeat himself once. You can ask him twice. But you can't ask him a third time. You start to sound rude. So I'd just nod my head, but I didn't know what he was actually saying." Thus spoke a President, who already suffered from partial deafness, about the intelligence chief he could not understand. One wonders what Casey might have been proposing that the President was agreeing to with his uncomprehending nods.

35.

"The Last of the Great Buccaneers"

After the brain surgery, and despite radiation treatment, Casey went into a steady decline. On March 27, Sophia decided to bring him home to Mayknoll.

She had cable television installed so that Bill could watch one channel he particularly enjoyed, C-Span, the live coverage of Congress. It was impossible to know how much of what he saw penetrated, shut off as he was from the power to communicate. Owen Smith recalled, "If Sophia or Bernadette tried to interrupt C-Span for their favorite soap operas, Bill would start banging on his chair."

He had labored, on and off, for ten years over the book on the OSS. His last offer had been the $100,000 advance from William Morrow and a $50,000 guarantee for promotion. But now, with Iran-contra shadowing the author's name, the publishing house started dragging its feet. Sophia was getting annoyed with Morrow. This book was to be a tribute to her husband, as writer and historian along with his other gifts. She decided to give the rights to a more appreciative publisher, the conservative house of Regnery Gateway, which ultimately published the book under the title *The Secret War Against Hitler.*

Casey continued to fail. On April 25, his breathing became so labored that he had to be taken to Community Hospital in nearby Glen Cove.

On May 5, the first witness in the congressional investigation of the Iran-contra affair, Richard V. Secord, was called to testify. Less than twenty-four hours later, Bill Casey was dead of pneumonia. The security detail went to Mayknoll and yanked out the secure phone and the Agency safe. A watch that had lasted almost six and a half years was ended.

News of Casey's passing reactivated the rumor mill. He had been

so wily, so crafty for so long, that even in death he provoked conspiratorial speculation. One story making the rounds in the Washington press corps had it that the Senate intelligence committee had
dispatched a staff member to the Nassau County coroner's office to
make sure Casey was dead.

His farewell from this world was to prove as tempestuous as his
life in it.

The funeral mass was scheduled for Saturday, May 9, at 1:45 p.m.
at Casey's home parish, Saint Mary's, in Roslyn Harbor. The day was
bright, with the sun vivid above and a fair breeze blowing in from
Long Island Sound. The President and Mrs. Reagan, both in black,
sat in the front pew. Also present were former President Nixon; Ed
Meese; Caspar Weinberger; Frank Carlucci; Charles Wick; the new
DCI, William Webster; Ollie North; and a large representation from
the OSS and the CIA.

The guests were getting edgy. The diocesan bishop, John McGann,
was to say mass, and the bishop was already more than twenty-five
minutes late. Sophia Casey had expected her parish priest, Father
Fagan, to officiate. The call from Bishop McGann had come as a
surprise to her. Nancy Reagan seemed particularly upset as the First
Family unmajestically cooled its heels. Ronald Reagan appeared
completely at ease.

Jeane Kirkpatrick used the time for last-minute changes in the
eulogy she was to deliver. Sophia had asked her to do it, and Kirkpatrick had been honored. "The first thing I did was phone Bob Gates
to send me some of Bill's recent speeches," she recalled. "Then I sat
down at the kitchen table, where I do my best work, and I wrote it."

In her text she noted that yes, "some mean-spirited, ill-informed
comments have been written and spoken in the last days. . . . These
comments would not have overly disturbed our friend. . . . Casey
could take the guff required to support unpopular ideas. . . . He lived
his life to the hilt and left it in the spirit of the man who said, 'I am
surrounded by my family. I have served my country. I have reliance
upon God, and I am not afraid of the devil.' "

Casey had summed up his own motive force in his speech five years
before to the Friendly Sons of Saint Patrick. "Some things," he had
said, "are right and some things are wrong, eternally right and eternally wrong." The Catholic church, if its communicants will give it
unquestioning faith, does provide, in return, certainty in an uncertain
world. His church gave Bill Casey lifelong certitude. His ideas of right
and wrong were indeed unambiguous. His was a world of Good or
Evil, "free" or communist, with us or against us. Moral simplification

was the way a sophisticated and convoluted intelligence coped with the bafflements and perversities of life—a quintessentially Catholic solution. As one friend put it, "Bill believed in the American flag, the Catholic Church, and nothing else." The judgment was incomplete but not inaccurate.

Bishop McGann arrived. He explained that he had been tied up in traffic. McGann turned to face the congregation and deliver the homily. He greeted the President, the other dignitaries, and the Casey family. He lavished praise on Bill Casey for his devotion to his church, his work for the diocese, his life of public service.

Bishop McGann paused before he plunged ahead:

His convictions about the fundamentally moral purpose of American actions, I am sure, made incomprehensible to him the ethical questions raised by me as his bishop, together with all the Catholic bishops of the United States, about our nation's defense policy since the dawn of the nuclear age.

I am equally sure that Bill must have thought the U.S. bishops blind to the potential of a Communist threat to this hemisphere, as we opposed—and continue to oppose—the violence wrought in Central America by support of the contras. . . . I cannot conceal or disguise my fundamental disagreement on these matters with a man I knew and respected.

The air virtually crackled with the stiff silence these words produced.

When Jeane Kirkpatrick rose to speak, her prepared text sounded like a rebuke of the bishop: "Some mean-spirited, ill-informed comments have been written and spoken in the last days. . . ." And when she finished, her praise of Casey provoked a rare burst of applause in a church.

Outside, afterward, the mourners milled about, muttering against a priest injecting politics into a religious service. Geoff Jones, executive director of the Veterans of the OSS, went home and dashed off a letter to the bishop. He concluded two pages of respectful outrage with, "Your Grace may recall from your seminary days, 'De mortuis nil nisi bonum' "—speak only good of the dead.

The headlines over the *New York Times* front-page story the next day read: BISHOP AT CASEY RITES QUESTIONS CONTRA AID. The *Daily News* read: SHOCKER AT CASEY RITES—L.I. BISHOP CAME TO BURY NOT PRAISE CIA HEAD. The furor was of a piece with the rest of Casey's life, confirming the adage that nothing happens to people that is not just like them.

He had gone through Langley like a gale-force wind that blew for six straight years. "Casey had that rare capacity to move things that are almost immovable," Clair George observed. "I never met anybody like him." The chief of his security detail reminisced, "If I close my eyes, I see him always moving, always calculating, never wasting a word or motion that wasn't designed to move something forward, something not always visible to the rest of us." "Casey was forever tiptoeing on the edge of disaster," George Lauder remembered. "We were always pulling him back. And I used to think, someday there won't be anybody to pull him back." To Bob Gates, "Bill Casey was the last of the great buccaneers."

David Durenberger, who tangled often with Casey, concluded, "I think of Bill in terms of lost opportunity. He was excellent on Afghanistan, Africa, Libya, terrorism. If he hadn't gotten himself hung up on Nicaragua, he would have been a great DCI. On a scale of ten, I would have rated him a nine."

He had managed to take a staff job, the President's intelligence officer, and elevate it to coauthor of Reagan-era foreign policy. No DCI ever had achieved or even attempted that role before, not even the fabled Allen Dulles in any comparable degree. "Casey defined the foreign policy agenda," Bob Woodward decided. "He got it because there was a great vacuum between the State Department and Defense. They couldn't agree. And so Casey said, 'Let's do it covertly.' . . . He was, when you really look at it, the most important person in the government other than Ronald Reagan."

Was that good, that an intelligence chief wielded so much influence? Certainly it was from the standpoint of Casey's ambitions. Foreign policy-making was the role he had coveted from the time he plunged into Nixon's failed campaign of 1960. But for the country, were Casey's simultaneous roles as intelligence officer and clandestine foreign minister healthy? "When you combine an intelligence gatherer and a policymaker," Senator Pat Leahy observed, "the objectivity of the former inevitably suffers from the subjectivity of the latter." Indeed, Durenberger dropped his grade of nine to a two when Casey's policy role was added. "There's danger," Durenberger believed, "when your eyes and ears become your brain. You start seeing what you want to see."

In the end, the judgment on his performance at the CIA lies in the eye of the beholder. To his fiercest partisans, his pugnacious anticommunism and his reinvigoration of the CIA left a glowing legacy.

To his critics, Casey offered a telling example of the stunting effect of chronic Cold War thinking on an otherwise fine mind. Inevitably, with the exposure of Iran-contra, he would be remembered most as one of the leads in a political immorality play.

He was a far better man when he turned on his brain rather than his emotions. Casey foresaw the emerging dominance of the information age early in his tenure as undersecretary of State for economic affairs. He correctly perceived that the Soviet Union, in order to survive in that age, would have to accept the free flow of information, and that *glasnost* must inevitably loosen the USSR's bonds over its own people and its satellites. He recognized that Mikhail Gorbachev, who accepted that reality, was a different breed of Soviet man, a leader who would be more concerned with saving his country from economic oblivion than with rescuing the world from Western capitalism. Yet when it came time to act, these admirable insights of Casey's would be lost in the blinding light of his fierce anti-communism.

His tenure at the CIA, however, was only the fiery tail of a long comet. It was a life begun as a social worker bent on saving the world from poverty and materialism and ending as a multimillioniare, conservative spy master. Yet, once he had found his philosophic bearings, a steel thread of consistency ran through his professional life. Whether at the Research Institute of America or the OSS, piling up a private fortune or heading the SEC, running a successful presidential campaign or directing the CIA, the lawyer, the advocate was always dominant. He conducted virtually all his enterprises like law firms: you determine your client's best interests, and then you do whatever the law, stretched to the outermost, allows in pursuit of that objective. Casey did not compartmentalize. There was not one way to run the Export-Import Bank and another way to conduct venture capitalism. Even the CIA was another Casey law firm. Here the client was the United States, and you did whatever you could get away with to advance the client's presumed advantage. And always hovering in the background was the spirit of the symbolic senior partner, the formative figure in Casey's life, William J. Donovan, urging softly: Risk. Dare. Break the mold. Remember, the perfect is the enemy of the good. John Shaheen had once told Casey, "Bill, you're the closest thing to the General yet." "That," Casey answered with a devilish grin, "is the nicest thing anybody ever said about me."

The words he inspired from those who knew him over a lifetime or after a single encounter include "appealing," "appalling," "thoughtful," "ruthless," "kindly," "tough," "charming," "abrasive," "understanding," "impatient," "straightforward," "cunning," "direct," "manipulative," "approachable," "intimidating," "an enigma."

This complex soul was laid to rest at Holyrood Cemetery, a few miles from the Roslyn Harbor he loved. After the funeral mass, Bill Casey's family and friends gathered at Mayknoll to toast the departed in the Irish tradition, with good food and drink and memories of the friend who was no more.

Appendix

When the author questioned Bob Woodward about his 1987 hospital visit with Casey, the following dialogue ensued (ellipses indicate pauses).

JP: You were first turned away from Casey's room before his January 28 resignation. How many days after that did you get in?

BW: What I've decided on, on that, because I've made clear somebody has helped me in this . . . and . . . I'm not going to go beyond what's in the book. It's become a kind of witch hunt in the CIA.

JP: The CIA contends they had security around the clock at Casey's door. The contention of Ferdinand Frank, the Georgetown Hospital security chief, is that he had his people on the door also. When you see Casey, do you get past security, or is there no security?

BW: Well, that opens other questions. I am protecting somebody who helped in . . . in a rather . . . you know. I think Sophia made a mistake. I know she's wrong in making the assertion she does that would make this kind of an issue, because, obviously, Casey was willing to see me, as I've said before. It was not like somebody walking in off the street. Her assertion, that she and Bernadette were there, is just not true.

JP: You're saying that when you were in the room . . . let's forget about the security, which you don't want to comment on . . . but when you're in the room, there's nobody but you and Bill?

BW: Certainly not Bernadette or Sophia.

JP: Were you in a white coat?

BW: Obviously not.

JP: I have to ask these things.

BW: A green coat [*laughingly*]. Maybe you will be able to resolve it. Maybe, ah . . .

JP: I'm talking to the only man on earth to have the answer here.

BW: I can assure you it happened exactly the way it has been described. And if you read it in the context of the book . . . and . . . look . . . as I also said before . . . it's . . . there's lots of scenes . . . read the last page . . . and seeing who's doing this . . . seeing who's doing that . . . and twenty words, nineteen words in four or five minutes . . . I'm not gonna go beyond what's in the book. But I knew what a devastated man he was physically. I mean, I've seen people, you've seen people in the hospital going through things . . .

JP: You're not maintaining that you were necessarily alone. . . .

BW: That's right.

JP: Okay. Can you tell me this—how long did this conversation last?

BW: I think about four or five minutes. But . . . that's my best esti-mate . . . you know . . . how long have we been talking?

JP: Okay. Another have-to-ask question. If you are in a court of law, and for some reason you had to prove you did this thing, by the rules of evidence, what evidence would you present?

BW: Well, I'm not in a court of law. And I don't . . . I mean, it hap-pened. And, it's . . . I urge upon you to not . . . I mean, ask what ques-tions you would, but to not . . . that it's some kind of momentous event. It's one page in the book. I think I owed it to him. It hap-pened. . . . If you'd been there you'd say, "You got it exactly right." That's exactly what he said. And that it's exactly what it is. You know, you'd come out and you'd say, "It's what it is" and . . . I would have loved to have gone back and tried to talk to him again . . . but . . .

JP: Let me put it this way—were you in this court-of-law situation, you would have the evidence?

BW: Well, if there were an investigation . . . and somebody were . . . I mean, who would be under investigation? Casey . . .

JP: I mean, whether or not you want to divulge it, you do have . . . you could make a hard case that you did this thing?

BW: I'd swear to it. And somebody helped me who could . . . if that person were willing to be honest . . . would be forced to testify, "Yes, this happened." . . . But, you know, you ought to . . . who were those guys? . . . There was a piece done that has a couple of interesting things in it . . . *The Washingtonian* . . .

JP: David Halevy and Neil Livingstone.

BW: That's right. In there, they talk to all the people around him and they talked to Sophia. And they say that Sophia and Bernadette say that they were there all the time except at maybe hour intervals when they weren't there.

JP: The other thing that I must ask about that situation is . . . On his best day, Bill Casey was hardly Edward R. Murrow in his diction. I've talked to maybe ten people who visited Casey at about the time you're talking about, including his son-in-law, Owen, who was there many times, Don Regan, others, all of whom said they never carried on any kind of meaningful communication with Casey. They would say things and hope by the expression in his eyes, he would seem to comprehend. But they never understood a word he said. Don Regan told me he said "mumble mumble mumble."

BW: To begin with the first part of your question, he was hard to understand before this happened, but not that hard once you got to . . . and I would . . . and when I would have long conversations with him, my rule was . . . I would ask . . . I would try to say . . . instead of saying "Huh?" I would say, "Could you repeat that? I don't understand you." And then he . . . as you know, he could talk clearly when he wanted to. Have you talked to Gates?

JP: Sure have.

BW: What does Gates say?

JP: He's the only—

BW: Can I tell you this? Gates came up to the *Post* in front of fourteen or fifteen people at lunch and said Casey was lucid . . . lucid.

JP: When was this?

BW: This was before Casey died and after he had resigned. And it was after Gates's nomination was withdrawn. And if you talk to any doctor about this, if you want to make this an issue . . . you know, it's like somebody will have good moments and days and good parts of the day and bad parts of the day and so . . . you know . . . I don't . . . He said those things as I reported.

JP: Those are verbatim words?

BW: Those are verbatim words. And so why would Gates come and say "Lucid, lucid"? Not just . . .

JP: Look, Bob, nobody among these ten people I've talked to—not one of them—said that Casey had lost his marbles. They said they couldn't understand him . . . he would feel this frustration trying to get out the thoughts that his mind could develop . . . but couldn't be expressed. He couldn't articulate. Okay?

BW: Well, you can talk to . . . you know . . . there are certain times of the day . . . I'll leave it to your ingenuity . . . when somebody in that condition who's gone through that can be much more lucid than at other parts of the day.

JP: I want to ask one last question on that subject. Did you submit the hospital visit story to the *Post?*

BW: Yeah . . . uh . . . uh, submit it? Uh, I told all the editors about it soon . . . right after it happened. And it was just . . . uh . . . and I said, you know, "I'm gonna use it as the last part of my book."

JP: You didn't submit it as a news story to your paper?

BW: How do you submit it as a news story? . . .

JP: I don't know. . . .

BW: I mean, I did. . . . There's so many, as you well know, so many pages in your book . . . that . . . how is that a news story? And I maintained that, you know, that it's exactly what happened. And if you read it kind of dispassionately, you say, well, you're willing to accept that that's what happened. What does it mean? The nod, the grunt . . . you know, the nineteen or twenty words or whatever it is. I make very clear that it was a sick man at the end.

JP: What I guess I'm getting at, Bob, is at some point after this happened did you sit down and write a news story for the *Post* about it?

BW: Literally write it out? Maybe at some point I tried to see it work as a news story.

JP: You talked it over with your colleagues?

BW: Well, I told everyone about it.

JP: Is there a written story submitted at some point where Bradlee or somebody says, "Well, maybe we can do this as a news story, maybe we can't"? Was it discussed as a news story?

BW: No. Because it's so obvious. What do you do? Say, "Casey, having just undergone this operation, nodded when asked about . . ."? You know . . . I mean, you've written books and been in this business. Bear with me on this. It's one of those things . . . you know . . . deathbed confession. As you know, it wasn't his deathbed. He got better and went home . . . comparatively . . . and then went home here, didn't he? And then went up to Long Island and was hospitalized there. So it's not his deathbed. The point you should know, which I'm sure you're aware of, is that the *Post* ran the story . . . as an excerpt from the book. As we planned always. And it's . . . well, you know . . . recorded . . . that I wrote this and submitted it to my publisher well before he died. That we were going to use it no matter what happened. That it . . . you know . . . that's the way it is . . . I wish it were more clear . . . I never . . . That's what happened. . . . My conviction? That I got it exactly right and, yeah . . . there is a kind of . . . in the nod . . . but, of course . . . yes . . . and he'd had an operation. I made that clear.

JP: But a story was not run by the *Post* at the time.

Index